Autistic Spectrum Disorders

Understanding the Diagnosis and Getting Help

Beijing • C • *Taipei • Tokyo*

Autistic Spectrum Disorders: Understanding the Diagnosis and Getting Help
by Mitzi Waltz

Copyright © 2002 Mitzi Waltz, All rights reserved.
Printed in the United States of America.

Published by O'Reilly & Associates, Inc., 1005 Gravenstein Hwy North, Sebastopol, CA 95472.

Editor: Linda Lamb

Production Editor: Tom Dorsaneo

Cover Designer: Kristen Throop

Printing History: July 1999, First Edition under the title *Pervasive Development Disorders*

Many of the designations used by manufacturers and sellers to distinguish their products are claimed as trademarks. Where those designations appear in this book, and O'Reilly & Associates, Inc. was aware of a trademark claim, the designations have been printed in caps or initial caps.

This book is meant to educate and should not be used as an alternative for professional medical care. Although we have exerted every effort to ensure that the information presented is accurate at the time of publication, there is no guarantee that this information will remain current over time. Appropriate medical professionals should be consulted before adopting any procedures or treatments discussed in this book.

Library of Congress Cataloging-in-Publication Data:

Waltz, Mitzi.
 Autistic spectrum disorders : understanding the diagnosis and getting help / by Mitzi Waltz.—
2nd ed.
  p. cm.
 Includes bibliographical references and index.
 ISBN 0-596-50013-0
 1. Autism—Patients—Rehabilitation. 2. Autism in children. I. Title.

RC553.A88 W356 2002
618.92'898203--dc21   2002066219

[M]

For Ian

Table of Contents

Preface

WHEN IAN WAS 2 YEARS OLD, he communicated with grunts, shrieks, and—only occasionally—sounds that resembled words. He insisted on watching the same videos over and over. Eye contact was hard to get, but if he wanted your attention *now*, he would literally grab your head and turn your face toward his own. He was a very cuddly, loving child at home, but seemed to shy away from intense sensations everywhere else. A trip to the grocery store was overwhelming; a visit with the dentist was impossible. His moods were mercurial, with quick laughter and equally quick temper tantrums. He was clumsy, constantly banging into furniture and falling, often with no sign of pain.

His father and I loved our beautiful little boy, but we knew something was not quite right.

Starting with his well-baby checkup at the age of 6 months, I expressed concerns about his development. The answer was as always, "Give him time—babies develop at their own rate. He's so big and healthy, and cute, too!" If you're reading this book, you've probably heard that one before. It's the answer an overanxious parent with a late bloomer needs to hear, but for many others it's false reassurance.

When Ian was almost 3, I was finally able to schedule a speech and hearing assessment at a nearby teaching hospital. His hearing was just fine, but the speech pathologist said our developmental concerns were justified. She collared a doctor in the corridor and asked him to take a look at Ian's shambling gait. "Looks like mild cerebral palsy to me," he said. "You should give Early Intervention a call." Then he walked away.

We were devastated.

Unfortunately, medical notes made at this evaluation were not shared with us at the time. We obtained them later, and found that the speech pathologist had expressed worries about Ian's social skills and eye contact as well. She thought he might be autistic—but that information was not conveyed to us or to his Early Intervention program.

Early Intervention, a service of the public schools for children with disabilities, provided Ian with an hour and a half of special education preschool three days a week. He received some speech therapy, which did seem to help jump-start his speech. He also got occupational therapy and physical therapy services. His muscles, previously hypotonic (weak and floppy), got a little stronger. The occupational therapist helped him better handle sounds, touches, and other sensations.

Meanwhile, I read everything we could find about cerebral palsy. Some things fit—the speech delay, the gait—but other things didn't. For one thing, Ian's behavior was becoming increasingly obsessional and repetitive. There was nothing in the cerebral palsy literature about toddlers who could watch a ceiling fan rotate for an hour. He was a real handful to manage, too, always into something and yet paying little attention to much of what went on around him. He went through periods where he made odd sounds or movements, and his tantrums were downright scary.

We worked for six years to finally get a real diagnosis for Ian, and when it came, it didn't explain much. He didn't have cerebral palsy after all. He was diagnosed with "pervasive developmental disorder, not otherwise specified" (PDD-NOS), a form of autism.

There was a certain relief in finally having an explanation of sorts for my son's differences, but now a new set of questions kept me up at night: What did PDD-NOS mean? Had my husband and I done something to cause Ian's problems? Was there treatment? Could he get better, or had the delay in diagnosis ruined his chances? What would his life be like?

At least a quarter of a million families in the United States alone face the same dilemma. Experts estimate that 1 out of every 1,000 children has a pervasive developmental disorder, a category of conditions also known as autistic spectrum disorders, and the numbers appear to be growing. In some areas, rates approaching 1 in 150 children have been reported—and because these conditions are twice as common in males, that translates into rates as high as 1 in 100 boys.

Of these children, one third will be diagnosed with autism itself. The rest do not meet all the diagnostic criteria for autism, but often benefit from therapeutic and educational techniques designed for autistic children.

A few notes about this book

The intention of this book is to bring together all the basic information needed by parents of a child or adult who has been diagnosed with an autistic spectrum disorder, adults with these challenges who want to gain more insight and self-help skills, and professionals working with individuals on the autistic spectrum. The first two chapters provide a broad overview of the entire family of pervasive developmental disorders, a category that includes autism and a range of related conditions. Subsequent chapters cover diagnosis, treatment, insurance, school, family issues, and building a support system.

The final two chapters of this book provide an inside look at life on the autistic spectrum, with personal narratives from affected children and adults about how they see the world; what they need from family members, professionals, and friends; and how they cope with these challenging conditions. Their perspective is unique and, in my opinion, crucially important. Information on planning for adult life with autism is included.

Several appendices provide extensive resource lists, including books, web sites, organizations, research centers, medications and supplements, and diagnostic tools. A glossary of acronyms is included as well, along with an overview of current research on the genetics of autism.

Although autistic spectrum disorders are more common in males than females, they are not exclusive to one gender. I've tried to alternate between pronouns when talking about patients.

I've done my best to provide accurate information about resources in the English-speaking world, including North America, the United Kingdom, the Republic of Ireland, Australia, and New Zealand. Autistic spectrum disorders are a universal phenomenon, however, and occur in all races and nationalities. Readers in other parts of the world may be able to find current data about local resources (including information available in languages other than English) on the Web. Many useful web sites are listed in Appendix A, *Resources*. Some information will be skewed toward North American or UK readers, but most will be useful to all.

Throughout the text I present information from the latest medical research. This information is not intended as medical advice. Please consult your physician before changing, stopping, or starting any medical treatment. Some of the health information provided comes from small studies or is controversial in nature. Neither the author nor O'Reilly & Associates endorse any particular medical or therapeutic approach, and readers are encouraged to carefully examine claims made by health care facilities, pharmaceutical firms, supplement manufacturers, therapists, and others before implementing new treatments.

The words of other parents and patients are presented throughout this book. These quotes are offset from the rest of the text and presented in italics. In many cases, the names and other identifying details have been changed at the individual's request.

Acknowledgments

Many people deserve credit for helping me create this book. My first thanks go to the many parents of children with autism and adults on the autistic spectrum who took the time to answer my questions. Your replies opened my eyes to issues I hadn't considered, and guided the structure and content of this book. I hope that the questions you asked in return have been fully answered in the text—and that this book will be helpful to you in your daily lives.

Dr. Stephen M. Edelson of the Center for the Study of Autism and Dr. Bernard Rimland of the Autism Research Institute have devoted their careers to researching the autistic spectrum and helping children with autistic spectrum disorders, and their assistance is very much appreciated. Dr. Randi Hagerman and Dr. Thomas Anders of the M.I.N.D. Institute at the University of California at Davis, Dr. Marc Potenza, Dr. Douglas Beer, Dr. Maria A. Pugliese, and Dr. Michael J. Goldberg, among others, granted me interviews. Eric Schopler and Western Psychological Services allowed me to use an excerpt from the Childhood Autism Rating Scale.

Paul Shattock, director of the Autism Research Unit at the University of Sunderland; Dr. Edelson; Dr. Stewart H. Mostofsky of the Kennedy-Kreiger Institute; and Rosemary Kessick of Allergy Induced Autism reviewed the manuscript of this book before publication. Dr. Goldberg, parent/researcher Susan Owens, parent/author Elizabeth Gerlach, and parent/education advocate Sheryl Lilly reviewed the first edition of this book, helping me correct numerous omissions and errors. I would also like to thank Bette Moske-Koski of Network for Special Education.

Everyone at O'Reilly & Associates has been wonderful to work with. Much deserved thanks go to Linda Lamb, Shawnde Paull, Deanna Blevins, Edie Freedman, and all of my publisher's extraordinarily professional editing and production staff.

Despite the inspiration and contributions of so many, any errors, omissions, misstatements, or flaws that remain are entirely my own.

Ian at age 11

Since the first edition of this book appeared three years ago, I have heard from many readers. Each shared wonderful stories about their children, and they always ask how Ian is doing these days, too. I'm happy to report that he has had a wonderful three years at a very supportive elementary school, making great strides academically and personally in a special education class.

His father and I were once told that the best we could hope for was "survival reading skills," but he's now plowing through the "Harry Potter" books like other children his age. Last year he participated in statewide academic testing and tested at or above grade level in every subject but writing, which continues to really challenge him. Perhaps more importantly, Ian's speech becomes clearer every year, and he has learned to make friends.

Last fall he embarked on a new adventure with his father and myself—we moved to England, where I am completing a doctorate in health sciences at the University of Sunderland. I'm excited about being directly involved with the work of the Autism Research Unit, but Ian is excited about seeing real Roman ruins, visiting Loch Ness, and seeing English football matches.

He's a bit disappointed that he's not going to Hogwarts School with Harry Potter, but we're very excited about his progress so far at his new school. This is the first time he's been in a regular, mainstream class, but so far he's doing well with just a little extra support. His writing has finally become legible, although he finds it hard to write more than a paragraph at once.

Few behavior problems crop up at school now, but he can still be challenging at home, especially now that adolescence is rearing its head.

In the fall, Ian will start secondary school. He fully expects to go to college, where he wants to study cryptozoology, classics, or both.

Ian has become an interesting young fellow, very bright and capable. That's my hope for all children and adults with autistic spectrum disorders—that each one can make the most of his or her special interests and talents, and that the world can be made ready to accept each one as a unique, wonderful individual.

—Mitzi Waltz
University of Sunderland
England
June 2002

If you would like to comment on this book or offer suggestions for future editions, please send email to *guides@oreilly.com,* or write to O'Reilly & Associates Inc. at 1005 Gravenstein Hwy North, Sebastopol, CA 95472, in the United States.

CHAPTER 1

The Medical Facts About Autism

AUTISM IS A LABEL OF CONVENIENCE created by psychiatrists. It is used to describe a spectrum of neurological conditions that can affect a person's speech and communication, emotional growth, social skills, and physical and mental abilities.

Researchers believe that autistic spectrum disorders (ASDs) are rooted in a complex combination of genetics, individual brain wiring, and environmental factors. As of this writing, no genetic test can predict these conditions, and doctors are not sure if anything can be done during pregnancy or infancy to prevent them. They are not caused by poor parenting, abuse, or economic deprivation. Although there is no cure, effective treatment is possible in many cases, and promising research is underway.

This chapter explains what's known about autistic spectrum disorders. It discusses the various diagnoses that come under the ASD umbrella and how they are used by physicians, including the frustrating process of diagnosis by elimination. It covers basic neurology as it relates to this topic, including differences in brain chemistry, structure, and electrical activity that may be involved. It also covers genetic and other factors, and winds up with a brief discussion of where research is heading.

A medical puzzle

Autistic spectrum disorders are a medical puzzle. Although the symptoms can be seen, they are hard to define medically or treat. They aren't the same as mental retardation or emotional disturbance, although their symptoms can mimic these conditions or coexist with them. In fact, although ASDs are classified as psychiatric conditions, they do not usually respond to the medications or talk therapies used to successfully treat other psychiatric problems.

Unfortunately, autistic spectrum disorders are not rare. For many years, the accepted rate of autism in the United States was about 1 in every 1,000 children, but this statistic has been called into question over the past decade. Recent epidemiological data indicate that the rate is approaching 1 in 150 children in some geographic areas—and because these conditions disproportionately affect boys, that means as many as 1 in 100 boys may be affected. Doctors do not agree on whether the increased rate is because of better diagnostic techniques or because of a rise in actual numbers of people with autism and related conditions, although many of the best-known autism researchers believe there is persuasive evidence for an actual increase. In particular, recent prevalence research around the world agrees that more cases of autism are occurring.[1]

Autistic disorder (autism) is the best known ASD, but less severe forms of the disorder are at least twice as common—and much more vaguely defined.

Roni, mother of 5-year-old Steve (diagnosed as having "atypical autism"), explains,

> The most frustrating thing about the diagnosis is that Stevie has mild
> [autistic] traits and is nonverbal, but he does not totally behave in the
> autistic mold. Therefore he does not fit in with certain parameters
> outlined by clinicians and school districts.

Parents of a young child with an undiagnosed ASD may suspect any number of things, from learning difficulties to severe allergies. Doctors may be just as befuddled, trying out labels such as the following:

- Atypical
- Pathologically shy or withdrawn
- Severe emotional disturbance
- Mental retardation/learning difficulties
- Developmental delay
- Autistic-like
- Autistic tendencies
- Severe communication disorder
- Developmental language disorder
- Nonverbal learning disorder
- Apraxia of speech
- Speech and/or gross motor dyspraxia
- Obsessive-compulsive disorder (OCD)
- Central auditory processing deficit (CAPD)

- Severe attention deficit disorder (ADD) or attention deficit hyperactivity disorder (ADHD)
- Deficits in attention, motor control, and perception (DAMP)
- Atypical or mild cerebral palsy

One or any combination of these terms may be used in an attempt to describe a child—or, eventually, an adult—who tends to be socially inappropriate and emotionally immature, often seems unaware of his or her surroundings, may not be able to speak or move normally, has great difficulty with social relationships, and may behave in obsessive, compulsive, repetitive, or unusual ways. These are the defining traits of autistic spectrum disorders. The final diagnosis is based on the level of severity and impairment, as well as on any information the family can provide about possible causes.

For example, Cindy, mother of 15-year-old Jeff, is still searching for a diagnosis for her son, whose autistic traits may be secondary to brain damage:

> When Jeffrey was 4 years old, a pediatric neurologist wrote "static encephalopathy." When he was 7 years old, another pediatric neurologist wrote "bilateral brain damage with secondary mental retardation." Just this month, I had a PhD in the psychiatric department review Jeff's history, test results, school and medical records, interview him, and interview me. He wrote in his report "typical of autism." That's as close as I am at this time.

The problem with labels

Neither autistic spectrum disorder nor its official synonym, pervasive developmental disorder, is a very descriptive term. "Autistic spectrum disorder" implies a definite relationship with so-called classical autism, which may be misleading for someone who has Rett syndrome (described later in this chapter), for example. The word "pervasive" isn't quite accurate, because individuals are usually not affected in every aspect of their lives or every body function. "Developmental" is a bit of a misnomer as well, because the problem doesn't really lie in how or how fast the person's abilities are manifested. On the one hand, there may be true delays in the emergence of speech, physical capabilities, social relationships, or emotional function. On the other hand, some abilities may never appear at all. Each person on the autistic spectrum is an individual with a unique pattern of symptoms, and no diagnostic label can really capture that fact.

Eight-year-old Theron has been diagnosed with pervasive developmental disorder, not otherwise specified (PDD-NOS); psychotic disorder; and borderline intellectual functioning. His mother, Ann, puts it this way:

> The most frustrating thing about his diagnosis was that it was put
> to me like it was the end of the world. He'd never do this, or that. And
> PDD-NOS is not an answer. It's too vague. He fit all the criteria for
> autism. [PDD-NOS] didn't come with a set of instructions.

Most doctors who have worked with people on the autistic spectrum for a long time know that there are wide variations and many subtypes, most of which have not yet been defined and named. At least some subtypes probably fall into the newly proposed diagnostic categories of multisystem neurological disorders or regulatory disorders, both championed by Dr. Stanley Greenspan and his allies in the fields of child psychiatry, psychology, and neurology. (You'll find Greenspan's excellent books listed in Appendix A, *Resources*.) These categories haven't won official acceptance yet, but they're a closer fit for many than the existing terms.

Defining autistic spectrum disorders (ASDs)

In the US, "pervasive developmental disorder" is the official term used to describe ASDs. It appears in the *Diagnostic and Statistical Manual of Mental Disorders* (the *DSM*), a regularly updated book used by psychiatrists and other physicians to define psychiatric conditions.

Perhaps ASDs shouldn't be in the *DSM* at all. Other neurological disorders, such as epilepsy and Alzheimer's disease, are considered medical issues, despite the effects they can have on behavior or thought. But for reasons that are unclear, our medical system has chosen to set the brain apart from all other organs of the body. When your heart isn't working properly, you go to see a medical doctor. When your brain is not functioning well, the first person you probably see is a counselor, social worker, psychologist, or psychiatrist. Of these, only the psychiatrist is an MD. Many other professionals still seem to believe that because the brain can think, all its ailments, too, can be controlled through better thinking.

When it comes to autism, this faulty conclusion has led to horrific results. Fifty years ago, the now discredited theories of Bruno Bettelheim held sway among doctors who saw patients with ASDs. Bettelheim believed that emotionally unavailable or abusive parents created autistic children. Parents were encouraged (and sometimes forced) to institutionalize children with autism and similar conditions. The institutions were unable to do much to help these children, but Bettelheim and other doctors claimed that was because irreparable damage had already been done in infancy.

A few doctors and social workers still hold such theories—and if you should happen to encounter one, run away quickly! Ancient research is still trotted out occasionally and used to attack parents, but there's not a shred of expert support for such theories anymore. Although medical science has not definitively identified the factors that cause ASDs, it is known that parenting style is not one of them. Extreme child abuse and neglect can cause symptoms that could be mistaken for autism—for example, the incessant self-rocking sometimes seen in understaffed orphanages where infants are left to fend for themselves—but that's an entirely separate issue.

It's certain that genetic inheritance plays a prominent role in autism, but only some children in families with a history of autistic spectrum disorders end up having difficulties. It's definitely not as simple as just inheriting a gene, or even a couple of genes. Many researchers believe that the genes involved usually convey only a sus-ceptibility, and that it then takes something else—an infectious disease, immune system problems, allergies, perhaps even exposure to heavy metals or environmental pollution—to make symptoms emerge.

In this model, autistic spectrum disorders resemble diabetes. A few people have an inherited insulin deficiency that always leads to diabetes in early childhood. Others inherit a strong genetic susceptibility to diabetes, experiencing it as an autoimmune condition set off by environmental factors such as diet. Others become diabetic almost entirely because of a combination of poor diet and advancing age, although a weak genetic susceptibility may also play a part. Although autistic spectrum dis-orders almost always start before the age of 3, the picture of how and why they occur is probably equally varied, if not more so.

A crash course in neurology

The brain is the most complex and least understood organ in the body. It is the focal point of the central nervous system (the CNS), which also includes the nerves of the spine. The CNS receives, processes, and sends billions of signals every day by way of chemicals and electrical impulses. Neurologists (physicians who specialize in studying and treating brain disorders) are only starting to identify how these processes work, and what is known right now can be woefully inadequate when something goes awry.

Most of the medical information presented in this chapter is derived from studies of people with the most severe forms of autism. The findings are believed to apply across the entire spectrum, although there are differences according to the severity of each individual's symptoms. There may also be some special, as yet unknown, factors involved in various ASDs.

Brain structure basics

The brain has several parts, all of which work together to control body functions, produce thought and emotion, and store and retrieve memories (see Figure 1-1). Researchers are not even sure which parts of the central nervous system are affected by ASDs, although a clearer picture is emerging every year.

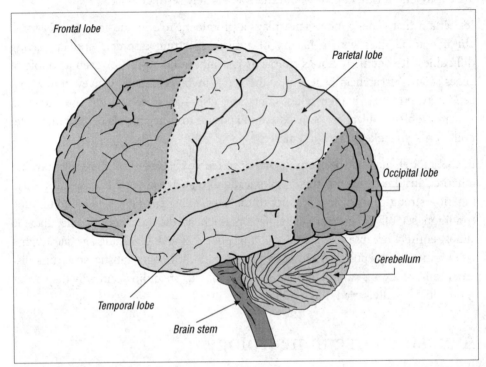

Figure 1-1. Parts of the human brain

The brain is mostly made up of two kinds of cells. The first kind, neurons, do the hard work of transmitting information. The second, glial cells, are twice as numerous as neurons. Glial cells have the less glamorous jobs of making sure the neurons have enough nutrients and other chemicals, repairing the brain if it is injured, and confronting bacteria and viruses that may try to attack the brain. Obviously, problems with either type of cell could be involved in ASDs, and if one type of cell is affected, that would change how the other type functions as well.

Brain differences in ASDs

There are only two ways to find out whether the brains of people with autism differ from the average in any way: scanning the brains of living people, and examining the brains of people with autism who have died. These two methods provide different types of information. Brain scans can provide some information about structure, but can also show chemical and electrical processes. Autopsies reveal more detailed information about structure, including cell structure.

As autism is not a deadly condition, there have been few autopsy studies. Some brain autopsies have indicated differences at the cell level in the brains of people with autism. Neurons in the limbic system of the brain seem to be smaller and closer together, whereas neurons in other areas of the brain may be larger or smaller than usual. The cerebellum appears to have fewer Purkinje cells, a particular type of neuron.[2] Differences seen in autopsies may depend on the age of the person, with brains from autistic children tending to be larger than normal and brains from autistic adults smaller than usual.

One 1997 autopsy study did find damaged areas in the brain stems of people with autism, which could explain the higher-than-normal number of minor ear malformations in this population as well. This study was spurred by the observation that when pregnant women used the dangerous drug Thalidomide, to prevent morning sickness, one third of the children exposed to it in the womb between the 20th and 24th day of fetal development were later diagnosed as autistic. Both the brain stem and the ears form during this four-day period.[3]

Another current theory is that the development of some brain cells or structures is slower than normal or never completed in people with ASDs, or conversely, that there are problems with the normal "pruning" process during brain development.[4] Pruning is what occurs when unused brain cells or circuits are discarded.

Very recently, researchers using computerized tomography (CT, or CAT, for computerized axial tomography), magnetic resonance imagery (MRI), and single-photon-emission computed tomography (SPECT or NeuroSPECT) scans have looked for subtle differences in the brains of living people with autism. Although these technologies can't be used to diagnose ASDs just yet, early reports indicate that the parietal, temporal, and occipital lobes are larger in volume than expected, and that there are signs of unusual activity patterns. There may also be differences in the size of the cerebellum.[5]

Researchers are careful to say that certain types of brain damage, such as lesions on the temporal lobe or damage caused by infection, can cause "autistic-like" symptoms.

Although research continues into differences in brain structure, most doctors are more concerned with how the brain actually functions. It's a pretty adaptable organ, after all—with proper medical care, people can often recover from strokes, accidents, or illnesses that cause brain damage, because the brain is built to route around problems whenever possible. It seems that where ASDs are concerned, relatively minor structural or chemical differences may be influencing how brain cells communicate with each other, with the CNS, and with the body as a whole. Learning more about these differences may help researchers develop new treatments as well as improving medical knowledge.

Neurotransmitters: The brain's telephone system

Neurons are the brain's internal communication centers, but they don't trade messages directly. Neurons have a central cell body with long "arms" called axons, and smaller tentaclelike structures called dendrites (see Figure 1-2). Inside a neuron, all the messages are sent via electrical impulses. Where two neurons meet to swap information, however, there's a small space between them called the synaptic cleft. Electrical impulses have to be translated into neurotransmitters, chemicals that cross the synaptic cleft and are then retranslated into electrical signals on the other side (see Figure 1-3).Much has been learned by accident about the role of neurotransmitters in ASDs. For example, autistic symptoms improved in some patients when they were taking medicines for something else, such as depression. Targeted studies of medications now indicate that several kinds of neurotransmitters have something to do with ASDs.

Many different neurotransmitters are at work in the human brain and body. Neurotransmitters are site-specific chemicals that can be absorbed only by certain cells and at certain spots. This site-specific absorption ensures that only the right kinds of messages get through. Neurotransmitters are also used and absorbed differently in various areas of the body, and sometimes turned into other kinds of chemicals.

Neurotransmitters that appear involved with ASDs are described as follows:

- **Serotonin.** Serotonin, also called 5-hydroxytryptamine or 5-HT, controls sleep, mood, some types of sensory perception, body temperature regulation, and appetite. It affects the rate at which hormones are released and has something to do with inflammation. Studies have shown that autistic people tend to have increased amounts of serotonin in their blood.[6] They may produce, absorb, or metabolize serotonin differently, although researchers are still trying to determine how.

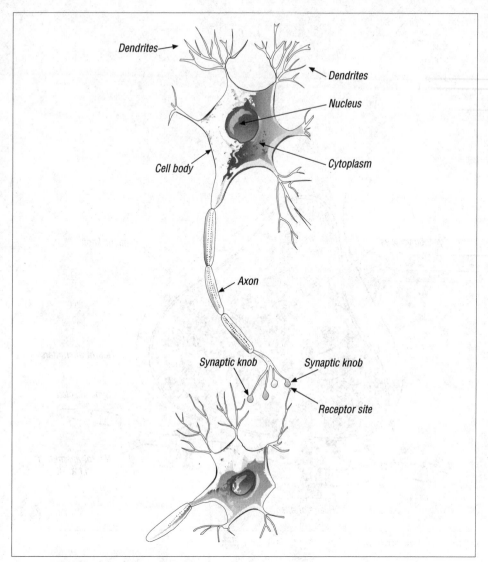

Figure 1-2. The structure of a neuron

- **Dopamine**. Dopamine, sometimes abbreviated as DA, helps control body movements and thought patterns, and also regulates how hormones are released. Although medications that block dopamine have been useful to some people with autism, researchers are not sure why.[7] Perhaps there are differences in how these people create or use dopamine.

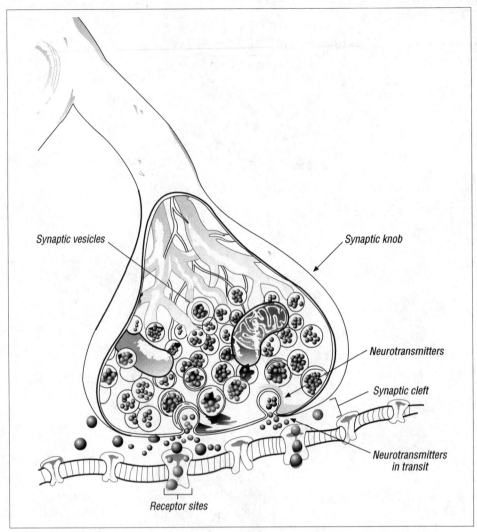

Synaptic vesicles

Synaptic knob

Neurotransmitters

Synaptic cleft

Neurotransmitters
in transit

Receptor sites

Figure 1-3. Neurotransmitters crossing the synaptic cleft

- **Norepinephrine.** Norepinephrine is used by both the CNS and the peripheral sympathetic nervous system (the nerves that communicate with the rest of the body). It governs arousal, the "fight or flight" response, anxiety, and memory. There seem to be small differences in how autistic people make and process norepinephrine.[8]

Medications that change how much of certain neurotransmitters are produced, or how these chemicals are absorbed in the brain, produce changes in autistic symptoms—that's one of the clues that have let researchers know which chemicals have something to do with the condition. These medicines don't cure the underlying disorder, but in some people they can create major improvements in behavior and emotional stability. See Chapter 5, *Medical Interventions,* and Appendix E, *Medication Reference,* for more information about these medications and how they work. Physical activity, exercise, diet, vitamins, and herbal supplements can also affect these neurotransmitters. That's one of the reasons you need to be as careful about choosing alternative treatments as you are about prescription drugs. For more information about nonpharmaceutical treatments for ASDs, see Chapter 6, *Therapeutic Interventions,* and Chapter 7, *Other Interventions.*

Electrical miswiring

The brain's electrical system is intimately intertwined with its chemical messaging system. Problems can occur when uncontrolled surges of electricity, called seizures, take place inside the brain. Seizure disorders (epilepsy) are common in people with autism. By young adulthood, between a quarter and a third of autistic people have experienced identifiable physical seizures.[9]

Many more people with ASDs may experience other types of seizures, some of which are hard to recognize, even with sophisticated monitoring equipment. For example, some doctors believe that the inexplicable temper tantrums some people with ASDs have may be related to seizures occurring deep within the frontal lobe.

If seizures are suspected, you should see a neurologist. Neurologists usually rely on evidence gathered from an electroencephalogram (EEG). Unfortunately, EEG equipment is not sensitive enough to easily detect all types of seizures in all parts of the brain. Chapter 2, *Categorizing Autistic Spectrum Disorders,* and Chapter 5 present more information about the connection between seizures and autistic spectrum disorders, and explain how seizure disorders are treated.

Genetics and ASDs

Autistic spectrum disorders do run in families, but although the genetic connection is fairly strong, the pattern of inheritance is unknown. Many parents of children diagnosed with ASDs recognize a little of themselves when they look at their child's symptoms, or can recall close relatives who seem to have been somewhere on the autistic spectrum.

Often parents worry about whether their other children will also have an ASD. The current wisdom is that parents of a child with autism have a 3 to 4.5 percent chance of having a second child with autism, about 50 times the normal risk.[10] Other studies have indicated that a greater number of autistic children's siblings have some degree of autistic tendencies, rather than autism per se.[11] In some cases there are no known relatives with even mild autistic tendencies.

Several teams of researchers around the world are searching for genes that contribute to autistic spectrum disorders. In 1997, one group of genetic researchers announced that the first of the three to five genes believed to cause most autistic spectrum disorders had been tentatively located on chromosomes 7 and 16.[12] A genetic mutation associated with speech and communication disorders, and particularly with apraxia of speech, has also been located on the same general area of chromosome 7 previously linked to autism.[13] Appendix D, *The Genetics of Autism,* shows current findings from genetic research in graph form.

One distinctive ASD subtype, Rett syndrome, is caused by a defective gene on the X chromosome. One identified gene, called MeCP2, plays an important part in brain development before birth. Because males have only one X chromosome, it appears that inheriting the MeCP2 gene is such a catastrophic event that such males rarely survive to birth. With two X chromosomes, females can carry the gene without developing symptoms (if the faulty copy is turned off), or may have symptoms ranging from mild to severe.[14] Chapter 2 provides more information about Rett syndrome.

Although the Rett syndrome gene itself is found in only one subgroup, the way it works may provide clues about other autistic spectrum disorders. For example, about 20 percent of people with Rett syndrome–like symptoms do not have the MeCP2 gene.[15]

Several genetic disorders are known to be associated directly with autism. Of these, fragile X syndrome (FRAXA) and tuberous sclerosis are probably the most important. Somewhere between 2.5 and 10 percent of people with autism have a fragile site on their X chromosome.[16] These individuals usually have some degree of mental retardation, and their autistic features are a little different from those of others on the spectrum. When neurologists suggest genetic screening for children they suspect may be autistic, what they are usually checking for is FRAXA.

Tuberous sclerosis is a relatively rare disorder (about 1 out of 6,000 people) that affects the brain, the skin, the eyes, and other organs of the body with varying degrees of severity. As many as half of all children diagnosed with tuberous sclerosis have autistic features. Most have epilepsy, and many are mentally retarded. Tuberous sclerosis can be caused by two different genetic defects, one on chromosome 9 and one on chromosome 16. Only one of these genes is necessary to cause the condition, although unknown genetic or environmental factors may also determine who develops the disorder. The link between tuberous sclerosis and autism may be physical rather than genetic. A 1997 study published in the medical journal *Lancet* stated that patients with both tuberous sclerosis and an ASD whose brains were imaged had tubers (a tumorlike growth characteristic of tuberous sclerosis) in their temporal lobes, and had more tubers in their brains in general than those patients without autistic features.[17]

Two genetic disorders caused by mutations on chromosome 15, Prader-Willi syndrome and Angelman syndrome, also correlate with autism and other ASDs. These are discussed briefly in Chapter 2. Some children with duplicated areas on chromosome 15 also have autistic features.

Several other neurological disorders occur more frequently in people with ASDs and their relatives than in the general population. Affective disorders—depression and bipolar disorder (manic depression)—are especially high in these families. Other problems reported more often include ADD/ADHD, phobias and other anxiety disorders, obsessive-compulsive disorder, and Tourette's syndrome. All these conditions are believed to be associated with genetic differences, but the genes have not been definitively identified for any of them. Direct genetic or functional relationships to ASDs may eventually be found, or these links may turn out to be circumstantial.

Genes can cause the brain to develop or work in ways that are outside the norm, and they also affect how the rest of the body works, including the endocrine (hormonal), metabolic, and immune systems. The late autism researcher Dr. Reed Warren's work suggested that some of the genes connected to autism might control immune system function.[18]

When researchers finally find all the genes that contribute to autism and related conditions, it may be possible to develop screening tests—although using such tests will certainly raise ethical issues. It may also be possible to develop some sort of gene therapy that could actually cure ASDs, although today this type of medicine is only in its infancy. More likely, understanding how these genetic differences actually affect people may help researchers design treatments that address things such as metabolic or immune system problems.

Other factors

Although genetic predisposition is almost surely a precurser to ASDs, other factors may also play a part. These may also be genetically based, or they may be purely environmental. Factors linked to ASDs include metabolic differences, gastrointestinal problems, infection, and exposure to toxins.

Although much is not yet known about these factors, parents may be heartened to know that researchers and advocacy groups are investigating these links.

It has long been noted that gastrointestinal (GI) problems, chronic diarrhea (sometimes alternating with constipation), and food intolerances or allergies are much more common in people with ASDs. This may mean that metabolic differences are involved. Because metabolism and digestion have genetic roots, are linked to the body's neurotransmitter system, and can be disrupted by a number of other factors, this is not necessarily a separate issue—but improved understanding of how metabolic differences affect people on the autistic spectrum can contribute to new treatment possibilities.

Amy, mother of 7-year-old Jared, is one of many parents who have observed these clues and noted their relationship to other issues, such as immune system function:

> We always knew, because of observing our son, that all of his behavioral difficulties were something metabolic—problems happened right after eating.
>
> Jared also has a history of heavy antibiotic use. At 11 months old, he had an infected benign tumor on his tongue. He developed a massive staph infection throughout his body, and was on a very strong antibiotic for a full year. All of his developmental problems occurred after that.

Among the metabolic disorders known to be associated with autistic features are phenylketonuria (PKU), histidinemia, and Lesch-Nyhan syndrome. In the US and Europe, PKU tests are routinely given to newborns. Tests are available for the other two metabolic disorders mentioned, although they are rare enough that physicians are reluctant to order testing without additional evidence.

Environmental factors, such as infection and exposure to toxins, probably play a role as well. Children who inherit particular types of genetic fragility may respond to certain kinds of bacteria, viruses, or toxins in unusual ways. For example, a recent study at the National Institutes of Health (NIH), which is discussed further in Chapter 5, has found a link between obsessive-compulsive disorder and Tourette's syndrome (a tic disorder) in some children infected with the same common streptococcus bacteria that cause strep throat or ear infections.[19] Members of the NIH research team think this link may extend to some children with ASDs, and an early look at this population indicates that they are correct.[20]

There are also many anecdotal reports of infection during pregnancy with rubella, herpes, Epstein-Barr virus, cytomegalovirus, HIV (human immunodeficiency virus, which leads to AIDS), and other agents, followed by the birth of children with ASDs.[21] Other parents have reported that autistic features emerged after an illness in infancy or early childhood, or shortly after vaccination.[22,23] When blood tests are done, some children with autism turn out to have surprisingly high levels of heavy metals, such as mercury or lead.

A recent study found correlations between significant levels of antibodies to the measles virus (measles-IgG) or the common human herpes virus (HHV-6-IgG) and/ or the presence of antibodies to the person's own myelin basic protein (anti-MBP) and/or neuron axon filament protein (anti-NAFP) in autistic subjects. Not all people with autistic spectrum disorders have these antibodies, but in those who do, it indicates the possibility of an autoimmune disorder that may be triggered by a virus or vaccine.[24] Dr. Andrew Wakefield's research in the UK has also implicated the measles/mumps/rubella (MMR) vaccine in regressive autism acccompanied by severe GI tract problems.[25]

There have been a number of reports linking ASDs with other environmental factors, ranging from cocaine use during pregnancy to living near centers of industrial pollution.[26] There's no proof, but these links may hold true for individual cases. The recent identification of possible geographic ASD clusters raises the ominous possibility that at least some cases may be caused or exacerbated by unknown environmental or infectious factors.[27]

You are not alone

Autism and related disorders affect at least a quarter of a million people in the US, one third of whom are children. According to researchers, there may be as many as twice that number who fit the diagnostic criteria, but who remain undiagnosed or misdiagnosed. Extrapolate these numbers to get a worldwide figure, and you can see that ASDs are not a minor medical problem.

There are probably other families in your community who are experiencing the same challenges that you face. It can be hard to connect, because the behaviors associated with ASDs can keep families isolated from each other. But even people who live in remote areas of the world can now make contact by joining support groups, subscribing to newsletters, or using the Internet. Chapter 10, *Family Issues and Support,* focuses on building these connections, which are essential for families, people with ASDs, and professionals who work with this population as well.

You can help

Parents are sometimes afraid to ask the question that keeps them awake at night: What will happen to my child? Teens and adults with ASDs may feel discouraged about their future in the world as well. At this time there is no cure for any form of autistic spectrum disorder, but there are medications, therapies, and educational techniques that address symptoms and improve the lives of people with ASDs. In some cases, the results can be spectacular—although subtle deficits and differences will probably remain, the properly treated individual can live a rich, enjoyable, and independent life.

For parents like Roni, that is the main goal:

> My hopes for Stevie are that he reaches adulthood and is able to
> function on his own, make his own decisions, hold down a job, drive
> a car (which he tries to do now at age 5), and have the communications
> abilities to enable him to do this.

As for the residual differences, who wants a world of cookie-cutter humans? People on the autistic spectrum are all unique and wonderful individuals, many with special talents to share, and each with a right to be accepted just as he or she is.

Today, only about one third of those diagnosed with an autistic spectrum disorder achieve full independence as adults, but that statistic is changing rapidly. Because of accumulating medical knowledge, new types of education programs, and the efforts of determined advocates for children and adults with disabilities, we are going to make the future much brighter for newly diagnosed children—and adults with ASDs will also benefit from these developments.

Adults with autism and related conditions are now working together to improve their status. Through support groups, web sites, online discussion groups, and self-advocacy work, they are trying to access better medical care, accept their differences, and find opportunities to use their often considerable abilities.

Best of all, current research into the possible causes of ASDs may hold the secret to real healing. Interest in the medical and research communities is growing, as evidenced by the National Institutes of Health's intensive, multiple-site autism research program, increased research-grant awards for autism-related studies around the world, and improved information about these disorders in medical textbooks.

It's important to keep abreast of the latest research into autistic spectrum disorders. There probably won't be one big breakthrough, but many small steps can lead to the same destination as one giant leap.

CHAPTER 2

Categorizing Autistic Spectrum Disorders

THIS BOOK BEGAN BY EXPLAINING what the autistic spectrum disorders are in general. This chapter gets down to specifics. If you're trying to make sense of a diagnosis, this chapter can help.

Along with autistic disorder (autism), the autistic spectrum disorders include Asperger's syndrome, childhood disintegrative disorder, fragile X syndrome, Rett syndrome, and "pervasive developmental disorder, not otherwise specified" (PDD-NOS). Some doctors use other diagnoses, particularly atypical autism or autistic spectrum disorder. This chapter describes each of these in some detail.

This chapter also describes other conditions that share some symptoms with the autistic spectrum disorders. These may need to be ruled out before a diagnosis is made, although these conditions may also coexist. Finally, it offers a brief discussion of diagnostic categories under development that may more accurately describe some individuals.

About categories and labels

The diagnostic merry-go-round is incredibly frustrating. It's especially hard to wait for another appointment, another referral, another opinion, when you feel that the opportunity to help a child is slipping away with every passing day.

It might seem that categorization doesn't do much in the here and now, but it's actually a very important task. A great deal of information is now available about helping people with ASDs, but there are such large differences between people on the spectrum that one-size-fits-all treatments are a mistake. It could be that people with one subtype will respond amazingly well to a particular medication, whereas others do not. Another subtype may respond to a special diet, whereas others do best with other therapies.

Incorrect diagnosis, however, can lead to incorrect—or even harmful—medical treatment.

Strategies and medications that work with specific symptoms can be used across the spectrum, no matter what subtype a person has been diagnosed with. For example, if a child with Asperger's syndrome is repetitively hitting herself in the head to the point of injury—a behavior more common in people with autistic disorder—methods used to stop this activity in more impaired autistic people might be just the thing to try. Getting the right diagnosis is important, but when it comes to treatment, you have to look at the person and his or her actual symptoms, not just the label.

Today's labels are also far too general. Each person with an autistic spectrum disorder diagnosis is neurologically impaired in one or more ways, but other systems may be unaffected. The degree of impact can also vary from mild to severe. For example, one person may have a severe speech delay but only mild social deficits, whereas another may be unable to form social attachments at all but may have relatively normal speech patterns.

As you read through these descriptions, you may notice that only parts of these diagnoses apply. A child may have the kind of topic fixations you'd expect with Asperger's syndrome, for instance, but also have a significant speech delay. Unless a person meets all the criteria for one of the specified ASDs, proper practice is to place him or her in the PDD-NOS (or atypical autism/autistic spectrum disorder) category.

Doctors and other professionals also use terms such as "high functioning" and "low functioning" to distinguish between people with autistic disorder. Most clinicians define "low functioning" autism as being nonverbal, having some degree of mental retardation, and perhaps having "difficult" behaviors or problems with toileting and other basic self-care skills. Most clinicians define "high functioning" autism as having an adequate amount of functional speech or the ability to use some other method of communication, some social ability, and at least basic self-care skills—although another clinician might call this picture PDD-NOS. There is no set definition for these terms, so if you are not sure what they mean, ask the person who is using them.

Finally, someone may start out with one diagnosis, such as autistic disorder, and end up with another one several years later when new symptoms emerge or old ones disappear. In many cases a very young child diagnosed with autistic disorder later "moves up" to PDD-NOS, atypical autism, or even no ASD diagnosis at all. Sometimes the first diagnosis was simply wrong, but other times the person has made truly remarkable progress. That's what parents and professionals are all hoping for, and, with luck, studying these cases can show the way to that goal.

Autistic symptoms can also get worse. This is particularly true when severe or untreated seizure activity occurs. In addition, if an individual with ASD suffers neglect or abuse, as has happened to many institutionalized children, a promising future becomes less likely—although it is never too late to try.

One family's experience

One family's long journey toward diagnosis took four years of trekking from doctor to doctor. Seven-year-old Joshua was given the following diagnoses:

- PDD-NOS. "The psychologist who gave this diagnosis said Joshua would probably never be able to live independently," says his mother, Krista.

- Disturbed. "The HMO child psychiatrist who gave this diagnosis had white plastic bags full of sweets all over his office floor," Krista notes, with more than a touch of residual ire in her voice.

- Severe communication disorder, ADHD (attention deficit hyperactive disorder), and possible Tourette's syndrome. "The developmental pediatrician and neuropsychologist at Children's Hospital gave this diagnosis, saying that PDD was wrong, that they'd seen specialized cases like Joshua's enough to know," Krista says.

- Rolandic epilepsy.

- Receptive and expressive language aphasia, central nervous system dysfunction, and ADHD.

In the past four years, Joshua has been through many medication trials, including stimulants, antidepressants, antipsychotics, and other drugs, none of them particularly helpful. He has undergone tests for allergies, metabolic disorders, chromosome abnormalities, hearing problems, and seizures.

Joshua sees a speech therapist, an occupational therapist, an adaptive PE (physical education) specialist, and a behaviorist, and is taught by a special education teacher. He attends school in a mainstream second-grade class. He has been variously described as intelligent, easily distracted, obsessional, unusual, sweet-natured, and overly emotional.

Krista explains,

> *Aside from the extreme attentional problems, the most difficult*
> *thing to deal with is his extreme variability. On good days, he does*

everything well: reads well, talks well, takes disappointment well.
On bad days, he can't do anything. He can't talk, he can't read, he
can't tolerate frustration, he can't perform at all. Everyone who works
with him knows this is a child with a great deal of potential who
presents different facets of himself as puzzles that are unresolved and
unaccounted for, bewildering.

How do you label a child like Joshua? It isn't enough to enumerate the symptoms and then say, "Let's just think of him as Josh."

George is the father of 6-year-old Jeremy, diagnosed with PDD-NOS. He says,

What does having [the description of his condition as] "just Jeremy"
do for my son? Are there schools for "just Jeremy"? Is anyone
developing medications for "just Jeremy"? I do see him as an
individual first—he's my son. But the rest of the world can't and
won't. I want to make sure he gets as much help as we can get him.

Autistic spectrum disorders defined

These ASDs are listed in alphabetic order, not according to how common they are or their severity. You may also want to see Appendix G, *Diagnostic Tools,* which includes questionnaires and rating scales that professionals use to make a diagnosis.

When faced with a difficult diagnosis, less experienced professionals sometimes use videos that illustrate typical behaviors associated with each autistic disorder. The wringing hand movements seen in girls with Rett syndrome, for example, are much easier to recognize once you've actually seen them. Medical libraries or a local organization for families coping with autism may have a video diagnostic aid available.

Most doctors are careful to avoid misdiagnosis whenever possible, but accuracy depends on how many patients on the autistic spectrum they've seen, whether or not they keep up to date on research, and how comfortable they are with the admittedly limited DSM-IV criteria.

Some doctors are quick to say "autistic" where another might prefer "atypical," simply because they feel they know it when they see it, or because they don't think "atypical" gives families enough information to plan treatment. Some doctors don't have the background to hazard a guess at all.

Dr. Stephen M. Edelson, director of the Center for the Study of Autism in Salem, Oregon, observes,

> *Most pediatricians don't know what autism is. Many physicians are*
> *afraid to use the word "autism," but all of the parents I've talked to*
> *say they want to know the truth.*

As a result, some people who probably meet all the criteria for autistic spectrum disorders receive a more vague diagnosis than they should.

The following sections describe each ASD. They are in alphabetical order, not arranged by severity or rate of frequency.

Asperger's syndrome

Asperger's syndrome is also called Asperger's disorder, and often abbreviated to AS. Some people with AS call themselves "Aspies" for short.

Asperger's syndrome is characterized by strong interests in a limited number of subjects or activities, interests that become full-fledged obsessions, and by extreme difficulty in understanding social cues and building relationships with others. People with AS are rarely retarded and are often quite intelligent. However, social skills just don't come naturally to them. They don't seem to have language delays; in fact, many are very early talkers and early readers (a symptom known as hyperlexia). Most do have speech differences, most noticeably a tendency to lecture endlessly on topics of special interest like a pedantic "little professor." Some, but not all, are physically awkward.

Serena, mother of 9-year-old Tom, describes her son:

> *Tom has an odd way of walking and moving. He loves to shoot*
> *hoops with his older brother, but he's very uncoordinated. He has a*
> *passion for insects that borders on the bizarre. Remember the scene in*
> Close Encounters of the Third Kind *where the Richard Dreyfuss*
> *character just had to build the model of that mountain? That's Tom in*
> *full effect.*

Many people with AS are highly successful in careers, such as computer programming and engineering, that both minimize contact with other people and make use of their special interests. Others find their progress hampered by social difficulties, or by additional conditions such as depression and severe anxiety, which are fairly common in this group.

Atypical autism

The condition named atypical autism is also called atypical PDD, autistic tendencies, autistic-like behavior, or merely "atypical."

Atypical autism is most often used to describe a child whose symptoms resemble Asperger's syndrome, but who doesn't meet all the criteria, such as a child with extreme topic obsessions but also a severe speech delay. It is also applied to people who have a mix of normal features and autistic-like behavior. For example, a child may show age-appropriate behavior and skills at most times, but occasionally revert to rocking, show tantrum behavior, and have stereotypic movements that are consistent with autism.

Jennifer, mother of 3-year-old Joseph, is as mystified by her "atypical" son's characteristics as his doctors are:

> *What do you do when your child stumps the experts? My son still doesn't have a diagnosis because no one, educator or doctor, can find anything that really fits. I guess that's why they sometimes just have to call it atypical autism.*
>
> *The most frustrating part is not knowing what the future holds or even what the true diagnosis is. Some days it seems like it would be easier if he had a condition that was visible at birth or could be determined by blood test. These atypical autisms are largely invisible, and the behavioral symptoms shift constantly. He'll have a good few weeks, and I start to doubt the diagnosis, and think that maybe the social problems are secondary to a language disorder and will disappear as his language improves. Other times it seems like he's from another planet. It's a roller coaster that never ends.*
>
> *It has been a source of tension in the family because, with my son at least, diagnosis is not clear-cut. He is not classically autistic and is, in fact, very affectionate and related to his family, both immediate and extended. There are those in the family who think nothing is wrong and we are stigmatizing him by seeking help, and others who think he is just poorly disciplined and out of control.*

The terms "atypical autism" and "atypical PDD" are used interchangeably by some diagnosticians. It's very likely that some children who do not meet the usual criteria for autism may be part of subtypes that have not yet been fully delineated.

Autistic disorder

Autistic disorder is what most people think of as autism, and is also called classical autism or Kanner's syndrome. Some people with autism call themselves "Auties" for short.

Autism is a neurological disorder that features marked impairment in social interaction and communication, as well as restricted, repetitive patterns of behavior, activities, or interests. It is often, but not always, accompanied by some degree of mental retardation. When the term "low-functioning autism" is used, retardation is generally present and symptoms are usually more difficult to remedy. High-functioning autism blends into PDD-NOS territory, with autistic traits less prominent and capabilities higher.

Some children with autism are different from birth. Others seem to be developing normally for a year or two, then either stop making progress or even regress by losing previous skills.

Lynda, mother of 8-year-old Candy, says,

> We had suspected that Candy was autistic since she was a baby. When that was confirmed by testing, we found out at the same time that she's moderately mentally retarded. She walks on her toes most of the time and usually avoids eye contact, but she does have relationships with people, on her own terms, anyway. Definitely with us and with her classroom aide.
>
> She is very sensitive to certain sounds, to clothes, and to many other physical sensations. She used to hit her ears over and over because noises drove her crazy, but now she wears headphones and they help. When she was a toddler, her favorite "game" was lining up stuffed animals on her bed for hours on end. If you interrupted, she would tantrum.
>
> She seems to enjoy using a computer at home and at school, and has begun to say a few words. She also tries to communicate in other ways at least some of the time, including using the signs for "potty" and "eat." It's been a tough fight, but we are thrilled with even these small steps. If she can go from nonverbal to verbal, and from no eye contact to limited eye contact with certain people, we know she can do even more.

With intensive help, children with autism can often improve a great deal. Some will make such gains that the diagnosis will no longer apply. Others don't respond to treatment—and no one knows why.

About half of children with autism respond very well to intensive behavioral intervention, some are helped by medications, and others seem to make progress with special diets, vitamin supplements, or occupational therapy that includes sensory integration work. This indicates that, as with the other ASDs, there is probably no single cause for autism. No single treatment will work for everyone, but with early diagnosis, therapeutic intervention, and lots of love, slow and steady improvement is the norm.

Childhood disintegrative disorder

Childhood disintegrative disorder is a heartbreaking mystery. Most parents notice that something is different about babies or toddlers later diagnosed with an ASD. But not with this variant, in which the losses occur sometime before 5 years of age, but after a time of seemingly normal development. Although many of these children can be helped with the same interventions used for autism, studies have shown that others tend to get worse with time instead of better, despite efforts at intensive therapy.

Elena, mother of 5-year-old Armando, was shocked by his rapid regression:

> Until a year ago, Armando had a great sense of humor, a mischievous smile, and a nonstop motor mouth. He spoke in full sentences, had regular conversations with me and his brothers, and played every day. But around last January, something happened. He began to "lose" words, and talked less and less. We would find him rocking in the corner, or hiding under the sofa cushions instead of playing outside. He threw tantrums whenever his routines changed. He no longer speaks, he doesn't want to be held, eye contact has all but disappeared. He doesn't even seem to care that we're here.

It seems likely that childhood disintegrative disorder has a different cause from other ASDs, although it hasn't been found. This disorder could be caused by some sort of virus, for example, or by undetected seizures that cause brain damage or scramble how the child interprets the world (see the discussion of Landau-Kleffner syndrome later in this chapter).

Fragile X syndrome

Fragile X syndrome is also called Martin-Bell syndrome, and may be abbreviated as FRAXA.

Fragile X syndrome is the most common inherited form of mental retardation, occurring in about 1 in 2,000 males and a smaller percentage of females. It is diagnosed with a genetic test that looks for one or more breaks in a particular spot on the X chromosome.

About one third of fragile X boys show ASD-like characteristics. Some meet the full criteria for autism, but most tend toward the milder end of the spectrum.

Male patients have a characteristic fragile X "look." Often this clue helps physicians make an early diagnosis. As with autistic disorder, the degree of impairment depends a lot on the degree of mental retardation.

Peter, father of 12-year-old Benny, tells about his son:

> Benny is mildly retarded, but he gets along okay. He goes to a regular school, and he gets extra help from a reading specialist. His teacher helps him keep on track with an agenda book, a daily homework reminder, and a few other adaptations.
>
> He is an unusual-looking kid. The first thing you notice is his long, horsey face and prominent chin. His jug-ears are set low, and he often sits in postures that other kids can't master. They love watching him in gym class, where he can show off his double-jointedness to full effect.
>
> He does have a habit of repeating what was just said to him, and he talks in a high-pitched, super-fast voice. We're working on that in speech therapy twice a week.

Characteristics of fragile X syndrome in boys include prominent or long ears, a long face, delayed speech, macroorchidism (large testes), hyperactivity, tactile defensiveness, and gross motor delays.

Much less is known about girls with fragile X syndrome. Only about half of all females who carry the genetic mutation have symptoms themselves. Of those, half are of normal intelligence, and only one fourth have an IQ under 70. Few fragile X girls have autistic symptoms, although they tend to be shy and quiet.

Pervasive developmental disorder, not otherwise specified

"Pervasive developmental disorder, not otherwise specified" is also called PDD-NOS, PDD, NOS, autistic tendencies, or autistic-like behavior. When people say someone has PDD, they usually mean that he or she has been diagnosed with PDD-NOS.

The term PDD-NOS is most often used to describe people who meet some, but not all, of the criteria for autism. Either the person is not impaired in all three areas considered when a clinician is making a diagnosis of autism (social development, communication, and activities and interests), or the problems are very slight in one or more area.

Sometimes a doctor chooses a diagnosis of PDD-NOS simply because the child attempts to communicate, with or without speech, or has a strong bond with his or her parents. This reflects many physicians' lack of knowledge about autism, which does not rule out communication or relationships.

Judy describes her 5-year-old son Steve, a child whose PDD-NOS diagnosis may well be apt:

> Steve did not speak until he was 4, and still shuns conversation most of the time. When he does speak, it's often in a whisper. He prefers playing beside other children to playing with them, but in the past year he has started to describe one boy in his small kindergarten classroom as his friend, and to tag along behind him on the playground.
>
> He's a handful, but we have a warm relationship with our son. He does have unusual behaviors and interests, but the level of perseveration and obsession varies. There are times when he seems almost normal—and times when he seems almost unreachable.

Obviously, there is a gray area between where PDD-NOS ends and high-functioning autism begins. This is a judgment call for clinicians. The best of them simply call it as they see it, without regard for either the supposed stigma of the autism label or the vagueness of the PDD-NOS label.

Rett syndrome

Rett syndrome is a genetic disorder. Several types of genetic mutations affecting the MECP2 gene on the X chromosome have been identified. These appear to be responsible for about 80 percent of cases, and genetic testing is now available through a few special clinics. Work is continuing to uncover the gene or genes responsible for the remaining 20 percent of cases.

Rett syndrome is not obvious at birth, but usually becomes so between the age of 6 months and 18 months. The child's torso and limbs may shake, her gait will be wobbly and rigid, and she may have difficulty with breathing and eating.

Children with Rett syndrome are almost always female, although similar symptoms have been seen in a few boys. These children tend to grow slowly and remain short as adults, and they have a small head (microcephaly). There is always some degree of mental retardation, generally ranging from severe to profound. About 80 percent of girls with Rett syndrome also have epilepsy. The degree of impairment seems related to the severity of genetic mutation.[1]

Girls affected by Rett syndrome always seem to be wringing their hands. Although they may have social avoidance problems in early childhood, these tend to lift by the grade school years.

Rose, mother of 4-year-old Kinesha, explains how Rett syndrome has affected her child:

> Kinesha was a quiet but normal baby, but when she was about 11 months old she started to rock and shake her body. She wasn't developing on schedule anymore, either. When we took her in and asked her pediatrician about it, she [the doctor] recognized Rett syndrome right away.
>
> Now she walks stiffly and on tiptoe, she sleeps at odd hours and never seems to be on schedule, and her hands are always in motion. She grinds her teeth so often that we had her fitted with a dental guard. She is profoundly mentally retarded, so much so that potty training is still a long way away.

Some girls diagnosed with Rett syndrome do recover some abilities that were lost. This is rare, however, and may represent yet another subtype.

Other possibilities

There are a few other conditions that doctors like to rule out before diagnosing a child as having an autistic spectrum disorder, or a disorder that they may mistake for an ASD.

If speech delay is present, hearing is usually the first thing checked, followed by an examination of the muscles and structures in the mouth and throat. If everything seems in working order, the doctor can discount the possibility of a hearing problem or a birth defect that might be affecting expressive speech.

Children with severe communication disorders sometimes show symptoms that look a lot like ASD. Many children with developmental verbal dyspraxia, oral-motor apraxia or apraxia of speech, dysphasia, or aphasia have sensory integration issues or gross motor problems, for example. A speech and language pathologist is qualified to evaluate and treat speech disorders.

It's important to note that a diagnosis of a communication disorder does not rule out the possibility of an ASD—the two can coexist in one person. Apraxia, for example, is common in people with fragile X syndrome. This common misconception has been responsible for wrongful denial of speech services to many children.

In some cases, a doctor may consider selective mutism (previously known as elective mutism). In this very rare psychological condition, a person with the ability to speak chooses not to do so, either as a result of some great trauma or as an expression of a social phobia. Normally a clinician would investigate this possibility only if parents report that the child's speech was developing normally up to a certain point, then stopped. If the child's background is unknown, as in the case of an adopted child with no speech, selective mutism should also be ruled out. This disorder is treated by skilled and gentle psychotherapy and family therapy if related to trauma, and by behavior therapy and medication if related to social phobia.

Alternatively, a diagnosis of mild cerebral palsy may be a better fit. Cerebral palsy is caused by brain damage. In its most severe forms, it affects mobility, but sometimes it affects primarily speech production. These children may have just a few signs of gross and fine motor problems, such as a knock-kneed, flat-footed gait. A neurologist can rule out cerebral palsy with exercises that test how well the brain–body connection is working. Some people with cerebral palsy have sensory integration problems that can lead to autistic-like behavior.

At one time the terms "autism" and "childhood schizophrenia" were used interchangeably. Today, we know they aren't the same thing at all. It's rare for schizophrenia to emerge during childhood, but it does happen. Schizophrenia is also a neurological disorder. People with this condition have hallucinations and delusions, and tend to have what psychiatrists call "flat affect"—not much personality. Like autistic children, schizophrenic children may shun eye contact and physical contact, have limited social skills, and behave in unusual ways. They may have self-soothing behaviors that look autistic, such as repetitive rocking, and may develop self-abusive behaviors. Medications are now available that can help most children and adults with schizophrenia.

Some people with autistic features better fit the criteria for childhood or adult bipolar disorder (manic depression), obsessive-compulsive disorder (OCD), Tourette's syndrome (TS), or very extreme ADHD. People with these diagnoses sometimes report sensory sensitivities that could make them look autistic—for example, avoidance of eye contact or touch—unless properly treated. Obsessions and compulsions are certainly common across the autistic spectrum. The vocal and physical tics that characterize Tourette's syndrome are not that dissimilar from the stereotypic movements and repetitive sounds made by some people with ASDs. Medications, interpersonal or behavior therapy, and adjustments to school programs can usually help children with these problems.

As with communication disorders, the presence of a different neurological disorder does not necessarily rule out the presence of an ASD—many people have more than one. Alphabet soup diagnoses such as ADHD/OCD/TS/Asperger's syndrome, or apraxia of speech/ASD/OCD are not that uncommon. There is considerable overlap among these neurological conditions, all of which are more common in families where someone has an ASD than in the general population.

Often a person who seems to be on the autistic spectrum is tested for seizures, both to rule out Landau-Kleffner syndrome (discussed later in this chapter) and to make sure that aggressive or self-injurious behaviors are not caused by seizure activity. Seizures can cause brain damage, so it's important to pursue diagnosis and treatment if they are suspected. Some of the signs to look out for are staring spells, times when the child seems confused or in a daze, inexplicable falling episodes, or convulsions.

Of course, if you have a history of epilepsy or seizures in your family, be sure to let your doctor know.

Some researchers have reported that brain lesions or tumors, or brain abnormalities such as a missing or atrophied cerebellum, can cause autistic symptoms. Neurologists can use brain-scanning technology to locate these, and may be able to remove a tumor or lesion surgically. Obviously, abnormalities in brain structure cannot be helped, although some people who are missing parts of their brains go on to function quite well. These causes for autistic symptoms are believed to be very rare.

Rare conditions with autistic-like features

The following disorders are so rare that an otherwise knowledgeable neurologist may never have seen a case—and may therefore miss one when it comes through the door. A very few children said to have an ASD may actually have one of these disorders. If everything seems to fit, it's worth talking to your doctor about and researching further. Appendix B, *Support and Advocacy,* includes sources for more information about these conditions.

Angelman syndrome

Angelman syndrome is a disorder caused by genetic differences on chromosome 15 in the 15q11–q13 region. It's not a subtype of autism, but some people who have it exhibit autistic-like behaviors, including hand-flapping, severe speech problems, attention deficits, and hyperactive behavior. Some are aggressive or self-abusive, and most such children also have epilepsy.

People with Angelman syndrome usually have distinctive facial features, including a wide, upturned mouth with a thin upper lip, and deep-set eyes. They often have very pale eyes, hair, and skin.

Children with Angelman syndrome are gregarious and love to laugh. They walk and move stiffly, and most are severely mentally retarded.

Cornelia de Lange syndrome

Also called Brachmann-de Lange syndrome, Cornelia de Lange syndrome may be abbreviated to CdLS or BDLS.

Cornelia de Lange syndrome is a very rare genetic disorder. It may be caused by a mutation on chromosome 3. Genetic testing is available from specialized centers. Its hallmarks are low birth weight, developmental delay, a small head that may also be short and wide, a broad pug nose, long eyelashes that curl, and thin, arched eyebrows that may meet. Other physical differences may be present, including malformations of major organ systems and limbs, webbed toes, and gastrointestinal reflux.

People with CdLS are usually, but not always, mentally retarded. Like people with autism, they often have stereotypic behaviors (mouthing of hands and objects is especially common), perseverations, and self-injurious behaviors.

Landau-Kleffner syndrome

Landau-Kleffner syndrome is a seizure disorder that results in loss of speech (aphasia) some time after 18 months of age. It is twice as common in males. It can be hard to diagnose, because the seizures are deep within the brain, occur during sleep, and may not show up on a one-time EEG test. If Landau-Kleffner syndrome is suspected, the physician may order a 24-hour or 48-hour EEG test, using a mobile unit.

As with childhood disintegrative disorder, which it resembles, no one is sure what causes Landau-Kleffner syndrome. Some cases definitely start after a known head trauma, but others are a mystery. Researchers suspect that a virus or immune system problem may be part of the picture for some patients.

Kim, mother of 7-year-old Brad, tells her son's story:

> Brad was diagnosed with a form of cognitive epilepsy called
> continuous spike wave syndrome, which is a variant of Landau-
> Kleffner syndrome. He also had an intraventricular hemorrhage at
> birth with VP shunt placement at one year of age. His hallmarks are

> *atypical PDD, autistic regression, cognitive and neuropsychological regression, and expressive language problems. There are so few cases known about that I have no idea what the future holds.*

This disorder can sometimes be successfully treated with antiseizure medications and/or corticosteroids. A few doctors try brain surgery, which may be effective in some cases. The later speech was lost, the better the prognosis.

Prader-Willi syndrome

Prader-Willi syndrome is a genetic disorder that sometimes occurs with autism or includes autistic-like features. It is caused by a deletion on the long arm of chromosome 15. Genetic testing is available from specialized centers.

The main perseverations seen are with food and eating. Sexual characteristics may be underdeveloped, as are the muscles. Most people with Prader-Willi syndrome are mildly retarded and have speech and movement problems. Temper tantrums, skin-picking, and sleep difficulties are also frequently seen.

Medication does not seem to help this population very much. It's likely that there is a metabolic disorder involved that governs how food is absorbed and whether the stomach feels full, but no one has yet discovered how to address the problem. Special diets and behavior modification can be useful for maintaining health, and for improving performance at school and in the community.

Williams syndrome

Williams syndrome is a rare genetic disorder caused by a deletion of genetic material on chromosome 7. Genetic testing is available for diagnosis.

Many people with Williams syndrome exhibit autistic behaviors, including hypersensitivity to sounds, extreme food likes and dislikes, and perseveration. They usually have developmental, gross motor, and language delays, and may have heart or blood vessel problems, high blood pressure, and elevated calcium levels.

These sociable, often quite animated people have unique facial features that can be described as "pixielike," including almond-shaped eyes, perfect oval ears, a broad mouth with full lips, and a narrow face with a small chin.

Newer classifications

Currently, researchers are trying to do a better job of categorizing ASDs, based either on groups of symptoms or on known or suspected causes. None of the potential ASD subtypes or alternative diagnoses discussed in this section have made their way into the *DSM-IV*, but you may still hear these terms from a doctor or educator who's been checking out the latest research. You might also find these ideas discussed in some of the books and online sites listed in Appendix A, *Resources,* or hear about them in parent support groups.

Dr. Stanley Greenspan, a child psychiatrist and researcher with George Washington University Medical School, has focused in on the autistic spectrum disorders and related developmental problems of children. He has also joined the crowd asking for a more specific diagnostic system, proposing the term "multisystem neurological disorder" (MSD) as an alternative. MSD could be used to describe children who, despite communication difficulties, perseverative behavior, and other characteristics of autism, have the capacity for building social relationships. The term "multisystem" is certainly more accurate than "pervasive" when it comes to expressing the variances between patients. "Neurological" is also much more accurate than "developmental."

Dr. Greenspan has also coined the term "regulatory disorders" to describe children whose basic problems lie in regulating attention, sensation, information processing, and movement. This category would include ADD/ADHD, some conduct disorders, and some children at the milder end of the autistic spectrum. He describes five types of regulatory disorders: sensitive/fearful, defiant, self-absorbed, active/craving, and inattentive.

Perhaps the best thing about Greenspan's research is its emphasis on uncovering underlying issues and helping each individual to reach his or her full potential. He is a champion of floor-time play therapy, which is discussed further in Chapter 6, *Therapeutic Interventions.*

Deficits in attention, motor control, and perception (DAMP) is a term used by a few researchers, primarily in Scandinavia, to describe conditions much like Greenspan's regulatory disorders.

Other classifications in popular use are based on similarities between patients, and may represent ASD subtypes. These terms and concepts are controversial in some circles, and relate to the concept of autism as an autoimmune or metabolic disorder. They include:

- Allergy-induced autism (sometimes called cerebral allergy), in which autistic symptoms appear to be caused or exacerbated by allergies, and diminish when allergies are treated.

- Autistic enterocolitis, a term used by Dr. Andrew Wakefield and others to describe children who after a period of normal development experienced autistic regression coupled with severe bowel problems. Symptoms are believed to follow either measles infection or administration of the MMR vaccine.

- *Candida*-caused autism, a variant that seems to respond extraordinarily well to diet and medications that inhibit the growth of *Candida albicans* yeast in the body.

- Neuro-immune dysfunction syndrome (NIDS), a variant in which unusual immune system function seems to be tied to autistic symptoms.

- Vaccine-related autism (also called vaccine-related encephalopathy), in which the onset of autistic symptoms appears to be caused by or related to a severe reaction to childhood immunizations, particularly the MMR vaccine (see also autistic enterocolitis).

Parents in the UK may also hear about pathological demand avoidance (PDA) syndrome. This is not an autistic spectrum disorder, but is sometimes mistaken for one because of some overlapping symptoms. Children with PDA avoid ordinary demands of life, such as adult direction and sociability, display obsessive behavior and mood swings, and may show a variety of minor neurological differences. PDA seems to affect girls and boys equally, and responds to different educational and therapeutic strategies.[2]

CHAPTER 3

Getting a Diagnosis

PEOPLE WITH AUTISTIC SPECTRUM DISORDERS need a medical diagnosis to get appropriate medical help, access to therapies, and special education. This chapter—which will be of most use to parents, other direct caregivers, and adults who suspect they may have an ASD—discusses how to navigate the diagnostic process. Topics covered include starting within either the medical, Early Intervention, or school system; choosing an evaluation facility and professionals; what to expect during the diagnostic interviews and testing; and how to make the process easier and more productive.

Who diagnoses ASDs?

The journey to a diagnosis can begin in several different ways, but for most it starts in the office of a pediatrician or general practitioner. For others, a mental health practitioner (counselor, social worker, psychiatrist, or psychologist) is the first person contacted. Some children are referred for help by a day care worker, a teacher, or other school personnel. A few, mostly people who already see a neurologist because of epilepsy or another known brain disorder, are diagnosed by a specialist without going through any preliminaries at all.

It's important to note that only a medical doctor can make a medical diagnosis, although a psychologist or neuropsychologist (a psychologist with special training in neurological differences) is also qualified to diagnose autistic spectrum disorders. School counselors, speech therapists, teachers, and other nonphysicians—including parents—may well be correct when they recognize autistic symptoms, but they can't officially make the call. If you suspect that your child, your student, or someone you care about has an ASD, the most helpful thing you can do is assist him in getting an appropriate diagnosis. For professionals and parents alike, that means finding a specialist with experience in diagnosing autistic spectrum disorders.

Ideally, diagnosis is done by a team of specialists working together (see the section "The multidisciplinary evaluation" later in this chapter), and is accompanied by a report detailing treatment suggestions and referrals.

Starting with a pediatrician

Usually, the first person to hear the concerns of a young child's parents is a pediatrician. In this age of managed care, the pediatrician takes on more importance than ever. Not only is she the doctor who knows the most about how a particular child's development has progressed and how it compares to the norm, but she is almost always the primary care provider (PCP) designated by the parent's health insurance plan. She generally serves as a gatekeeper to advanced care, making referrals to specialists as needed.

Everything in the following three sections applies to general practitioners (GPs) as well as to pediatricians, so adults seeking diagnostic services should follow the same procedures with their GP or other primary care provider.

In an ideal world, pediatricians would be quick to see the early signs of ASDs and would guide parents toward the best medical resources available. Sometimes that's how it works.

For Sarah, mother of 2-year-old Elaine, help came quickly:

> Elaine's pediatrician recognized developmental problems quite early. He said that she did not speak because she couldn't, not because she didn't want to, and advised me to have her seen by St. Mary's Hospital for Early Intervention. At St. Mary's, Elaine was seen by a neurologist, a speech expert, and countless doctors. They couldn't agree on a label—only the neurologist felt certain that it was PDD-NOS. Luckily, they did agree on recommendations for treatment.

Because parents know the most about their child, they play a key role. To ensure a proper diagnosis, make your concerns crystal clear. That isn't always easy. Many pediatricians complain that parents seem almost apologetic about being in their offices, don't ask enough questions, and don't volunteer important information unless asked. By and large, that's learned behavior, ingrained over a lifetime of rushed appointments with harried doctors.

It's true that the typical sore throat appointment is a 10-minute affair these days, but when you have greater concerns it's okay to ask for more one-on-one time with the doctor. There's no need to feel guilty, because doctors are accustomed to scheduling longer sessions for some types of appointments. Practitioners should reassure parents about this point.

You're not asking the pediatrician to diagnose an ASD, you're looking for a referral—but before a referral can be approved, the pediatrician must be sure that specialized diagnostic help is required. Ask for a consultation appointment of at least 30 minutes (more would be nice).

Why do you need to go beyond the pediatrician? Because while pediatricians are indeed experts in the typical problems of children—croup, the flu, pinworms, diaper rashes, and all the rest—they receive very little training in neurological or psychiatric disorders. In fact, a study by Elizabeth Costello, PhD, associate professor of child and adolescent psychiatry at Duke University, found that in one large HMO (health management organization), the pediatricians were able to diagnose only 17 percent of the children who presented with psychiatric disorders. In addition, that 17 percent tended to be children with the most common problems, including bedwetting and learning disabilities.[1]

Pediatricians also have their own opinions about disability. Some know very little about available services, and assume that only the severely disabled are eligible for assistance. This can encourage them to delay diagnosis.

Jennifer, mother of 3-year-old Joseph, found this reluctance frustrating:

> We began asking our pediatrician questions about Joseph's language regression at 15 months, but she ignored our concerns because she felt his skill with letters and numbers precluded any developmental disability. She actually discouraged us from seeking Early Intervention when he was 24 months old. She said we might be uncomfortable since "the other children are more severely impaired."

Use your consultation appointment as efficiently as possible. Accurate, detailed records are the most important thing you can contribute. These should include the usual "baby book" milestones (first step, first word, and so on) as well as notes about anything unusual you have observed. Areas the pediatrician is likely to ask about include patient and family medical history, speech abilities, relationships with family members and peers, play patterns, and interests. You may want to consult the diagnostic questionnaires in Appendix G, *Diagnostic Tools,* to see the kinds of questions a doctor might ask.

Keeping a daily diary is a good way to prepare for a diagnostic evaluation. Many families have learned a great deal during this process as well. If possible, record activities, diet, and behaviors each day for a period of two weeks or more, with the time and duration of activities and behaviors noted. Not only can this diary provide a very complete picture of the child to a professional, but it can also help to identify patterns. Some families have identified food allergies this way, or collected data they needed to create the most beneficial daily routine for their child.

If the child has seen other doctors, releases must be signed to transfer any useful records to the pediatrician. Older children may have school records that would be helpful, and these can also be transferred if a signed release is on file. Transfers always seem to take longer than you would expect, so get releases taken care of early, and make sure records were sent and received. Alternatively, if you have your own copies of these records (and you should), you may photocopy and deliver them yourself.

If possible, provide your information to the pediatrician at least a week before the consultation appointment. Include a request that she read the material in advance and review the patient's medical file before the meeting. The goal is to put your child's case on the pediatrician's front burner and to ensure that when the appointment takes place, the details are fresh in her mind.

You should also summarize your concerns in writing. The records already mentioned can help you gather your thoughts. You don't have to be an eloquent writer to express what worries you. If you prefer, you can jot down a simple numbered list rather than writing whole paragraphs. It may help to compare your child to his or her siblings or to other children in the day care center, school, or neighborhood. Some parents send a summary of concerns to the doctor in advance; others prefer to use it as an agenda for discussion during the consultation session.

You may also want to discuss your concerns in advance with an advice nurse or another person who works closely with the pediatrician, such as a physician's assistant. In large medical practices or HMOs, nurses are an important part of the organization. They can be allies when you need a specialist referral or even just a listening ear.

As you prepare for it, keep in mind that the consultation appointment is only a preliminary step toward your real goal: a multidisciplinary evaluation.

The consultation appointment

A consultation appointment is different from a regular visit to the pediatrician. Unless the doctor happens to notice something of medical concern, there is no need to do the usual physical exam. In fact, the appointment may take place in a meeting room or office rather than in an examination room.

When you come, bring any records you have gathered, copies of your earlier letter (just in case it never reached the doctor), your summary of concerns, and any questions that you want to ask. Bringing a small notebook can help you keep a record of the discussion. If your child tends to be difficult to manage, bring a bag of toys or books that are likely to help keep him calm. Parents may want to choose playthings that can help the doctor see where the child is developmentally, such as a doll or stuffed animal.

If the consultation seems to be getting off to an awkward start, begin by referring to your summary of concerns or your list of questions. Always keep your goal in mind: You're there to make a case for referral, and your observations are the evidence you need to convince the pediatrician. Think of yourself as a salesperson, trying to persuade a customer. You want to be the one in charge of this meeting, and keeping that image in your mind can help.

Most pediatricians use the consultation appointment to listen to your concerns, discuss the issues raised, and recommend the next course of action. Some will use a set of general screening questions about behavior and development. For children, the Pediatric Symptom Checklist is one of the most common screening tools used. It's a list of 35 questions created by Dr. Michael S. Jellinek of Harvard Medical School, and has proven about 95 percent effective at catching psychiatric disorders in children.

Checklists and guidelines are great, but there's really no substitute for knowledge and experience. As parents interviewed for this book make painfully clear, some pediatricians are reluctant or unable to recognize ASDs, even when faced with a nonverbal 3-year-old who spends the entire consultation appointment screaming or disassembling the doctor's scale. You may hear phrases like "Your child just needs to be disciplined more strictly," "He'll grow out of it," or "Let's wait and see." There are several responses you can make:

- Go back over your evidence, showing that your child is having more than one developmental problem, and explaining how it is affecting her life. If you feel comfortable doing so, you may also want to mention how it is affecting your family life.

- Set a "wait and see" timetable. Ask the pediatrician which important milestones (such as meaningful speech) should be passed within the next three months, and secure a promise that if these goals have not been met, a referral will be made. This approach may be appropriate for very young children whose possible impairments are subtle.

- If the pediatrician says he knows nothing about autistic spectrum disorders, suggest that he do some research. The organization First Signs, online at *http://www. firstsigns.org,* sends out an excellent kit for pediatricians that includes diagnostic information in written form and on video. You might even order one for the doctor yourself.

- Ask the reluctant pediatrician for a referral to a developmental pediatrician (see following discussion).

- Go up the chain of command in the health care organization, if you are using a managed care or HMO practitioner. There's usually a board that takes complaints under consideration. You can petition the board to approve your referral even if the pediatrician refuses. Usually this is done in writing.

- Ask the doctor to put his refusal to refer in writing. This may not be something he'd like to commit to paper, so you might end up getting the referral after all.

- If the doctor does put his refusal in writing, you could call your diagnostic facility of choice and set up an appointment with the appropriate evaluation team directly. Be prepared to pay for this visit out-of-pocket. If the team confirms your suspicions, you should be able to bill your insurance company for reimbursement because an appropriate referral was refused.

- If the pediatrician won't refer, but won't put his refusal in writing either, you can still "self-refer," but it will be harder to get reimbursed. You should send a letter to the pediatrician explaining why you have made this choice over his objections. Send a copy to your insurance company as well. This creates a paper record to support a claim for improper refusal later on.

Referral to a developmental pediatrician, a doctor who specializes in treating the health problems of children with developmental delays or handicaps, presents a less expensive alternative. For you, seeing another pediatrician may seem like one more hurdle to jump on the way to the diagnostic team. Your reluctant pediatrician, in contrast, will probably like the idea. If your concerns are valid, the developmental pediatrician can explain the reasons to your regular pediatrician, and can provide information about the best resources available locally for full diagnosis and treatment.

Developmental pediatricians are much more familiar with neurological problems, medications, and current research on disabilities. They tend to work closely with specialists, including neurologists, psychiatrists, and therapists of various types. In fact, you may want to continue seeing the developmental pediatrician for continuing care.

Roadblocks to referral

Most doctors in the United States share the risks and expenses of caring for special needs patients, including specialist referrals, with business partners or an HMO group. Doctors who make too many referrals can face financial penalties, even if the extra services were absolutely necessary. Physicians may also feel constrained by directives from insurance companies, which want to minimize expenses. Chapter 8, *Insurance,* discusses the insurance system in greater detail, but it's sufficient to say that the health care structure in America can make it more than a little difficult to convince your pediatrician to send you to an expensive facility.

Low-income Americans who are uninsured face the biggest roadblock of all: lack of access to health care. They may be able to obtain diagnostic help through the school district (see the section "Starting with the school district," later in this chapter) or through public Early Intervention programs for preschool children. The school district may also provide some diagnostic and therapeutic assistance, especially in the areas of speech, occupational, and physical therapy, if it relates to classroom performance. Special medical programs are available for low-income families and for children with handicapping conditions. Both Chapter 8 and Chapter 10, *Family Issues and Support,* provide many ideas for getting ongoing medical care for people with ASDs who are not covered by private insurance.

In Canada and Europe, where the single-payer system of nationalized health care predominates, doctors have a different set of constraints on their ability to make referrals. Resources are focused on providing basic health care to everyone, so specialists are rarer and harder to get an appointment with than in the US. People may be forced to pay out-of-pocket expenses to doctors who practice outside the national health-care scheme. These expenses can be considerable. Some families have been able to gain more timely access with help from a sympathetic social worker or health visitor, or have called on disability advocacy groups for assistance.

In countries where neither the private insurance nor the single-payer model predominates, parents should seek out—and pay for—a specialist directly, without going through a preliminary consultation appointment. Reduced-fee or free help may be available through state-run hospitals and clinics, medical facilities run by religious orders or charities, or individual physicians who are willing to take a case at a lower cost than usual.

Starting with Early Intervention

All US states, Canadian provinces, and Australian states have Early Intervention (EI) programs that identify, evaluate, and assist children with developmental disabilities, including ASDs. New Zealand and all European countries also have publicly funded programs available for young children (in the UK, Sure Start is the main one). Similar services are available in the more developed countries of Asia, Central and South America, and Africa.

These programs are not identical, however—in fact, they can differ drastically between states, or even between cities in the same state. Some are very aggressive about reaching out to families, whereas others have such a low profile that parents may not know they exist until the child is too old to benefit. Some provide screening and referral services only, whereas others offer (and pay for) full multidisciplinary evaluations. Many provide ongoing direct services, such as speech therapy or applied behavioral analysis (ABA) sessions. Services may be very limited outside major urban areas.

Early Intervention services may be offered in the child's home, at a special disabilities center, in a public school, in a hospital or clinic setting, or at multiple sites. In the British model, which prevails in the UK, New Zealand, and Australia, most services are home based. According to parents, Australia's EI services are extraordinarily flexible and extensive—perhaps the best available anywhere, at any price. Canada and the US both tend toward a school- or clinic-based model of EI service.

When home-based programs are available in the US or Canada, that fact is rarely advertised. However, there are families in the US who receive home-based ABA programs, speech therapy, occupational therapy, and much more for a child with an autistic spectrum disorder, and who pay no or very low charges for as much as 40 hours of direct service per week in their own homes. Needless to say, these parents have been willing to try everything possible to meet their children's needs. It's not uncommon to find that children in the same city or county are receiving very different levels of services.

The common denominator in Early Intervention programs seems to be that you either get what they offer, or you get what you demand. Practitioners are not as well paid as those in the private sector (and therefore more likely to quit suddenly, to refuse additional work, or to be substandard), and waiting lists can be long. But smart parents can use EI resources to accomplish a great deal on behalf of their children, or to supplement what they're able to pay for privately.

Some EI programs provide excellent services for young children, and the best of them involve the whole family in finding innovative solutions to behavioral and medical problems. At the very least, EI can put you in touch with community resources. Even families with excellent private insurance should contact their local EI program as early as possible.

For most families, the point of entry for Early Intervention programs is a public-health clinic or hospital, or the school district's special education department. Your state or county health and human services or social services department may also be able to help you access EI services. Depending on local regulations, assistance for people with autistic spectrum disorders may be coordinated by specialists in behavioral/mental health or in developmental disabilities. In either case, service coordinators are usually social workers.

You may be assigned a caseworker whose job is to inform you about services, hear and respond to your concerns, and coordinate both evaluations and the provision of direct services. Caseworkers may have 100 or more clients, so you will have to be a bit pushy to get your case on their agenda. In fact, you'll find that most of the work will have to be either done by you or double-checked by you. Most caseworkers you will come into contact with are truly caring and decent people—they're simply overburdened to the extreme.

As with a private pediatrician, your job will be to convince the caseworker or other EI representative that your child needs a multidisciplinary evaluation. The same tactics apply. There is one difference: in most cases, you have a *right* to demand an EI evaluation. Don't be afraid to exercise that right.

The evaluation should be identical to the kind of multidisciplinary evaluation discussed later in this chapter. If the process is under the auspices of the local special education department, it may include additional testing for learning disabilities, reading level, and other school-oriented factors.

Starting with the school district

Sometimes parents of an older child with mild autistic features are approached by concerned school personnel. First-time parents may not have known their child needed help, or their earlier questions about the child's development may have been rebuffed. Teachers, aides, school counselors, speech therapists, and other nonphysicians cannot diagnose, but they can help families access resources—sometimes including medical diagnosis and even treatment.

Ten-year-old Mikael was diagnosed after a school referral, says his mother, Galena:

> Mikael was not thrilled about spending three days with a school-district evaluation team, but I was. After he had struggled with severe school and social problems for four years, a teacher finally recognized that he was more than just shy. Mikael's fourth-grade teacher had worked with two autistic boys in college. "I don't want to scare you, but he does some very

similar things, and he seems to think and learn in the same way they did,"
she told me. "I know he's not autistic, but he's similar somehow, and
finding out more can help me teach him."

She gave me some information from the district's special education
office, and we got in touch with a school psychologist. The psychologist
set up classroom observations, interviewed us, and spent some time with
Mikael. In the end, her diagnosis was PDD-NOS, and the special
education team designed some modifications to help Mikael succeed.
She also referred us to a local psychiatrist who had worked with similar
children.

Schools take a different approach to disabilities than medical practitioners. Their concern is with how the problem affects educational performance, not what caused it or how to treat it. Chapter 9, *School,* discusses special education services in detail; this section simply explains how parents can use a school-based evaluation to obtain a diagnosis.

Schools are required to perform a special-education evaluation at the request of a school-age child's parents, or at the request of school personnel and with parental permission. To start the process, request a special-education assessment, preferably in writing. Let the district know that you expect to receive an assessment plan within 15 days of its receipt of your referral letter. Keep a copy of this letter and of all correspondence with the district.

In most districts, evaluations are carried out by a team, which may include a classroom teacher, disability specialist, occupational therapist, speech-and-language pathologist (SLP) or speech therapist, psychologist or psychiatrist, and other personnel. Larger school districts may have one or more autism specialists; major metropolitan areas (as well as state or regional education offices) may have an entire autism team. When you make initial contact with your district, ask if you can speak with one of these specialists.

If the school district requires a doctor's diagnosis as part of the special-education evaluation, the district must pay for that diagnosis if it has not already been obtained. Districts may work closely with regional education centers, Early Intervention programs, and child-development programs to perform medical evaluations.

Schools tend to lean heavily on standardized tests. On the positive side, that helps ensure that evaluations are more objective than purely observation-based judgments might be. On the not-so-positive side, no standardized test is purely objective. As a result, US federal law limits how schools can use tests to evaluate and place students, and other countries are following suit. These rules include the following:

- Tests must be selected and administered so as not to be racially, culturally, or sexually discriminatory.

- Tests must be administered in the student's primary language or other mode of communication, such as sign language.

- Tests must be validated for the specific purpose for which they are used.

- Testing must assess specific areas of educational need, rather than producing a single intelligence-quotient (IQ) score.

- No single procedure can be used to determine an appropriate educational program for a student.

- When a student has impaired sensory, manual, or speaking skills, the tester must ensure that results accurately reflect the student's aptitude or achievement level rather than the student's impaired skills, unless the test is intended to measure those skills.

- Students must be assessed in all areas related to a suspected disability including, where appropriate, health and development, vision, hearing, gross and fine motor abilities, general ability, academic performance, self-help, orientation and mobility skills, vocational aptitude and interests, and social and emotional status.

- Parents must give informed consent for student-evaluation procedures.

State special-education regulations may add more items to this list. California, for example, requires that psychological assessments be performed by a credentialed school psychologist trained to assess cultural and ethnic factors that may affect diagnosis. States are required to make these rules available to parents, so if you have a concern about testing procedures, call your local or state special-education office and request a copy. Federal, state, and local regulations may also be available from disability advocacy groups or on the Internet.

Parents in the UK and other countries should contact their local education authority for information about similar regulations. In general, most countries other than the US make educational policy at a national level.

All tests that the district plans to administer should be listed on your assessment plan and arranged according to areas of function to be tested. If you think one of the tests chosen is inappropriate, don't sign the Consent for Assessment form that comes with this plan until the issue is resolved.

You can ask that specific tests or types of tests (for example, a nonverbal intelligence test) be used. If the district doesn't have a qualified person to administer a test, it can contract with a community provider at no charge to you.

Choosing an evaluation facility

If it's clear to your doctor, Early Intervention provider, or school district that something is amiss and deserves expert attention, you may move quickly from discussing your concerns to the next step: choosing a setting and date for the formal team evaluation.

Don't assume that the first person to validate your concerns knows the best place to go. If you've heard information about local facilities, positive or negative, feel free to share it. Ask what the outcome has been for other families referred to a facility. If references are available, check them out. You could schedule tours of one or more facilities before making a choice.

Those who live in rural areas may want to request a referral to a regional child-development center instead of opting for an ad-hoc evaluation team made up of local professionals or an inexperienced school-based team. All US states and Canadian provinces maintain such centers, which are usually affiliated with a public medical school or teaching hospital. In the UK, your regional NHS office should be able to locate the closest facility.

If you can't identify a site within a reasonable distance of your home, call the national autism organization in your country or, better yet, contact a nearby state or local chapter. If you're an Internet user, mailing lists and chat sites are good resources for getting names of and opinions about diagnostic facilities.

If you, your doctor, or the school district needs to do some legwork before choosing an evaluation site, make sure to set a date for finalizing the decision. It shouldn't take more than a week or two to get things set up (usually, it's just a matter of making a couple of phone calls). Write this date down, and ensure that the other party also has it in writing.

If you do agree on an evaluation site at the consultation, make sure the referral process starts immediately. It's an unfortunate fact that many of the best facilities have long waiting lists. A three-month wait is not unusual in the US, and some specialists in the UK are booked up for as long as a year in advance. You want to get your name on that waiting list as soon as possible.

No one should have to wait months, even years, just to get a diagnosis. There are strategies you can use to move up the list at a diagnostic facility:

- **Keep on top of the process.** You wouldn't believe how often important paperwork, referral forms, and case files are misplaced or never sent. Make sure all the necessary materials are sent and received.

- **Make personal contact with someone at the facility.** Nurses, secretaries, even the intake specialist can become your advocate if they know who your child is and why she needs to be seen soon. Be more to the staff than just a name on a list.

- **Ask if the facility keeps a cancellation fill-in list.** This is a roster of patients willing to come in on short notice in case of a cancellation. If this option is practical for you, it may save you months of waiting.

Choosing the evaluation team

As good as some experienced practitioners are at recognizing developmental disabilities, it's important to work with a team of professionals if you can. The multidisciplinary approach (also called the team-based model) is widely accepted as the best, most-thorough method for diagnosing complex disorders such as ASDs.

Each person on the team will have a slightly different perspective and area of expertise, and the group will collectively have more background and experience than any single person in it. Ideally, the team will be personalized to meet the needs of each child. Any number of specialties may be represented, including developmental pediatrics, psychology, psychiatry, neurology, audiology, speech and language pathology, physical therapy, and occupational therapy. Some facilities have one or more clinicians who specialize in autistic spectrum disorders, and who coordinate all multidisciplinary evaluations in that specialty.

Your list of concerns can help you insist on specialists to include. If lack of communication tops your list, make sure there's both a speech-and-language pathologist and an audiologist involved. If seizures are a worry, a neurologist must be part of the team. If obsessive-compulsive behaviors are the most urgent symptom, that's a psychiatric issue, requiring a psychiatrist. The idea is to cover all the bases.

If the multidisciplinary evaluation will take place in a school setting, the team may not include a medical doctor. You can request that one be included (back up your request with good reasons, of course). School districts routinely contract with local physicians, psychiatrists, neurologists, and medically oriented testing specialists. The school district cannot charge you for medical testing and diagnosis if it has ordered it. Some districts will try to bill your insurance, although parents have successfully challenged this practice.

The evaluation team needs a leader. The leader will be your main contact during the evaluation process, so it needs to be someone who has time to talk. Often the team selects whichever clinician has the most expertise as its de facto or official leader—the neurologist or psychiatrist, say—but that's not always ideal. These practitioners can be extraordinarily busy, too busy to discuss the team's findings for hours, too busy to field frantic phone calls two months later, and definitely too busy to give hugs and encouragement. The experience of many parents interviewed for this book indicates that social workers, special education caseworkers, and developmental pediatricians tend to make the best team leaders. They're trained in the interpersonal skills necessary for the job, and they tend to use less medical jargon when talking to families and patients.

In some cases, you may be able to request (or refuse) to have specific people be part of the team. You can use the same resources mentioned previously for finding information about evaluation facilities to get a list of practitioners' names. Personal recommendations from others in your situation are an excellent indication of expertise.

One size does not fit all when it comes to diagnosing ASDs. A psychiatrist whose specialty is treating adolescents with depression is probably not an expert on autistic spectrum disorders, and a speech and language pathologist who only works with kids who stutter and lisp may be in over his head. If you have a chance to ask the team members about their experience with ASDs before the evaluation, do so—you may find that one or more is not a good fit for the job.

It's okay to say no. If a team member is rude to you on the phone, makes you feel unwelcome or uncomfortable, or gets poor marks from other families, ask for someone different. With luck, an acceptable replacement will be available.

The multidisciplinary evaluation

Multidisciplinary evaluations take time—lots of it. Although some public EI programs claim that a multidisciplinary evaluation can be completed in as little as two hours or a single afternoon, most hospital-based programs take one to two days, or even longer, to do a full evaluation. This provides enough time for observing the person, conducting interviews, administering standardized tests, and comparing notes. It's essential that the evaluators make time to talk about what parents have observed over years of being with their child on a daily basis, and to speak with older patients one-on-one.

You can ask how many people will be working with you or your child on each day, including assistants; how long each section of the evaluation process will last; and whether a parent, caregiver, friend, or other advocate may be present during all parts of the procedure.

Multidisciplinary evaluation schedules

The typical multidisciplinary evaluation schedule can be exhausting. Children with ASDs tend to act up or withdraw in new situations anyway, and are not very amenable to being poked and prodded by strangers. This may give the clinicians a chance to see your child at his worst—which could be good or bad, depending on how they use that opportunity. Adults with ASDs tend to have more coping skills, but may need to arrange for a "time out" procedure in advance, just in case the process gets too overwhelming.

A typical day of multidisciplinary evaluation might look like this:

> 9 to 9:30 A.M.—audiological exam
>
> 10 A.M. to 12 P.M.—speech and language evaluation
>
> Break for lunch
>
> 1 to 2 P.M.—occupational therapy evaluation
>
> 2:15 to 3 P.M.—psychiatric observation and interview
>
> 3:15 to 4 P.M.—neurological exam

The schedule depends on the patient and the team. Some programs feature a full nutritional or metabolic workup, for example, whereas a research facility may insist that every patient undergo several basic tests in addition to tests related specifically to ASDs.

Typical multidisciplinary evaluation tests

Each team member will use some kind of standardized instrument to measure the person's function against established norms. They may also make use of questionnaires, formal or informal observations in one or more settings, and special equipment.

- Audiology tests may require the person to wear headphones and point to the location of a sound, or they may involve measuring brain stem response to sound. Audiologists will probably have to involve parents in the process with young children. Some audiologists provide computerized reports showing the range of hearing.

- Speech and language pathologists (SLPs) employ flash cards, questions, toys, and games to elicit sounds and speech, then grade the performance in standardized ways. There are a number of standardized tests for gauging speech and communication skills. The SLP should also ask parents many questions about actions, gestures, sounds, and words their child uses to communicate.

- Occupational and physical therapists will ask the patient to try various activities, such as throwing a ball to the tester or walking along a low balance beam. To rate the individual for sensory impairments or problems, OTs might use the Sensory Integration and Praxis Tests (SIPT). Parents or adult patients may answer written or verbal questions.

- Psychiatrists and psychologists use checklists, questionnaires, observations, and conversations to make their diagnoses. They may also administer standardized tests.

- Neurologists employ simple physical tests that can indicate brain dysfunction and can also call on an array of high-tech tools. If seizures are suspected or if the facility has a research orientation, an electroencephalogram (EEG) and possibly other types of brain-scanning technology may be brought to bear.

The tests and other measures schools use to assess children with suspected ASDs may be somewhat different from those used in a medical setting. Interviews with parents are usually the starting point. Checklists or questionnaires may be used in interviews, including autism-rating scales. Parents will be asked many, many questions about their child's development, abilities, difficulties, and learning style. The records and daily diary discussed earlier in this chapter will prove invaluable in the parent interview.

Children may be observed in a classroom or playroom setting, in an office setting, or at home. It's best if the child is observed in more than one place—many children on the autistic spectrum never speak at school, but do use some words at home, for example.

Test instruments for diagnosing ASDs

Hundreds of standardized tests, questionnaires, and observation plans are available for rating behaviors, abilities, and other factors that could be related to autistic spectrum disorders. The lists in the next sections provide a little information about some of the tests most commonly encountered, but they are by no means complete.

In the US, most standardized tests are developed by commercial publishers, often in concert with university researchers. There is a great deal of competition among firms that publish tests. In most European and Asian countries, as well as Australia, public schools and medical facilities may be required to use special national assessment tools developed by government bureaus instead of, or in addition to, commercially developed instruments. In the interest of keeping this book's length manageable, these tests have not been listed.

Thankfully, no one will be given all these tests! The evaluation team members will choose tests that are appropriate for the person's developmental level and provide the most information about areas of strength and weakness.

If you encounter an unfamiliar test, or if you're not sure how to interpret a test score, don't be embarrassed to ask questions. The results returned by these instruments tend to be nearly incomprehensible unless you've had training.

Sometimes the results of a test will seem very wrong. Many parents have been dismayed when their children were rated as retarded by an IQ test, for example, when they appeared to have normal or even superior abilities in at least some areas of intellectual function. Although it's true that parents tend to see their own children in the best light, it's also true that they have more information about the child's capabilities than a tester who has met with the child only once. It's often worthwhile to try a different test that measures roughly the same set of capabilities, but in a different way.

Make sure the testing conditions work for the person. Obviously, nonverbal people will score poorly on a test that requires verbal responses, and people with sensory difficulties may be unable to complete a test given in a noisy ward. You'd be surprised how often evaluators overlook such basic factors.

Audiological tests

Audiological tests ensure that communication and social deficits are not being caused by hearing loss or an auditory processing disorder. Autistic spectrum disorders can also occur in people who are deaf or hearing impaired, however, and if so the hearing problem will need to be addressed along with other symptoms to achieve progress.

Some audiological tests can also detect auditory over- or under-sensitivity, which is often an issue in people with ASDs. Tests include the following:

- **Acoustic impedance testing**. This test measures middle ear function, and can detect the presence of fluid or abnormal structure. The results are presented as a diagram called a tympanogram.

- Auditory brain stem response/brain stem–evoked response (ABR/BSER). For this test, sounds are piped directly into a sleeping patient's ears through headphones. The brain's electrical response to these tones is then measured electronically. It's used most commonly with infants and nonverbal children, and can determine the extent of a hearing loss or auditory processing problem.

- Bone conduction. In this basic audiology test, a device called a bone vibrator is placed behind the ear to determine the softest level heard when bypassing the outer and middle ear to stimulate the inner ear directly.

- Comprehensive central auditory processing (CAP) testing. These tests determine how thoroughly a person processes auditory information. A comprehensive battery might include one or more tests of central nervous system function such as the ABR, and measurements of auditory memory, sequencing, tonal pattern recognition, and information storage.

- Conditioned play audiometry (CPA). This is a basic hearing test for young children, using play activities to check function.

- Immittance audiometry. This test has three parts: tympanometry, which checks how the eardrum moves and the status of the middle and inner ear; acoustic reflex thresholds, which determine if there is a sensorineural or conductive hearing loss; and reflex decay, which determines if there is a hearing loss caused by problems in the cochlea or acoustic nerve.

- Oral myofunctional evaluation. This observation-based test determines the extent of tongue thrust when making some sounds.

- Pure tone testing. Using an electronic device called a pure tone audiometer, the audiologist makes a sound. The child is taught to perform some fun activity when she hears that sound. It measures whether children can discriminate between tones.

- Visual response evaluation/sound field testing. For this test, the infant or young child is held on a parent's lap in a quiet test booth. While a test assistant tries to get the child's attention visually, sounds come through a loudspeaker on the other side. Afterward, a visual cue (such as a light or moving toy) activates next to the loudspeaker.

Autistic behavior and symptom scales

These tests attempt to screen for or diagnose autistic spectrum disorders. They may also be used to determine the level and severity of autistic behaviors.

- **Autism Behavior Checklist of the Autism Screening Instrument for Educational Planning (ABC-ASIEP).** The ABC is a subtest of the longer ASIEP, and is used alone or in conjunction with four other ASIEP subtests. It consists of 57 behavior descriptions in five areas, and is used to conduct a structured interview with a caregiver. The score is presented as a scale of the existence and severity of autistic behavior, as contrasted to other disorders. It is less effective with high-functioning forms of autism than with "classical" autism.

- **Autism Diagnostic Interview-Revised (ADI-R, also called the Wing scale).** Administered more in the UK and Europe than in the US, the ADI-R is used to conduct a standardized parent interview. It's based on the World Health Organization (WHO) definition of autism. The score is expressed as a scale.

- **Autism Diagnostic Observation Schedule (ADOS).** This is a format for conducting a diagnosis via direct observation of the patient. Many evaluators consider the ADOS to be the "gold standard" in autism-testing instruments. It is highly accurate and less subjective than some others. The score is expressed as a scale with defined variances.

- **Behavior Observation Scale for Autism (BOS).** The BOS checklist is a direct-observation format intended to help evaluators distinguish autistic spectrum children from normal or mentally retarded patients. Score is expressed as a scale.

- **Behavior Rating Instrument for Autistic and Other Atypical Children (BRIAC).** This observation-based diagnostic tool looks at relationship to an adult, communication, drive for mastery, vocalization and expressive speech, sound and speech reception, social responsiveness, and psychobiological development. Additional scales are available for nonverbal and/or hearing-impaired children. Scores are expressed as scales.

- **Childhood Autism Rating Scale (CARS).** The CARS is a direct observation format for evaluating the behavior of children and adolescents. Results can be scored on two scales, one with a range from "age appropriate" to "severely abnormal," the other with a range from "not autistic" to "mild-moderate autistic" to "severely autistic." An excerpt from the CARS is included in Appendix G, *Diagnostic Tools*.

- **Gilliam Autism Rating Scale (GARS).** Three GARS subtests cover behaviors and their frequency in the areas of stereotyped behaviors, communication, and social interaction. A third subtest asks parents about developmental disturbances in the child's first three years. Scores are expressed as scales and percentages.

- **Parent Interviews for Autism (PIA).** This set of questions for parents is frequently used when diagnosing younger or nonverbal children.

Behavioral, psychiatric, and neuropsychiatric tests

Some of the tests discussed in this section are highly clinical instruments used for differential diagnosis (for example, to distinguish autism from schizophrenia), and also to diagnose coexisting disorders, such as depression, bipolar disorder, and ADHD. Others are more subjective, and are used by teachers and other nonphysicians to rank behavior problems or uncover emotional difficulties.

Like the Rorschach blot interpretation test, which is rarely used anymore, tests for emotional disturbance that ask patients to draw and interpret what they've drawn are highly subjective. These so-called projective tests have little use in diagnosing autistic spectrum disorders, but are routinely administered nonetheless, especially in school settings. Drawing-based tests don't make proper allowances for fine motor issues, among other things. Projective tests should never be used to diagnose a condition.

- **Aberrant Behavior Checklist (ABC).** One of the most popular behavioral checklists, the ABC also has a good reputation for accuracy. Versions are available for children and adults, and it is set up to account for mental retardation when assessing behavior problems in the home, school, or workplace. Scores are expressed as scales in the areas of irritability and agitation, lethargy and social withdrawal, stereotypic behavior, hyperactivity and noncompliance, and inappropriate speech.

- **Achenbach Child Behavior Checklist (CBC).** The CBC is available in versions for girls and boys of various ages. Six different inventories are used, including a parent report, teacher report, youth report (if practical), and structured direct-observation report. It looks at the child's behaviors in several areas, including withdrawal and anxiety. The results are classified as clinically significant or normal.

- **Attention Deficit Disorders Evaluation Scale.** Versions of this questionnaire about behaviors linked with ADD/ADHD are available for parents to fill out at home or in a clinical setting, as well as for direct use with older children and adults. Scores are expressed as a scale.

- **Behavior Assessment System for Children (BASC).** This set of tests includes a teacher rating scale, parent rating scale, and self-report of personality. The BASC attempts to measure both problem and adaptive behaviors, as well as behaviors linked to ADD/ADHD. Scores are expressed as a scale keyed to a norm.

- **Conner's Rating Scales (CRS).** Parent and teacher versions of this test are intended to uncover behaviors linked to ADD/ADHD, conduct disorders, learning disabilities, psychosomatic complaints, and anxiety, among other conditions. Scores are scaled and plotted graphically.

- **Draw-a-Person.** This is a projective psychological screening procedure in which a person is asked to draw three human figures: a man, a woman, and himself. The drawing is then rated on a scale, with differences in ratings according to gender and age. Ratings are subjective interpretations, not objective measures.

- **House-Tree-Person Projective Drawing Technique.** In this projective test, the person is asked to draw a house, a tree, and a person, and then is asked a series of questions about these drawings. Sometimes these drawings are separate, sometimes they are done on a single page. Ratings are subjective interpretations, not objective measures.

- **Kinetic Family Drawing System for Family and School.** In this projective test, the person tested draws her family doing something or her class doing something. Then she is asked questions about what's going on in the drawing. Ratings are subjective interpretations, not objective measures.

- **Luria-Nebraska Neuropsychological Battery (LNNB), Luria-Nebraska Neuropsychological Battery—Children's Revision (LNNB-CR).** The LNNB-CR contains 11 scales with a total of 149 test items, which are intended to measure motor skills, rhythm, tactile, visual, receptive speech, expressive language, writing, reading, arithmetic, memory, and intelligence. Each test item is scored on a scale, and a total scale for all items is also derived. The adult LNNB also tests the maturation level of the frontal lobe tertiary zones.

- **Pediatric Symptom Checklist (PSC).** A simple questionnaire about behavioral symptoms, the PSC is commonly used as a screening tool by pediatricians. Score is expressed as a scale.

- **Psychiatric Assessment Schedule for Adults with Developmental Disability (PAS-ADD).** Used primarily in the UK, this is a self-reporting questionnaire used to assess psychiatric states in people with developmental delay, learning disability, neurobiological disorders, or senility, among other conditions. Score is expressed as a scale.

- **Reitan-Indiana Neuropsychological Test Battery (RINTB), Reitan-Indiana Neuropsychological Test Battery for Children (RINTBC), Halstead-Reitan Neuropsychological Test Battery for Children (HNTBC).** These widely used neuropsychological tests look for signs of brain damage. The RINTBC contains the following tests: Category, Tactile Performance, Finger Oscillation, Sensory-Perceptual Measures, Aphasia Screening, Grip Strength, Lateral Dominance

Examination, Color Form, Progressive Figures, Matching Pictures, Target, Individual Performance, and Marching. The HNTBC adds the Seashore Rhythm Test, Speech Sounds Perception, Finger-Tip Number Writing Perception, and Trail-Making, but omits some other tests. The RINTB is very similar. Results are expressed as a scale (the Neuropsychological Deficit Scale or the Halstead Impairment Index). Information on right–left dominance and performance patterns may also be derived.

- **Vineland Adaptive Behavior Scales.** These tests measure personal and social skills from birth to adulthood, using a semistructured interview with a parent or other caregiver. Versions are available for children of all ages and for low-functioning adults. Social and behavioral maturity in four major areas—communication, daily living skills, socialization, and motor skills—is assessed. Responses are rated on a 100-point scale for each area, and a composite score is also provided. Scores can be translated into developmental or mental ages.

Intelligence, developmental, and academic tests

Intelligence is a tricky concept, especially because repeated studies have shown that children's IQs can and do change when they are measured differently, or when the child is taught differently and then retested. Most IQ tests also carry some cultural, racial, language, and/or gender bias, although testing companies are trying to create better tests. However, because this bias has inappropriately placed nonhandicapped students from ethnic minorities into special education in the past, it is no longer legal to use IQ tests alone as an evaluation tool in US schools.

In some school districts IQ testing has been supplanted by tests that measure adaptive behavior, which can be loosely described as how well and how quickly a person can come up with a solution to a problem and carry it out. These provide a more realistic measure of "intelligence" as most people think of it, as opposed to measuring cultural knowledge.

Developmental tests rank an individual's development against the norm, often resulting in a "mental age" or "developmental age" score. Some of the tests listed in the "Behavior, psychiatric, or neuropsychiatric tests" section in this chapter also chart a person's developmental stages.

Academic testing is a must during the special education evaluation process. It's also used with adults to provide clues about undiscovered learning disabilities or to design adult learning programs. Some clinicians like to compare the results of these three types of tests, a practice that provides a picture of actual achievement against the background of supposed innate capability.

Sometimes instead of one of the commercial tests listed, a local, state, or national academic test is used to rate a child by grade level.

- **Adaptive Behavior Inventory for Children (ABIC).** This standardized measure of adaptive behavior uses a questionnaire format, with a parent or other caregiver providing the answers. It includes subtests called Family, Community, Peer Relations, Nonacademic School Roles, Earner/Consumer, and Self-Maintenance. Used with the WISC-III IQ test and a special grading scale, ABIC is part of the System of Multicultural Pluralistic Assessment some districts use to make more sensitive assessments of racial minority children. Results are expressed on a scale.

- **Battelle Developmental Inventory.** This test ranks children's adaptive skills (self-feeding, dressing, and so on) as a percentage of his chronological age. The score may be expressed as a percentage, such as "between 40 percent and 55 percent of his/her chronological age," or as a single-number standard deviation.

- **Cattell Scales.** This test rates the person's developmental level. The score is expressed as a mental age (MA).

- **Children's Memory Scale (CMS).** The CMS is intended to provide a complete picture of a child or adolescent's cognitive ability, and is often used with children who have acquired or innate neurological problems. Areas screened in six subtests include verbal and visual memory; short-delay and long-delay memory; recall, recognition, and working memory; learning characteristics; and attentional functions. It rates skills in all areas and links them to an IQ score.

- **Developmental Assessment Screening Inventory II (DASI-II).** This screening and assessment tool for preschool children does not rely heavily on verbal or language-based skills. Its scores rate the person's developmental level.

- **Developmental Profile II.** This developmental skill inventory for children up to 9 years old (or older people whose developmental levels fall within that range) is based on an interview with a parent or other caregiver. It covers physical, self-help, social-emotional, communication, and academic skills. Scores are provided as an individual profile depicting the functional developmental age level in each area.

- **Kaufman Assessment Battery for Children (Kaufman-ABC).** A nonverbal IQ test, the Kaufman-ABC measures cognitive intellectual abilities in children aged 2 ½ to 12. It's one of the best tests for use with nonverbal children without significant fine motor problems. Scaled scores are provided for overall ability (the mental processing composite) and for simultaneous and sequential processing.

- Learning Potential Assessment Device (LPAD). This test of cognitive function uses different assumptions from some of the other IQ tests, and was designed for use primarily with learning-disabled or developmentally disabled children. It provides several scaled scores, with interesting ideas about interpreting and using them.

- Leiter International Performance Scale—Revised (Leiter-R). This nonverbal IQ test has puzzle-type problems only covering the areas of visual, spatial, and (in a few cases) language-based reasoning. It produces scaled results.

- Peabody Developmental and Motor Scales (PDMS). These tests use activities, such as threading beads or catching a ball, to gauge the level of physical development, as well as motor capabilities and coordination. They can be used to test large groups of children. Scores are expressed on a scale interpreted as an age level, so raw numbers may be followed by notations such as "below age level by five percentiles" or "above age level."

- Peabody Individual Achievement Test (PIAT). These short tests measure performance in reading, writing, spelling, and math. Scores are expressed as a grade level.

- Stanford-Binet Intelligence Test Fourth Edition (S-B IV). This intelligence test is sometimes used with young or nonverbal children. The score is expressed as an IQ number or as a scale.

- Test of Nonverbal Intelligence 3 (TONI-3). This short, nonverbal IQ test for children over age 5 presents a series of increasingly difficult problem-solving tasks, such as locating the missing part of a figure. The score is expressed as an IQ number or age equivalent.

- Vineland Adaptive Behavior Scales. A standardized measure of adaptive behavior, the Vineland scale tests problem-solving and cognitive skills. Scores are presented as a scale, IQ-style number, or age equivalent.

- Weschler Preschool and Prima Scale of Intelligence (WPPSI), Weschler Intelligence Scale for Children-Revised (WISC-R), Weschler Intelligence Scale for Children-Third Edition (WISC-III), Weschler Adult Intelligence Scale (WAIS-R). The Weschler Scales are intelligence tests that use age-appropriate word-based activities and mechanical, puzzle-type activities to test problem-solving skills. They return scores for verbal IQ and performance IQ, which may be broken down into several categories. This IQ test is frequently used while diagnosing autistic-spectrum disorders, because a significant discrepancy between verbal and performance IQ is considered symptomatic of ASDs.

- **Wide Range of Assessment Test—Revision 3 (WRAT 3).** This standardized test determines academic level in reading, writing, spelling, and math. Scores are expressed as raw numbers or grade level equivalents.

- **Woodcock-Johnson Psycho-Educational Battery—Revised (WJPEB-R, WJ-R).** An individual test of educational achievement in reading, writing, spelling, and math, the WJ-R has many subtests that can be given as a group or separately. Standard scores are derived that compare the test taker against US norms and that can also be expressed as an age or grade-level equivalency. One popular subtest, the Scales of Independent Behavior-Revised (SIB-R/Woodcock, Johnson Battery, Part IV), is a standardized measure of adaptive behavior. SIB-R scores are raw numbers similar to IQ scores, but may be shown as a grade or age equivalency.

Occupational therapy tests, including sensory integration

Occupational therapists for children usually evaluate life or school-related skills, such as the ability to hold a pencil and write. OTs for adults may look at life skills or work-related skills. Much of this evaluation is based on direct observation rather than standardized instruments. For example, the OT might ask the patient for a handwriting sample, or watch her perform typical daily tasks such as opening a door.

Sensory integration (SI) evaluations determine how well the body's sensory systems process information and how they regulate sensation and movement. These tests are usually administered by an OT. Most school OTs use informal, observational measures to look at SI issues.

- **Developmental Test of Visual-Motor Integration (Berry-Buktenica Test).** This test consists of geometric figures, arranged in order of increasing difficulty, which children must copy. It works well with kids who have short attention spans. Scores are expressed as a raw number and can be translated into a percentile.

- **Bruiniks-Oseretsky Test of Motor Proficiency.** In this standardized test of gross and fine motor proficiency, the tester asks the patient to try a number of simple physical activities and puzzle-type tests, including running, walking on a balance beam, and catching a ball. Results are scored, and then scaled from "much below average" on up.

- **McCarthy Scales**. This simple set of tests rates arm and leg coordination. The raw score is scaled to a percentile.

- **Sensory Integration and Praxis Tests (SIPT)**. Combining standardized testing, parent interviews, and structured observations, the SIPT examines how the child responds to sensory stimulation. It collects information related to posture, balance, coordination, eye movements and play. This battery of tests takes from one-and-a-half to three hours, and is too long and difficult for some children under age 6. Results are expressed numerically, and usually also in a narrative report.

- **Southern California Sensory Integration Test (SCSIT)**. This earlier version of the SIPT test is still in use by some OTs. Results are expressed numerically, and usually also in a narrative report.

Speech and language tests

These tests are usually administered by speech and language pathologists. Pervasive developmental disorders can coexist with speech and communication disorders, or one can be mistaken for the other. Comprehensive speech and language testing is important for designing treatment plans, no matter what the eventual diagnosis is. Standardized, qualitative measures such as the ones listed here are usually accompanied by informal observations and attempts at conversation (qualitative assessments). These are intended to find out how the person uses speech in a more natural setting, and may be presented in the report under the heading "language sample analysis" or something similar.

Along with test scores and a language sample, the speech and language evaluation will probably include observations made by the SLP about issues such as vocal tone (nasal or otherwise unusual voice qualities), stuttering and other fluency problems observed, and any abnormalities seen in the physical structures used to produce speech.

It is possible to do speech and language testing with nonverbal people. In these cases, the examiner looks at other forms of functional communication, including the use of gestures, formal sign language, pictures, and augmentative communication devices.

Standardized tests help the SLP rate various components of speech and language, including the domains of pragmatics (rules that govern the use of functional language to communicate), semantics (the rules that govern language content, including word meaning and word order), syntax (grammatical rules), morphology (rules governing the formation of words from smaller parts), and phonology (rules associated with a particular language's sound system).

Comprehensive testing will look for problems in both expressive and receptive speech, and also for discrepancies between the two. Tests you may encounter include the following:

- **Assessment Link between Phonology and Articulation Test (ALPHA).** This verbal test assesses speech sound-production skills. The tester notes pronunciation and other errors as the patient says common words. Results are returned as a raw score, percentile, performance rank (from "profound disability" on up), and scaled against a norm.

- **Boston Naming Test.** This test assesses expressive vocabulary knowledge, as well as the ability to recall and retrieve word labels. Results are returned as both a raw score and an age equivalency.

- **Clinical Evaluation of Language Fundamentals—3 (CELF-3).** This is a standardized test of basic communication capabilities. Results are expressed as a raw score, which can be interpreted further with the test guide.

- **Hiskev-Nebraska Test of Learning Aptitude.** Developed for assessing the communication capabilities of deaf children, this nonverbal test is also useful for some autistic spectrum children who do not speak. Directions are pantomimed.

- **Mayo Test for Apraxia of Speech and Oral Apraxia—Children's Battery.** This checklist helps SLPs assess motor speech skills, such as the ability to blow, move the lips, and make other movements that generate sound.

- **Peabody Picture Vocabulary Test—Revised (PPVT-R).** This standardized test measures receptive vocabulary knowledge. Scores are returned as raw numbers, percentile, and age equivalent, and can be interpreted further.

- **Preschool Language Scale.** This test for children under age 7 requires picture identification skills. It assesses receptive and expressive speech. Scores are expressed as a scale, and can be translated into a language age.

- **Sequenced Inventory of Communication Development (SICD-R).** Generally used for screening, the SICD-R works with children of all developmental levels. It employs a box of miniature real objects, such as a tiny basket and a little car, to elicit speech or signs of recognition. The instructions include hints for assessing autistic, hyperactive, and other "difficult" children. Subtests in three areas of receptive speech (awareness, discrimination, and understanding) and five areas of expressive speech (imitation, initiation, response, verbal output, and articulation) can be given together or separately. Scores are scaled against a norm.

- **Test of Language Competence (TLC).** This test for school-age children assesses understanding of semantics, syntax, and pragmatics in communication. It's said to be especially good at picking up the subtle deficits in understanding figurative or abstract language that are common in people with ASDs. Scaled scores compare the test taker to a norm.

- **Test of Language Development—2 Primary (TOLD-2).** This rather laborious test for children ages 4 through 9 assesses both receptive and expressive language, including vocabulary, phonology, syntax, and semantics. A composite score is generated, as are scores for each of several subtests.

- **Test of Language Development—2 Intermediate (TOLD-2).** Similar to the Primary TOLD-2 test, this is for older school-age children. It covers more advanced language use and includes subtests on sentence combining, vocabulary, word ordering, generals, grammatical comprehension, and malapropisms. A composite score is generated, as are scores for each of several subtests.

Making the most of test time

Environmental factors affect test scores, so test givers should do their best to make evaluation pleasant. Proper lighting, good sound, comfortable seating arrangements, a low level of visual or auditory distractions, and other factors can improve performance. Needless to say, the corner of a busy classroom or an echoing gymnasium is not an ideal testing environment for anyone.

Despite the team's best efforts, your evaluation experience may not be very enjoyable. It's stressful to take the tests, there may be long waits between tests, and nerves soon start to fray. The situation will really deteriorate if the person being tested hits the sensory overload threshold. For people with severe sensory issues, be sure to build in extra time to relax and calm down between tests, or even during long tests. The more prepared everyone is, the better it will be.

It's essential that the team leader has all medical, social, and school files needed at hand, permitting team members to get background information quickly.

Caregivers need to receive a schedule for the evaluation in advance, allowing them to prepare the person for this sequence of unfamiliar events. Parents should pack a big bag of tricks to help their child participate as much as possible. Most kids get balky and uncooperative well before lunch, but the promise of carrying along a favorite toy or getting a treat can make a big difference. Small snacks, such as M&Ms or crackers, may also prove useful for reinforcing good behavior. Some children perform more readily when held in a parent's lap or when the parent is in the same room. Some, however, act out more when the parent is present. If the latter occurs, it's no indictment of parenting skills—it probably just means that, when alone with a tester, the child feels more inhibited.

Sometimes neither parents nor testers are successful at gaining a child's cooperation. One of the hallmarks of ASDs is "shutting down" when overwhelmed, so this should be no surprise. Talk to the team leader in advance about what will happen if non-compliance keeps an evaluation from being finished. Don't let the team simply blow off part of the evaluation because it's "too hard on the child." Brainstorm some solutions to the problem instead, such as breaking the process down into small parts with play or rest in between.

Histories

Narrative histories written by the patient, a caregiver, or a practitioner as a result of interviews are also an important element in most multidisciplinary evaluations.

These histories can include the following types of information:

- Developmental
- Family
- Medical
- School/academic
- Social

A developmental history talks about when and how the person met common developmental milestones, such as walking, talking, and tying shoes. For adults, the developmental history may get into social-emotional development issues as well.

A family history includes information about current family structure, such as who lives in the home and whom the person is closest to. In addition, someone on the team will probably ask a long list of questions about psychiatric problems and developmental disorders experienced by other people in the extended family. Because autistic spectrum disorders have a definite genetic background, these questions are very necessary.

A complete medical history collects information about all medical conditions, not just psychiatric diagnoses. It should include lists of current and past medications, treatments, and hospitalizations.

Sometimes a school team will prepare a history that concentrates on how well a child has done in school academically and socially. It generally includes information about any significant behavior, learning, or interpersonal problems observed over the years.

A social history tries to put the person's life in context, and may include aspects of the other reports. Social histories tend to read like a brief biography, starting out with the circumstances of birth and touching on developmental milestones, problems and accomplishments of childhood, family structure and stresses, and socioeconomic, ethnic, religious, and other cultural issues, if relevant.

The evaluation report

The evaluation process itself doesn't mean much to those who are seeking answers. It's the result of the evaluation—the finished report—that puts it all together. This report should not be made up of raw scores. All the actual data collected should be included, but it must be accompanied by explanations of what the scores mean in real life situations, including both home and school or work environments.

The report should be as jargon-free and understandable as possible. If it doesn't make sense to you, ask that it be rewritten or, at the very least, explained verbally. In the case of Early Intervention or special education evaluations in the US, the report must be translated into the person's or caregiver's primary language, if it is not English.

To be truly useful, the report should also include recommendations for addressing those areas of weakness and difficulty uncovered, and for building on areas of strength. It should include specific service recommendations, not just vague state-ments like "George's sensory defensiveness should be addressed." For example, George's report could instead suggest specific types of sensory integration therapy, note the goals of that therapy, and list local service sources.

In areas where direct EI services are offered, the report may include a complete list of all services available, or just those that the evaluation team thinks would be useful to your child. Remember, other services (and particularly home-based services) may be available but not listed. Typical offerings include special preschool classes, speech therapy, occupational therapy, and parent training.

The report should offer a very clear picture of where the individual functions right now in all important areas, including communication, socialization, physical skills, and academic or work skills as applicable. This picture will be the baseline against which future therapies and interventions will be measured, so accuracy is a must. If you disagree with any part of the assessment, speak up.

Parents will probably need to fill out a release form to get their own copy of the full evaluation report. Check the report over to make sure everything's there. Evaluators will soon be moving on to look at other people, so ask any questions as soon as you can.

You can supply a copy of this report to anyone you choose, either by delivering it personally or by signing a release/request form. Pediatricians, therapists, classroom teachers, the special education department, and others may be on your list of people to receive the report. However, you are not required to provide the report to anyone else. You may need to follow up personally to ensure that the report is delivered to the parties of your choice. Paperwork seems to have a way of getting lost.

In most countries, special education (SE) evaluations and Early Intervention evaluations have a legal aspect in addition to their diagnostic purpose: They include a determination of eligibility for public services. In the US, an SE evaluation report must meet the federal criteria that follow:

- It must state whether the student needs special education and related services.

- It must clearly state the basis for making this determination.

- Relevant behavior noted during observation of the student in an appropriate setting must be described.

- The relationship of that behavior to the student's academic and social functioning must be described.

- It must summarize any educationally relevant health, developmental, and medical findings.

- For students with learning disabilities, it must state whether there is a discrepancy between achievement and ability that cannot be corrected without special education and related services.

- It must include a determination concerning the effects of environmental, cultural, or economic disadvantage, where appropriate.

- It must state if there is a need for specialized services, materials, and equipment for the student with a low-incidence disability. (*Note:* The autistic spectrum disorders are considered low-incidence disabilities under current education law, despite their actual prevalence.)

In other countries, the results of an SE or EI evaluation may be more or less binding, and different formats and data may be required in the final report. School officials or disability advocates should be able to help you find out about pertinent regulations and requirements.

About adult diagnosis

Twenty or even ten years ago, few children on the higher functioning end of the autistic spectrum were diagnosed. Accordingly, many teenagers and adults fit the profile but have never been diagnosed, and others have so far gone through life with a misdiagnosis of a psychiatric condition, mild mental retardation, minimal brain dysfunction (MBD is the old term for ADD/ADHD-like conditions), severe ADD, apraxia or dyspraxia of speech, or another inappropriate label.

Adults presenting with undiagnosed ASDs have frequently been frustrated for years in their attempts to receive help. They may have been mistreated by family members and peers, have often been unsuccessful in school and work, and may have been given large doses of useless or even harmful medications in the past. As a result, some rarely see a physician or psychiatrist unless they are in acute crisis. Others may present with constant physical complaints (not necessarily psychosomatic, although they may be dismissed as such), but keep the other issues under wraps.

Many suffer from more noticeable comorbid problems, particularly depression and obsessive-compulsive disorder. Often it's these that bring an adult into the doctor's office, not the sensory difficulties and processing problems that have been with him for life. Practitioners savvy enough to recognize the symptoms may be able to effect great change in the lives of adults with undiagnosed ASDs.

Unfortunately, most of the diagnostic tools commonly used to pinpoint autistic spectrum disorders are geared toward use with children. Physicians may be able to access a person's childhood records and make a retrospective diagnosis based on the data they contain. Alternatively, they can use one of the autism-rating scales (asking the patient to answer based on his entire life, not simply current experiences) in conjunction with adult IQ testing and other measures, such as the SIPT test for measuring sensory integration dysfunction. Of course, many adults will not be able to answer the rating scale questions about infancy and toddlerhood, and memories can be faulty. If the person provides permission and a family member is available, an interview with a parent or older sibling may be able to clarify things.

Literate adults tend to self-diagnose, and may even bring the book that "finally explained why I'm the way I am" in to the doctor. As a way of gently explaining about ASDs, practitioners working with people who might be particularly sensitive to being mislabeled again may want to suggest that patients look at books written by adults on the autistic spectrum. Books by Donna Williams and Temple Grandin, among others, can be real eye-openers. Other adults may prefer a "just the facts" approach to these personal accounts. Practitioners might refer them to a book such as this one or provide short, printed summaries explaining how ASDs are diagnosed and treated.

Nonliterate adults with ASDs also deserve a sensitive and thoughtful approach. Working with an occupational therapist who is knowledgeable about sensory integration issues can be very helpful. Practitioners or family members may be able to read printed materials to the person, and can facilitate as much discussion as is possible. Affected adults may need to bring a family member, friend, advocate, or sign language interpreter to the consultation and evaluation sessions. Practitioners should encourage them to do so.

For practitioners, it's important to recognize how intrusive the diagnostic process for ASDs can be. Most adults do not like to answer questions about embarrassing subjects, such as toileting, obsessive-compulsive behavior, social difficulties, or bad school experiences. It's one thing to volunteer such information to a trusted friend or counselor; it's quite another to respond to a cold questionnaire offered by an unfamiliar professional. It may take time to build a relationship that allows for this kind of probing.

An adult needs to be an equal partner in the diagnostic team, just as parents should be when a child is diagnosed. If you are an adult who suspects that you might have an ASD, do your best to compile the same records of childhood milestones and difficulties that a parent might bring to a child's evaluation. You may want to get help from a disability advocate if getting these records is difficult.

If you have sensory issues that have made getting health care difficult in the past, such as an extreme sensitivity to flickering fluorescent lights or medical smells, it's okay to ask that the consultation appointment take place in a setting that won't be too stressful. In some cases, public health providers (particularly social workers) will even make house calls. It may put your mind at ease to know that many types of therapy for ASDs, including occupational therapy and speech therapy, can be done in your home or another nonclinical setting. Good therapists can give you "homework" to do on your own, as well.

You can choose to bring a family member, friend, advocate, or interpreter to the consultation appointment, and to any evaluation and testing appointments. This is a good idea if communication is an issue or if you tend to get intimidated by doctors. Writing down your concerns and questions in advance is definitely an excellent plan. You may even want to send them to the physician or evaluation team in advance of your appointment.

About misdiagnosis

Reluctant pediatricians aren't the only problem you may face on the way to diagnosis. Misdiagnosis is common, as is attribution of ASD symptoms to another known health condition, to medication, or to psychiatric or family problems. This often prevents patients from seeking the help of a specialist when it's needed.

Kim, mother of 7-year-old Brad, lost years of precious time before his diagnosis with Landau-Kleffner syndrome:

> *Brad did not receive a diagnosis until he was 7 years old, when his neurologist at a university hospital clinic made the call. Until then, his difficulties had been chalked up to side effects of his epilepsy medication, or aftereffects of a hemorrhage he suffered at birth.*

If you or your child have other known health problems, be sure to list them in your pre-consultation letter—and explain why you don't think they're the cause of the problems you're investigating. The physician may not agree, but stick to your guns about getting a formal assessment. Tell the doctor that when the diagnostic team's members take a look, they can make a better judgment about the various factors involved.

Robin, mother of 5-year-old Nicole, says,

> *Nicole was diagnosed a year ago by a psychologist at a regional child development center. At first, the diagnosis was "expressive/receptive language delay," but as the doctor learned more about Nicole, he changed it to "mild autism, high-functioning." She had previously been labeled as having a language disorder by the school district's Early Intervention assessors. I felt valuable time was lost for Nicole by that misdiagnosis.*

Misdiagnosis seems to be most common when families rely on a single professional, particularly when that person's training is in special education, psychology, or speech therapy alone, or when a physician has little experience with or interest in developmental disabilities.

Parents also need to know that doctors' answers generally reflect their area of expertise. Psychiatrists are rarely in the know about gastroenterology or immunology, and vice versa, even though problems in one physical system can affect another. If you ask questions of the wrong professional, you can pretty much expect to hear a negative answer, or to hear that some other specialty's perspective on ASDs is bunk.

What to do if you don't agree

You don't have to agree with the evaluation team's diagnosis, or its recommendations. Before you fire off an angry letter, go over the report with your spouse, a trusted friend, or a disability advocate to make sure you understand what they're saying, and that the problem is not just a difference in perspective or terminology.

Chapter 9 goes over the legal procedure for appealing a special education evaluation, including choice or denial of therapies. Insurance companies, HMOs, universal medical-care schemes, and medical facilities all have formal appeal boards. Just as with a doctor you pay privately, you can always ask for a second opinion. It may be hard to get the insurance company to spring for more than one multidisciplinary evaluation, however, so your next visit might be with a neuropsychologist, neurologist, or psychiatrist only.

Make any appeal or request for a second opinion in writing, and keep copies of this and all other correspondence with your doctor, HMO, or insurance company.

Occasionally team members strongly disagree. Under normal conditions, they work hard to iron these out before writing their report, so you'll be none the wiser. However, sometimes these disagreements pop up in the conclusions or recommendations section, or a dissenting opinion may even be attached to the final document.

Unless the dissenter seems to be way out in left field and therefore easily ignored, this puts you in a bad situation. You don't want to be drawn into a dispute between evaluators. You may need to call in a referee: a medical review board or a practitioner who can reassess the person and issue a second opinion.

The diagnostic process can be full of fear and worry, but no matter what the verdict turns out to be, most people are relieved to finally have a name for what's wrong. Plain talk can hurt at first, but a sugar-coated diagnosis has never helped someone get needed services.

Sally, mother of 5-year-old Dhylan (diagnosed PDD-NOS with autistic features) put it this way:

> I personally despise the diagnosis—I call it "Perverse Diagnostic Denial, Not Otherwise Specified." Doctors are too afraid to use the "A word," they think they might break our hearts. They don't realize that our hearts were broken long before we took this child to the doctor for evaluation. We need a firm diagnosis of autism. There are

more benefits and programs for those given a correct and definitive diagnosis.

No matter how depressing the test scores or reports may seem, keep in mind that they measure only where the person concerned is today. There is hope, there is help, and things will get better.

That's what the next three chapters of this book are all about.

CHAPTER 4

Getting Started

THIS CHAPTER COVERS HOW YOU CAN MOVE from the shock of an ASD diagnosis to actively helping the person affected. It includes many quotes from people with ASDs and their families, because they have good advice to share. Their main message: You can't let a diagnosis paralyze you, nor can you let it take over your relationship with your child or your family's life. Sections discuss dealing with difficult emotions, setting goals, and creating your own plan to meet those goals.

Whenever possible, adults with ASDs should set their own goals, and make their own plans to meet them. Some may need assistance with tasks such as carrying out research, making official phone calls, and handling extensive paperwork. If you are an adult with an autistic spectrum disorder and resources are hard to find in your community, the ideas discussed in this otherwise parent-oriented chapter may be helpful. In addition, adult-oriented support groups and the Internet can put you in touch with local or nationally known professionals and help you meet supportive people.

Professionals should find the information in this chapter useful for guiding clients and their families through the difficult postdiagnosis period, and for helping them make and carry out plans.

Changing dreams

Coming to terms with a child's permanent disability is like grieving. All people go into the job of parenthood with hopes, dreams, and plans. Even before a baby is born, mothers and fathers fantasize about cheering at soccer games, enjoying family vacations together, watching their progeny graduate from college.

A autistic spectrum diagnosis changes those dreams. It's as if that child you dreamed about has actually died, or been stolen away and replaced by another. People go through all the stages of fear, sadness, anger, and acceptance that make up the grieving process before they finally deal with the diagnosis and move on.

Fear

After a diagnosis, the first emotion that sweeps over most parents is absolute fear and panic. For some people, it's such an overwhelming feeling that they go numb inside, unable to cope with the frightening level of intensity.

Peter, father of 3-year-old Morgan, has felt trapped in this stage since his son's diagnosis:

> It's been three months since the diagnosis, and I'm only now able to say the letters "PDD-NOS." I can't talk about it with anyone, not even [my wife] . . . in fact, she's been yelling at me a lot, saying that I must not care, because she's carrying the whole load right now.
>
> The truth is that I care too much, and I just don't know what to do. I don't know if my boy is going to be okay, I don't know if I'm going to be okay, I don't know if this marriage is going to be okay. Some days I want to run away. I keep wishing this was a dream, and I'm going to wake up and everything will be normal again. And then I wake up, and it's so not-normal, and there's nobody among our old friends or at work who I can talk to about it.

Some people feel like they need permission to scream, cry, and say the angry, hurt words that want to come out. If your partner seems to have shut down, maybe the best thing you can do is grant that permission—and get out of the way! People do cope differently. It's just a fact of life.

Make time to sit down and talk with your partner, a close friend or relative, a trusted clergy member, or a counselor. Just getting your feelings out in the open can lift your burden perceptibly.

It may be hard to find someone to talk to about these issues, especially if you are a single parent or your relationship is already stressed. Support groups (see Chapter 10, *Family Issues and Support*) were created for exactly this purpose. You might also try pouring your feelings out in a journal.

No matter how you choose to do it, expressing fears lets them out. Once they are no longer a secret, you can examine them, see which ones are realistic and which are not, and make a plan of action. As long as they are held inside, you're expending your energy to keep them pushed down—and it never works.

Here are some of the worries expressed by parents who were interviewed for this book. You may recognize your own worst fears in their statements.

I am fearful that he will never progress past early school level. He probably gains two months for each year of age (currently tests at about age 3 level, except for speech, which is worse). This will eventually slow down. If he isn't helped within two years, he will be institutionalized or our family will dissolve.

· · · · ·

My fears are that he will be unable to defend himself, and that my daughter will have to give up certain things to care for him.

· · · · ·

When I think of Doug as an adult, it really scares me. Each day that he gets older, so do I, and I'm finding that he's getting to be so strong. I know Doug is going to be a big boy, probably near six feet tall. Sometimes now I can hardly handle Doug when he's upset, especially in public, and my worst fear is that I'm going to have to find someplace else for Doug to live. I do know that when Doug enters puberty it is going to be the big turning point. Either he is going to mellow or get more aggressive. And I'm seeing him starting to get more aggressive.

· · · · ·

My fear is that his life will always be stressful and difficult, that he will be alone.

· · · · ·

I am so scared that my son will never know the joys of having a family or friends. I also worry that he won't ever be able to support himself.

Some parents find that their fear turns into uncontrollable, immobilizing panic or that their crying won't stop. Depression is not an abnormal response to this diagnosis; in fact, you should expect to feel depressed at times. If it goes on too long or is too difficult to cope with, see your doctor. Medical treatment and counseling can help.

Relief

Particularly if the diagnosis was a long time coming, your first reaction may be a happy one. That's something that outsiders will find hard to comprehend.

Jamal, father of 7-year-old Lisa, explains:

We had been to six doctors with Lisa before someone took the time to find out what was really wrong. We got told all kinds of things, some of which are really incredible, like that it couldn't be autism because it only occurs in boys, or it doesn't exist in black children. The first five doctors

we saw were all quick to label her as mentally retarded, and just as
quickly they said she wasn't like any other retarded child they had seen
because she could read, but was not potty trained and rarely spoke.

There seemed to be a lot of suspicion about us as parents, assumptions
that Monica had done drugs when she was carrying her or that we were
abusive. It was such a relief when we found [our current psychiatrist],
both of us just broke down and cried in her office when she explained
about atypical PDD.

Newly diagnosed adults are particularly likely to experience the relief reaction. People who have spent years in near-useless therapy, who have been prescribed the wrong psychiatric medications, or who have struggled with difficulties in school, work, and life for a long time are in need of information and answers. When an explanation finally comes, it's as if the clouds have parted.

Bill, age 43, was diagnosed with Asperger's syndrome as an adult:

I was so happy, I felt like I was floating. For the first time in my life, a
doctor had said something to me besides "you're crazy." It gave me hope.

Bewilderment

When it comes to PDD-NOS, atypical autism, "autistic tendencies," and similar vague labels, postdiagnostic feelings of relief may be short-lived, however. If you run from the doctor's office to the nearest library, bookstore, or Internet site in search of information, you'll probably come up dry. Many doctors do not even explain that pervasive developmental disorders and autistic spectrum disorders are one and the same, leaving families to search through books on developmental disabilities rather than books on autism.

Joe, father of 7-year-old Kyle, expresses his bewilderment:

It is frustrating not knowing what PDD means, and then dealing with
the stigma of autism. And then you discover this is not a diagnosis, but
merely a label for those whose symptoms are alike. There are many
causes of PDD/autism—why so few labels?

A label is not the same thing as an explanation. Even with cancer, an illness whose actual cause is rarely known, there is an explanation available about what's going on in the body and how treatments are supposed to change the situation. Doctors can explain what a cancer cell is, how it grows, and how it can be destroyed with radiation or chemotherapy. This information may be frightening, but it at least gives you a handle on what's happening.

With autistic spectrum disorders, there's no such surety. For now, there's no tissue biopsy, brain scan, or blood test that can show the presence or extent of the condition. Treatment options are scattershot, often seemingly based on guesswork, chance, and luck. It's hard to explain ASDs to your family and friends, not to mention curious strangers.

As one mother puts it:

> People do ask what's wrong with my son, and I have said a lot of different things. Children are very quick to ask, actually, which is kind of embarrassing to him. I usually explain that he couldn't talk until he was almost 3, so he's still learning. Kids seem to accept that, and not to assume that it means he's retarded.
>
> To adults I've said, "He's wired differently," and that's probably closest to the truth. I've said he's "mildly autistic," whatever that means. I've said, "He has some neurological problems." I always try to add that he's really smart, especially if he's standing right there. If he was retarded as well as having PDD-NOS, I wonder how I would handle these questions?
>
> I know he hates it when people notice that he's different.

Guilt

Guilt is a killer. It poisons relationships, prevents forward movement, and can result in a downward spiral of recrimination, self-blame, even self-hatred. It is in no way productive. It is, however, a very common reaction to any type of neurological diagnosis.

Elizabeth, mother of 4-year-old Tommy, says what many parents have felt:

> I'm stuck in this stupid guilt trip, going over and over everything that I might have done wrong when I was pregnant. I've even blamed my husband—we think the genes were inherited from his side of the family, because he also has a nephew with autism—and then felt horribly guilty for doing it. I can't even begin to tell you how many times I've woken up in the middle of the night, obsessing over having smoked pot in college (eight years before our son was even conceived), having one glass of champagne at a wedding during my pregnancy, allowing Tommy to have his immunizations.

Intellectually, I know I didn't cause his problems, but deep down, I can't shake the feeling that I did.

Guilt may be the most paralyzing emotion of all. If you can't move beyond this, do not hesitate to seek professional help from a counselor or psychologist, preferably one who has experience with families affected by disability.

Guilt feelings are one thing you have in common with every parent whose child is less than perfect. Parents tend to take on all the blame for their children's faults, even for medical problems that are beyond anyone's control. It's terribly unhealthy to allow this to affect you. It's simply unrealistic. In families where one child has an ASD, most other children do not, despite being raised by the same people in the same environment.

Perhaps the worst guilt hits when you read an article or medical study that indicates a cause for autistic spectrum disorders over which you actually did have some control. Studies that have linked autism and the MMR (measles-mumps-rubella) vaccine are a perfect example of research that makes parents beat up on themselves. Just remember that as of this writing, all current research on the causes of ASDs is in its preliminary stages, and it's not fair to berate yourself over a hypothesis. Besides, when you chose to immunize your child, adopt a vegetarian diet during pregnancy, give your toddler milk, or whatever past action you fear may have caused harm, you did so with the intention of protecting him, not hurting him. No parent can be held responsible for ill effects that could not have been predicted.

Certainly no one should feel guilty over being the bearer of "bad genes." If guilt feelings in this area are carrying over into your decisions about having more children, you should see a genetic counselor to assess the likelihood of having a second child with a ASD. Genetic counseling services are available at most major hospitals, and referrals are often available through support and advocacy agencies. Genetic counseling organizations are listed in Appendix A, *Resources*.

If it makes you feel any better, the same families that appear to have a higher risk of having children with autism also seem to have a higher chance of producing artists and geniuses.

Anger

Guilt has a tendency to segue into anger, especially for parents of older children. If the diagnosis comes after your child is no longer eligible for Early Intervention services, or if your child has already suffered ostracism, punishment, or improper medical treatment, you really do have a right to be mad.

Renée, mother of 14-year-old John, says,

> John is 14 years old, and was diagnosed with atypical PDD last summer. If you knew how many doctors we've seen, and how many times he has been suspended from school, punished, shamed, and made fun of, you would understand why I am mad! I have spent most of his life taking him to doctors. Why didn't someone have the decency to agree with me that his problems went way beyond ADHD, and help us do something?
>
> He has missed out on so many opportunities, and arguments over his "bad behavior" were what led to my divorce. There are some teachers I would literally like to strangle for the harm they did to my son. And what can we do now? It seems like all the good programs are for toddlers.

If you're feeling uncomfortable about the rage bubbling up within you, you may be surprised to hear that it can actually be a productive emotion. Most people, particularly women, try hard to suppress feelings of anger. Hateful words and actions can certainly be damaging forces. However, anger is often the best fuel for action.

Newly diagnosed adolescents and adults may also react with anger. Often it's directed at their parents, who they feel should have known, should have sought more information, or should have reacted differently to their symptoms. Older adults with ASDs frequently fear that they'll never fit in, that their whole life will be a series of failures, that they may be too "disabled" to ever achieve their dreams. These fears produce an anger that's rooted in frustration.

At least one anger-producing misconception can be put to rest: it's never too late for appropriate therapies, lifestyle changes, and medications to improve a person's life. Although it's true that starting early is best, you can only begin where you are. Take that anger and make it work for you. Let it be the armor you wear as you weather battles with the school system, the medical system, and people who just don't understand.

From reaction to action

People sometimes talk about the stages just described as if they're something you work through once, then move on from. It's not like that. Feelings of depression, anger, guilt, and more will keep recurring through the years. On the positive side, after the postdiagnosis "nightmare" period, these flare-ups of emotion eventually blend into the rhythms of daily life. They'll be balanced by more enjoyable emotions and activities. Before long, you'll have changed your schedule, your daily goals, and many other factors in your life to accommodate new realities. It's not going to be easy, but at some point you'll realize that all this seems normal now.

There's no special trick to getting from here to there, but purposeful, goal-oriented activity is usually what helps people move on.

Setting goals

ASDs affect so many aspects of a person's life that it's hard to set priorities for which areas of function should be addressed first. It's also hard to generalize about people with ASDs—one may have excellent verbal skills but need targeted work on social skills, whereas another may be struggling with toilet training and basic communications skills.

The following goals have been pulled from parent interviews, the author's personal experiences, individualized family service plans (IFSPs) and individualized education plans (IEPs), treatment plans, and other sources. In each category are lists of goals for people with varying levels of ability and proficiency. You may want to use these as a menu for creating your own list of goals, which may differ from these suggestions.

Remember to prioritize your list. Priorities should be those of the affected person whenever practical. A general guideline for setting priorities is to start at the top of the following list, and work your way down:

1. Health and safety
2. Communication
3. Social
4. Academic/vocational

Some might question putting "social skills" before academic and vocational issues, but in truth, without the ability to be marginally appropriate in the social situations of school and work there is little likelihood that the person with an ASD can acquire or apply academic and vocational skills. However, social, academic, and vocational skills are often learned in concert with one another. In fact, all these categories overlap to some extent—once learned, communication skills are the bedrock for socialization and academics, for example.

Please note that many goals on these lists apply to caregivers, not to people with ASDs themselves. Parents, too, must learn new skills to make it easier for those in their care to progress.

Always start with the most simple goals possible. Take your cue from these necessarily general lists, but make your list specific—for example, "reduce spitting in class" is a more workable goal than "make John stop spitting."

This is part of the approach used in applied behavioral analysis (ABA), which breaks down desired or problematic behavior into discrete skills and works on each one with intense drills. The ABA approach has a proven track record, although other training methods may be more appropriate for some children and some skills. The ABA approach is probably best for basic skills, such as maintaining eye contact, that form the building blocks of higher level skills. Chapter 6, *Therapeutic Interventions,* discusses ABA and similar programs in greater detail.

Health and safety goals

The most basic goals are the ones that ensure safety, basic health, and personal hygiene. For some, special teaching materials may be available that are geared to the needs of people with disabilities and their families. For others, you may be on your own when it comes to designing a program.

- Obtaining basic medical care (not necessarily related to disability) for patient and for caregivers
- Obtaining expert medical care (neurological, psychiatric, and so on)
- Controlling seizures
- Providing proper nutrition
- Testing for allergies, if indicated
- Creating a crisis plan in case of a behavioral/mental health emergency
- Managing medication, with special attention to monitoring effectiveness, side effects, and interactions
- Writing a school treatment plan, if warranted
- Reducing tantrums/rage behaviors
- Ensuring that the patient is not physically or sexually abused
- Ensuring that the patient does not abuse or injure others by biting, hitting, kicking, pushing, throwing, and so on
- Learning about "good" and "bad" touches to protect against abuse
- Learning parenting and disciplinary skills that are effective and nonviolent
- Extinguishing self-abusive behavior

- Protecting the person from self-abusive behavior with helmet, pads, or other devices

- Improving awareness of pain and other sensations

- Installing and using child-safety devices in the home to prevent accidents

- Preventing running away by installing and using fences, locks, alarms, and other security devices

- Learning safety rules for crossing the street, playing, and home activities

- Learning to say, write, or otherwise tell (by pointing to an ID bracelet, for example) name, address, and phone number

- Toilet training

- Learning menstrual health and self-care skills

- Learning about sexual health and safety

- Avoiding drugs and alcohol

- Learning about prescription-drug interactions with alcohol and street drugs, and avoiding abuse, misuse, and theft of prescription drugs

- Gaining basic health-related self-care skills, including washing and other sanitary habits

- Gaining advanced self-care skills, such as choosing a nutritious diet, cooking, laundry, basic repairs and mending, and housework

- Medical self-management, including learning about medications and medication interactions, talking to doctors about symptoms, and monitoring coexisting health problems such as diabetes or asthma

Communication goals

For many of these goals, progress will be measured by the person's ability to maintain a communication activity over ever increasing lengths of time. For example, it could take months of structured work to get eye contact when requested, even with a small treat or other reward. Once that goal has been met, you might move on to exercises that lengthen the amount of eye contact. Finally, you might gradually replace the tangible reward with a smile or hug.

Many books about speech disorders claim that there is a "window of opportunity" for learning to speak, and that it closes around the age of 7. Although it is certainly easier for most people to learn to speak (or otherwise communicate) during this time period, it's also true that parts of the brain can always be retrained. Just as adults can learn to speak again after a stroke, some nonverbal children can and do surprise the experts by gaining speech at a late age. Many adults who have never been able to communicate can, with help from an expert or appropriate medical intervention, learn to use gestures, signs, communication devices, and even words at an advanced age.

Experienced speech and language pathologists say that the "total communication" approach works best. It entails using and rewarding all forms of communication that a person is capable of, including gestures, behaviors, sign language, augmentative communication devices, sounds, and words. Chapter 6 provides more detailed information about improving speech and communication skills.

Goals to consider include the following:

- Eye contact
- Attention
- Ability to be peacefully redirected to a new activity
- Pointing
- Use of picture-based communication book
- Sound production (not necessarily for communication)
- Use of basic sounds or gestures to communicate needs
- Improved oral motor function for apraxic/dyspraxic children
- Reducing echolalia and palilalia
- Use of basic sign language (Makaton, American Sign Language, or other)
- Use of simple augmentative communication devices
- Use of simple, single words
- Use of two-word combinations
- Use of simple sentences
- Use of fluent sign language (ASL or other)
- Use of full-featured augmentative communication device
- Therapy for stuttering, cluttering, and other speech patterns
- "Floor time" interactions aimed at opening and closing circles of communication
- Improving quality of speaking voice
- Improving the "flow" of speech (prosody), or reducing odd speech patterns

- Using a variety of facial expressions

- Understanding common facial expressions

- Decoding "body language"

- Understanding and using high-level speech, including idioms, analogies, and slang

Social goals

Most kids seem to pick up social skills by osmosis, but those with ASDs do not. Social skills must be explicitly taught, and reinforced over and over. For some children, successful social interactions or play may be their own reward, but they are not for others. Most children on the autistic spectrum are confused by the complexity of the social scene, prefer to interact according to their own rules, and may appear socially "clueless." Flexibility can be learned, however, if it's approached in a spirit of fun—and if you are relentless in encouraging it.

Remember that many people prefer one-to-one relationships or solitary pursuits over group activities. Some people will never find team sports, clubs, dances, or even shopping at the mall enjoyable, and that's okay. Encourage activities that can be solitary or shared with just one friend, such as bowling, swimming, running, working out, art, model building, carpentry, working on cars or machines, sewing, cooking, card games, puzzles, and computing. One good friend can be more valuable than a crowd of acquaintances.

Adolescents and adults with ASDs may seem to have skipped their lessons on grooming, dressing, manners, and social behavior. In truth, few schools or families provide actual lessons on these topics—and this is a population that wants them. Books on etiquette and comportment may be much-appreciated gifts, if they are given with kindness. Activities that provide specific information about proper social interactions, such as religious training, Scouting, special classes, even theater classes, can be very beneficial.

Social goals to consider include the following:

- Eye contact

- Attention to another person's play activity

- Parallel play

- Learning to handle and process appropriate social touch and gaze

- Reducing impulsivity

- Reducing inappropriate touch or gaze habits

- Reducing the intensity and frequency of repetitive behaviors or obsessive-compulsive activity

- One-on-one play with and directed by an adult

- One-on-one play with a peer, directed by an adult

- One-on-one play with a peer, closely supervised by an adult

- One-on-one play with a peer, loosely supervised by an adult

- Group social activities, directed by an adult

- Play activities "supervised" by older or more advanced peers (or siblings)

- Finding play group opportunities

- Understanding and practicing the concepts of taking turns and sharing

- Building basic conversational skills

- Finding and cultivating interests or activities that the patient can share with peers

- Giving and receiving compliments

- Role-playing or discussing hypothetical social situations

- Communicating online

- Joining clubs or affinity groups with peers, such as Scouting or religious organizations

- Religious and ethical education

- Involving the extended family in care and support of people with ASDs

- Learning the rules of playground games

- Learning sports, board games, dancing, and other social activities

- Improving personal hygiene and dress for social reasons

- Initiating social interactions

- Handling teasing and negative attention

- Gaining emotional flexibility, the ability to handle changing situations

- Learning about and using humor and jokes

- Understanding how other people feel, and using it to anticipate their reactions

- Friendships, including both formal, arranged "friendship clubs" and self-chosen friends

- Learning to avoid being misled, abused, or taken advantage of by friends and acquaintances

- Learning the "rules" of workplace social relationships

- Learning sexual ettiquette: understanding the meaning of consent and the right to say no, as well as understanding socially acceptable sexual behavior

- Learning the rules of dating and marriage

Academic and vocational goals

In the academic area, your goal should be the best performance that the affected person is comfortably capable of. Your expectations should be at grade level unless the presence of mental retardation or learning disabilities puts the child at a disadvantage. Even with these added factors, don't assume that the person cannot learn—it may simply be necessary to try another method of teaching.

As students with ASDs enter high school, parents need to make sure that they are earning enough credits to graduate. This is not always the case for students in self-contained special education programs. Some of these operate on the assumption that special education students will not be going on to college, so graduation per se is unimportant. This may not be the case, though, and a so-called IEP diploma is even less compelling to college admissions officers than a general equivalency diploma. However, special education students can have up to four additional years to complete their graduation requirements. Summer school, classes at the local community college, correspondence courses, and classes delivered via television, radio, or the Internet have saved many a diploma.

A new issue in some areas of the US is a trend toward test-based graduation. Some states that have instituted tests as part of their graduation process or for a special, higher level diploma have refused to allow accommodations for special education students. Without a doubt, this practice is illegal—but you may not have time to challenge it in court if graduation day looms near. If accommodations are refused, protest loudly, but also pursue any resources or special tutoring that could help your child pass the test.

Today, quite a few people diagnosed with an autistic spectrum disorder in childhood attend trade school, community college, university, and graduate school. They are entitled to special education assistance through age 22, and should be able to access services for the disabled at all publicly funded institutions. These services may include academic counseling, tutoring, mental health care, peer-mentoring programs, and other supports to improve their chances of success.

Another area where students with ASD may need enrichment is education for daily living skills. Laundromat 101, Borrowing the Car for Beginners, and Balancing the Checkbook are all "classes" that parents must teach. Try to build in flexibility as you teach these topics, as many autistic spectrum individuals learn how to do something like washing the dishes one way (such as in your sink, with the blue soap), but can't seem to generalize the skill to a new situation (such as in their new apartment's sink, with the pink soap). Chapter 9, *School,* covers more specific education issues.

Possible academic and vocational goals include the following:

- Assessment and testing for Early Intervention
- Assessment and testing for special education
- Testing to determine current academic levels
- Testing to determine learning style (visual, auditory, and so forth)
- Testing for learning disabilities
- IQ testing, if indicated
- Creating a curriculum to address deficits
- Writing an IFSP or IEP
- Addressing sensory issues in the classroom, such as loud noises or poor lighting
- Learning to recognize letters and numbers
- Learning to read simple words
- Learning to read at an intermediate level
- Advanced reading skills
- Understanding difficult literary concepts, including metaphors and fantasy
- Keyboarding skills
- Printing, typing and/or writing letters
- Printing, typing and/or writing words and sentences
- Learning basic mathematical concepts
- Intermediate math skills
- Advanced math skills

- "Kitchen science" activities
- Structured science activities and basic scientific concepts
- Intermediate scientific knowledge
- Advanced scientific exploration
- Computer basics
- Intermediate computing skills
- Advanced computing skills, including programming and graphics for those interested
- Learning to use the library and reference materials
- Shopping and home economics
- Money management
- Learning to read maps
- Learning to use public transportation
- Learning to ride a bicycle
- Learning to drive
- School-to-work transition planning
- Vocational aptitude and interest testing
- Exploring career ideas, including internships and other work experiences
- Identifying and working with mentors in fields of interest, job shadowing
- Signing up for vocational assistance programs
- Paid or unpaid employment using a job coach
- Paid or unpaid employment with regular supervision only
- College placement testing (PSAT, SAT, ACT, A levels and AS levels, national exams, and so forth)
- Identifying resources for success in higher education, including tutors, disability assistance programs, scholarships, classroom assistance, test and coursework modification, and so on
- Trade school
- Community college
- Four-year or longer university programs

Other goals

This category is here because some goals are multifaceted, or don't quite fit into the other lists. These include:

- Planning and setting up a home ABA program to address multiple areas
- Obtaining funding for ABA, therapy, or private school
- Finding transportation or scheduling help to manage therapy and medical appointments
- Finding community resources for respite care
- Finding community resources for day care or after-school care
- Organizing medical and school records
- Setting up "house rules" and consequences to make living together easier
- Reinforcing desirable behaviors with praise and rewards
- Finding new rewards and incentives
- Limiting television and/or computer time, if it has become a problem
- Finding family activities that everyone can enjoy
- Making time for parents to be alone, or alone together
- Working with partner to ensure that you have mutual goals and agree on plans to meet them
- Setting aside special time for siblings to get the attention they need
- Finding support resources for siblings
- Signing up for TANF (Temporary Assistance for Needy Families), Social Security Disability Income, and Medicaid (or equivalent social support programs, for those outside the US) if needed
- Planning related to financial and inheritance issues
- Researching supported living options and getting on waiting lists
- Researching residential living options and getting on waiting lists
- Researching independent living options, with or without support or supervision
- Advocating for yourself or for other people with ASDs
- Coordinating support for other families

Creating a plan

Now that you have a list of goals, prioritize them. You simply can't achieve every-thing at once. Break each major project down into small parts. When you match these parts to specific resources, timetables, and activities, you have a plan of action.

Even though it's a pain, planning is incredibly important to both your success and your peace of mind. Plans give you concrete tasks to attend to, and as the details fall into place, you'll see that things can and will get better. Plans give you a regained sense of control.

Your plan might resemble the kind of individualized education plan discussed in Chapter 9, or it might look like a schedule. Look at least three months ahead with specifics (big goals can go on up to adulthood and beyond).

Here's one part of a plan written for a 7-year-old boy with PDD-NOS:

> *Goal: Reducing rage behaviors*
>
> *Activities:*
> - *Try to identify rage triggers, and eliminate when possible.*
> - *Work on redirection skills.*
> - *Possible medication change, explore this with psychiatrist.*
> - *Work on learning self-soothing behaviors (OT can help with this).*
> - *Set up "quiet area" in room to go to when agitated.*
> - *Look into possible link to eating and sleeping habits—changes? Appointment with allergist?*
> - *Ask about other parents' coping strategies at next support group meeting.*

As you can see, each item on the activities list looks at a different way to address the problem. Maybe one will be the obvious solution, maybe it will take all of them together—or maybe the beleaguered parent will still be at his wits' end when that support group meeting in the last item rolls around. The important thing is that the parent has identified things to do and named people who can help. The next step, setting a timetable, is almost automatic.

Making your plan happen

Whether you're a parent, a therapist, a teacher, or an adult with an ASD, you will need help, as the preceding example makes clear. You can pay for help, you can rely on family and friends, or you can look into free or low-cost community resources and official support groups.

As you look at your first plan, you'll probably notice some areas where extra hands and hearts will be crucial: for example, running a home ABA program for 30 hours per week is not a job for one. Finding community resources can be an uphill struggle, but even in the smallest of towns there are good people who can help. If trained professionals are not an option, go to the folks who have the most spare time and energy: teenagers, college students, and senior citizens. Families have found unexpected gems at the retirement home or high school.

In big cities, the resources are usually there for the plucking. The problem is finding out about them, and coming up with the cash. Programs change rapidly, and sometimes people from one program don't like a different one. When parents or adults with ASDs put their heads together, however, resource lists seem to magically materialize and grow. Chapter 10, *Family Issues and Support,* offers more concrete suggestions on diving into the local talent pool.

Holly, mother of 3-year-old Max, plans to share what she has learned:

> *It's like pulling teeth to find community resources. Each person gives you little bits and pieces, but no one has a whole local resources guide. I will eventually, and I will give it to the ASA and a few others to distribute it. Maybe I'll put it on the Web!*

If you have persistent problems with follow-through, chances are you've bitten off more than you can chew. Try easier goals and smaller steps at first. You may also need to reward yourself for attaining goals, especially if the end result is not its own reward.

Some parents may also need to deal with clinical depression, anxiety, marital conflict, or other personal problems before they can handle intense activity on their child's behalf. If that's the case, do what you need to do to be effective and capable, and try to find someone to fill in for you in the meantime.

Keep your eyes on the prize

Today's goal may be as small as maintaining eye contact for two minutes, but never let go of the big picture. Striving for the best future, even saying out loud that you're working toward a cure when that's supposed to be an impossibility, is what makes today's minuscule, difficult steps manageable.

You may have let go of some very specific dreams for your child on accepting this diagnosis, but certain goals are universal to all parents, and for all children. Here are some personal hopes that parents of children on the autistic spectrum would like to share with you.

> *I pay for Sarah's prepaid college tuition every month. It will be paid off in a year! I want her to function and live a normal adult life.*

> • • • • •

> *I would love for Dhylan to have the rights of life, liberty, and the pursuit of happiness. I would love for him to be accepted by his peers, to marry, and to live independently. I would love to see him live up to his potential, and for others to allow him this privilege. I dream the same dreams for him as I do for my other seven children. If we don't set our goals high, we fail him.*

> • • • • •

> *I would like to see Jesse go to college one day, be successful in a career, and have a faith in God.*

> • • • • •

> *My hopes are that he will be able to have a career that takes advantage of his amazing talents, much like [autistic animal-behavior expert] Temple Grandin.*

Are these parents foolish to dream of marriage, college, a normal adult life for their children? No. Dreams are not the same thing as expectations: they are an expression of your hopes, and they should always be about the possible, not the merely probable. If someone tries to dash your dreams with unkind words, keep moving forward. More is learned about autistic spectrum disorders every day, so no one can tell you with any certainty what your child's life will be like 10, 20, or 30 years from now. Your child may not reach all the goals you set, but your dogged determination and hard work will ensure that he gets just as far as he can go.

And that's all that any parent can do.

CHAPTER 5

Medical Interventions

MEDICAL APPROACHES TO TREATING autistic spectrum disorders begin with physical and mental health assessment. They may include the use of seizure-control strategies, including antiseizure medication, prescribing other types of medication to address specific symptoms, case and medication management, and services provided by special health care workers, such as speech therapists and physical therapists.

This chapter discusses how psychiatrists and other doctors currently treat ASDs. It also covers medical tests and lists commonly used medications, which are described in greater detail in Appendix E, *Medication Reference*. Treatments that appear to help some people with ASDs by strengthening the immune system are also covered. Chapter 6, *Therapeutic Interventions,* talks about speech therapy, physical therapy, occupational therapy, behavioral approaches, and more. Information about special diets and supplements that may complement medical treatment is in Chapter 7, *Other Interventions.*

Assessment and testing

There is no medicine that can cure ASDs; indeed, as of this writing no drugs have gained official approval for addressing the symptoms of autism, although many approved for other conditions are used. So far, drugs appear to work reasonably well for individual symptoms—obsessive-compulsive behavior, for example—but have not been shown to reach the core symptoms of autism, such as impaired social related-ness or communication problems.

If you have prepared a plan of action that sets priorities for areas of greatest concern, as described in Chapter 4, *Getting Started,* share it with the physician who will set up the treatment plan. Bring any recent evaluations, and also a list of past medications, therapies, diets, and supplements. Include dosages, dates used, and effects, if any.

Responsible doctors take a top-down approach: Medication is prescribed only for symptoms causing the most distress, preferably after nondrug alternatives have been tried or in concert with such treatments. At your first assessment appointment with a physician who treats autistic spectrum disorders, you might receive a list like the following:

Interventions Prior to Using Medication

1. *Education*

2. *Applied behavior modification (ABA)*

3. *Speech therapy*

4. *Sensory integration (SI) therapy, including deep pressure, skin brushing, and vestibular stimulation*

5. *Relaxation therapy*

6. *Structured teaching (TEACCH)*

7. *Auditory integration training*

8. *Vitamin B_6 plus magnesium*

9. *Dimethylglycine (DMG)*

10. *Allergy evaluation, including food sensitivities*

11. *Casein-free and gluten-free diet*

12. *Social stories*

These terms may sound like Greek to you now, but all the techniques listed can play an important part in helping people with ASDs. These approaches are covered in later chapters. That they are recommended first by many clinicians indicates how important it is to look at the roots of problem behaviors before medicating the person exhibiting them.

Even the most distressing problems, such as head-banging and other forms of self-injurious behavior (SIB), may be a form of communication. In fact, head-banging is often associated with ear infections, and may go away if the underlying infection is treated rather than the behavior. Likewise, in some people with ASDs hyperactivity is related to having an unresponsive sensory system, and can be ameliorated with sensory integration therapy rather than stimulant medications. Unlike Ritalin, sensory integration has no side effects to worry about. The functional behavioral-analysis techniques described in Chapter 6 can help you find the roots of problem behaviors and lead you toward tools for addressing them. Sometimes those tools are medical, sometimes not.

The assessment process should be followed by a discussion of strategies, including both the medical strategies discussed in this chapter and nonmedical alternatives. This strategic plan should also consider seemingly unrelated health issues. Many people have found that what seemed a purely psychiatric symptom actually had roots in mundane physical problems.

Lucy, mother of 13-year-old Richard, has had many such experiences:

> *My son experiences auditory hallucinations, but after one and a half days on antibiotics, the voices are nearly gone. He is feeling great, and was able to participate normally in classes today.*
>
> *Who would have thought . . . an outer ear infection leading to voices! Which makes me really, really wonder—if ulcers are now known to be caused by bacteria in most cases, how many people classified with "mental" illnesses might show significant improvement if they went through a round or two of antibiotics? And what if I had taken him directly to the psychiatrist to deal with the voices, rather than the pediatrician, who looked in his ear? He would have sat across the desk from the doctor, who would have advised increasing the dosage of the psychiatric drugs.*
>
> *I know this can't be the answer for everybody. But how many people are being evaluated on the basis of their "mental" symptoms, without their "physical" symptoms being considered simultaneously?*

Help your doctor by answering questions as completely as possible during the assessment and planning process. Ask whether medical testing, a metabolic workup, genetic screening, an immune system test battery, or allergy testing should be pursued, based on the symptoms you have seen.

If your doctor isn't sure how to proceed, the *DAN! Clinical Options Manual* may be helpful. See the section "Autism studies" later in this chapter for more information on the DAN! (Defeat Autism Now!) organization. If your doctor seems interested only in prescribing medications, or if follow-up is not handled well, find another physician.

Blood tests and EKGs

With some medications, such as the antiseizure drug Depakote, regular blood tests are required. These tests make sure the medication is at a therapeutic level (the dosage at which it is effective without causing harm) or check liver function by measuring the level of certain enzymes.

The information sheet insert that comes with a medication will tell you if blood tests are needed, as will your doctor. Experienced doctors have found that repeated blood tests are rarely needed on otherwise healthy people whose medication is effective.

Heart or liver problems make regular blood tests more important. Sometimes blood tests are also needed to check immune system function.

Good phlebotomists (blood draw specialists) do not cause bruising or more than a twinge of pain when they do their job, but people who respond strongly to unusual sensations still find blood draws difficult. An occupational therapist can teach techniques for desensitizing the area from which blood will need to be drawn. Numbing ointments such as EMLA cream can also help, although in some cases they cause the veins to constrict.

Lucy, mother of a child who has had frequent blood draws, shares her tips:

> *Tip 1: Use butterfly needles. Much tinier, take longer to draw the blood, but far less pain involved.*

> *Tip 2: Listen to the kid. Seems obvious, but you'd be surprised how often the technicians don't bother with it. If the kid says he has the best veins in his left arm, start looking for a vein in his left arm. If he says he can keep the blood flowing sitting up better than lying down . . . let him sit up. One of my sons has unusually deep veins; every technician seems to have to learn this the hard way. We are grateful for the occasional tech who believes him and doesn't assume the previous techs just didn't have his or her "magic touch."*

> *Tip 3: Have some small reward available for afterward. Even a small container of fruit juice is much appreciated after a blood draw.*

Understanding blood test results

The liver is the body's center for eliminating toxins, and because many medications used to treat seizures or ASD symptoms include or produce toxins, they can stress the liver. Routine blood tests can check the levels of liver (hepatic) enzymes. These enzymes result from the death of liver cells. The liver is constantly regenerating itself, so some of these enzymes should always be present. When a medication is metabolized by the liver, the enzyme level will be a bit higher than usual. Doctors look out for levels that are much too high.

The following three liver enzymes are most commonly checked.

- AST (aspartate amino transferase). AST is also known as SGOT (serum glutamic-oxaloacetic transaminase) or aspartate transaminase.

- ALT (alanine amino transferase). ALT is also known as SGPT (serum glutamate pyruvate transaminase) or alanine transaminase.

- GGT (gamma glutamyl transpeptidase).

For people in good health, the levels of these three liver enzymes are usually below 25. Simply taking certain medications can double the level of liver enzymes. If the level goes over 70, that's generally considered cause for concern. If a person has known liver problems or is experiencing health problems that could be caused by liver problems, a doctor might also be concerned about levels between 35 and 70. High liver enzyme levels can also indicate heart problems.

The following tests are used to check immune system function:

- WBC count. WBC stands for white blood cells, also known as lymphocytes. A properly functioning immune system has a healthy number of white blood cells, but a very elevated number can indicate the presence of infection. A very low number can indicate either a suppressed immune system or an infection that has overwhelmed the body's defenses. The WBC count is included in a CBC count, described next.

- CBC count. CBC stands for "complete blood cell," and as the name indicates, this test measures the numbers of various types of cells that should be present in the blood. It returns levels for red and white blood cells, blood platelets, and subgroups of these cells. Typical, normal values returned from a CBC count are listed in the following table.

CBC test component	Expected result
WBCs (white blood cells)	5,000 to 10,000 WBCs per cubic millimeter of blood
HGB (hemoglobin)	12 to15 grams per 100 cubic centimeters of blood
Hct (hematocrit)	31 to 43 percent of whole blood
RBCs (red blood cells)	4 to 5.2 million RBCs per cubic millimeter of blood
Platelets	130,000 to 500,000 platelets per cubic millimeter of blood
MCV (mean corpuscular volume)	74 to 85, an expression of the average size of red blood cells

Normal CBC values depend on a person's age, size, state of general health, and medications used. Individual variations can occur, and may not indicate a problem. If the results on this or any other blood test seem to fall outside the normal range, ask the doctor whether it should be a concern or not.

Electrocardiogram (EKG)

Sometimes heart function should be tested before a drug is started. Heart function is usually assayed with a regular blood pressure test, a physical exam, and an electrocardiogram (EKG).

The EKG can be done in the doctor's office, and because it uses wires that stick on the chest with an adhesive patch or gooey substance, it doesn't hurt at all. You have to lie still, however, so it's a tough test for wiggly children.

Seizures and seizure detection tests

Seizures are common in people with ASDs, and can affect not only general health but also behavior, development, and mental state. Seizures occur when nerve cells fire off abnormal electrical charges. This can happen for many different reasons. The two general classifications of seizures follow, broken down into subcategories.

- **Generalized seizures** affect the whole brain.
  - Absence seizures are sometimes called *petit mal* seizures, although this term may be applied to other types of "mild" seizures as well. These brief events are characterized by blank staring and sometimes small, repetitive movements (automatisms).
  - Myoclonic seizures are jerking movements of muscles or muscle groups.
  - Atonic seizures, also called drop attacks, are seizures in which the person has a sudden loss of muscle tone and cannot stand or sit upright.
  - Tonic/clonic seizures, formerly called *grand mal* seizures, are the best known and most obvious type of seizure. The body is rigid during the tonic phase, and jerks during the clonic phase. Tonic/clonic seizures are often followed by a "foggy" feeling, headaches, or sleep.
- **Partial seizures**, also called focal or local seizures, affect only part of the brain.
  - Simple partial seizures affect one part of the body, or several body parts on one side only, which may twitch uncontrollably. Alternatively, the person may see, hear, or smell things that are not there, or have a sudden flood of emotions. The person may feel confused and unsure of where she is. She will, however, be conscious.
  - Complex partial seizures are like a simple partial seizure, but with loss of consciousness. The person may walk, talk, or move around, but won't remember doing so afterward.

- **Status epilepticus,** a dangerous and possibly life-threatening condition, occurs when multiple seizures happen one after another, without regained consciousness in between. People in the throes of status epilepticus need emergency medical care. Thankfully, this type of seizure activity is very rare.

Seizures may be present from infancy or begin later in life. The onset of puberty is a particularly likely time for seizures to begin in people with ASDs, possibly because of increased hormonal activity in the brain. No matter when they occur, seizures can have a profound impact.

Dr. Stephen M. Edelson, director of the Center for the Study of Autism, explains:

> One has a better idea of a person's prognosis when he or she reaches puberty. It is estimated that 20 to 25 percent experience seizures for the first time around puberty. This can range from grand mal seizures to subclinical seizures. I have known a few individuals who were not treated for these seizures, and they went from high functioning to low functioning.

Diagnosis of seizure disorders

If seizures of any type are suspected, your general practitioner should refer you to a neurologist, preferably one who specializes in epilepsy. The primary test for seizure activity is the electroencephalogram (EEG), which records electrical activity in the brain. Electrodes are placed on the person's scalp to detect electrical impulses, which are carried to the EEG machine by wires. A printer attached to this device prints out this activity as wavy lines. By looking at this graph, EEG technicians can see where abnormal activity is taking place.

Most EEGs take one or two hours. The EEG technician may try to get a reading asleep, at rest, wide awake, during deep breathing exercises, and while a light is flashing. The test is not painful at all, and some little kids think it's "cool," in a Frank-enstein's laboratory kind of way.

If the short EEG is inconclusive, the doctor may order a sleep-deprived EEG. As the name indicates, the person needs to be awake but bone tired for this test. Parents can take turns keeping a child up all through the night, then bring him to the test site first thing in the morning. You can imagine how much fun this will be with a willful, cranky child! Movie marathons, midnight bowling, and shopping trips to the all-night convenience store are among the carrots that have kept some young ones (and many sleepy adults as well) awake. The idea is for the exhausted person to drop into a deep sleep right away, and it usually works.

But even this procedure may not show clear evidence of seizures. In cases where the doctor still suspects seizure activity, she may order 24-, 36-, or 48-hour EEG monitoring. This procedure can be done at home with a portable EEG unit or in a hospital setting. The portable units are certainly more convenient, but they're rather cumbersome, and wires have a tendency to come loose. If they do, the test must be redone.

Other types of brain scans include magnetic resonance imagery (MRI), single-photon emission computed tomography (SPECT, also called NeuroSPECT), and positron emission tomography (PET). An MRI shows physical changes associated with seizure activity; SPECT scans show cerebral blood flow, which may be a helpful clue to areas where neural activity is abnormally high or low; and PET images show changes in cerebral metabolism.

Temporal lobe epilepsy, usually now called complex partial seizure disorder, is hard to diagnose. People with temporal lobe epilepsy experience odd states of mind rather than the easier-to-recognize physical seizures that result from activity in the parts of the brain that govern movement. During a temporal lobe seizure, the person's environment may suddenly seem "unreal," for example. Objects and sounds may take on a hallucinatory quality. Strong emotions, such as fear or disgust, may come on in a rush, and with no relationship to reality. Actual auditory and visual hallucinations may occur, often similar to the classic migraine aura or epileptic aura that brings visions of patterns and colors, or the person may smell or taste things that are not there. Some describe an internal sensation that "flows up" from their stomach to their head as a seizure begins.

Still more difficult to detect are seizures that occur deep within the brain. Diagnosis of hidden events is hit-and-miss: it would be surprising if one just happened to occur during an expensive brain scan, or even during an EEG.

Coping with seizures

Seizures can occur in anyone as a result of fever or injury, so everyone should know the following basic first aid steps:

- Move the person to the floor, and make sure anything nearby that could cause injury is moved.

- Turn the person on her side to prevent choking. *Never* put an object in the person's mouth "to keep her from swallowing her tongue"; there's no chance that she will swallow her tongue.

- Loosen any tight clothing.

- Stay with the person until the seizure ends.

- Help the person get comfortable as she recovers from the seizure.

- If a seizure lasts more than 5 minutes, or if seizures continue to follow each other during a 10-minute period, call for emergency medical help and wait with the person until it arrives.

Some medications and herbal supplements may lower the seizure threshold, causing seizures in patients who have not experienced them before, or worsening seizure activity in those who have epilepsy. Be sure to tell the doctor if seizures have happened before, or if they occur during medication or supplement use.

Medication tips

Ask for the results of any screening tests, medical tests, and therapeutic blood levels, as well as for copies of prescriptions and other information collected as part of the assessment and follow-up care. A physician's assistant or nurse should be able to help you read these records and interpret test results.

Many people have caught potentially harmful errors by examining this paperwork. Common mistakes include drugs prescribed in different doses from those the physician intended, misinterpreted blood tests, and blood samples assessed with the wrong test.

Karen, mother of 8-year-old Louis, caught an error just by looking:

> I was cutting my son's pills today to put them in his weekly pill holder, and something looked odd. I called the pharmacy, and they sent someone to pick up the pills and take them back. When the delivery man came back, I noticed that indeed the Clonidine pills looked normal now. I called the pharmacist. "Sure enough," he said, "right medicine, wrong strength." Please remember, if it looks odd, ask. And also remember to look.

Keep track of unusual symptoms that could be medication side effects, and immediately report any of concern. Most people remember to do this when a prescription is new, but grow lax in their observations over time. That's a mistake, because little information is available on the long-term effects of many psychiatric drugs. "The first data that's collected is the short-term efficacy and side effects," explains Dr. Marc Potenza, a Fellow at Yale University's Department of Psychiatry who has researched and written about medications for ASDs. Potenza adds that drug studies rarely last for long, because long-term studies are expensive, time consuming, and not required to gain official approval for a drug.

In other words, patients who use a medication during its first 10 or 20 years on the market *are* the test group for long-term use.

Dosage details

Selecting the correct dosage for an individual is more of an art than a science. Doctors who are unfamiliar with a particular medication usually follow the manufacturer's guidelines on dose according to the person's weight and/or age. These guidelines are intended to keep doses within safe and effective levels.

Each person's body chemistry is different, however, and people with neurological disorders can have rather unusual responses to medications. For example, people with ASDs can be hyperactive, but they tend to respond very differently to stimulants such as Ritalin from the way people with ADHD alone respond. People with ASDs may have exquisite sensitivity to medications or require larger doses than would normally be used. This makes life very difficult for those who want to be careful medication consumers.

Doctors can take simple steps to lessen the chance of medication difficulties. Dosages are often too high to start with, or medications are increased to the full therapeutic dose over just a few days. For many people, this strategy ensures difficult side effects and makes noncompliance (abandonment of the medication) more likely. Gradual titration (increase in dosage) over a period of weeks can make all the difference, although this strategy has its own drawback: people are less likely to see dramatic, positive effects right away.

Sometimes, when a medication doesn't seem to be working the dose actually should be *lower*, not higher. In people with ASDs, this effect has often been observed with the selective seratonin reuptake inhibitor (SSRI) antidepressants. It could be that a low dose of these drugs helps to balance brain chemistry, whereas a higher dose actually throws it out of whack in the opposite direction.

It doesn't help that drugs often come in one size only, and that the available doses may be too high for extrasensitive people. Options that can help include the following.

- A number of psychiatric medications, including Prozac, Haldol, and Risperdol, are available in liquid form. Liquids can be measured out in tiny doses and increased very gradually. Liquid medications can be easily administered to children with swallowing problems and to those who refuse pills. You may even be able to mix the liquid with food or drinks (check with your pharmacist first).

- Some medications can be broken into fractions. Pill splitters are available at most pharmacies. Before you do so, however, make sure it's okay to split a medication: Time release medications and some pills with special coatings will not work properly when broken. Generally speaking, if the pill is scored down the middle, you can definitely split it. If it isn't, ask your pharmacist, or call the manufacturer's customer hotline.

- Some pills that are too small or oddly shaped to split can be crushed and divided into equal parts. Again, ask your pharmacist before doing this, as it's hard to get precise doses with crushed pills. Tiny mortar-and-pestle sets can be found at health food or cooking shops. You can buy empty gel caps to put the powder into, or you may be able to mix it with food or drink.

Some medications come in patch form. Tempting though it may be, don't cut these patches to get a smaller dose or to move up to a larger dose gradually. Doing so will keep the medication from being absorbed properly.

Compounding pharmacies can make medications to order in their own lab—for example, they can make a liquid version of a substance normally available in tablet form only. These pharmacies are especially helpful to individuals with allergy problems. Many pills and syrups contain common allergens, including eggs, soy, corn, and dyes. If a hypoallergenic version isn't available from the manufacturer, seek out a compounding pharmacy. If there isn't one where you live, several allow people with valid prescriptions to order over the Internet. Just use a search engine like AltaVista (*http://www.altavista.com/*) or Google (*http://www.google.com/*) to search for the term "compounding pharmacy." As always with Internet-based or mail order businesses, check references before you pay for goods or services.

Be careful to follow medication instructions about eating or drinking. Also, avoid taking medications with grapefruit juice, which can prevent the breakdown of certain medications.

Prescription notes

You may see some odd initials on your prescriptions or pill bottles. Most of them stand for Latin words, so they are hard to figure out on your own. The most common abbreviations used by doctors and pharmacists follow.

Abbreviation	Latin term	Meaning
ac	ante cibum	Take before meals
bid	bis in die	Take twice a day
gtt	guttae	Drops
pc	post cibum	Take after meals
po	per os	Take by mouth
prn	pro re nata	Take as needed
qd	quaque die	Take once a day
qh	quaque hora	Take every hour
qid	quater in die	Take four times a day
q(number)h	quaque (number) hora	Take every (number) of hours
q hs	quaque hora somni	Take at bedtime
q day	quaque day	Take once per day
tid	ter in die	Take three times a day
ut dict.	ut dictum	Take as directed

In the US, most pharmacies also use colored stickers and letter codes to let you know about medication side effects and risks. If the picture or wording doesn't make sense to you, ask your pharmacist to explain.

Withdrawal procedures

If a person with ASDs is on medication but still having great difficulty, a physician may ask that all medication be withdrawn, to get a baseline look at which symptoms are being caused by the disorder and which are caused by over-, under-, or mis-medication. If not managed well, this process can be exceptionally trying for patients and families. Very few medications can be stopped cold without causing distress—and with some, such as Clonidine, stopping suddenly can be life-threatening.

Ask your doctor if there are any symptoms you might expect during the withdrawal period. She may be able to recommend over-the-counter or dietary remedies for likely problems, such as diarrhea or nausea. With children, nonmedication strategies should be decided on in advance to deal with problem behaviors that may occur as drugs are tapered off.

Gradual withdrawal is almost always the best approach. Patients should be carefully monitored for signs of trouble. In some cases, medication withdrawal may need to take place in a hospital setting.

Abandoned "breakthrough" drugs

It seems that every year some compound is touted as a wonderful new treatment for autistic spectrum disorders, often based on only a few cases in which it seemed beneficial. Such reports usually result in a stampede of people desperate to try the new drug. Unfortunately, several medications that have been tested for use in autism have eventually been found wanting. Some of these showed much promise initially. Accordingly, it's important to avoid jumping the gun when you hear about new drugs.

Here is a list of medication dead-ends to date:

- **Fenfluramine hydrochloride.** Sold under many brand-names, including Pondimin, this amphetamine was the "Fen" in the dangerous and discredited weight loss drug Fen-Phen. It has been removed from the market in the US.

- **Imipramine.** Also known as Tofranil, this tricyclic antidepressant didn't work well for autistic patients in studies.

- **Methysergide.** Sold as Sansert, an antimigraine medication, methysergide is derived from the ergot fungus.

- **Lysergic acid diethylamide.** Better known by its street name, LSD, this ergot-based compound has been shown to affect the serotonin system. Despite that silly film *Tommy,* in lab tests its effects were not useful for autistic symptoms.

Although a few patients may have experienced positive effects from some of these drugs, they are no longer recommended for use. These abandoned "breakthroughs" should be remembered whenever a new miracle drug is reported. It's better to stick with the tried and true until clinical trials have been completed—and even then, caution should be your watchword.

Medications

Although the US Food and Drug Administration (FDA) has never approved a drug for the treatment of autistic spectrum disorders, many people with ASDs do take medication prescribed for specific symptoms. Drugs may be suggested to address symptoms such as difficulty in focusing, hyperactivity, self-abusive behavior, depression, anxiety, and uncontrollable aggression. This section discusses the major types of drugs currently used, and explains why they work for at least some people with ASDs. See Appendix E for more detailed information.

Most of the brand-names provided in this chapter are those used in the US. Brand-names and formulations may vary in other countries, and some drugs may not be available elsewhere. Conversely, there may be new medications approved for use in Asia or Europe that have not made it to North America yet. If you're curious about an unfamiliar medication, look it up by its generic name to find the names of non-US equivalents, or ask your doctor whether something similar is available where you live.

Sometimes medications that have not been formally approved by government regulators are available under "compassionate use" laws, including medications that normally would be available overseas. These laws rarely apply to ASDs. Some unapproved drugs may be made available to participants in human research trials. It is sometimes possible—if not absolutely legal—for a physician in one country to prescribe a medication available only overseas, and for patients to then have the prescription filled at an overseas pharmacy.

Most of the drugs used for ASDs affect the neurotransmitters, particularly serotonin and dopamine. They include antidepressants, antiseizure drugs, neuroleptics, and stimulants, among others. Unless otherwise noted in the next discussion, most of these medications have not been specifically tested on people with autistic spectrum disorders.

You might wonder why medications have not been created specifically for autistic symptoms. Truthfully, with the past decade's explosion of drugs that work on neurotransmitter systems, researchers have barely completed preliminary research on medicines already discovered that might help people with ASDs.

Potenza notes that more research is needed:

> Investigation is still warranted into the drugs that we do have available to see in which clinical population drugs are going to be effective. There have been significant advances in regards to our abilities to target specific symptoms.

It's likely that the next decade will bring psychiatric medications that target specific neurotransmitters more precisely, improving the quality of medical treatment and reducing side effects. As this book went to press, at least two pharmaceutical companies were working on treatments specifically for autism.

Antidepressants

Some people with ASDs are clinically depressed, but that's not the only reason these drugs are increasingly prescribed for people with autistic spectrum disorders. Low levels of serotonin, or problems in regulating the use of serotonin, are believed to be one of the root causes of autistic symptoms. Antidepressants may also affect the production or use of other neurotransmitters. And these drugs do not affect the brain alone: The same neurotransmitters are also involved, if not always so directly, in carrying regulatory messages to the immune system and the gastrointestinal tract. They can even change the way a person perceives pain. Properly used, antidepressants can create global changes.

Today's antidepressants are much more advanced than those used just a decade ago, but they're still a blunt instrument for attacking brain dysfunction. There are several different types, and within each group related medications may function quite differently. That's why you shouldn't write off a whole family of drugs just because one was a disaster. A slightly different medication may work.

All the antidepressants should be used with care. Check package inserts and pharmacy information sheets to avoid interactions with other medications. Be sure to tell your doctor about any over-the-counter drugs you use, even aspirin, herbal medicines, or supplements.

Selective serotonin reuptake inhibitors (SSRIs)

The brain is chock-full of serotonin receptors, tiny sites that bind with serotonin molecules to move chemical impulses through the brain. The SSRIs block certain receptors from absorbing serotonin. Researchers believe this results in lowered or raised levels of serotonin in specific areas of the brain. Over time, SSRIs may cause changes in brain chemistry, hopefully in the direction of improved neurotransmitter balance. SSRIs may also cause actual changes in brain structure with prolonged use. There are serotonin receptor sites elsewhere in the body as well, so SSRIs can affect saliva production, appetite, digestion, skin sensitivity, and many other functions.

The following five drugs (generic names given first, followed by brand-names in parentheses) are currently considered to be in the SSRI family:

- fluoxetine (Prozac)
- fluvoxamine (Luvox)
- paroxetine (Paxil)
- sertraline (Zoloft)
- citalopram (Celexa)

These medications are not identical in either their chemical composition or their effects on the brain. Prozac and Zoloft tend to have an energizing and focusing effect as well as to reduce depression, for example, whereas Paxil may calm anxious or agitated patients who are also depressed. Each SSRI has major or minor side effects of its own—see Appendix E for details. Of the SSRIs, only Luvox, Prozac, and Zoloft have been clinically tested as treatments for ASDs.[1,2,3] Each showed strong benefits for at least some people.

Tricyclic antidepressants

Before Prozac became famous, the tricyclic antidepressants were the wonder drugs for depression and obsessive-compulsive disorder (OCD). They are still the best choice for some people, although today doctors usually try an SSRI or two first. One, clomipramine, has been tested as a treatment for ASDs.[4]

The tricyclic antidepressants work by inhibiting the uptake of various neurotransmitters at adrenergic nerve terminals, resulting in an increase of monoamine neurotransmission. There are several tricyclic antidepressants, many of which combine more than one active drug. They include the following:

- amitriptyline (Elavil)
- amitriptyline/perphenazine (Etrafon, Triavil)
- amitriptyline/chlordiazepoxide (Limbitrol)
- amoxapine (Asendin)
- clomipramine (Anafranil)
- desipramine (Norpramin)
- doxepin (Sinequan)
- imipramine (Tofranil)
- nortriptyline (Aventyl, Pamelor)
- protriptyline (Vivactil)
- trimipramine (Surmontil)

Of these, only clomipramine and nortriptyline are used with any regularity by people with autistic spectrum disorders. Clomipramine is particularly helpful for treating obsessive-compulsive behaviors. Tricyclic antidepressants may help with nighttime bedwetting, appetite, sleep, alertness, anxiety, and hyperactivity.

MAO inhibitors

Three monoamineoxidase inhibitors (MAOIs) are currently available in the US. These medications, which address depression by inhibiting the metabolism of the neurotransmitters serotonin, norepinephrine, and dopamine, are

- moclobemide (Aurorex)
- phenelzine (Nardil)
- tranylcypromine sulfate (Parnate)

MAOIs are rarely prescribed, as they can have unpleasant and even life-threatening interactions with many other drugs, including common over-the-counter medications, and with many foods. They have not shown special benefit for people with ASDs.

Buproprion

The drug buproprion (Wellbutrin, Zyban) is a unique aminoketone antidepressant. It appears to have mild effects on serotonin, dopamine, and norepinephrine, and also seems to be a mild general CNS stimulant. It may help with symptoms of depression and ADHD. It has not been studied for autism.

Lithium

Lithium, sold as Eskalith, Lithane, Lithobid, Lithonate, and Lithotabs, differs from all other antidepressants. Lithium can control bipolar disorder (manic depression, which is characterized by extreme mood swings). Made from a naturally occurring salt, lithium is probably the oldest psychiatric remedy on Earth. Natural lithium springs were frequented by Native Americans and ancient Europeans alike.

One small study indicated that some people with ASDs and mood swings may benefit from lithium carbonate.[5]

Mirtazapine

Described by its manufacturer as a noradrenergic and specific serotonergic antidepressant (NaSSA), mirtazapine (Remeron) affects the neurotransmitter noradrenaline as well as some serotonin receptors. It has both energizing and antianxiety effects. A rcent study showed modest benefits for people with ASDs.[6]

Nefazodone

Nefazodone (Serzone), another unique antidepressant, blocks the uptake of serotonin and norepinephrine in the brain. It also increases the levels of two natural antihistamines in the bloodstream. It has not been studied in people with autism, although anecdotal reports indicate it is being used.

Reboxetine

Reboxetine (Vestra, Edronax) is a brand-new antidepressant classified as a nontricyclic selective norepinephrine reuptake inhibitor (selective NRI). It has not been studied in people with autism, although anecdotal reports indicate it is being used.

Venlafaxine

The antidepressant venlafaxine (Effexor, Effexor XR) is also in its own category. It limits absorption of at least three neurotransmitters: serotonin, norepinephrine, and dopamine. Some people who have not tolerated SSRIs well have had better results with Effexor. A brief open trial showed benefits for people with autism.[7]

"Natural" antidepressants

Herbal medications and supplements are covered in more detail in Chapter 7 and in Appendix F, *Supplement Reference,* but it's important to know that some natural substances may act on the neurotransmitter system like prescription antidepressants. Be sure to tell your doctor about *any* supplements, herbal medications, or folk remedies you add to the medication regimen.

Perhaps one of the most important natural antidepressants is sleep. Researchers speculate that at least some of the positive effects attributed to antidepressants are actually caused by their sleep-inducing powers. Improper sleep disturbs mood: Too much can be the first sign of impending depression, whereas lack of sleep can herald manic behavior. People with ASDs frequently have unusual sleep schedules, sleep disturbances, or full-fledged sleep disorders. Medications, exercise, relaxation techniques, and scheduling adjustments can help them get control over these problems. Proper sleep can make a huge difference, and it's best if it can be achieved without drugs.

Daily activities can be powerful mood enhancers as well, from eating a healthful diet to cultivating interests that occupy the troubled mind. Scheduling, even right down to 15-minute blocks, can provide daily motivation and the reward of purposeful activity.

Antianxiety drugs

Most drugs prescribed for anxiety are in the benzodiazepine family of tranquilizers. Some of these medications may also help to prevent seizures and ease depression. They include the following:

- alprazolam (Xanax)
- chlordiazepoxide (Librium)

- clonazepam (Klonopin)

- clorazepate (Tranxene)

- diazepam (Valium)

- lorazepam (Ativan)

- oxazepam (Serax)

- prazepam (Centrax)

Doctors try to avoid prescribing tranquilizers for long-term use. These drugs slow down CNS activity, they often don't mix well with some other medications, and they can be addictive. However, for patients with severe anxiety, benzodiazepine tranquilizers can be very effective. Some people can take these on an "as needed" basis, avoiding medication dependency. One study found that children with autism had paradoxically negative responses to Valium.[8] Many caregivers have noted unusual reactions to benzodiazepines used to sedate people with autism for dentistry or medical procedures.

Buspirone (BuSpar) is a nonbenzodiazepine antianxiety drug and tranquilizer. Because it doesn't carry the addiction risk of a benzodiazepine, it may be preferable for some people. Small studies have shown that BuSpar may be useful for reducing aggressive behavior, hyperactivity, and stereotypic movements in some people with ASDs.[9,10] However, anecdotal reports indicate that some patients find this medication difficult to tolerate.

Sometimes BuSpar is added to an SSRI to prolong its effectiveness.

Antiseizure medications

Although seizures are not part of the DSM-IV definition of pervasive developmental disorders, many people with ASDs have seizures, and seizures can have a deleterious effect on neurological function. In some cases, seizures may be the root cause of an ASD, as in the case of Landau-Kleffner syndrome.

Seven-year-old Kyle has been diagnosed PDD-NOS with autistic features, and seizures are definitely part of his overall challenges. His father, Joe explains:

> Kyle was on Depakote for seizure control [from] ages 5 to 7. This
> controlled seizures. One seizure, in which he was nonresponsive for 20
> or 30 seconds, caused our son to lose all expressive language for a week.
> Other symptoms of minor seizures included rapid eye movements back
> and forth for two to four seconds, followed by laughter or crying. These

> were controlled by Depakote, which may have helped preserve gains
> made by taking prednisone.

Seizure control is usually the first line of medical treatment when epilepsy occurs with ASDs. Commonly used antiseizure medications include the following:

- carbamazepine (Tegretol)
- clonazepam (Klonopin)
- ethosuximide (Zarontin)
- ethotoin (Peganone)
- fosphenytoin (Cerebyx)
- gabapentin (Neurontin)
- lamotrigine (Lamictal)
- mephenytoin (Mesantoin)
- phenobarbital (Luminal, Solfoton)
- phenytoin (Dilantin)
- primidone (Mysoline)
- topiramate (Topamax)
- valproic acid (Depakene) and divalproex sodium (Depakote, Depakote Sprinkles)

Tegretol and Depakote are probably the antiseizure drugs used most commonly in people with ASDs, mostly because there is quite a bit of information available about how these drugs work in concert with other psychiatric medications. A recent study of Depakote in people with autism found substantial benefits, particularly for those subjects with abnormal EEGs (but not necessarily with a diagnosis of epilepsy).[11] A case study of Depakene treatment in autistic twins with absence seizures also presents positive responses, and notes that the boys' autistic symptoms receded as seizure control improved.[12] However, when pregnant women take valproate drugs, their children run a higher risk of autism-like symptoms.[13]

Antiseizure drugs are often prescribed in combinations, as two can be more effective together than one. However, this increases the risk of side effects. Treatment with a single drug is believed to be the best choice when possible.

Some forms of epilepsy may also be treated with a combination of steroids, such as prednisone, and antiseizure medications. Steroids tend to cause weight gain and mood swings, and they suppress the immune system. Unless nothing else works, steroids should be avoided.

Gabapentin (Neurontin)

This relatively new antiseizure drug has been getting rave reviews from adults with epilepsy. It appears to have fewer side effects than the rest, and can be used as an adjunct to these and other drugs. Not only does it provide seizure control, but it also helps level the mood swings experienced by some patients with bipolar disorder or severe episodic aggression. It has not yet been studied for use in autism.

Other ways to address seizures

Adolescent and adult patients with seizures can often make lifestyle changes that reduce the number or severity of episodes, and parents can learn ways to help children. One of the most important steps is becoming aware of environmental triggers. Avoiding certain types of carnival rides, uncontrolled stress, and disco dances with strobe lights, for example, can be helpful. Learning relaxation techniques, such as meditation or biofeedback, is another good step.

Some people with seizure disorders have reported beneficial effects from special diets and supplements, particularly from vitamin B_6, and the supplements lecithin and DMG. These are discussed in Chapter 7. One intervention that can help in extreme cases is the ketogenic diet. This high-fat, low-protein, low-carbohydrate regimen has proved very useful for some people with epilepsy, although it should never be undertaken without medical supervision.

In a very few cases, seizure disorders cannot be controlled with medication, diet, or other efforts. Surgery may be considered. A new procedure involves implanting in the chest a small device called a vagus nerve stimulator. People with uncontrollable epilepsy must take steps to prevent harm during a seizure. They may need to wear a helmet, change their surroundings, and avoid driving.

Antiseizure drugs for aggression or SIB

Physicians may also prescribe antiseizure medications, particularly Depakote or Neurontin, to treat uncontrolled aggressive or self-injurious behavior (SIB) rather than seizures per se. Sometimes this approach works, perhaps because the aggressive episodes are set off by seizures deep in the brain. These subclinical seizures may be affecting areas of the brain that control behavioral inhibition, emotion, or the "fight or flight" response. It's also possible that some antiseizure drugs have other, as yet unknown, effects on brain chemistry.

Stimulants

The stimulant drugs have a generally energizing effect on the "normal" brain and body, but in many hyperactive individuals they appear to even out brain activity, calming such people down and allowing them to focus their attention more appropriately. It's believed that these drugs increase how much dopamine and norepinephrine are released from the sympathetic nervous system, and inhibit uptake of these neurotransmitters by the caudate nucleus. They also increase the blood flow to all parts of the brain.

Stimulants are the drugs most frequently prescribed to children with ASDs, despite the fact that no studies of stimulant use have been done in this population. In fact, the Autism Research Institute's database indicates that many people with ASDs have bad reactions to stimulants, including increased hyperactivity, aggression, and stereotypic behaviors or tics. Out of 2,788 parents of ASD children who replied to a survey about treatment outcomes, 45 percent reported that Ritalin made their autistic children's behavior worse, with 27 percent reporting no change and only 20 percent seeing improvement.[14]

For that 20 percent, stimulants may be appropriate. Start with a small dose and titrate very slowly for the best effect.

Amy, mother of 7-year-old Miles (diagnosed PDD-NOS and ADHD), says,

> *Miles has been on Ritalin since the age of 5. It has enabled him to learn in a classroom environment, and to reduce the incidence of unsafe behaviors. We tried Dexedrine for about three months; it depressed Miles's mood significantly.*

In 2001, the National Institute of Mental Health launched a comparison study of Ritalin and another drug used for ADHD, guanfacine (Tenex), in children with ASDs. No results had been released when this book went to press.[15]

Some people (including quite a few doctors) swear that the brand-name Ritalin is superior to its generic counterpart. It may be worth trying the brand-name version if the generic didn't work well. Stimulants include the following medications:

- dextroamphetamine sulfate (Das, Dexampex, Dexedrine, Dexedrine Spansules, Dextrostat, Ferndex, Oxydess)

- dextroamphetamine/amphetamine (Adderall)

- methamphetamine (MTH)

- methylphenidate hydrochloride (Ritalin)

- pemoline (Cylert)

These drugs all work pretty much the same way, but for different lengths of time and with varying danger of the dreaded "rebound effect." This phenomenon's symptoms range from manic-like euphoria to depression or aggression.

The rebound effect can be prevented with careful dosing. Ritalin is the shortest-acting stimulant, and the one associated with the greatest amount of rebound trouble. Doctors often ask that it be given at 2.5- to 3-hour intervals, with half of a regular dose at bedtime to permit better sleep. A sustained release version (Ritalin SR) is available, but gets low marks from patients when used alone.

Dexedrine lasts four to six hours, and the Dexedrine Spansule formulation can maintain its beneficial effects for up to eight hours.

Adderall is not as well known as Ritalin, but it may be a better choice for many people. It time-releases different amphetamine compounds smoothly over several hours, resulting in less chance of rebound.

Cylert has a long action period, but is rarely used unless all the others have failed to have positive effects. Regular liver monitoring is a must with this drug.

Stimulants and tic disorders

There is a persistent myth that stimulants can cause tic disorders, including Tourette's syndrome. Studies indicate that this is not so: Many children diagnosed with ADHD before the school years go on to show signs of a tic disorder later on, often around the age of 7, regardless of whether stimulants are used or not. The two conditions appear to be related, as they often occur in the same families or the same individuals. Stimulants are often prescribed around age 5, hence the appearance of a "cause and effect" relationship between stimulants and tics.

It is possible that stimulants cause tics to appear sooner than they would have otherwise or that they make tics worse. Many people with Tourette's syndrome avoid stimulants for this reason.

Over-the-counter stimulants

Some patients and parents have experimented with over-the-counter stimulants, particularly phenylpropanolamine (PPA). PPA is present in "diet pills," usually in combination with caffeine. PPA is also found in a number of common medicines, especially cold remedies. Although benefits have been reported anecdotally, these medications can be dangerous if misused or mixed with other drugs. They are certainly not advised for anyone with a heart condition or whose heart function has never been tested.

Side effects reported include high blood pressure, nausea, restlessness, anxiety, insomnia, irritability, and hallucinations. There have been cases of death, generally from heart attack, from OTC stimulants based on PPA, ephedrine (or the herb ephedra, also called *ma huang,* from which it is made), or even caffeine. Tell your doctor if you use these, and monitor side effects carefully.

Neuroleptics

The neuroleptics are also known by the slightly scarier name antipsychotics. These medications are used to treat a wide variety of serious mental illnesses, and they are certainly not limited to the treatment of outright psychosis. Most of these drugs affect dopamine production or absorption; some also work on serotonin or other neurotransmitters.

The very first neuroleptics were discovered in the 1950s and 1960s, and represented the first major breakthrough in medical treatment for mental illness. However, when the results of long-term use and overdose were discovered the excitement was short-lived.

Many of these older medications are still prescribed for people with ASDs, particularly Haldol, which was one the first medications found to help with major behavior problems in people with autism.[16] The older neuroleptics include the following:

- chlorpromazine (Thorazine)
- diphenylbutylpiperidine (Orap, Pimozide)
- fluphenazine (Prolixin, Prolixin Decanoate)
- haloperidol (Haldol, Haldol Decanoate)
- loxapine (Loxipax, Loxitane)
- mesoridazine (Serentil)
- molindone (Moban)
- perphenazine (Etrafon, Trilafon, Triavil)
- prochlorperazine (Compazine)
- thioridazine (Mellaril)
- thiothixene (Navane)
- trifluoperazine (Stelazine, Vesprin)

Knowledgeable physicians no longer use these drugs first. If anything this strong is needed, the atypical neuroleptics are infinitely preferable.

The atypical neuroleptics are recent discoveries. They blend functionality against schizophrenia, psychosis, self-injurious behavior, painful tics, and other major mental health symptoms with far fewer side effects and dangers than their ancestors—although they still carry many risks, and should be used only when alternatives have failed. People currently taking older neuroleptics should definitely ask their physician about switching. The atypical neuroleptics include the following:

- clozapine (Clozaril)
- olanzapine (Zyprexa)
- risperidone (Risperdal)
- quetiapine (Seroquel)
- ziprasidone (Zeldox)

Of these, Risperdal has gotten the most attention as a drug for ASD-linked symptoms. A recent study found marked benefits from both short- and long-term Risperdal use by people with ASDs—but also noted that side effects occur with worrying frequency.[17]

Excessive weight gain is a common problem with both older and atypical neuroleptics. Each drug in this family is associated with a varying risk of major side effects.

Other medications

A few medications that don't fit into one of the preceding categories have proved useful for some people with ASDs, or are currently being investigated.

Antihypertension medications

Two drugs more commonly used to treat high blood pressure—catapres (Clonidine) and guanfacine (Tenex)—are sometimes effective against hyperactivity and tics. Clonidine or Tenex are often used when stimulants don't work or can't be combined with other necessary medications. Both may also help curb aggression. These "alpha blockers" act on the nervous system to dilate blood vessels, presumably increasing the flow of blood in the brain as well as in the rest of the body. One small trial of Clonidine in boys with autism and hyperactivity showed modest benefits.[18]

Clonidine is available in pill or patch form, although only the pill is available as a less expensive generic. The patch is easier to use, and and less likely to cause sleepy "crashes" as the medication is first absorbed in the bloodstream. The crash effect can interfere with school or work.

As Rachel, mother of 11-year-old William, says,

> The Clonidine pill was definitely a wash. Our son was out like a light by 10 A.M., and napped for well over an hour. We saw great improvements in his ability to pay attention, stay on task in class, and clamp down on his own inappropriate, impulsive behavior, but we had to go to the patch instead so he wouldn't sleep through first grade. The patch tends to fall off before it should, but it's a much smoother medication.

When using the Clonidine patch, place it on a part of the body where it's likely to stay and be properly absorbed. Adults usually prefer the upper arm. For children, try hard-to-reach areas on the back. The foam-like overlays packaged with this medication don't work very well. Clonidine users report that the best overlay is the transparent film dressing Tegaderm, although it's expensive. They haven't worked for everyone, but the extra-large semitransparent "Tattoos" bandages made by Nexcare often do a good job at a lower cost.

Both Clonidine and Tenex can affect heart function and blood pressure, so regular monitoring is a must. Neither medication can be stopped suddenly, because of the risk of a dangerous drop in blood pressure.

Opioid blockers

These medications are more often used as part of a comprehensive detoxification program for addiction to drugs and alcohol, but they can sometimes address certain symptoms of ASDs. This use fits the "opioid theory" of autism, which presumes that some of the problems with attention, sensation, and behavior are caused by abnormal metabolism of natural opiates produced within the body.

The opioid antagonist naltrexone (ReVia, Trexan, or NTX) has been used by autistic people in several studies, with mixed results. People in one subgroup of autism are definitely helped by this drug,[19] and it may be especially effective in cases of self-injury.

Medications under investigation

As this book went to press, a number of interesting clinical trials were underway or planned. Among the drugs being studied were antibiotics and antivirals, which are discussed later in this chapter; D-cycloserine (a substance normally used to treat tuberculosis), which acts on the glutamatergic N-methyl-D-aspartate (NDMA) receptor system and has shown benefit for people with schizophrenia; the hormone secretin; and other substances that may affect gastrointestinal function as a route to lessening autistic symptoms.

An intriguing anatomic study released in 2001 found striking differences in the nicotinic receptors found in the brains of people with autism.[20] This means that medications aimed at the cholinergic system, including drugs based on nicotine, may prove effective. Nicotine has already shown some benefit as a treatment for Tourette's syndrome, which is more common among people with autism than in the general population.

To find out about clinical trials, contact the National Institutes of Health in the US (*http://www.clinicaltrials.gov*), the National Health Service (*http://www.nhs.uk*) in the UK, or a similar agency in your country.

Welcome to the medical merry-go-round

Some people with ASDs have been on an incredible array of medications. The side effects can be as bad as the symptoms the drugs were intended to alleviate—or you may just get lucky and find the perfect fit. "Med trials" are indeed trying, especially when it's hard to find something that works.

Ann, mother of 8-year-old Theron, offers the following chronicle:

> *Medicines that we tried for hyperactivity:*
>
> - *Ritalin, Ritalin ER—no calming effect.*
> - *Dexedrine, Dexedrine Spansules—extreme increase of hyperactivity.*
> - *Cylert—hallucinations.*
> - *Dextrostat—increased attention span, less hyperactivity.*
>
> *Medications that we tried for impulsivity, aggression:*
>
> - *Tegretol, Navane, Desipramine, Clonazapam, Lithium, Mellaril, Tenex, Paxil, and Zoloft hyped him up; we also tried Stelazine, Trazodone, Pamelor, and probably many more I can't recall. None of these meds had any effectiveness.*
> - *Wellbutrin caused grand mal seizures, Wellbutrin SR did not.*
> - *Depakote levels his moods fairly well.*

- *Risperdal reduced auditory hallucinations well, Seroquel and Zyprexa had no effect.*
- *Prozac seems to stop some of the whining and complaining.*
- *DDAVP nasal spray stops the bedwetting, as did Imipramine for several years until immunity was built up.*

It's very important to keep careful records of all the medications you've tried, including information about whether it was a brand-name or generic formula, starting dose, dose titration, length and regularity of use, beneficial effects, and not-so-beneficial effects. You or your doctor may discern patterns when you look back over these records.

Frequently medications are rejected before getting a fair trial. Either they are started at too high a dose, causing unpleasant side effects, or they are given in combination with another drug that strengthens or weakens the new medication's effects. As noted in the section "Dosage details," earlier in the chapter, sometimes medication problems are actually allergic reactions to a dye or filler.

"Slow and steady" should be the words you live by when trying new medications. Start low, and gradually increase the dose. Keep notes. Research the possibility of interactions with other medications—no doctor can be aware of all interaction possibilities. Research resources include inexpensive books, such as *The Pill Book,* Internet pharmacology sites, your pharmacist, and package inserts. Several reliable resources are listed in Appendix A, *Resources.*

Case and medication management

One of the most difficult dilemmas faced by people with ASDs and their caregivers is obtaining adequate case management and medication management services. Ideally, one person can provide advice on both medications and other treatment options, handle referrals to speech therapists and other providers, make sure appointments and services are scheduled and delivered, and oversee the treatment process in a holistic manner.

Unfortunately, this ideal situation is rare. Often you must see several different doctors, who may not agree with or even read each other's reports. This can lead to medication interactions at worst, and lack of information about other treatment options at best. Of all the complaints I heard while researching this book, the need for informed case-management services came through the clearest.

Cindy, mother of 15-year-old Jeffrey, says,

> *I felt like I was having a nervous breakdown when he was 2 and I was doing research; again when I got the reports at age 7 and was trying to get speech and OT and special education; and now I feel that way again, fighting with [service provider], trying to be a "case manager" for my son, and figuring out what tests he needs, what specialist I should consult next, to satisfy them and get his eligibility. And now, I'm fighting with the school district too!*
>
> *In my dreams, one person would be assigned to manage the child's needs, from early identification through diagnosis. This person could help parents and child through the system to get the medical, psychological, educational, recreational, vocational, and independent living skills and services they need to become functioning, productive citizens, or help them be placed appropriately for their needs.*
>
> *This person could be a government employee, with power to dictate to the local school districts, to any private insurer, to any state or federal agency, to get the evaluations, the reports, the funding, etc., and to get help for the family, too.*

Families dealing with autistic spectrum disorders are under a lot of stress, and adding a second job in case management and medication research to the load is more than some can bear. There are options, although you'll probably have to squawk to gain access. Case management services may be available through one of the following sources:

- HMOs and managed care groups
- Health insurance companies
- Psychiatric, behavioral health, and developmental disorder clinics
- Government agencies in charge of mental health, developmental disability, or medical care (in the US, start at the county level; in the UK, contact your local Social Services department)
- Private charitable organizations for the disabled, such as Easter Seals or Mencap
- Special school-based programs that arrange for "wraparound" services in addition to classroom help

Some families actually hire someone to do case management, and bring this person to their meetings with doctors, school officials, and therapists as a sort of consultant.

No matter where you find a case manager, you may have to spend a great deal of time educating him or her. Jennifer, mother of 3-year-old Joseph, explains:

> I find that I often know more than my son's teachers, doctors, and case coordinator about hyperlexia and atypical autism—not a very confidence-building feeling. Perhaps there should be regional specialists in atypical autism who not only coordinate care, but put the parents in contact with each other.

The key to getting someone to help manage your case is *asking*. You may have to ask rather insistently, particularly if you're dealing with an HMO or managed care group. Be sure to remind bureaucrats that well-managed cases cost less in the long run, because patients improve more, and do so quicker. Good case management now will mean less need for expensive adult services later on.

Referrals to other treatment providers

Referrals are another hot-button issue. Obtaining speech therapy, occupational therapy, physical therapy, allergy testing, metabolic screening, EEGs and EKGs, and other specialist services is often more of a headache than it should be.

Psychiatric medications are a specialty in and of themselves. Managed care practices sometimes discourage pediatricians and general practitioners from referring patients to a psychopharmacologist (psychiatric medication specialist) or psychiatrist for medication management. There may also be disencentives for referring people for speech therapy, counseling, and other specialist services.

Dorthy, mother of 5-year-old Jesse, used a novel approach:

> It took two years to even get someone to listen. I was dismissed time and again as a nervous mother. I finally had to let Jesse loose in the doctor's office to get a referral.

You may have to petition an HMO or insurance company board for permission to use or extend your use of these services. You may need to write letters, make many phone calls, even contact government agencies. Your best hope is finding someone in the organization you're petitioning who will walk you through the necessary steps.

Unless you have a case manager, you'll need to keep track of specialist services yourself. Make sure appointments are scheduled when they should be, that test results get to the other members of the treatment team, and that direct services are actually delivered and meet the person's needs.

Addressing the root causes of ASDs

Doctors are beginning to experiment with doing more than merely treating the symptoms of autistic spectrum disorders, based on indications that at least some subtypes are caused by underlying immune system or metabolic dysfunction, an autoimmune disorder, or even an infectious disease. Although these concepts should be examined separately, it's probably not a case of "one or the other." All these factors could be intimately connected, and genetic differences lie at the root of most of them.

It helps to think of the central nervous system (CNS), the immune system, and the gastrointestinal tract as a holistic entity. All three are controlled by the same complex stew of hormones, neurotransmitters, and nutrients. When one system is not up to par, the other two will also be affected. In the case of serious illness, the impact can affect everything in the body.

Indeed, both personal and family medical histories of people with ASDs indicate that disturbances in all parts of this triad occur more frequently than in the general population. They appear to have a genetic predisposition to immune system dysfunction, as demonstrated by a higher rate of allergies, eczema, and chronic bowel problems that may be linked to infection.

The tendency in medical research is to study each physical process separately. Advances in immunology prompted by the AIDS tragedy, however, have encouraged more clinicians to see the interconnections between systems as significant. AIDS destroys the immune system, creates abnormalities in nutrient absorption and appetite that can lead to wasting syndrome, and eventually affects the central nervous system, sometimes causing dementia and other neurological problems. Physicians have had to work on all these fronts to bring people with AIDS back to health. That they are succeeding in many cases shows the value of this approach in the worst of circumstances, and makes it likely that similar successes can be realized in other illnesses that have pervasive effects.

In the case of ASDs, there are two fronts for action: genetics and environment. As of this writing there's no way to "turn off" genes that may lead to autism or to "turn on" genes that may be protective. However, growing knowledge of how the genes involved work may lead to measures for circumventing their effects. For example, if it's discovered that a child has a genetic fragility that couuld lead to immune system problems linked with autism, efforts could be made to build up the immune system, to avoid exposure to certain illnesses or substances, or both. If a child inherits a metabolic difference that could lead to autism, the diet can be changed to prevent difficulties.

PANDAS

Research that may bear fruit for people with ASDs is now occurring on a number of fronts. One of the first breakthroughs was the Pediatric Autoimmune Neuropsychiatric Disorder Associated with Streptococcus (PANDAS) project, steered by the National Institute of Mental Health's Dr. Susan Swedo. Swedo's group identified an auto-immune response to streptococcus bacteria as the trigger in some cases of childhood neuropsychiatric illness.[21] One of the researchers' most interesting findings was that a blood marker, B lymphocyte antigen D8/17, is associated with PANDAS. A diagnostic blood test was developed for use in research settings.

According to the PANDAS hypothesis, when some children are exposed to the common group A beta-hemolytic streptococcus bacteria, the same bacteria that cause strep throat, they develop antibodies that mistakenly attack the basal ganglia in the brain as well as the strep bacteria. These children's symptoms are consistent with obsessive-compulsive disorder (OCD) and/or Tourette's syndrome (TS). PANDAS researchers have also found that some children already diagnosed with OCD or TS have symptom flare-ups when they contract strep infections, although this may occur with other illnesses as well.

Although the initial NIMH study targeted OCD and TS only, it raised questions about the diagnosis and treatment of ASDs. First, both OCD and TS appear to have a genetic or medical link with ASDs, appearing fairly often in the same families. Second, both conditions are frequently secondary diagnoses in people who have a primary diagnosis of an autistic spectrum disorder. Finally, subtle social deficits, sensory integration problems, and other symptoms that might otherwise be attributed to ASDs also occur in some children with TS and OCD. So it came as no surprise to some observers when a research team at the Seaver Autism Research Center announced in early 1999 that the B lymphocyte antigen D8/17 marker was also found in 78 percent of the autistic children studied, and that its presence correlated strongly with severity of compulsive behaviors.[22]

Many parents interviewed for this book reported that their children have had chronic, recurring strep throat and/or strep-related ear infections. Some have reported obvious increases in stereotypic movements or tics, obsessive-compulsive behavior, aggression, withdrawal, and other "autism-like" symptoms during or following these infections.

Rachel, mother of 11-year-old William, says,

> My son, then age 7, was absolutely off the wall—aggressive, obsessive, and having his first bout of complex, full-body tics, which involved

making a yipping sound while whacking himself in the groin area. His facial tics got so bad that his chin was chapped from licking it. He was grinding and clicking his teeth, picking his nose compulsively until it bled. It was the pits! On a hunch, I took him in for a strep throat swab. It was negative, but I convinced his pediatrician to send him for a strep blood titer. It came back at 886, over four times the normal level of strep antibodies. His psychiatrist was very interested, especially when his symptoms subsided incredibly quickly when we started a course of antibiotics. When he had similar behavior problems four months later, we did the throat swab and the titer again. This time the throat test was positive and the titer level was 633. He took prophylactic antibiotics for a year, which seemed to help, and we explored the possibility of IVIG [intravenous immunoglobulin] therapy.

Dr. Douglas Beer, a research fellow at Rhode Island Hospital's Pediatric Neuropsychiatry Clinic, notes,

> *We feel [the PANDAS subtype] possibly represents a homogeneous subgroup of childhood-onset neuropsychiatric disorders, and I know our group is pretty much concentrating on continuing to do PANDAS-related research. PANDAS may represent a significant paradigm shift in terms of investigations into childhood neuropsychiatric illness. Of course, we wonder as well about other etiologic factors that may be out there.*[23]

Yet another clue is the surprising effectiveness of the "superantibiotic" vancomycin in temporarily helping some children with ASDs. Dr. Richard Sandler, a researcher at Rush Children's Hospital in Chicago, tried vancomycin on the group of children in his care, all with a history of persistent ear infections and repeated treatment with regular antibiotics. Sandler felt they might have developed symptoms from a "superbacterium" producing toxic substances. Although the children's symptoms did improve during treatment, all regressed markedly after the vancomycin was halted. The published results included a warning that for safety reasons vancomycin should not be used outside a research setting.[24]

Long courses of conventional antibiotics have been successfully used to treat PANDAS, a treatment that is routine for two related conditions, rheumatic fever and Sydenham's chorea. Some doctors have also successfully used antibiotics in treatment programs for autoimmune disorders, such as lupus and fibromyalgia.[25]

However, treatment with antibiotics carries risks as well as potential benefits. Overuse of antibiotics can lead to problems with *Candida albicans* yeast (see "*Candida* yeast and

ASDs," later in this chapter), and overuse can actually increase susceptibility to hard-to-treat infections. The use of vancomycin is especially worrisome, because it's the antibiotic of last resort for treatment-resistant infections.

Immune system differences

A number of recent studies on autism spectrum disorders—in particular, research performed by Dr. V. K. Singh, the late Dr. Reed Warren, and Dr. Gene Stubbs—have examined immune system abnormalities in people with ASDs. In the blood of people with autism, researchers have discovered antibodies to neuronal and glial filament proteins.[26] As with the misguided antibodies seen in PANDAS, these antibodies could damage or destroy parts of the nervous system.

Evidence also suggests that the immune systems of some people with autism are attacking their own myelin.[27] Myelin, a substance that covers the spinal cord and nerves, is necessary for conduction of messages by the nervous system.

Dr. Bernard Rimland (founder of the Autism Society of America and the first medical researcher in the US to seriously debate the concept of autism as a psychological disorder) and Dr. Stephen M. Edelson, both tireless advocates for autism research, have for years stressed the idea of a connection between ASDs and autoimmune or immune system dysfunction. In 1995, Rimland's Autism Research Institute was instrumental in getting doctors from all over the world to attend the first annual Defeat Autism Now! (DAN!) conference. Conference participants have since released the *DAN! Clinical Options Manual,* which any doctor can use as a reference.

Possible viral connections

It has long been known that autism-like symptoms can follow viral meningitis (viral infection of the membrane that protects the brain) or encephalitis (brain infection). Chapter 12, *Adults with Autistic Spectrum Disorders,* includes the story of one young woman whose ASD symptoms began after encephalitis at age 3. Problems are probably most likely if an infant is infected before birth, skewing both prenatal and later development.

Contracting multiple viral illnesses at once also seems to be a particular risk factor. One of the very earliest epidemiological studies to look at autism found that rates were markedly higher in children who caught both German measles (rubella) and mumps during the same time period.[28] These illnesses have become rare in the developed world over the past three decades, and this early clue has been largely forgotten.

Herpes viruses have also been linked to autism in some cases, including two published case studies.[29,30] There are several viruses in this large family, including the one that causes chicken pox. Some researchers have raised particular questions about the cytomegaloviruses, which are part of this group.[31,32] These viruses have also been connected with other neuropsychiatric illnesses, including Tourette's syndrome.

Herpes viruses can infect a person without causing notable illness. However, these viruses can also live on in dormant form for years, waiting to make their move when the immune system gets run down for some reason. Most adults are familiar with one such herpes virus: herpes simplex, the virus that causes cold sores. It reactivates when you have a cold, and sometimes even when you're just under stress.

Parents of children with ASDs point to the high prevalence of otitis media (ear infections)—and particularly otitis media that does not respond to antibiotics—in this population as evidence for viral causes. Otitis media is usually caused by bacteria, especially those in the streptococcus family. One third or more of ear infections are viral in origin, however, and these cannot be cured with antibiotics.[33] Some children with ASDs have had more than 20 ear infections treated with antibiotics to no avail.

If viruses are an issue in some cases of autism, what's to be done? That's a difficult question. Workups for viral infection are rarely performed unless a person is seriously ill. A very few children with ASDs have been tested for viral involvement, usually in research settings. If you have reason to suspect viral infection—for example, if a person with ASDs has ear infections that don't respond to antibiotics, has had encephalitis or meningitis in the past, or has had bouts of recurrent, unexplained illness—it can't hurt to ask for a workup.

In recent years some doctors have hestitantly experimented with antiviral drugs as a treatment for autistic symptoms. This is not an easy step to take. The very latest antivirals developed to combat the HIV virus are both highly effective and potentially dangerous, whereas older antivirals are less effective.

In the late 1990s pediatrician Dr. Michael J. Goldberg (in Tarzana, California) began testing antivirals with some patients:

> I'll bluntly say that we're looking at an illness affecting a lot of these kids. We're looking at a whole group of children where, with the right trigger—be it an immunization, a virus, or strep—you kick off a whole range of neuroimmune problems.

Goldberg says he has found surprising similarities between brain activity observed using the NeuroSPECT scan in adults with chronic fatigue immune deficiency syndrome (CFIDS) and children diagnosed with ASDs.

> I think [prognosis] depends on the age of onset. . . . With CFIDS, these are adults with mature brains, and then their brains start playing tricks on them. But when you're looking at kids, the brain is still evolving. If you shut it down, you're going to "lose" those children.

In other words, immune system impairments in people with ASDs, perhaps complicated by opportunistic infections, may skew the normal process of development and cause autistic symptoms.

Another recent study looked at amantadine hydrochloride, an antiviral drug that acts on the glutamatergic system. This is a system of neurons that use glutamine as their main neurotransmitter: proper glutamine activity is essential for memory and other basic thought processes. Minor improvements were seen in hyperactivity and inappropriate speech, leading the researchers to state that further investigation is warranted.[34]

Immunization issues

Any discussion of viruses and autism eventually leads to the thorny issue of childhood immunizations and autism. Although there is no proof positive as yet, case studies indicate that vaccines have been a "trigger" in the development of autism for some people. There are cases in which postvaccine encephalitis (inflammation of the brain) was medically diagnosed and then followed by autism-like behavior. Some parents report that their child had obvious and immediate problems, such as febrile seizures or catching one of the illnesses they had been vaccinated for. Others report a slower progress in which bowel problems often preceded neurological symptoms.[35]

In some people with autism, blood test results indicate an unusual response to childhood immunizations. Titers may reveal higher-than-normal amounts of antibodies to illnesses the person was immunized against in the past, as though a low-level infection began then and never quite left. Conversely, titers may show nothing at all, as though the person had never been immunized.[36]

There are three ways that vaccination could act as a trigger: activating autoimmune processes, actual infection, and heavy metal poisoning:

- Some children may react to vaccination not by strengthening the immune system against illness as hoped, but by sending it into overdrive. As with PANDAS, this could include developing antibodies that target neural tissue.[37]

- Alternatively, some children may not be able to cope with catching a mild case of an illness from a vaccine. Moreover, as indicated by the study cited earlier as showing increased harm from getting measles and mumps in short succession, the risk may increase with vaccines containing multiple viruses. For some the harm could be infection of the brain itself, whereas others' problems may begin with bowel infection that creates the right conditions for allowing opiate peptides through the gut wall, into the bloodstream, and on to the brain. British researcher Dr. Andrew Wakefield has published interesting studies on the potential links among measles (presumably from the MMR vaccine), GI tract problems, and autism.[38] His research continues, and replication studies have been promising.[39] One genetic difference observed in some people with autism relates to decreased production of the neurodevelopmental protein reelin in the presence of viral infection.[40] (Reelin is also involved in the metabolism of heavy metals.)

- Finally, some vaccines contain the preservative thimerosol, a derivative of mercury that could cause direct neurological damage. The majority of vaccinated children are not harmed by the small amounts of thimerosol used, but people who inherit genes associated with autism may not be so lucky. One genetic difference observed can adversely affect a person's ability to metabolize heavy metals such as mercury, allowing this known neurodevelopmental poison to embed itself in the body and cause harm. There could also be other harmful substances in certain vaccines. See the section "Chelation" in Chapter 7 for more information on how doctors can help with this issue.

Because vaccination is important for public health, no responsible professionals want to recommend it be abolished. However, it may be wise for children who are "at risk"—for example, those who have autistic siblings or close relatives—to opt for single-illness vaccines spaced widely apart, ensuring that the child is healthy both at the time of vaccination and after. Vaccines might be delayed until after the most crucial period of development, as is already recommended for children with chronic brain disorders, and certain kinds of immune system problems.[41]

Developing safer vaccines and encouraging the prudent use of these health promotion tools is important for everyone's health. Already the US Food and Drug Administration has recommended removing thimerosol from vaccines.[42] It is hoped that other countries will follow suit. Research into the long-term effects of vaccines has not been done, but the persistent questions raised about the role of the MMR vaccine in autism might just make it happen.

In the meantime, parents are left wondering what they should do. Joe, father of 7-year-old Kyle, says:

I think the diagnosis of PDD and autism is a simple way of ignoring the problem and not seeking the real cause. In our son's case, his immune system is out of whack. [He has] very high pertussis and polio titers.

People whose immune systems are in good shape have little to fear from routine immunizations. Others should consult with their physician, or perhaps a specialist. No matter what decision is made, there are risks: It seems evident that if the MMR vaccine (or any other vaccine) can cause neurological problems, infection with the actual diseases it's intended to prevent can also do damage.

Allergies

Sometimes autistic spectrum disorders appear linked to, or just exacerbated by, severe allergies. People with ASDs have occasionally made spectacular progress by simply removing allergens from their diet and environment.

Allergies are a type of autoimmune disorder. When you have an allergy, your immune system kicks into hyperdrive while it tries to rid itself of the perceived toxin, making you feel awful in the process. Common signs of allergies include skin rashes, including eczema; runny noses that are unrelated to colds or viral infections; and puffiness or swelling of the face or of areas that came in contact with the allergen. Swelling of any sort is a potentially dangerous reaction, because if it spreads to the throat you can have trouble breathing. Uncommon signs of allergies, according to some (but not all) allergists, can include behavior disturbances.

The concept of allergy-caused autism got a lot of publicity when Mary Callahan's book *Fighting for Tony* was published in 1987. Callahan, a registered nurse, used a combination of a dairy-free diet, floor-time strategies to increase attention and socialization, special education, and dogged determination to end her young son's severe autism-like behaviors. It may well be that so-called cerebral allergies (reactions to foods and other substances that affect brain chemistry) represent a subtype of autistic spectrum disorders. Dr. Doris J. Rapp's *Is This Your Child? Discovering and Treating Unrecognized Allergies in Children and Adults* provides quite a bit of observational information about allergies and behavior problems. See Appendix A for resources.

However, as noted in the following section, "Metabolic disorders," some people have surprisingly severe reactions to foods without having actual allergies.

People with ASDs can have allergies without one medical problem causing the other. It's important that this and other aspects of routine health care be dealt with. Tackling allergy problems, particularly serious or asthmatic allergic reactions, has improved function in some children and adults with ASDs, simply by boosting general health and physical comfort.

You may have to search for an allergist who is familiar with the possible links between allergies and ASDs. Allergists can perform tests, recommend treatments, and suggest ways to reduce allergens in your diet and environment.

Do be careful to find a reputable provider—this is one area of medicine where crackpots still seem to roam free, according to several parents interviewed for this book. The best practitioners are board certified in their specialty, and do not propose that allergies are the root cause of all medical problems.

Be extra careful about mixing allergy medications with psychiatric drugs, and watch out for behavioral side effects. Asthma inhalers and antihistamines make some people feel nervous or "foggy," and can increase hyperactivity. Steroids and the steroid inhalers used for some forms of asthma are especially likely to have an impact on behavior. If medication is needed, use it—steroid inhalers, for example, can prevent mild asthma from progressing, and stave off lung damage. Just be aware that drugs may cause unusual symptoms, and that these should go away once the course of medication has ended.

Metabolic disorders

The story of phenylketonuria (PKU) is inspiring. A group of parents was so angered by the lack of medical research into their infants' unexplained mental and physical decline that they forced researchers to find a solution. The culprit turned out to be difficulty in processing a protein called phenylalanine. Normally this protein is converted to the amino acid tyrosine. In people with PKU, phenylalanine builds up in the bloodstream instead, eventually causing brain damage, mental retardation, and neurological symptoms. Today most babies are screened for PKU with a blood test at birth, and children can be safeguarded by following a special diet. In fact, you may have noticed labels on diet soda and other items that warn phenylketonurics to avoid the product.

What had been a mysterious attacker of young brains turned out to be a treatable metabolic disorder. Metabolic disorders are differences in how the body breaks down or uses food and other substances. Some are fairly common, and not all that serious—lactose intolerance in adults is more uncomfortable than life threatening, for example, and can be easily addressed.

Some people with ASDs may have metabolic disorders that are unrelated to their autistic spectrum diagnosis, whereas in other cases a metabolic disorder may be a very important piece of the puzzle. Other people with ASDs do not seem to have any metabolic differences from the general population.

Sulfation chemistry

Metabolic processes are complex. Dr. Rosemary Waring, a UK biochemist, is doing pioneering work on the sulfation chemistry differences found in people with ASDs. According to her research, some people with ASDs appear to be short on sulfate, the essential substrate of a sulfotransferase enzyme called phenolsulfotransferase (PST), which breaks down phenols and amines. The PST enzyme transfers a sulfate ion from the enzyme phosphoadenylyl sulfate (PAPS) to a phenolic compound, which should then detoxify the phenolic compound and prepare it for removal from the body. If the PAPS enzyme is short on sulfate, or if the body didn't have enough magnesium available to build the PAPS molecule in the first place, this process is short-circuited. As a result, toxic phenolic compounds build up in the body.[43]

Sulfate is also essential for a number of other detoxification processes, including activating and deactivating certain hormones and neurotransmitters. Other sulfotransferases have the job of maintaining the integrity of the gut wall by surrounding cell surfaces with sulfated sugars attached to a protein core. These are called glycosaminoglycans (GAGs) or mucopolysaccharides. GAGs are released when inflammation occurs.

Supplementation with sulfation agents, such as MSM (methyl-sulfonyl-methane) and N-acetyl cysteine, may be helpful. Adding magnesium as a supplement may also help. Even adding Epsom salts to the bath can encourage better sulfation. People with sulfation problems should also be careful to avoid other things that overwork the sulfation system, including Tylenol, sulfa-based antibiotics, and exposure to certain toxic chemicals.

Leaky gut and opiates

As protein particles are digested, they form amino acid chains called peptides. Doctors used to believe that the GI tract could not be permeated by anything as large as a peptide. According to recent research, however, peptides can escape the GI tract when there is inflammation and damage to the gut wall—for example, when the GAGs are released because of inflammation, or when the gut is overcolonized by *Candida albicans*. This is referred to as the "leaky gut" phenomenon.[44]

Once in the bloodstream, these peptides could make their way into the brain via "leaky" regions in the blood–brain barrier, which may also be weakened by the same processes. Sometimes the brain may be fooled into thinking these peptides are natural opiates, which play many roles in the body, including modulating various brain functions. These peptides could be mistakenly allowed to bind to sites in the brain, a process known as "molecular mimicry."

Alternatively, the immune system may decide to attack both these "foreign invaders" and the brain chemicals that they mimic.

Some people with ASDs seem to have an extreme difficulty in handling the protein casein, which is found in all milk products, and/or gluten, the protein found in wheat and some other grains. The peptides produced by breaking down these proteins are particularly similar to opiates. Quite a few people have experienced improvements in behavior, attention, and general ability when one or both of these proteins was eliminated from their diet.

In some cases of autistic spectrum disorders, there is a diagnosis of actual celiac disease (sometimes called celiac sprue). This serious form of malabsorption results from inflammation of the small intestine's lining. Inflammation can be caused or exacerbated by an overgrowth of *Candida* yeast (see the section "*Candida* yeast and ASDs," which follows), or can result from the use of antibiotics, operations, autoimmune activity, or other factors. Celiac disease is characterized by difficulties with digesting many everyday foods, followed by chronic diarrhea or unusual stools.

Candida yeast and ASDs

Overgrowth of *Candida albicans* is a persistent problem for many people, especially those who have taken a lot of antibiotics and those with impaired immune systems. It's normal for some *Candida* to be in your system, but when there's way too much of this fungal organism, it's a sure sign that your body's self-righting system is awry. Too much *Candida* can lead to yeast infections of the skin, the mucous membranes in the mouth ("thrush"), and the GI tract, as well as vaginal yeast infections and diaper rash. Some people with autistic spectrum disorders have experienced symptom improvement when yeast overgrowth is treated.

This doesn't mean that *Candida* overgrowth causes autism, however—if it did, autistic behavior would probably be seen in women with chronic vaginal yeast infections, just to give one example. Beware of any doctor who tries to pin the blame for ASDs on yeast overgrowth alone. Overgrowth is a symptom of underlying dysfunction, an opportunistic beastie that can make symptoms worse, but there's no evidence that *Candida* yeast can actually be a causative agent for ASDs.

In a few cases, treatment for *Candida* overgrowth appears to have made a major difference. If the problem can be documented, it's worth a try to eliminate it. See the section "Antifungals" later in this chapter for treatment information.

Medical testing to find reasons

Many neurologists and psychiatrists try to dissuade people from looking for the root causes of neuropsychiatric disorders. They may be aware that a connection is possible, but they also know that thoroughly investigated treatment options are few. There is some wisdom in this approach, especially because interventions such as ABA, floor-time play therapy, sensory integration, and psychiatric medication work, and work well, for so many.

However, as research into autistic spectrum disorders continues, more people are willing to spend time and money on a search for specific causes (and, by extension, specific treatments). Testing for autoimmune disorders generally begins with the blood. Immunologists, rheumatologists, and other doctors can use a number of tests. Because every person with ASDs is unique, you'll need to discuss test options with your physician. Here are some of the tests that physicians might use:

- **Blood count.** Depleted white blood cells may indicate that a virus or other infection is active somewhere in the body.

- **Sedimentation rate.** This test measures how quickly the red cells separate from the serum in a test tube. With normal inflammatory or autoimmune diseases, they separate quickly. Some clinicians have reported a very low "sed rate" in 35 to 40 percent of children with ASDs, indicating that a contradictory type of autoimmune reaction could be taking place.

- **General chemistry panel.** Generally abbreviated as "Chem," and followed by a number that indicates how many tests were performed (Chem-16, Chem-25, and so forth). The basic Chem panel checks levels of glucose (blood sugar), blood urea nitrogen (BUN), creatinine, and electrolytes (including sodium and potassium).

- **Immune panel test.** This general screen may include a search for antibodies, mitogen, antigen, and lymphocyte surface markers, and blood tests for various specific markers for immune dysfunction.

- **Antineuronal antibody (ANA) screen.** The ANA looks for antibodies to brain tissue in the bloodstream. Their presence is a general indicator for a variety of autoimmune disorders, such as lupus. Note that the antinuclear antibody test, also abbreviated as ANA, may also be ordered. This test is used to screen for several autoimmune inflammatory diseases.

- **Tests that look for unusual levels of specific viral antibodies.** Targets include those associated with the Epstein-Barr virus, other human herpes viruses (HHV6, HHV7, HHV8, HSV-1, HSV-2), cytomegalovirus (CMV), rubella (German measles), or measles. If PANDAS is suspected, titers for group A beta-hemolytic streptococcus (ASO or ASLO) bacteria can be done.

- **Tests to check for immunoglobulin G (IgG) subclass abnormalities (IgG1, IgG2, IgG3, IgG4).** These are found in patients with increased susceptibility to viral or bacterial infections because of a compromised immune system, autoimmune diseases, and immune-mediated neurological disorders. It's possible to plot the distributions of IgG subtypes against patterns associated with specific viruses or conditions.

- **Amino acid profile.** Markers for an impaired immune system include low amounts of the amino acids lysine and arginine.

- NeuroSPECT. This brain scan shows the diffusion of blood through the brain, indicating areas of low and high activity. In some people with ASDs, findings include low activity in the temporal lobe and sometimes in other regions of the brain.

- **Allergy tests.** These can include the common skin test (mostly for environmental allergens), the RAST (Radioallergosorbent Test) test generally used for food sensitivities, and more precise tests of blood, stool, or urine samples.

- **Tests for celiac disease.** These may include blood tests for IgG and IgA gliadin antibodies (IgA AGA, which is the most specific of these two tests); IgA reticulin antibodies (IgA ARA, R1 type, a highly specific test); and IgA endomysial antibodies (EmA).

- **Urine testing for abnormal metabolism of gluten and/or casein.**

- **Tests for *Candida albicans*.** Possibilities include microscopic stool exams, or blood serum or urine D-arabinitol (a *Candida* metabolite) levels. Although not definitive, elevated immunoglobulin M (IgM) levels suggest active or recent infection. IgG antibodies may be present long after the candidiasis is cured, so they don't necessarily mean anything. Remember, it is normal to find some *Candida* in the body. Only severely elevated findings should be a cause for concern.

- **Colonoscopy.** For serious GI tract problems, this invasive test is performed by a gastroenterologist.

A multifaceted immune panel can turn up many small pieces of evidence that, taken together, indicate a compromised immune system. Findings that may mean trouble include elevated CD4 and CD8 counts, or very low CD8 counts; low levels of natural killer (NK) cells; and elevated numbers of B cells, which produce antibodies to disease.

Treating immune system–linked ASDs

The primary goal in treating immune system dysfunction that may be related to ASDs is to clear away any problem that may be obscuring your view, in addition to promoting the person's general physical well-being. It's not unlike looking for a baseline by withdrawing psychiatric medications, as described earlier in this chapter: Clearing up these problems lets you see what's immune related, what's purely neurological (based on brain damage or dysfunction), and what's emotional or behavioral.

The National Institute of Mental Health's preliminary treatment protocol for PANDAS provides some suggestions as to how this and other autoimmune-linked neuropsychiatric disorders might be addressed.

PANDAS treatment options currently include the following:

- Intravenous immunoglobulin (IVIG) infusion
- Plasmapheresis (therapeutic plasma exchange, or TPE)
- Prophylactic antibiotics (particularly amoxicillin) to prevent reinfection with strep
- Immunosuppression

All four of these treatments are controversial, and each carries significant risks.

IVIG transfusion

Intravenous immunoglobulin G (IVIG, sometimes also called IVGG) is made from blood taken from thousands of human donors. It has been used to treat immunological disorders since 1980 and is similar to the substance RHogam that some Rh-negative women take during pregnancy.

IVIG is administered via a transfusion, which can take several hours and takes place in a medical facility.

IVIG is expensive and difficult to obtain, so difficult that even NIMH has not been able to arrange for a steady supply for its PANDAS project. In addition, IVIG is not absolutely safe.

Because IVIG is a blood product, there is a risk of blood-borne infection, even though the plasma donors whose blood is used are screened. When IVIG first became available for use in clinical studies, several people contracted hepatitis B or hepatitis C. A solvent/detergent viral inactivation step was then added to the preparation process, which is now believed to be effective against hepatitis A, B, and C, as well as HIV-1 and HIV-2, HTLV-1, HBV, and HCV viruses. This process is used in three commercial IVIG preparations: Venoglobulin S, Polygam, and Gammagard. Batches of IVIG in these preparations are also "DNA fingerprinted" to look for other viruses and traces of viruses.

There have been official warnings about "stealth viruses" that may be present in IVIG (according to the National Institutes of Health, there are probably hundreds of obscure viruses, some of which may be relatively benign, and some of which may cause harm). Certain lots of IVIG were taken off the market when some of the original plasma donors went on to develop Creutzfeldt-Jakob disease, an extremely rare and deadly neurological disorder related to bovine spongiform encephalopathy (BSE, or "mad cow disease"). There isn't a common test to screen plasma for this disease just yet, so the US Food and Drug Administration has increased its scrutiny of IVIG production and sale. The status of IVIG safety in other countries is unknown.

There is also a risk of side effects from IVIG therapy that are not disease related, including heart attacks from increased serum viscosity (stickier blood), infection from IV lines, nephrotic syndrome, and low blood pressure.

No one is exactly sure why IVIG appears to work against some neuroimmune illnesses. Possibilities that researchers have suggested include the following.

- IVIG decreases the toxic effects of natural killer (NK) cells.

- IVIG binds to autoimmune antibodies.

- IVIG binds to B-cell surface immunoglobulin, blocking the action of autoimmune antibodies.

- IVIG makes T-suppresser cells work harder, resulting in fewer B-cell autoimmune antibodies being produced.

- IVIG binds to complement, limiting the amount of complement available to bind to autoimmune antibodies. Complement is a substance in the blood that assists the immune system.

- IVIG use in high doses triggers a feedback-based inhibition of antibody production.

A few autism researchers and clinicians have been exploring the use of IVIG, and have gotten encouraging results in some cases. As of this writing, a series of multisite trials is underway. The dangers just mentioned have slowed this activity down, however, as has the shrinking supply of screened IVIG.

Plasmapheresis

Therapeutic plasmapheresis (TPE) is an invasive procedure for removing toxins, metabolic substances, and certain parts of blood plasma that may cause disease, including complement and antibodies. The patient's blood is removed, the plasma is separated out, and the remaining blood elements are combined with a plasma replacement and put back into the patient. Currently, between 10,000 and 15,000 patients with neurological disorders are treated with TPE in the US each year. Response rates reported vary depending on the condition treated.[45]

Plasma exchange takes place in a medical facility and is usually repeated several times over a period of weeks for maximum effectiveness. It rarely produces permanent improvement, although the initial response may make successful pharmaceutical treatment possible.

As with IVIG, there is a possibility of infection at the IV insertion sites. Both serious and fatal reactions have been reported, primarily cardiac and respiratory arrest. The risk of such reactions is probably higher if human plasma is used as the replacement fluid, because it could transmit a new infection.

Its potential for complications makes physicians leery of using plasmapheresis unless absolutely necessary. If this option is chosen, attention to detail is very important, particularly in mixing the replacement solution.

Prophylactic antibiotic therapy

Prophylactic antibiotic therapy, the long-term use of antibiotics to prevent infection, was described earlier in this chapter.

If antibiotics must be used, they should be accompanied by probiotics, such as *Lactobacillus acidophilus,* to rebuild friendly intestinal fauna. Your physician can suggest supplements and dietary changes to minimize any detrimental impact from antibiotics.

Immunosuppression

To treat other autoimmune conditions, suppressing the immune response with drugs is a common strategy. Obviously, the primary danger here is that resistance to dangerous diseases could be dampened. This treatment would not normally be supported in cases where a compromised immune system is already a possibility.

Immune system modulators

AIDS research has resulted in many new medications that could be called "immune system stimulants" or "immune system modulators." The majority of these drugs have side effects that make them undesirable, except for patients faced with a life-threatening immune deficiency. Others may deserve a trial for treating immune system–linked ASDs. As the saying goes, "your mileage may vary" with these medications and supplements.

Immune modulators currently used by some patients include the following:

- Kutapressin, a porcine liver extract comprised of very small proteins or polypeptides. Kutapressin inhibits human herpes viruses (its best known use is as a medication for herpes zoster, or shingles) and reduces inflammation. It is given in intramuscular injections; can be rather expensive, because the supply is currently limited; and may not be a long-term solution for herpes infection.

- Dimethylglycine (DMG) is a vitamin-like supplement that appears to mildly boost the immune system, possibly by increasing the number of natural killer (NK) cells. DMG has a fairly long track record as a treatment for autistic symptoms, including some success in clinical trials. According to the ARI's Rimland, "Many parents have reported that, within a few days of starting DMG, the child's behavior improved noticeably, better eye contact was seen, frustration tolerance increased, the child's speech improved, or more interest and ability in speaking was observed."[46]

- Inosine pranobex (Isoprinosine), an older antiviral, is also active against human herpes virus and other infections. It is a relatively weak immune modulator.

- Acyclovir (Zovirax) is a potent antiviral that works against several human herpes viruses, Epstein-Barr virus, herpes zoster, varicella (chicken pox), cytomegalovirus, and other viruses.

- Foscarnet is another antiherpes drug (and unfortunately, rather toxic).

- Ampligen is a nucleic acid (NA) compound that apparently heightens production of the body's own immunological and antiviral agents, such as interferon. It is expensive, is administered via intravenous infusion, and is not available to all patients or in all countries.

- SSRIs antidepressants were discussed earlier in this chapter. They may affect neurotransmitters in ways that not only address depression and other neurological disorders, but that also directly or indirectly regulate the gastrointestinal and immune systems. When used for this purpose, they are often given at very low doses.

Roni, adoptive mother of 5-year-old Stevie, says,

> *Stevie has been on DMG and Super NuThera [a B₆/magnesium*
> *formula] for almost 200 days. The biggest improvement has been his*
> *immune system: fewer runny noses, ear infections, and colds. He began*
> *to speak a few words, but no miracle in the speech department. Calmed*
> *him down some and I believe helped improve eye contact. Hard to*
> *pinpoint that one, because the more he began to feel comfortable with me*
> *and trust me, the better the eye contact and behavior.*

When immune modulators are employed to improve the function of people with ASDs, they are not used in the same ways or at the same doses as in fatal immune system diseases, such as AIDS. The goal is to normalize the patient's system, not hit it with "big guns" that provoke an overwhelming reaction.

Secretin

Secretin is a hormone normally produced when acid stimulates the mucosa of the duodenum, increasing the secretion of bicarbonate ions by the pancreas. It also acts on the peripheral nervous system to slow down stomach activity, presumably giving food more time to digest. In addition, secretin does appear to have some activity in the brain. Specifically, in animal studies it was found to be active in the amygdala, hippocampus, and cerebellum: precisely the areas where abnormality has been seen in people with autism. It is approved for use in the US to diagnose certain gastro-intestinal disorders.

Because autism-like symptoms are not characteristic of conditions that include a known deficiency of secretin, administering secretin is a somewhat surprising therapy. It is possible that one subtype of autistic spectrum disorders—perhaps one hitherto unidentified—does respond to secretin. One theory is that secretin is one part of a larger chemical system within the body, and that administering the hormone leads to a cascade of actions that may be beneficial. Further research may find a different way to activate this same system.

Secretin is normally administered by infusion (slow injection), and most families who reported positive results did repeated infusions. Some doctors and parents have been quietly experimenting with other methods for using secretin, including oral adminis-tration and devising methods to administer secretin through the surface of the skin. Homeopathic secretin is also available, but would not be expected to be helpful, as administering secretin in this way goes against the basic principle of homeopathic medicine. That said, some families have reported benefits from homeopathic secretin.

Several scientific studies of secretin are currently underway, including multisite, double-blind (or double-blind crossover) studies. Early research results have been mixed. Some trials found no effect, others noted improvement in some children but not others. Most of these trials used only a single dose of secretin.

A summary on secretin studies can be found online at *http://www.secretin.com*. A US manufacturer of synthetic secretin, Repligen Corporation, has funded several studies and offers information on the web at *http://www.repligen.com*. Repligen is currently looking into how secretin affects the amygdala, hippocampus, and cerebellum in humans.

Some doctors have expressed concerns about secretin treatment as it is currently done. First, the secretin that most families have used is porcine (pig) secretin from Ferring Pharmaceuticals Inc. It is not an exact match for human secretin. Synthetic human secretin is available, but not yet in common use. That said, the porcine product has been in use for years as a diagnostic aid, with no major side effects noted.

Second, some parents have reported doing secretin infusions at home or in clinic offices that lacked resuscitation equipment. This is not a good idea because of the riskiness of any intravenous procedure. The proper dose and administration schedule for secretin as a treatment for ASDs have also not been established.

Rumors have swirled about secretin over the past couple of years, most of them false. For example, some parents were informed that the substance was no longer being made, or that there was a shortage. There was a temporary shortage, but it was soon ameliorated. Others were told that the US Food and Drug Administration had banned secretin, or that secretin had been linked to serious adverse effects—including death—in some autistic children. There have been some reports of adverse effects, but there have not been any deaths or life-threatening effects. The FDA has specifically permitted Ferring to increase the secretin supply in the US as long as it does not actively promote secretin as a treatment for autism.

Sadly, con artists have also gotten involved. Some outfits claiming to sell secretin by mail-order or over the Internet have proved to be a sham, and products of unknown origin are being sold as equivalent to the Ferring formulation.

Hospitals and clinics have become aware that parents of children with ASDs may be seeking secretin as a treatment rather than as a diagnostic tool. Unfortunately, this has led some facilities to refuse to administer secretin to such children for GI disorder tests—even in cases where the child has long-standing gastrointestinal problems. If this happens to you, you will probably need to appeal the ban. (If treatment rather than diagnosis actually was your goal, you could seek another source.)

Pepcid AC

Pepcid AC (famotidine) is one of several H2 blockers commonly used to treat acid reflux and other common stomach complaints. As a histamine type 2-receptor antagonist, famotidine competitively inhibits the binding of histamine (HA) to HA receptors on the gastric basolateral membrane of parietal cells, reducing the secretion of gastric acid. It may help heal the gastric mucous membranes and protect them from irritants. It is known to affect the CNS, although the exact mechanism has not been extensively studied.

Pepcid AC is available as an over-the-counter medication. In one study, it was found to help some autistic children who had social deficits. However, it may increase the growth of *Candida* yeasts, which thrive when there is less gastric acid in the digestive system.

You should tell your doctor if you plan to use Pepcid or another H2 blocker, such as cimetidine (Tagamet) or ranitidine (Zantac), whether your intended purpose is addressing autistic symptoms or reducing GI distress.

Incidentally, cimetidine was recently shown to have some antiviral activity as well as efficacy for GI tract problems, and the same may hold true for other H2 blockers.

Antifungals

Medications commonly used to reduce an overgrowth of *Candida albicans* and other yeasts include the following:

- nystatin (Mycostatin, Nilstat)
- fluconazole (Diflucan)
- itraconazole (Sporanax)
- ketoconazole (Nizoral)
- miconazole (Monistat)
- terbinafine (Lamisil)

These drugs may kill not only *Candida*, but also other harmful fungi, including dermophytes, aspergillus, and cryptococcus. Miconazole preparations and Lamisil tablets are used to treat topical fungal infections, such as diaper rash, athlete's foot, and vaginal infections.

Diet can also be a powerful tool against *Candida*. People who have chronic yeast infections may choose to avoid sugars and many carbohydrates, which seem to make the problem worse. Chapter 7 covers dietary recommendations.

Surgery and ASDs

No, there's no operation that can cure ASDs. However, if someone on the autistic spectrum needs surgery for other reasons, there are a few things you should know.

First, the surgeon, anesthetist, and others taking part in the operation will need some basic information about the diagnosis and any unusual behaviors they may see. For example, if a child has difficulty making eye contact, lack of eye contact should not be considered a sign that the anesthetic is taking effect.

Second, if possible, a parent or other familiar person should accompany the patient during initial anesthesia and meet the patient in the recovery room. Building as much predictability into the surgery process as possible is a good idea. Familiar clothing, toys, and foods in the hospital can also go a long way toward making the stay comfortable.

Finally, some people with ASDs have unusual reactions to anesthetics. Be sure to share any salient information with the anesthetist, including the names and dosages of all drugs, herbal remedies, and supplements the patient uses.

Dental care and ASDs

Dental care is a nightmare for many people with ASDs. Sensory hypersensitivity can turn a routine cleaning into a torture session, and serious dental work can be additionally complicated by unusual reactions to anesthesia.

However, the dentist is a more important part of your medical treatment plan than you might think. Your dentist may be the first professional to notice certain types of health problems. Vitamin deficiencies and dietary problems tend to show up in the mouth first, with certain types of dental caries patterns, receding gums, bleeding, and other symptoms. The dentist may also be the first to notice signs of infection or disease.

Finding and working with a dentist can be difficult. United Cerebral Palsy (UCP) can help, as can the ARC (formerly known as the Association for Retarded Citizens) and other large organizations that work with people who have other disabilities. Dental problems are characteristic of many disabilities, from Down syndrome to cerebral palsy. These groups usually have referral lists of sympathetic dentists.

There are a few special dental problems to watch for, particularly tooth grinding and clenching. Medication (especially antidepressants) can help. However, sometimes these behaviors are evoked by the sensation of dry mouth that these very medications create. A plastic dental guard can be prescribed, made by the dentist, or even purchased over the counter. These are especially useful for nighttime tooth-grinders. Without intervention, tooth grinding and clenching can lead to loss of enamel, chipped teeth, jaw pain, or loss of teeth.

Dental decay can also have behavioral effects, including self-injurious behavior. Infections in the mouth are among the most painful around, and the most likely to cause general unpleasantness in the body. They can make eating painful, too, so think of tooth trouble when foods are suddenly refused.

Vision care and ASDs

People with ASDs do have a higher incidence of eye problems, including strabismus (crossed eyes), photophobia (extreme sensitivity to light), Duane syndrome, abnormal retinal activity, reliance on peripheral vision, tunnel vision, and stereotypic behaviors that involve the eyes, such as flicking fingers in front of the eyes repetitively or fixating on patterns of light and shadow. Even the most "behavioral looking" of these symptoms, such as "stims" that involve the eyes, are medical symptoms. For example, some people who have self-injurious behaviors involving their eyes improve when given calcium supplements, and no one knows how much of the common difficulty with sustained eye contact seen in some people with ASDs is caused by eye sensitivity or physical difficulty with focusing.

Some high-functioning autistic adults have described their own visual disturbances, ranging from difficulties in processing and making sense of what they see, to "seeing" sounds. Some of these effects resemble those of hallucinogenic drugs. Not only can visual disturbances make the world seem a scary place, but they can also interfere with learning to read, write, and do math on paper.

Regular vision care is a must, and the best provider will be one familiar with autistic spectrum disorders. If possible, find a behavioral optometrist—an eye doctor who understands the interplay between vision problems and behavior. These optometrists may recommend vision therapy via exercises or the use of prismatic lenses. Again, groups such as United Cerebral Palsy, the ARC, or local autism advocacy organizations can be great resources for finding a sympathetic and resourceful optometrist. The College of Optometrists in Vision Development (888-COVD-770, *http://www.covd. org*) and the Optometric Extension Program Foundation (949-250-8070, *http://www. oep.org*) also provide referrals to behavioral optometrists.

Some children with ASDs have more than the usual trouble with maintaining their contacts or glasses. These expensive items may be broken, scratched, or lost with maddening regularity. First, make it clear that these items are very important and, if you think it will make a difference to how the child thinks of them, very expensive! Make sure that the glasses fit well, and are at the correct strength, and that the child likes the style. Ask if there's a problem with glasses-smashing bullies at school (an all-too-common pest). You may want to try sports glasses, which come with a built-in strap and are practically indestructible. Most opticians have these in stock, or they can be special ordered. Otherwise, attaching a cool-looking sports strap of the sort used with hip sunglasses may keep them hanging around a little while longer.

Some people with ASDs, including author Donna Williams, claim that special colored lenses have helped them reduce visual processing problems. The Irlen Institute (*http:// www.irlen.com/,* or see Appendix A) developed such lenses, and many eye specialists do recommend them, although they are rather expensive.

It should be noted that the Irlen system and the prismatic lenses used by some behavioral optometrists do not have universal support in the eye care field—in fact, the American Academy of Pediatrics, the American Association for Pediatric Ophthalmology and Strabismus, and the American Academy of Ophthalmology issued a joint statement in 1992 disavowing the use of colored lenses and prismatic lenses to treat neurological problems.[47]

In some cases, adults with ASDs may want to consider eye surgery to address near-sightedness if broken or lost glasses are a persistent problem.

Coping with self-injurious behavior

As explained earlier in this chapter, self-injurious behavior (SIB) needs to be viewed as a medical issue, not a behavior problem. Just as SIB can result from untreated medical problems, including the dental and eye problems just mentioned, it can cause medical problems. Sad to say, through SIB children have put out their own eyes, caused permanent scarring, and damaged their bodies in any number of ways.

SIB can be a form of communication, a way of saying "I hurt," especially for nonverbal children or those who have a very hard time being understood with words. It may also be a way of stimulating an underactive dopamine system, one that feels little sensation normally and perceives as almost pleasant sensations that would be painful to someone else. It's essential to examine SIB carefully to find the cause. The behavior analysis techniques discussed in Chapter 6 can help. As this book went to press, Dr. Edelson from the Center for the Study of Autism was preparing a video on successful interventions for SIB. If SIB is a concern, this could be an excellent resource.

Behavior modification (ABA or other forms) has great effectiveness against SIB. Even if you don't subscribe to this approach as a general treatment for ASDs, make it part of your plan for dealing with SIB if it crops up. In addition, if you eschew pharmaceutical medication as a general treatment, please consider it if your child is in danger of harming himself or others. Naltrexone (ReVia), an opiate blocker, has been very helpful for some people with SIB.

Until SIB has been dealt with medically or behaviorally, take careful steps to minimize any damage. Helmets and other protective devices are available by prescription, through hospitals, and from mail order catalogs to safeguard the head, eyes, genitalia, and other body parts that may be at risk. You may also need to use "childproofing" measures that keep potentially dangerous items under wraps. Chapter 10, *Family Issues and Support,* shares ideas that other families have used to keep people with ASDs safe at home and in the community.

Alternative and complementary medicine

Many people see alternative medical practitioners instead of a traditional (allopathic) doctors, whereas others blend the two: a practice known as complementary medicine. These specialists—including naturopaths, homeopathic physicians, chiropractors, practitioners of Asian and Ayurvedic medicine, and acupuncturists—may have different ideas about treating ASDs than those presented in this chapter. Chapter 7 discusses a number of specific therapies.

Be sure to check the credentials of complementary practitioners, and before trying a treatment look for hard evidence that it is effective for the symptom at hand. There is much value in these approaches for some people with ASDs, but alternative and complementary therapies are not appropriate for all.

Make sure all your health care practitioners know what you're doing. If you can, get them to talk to each other. It's certainly not universal, but many Western doctors are gaining a great deal of respect for the track record of their alternative counterparts in treating chronic illness.

Be careful about the herbal remedies you try. In the US, supplements are not regulated for content or potency. For example, the *Los Angeles Times* in 1998 commissioned independent lab analysis of ten major brands of St. John's wort extract. Three proved less than half as potent as their labels claimed, and four others were less than 90 percent potent.[48] Until there are firm standards, either voluntary or government imposed, consumers must educate themselves well.

Autistic spectrum disorders are becoming less of a puzzle. Medical treatment is a real possibility for an increasingly large number of children and adults. When coupled with educational, behavioral, and other interventions, the rate of success is promising.

CHAPTER 6

Therapeutic Interventions

THE MOST IMPORTANT ROLE OF MEDICATION in a well-conceived treatment program is to help a person be available for, and capable of, other therapies. Many types of therapeutic intervention can be useful to individuals with autistic spectrum disorders, and unlike most of the biomedical interventions available today, these methods can create permanent change.

In this chapter, we'll discuss most well-known therapies used by and for people with autistic spectrum disorders. Therapeutic interventions that may be recommended by physicians or schools (or that you may hear about in the press) include the following. These are listed and described alphabetically, not in order of their efficacy.

- Animal-assisted therapy
- Applied behavior analysis (ABA, "the Lovaas method")
- Auditory system therapies, including auditory integration training (AIT)
- Augmentative communication (assistive technology), including Picture Exchange Communication System (PECS)
- Behavior modification programs other than ABA
- Dance, music, or art therapy
- Facilitated communication
- Floor-time play therapy ("the Greenspan method")
- The HANDLE Institute approach
- The Linwood method
- Occupational therapy
- The Options Institute method ("Son-Rise")
- Physical therapy
- Pivotal response training (PRT)
- Play therapy
- Relaxation techniques

- Psychoanalysis or counseling (talk therapy)
- Sensory integration (SI)
- Social skills training
- Snoezelen
- Speech therapy

Therapeutic choices

For most people with ASDs, there's no single best approach. You can combine therapies, taking what's best and most applicable to the individual from each. There's no need to be a slave to one method.

However, proponents of various methods are very attached to their favorites, and may downplay the merits of competing ideas. This can make it hard for you to judge programs objectively. One thing is certain: If someone tells you, "This is the *only* way to help people with autistic spectrum disorders," that person is probably more interested in the program itself than in the person who might benefit from it.

Just as you should beware of zealotry on behalf of one approach, watch out for "one size fits all" programs. Therapeutic programs, whether they involve speech therapy, counseling, or teaching methods, must be *individualized*. Even when a program brings together groups of children or adults, such as a social skills club, each person in the group should have his or her own goals, and each may require different teaching methods.

Animal-assisted therapy

Quite a few autistic spectrum individuals report a feeling of special empathy with animals. Clinicians such as Dr. Oliver Sacks (the author of *Awakenings* and other popular books on neurology) have even speculated that, for these people, their extra depth of understanding could be a unique form of intelligence. It can also be a springboard to skills needed for human interaction.

Most people are aware of the therapeutic potential of pet ownership. A strong bond with a pet can help people learn compassion and feel less lonely. The simple act of stroking a pet can calm a racing heartbeat or a troubled mind. Some animals are also natural experts at therapeutic touch, cuddling or nuzzling just when it's most needed. Because animals communicate without words, nonverbal people and those with auditory sensitivities sometimes prefer their company to that of noisy, jabbering humans.

This knowledge is applied by professionals working in the field of animal-assisted therapy. Programs include therapeutic horseback riding (hippotherapy—*hippo* is the ancient Greek word for horse), bringing animals to visit children in schools, homes, or residential centers, and even "dolphin therapy," whose proponents claim that interacting with these intelligent marine mammals offers benefits for people with ASDs.

Be careful of animal-assisted therapy programs that charge a lot of money or make extravagant claims. Pets, including school pets as well as animals kept at home, are a great idea for individuals who are not likely to injure an animal. Not all people with ASDs like animals, and certain animals (such as high-strung breeds and those likely to bite) are unsuited for the job.

People with ASDs who have seizure disorders may be able to gain yet another benefit from canine company. Some dogs can be trained to recognize seizures and provide assistance to people who live alone. The Epilepsy International web site (*http://www.epiworld.com/*) has more information about seizure dogs, as do most local epilepsy support associations.

Applied behavior analysis

Applied behavior analysis (ABA) has the longest and best documented track record of any therapeutic intervention for children with autism. Developed by Dr. O. Ivar Lovaas, a pioneering clinical researcher at the University of California at Los Angeles (UCLA), it is an intensive intervention system for autism based on principles borrowed from behavioral modification. ABA is sometimes called discrete trial training, as it is structured around short drills called discrete trials.

The details of ABA are considerably more complex than the following brief description. Consult other resources before you design or implement a program.

1. Observe the behaviors you want to change, replace, or initiate. Take a baseline measurement of where the person is right now. Chart behaviors and their antecedents: what leads up to a behavior, where it occurred, and when it occurred.

2. If you want to change or replace a behavior, make a hypothesis about what the behavior might be intended to communicate. Next, design an intervention based on this hypothesis. Have a positive goal, not a negative one (for example, "Jimmy will make eye contact when requested," not "Jimmy will stop avoiding eye contact"). Break this goal down into small steps, and design a separate, progressive drill to address each step in turn.

3. If you want to initiate a behavior, make a goal and break it down into its smallest components. Address each component in a set of separate, progressive drills. Dr. Lovaas recommends starting with speech skills for the first few months, and following with drills for social interaction skills.

4. Apply the intervention, using positive reinforcement for each instance of desired behavior. Because drills are short and repetitive, the rewards must be small and frequent. Small pieces of food, hugs, play activities, and verbal praise have all been employed as reinforcers. The reinforcer must be something the child really wants. Some practitioners use negative reinforcers (aversives) when undesired behaviors occur. Whether you choose to do so is a matter of philosophy and, perhaps, what works best with a specific person. Although Dr. Lovaas's early experiments included the use of mild electric shock and other physical aversives, these are no longer employed in his program or recommended by reputable practitioners: Today, a negative reinforcer might be a loud "no," a frown, or restricting access to a desired activity.

5. Assess the effectiveness of the intervention, and adjust it if necessary.

In 1987, Dr. Lovaas's team reported good outcomes in 47 percent of the children who completed his program, based on a well-designed study.[1] Since then, hundreds of ABA practitioners have been trained, and thousands of parents have applied Lovaas's methods themselves. ABA techniques have been carefully honed by practitioners, many of whom now report that better than half of the children they work with experience good results.

What constitutes "good results?" For Lovaas, it was approaching normal functioning, including being capable of self-care and mainstream education. For some parents, ABA has been a truly incredible experience. Catherine Maurice, mother of two children diagnosed as autistic, details the miracles wrought by a well-designed, firmly implemented home ABA program in her book, *Let Me Hear Your Voice* (Fawcett Books, 1994). Both her children are now mainstreamed and, she says, no longer meet the criteria for autistic disorder. Most parents who implement ABA programs do not have the dramatic results reported by Maurice and some other parents. However, it's safe to say that ABA *does* work, and works well, for a very significant number of children.

Holly, mother of 3-year-old Max, says,

> *ABA is the most effective of the therapies we have tried. I believe that ABA is also the stepping-stone to being able to accept and benefit from other therapies.*

Lovaas and other ABA experts recommend a very intensive program when working with children who have a diagnosis of autistic disorder. Forty hours per week of one-on-one, structured intervention is the standard. Lovaas's own research (which has been replicated by others) has shown that neither 10 hours per week nor 20 hours per week is "enough." However, his clinical research was done primarily with moderately to severely autistic children. For children who already have some of the basic skills that ABA practitioners work many months to initiate with more severely affected children, mixing a smaller amount of ABA work with other interventions *may* be sufficient. This has been the case for some families who have tried a modified ABA approach, but it has *not* been clinically tested. Many families whose children have a PDD-NOS, atypical PDD, or a similar diagnosis choose to follow Lovaas's recommendations to the letter, providing 30 to 40 hours per week of ABA work.

Catherine Maurice has edited an ABA manual that gets rave reviews from many families, *Behavioral Intervention for Young Children with Autism* (Pro-Ed, 1996). Dr. Lovaas's *Teaching Developmentally Disabled Children: The ME Book* (Pro-Ed, 1981) is also considered a classic for teaching ABA concepts, although parts are somewhat outdated. He has recently written a new book, *Teaching Individuals with Developmental Delays: Basics* (Pro-Ed, 2002). Videotapes available from Pro-Ed show ABA techniques in action.

There is an Internet mailing list for parents and professionals using ABA techniques, the Me List (see Appendix A, *Resources*). Parent Richard Saffran maintains a web-based resource site (*http://members.tripod.com/~RSaffran/aba.html*) that can lead you to additional resources, including information about insurance coverage for ABA programs, a list of credentialed practitioners, and specific instructions for setting up a home ABA program. The Lovaas Institute for Early Intervention (*http://www.lovaas.com/*) also has many links to practitioners, including ABA-friendly programs in Spain, Iceland, Norway, and the UK. There are now several "Lovaas replication sites" in the US, programs whose practitioners and methods duplicate those used in the original UCLA program.

Sarah, mother of 3-year-old Elaine, says,

> I have a home program based on discrete trials geared around speech.
> Behavior modification works great with Elaine, as it does with all people.
> We all work for rewards.

Family participation is very important in most ABA programs, although these techniques can be applied in school or residential settings as well. Most families using ABA techniques run a home-based program relying on themselves, other family members, community volunteers, students, and sometimes paid practitioners. Training in

ABA techniques is often available at state or regional autism conferences, or through firms that specialize in training parents and providing trained paraprofessionals for home ABA programs. Qualified consultants can help families set up programs and provide ongoing supervision.

Dr. Lovaas has noted that follow-up is also very important when using ABA programs. When children have made sufficient gains to be in preschool or school, he strongly encourages full inclusion in a mainstream classroom, with continued social skills instruction geared toward group situations.

Some Early Intervention programs and school districts do support and fund ABA programs. Because ABA has been clinically proven to work, many parents have sucessfully gone to court to force school districts to pay for and implement ABA programs.

ABA drawbacks

No program is perfect, and ABA certainly has its detractors. The most common criticism you may hear is one based on lack of knowledge: Quite a few people still think that ABA programs rely on physical punishment to get compliance. As noted earlier, this is no longer true.

Others (including some adults with high-functioning autism) feel ABA is much like animal training, encouraging children to develop robotlike behavior in exchange for bits of food. Parents who have actually implemented ABA programs reply that nothing could be further from the truth. The goal of ABA is not Pavlovian response, but the emergence of skills that build the ability to respond naturally, expressing the person's own needs and ideas.

You may also hear that ABA is only for preschool children or for those with severe autistic behaviors. This is certainly not the case.

Some parents do not turn out to be good ABA practitioners. It takes a lot of stamina and dedication. If a parent is struggling with depression or physical illness, it can be especially difficult. Sharing the duties with your partner, other family members, volunteers, or paid helpers can lighten the load. Parents doing ABA certainly need to take special care of their own physical and mental health, and will need to arrange for at least some time off—time for an occasional dinner out, an evening class, or a quiet walk in the park.

Finally, the time commitment required to implement 30 to 40 hours of ABA is considerable. Lovaas requires families entering his program to commit one parent to working nearly full time with their child—something that's not always easy in this age of single-parent and two-earner families. Many families have made considerable sacrifices, both personal and professional, to make ABA work. Not every family has the ability to make that choice. And if you are paying for ABA specialists to work with your child daily, the cost can be very high.

Similar programs

Lovaas was the first to report good results from a well-designed, well-documented study of intensive intervention with a large number of autistic children. Other programs use some similar methods.

Martin A. Kozloff developed a program that also used behavior modification techniques, but in a less stringent manner than Lovaas's ABA program. Kozloff's approach also includes motivators for parents to encourage them to complete training sessions, and intensive counseling work with families. As described in his books *Reaching the Autistic Child: A Parent Training Program* (Research Press, 1973) and *A Program for Families of Children with Learning and Behavior Problems* (Wiley, 1979), Kozloff's program might be well suited for families experiencing significant internal stress, or whose parenting skills need help and support. If implemented as written, it should provide a particularly supportive structure, although some aspects might be perceived as coercive or blaming. The author is not aware of any programs currently using the Kozloff approach.

Pivotal response training (PRT), described later in this chapter, also shares some characteristics with ABA.

Dr. Stanley Greenspan's "floor-time play therapy" program, described later in this chapter, also relies on one-to-one interactions that build basic communication and social skills. Like ABA, it has been clinically successful with many autistic spectrum children.

Some families may prefer the less regimented approach of PRT or floor-time play therapy, or may want to mix and match.

Auditory system therapies

Extreme sensitivity to sounds and other stimuli may be responsible for some autistic behaviors. Loud, sudden noises, or sounds in certain frequencies, can be excruciating. Incidentally, similar methods are used to combat tinnitus (ringing in the ears).

Based on principles first developed by French hearing specialist Guy Bérard, AIT involves listening to particular sounds through earphones to retrain the hearing mechanism. The process is somewhat time consuming.

Another auditory therapy is called the Tomatis method.

AIT (auditory integration therapy) is the topic of *The Sound of a Miracle* by Annabel Stehli. Stehli's book is the story of her autistic daughter Georgie's success with Dr. Bérard's auditory training methods. AIT has been a contributing factor to improved comfort and reduced symptoms for many individuals with ASDs.

Quite a few audiologists and other professionals currently offer AIT. For more information, contact the Society for Auditory Intervention Techniques *(http://www.sait.org/)*, has sponsored several studies of the method, or see the list of practitioners available through the Autism Research Institute *(http://www.autismresearchinstitute.com)*. The Autism Society of America's web page on the topic, *(http://www.autism-society.org/ packages/auditory_based_techniques.pdf)*, includes a number of informative articles and another list of practitioners, maintained by Annabel Stehli's Georgianna Foundation.

In an interesting twist, it may be possible to do an AIT-like program at home. A CD series called EASe, for Electronic Auditory Stimulation effect, has been developed by Vision Audio Inc. *(http://www.vision-audio.com/)*. You can listen to the EASe CDs using good-quality home equipment, following a prescribed course. No research results on this product are yet available, but it could provide some help for people who can't access a full-fledged AIT program. A number of autism support groups have purchased the EASe CDs, so you may be able to borrow them from a group in your area.

Similar software products are already available for retraining the brain's auditory processing mechanism. These do not reduce sound sensitivity, but help the individual differentiate the sounds of speech from one another. Perhaps the best known product is FastForward, developed by Scientific Learning Corporation *(http://www. scientificlearning.com/)*. FastForward is based on the research of Dr. Paula Tallal and Dr. Mike Merzenich (Dr. Merzenich was also a codeveloper of the cochlear implant for deafness), and was rigorously tested at Rutgers University for use in speech and auditory processing disorders. It uses video game techniques to bring users through a series of exercises said to increase temporal processing (acoustics) and language processing.

During clinical trials, FastForward was administered to a group of children with autistic spectrum disorders, most of whom were diagnosed with autistic disorder. Compared to children with attention deficit disorder (ADD) or central auditory processing disorder (CAPD) alone, the children with ASDs made the most impressive gains. The ASD group started out more impaired than the other two groups, but improved auditory performance more than 200 percent in an eight-week trial. However, the auditory and language skills of the ADD and CAPD groups moved into the low end of the "normal" range after treatment, whereas those of the ASD group were still classified as impaired.[2] This difference may have been caused by disparities within the ASD group, however—autistic spectrum disorders have multiple causes, so some children may achieve excellent progress with FastForward or similar programs, whereas others will experience no gains at all.

The FastForward software is available only to clinicians, and these purchasers must be trained to use it properly before they can obtain it. A list of licensed clinicians (mostly speech therapists and audiologists) is available from Scientific Learning Corporation. The program is time consuming, and many clinicians charge $1,000 or more to administer it over a period of weeks. Some school districts have also purchased the software. Home-based programs are available that use the Internet to keep parents and clinicians in touch, and are less expensive.

If you are interested in FastForward, you might want to purchase a tape of a speech by SLPs Karen Supel and Christina Rogers called "Using FastForward with Children with PDD." It is available from the Autism Society of America, which sponsored Rogers and Supel's presentation at its 1998 conference.

A less advanced program called Earobics from Cognitive Concepts Inc. *(http://www. cogcon.com/)* can be purchased for home use and is much less expensive. You might try Earobics first and move on up to FastForward if this approach seems to be beneficial.

Augmentative and alternative communication

Most school districts and hospital rehabilitation centers have specialists in augmentative and alternative communication (AAC), sometimes called assistive technology. These experts use methods and devices that open up new communication possibilities for nonverbal or speech-impaired people.

If you've ever seen British physicist Stephen Hawking "talk" with the assistance of his computer, you know what the very finest augmentative communication devices can do. A wide variety of products is available—and in some cases, the cost (which can be considerable) is covered by private insurance, government medical plans, or school districts.

Information about these devices, including a list of companies that make them, is available online at *http://www.abledata.com/,* a site maintained for the National Institute on Disability and Rehabilitation Research. Some products cost less than US $100 and produce a limited vocabulary of words. You may even be able to find a computer-like "toy" at a local toy store that can do rough sound synthesis of a few letters together or of simple words. Other devices are programmable: Parents or clinicians can choose or record the desired words ("potty," "go," "drink," and so on) and map them to an appropriate picture on a keyboard or a screen. At the high end, AAC devices can help a brilliant scientist like Hawking deliver a complete lecture.

Augmentative communication actually predates the computer age, however. Before machines could synthesize sound, nonverbal people used gestures and drawings to let others know their thoughts and needs. Schools often use PECS (Picture Exchange Communication System) to help young children with severe speech disorders communicate. Developed by Lori Frost and Andrew Bondy, PECS uses specially designed pictures to symbolize words and concepts.

PECS and similar commercial products are available for use at home, school, and work. Parents and professionals can also create their own customized picture books. These are a great way to stimulate "conversation" with a nonverbal person by offering acceptable choices in the form of pictures.

Health concerns aside, many parents swear by the picture menus available at fast-food restaurants like McDonald's. Children tend to be enthusiastic about getting a desired food or drink by pointing to a picture. You can extend this practice by creating "menus" of your own, using PECS or similar drawings, pictures cut from magazines, or photographs. You might create a menu of food choices at home, clothes to wear to school, or activity choices.

Homemade picture books can also be used to schedule activities. By putting pictures in order, perhaps with a ring binder, people can truly visualize the day's plans. Many people with autism are visual thinkers by nature, and learn best when they can see (and touch and smell) as well as hear something.

When using picture-based AAC systems, include the written and spoken word. Some children will never be verbally proficient, but seeing and hearing words with pictures of the items or activities they represent help them make essential associations they need to develop their communication skills as fully as possible. For children who do make some attempts at speech, gradually insist that they approximate the word's sound rather than just point at the picture.

Some people on the autistic spectrum learn to read, or at least to recognize the shapes of some words, before they can speak. You might try labeling objects around your home with their names in large letters, pointing to the labels and then saying the words whenever possible. Keep books around that have a single picture and word on each page, and read them with your child whenever you can. As always, build on skills that come easily for your child, to help her gain others that come only with great effort.

See the section "Total communication" later in this chapter for more on sign language as a communication strategy.

Behavior modification programs other than ABA

In its broadest sense, "behavior modification" includes any system of controlling behavior by means of rewards and punishments. Ever since the work of psychologist B.F. Skinner became widely known, behavior modification techniques have been used in schools, institutions, prisons, and workplaces. .

These programs can be highly effective, but until the advent of specially targeted ABA techniques there was a notable lack of success with people who have autism. Part of the problem was poor understanding about autism and related disorders. In many cases, people with ASDs who were placed in residential schools or hospitals were punished for such "willful" acts as not speaking, making repetitive motions, or behaving in self-abusive ways. Because the people in charge of these behavior modification programs did not know the characteristics of autism and did not look at behavior as a form of communication, these people with ASDs frequently regressed rather than ending their behaviors.

If you are considering a school or residential center that employs behavior modification, make sure the staff thoroughly understands autistic spectrum disorders and ABA-style techniques. Even the simplest behavior modification ideas, such as "token economies" or other reward systems, must be adapted to meet the needs of people with ASDs.

One area where behavior modification techniques can be helpful is in designing a plan for home discipline. Parents who are frustrated with problem behaviors can apply these techniques, even with older children or adults. Training or a behavior consultant may be available through social service agencies.

Debbie, mother of 11-year-old Doug, explains:

> Doug is getting what's called wrap-around services. This is where a therapeutic support staff person comes to the house, and we target certain behaviors to try and get Doug to stop doing them. The behavior is whatever Doug seems to be doing for a certain time, such as throwing things when he's upset, or things like getting him to sit at the table and eat his meals.

As with ABA, behavior modification programs for people with ASDs usually work best when incentives, not punishments, are employed.

Dance, music, or art therapy

There is no proof that dance, music, or art therapy has curative value for people with ASDs, but these activities often draw out hidden talents and bring a sense of joy and accomplishment.

Each also builds important skills. Dance, for example, teaches a sense of rhythm, relies on counting and imitative skills, and can help people develop their sense of balance. Music has mathematical underpinnings, and art can be an alternative form of communication even as it builds fine motor skills and imagination.

Well-trained dance, music, and art therapists are aware of what they're teaching along with the activity, but integration into mainstream or adapted classes in these subjects can also be enriching.

Some autistic spectrum people have "splinter skills" in one of these areas, and are able to develop their talents into a lifelong hobby or even a career.

Facilitated communication

You may have heard of facilitated communication (FC), a form of assistive communication in which a trained aide helps a nonverbal person type by supporting his hand. Unfortunately, scientific studies have shown that the words and ideas generated almost always arise with the aide, not the person being assisted.[3] Reputable researchers have gone so far as to call FC a fraud and to accuse its boosters of giving families false hope. See "Spotting a scam" toward the end of this chapter for more on that topic.

In a few instances, a previously nonverbal person has learned to type independently after starting with FC-style supported typing. Nevertheless, it would be wiser to seek the help of an occupational therapist or an assistive/augmentative communication professional. Occupational therapy can help build the muscles needed for typing, and some OTs and physical therapists can devise support splints. A wide variety of AAC systems for typing are available that work well for people with limited hand strength or poor muscle control.

Floor-time play therapy

Dr. Stanley Greenspan of George Washington University and the Washington Psychoanalytic Institute is the primary proponent of a relationship-based, interactive, individualized form of therapy that he calls floor-time play therapy. It uses developmental principles to help children build social, emotional, and communication skills from the ground up.

Floor-time interactions are less like ABA drills and more like play, even when they carry the same content and intention. The parent or therapist tries to engage the child's attention, and rewards the engagement when it occurs. Floor-time therapy is a one-on-one experience that involves getting right down to the child's level to encourage interaction, by any playful means necessary. If a child tends to line up miniature toy cars in endless lines, for example, Dad might try to find out what happens when car No. 3 in the line drives away noisily. If a child babbles the same sound over and over, Mom might try joining in with a silly look on her face, then varying the tune and the movements. If one strategy doesn't work, you try another. As interaction increases and the child begins to initiate activities, the parent follows the child's lead, always trying to keep attention focused on interaction and communication.

Greenspan suggests that floor-time principles be made the basis for Early Intervention and school programs for children with ASDs, and that they be used by other types of therapists who need to engage the child for their purposes. He recommends that parents or their assistants complete between six and ten 20- to 30-minute floor-time sessions every day.

Jennifer, mother of 3-year-old Joseph, says,

> One-on-one teaching has worked very well. I have been using
> Greenspan's floor-time model at home with [Joseph] with great success.
> He is even beginning to use some imaginative play. Any method that is
> visual rather than auditory also works well.

Greenspan reports that 58 percent of the children with PDD-NOS or autism who participated in his program for two or more years showed "good to outstanding" outcomes, as measured by no longer scoring in the autistic range on the Childhood Autism Rating Scale (CARS) and by detailed observation. About 24 percent made a "medium" level of progress, described as having lost many "autistic" behaviors (perseveration, self-absorption, self-stimulation), but having continued difficulty with symbolic communication. Only 17 percent continued to have fairly serious problems, despite whatever small gains they may have made in the program. These judgments were based on file review of 200 cases, formal testing, and videotaped observations over a period of years.[4]

Greenspan notes that the most successful children were those who fell on the low end of the CARS scale before intervention, that is, those more likely to be labeled PDD-NOS or atypical autism rather than autistic disorder. This indicates that the floor-time approach may be especially useful for children whose higher level abilities and needs don't fit as well with the ABA approach.

Somewhat controversially, Greenspan also reports that although a comparison group of children in ABA-style programs for over 30 hours per week made significant gains over those receiving "traditional" (school-based Early Intervention and perhaps medication) interventions, most continued to have significant difficulty with higher level, spontaneous thought and action. However, Greenspan has since said publicly that the ABA approach can work very well with some children (including those with the most severe autistic characteristics) and that parents and practitioners should judge each model according to its merits for the individual.

Greenspan's program is not much like the psychoanalytic model of play therapy described later in this chapter, but like ABA, it does have some cousins. Filial therapy, in which parents take turns initiating structured interactions with their child, is certainly similar. Some institutions and day treatment centers are based on the concept of milieu therapy, where all interactions between staff and resident, between residents, or between residents and parents are seen as potentially therapeutic. These approaches are less structured than the floor-time model and could be incorporated with it, particularly for older children.

The Options Institute method described later in this chapter also has similarities.

The HANDLE Institute approach

The Seattle-based HANDLE Institute, founded and directed by Judith Bluestone, works with children and adults who have neurological problems or injuries, including ASDs. The acronym HANDLE stands for "Holistic Approach to Neuro-Development and Learning Efficiency."

HANDLE conducts a comprehensive two-part diagnostic interview, including structured observation, after which a series of simple exercises is recommended. These provide what Bluestone calls "gentle enhancement" to retrain and rebuild the nervous system. Videotapes are made at the initial visit and any follow-up visits to help parents or adult clients assess progress. The exercises are similar to activities used in sensory integration and occupational therapy programs.

Some parents report that they found HANDLE's promotional materials too boosterish for their taste, but others who did try the program praised its individualized approach. These parents said the exercises were easy to fit into their family life and, most importantly, helpful.

There have been no scientific studies of the HANDLE method to date. A great deal of anecdotal evidence suggests that the HANDLE Institute's methods can help at least some people with ASDs improve their ability to function. Other centers and clinics advertise similar services, but HANDLE has one major advantage: Its services are primarily in the area of evaluation and program design. The exercises themselves are performed at home. As a result, it is considerably less expensive than some other therapeutic resources.

As of this writing, HANDLE-trained providers are practicing in Seattle and several other cities in Washington State; Oregon City, Oregon; a few other US and UK cities; and Hadera, Israel. See *http://www.handle.org* for more information.

The Linwood method

The Linwood method was developed by Jeanne Simons, director of one of the first high-quality residential programs for autistic children in the US, Linwood Children's Center. Founded in 1955, Linwood used what would be called a milieu therapy approach today—every interaction and event was part of a holistic therapeutic process.

Simons describes her program in *The Hidden Child: The Linwood Method for Reaching the Autistic Child* (Woodbine House, 1987). The title—and the time period in which Simons did her work—might lead you to believe that her approach was psycho-analytical, but it actually had much in common with the sensory integration, behavior modification, and floor-time approaches used today. Children's behavior was observed, and caretakers worked hard to find and address the motivations for disturbing or dangerous behaviors. Sometimes they found a psychological cause, as in the case of one boy who developed a fixation with people's birthdays when his parents changed his own "official" birth date because of his small size, to avoid comment from nosy neighbors. More often the problem was sensory or developmental in nature, and staff members worked out wonderfully thoughtful programs to address these deficits.

Although Simons wrote her book to address the needs of residential centers and schools, her careful observations and suggestions can be useful to parents as well. Her chapter on language has some particularly excellent ideas, especially for devising conversation skills training programs for older children.

If you are considering residential placement, a school that follows Linwood's approach (along with providing modern medical, educational, occupational, and physical therapies) might be an excellent choice.

Occupational therapy

Occupational therapy (OT) builds fine motor and gross motor skills with special exercises, and also works to ameliorate deficits in the body's sensory systems. Schools and hospital rehabilitation centers provide OT assessments and treatment, as do private occupational therapists, who may work out of a doctor's office or clinic, or practice independently. Some deliver services in the home, particularly for very young children or those with mobility impairments.

Schools and medical centers tend to have different goals for OT. At school, the goals are typically educational: developing correct pencil grasp, for example, or working on the sense of balance to permit inclusion in physical activities. In a medical setting, occupational therapists work with people who have brain injuries or birth defects, as well as with people who have neurological problems. Their goals are usually broader, and their repertoire of skills is often (but not always) wider. The two approaches should be seen as complementary.

Dorthy, mother of 5-year-old Jesse, says his OT program focuses on basics:

> Jesse sees an OT two times a week for about 45 minutes each time, in conjunction with a speech therapist. His OT is currently helping him with life skills—face washing, buttoning shirts, eating with a fork.

There are many OT techniques, including sensory integration, which is described in greater detail later in this chapter. Each person's program should be individualized, based on thorough assessment. Typical OT exercises might include working on pencil grasp by writing out letters using instruments of various sizes and shapes, or using small pieces of equipment, such as an elastic band for building up the arm muscles. Other exercises rely on large equipment, ranging from huge "therapy balls" to swings attached to the ceiling. Children may toss bean bags while swinging, walk on a balance beam, or scoot along on a roller board to build specific muscle groups and sensory skills.

Done right, OT is lots of fun. A talented occupational therapist who enjoys children probably has more motivational tricks up his or her sleeve than any other practitioner you'll come into contact with.

Joe, father of 5-year-old Kyle, tells about his son's occupational therapy experience:

> Our son received OT at preschool until being home-schooled this year. The OT helped him learn to suck on a straw, put on clothes, etc. She also worked on calming him, using brushing and vestibular motion. Our son liked this person more than other therapists.

The best occupational therapists see teachers, parents, and especially the people they work with as a team. They can teach home activities for building specific muscles or skills, for self-relaxation, or for handling sensory overload.

Occupational therapy can be easily adapted to meet the needs of both children and adults—in fact, adults who attend sessions at a local rehabilitation center will find they have plenty of company. The equipment used with adults is similar, but sometimes the OTs encourage more repetition and drill with adults than they might with children. If as an adult with an ASD you feel your abilities are being overtaxed, let the therapist know. Because you're there to work on deficits that have been with you for many years rather than for postaccident or poststroke care, there's no rush.

The Options Institute method ("Son-Rise")

Barry Neil Kaufman's books, *Son-Rise* (Warner Books, 1976) and *Son-Rise: The Miracle Continues* (H. J. Kramer, 1995), are documentaries of the grueling process he and his wife underwent to help their severely autistic son, Raun. Kaufman literally locked himself in a room with his son for hours on end for almost three years, observing Raun, following his lead when he could perceive an initiative, and trying to "bring him back to the world."

Raun Kaufman is grown now and has graduated from college. The Kaufmans remain heavily involved in the treatment of autism, however, through the Options Institute (*http://www.son-rise.org*) in Sheffield, Massachusetts. Satellite centers have opened in Holland and the UK. Although the Options program is quite expensive, some parents say it has been helpful. Its primary principles are unconditional love and acceptance.

Joe says this aspect of the Options Institute approach was worthwhile:

> *The Options Institute taught us how to interact with a nonverbal child and gave advice on coping. Our son responds well to the Options approach, which lets the child direct activity and encourages speech and interaction. We suspect our Options training has helped our son be non-self-injurious.*

The Options program is somewhat controversial in the autism community, both because of its price tag and because of its philosophy. Few parents can go to the extremes that Barry Kaufman did with Raun, no matter how admirable and successful, and not everyone is comfortable with his ideas about autism and how to treat it. The program has also not published research results in journals, as one would normally expect for an intervention that makes such claims. But for those who feel inspired by Kaufman's ideals, the Options Institute holds weeklong parent-training programs on a regular basis, and also offers seminars, individual sessions, and program design assistance.

Physical therapy (PT)

Physical therapists are trained to work in schools, hospital rehabilitation centers, and private practice. Some, particularly those working in Early Intervention programs, may deliver services in your home. PTs use equipment and exercises to help people overcome mobility impairments or handle the effects of accident or injury. Most PTs work primarily on gross motor issues: problems involving the major muscles and their movements, such as crawling, walking, and bending. They can also devise exercises that reduce chronic pain from injury, overstress of muscles, or birth defects.

Many people on the autistic spectrum will never need the services of a physical therapist, but some do. PTs can help with gait problems, low muscle tone, strength deficits, and related issues.

As with occupational therapy, physical therapy at school and in a medical setting may look quite different. PTs in Early Intervention programs often have access to large equipment, such as slant boards, scooters, and walking bars; PTs working in regular K–12 schools may not. Hospital- and clinic-based programs are usually equipment rich. Not all problems require fancy equipment, however, and a talented PT can get a lot done without it.

Whether the work is done in school, in a clinical setting, or at home, it's important to have clear goals. The exercises can be difficult at times, although PT has the potential for being fun if you're working with a gifted practitioner. Regular progress reports are a must, and should be written in clear language. For nonverbal or very young people, practitioners should work out a system in advance for indicating that something hurts.

Pivotal response training

Pivotal response training (PRT), like ABA, is based on discrete trials. PRT was developed by Robert L. Koegel and Laura Schreibman. Instead of concentrating on small, individual behaviors, PRT trials focus on encouraging "pivotal" behaviors, such as motivation and initiating activities, that could produce a global change. Trials take place in a natural play or school setting. In this way, it is similar to floor-time play therapy—one might say it melds elements of both these proven approaches.

Clinicians at the University of California at San Diego's Autism Research Laboratory have published results indicating that the PRT approach works in a classroom setting for improving social behavior in children with autism.[5] Some information is available on the Web at *http://psy.ucsd.edu/~vcestone/PRT2.html,* and a parent training manual is available.

PRT was previously known as Natural Language Paradigm.

Play therapy

For children, play is a mode of communication, and a vehicle for working out ideas about social roles, fears, and relationships. Counselors working with young children often use hand puppets, stuffed animals, dolls, and sand tables with small figurines to encourage them to "talk" by playing.

Because one hallmark of autistic spectrum disorders is limited and repetitive play, traditional play therapy would seem an unlikely treatment. However, some therapists still rely on it, usually with predictably uneven results, or none at all. The book *Dibs: In Search of Self* (Ballantine, reissued 1990) by play therapy pioneer Virginia M. Axline has unfortunately been influential. Widely read by psychology students, the book never mentions that the child "Dibs" is obviously on the autistic spectrum. Instead, the parents are blamed for his "emotional disturbance," and he is "saved" by his dedicated therapist.

Traditional play therapy may be worthwhile for working with nonverbal children who have had life traumas in addition to ASDs, because with a well-trained therapist, play can provide clues and an avenue for communication. However, unless it is incorporated into a structured program, such as the floor-time program described previously, it is unlikely to be useful in general.

Psychoanalysis or counseling (talk therapy)

Long-term psychoanalysis is out of vogue these days, although it can help some adults understand how they think. There's nothing wrong with a little self-understanding, but it doesn't really have a role to play in the treatment of ASDs.

Cognitive-behavioral therapy (CBT) can be useful to adolescents and adults who are dealing with personality, self-esteem, or behavior problems, or with life crises. Some clinicians are using this approach to help people with Asperger's syndrome or high-functioning autism.[6] Using CBT techniques, the therapist and client work together to combat obsessive-compulsive behavior, anxiety, and depression. CBT relies on developing awareness of thought patterns that aren't functional ("all or nothing" thinking, for example) and using both therapy sessions and "homework" exercises to work on moods and behaviors.

Finally, family counseling or therapy is frequently a part of school or residential center programs for treating autistic spectrum disorders. Efficacy depends on the skills, background, and knowledge of the therapist, as well as on what goals counseling or therapy is intended to meet. As discussed in Chapter 10, *Family Issues and Support,* raising a child with an ASD, caring for an adult on the autistic spectrum, or being an adult with an ASD can be stressful. Family therapy sessions can give all family members a chance to unload their negative feelings on a professional instead of each other, learn new coping skills, and gain valuable knowledge about helping the affected individual while avoiding burnout.

Relaxation techniques

People with ASDs report that their bodies sometimes send them misleading signals, failing to warn them when they are in true danger or, worse yet, kicking in with a "fight or flight" adrenaline response for no good reason. This feeling can be disturbing, and it's even harder for young children to cope with. Self-stimulatory behaviors, such as hand-flapping or rocking, can be a reaction to these tense and unpleasant sensations.

Many programs working with people on the autistic spectrum teach relaxation techniques. These range from high-tech (biofeedback) to old-fashioned (meditation or prayer). Deep breathing, counting, using a device like author Temple Grandin's "Hug Machine," exercises in guided imagery, self-hypnosis—these are all effective for some individuals. Vestibular stimulation using swings or exercises can also be a useful relaxation technique (see "Sensory integration," later in this chapter).

Because having the ability to self-calm is so essential, both children and adults with ASDs should get some kind of relaxation training. Sensory integration and auditory integration training can help tune down the overamped arousal system once and for all. What works best will depend entirely on the individual.

Sensory integration

The theories behind sensory integration (SI) were first developed by an occupational therapist and researcher, Jean Ayres. Many OTs are at least familiar with the principles of SI, and some have special training or certification. Sensory Integration International (*http://home.earthlink.net/~sensoryint/*) is one group that can provide parents with a list of trained therapists and evaluators.

Sensory integration work is based on the idea that people with motor or sensory problems have difficulty processing the information they receive through the various senses. Just as auditory integration training attempts to desensitize the sense of hearing, SI exercises are intended to reduce sensory disturbances related to touch, movement, and gravity. These disturbances can occur in any or all of the following areas:

- **Processing.** How quickly (or if) the sensation reaches the central nervous system to be interpreted

- **Analysis.** How the person interprets the sensation

- **Organization.** How the person responds to her analysis of the situation

- **Memory.** How (or if) the person remembers similar sensations and proper responses from the past

Like other forms of occupational therapy, sensory integration work can easily be adapted to meet the needs of adolescents and adults. Some adults may be more comfortable doing an SI-style program of their own design in privacy, whereas others may want to see an SI specialist in a clinic or hospital.

Adults with sensory system dysfunction have devised all sorts of ways to reduce their exposure to difficult or painful sensations, although this avoidance can lead to increased isolation. For example, some adults with ASDs have installed expensive soundproofing in their homes, buy only soft cotton clothing, or have "picky" eating habits that have more to do with avoiding unpleasant textures than with taste. These coping strategies are admirable, but anyone who truly wants to break out of old life patterns without experiencing the discomfort of the past can look to SI techniques for help.

Disturbances can occur in either the traditional five senses (sight, hearing, smell, taste, and touch) or in less well-known senses that may actually have a greater effect on gross motor development. SI exercises generally work on these "whole body" senses, as follows:

- **Tactile.** Based in the system created by the entire skin surface and the nerves that serve it, this sense processes information taken in via all types of touch.

- **Proprioceptive.** Based in the muscles, ligaments, joints, and the nerves that serve them, this sense processes information about where the body and its various parts are in space.

- **Vestibular.** Based mostly in the inner ear, which acts as a sort of internal carpenter's level, this sense processes information about how the body interacts with gravity as it moves and attempts to retain its balance.

Most of us never think about these senses, unless they are suddenly disordered in some way, such as from an inner ear infection, a dizziness-producing carnival ride, or a leg that "falls asleep" and causes stumbling. For many people with ASDs, however, dysfunction in these sensory systems is the norm—in fact, for many people this sensory dysfunction is the most pervasive part of the disorder and may lead to its most disabling effects. Many behaviors commonly thought of as "autistic," including toe-walking, hand-flapping, and rocking, can be attempts to deal with sensory integration dysfunction.

Infants and young children learn to interpret the world around them through their senses. If the information comes in all wrong or cannot be processed properly, the world is a confusing place. Imagine trying to pay attention to your mother's lullaby if it sounded like an electric drill, or trying to play with a toy when your clothing was causing intense discomfort! The tactile, proprioceptive, and vestibular senses are our most elementary ways of relating to the environment—they're with us from the earliest nervous system development in the womb. Problems in this area are fundamental, because they interfere with the ability to learn the basic skills that are the building blocks for all others.

Luckily, sensory integration work can help most people with ASDs get better control of the information they take in. Please consult an occupational therapist who is trained in SI techniques if possible, or at least explore further by reading some of the SI-related books listed in Appendix A.

Rachel, mother of 11-year-old William, explains:

> For William, sensory integration was the key to progress in all other areas. He was sensory defensive sometimes, and that made it hard for him to be in his Early Intervention class, where there was a lot of touching. He was undersensitive to touch at other times and had low muscle tone, as evidenced by W-sitting [sitting in reverse "indian style", similar to a "W"], slack posture, and lack of strength.
>
> We did brushing and joint compression; the school OT added working on a balance beam and other equipment. It made a big difference in his life. He was just more comfortable in his body. We continue to use SI activities for calming and to continue that beneficial process.

SI activities are usually quite simple. Special equipment is not a must, although some parents have used swings, hammocks, and small items that can be obtained from catalogs (see Appendix A). The following lists offer a few examples of typical SI activities that may be done at home.

For tactile sensitivity problems (under- or oversensitivity), activities like those in the following list may help:

- The so-called Wilbarger brushing technique is based on the use of firm strokes with a soft surgical brush (available inexpensively from medical supply stores) on the back, arms, and legs. Brushing is interspersed with joint compression, in which the elbows, arm sockets, knees, and hip joints are pushed together firmly several times in succession. It's hard to explain this practice in print—it's really something you should be taught in person.

- Handling materials with a variety of textures, such as wet or dry sand, shaving cream, dry beans, and water. Children can be encouraged to play with the materials, even put them on their arms, legs, or face if appropriate.

- Using deep pressure massage or hugs.

- Making a "kid burrito" by rolling the child up tightly in a blanket, or a "kid sandwich" by (carefully) squishing the child between two gymnastic mats or sofa cushions.

- Parents and other caregivers should also avoid introducing people with tactile oversensitivity to unnecessary unpleasant sensations. Clothing problems are very common in this group, with tags and scratchy materials being frequent offenders. Incidentally, tactile undersensitivity is a common cause of hyperactive behavior.

For proprioceptive problems, the following exercises might be used:

- Swinging (clinics often use a big therapy swing that lets the person swing in a prone position)

- Jumping on a small trampoline

- The joint compression technique just mentioned

For vestibular problems, the next list contains suggestions:

- Walking on a balance beam

- Balancing on a large "therapy ball" as it moves

- OT work aimed at strengthening and developing gross motor skills (people with vestibular problems tend to have low muscle tone)

- Exercises that encourage "crossing the midline": using the left hand and arm on the right side of the body, and vice versa (for example, some kinds of dancing, and rocking from side to side)

- Stair climbing

Most of these exercises actually work on more than one sense at once. Activities can be combined and varied to keep SI work fun. Adults with long-term sensory issues may have a hard time getting started with an SI program, especially because some of the activities may seem childish or silly.

One special area of concern is oral tactile dysfunction. For years, parents have told their physicians that their children with ASDs had strange, limited food preferences. Many prefer bland, smooth foods, and self-select from only a few favorites: peanut butter, white bread, and applesauce only, for example. Although sometimes food preferences have their roots in allergies or metabolism, if texture appears to be the primary issue the problem is more likely to be oral tactile defensiveness. OTs can work to desensitize the nerves in the mouth, helping people gradually tolerate more textures and broaden their diet.

Sensory integration differences extend to eating habits. Some people with ASDs will stuff their mouths to the bursting point, for instance, and may not notice when food gets on their faces or hands. The issue here is tactile undersensitivity, and that can also be addressed by an OT.

Most speech therapists are also knowledgeable about sensitivity problems in the mouth and throat, and may be able to help.

In addition to exercises that reduce sensory defensiveness, or that help the undersensitive person integrate and process sensations, clinicians recommend making a sensory diet part of daily activities at home and at school. This means integrating soothing sensory experiences into daily activities at a regular interval. These activities could include the following:

- Slow, repetitive rhythmic movements, such as T'ai Chi, water aerobics, or using a rocking chair

- Firm pressure on the skin, from hugs, compression devices, or another source

- "Heavy work," such as moving furniture, carrying heavy bags, or lifting weights

- Activities done upside down, such as headstands or tumbling

The treatment methods recommended by Madeleine Portwood (*http://web.ukonline.co.uk/members/madeleine.portwood/index.htm*) for children with developmental dyspraxia are very similar to SI. Portwood is an educational psychologist with the Durham County Council in the UK, and the author of *Developmental Dyspraxia: A Practical Manual for Parents and Professionals* (Educational Psychology Service, 1996).

Social skills training

When social skills don't come naturally, they need to be taught. Social skills can be taught through one-to-one instruction or in small groups. Lessons should be reinforced by practice and, if they are well learned, will result in increased self-sufficiency and social success.

A typical social skills group might include children with and without disabilities, led by an adult who sets up activities designed to teach specific lessons. For example, board games are a great way to teach kids how to take turns, how to address unfairness, and how to handle winning and losing. Other lessons might include using role playing to practice ways to open and close a conversation with a new person, learning how to participate in playground games, learning strategies for handling teasing and bullying with aplomb, and more.

Because lunchtime and recess are frequently problem times for children with ASDs, several schools have set up "lunch bunch" groups that combine targeted work on social skills with etiquette lessons.

A social skills training program for adults could include anything from work on conversation skills to "finishing school"-style lessons on deportment. It should be geared to the needs of the individual.

Snoezelen

Snoezelen is a rather unique approach to the sensory difficulties experienced by some persons with autistic spectrum disorders, although it fits within a subset of occupational therapy called "multisensory therapy." It was developed in Holland, and although it has not made much impact as a treatment for people with ASDs elsewhere, it has been incorporated into dementia and Alzheimer's disease programs around the world.

The basic principle is creating a rich sensory environment. "Snoezelen rooms" may contain a variety of invitingly tactile surfaces, lights that move or change color, things to touch, relaxing sounds, and even scents. This environment should stimulate interest, promote exploration, and encourage relaxation and interaction. You can find out more on the Web at *http://www.swwf.com/*.

Speech therapy

Speech delay and/or dysfunction is considered a primary symptom of autistic spectrum disorders. Problems range from lack of speech because of an apparent inability to understand speech as a vehicle for symbolic communication, to motor problems that affect the production of clear speech, to problems with speech prosody.

A person on the autistic spectrum may also be affected by some other common speech disorder. In fact, they are far more common in people with ASDs than in the general population. Speech disorders come in many flavors. Here are the descriptive terms you will see most often:

- **Aphasia**. Difficulty in using oral language (expressive aphasia) or aural language (receptive aphasia). Can be characterized by pauses in speech or seeming to be "deaf" at times. Aphasia is usually associated with brain injury.

- **Stuttering**. Getting stuck on a sound, usually a single letter or syllable at the beginning of a word, and repeating it.

- **Cluttering**. Getting stuck on a complex sound, such as a word or phrase, and repeating it. Also characterized by a fast, fluctuating rate of speech.

- **Verbal dyspraxia**. Disordered speech because of underlying problems with muscle control. Also called developmental dyspraxia of speech.

- **Oral motor apraxia**. Lack of speech, or disordered speech, because of underlying problems with muscle control.

Technically, *apraxia* refers to the absence of speech, whereas *dyspraxia* refers to disordered speech. In the UK and some other countries, that's how these terms are used. In the US and Canada, however, the terms are used almost interchangeably, leading to much confusion. Be sure to ask what any diagnosis you or your child receives is actually intended to mean.

For a nonverbal person, simply producing sounds that have communicative intent is the initial goal of speech therapy. As people become verbal, oral motor problems, such as stuttering, may emerge. Speech therapy should be tailored to fit the individual. Stuttering, for example, can often be remedied in weekly group sessions with homework. Oral motor apraxia is a much more demanding condition, requiring intense, frequent sessions.

Language disorders

Even people with ASDs who speak, and speak well, can have language problems. Pragmatic language deficits—difficulty using language in context, such as in a conversation—are common in people with ASDs. The person's grammar, syntax, and conversational gambits may be limited, pedantic (as in Asperger's syndrome), or odd. The rate, volume, and rhythm of speech may be odd. Perseveration (frequent repetition of words or sentences, or getting stuck on topics) is not uncommon. The voice itself may be unusually raspy, hoarse, whispery, loud, or otherwise unusual. Speech therapists can address these problems, sometimes in individual sessions, sometimes in a group situation where the social aspects of language can be pointed out and practiced.

Two special language disorders are found primarily in people with autistic spectrum disorders, and are also common in people with Tourette's syndrome.

- **Echolalia.** The persistent repetition of words or phrases just heard. Some books on speech disorders still say that echolalia is "meaningless," but it can have communicative intent. For many young children with ASDs, echolalia is the first or only speech to emerge before intervention is tried.

- **Palilalia.** Repetition of your own words or thoughts (similar to perseveration, but with more of a compulsive quality).

A third language disorder, coprolalia, is experienced by about one tenth of all people diagnosed with Tourette's syndrome, usually as a transitory phase. Coprolalia is the inadvertent blurting of obscene or derogatory language, usually unrelated or only tangentially related to the situation at hand. Some people with ASDs occasionally evidence coprolalia, with or without a comorbid diagnosis of Tourette's syndrome.

The most common methods for dealing with coprolalia are substituting an inoffensive but similar word for the offending term (saying "fudge" or "ship" instead of the similar obscene word, for example), holding back the urge until the vocal tic can be released in private, or using medication that reduces tics. It's important that parents and professionals understand that coprolalia is a tic—a behavior that occurs because of a short-circuit in the impulse control system, not a truly volitional act. It is as difficult to control as an eye-blinking or finger-tapping tic, and should not be punished. Coprolalia causes extreme embarrassment, and most people who experience it are willing to try almost anything to make it disappear.

Speech therapy methods

Methods used by speech therapists (and by parents and teachers) depend on the problem at hand and differ depending on the setting. For oral motor apraxia, for example, speech therapists in medical centers may work "inside the mouth" using popsicle sticks, fingers, whistles, straws, and other items to help the person gain control over muscles of the mouth, tongue, and throat. SLPs in schools are less likely to do so, but may combine sound drills with adding speech activities to a child's regular classroom program.

For most people with severe communication disorders, one-to-one treatment is essential. Some school districts and health care facilities try to cut corners by delivering speech therapy in a group setting. This works well for less serious problems or for speech pragmatics, but is not sufficient for nonverbal, apraxic, or severely dyspraxic children.

There are all sorts of ways to encourage the production of speech, and they can be integrated into ABA, floor-time, or other types of therapeutic systems. Perhaps the best reference available is *Teach Me Language* (SKF Books, 1997), by Sabrina Freeman and Lorelei Dake. Freeman and Dake mix speech and language concepts tailored to the specific needs of autistic spectrum children with ABA teaching techniques, and their suggestions can easily be incorporated into home and school programs.

When doing speech therapy with children (and particularly with those who have ASDs), motivation can be a roadblock. Smart SLPs use speech games, flash cards, toys, hand puppets, and reinforcers of all sorts to keep sessions on track and encourage children to work harder. These aids are available to parents as well through catalogs (see Appendix A) or sometimes directly from the SLP. Songs and rhythm work well with some people.

William's mother says,

> Our son has severe oral motor apraxia. One thing he simply could not do is breathe through his nose, which caused prosody problems when he tried to talk and breathe through his mouth at the same time.
>
> After many frustrating speech sessions, his SLP found the perfect solution! She purchased a package of plastic "nose flutes," which whistle when you blow through your nose with your mouth closed. It took him a week to get the first sound out of one, but it was a fun challenge.
>
> One of the first things we noticed was less snoring, because he started breathing through his nose most of the time while sleeping.

Your child may get homework, often in the form of worksheets with sounds to attempt. Ask the SLP how to make these drills more fun. Adults in speech therapy may have homework too, sometimes drills, sometimes mouth exercises with a mirror.

Total communication

The best approach to working with nonverbal, barely verbal, or apraxic children and adults is what some speech therapists call "total communication." It involves not only relying on oral language to build communication skills, but also introducing gestures, sign language, and other visual communication systems even as you do speech therapy. A person who cannot communicate is cut off from others, and it has been conclusively shown that visual communication systems use the same brain circuits as oral communication does. In other words, using visual communication may help build up these weak circuits, laying the groundwork for oral speech. The goal of the SLP in this situation is to help the person make the transition from the visual to the verbal, first by connecting the two, and then by doing traditional speech work. Most experts in helping people with communication disorders endorse the total communication approach.

Dr. Stephen M. Edelson, director of the Center for the Study of Autism, says,

> There is research [showing] that teaching speech and sign language at the same time will increase the likelihood that the child will speak. Unfortunately, many behavior therapists teach only speech because they feel that sign language will become a crutch, and the child will rely on signs rather than speaking. There is no evidence to support this notion.
>
> Interestingly, when a person talks or uses sign language, the same area of the brain is activated. Thus, the procedure of teaching speech and sign language simultaneously may, in fact, be stimulating two neurological pathways that activate the same area of the brain.

Even Dr. Lovaas, who has long pushed a speech-only approach, is beginning to come around to the total communication point of view. If after a long time children in an intensive ABA program still have not begun to talk, he now recommends using PECS symbols or something similar to jump-start communication, according to parents.

Some people with autism have motor problems that do not allow them to develop easily understood speech. Sign language can give these individuals anything from a few essential signs to a complete and fluent language. There are actually several different sign languages, and there are even regional "accents." Beginners can start with readily available books or videos, and classes are available from community colleges, schools for the deaf, and other sources.

Speech and behavior

There is a strong link between speech problems and distressing behavior, as many parents can attest. The frustration of not being understood can build up to produce tantrums. It makes a person feel isolated, and it can make him more vulnerable to abuse.

Interestingly, poor communication abilities are cited by social scientists as one of the three factors most likely to lead to violent behavior in children, adolescents, or adults (the other two: male gender and abuse). Case studies of autistic spectrum disorders have shown that the development of speech correlates strongly with better outcomes.

Don't let these facts frighten you—let them motivate you. Don't let anyone tell you that a person is too old for speech therapy, unable to behave well enough to benefit from speech therapy, not intelligent enough for speech therapy, or simply a "late talker." Communication is the key to everything else.

Cindy, mother of 15-year-old Jeffrey, says,

> When his own brother and mother don't understand his speech, when he can't tell a story or explain a need, that must be so frustrating! And does he feel sad? Or lonely? Or depressed? I don't know. He doesn't have the expressive language to tell me.

When a child is experiencing behavior problems, communication problems are often at the root. It should be the first area addressed when searching for a solution. Behavior is communication, and for those who have difficulty expressing themselves with words, it can be the only form of communication available. We need to pay attention.

Who delivers, who pays?

If you have read this chapter, you've probably noticed that the most demonstrably effective interventions rely on one-to-one interaction for several hours every day. Parents, grandparents, even teenage or adult siblings can be trained to do much of this work, but it is exhausting. And many important interventions, such as speech therapy, do require college-trained therapists.

Indeed, one of the biggest issues around therapeutic interventions is who delivers them—and who pays for them. Insurance companies often refuse to provide anything, whereas schools tend to do as little as possible—and increasingly try to bill the parents' insurance for whatever the schools do deliver! Often families end up spending thousands of dollars for therapy delivered by private practitioners, when either their health insurance or the school system should have paid for it.

Start your search with your local Early Intervention program or school district. In the US, Canada, and most of Europe, these entities are charged with providing at least some assistance at no charge to the parents. Some programs in the US and Canada *do* pay for home-based ABA or similar intensive therapies for young children. It works, and the growing consensus among advocates for children on the autistic spectrum is that intensive, full-time programs should be the norm for all young children diagnosed with an ASD. Making that a reality will probably require government edicts or court cases.

In the meantime, parents whose budgets cannot bear the weight of paying for ABA, speech, OT, and groceries at the same time must find other resources. The first place to look is inward. Parents and other family members know their children better than anyone else. They understand what motivates them, what annoys them, what sparks a tantrum, and what special skills they have. Parents are the true experts, but they often labor under a burden of self-doubt, fearing they don't have the skills or energy to teach. Perhaps the most valuable investment is in training that provides you with the actual skills you need and with the self-confidence required to exercise them.

Parent training for ABA, floor-time play therapy, and similar programs is not always easy to find locally. You may have to attend an autism conference, or travel to a center that specializes in training practitioners and parents. Appendix B, *Support and Advocacy*, lists a number of resources that can help you get started. People who don't have access to classes can also use books as self-training aids. Online resources can put you in touch with people who have experience in various types of therapy.

Once parents have been trained, they can train others. These others can be paid, but many families have found volunteers who were more than willing to help out with a home-based program for a few hours each week. Family members have stood before their religious congregations to ask for help, contacted local high schools and colleges in search of willing students, put up notices on community bulletin boards, and contacted such organizations as Volunteers of America or Easter Seals. College students, especially those who need to complete a certain number of hours for a practicum requirement, are an especially excellent resource. Some senior citizens also have the time, patience, and desire to help that make a great volunteer.

It's been estimated that a 40-hour-per-week ABA program for a child with autistic disorder can cost as much as $30,000 to $60,000. Parents whose children have less severe difficulties can expect to pay less. But some families have successfully provided intensive, one-on-one therapeutic interventions—even for children who are severely autistic—using only their own labor and assistance from unpaid volunteers. Chapter 10 provides some additional ideas in this vein. Two parents interviewed for this book have done so despite having very low incomes, including one subsisting on disability benefit in the UK.

Professionals in the field caution parents against courting bankruptcy to provide high-priced help. Sometimes the most important interventions are those that cost the least. In a recent presentation to families, Dr. Stanley Greenspan noted that "a really good teenage babysitter, one who will play and interact with your child for a couple of hours, not just watch TV, can sometimes be a better investment than another hour of speech therapy."

As noted at the beginning of this section, schools and insurance companies may try to pass the burden off to each other. In 1997 and 1998, school districts asked a number of parents in the US for the first time to give them health insurance billing information, which the districts then tried to use to extract payment from insurance companies for speech therapy and other services provided by the school district. Because the special education laws specify quite clearly that schools are to provide a *free* and appropriate public education ("FAPE"), special education advocates suspect that this practice skirts the law. A number of families have successfully refused to provide this information for any purpose other than ensuring its availability in case emergency medical care is needed during school hours. To our knowledge, no one has yet taken a US school district to court over this issue, but it is likely to happen in the near future.

Why would you want to resist such requests? Other than the legal issue just noted, this practice can block your access to therapies provided in a medical setting. Most health insurers limit the amount of therapeutic services an insured patient can receive. Because schools and medical facilities take different, and yet complementary, approaches to speech, occupational, and physical therapy, you don't want to lose the opportunity to use both. If your insurer insists on calling ASDs "mental disorders," as so many still do, you may lose access to family therapy and other benefits because the school district has charged the insurer for counseling or social work services.

In addition, as discussed in detail in Chapter 8, *Insurance,* you may not want to share your child's educational diagnosis with your health insurer. Many companies do discriminate against people with autistic spectrum disorders, refusing them services that are provided to people with other diagnoses.

Some professionals do applaud the practice of school districts billing private insurance, arguing that insurers may be more willing to provide their own services if they will otherwise be forced to pay for school-based services whose quality and outcome they cannot control.

Evaluating programs and practitioners

Families and adults with ASDs can choose from many therapeutic models. Your decisions should be based on how comfortable you feel with a particular approach, the provider's reputation, published research, and whether it fits the person's needs.

Others who have tried an approach are your best resources for vetting programs and practitioners. Ask around at meetings of autism support groups, and seek out information about people like yourself or your child in particular. You can even ask in online forums, although it's best to request that all responses be made directly to you rather than to the entire mailing list. Some practitioners take part in these lists, too. Local service agencies, such as disability services offices or advocacy organizations, may be able to give you an opinion. Special education case managers are often familiar with both public and private programs in your area.

One thing you should never do is rely on the program itself for references. Almost every method attempted has produced a "success story" or two, even those that are generally considered to be discredited. If these are the only voices you hear, you aren't getting the full picture.

If a program claims to have documented proof of its efficacy, ask to see the studies themselves, not just their purported results. Sometimes results have been misinterpreted, and sometimes studies are so poorly constructed that the results are meaningless. If you're not sure about a study, take it to your physician or another knowledgeable adviser for a second opinion.

Evaluating practitioners

As you choose speech therapists and others to work with your child, be aware that even the most recent textbooks may have provided them with misinformation about autistic spectrum disorders. For example, the ninth edition of *Speech Correction: An Introduction to Speech Pathology and Audiology,* by Charles Van Riper and Robert L. Erickson (Allyn and Bacon, 1996), one of the most popular speech textbooks in current US use, classes autism under "emotional problems," describes autistic children as "strange . . . not of this world," and fails to so much as mention PDD-NOS, atypical PDD, Asperger's syndrome, or that there is a spectrum of autistic disorders at all.

If a therapist has been miseducated, it's not really fair to blame her. But it certainly is a hassle to have to educate professionals year after year, as so many parents must do. If the professional is resistant to new information, don't delay in finding someone else. In a school setting this can be difficult, and in rural areas you may have no alternative choices.

When bringing volunteers or paid aides for a home program onboard, make sure you feel comfortable with the person's approach, demeanor, willingness to listen, and work ethic. Pay attention to your intuition. If someone makes you feel uncomfortable, they are likely to have a similar effect on your child. Some parents have chosen to do criminal background checks on prospective aides.

Evaluating results

You can't evaluate results of a particular therapy if baseline data were not collected before it began, so that's an essential step. You should receive a report summarizing the results of a baseline evaluation before the therapist gets started. If you see something that doesn't ring true, bring it up now. Sometimes people perform differently in a clinical setting or with strangers from the way they do at home, and that's information the therapist can use.

You also need to keep a record of the interventions you're trying. We strongly recommend keeping a journal that tracks medications, therapy appointments, changes in diet, vitamins, and everything else you do (see Chapter 10), but it can be time consuming. At the very least, ensure that services are actually being delivered—not always an easy task with school-based programs—and ask the therapist how he will evaluate the effectiveness of his work.

If standardized tests are to be used as a measure of progress, make sure appropriate instruments are used, that you get a copy of the results, and that they are adequately explained.

Whenever possible, change or add therapeutic interventions just as you would medications: one at a time. It's hard to tell what change is responsible for an advance if you have made many at once.

Sarah, mother of 3-year-old Elaine, says,

> I really didn't know what to look for when I was in the Part-H program
> [an Early Intervention program]. I was willing to stick with the first
> speech person, and I really wish I had changed before Elaine turned 3.
> I wanted to at least give her a fair try . . . [but] after six months I looked
> for another SLP—much better results!

If you are truly dissatisfied with a therapeutic intervention after you've given it several months, talk to your practitioner. It could be that progress is occurring, but at a more subtle level than expected. It could also be that this is not the right intervention for this person, or that this practitioner is not the right person to work with this individual.

Spotting a scam

Whenever people are desperate, you will find someone seeking to take advantage of their desperation. These con artists can be hard to spot. Some sport the initials "MD" after their names, some have published books, others have the ability to make you feel warm and fuzzy inside as you listen to their spiel. They promise you the moon, but they can't deliver.

The field of autistic spectrum disorders has been home to many a false prophet. Not all have been strictly venal: Perhaps a therapy worked for one child, and they were sure it would for all. Perhaps an idea seemed as though it *should* work, and they truly wanted it to. Others are simply charlatans, well aware that they're selling snake oil. How can you avoid being taken in?

First, educate yourself about any therapy that you're considering. If you're told that it's backed by research, ask to see the published research. Real researchers publish their work in reputable journals, according to their profession (medicine, occupational therapy, speech therapy, and so on) where others in their field review the study before publication.

If a therapy is new, research may still be in progress. Ask the practitioner to contrast his approach to well-tested mainstream methods, such as ABA or sensory integration—nothing is ever so new that it has no relationship to what has gone before. Make sure the rationale behind a new approach makes sense to you and is safe.

If a therapy has been around for more than a couple years, be suspicious if no peer-reviewed research (or only badly done research) has been published.

Check out a practitioner's credentials, ensuring that they come from a reputable source, not a mail-order "diploma mill." Letters after a name can stand for a lot of things, not all of them useful. Some people add them just to fool you, like a certain US practitioner who follows his name with the misleading letters "PhC" (meaning PhD candidate) . . . and has done so for over a decade.

Learn the "buzzwords" used in a particular therapy, so you can sound knowledgeable when you ask questions. Con artists tend to dress up their wares in a lot of fancy terminology, in an effort to make it sound scientific or up-to-the-minute. People who do have something genuinely new to offer are usually happy to attempt a layperson's-level explanation. If you're told it's too complex or mysterious to explain, a red flag should go up in your mind.

Dr. Lovaas is widely admired by grateful families, and rightly so, but no one hangs on his every word. He's a good researcher, and an important guy in the field of autism, not a guru. That's as it should be. Watch out for therapies that seem to be hitched to a cult of personality. Some therapies do have such leaders: people who refuse to be questioned, who encourage parents to spend huge sums of money just to bask in their presence, and who accuse their critics of something close to heresy.

These ersatz gurus will tell you that theirs is the only method and discourage you from seeking any other kind of help for you or your child. Often they use coercive methods to bring you into their orbit, and cultlike techniques to keep you there. Some may even threaten to reveal privileged information about you if you leave. Others may claim that the person being treated will regress, and the blame will all be on you.

Money can be another red flag issue. Doctors and therapists deserve to get paid, but the cost of treatment should be in proportion to the cost of similar therapies. If speech therapy costs $50 per hour but "Therapy X" costs $500 per hour, that doesn't necessarily mean "Therapy X" is much better. Most reputable therapists who treat people with ASDs do so because they care. They want to make an adequate living, but they aren't expecting to live a lavish lifestyle on other people's misery. Ask about costs. If the answer sounds like mumbo-jumbo instead of a truthful accounting of expenses, find the door.

Be especially careful of any method that claims to *cure* ASDs. People do get better with proper intervention. They function better in the world, they feel happier, they're able to enjoy the benefits of more relationships and activities. A stranger might never know that they once carried the label of an autistic spectrum disorder. But subtle differences remain, and any therapist who claims she can make someone absolutely "normal" is shading the truth a little.

If you'd like an inside look at the issue of false therapies, the books *Facilitated Communication—A Passion to Believe: Autism and the Facilitated Communication Phenomenon* (Westview Press, 1998), by Diane Twachtman-Cullen, and *No Time for Jello* (Brookline Books, 1989), by Berneen Bratt, are recommended reading. The first takes the "facilitated communication" phenomenon to task, the second tackles the Doman-Delacato/Institutes for the Achievement of Human Potential "patterning" program. As these books make clear, smart people can be taken in, including idealistic young therapists who themselves end up bamboozled into the wrong camp.

Perhaps the most important thing you can do to avoid therapy scams is trust your own intuition. If it feels wrong, it probably is.

Don't call it therapy

Most children develop their gross and fine motor skills, their social capabilities, and their speech in the course of everyday activities. People with ASDs can also enjoy the therapeutic potential of typical activities.

Young children may not seem to be enjoying an activity at first, perhaps opting out of the action. Try to work up to it in small steps. For example, if your child shows an interest in collecting cards, introduce a card album, show her how to slip the cards into the pockets, and back away. Save the activities of trading cards with other kids, playing collectible card games, going to card stores, and attending card shows for other days.

Here are just a few of the fun activities that build important skills. Every kid should have these experiences. Whatever you do, don't call it therapy (even though it is).

- Playing card games and board games
- Swimming
- Playing on the playground, at the park, or in your yard
- Reading aloud (or silently), with an accent on the "what-ifs" of factual books and on fantasy
- Nursery rhymes, jump rope jingles, and hand games
- Simple group games such as London Bridge and freeze tag (see books on "New Games" for some cooperative play possibilities for groups)
- Using costumes and props for imaginative play
- Starting and maintaining collections of rocks, stamps, cards, or toys
- Building models and playing with construction toys
- Turning off the television and video games in favor of relating to one another
- Getting messy outdoors or in the kitchen

Finally, although therapy, medical appointments, taking pills, and eating special meals may be part of your child's life or your own, they shouldn't be the totality of it. Therapies should enhance life. Make time for relaxation, play, hugs, Saturday morning cartoons, and just watching the clouds go by. These moments work a sort of magic too, and they aren't to be missed.

CHAPTER 7

Other Interventions

BECAUSE MEDICAL SCIENCE HASN'T CAUGHT UP TO addressing the causes of autistic spectrum disorders just yet, many people experiment with herbal supplements, vitamins, chiropractic, homeopathy, acupuncture, and other complementary interventions. This chapter lists and defines most of the "alternative" treatments that you may hear about and explains how to evaluate the claims of practitioners and salespeople.

As with the medical and therapeutic interventions discussed in the preceding two chapters, exercise caution. If a substance or treatment has actual effects (not all will), its use should be taken as seriously as using a pharmaceutical medication that produces similar effects. Appendix F, *Supplement Reference*, provides more detailed information about some of these products.

There is no proof that any of these therapies or programs will help a specific person, but anecdotal evidence—and in a few cases, clinical trials—indicate that some individuals with ASDs may experience significant improvements.

Miranda was tentatively diagnosed autistic before her first birthday. Her mother, Maria, embarked on a journey through the world of complementary medicine:

> *At the age of 10 months, my daughter was described by the psychologist as follows:*
>
> *"This little girl has a very short, fleeting attention span. She gaze-averts, and makes only intermittent and relatively unmeaningful eye contact. She is a very hypotonic baby . . . intermittently unresponsive to sound, and is more responsive to inanimate than vocal input. She appears vacuous, and had many staring episodes, which were suggestive of a possible underlying seizure disorder. She flaps her hands, shakes her head, and does some other self-stimulating behaviors in a repetitive manner . . . "*
>
> *Her BSID II mental age was 4 months; motor age, 5 months. On the Gesell, at 42 weeks old, she ranged from a high score of 24 weeks on fine motor to a low of 13 weeks on personal/social. Very erratic.*

I only repeat all this because inevitably, there will be those who respond to our success with skepticism about her initial diagnosis. And because the CHAT [Checklist for Autism in Toddlers] is the earliest diagnostic tool I know of, at 18 months of age, you have every right to do so. However, if Miranda was headed for a confirmed diagnosis of an autistic spectrum disorder at a later date, I truly believe that in her case we have stopped or mediated the metabolic problems that were causing her symptoms, and perhaps prevented irreversible CNS damage.

We started DMG and then Super Nu-Thera first, and got better sleep patterns, more eye contact, and increased babbling. With her history of ear infections, we decided to have Dr. Shaw's test done, and actually started the antiyeast diet, probiotics, and MCT oil while awaiting the results. Eventually, we added Nystatin. After a nightmare two-week die-off period, the effects were like a fog had lifted from Miranda. Prolonged, meaningful, deep gazes into Mommy's eyes, dissolving into fits of giggles at funny faces, awareness of and interest in her environment, and finally, sitting unassisted.

The test came back with 18 levels high, some extremely so. Several were fungal metabolites, so we were vigilant about the diet, Nystatin, and supplements. We still see regression when Miranda has fruit, and had a terrible regression and actual fungal diaper rash when we tried rice milk (too much sugar). Miranda also had the gluten/casein peptides test done. She showed high IAG, an indicator of gut permeability, and gliadomorphin, but not casomorphin. At the time, she was still breastfed and I was avoiding dairy, so we opted to go both gluten-free and casein-free since the peptides are so similar.

Jump to the present. Miranda is 13 months old. Current interventions: gluten- and casein-free diet and antiyeast diet, MCT oil, DMG, and Super Nu-Thera, choline/inositol, and just started MSM. She drinks DariFree spiked with EFAs and rice protein powder. She is also in Early Intervention, getting PT, OT, and sensory integration, and tons of intensive interaction and floor-time [therapy] with a dash of ABA from Mom.

She's a clingy, cuddly, snuggly, affectionate child now. She imitates funny faces and sounds, claps when you say "Yaaaay!" She crawls around the house looking for me and calling "Mamamamamama," gets into all the cupboards, pulls up to stand on the furniture, drinks from a sippy cup.

> She passed the 7- to 10-month-old competencies in every area of her
> latest assessment (the IDA) and passed the 11- to 13-month-old
> competencies for social/emotional development.
>
> Believe me, we have a long way to go—I still worry about language
> development, her sensory issues, and when my little "doughgirl" will ever
> have enough muscle tone to actually walk, but she's here, in our world,
> instead of that foggy one she used to be lost in, and we continue to be
> amazed and delighted at her progress.
>
> Of course these same interventions won't help everyone, but I
> encourage you all to continue to be dedicated detectives. Find out the
> "why?" behind each treatment option, and look at your child's history
> to see if [he or she] might benefit. Sift, study, analyze, ask, try, compare,
> and never give up!

Other parents try alternative routes and find them lacking, sometimes because they
have been steered in the wrong direction, sometimes because there's nothing there to
find.

Kim, mother of 7-year-old Brad, says,

> We had problems, and small improvement. [We tried] zinc and a host
> of other minerals, such as calcium—no real help at all. Immunological
> testing showed nothing. Allergy testing showed environmental allergies
> to grass, leaf molds, and ragweed. No food allergies.

General holistic/alternative treatment systems

In the UK, the queen herself sees a homeopathic physician. Many insurance plans
cover chiropractic adjustments, at least for back trouble. And the oldest medical
systems—India's Ayurvedic medicine, Chinese herbalism, and the folk medicine of
native peoples around the world—undoubtedly feature some time-tested remedies
that Western medicine could adopt to its benefit. Following are brief descriptions of
the most common alternative medicine systems, in alphabetic order.

Acupuncture

Developed in China, acupuncture is based on the concept of *ch'i*, an energy force that
is believed to course through the human body. Acupuncture theory states that if your
ch'i is blocked, illness results. To undo these blockages, acupuncturists use tiny
needles inserted into the skin at specific points.

Modern acupuncturists use disposable needles to ensure sterility. Some also employ heat (moxibustion), noninvasive lasers, magnetic devices, essential oils, or electrical stimulation. Many have expertise in other Chinese or Western complementary therapies, such as herbal medicine.

If you do try acupuncture, you may encounter terms and practices that are unfamiliar to you. Acupuncture, and Chinese medicine in general, work from a different set of core beliefs from Western medicine. Ask your practitioner about anything you don't understand.

Studies funded by the National Institutes of Health have found that acupuncture does help some conditions, including chronic pain, and works well as an adjunct to other methods in the treatment of drug addiction. Some researchers think the needles influence the body's production of natural opioid chemicals and neurotransmitters.[1]

For people with ASDs, the areas of most interest regarding acupuncture are its potential effects on the GI tract and the nervous system. Reputable research indicates that properly applied acupuncture treatments may help regulate gastrointestinal functions, which could be good news for people with GI distress caused by medication.[2] Other studies have indicated (but not proven) that acupuncture may heal nerve damage.[3]

Acupuncture is used to treat autistic children in China. A team from the University of Hong Kong announced measurable success using tongue acupuncture with autistic children in 2001. They used brain imaging and observation scales to document changes.[4]

Ayurvedic and Chinese traditional medicine

Indigenous peoples everywhere have medical systems based on the use of herbal remedies. Two of these, India's Ayurveda and traditional Chinese medicine, have been systematized and studied to a great extent. The Ayurvedic medicine concept revolves around a life force called *prana,* whereas Chinese traditionalists talk about *ch'i,* as mentioned in the previous section on acupuncture.

Ayurvedic practitioners will give you a thorough exam and then tell you which "type" you are in their diagnostic system. Then they'll suggest an appropriate diet, lifestyle adjustments, and probably therapeutic meditation. They may also have various suggestions about cleaning out your digestive tract.

Chinese traditional practitioners take a very similar approach, although their dietary recommendations are usually less strict than a typical Ayurvedic plan.

There is a vast array of Ayurvedic and Chinese herbal remedies. Some of these concoctions are probably quite effective, whereas others could be dangerous to your health. If possible, try to find out exactly which herbs are in a potion, and check out their effects. For example, the popular Chinese herb *ma huang* (ephedra) is a common ingredient in traditional "nerve tonics." It is also a powerful central nervous system stimulant, and should be taken with extreme caution.

It is far safer to work closely with a practitioner who knows your state of health and can monitor you during treatment than it is to purchase Chinese or Ayurvedic remedies over the counter.

In the US, the primary certification agency for practitioners of Chinese medicine is the National Certification Commission for Acupuncture and Oriental Medicine. You can reach NCCAOM at (703) 548-9004 or on the Web at *http://www.nccaom.org*.

There is no US certification commission for Ayurvedic practitioners or Western herbalists. The most active group promoting Ayurveda in the US is the National Institute of Ayurvedic Medicine, which can be reached at (914) 278-8700 or online at *http://niam.com/corp-web/index.htm*.

As far as the author can tell from an extensive review of the literature in English, no medical researcher has ever surveyed or studied traditional herbal remedies for autistic spectrum disorders, although some people have tried them. It would be an interesting pursuit, and hopefully someone will do so.

Chiropractic

Chiropractors adjust the spine and related body structures. Their work in this area does seem useful to some people with back pain, and the International Chiropractic Pediatric Association reports that chiropractic adjustments brought about "positive behavior changes" in about half the children with autism treated in a 1987 study.[5]

Some parents report that their chiropractors have offered to treat their children with autism or other developmental disabilities at low or no cost. Results have been very variable—some children cannot tolerate the sensory experience of being "adjusted," others seem to enjoy it.

Homeopathy

Homeopathy is based on the principle that remedies containing infinitesimal amounts of substances that could cause the medical condition being treated can instead prod the immune system into action against the condition. Homeopathy is a fairly mainstream medical practice in the UK, although repeated studies have not verified that it works.[6]

In the US and Canada, homeopathic physicians are not licensed to practice medicine. However, some MDs and NDs do recommend homeopathic treatments. For information about homeopathic medicine and licensing for homeopaths in North America, contact the National Center for Homeopathy at (703) 548-7790 or on the Web at *http://www.homeopathic.org*. In the UK, the Royal London Homeopathic Hospital (020 7837 8833) is a top resource.

For autism, the homeopathic remedies mentioned most often by parents who prefer this approach—Bufo, Bufo rana, Bufo cinereus, Bufo vulgaris, and Rana bufo— contain small amounts of the toxin made by the bufo toad. Oddly enough, one presentation at the 1998 DAN! conference noted that a substance very much like this toxin had been isolated from the blood of some autistic children (not children who were taking these remedies, it should be noted).[7]

Some families have also tried homeopathic secretin, although this would seem to contravene the basic principle of homeopathic medicine.

Although homeopathic remedies can often be purchased at health food stores, responsible practitioners recommend seeing a homeopathic doctor before choosing remedies. The remedies are generally used only as part of an overall treatment plan that may include diet changes and stress reduction. Even if the remedies themselves are of no value, as many skeptics believe, you might benefit from the rest of the program.

Naturopathy

Naturopaths are licensed to practice medicine in some US states, Canadian provinces, and other countries. They are trained and licensed as naturopathic doctors (ND). Naturopaths tend to see themselves as "wellness promoters," not just treaters of disease. Their practice stresses preventing disease through diet, exercise, and vitamins. They may prescribe herbal remedies or Western pharmaceuticals (in states where they are licensed to do so) to people with illness, and may also suggest and/or administer complementary therapies such as hydrotherapy (special baths or wet packs) or massage.

Naturopaths vary in their personal philosophy about Western medicine. Some refer you elsewhere for ailments they feel are out of their league, others prefer to rely solely on nutritional and natural medicine.

People who want to try herbal remedies and nutritional interventions such as the ones mentioned in this chapter can choose a naturopath as their primary care provider. Take care when making a choice, however: In the US, some people calling themselves naturopaths have not completed an accredited program. Properly licensed naturopaths receive medical training roughly comparable to traditional ("allopathic") medical school, although with a different emphasis.

For information about finding a licensed naturopath in the US or Canada, contact the American Association of Naturopathic Physicians (*http://www.naturopathic.org*) or the Canadian Naturopathic Association (*http://www.naturopathicassoc.ca/*).

Orthomolecular medicine

The most famous proponent of orthomolecular medicine was its late founder, Dr. Linus Pauling. Best known for receiving the 1954 Nobel Prize for Chemistry and the 1962 Nobel Prize for Peace, Pauling spent his later life studying and publicizing the effects of megadoses of vitamins, particularly vitamin C. Many of Dr. Pauling's claims have not been substantiated, but his reputation as a scientist forced the medical establishment to take his ideas seriously.

Some MDs are firm believers in orthomolecular medicine, and Pauling's principles underlie the megadose vitamin concoctions in health food stores. See the section "Vitamins" later in this chapter for more information about how these are sometimes used by people with ASDs.

If a practitioner says she is an orthomolecular physician, that should mean she is a licensed MD or DO (Doctor of Osteopathy). You can check on the status of a physician's license with your state medical licensing board. If a practitioner says he is board certified, you can confirm that with the American Board of Medical Specialties at (847) 491-9091 or online at *http://www.abms.org/*. An appropriate board certification for an orthomolecular psychiatrist would be in psychiatry or neurology. Unfortunately, some people presenting themselves as orthomolecular physicians or psychiatrists are not licensed MDs or DOs.

Osteopathy

Osteopathic physicians are trained as primary care providers first, although they may then specialize as pediatricians, surgeons, allergists, and so on. They stress preventive care, and look closely at the role of body structure in the disease process. They sometimes adjust the musculoskeletal system to effect improvement.

In the UK, licensed osteopaths participate in the National Health program. They are licensed to practice medicine in all US states, and use the initials DO (Doctor of Osteopathy) instead of MD. You can find out if an osteopath is licensed to practice medicine in your state by calling your state medical board or state osteopathic board. You can find out more about DO certification and find a practitioner through the American Osteopathy Association at (800) 621-1773 or online at *http://www.aoa-net.org*.

One area of osteopathy-related treatment, craniosacral therapy, is often recommended for children with neurological challenges, including autistic spectrum disorders. Although developed by osteopath John Upledger, craniosacral therapy is practiced by trained members of other professions, including some occupational therapists and physical therapists. Upledger includes some accounts of beneficial use of this therapy for people with autism in his book *Your Inner Physician and You: Craniosacral Therapy and Somatoemotional Release* (North Atlantic Books, 1997).

Vitamins

Many physicians actually consider vitamins a first-line approach to autism. Clear and compelling clinical evidence suggests that at least some people with ASDs can benefit from taking additional B_6,[8] and the evidence for beneficial effects from some other vitamins is also reliable. The Autism Research Institute (ARI) has been an early and vocal booster of this approach, and has funded some of the research as well. People interested in pursuing vitamin therapy for autistic spectrum disorders would be well advised to contact ARI for the most recent information in this area.

In this section, only effects believed relevant to autistic spectrum disorders are mentioned. Vitamins and other supplements may have other health benefits as well. As always, approach these options with caution, and inform your primary care physician when you add vitamins to your personal health care prescription.

The B vitamin family

The B vitamin family includes the following:

- **Vitamin B_1** (thiamin) is needed to fight stress and metabolize glucose into energy. It is sometimes found to be low in autistic subjects. Severe thiamin deficiency is called beri-beri, a potentially fatal condition whose symptoms include pain, weakness, nausea, constipation, and neurological problems.

- **Vitamin B_2** (riboflavin) takes part in the conversion of tryptophan, and in the synthesis of your body's own antiinflammatory substances, the corticosteroids. If you follow a vegetarian diet, you probably should add vitamin B_2 to your diet as a matter of course. Three medications sometimes used for ASD symptoms—chlorpromazine, imipramine, and amitriptyline—inhibit the body's use of riboflavin. This effect may also hold true for clomipramine and perhaps for other antidepressants. Those using these medications should take B_2 supplements, particularly if they are on a gluten-free diet (in the US and some other countries, breads and other baked goods made with white flour are routinely enriched with vitamin B_2).

- **Vitamin B_3** (niacin) is believed to reduce inflammation and help the body cope with stress. It is also needed to help red blood cells carry oxygen and to build tissue, including nerve tissue. Severe niacin deficiency (pellagra) causes GI tract irritation and severe neurological problems. A small group of people diagnosed as schizophrenic recover when given niacin supplements,[9] which gave doctors treating autism (then thought to be the same as childhood schizophrenia) the idea of trying B vitamins. However, if you take antiseizure drugs, niacin may strengthen their action. If you experience "flushing" (spreading warmth and redness) when taking niacin, buffered "antiflush" niacin is available.

- **Vitamin B_5** (pantothenic acid) is necessary for normal antibody production and metabolism. B_5 deficiency is rare in people eating a typical Western diet, but when volunteers in one study were given a deliberately deficient diet they developed neurological and GI tract problems.[10]

- **Vitamin B_6** (pyridoxine) is needed to process protein, essential fatty acids, and stored starches. It also influences the production of neurotransmitters, particularly norepinephrine, dopamine, and serotonin. Deficiency markers include dry skin, nausea, depression, and neurological symptoms, including seizures. If you feel a tingling sensation in your hands or feet, stop taking B_6. For optimal absorption, B_6 must be given with magnesium.

- B_{12} (cobalamin) can be deficient in people who are not making a normal amount of digestive enzymes, such as those with GI tract disorders. It is also needed to build the myelin sheath that protects nerve fibers. Deficiency symptoms include pernicious anemia and depression. People with ASDs who test positive for autoantibodies to myelin protein and those with inflammation of the terminal ileum of the intestine (where B_{12} is absorbed) should probably supplement with vitamin B_{12}. Others may want to do so as well.

- **Folic acid** is required for your body to process the other B vitamins. It also plays a role in producing white blood cells and other immune system components, converting amino acids into proteins, and building the nervous system. Deficiency markers include slow growth in children, depression, and megaloblastic anemia. The antiseizure drug Dilantin competes with folic acid in the GI tract and in the brain, so people who take Dilantin should consult with a physician about taking folic acid.

When B vitamin supplementation works, the results can range from minor to major. It is one of several interventions with a good success rate among adults with ASDs, as Rebecca's story eloquently attests:

> *Nathaniel turned 20 in July. It seems like just yesterday that I was trying to imagine what it would be like when he grew up. The first studies on the effects of nutrition in autism were done about the time Nat was born. We heard about them, and even half-heartedly tried some nutritional things, but without any valid research to back it up we gave up almost before we started. Everyone thought we were crazy. We had no support. There was no Internet. The great thing is that it does exist now, the research is there, and we are learning that it is never too late.*

> *Nathaniel was doing okay for many years. When he started having some problems, we started looking for answers. We have had an incredible year. In the spring I talked to Dr. Rimland and decided that we should find a DAN! doctor (another thing that didn't exist 20 years ago). In the meantime, we started Nathaniel on B_6 and worked him up to 1,000 milligrams a day. It blew us away! He was a different person. We began to have conversations with him . . . for the first time in his life.*

> *We finally found a DAN! doctor an eight-hour drive away. The doctor decided to take him off of the vitamins for a couple of weeks so that he could do tests (we did everything but secretin). During the time that he was off the vitamins we saw a gradual loss of awareness, communication, and self-help skills . . . it was frightening. His new doctor decided to put him on different supplementation after he got the test results back. He lowered the B_6 to 500 mg and put him on a complete regimen of other things, which included SBOs, enzymes, niacin, super multiples, and CoQ10. At first I was apprehensive, because it seemed like he wasn't making the gains that he had been on the high dose of B_6, but now he has started to surpass where he was in early July. He is calling people by name, initiating thoughts of his own, expressing his desires.*

> *It's incredible to see this kind of thing in a small child. Imagine what it's like to watch it in a 20 year old. We're kind of in shock. It's a combination*

of joy and amazement, and guilt that we didn't do it sooner. We had no idea that something like this could happen.

Do all that you can. . . do all of the tests . . . spare no expense. This nutritional stuff is real. We're watching miracles right before our eyes. It's never too late, but the sooner the better!

B vitamin deficiencies may develop in any person during periods of extreme stress. The B vitamins are water soluble and are not stored up in any large quantity, so deficiency can materialize fairly quickly.

B_6 is the B vitamin shown to help most in autism, as evidenced by 18 studies of its use in this population (11 of them double-blind studies).[11] It's important to start the dose of B_6 low, and titrate it up slowly. Your doctor can help you make a dosage plan and monitor side effects. Side effects reported include hyperactivity, nausea, increased sensitivity to sound, bedwetting, and diarrhea. A few children become quite wild and aggressive when just starting B_6. If any of these side effects occurs, reduce the dose temporarily, and make sure the vitamin is accompanied with the correct amount of magnesium. B_6 and magnesium actually have a higher level of scientific support as a treatment for autism than any other biological intervention, including drugs.

Many people who are taking B_6 for ASDs use a multiple-B supplement. These are readily available. Super Nu-Thera, a multivitamin formula made by Kirkman Sales (*http://www.kirkmanlabs.com/*), has become very popular because it combines the B vitamins at the doses recommended by ARI with other nutrients that are believed helpful. Kirkman also sells DMG (described later in this chapter) and folic acid supplements in the ARI-recommended formulations.

Antioxidants

Antioxidants scavenge the bloodstream for particles called free radicals. Free radicals wreak havoc by damaging cells and causing inflammation of tissues. If autistic spectrum disorders have an autoimmune component, it stands to reason that antioxidants could be important for keeping the patient's immune system in balance. They include the following:

- **Vitamin A** (retinol) has antioxidant properties and also helps maintain the mucous lining of the intestines. People with celiac disease have a hard time getting enough A, and often experience a deficiency of this vitamin.

- **Vitamin C** (ascorbic acid) has shown benefits for some people with autism in megadoses.[12] Actual vitamin C deficiency, known as scurvy, is mighty rare these days. One population in which it does occur, however, is people who start using megadoses of C and then suddenly stop. The acidic nature of ascorbic acid can also contribute to kidney stones, but the buffered form, calcium ascorbate, is more easily tolerated. Vitamin C should be accompanied by vitamin E.

- **Vitamin E** (alpha tocopherol) is believed to be important for proper immune system functioning. People who take neuroleptics, tricyclic antidepressants, or other medications that carry a known risk for tardive dyskinesia should supplement them with vitamin E. It appears to have protective and symptom reduction qualities.

- **Beta carotene** is a nutrient related to vitamin A, and is found in dark green leafy vegetables and yellow-orange vegetables. It's best to get it through the diet rather than from a supplement.

- **Coenzyme Q10** (CoQ10, ubiquinone) is a vitaminlike antioxidant, one of the strongest available. It's part of the cellular process that uses fats, sugars, and amino acids to produce the energy molecule ATP (Adenosine triphosphate). It is said to boost immune system function and help heal GI tract problems.

- **Glutathione peroxidase** is an antioxidant peptide manufactured by the body itself. To make it, you need to have enough selenium, vitamin C, and vitamin E. There's no need to supplement directly with glutathione itself.

- **Selenium** deficiency occurs in some people with celiac disease and other autoimmune disorders. This mineral works best in its easily absorbed, chelated form (L-selenomethionane). The cooperation of vitamin E and selenium produces the antioxidant peptide glutathione peroxidase.

- **Zinc** deficiency occurs in some people with celiac disease, and has also been documented in people with autism.[13] You may want to use a supplement of this mineral in its easiest-to-absorb, chelated form (zinc aspartate or zinc picolinate).

- **Oligomeric proanthocyanidins** (OPCs, Pycogenol, grapeseed oil) are the active ingredients in several naturally occurring antioxidant compounds. Grapeseed oil is just what its name indicates, whereas Pycogenol is a brand-name formulation derived from maritime pine bark. Both have been tried by people with ASDs and other neurological disorders, with some reporting beneficial effects for seizure control, reduced aggression, and improved immune system function.

- **Cat's claw** (una de gato) is another herbal antioxidant, this one from the indigenous Mexican pharmacopeia. No information about benefits for people with ASDs is available at this time.

Vitamin cautions

Vitamins A and D are fat soluble, so they are stored in the body's fat cells for later use. Having a little put away for a rainy day is probably okay, but if you take too much, hypervitaminosis may develop. Symptoms of hypervitaminosis A include orangeish, itchy skin, loss of appetite, increased fatigue, and hard, painful swellings on the arms, legs, or back of the head. Symptoms of hypervitaminosis D include hypercalcemia, osteoporosis, and kidney problems.

If you plan to pursue vitamin therapies, purchase a basic guide to vitamins and minerals that includes information about toxicity symptoms. Some people metabolize vitamins and minerals differently and may be more or less susceptible to potential toxic effects. Along with your doctor's guidance, a good reference book can help you avoid problems.

Also, take vitamin company sales pitches and dosage recommendations with a grain of salt. The testimonials these companies produce are intended to sell their products, not to help you develop a treatment plan. For unbiased, individualized advice, consult a physician, or a licensed dietician or nutritionist who does not sell supplements.

Dietary supplements and herbs

Dietary supplements and herbal remedies are big business these days, thanks to articles and books touting the benefits of everything from garlic to herbal antidepressants. Here are some you may hear about in relation to autistic spectrum disorders.

Minerals

Several minerals are essential for optimal health. Some are also necessary to help the body use certain vitamins.

- **Calcium** is important for the regulation of impulses in the nervous system and for neurotransmitter production. Low levels of excreted calcium have been reported in some people with autism.[14]

- **Magnesium** lowers blood pressure and is also important for the regulation of impulses in the nervous system and neurotransmitter production. If you are supplementing with vitamin B_6, you will need to add magnesium as well.

- **Iron** (ferrous sulfate) deficiency in infants can inhibit mental and motor skills development, but too much iron can cause digestive and elimination problems, or even kill. Acoordingly, ensure that there is an adequate amount of iron-rich foods in a child's diet, but avoid iron supplements. Adult women and some older adults may need to add a small amount of iron to their diet in supplement form.

Enzymes and sulfates

The human digestive tract produces enzymes to digest various types of food. Protease acts on protein, amylase on carbohydrates, lipase on fats, pectinase on pectins (found in some fruits and other foods), and cellulase on fiber.

Other enzymes are produced to detoxify the body. One study, and some subsequent clinical research, has shown that many people with autism have detoxification enzyme activity that is lower than normal.[15] This activity, which relies on a steady supply of sulfate, is essential for maintaining the GI tract's mucous membrane and for moving toxins out of the body through hydrolation. If the mucous membrane in the gut is in good shape, the brain will be protected from a buildup of phenolic compounds, which can interfere with neurotransmission. If it is not, nervous system problems can ensue.[16]

Some people with a documented sulfation problem take the enzyme methyl-sulfonyl-methane (MSM), which may help them produce sulfate. It is hard to digest, however. Others have added the amino acid N-acetyl-cysteine (NAC), which is also said to have antispasmodic qualities. Another recommendation is taking frequent Epsom salts (hydrated magnesium sulfate) baths. Neither of these approaches is proven to work, but some people do seem to improve as a result. For those who would like to try the Epsom salts approach, add 1 to 2 teaspoons of Epsom salts to a bath. A few people have reported temporary side effects from Epsom salts baths. If no ill effects are seen, you can add more to future baths—some people use one to two cups. It's never a good idea to take Epsom salts internally unless recommended by your doctor, so make sure children don't drink the bath water.

Researchers have noted that dairy and gluten digestion difficulties would be expected in people with low sulfation, lending credence to the gluten-free/casein-free diet approach for these individuals.[17]

Food items that are high in phenols might also be removed from the diet with beneficial results. Among the many phenols are tannin, which gives tea and persimmons their tang; quercitin, found in green beans and rhubarb; and coumarin, found in cabbage, radishes, and spinach. Other items high in phenols include apples, grapes, avocados, and some other fruits; some artificial food colorings; many spices, such as cloves and sassafras; some preservatives, particularly the ubiquitous BHA (butylated hydroxyanisole) and BHT (butylated hydroxytoluene); some herbs used in antioxidant compounds and teas, including grapeseed oil and comfrey tea; chocolate, coffee, and red wine.

Phenols are also used in many manufacturing processes, cleaning products, insecticides, plastics, and chemical compounds. These products and their fumes should be avoided by people with extreme sensitivity to phenols.

Essential fatty acids

The essential fatty acid (EFA) linoleic acid and its derivatives, including gammalinolenic acid (GLA), dihomogamma-linolenic acid (DGLA), and arachidonic acid (AA), are also called omega-6 fatty acids. These substances come from animal fats and some plants. Another type of EFAs, omega-3 fatty acids, are found almost exclusively in fish oils. As the "essential" in their name implies, these substances are needed to build cells and also to support the body's anti-inflammatory response. They are the "good" polyunsaturated fats that improve cardiovascular health when substituted for the "bad" saturated fats.

The heart and blood vessels aren't the only beneficiaries of EFAs, however. EFAs appear to help the GI tract resist and repair damage, probably by restoring the lipid cells. Recent research in psychiatry has even found that omega-3 fatty acids can act as a mood stabilizer for some people with bipolar disorder.[18] Researchers believe that a proper balance between omega-3 and omega-6 fatty acids is also important for optimal health.

- **Evening primrose oil (EPO)** is one of the best EFA sources around, and as a result has become a very popular supplement. Other plant sources for omega-6 fatty acids include borage oil, flax seed oil, and black current seed oil. The omega-6 fatty acids in evening primrose oil have been reported to lower the threshold for frontal lobe seizures, however, so people who have seizures should exercise caution. All are available in gelatin caps as well as in liquid form.

- **Efamol and Efalex** are brand-name EFA supplements made by Efamol Neutriceuticals Inc. Efalex was specifically created to treat developmental dyspraxia in the UK and is widely touted as a supplement for people with ADD or ADHD as well. Efalex contains a mix of omega-3 fish oil, omega-6 EPO and thyme oil, and vitamin E. Efamol, marketed as a treatment for PMS (premenstrual syndrome), combines EPO; vitamins B_6, C, and E; niacin, zinc, and magnesium. Both of these commercial EFA supplements are now available in the US and Canada as well, and can be purchased by mail order. Unlike many supplements manufacturers,

Efamol adheres to strict standards and also sponsors reputable research. However, some people have difficulties with the thyme oil or EPO in this product.

- **EicoPro**, made by Eicotec Inc., is another brand-name EFA supplement you may hear about. It combines omega-3 fish oils and omega-6 linoleic acid. Eicotec is another supplements manufacturer known for its high manufacturing standards.

- **Equazen's eye q and OmegaBrite** from OmegaBrite Inc. are two more high-quality brand-name EFA supplements. There are certainly others available, including cod liver oil: Look for EFAs that have been toxicology tested and protected from oxidation.

- **Monolaurin** is made by the body from lauric acid, another medium-chain fatty acid that is found in abundance in coconuts and some other foods, including human breast milk. It is known to have antibacterial and antiviral properties. Monolaurin may be the active ingredient in colostrum, the "pre-milk" all mammals produce to jump-start a newborn's immune system. In some areas, cow colostrum is actually available in supplement form.

- **NutriVene-D** is a supplement, created for people with Down syndrome, that mixes EFAs, vitamins, and other substances.

Perhaps the most popular way to get extra EFAs is taking cod liver oil, or fish body oil (which may be better for you). Fish oils contain omega-3 fatty acids and vitamin A. Research into fish oils as a treatment for autistic symptoms was underway in both the US and England as this book went to press. For information on research directions, see the online presentation by Dr. Andrew Stoll at *http://www.up-to-date.com/dan/powerpoint/Stoll.htm*.

It's great if you can get your EFAs in food. Low-fat diets are part of the reason some people, especially those who are trying to lose weight, may not get enough EFAs. Many cold-pressed salad oils, including safflower, sunflower, corn, and canola oils, do contain EFA. When these oils are processed with heat, however, it may destroy or change the fatty acids. Oily fish (mullet, orange roughy, Atlantic salmon) are another great source, although, again, cooking may be a problem (and not everyone is a sushi fan).

Diabetics may experience adverse effects from too much EFA, and should consult their physician before supplementing with EFA products.

DMG

Dimethylglycine (DMG, calcium pangamate, pangamic acid, "vitamin B_{15}") is a naturally occurring amino acid that may help some people with autistic spectrum disorders with speech production, increased stress tolerance, seizure reduction, and immune system strengthening. Studies have been done in Russia and Korea with positive results for between half and 80 percent of the children given DMG, although they were not double-blind studies.[19]

A double-blind, placebo-controlled study of DMG as a treatment for children with ASDs did not find across-the-board benefits, although the research team noted that a subset of children did seem to respond positively.[20] This small trial used lower doses than are usually recommended. Another double-blind trial, this one in Taiwan, reported more positive outcomes; however, many of the initial group stopped treatment and were not included in these results.[21] More research is warranted into how (and for whom) DMG works.

Robin, mother of 5-year-old Nicole, says,

> We have only used DMG for speech, and B6/magnesium. We are seeing improvements in both Nicole's articulation and in her ability to put sentences together. She has gained quite a few new words, and is attempting to place them in short sentences, whereas before she only used single words and more of a pull-and-point method. She definitely is trying harder to "say the words!"

DMG changes the way your body uses folic acid, so you may need to also take that vitamin. Increased hyperactivity may result if folic acid is low.

Melatonin

Melatonin (MLT) is produced by the pineal gland and is responsible for helping the body maintain sleep and other biochemical rhythms. Studies have shown a deficiency or aberrant production of this hormone in autistic subjects,[22] and indeed, at least half of all people with autism have sleep disorders.[23] Melatonin supplements given about half an hour before bed may be useful for addressing these problems.

The effect may not be lasting, however. "Using melatonin for sleep worked awesome at first; now it is iffy," says Lesley, mother of 3-year-old Danielle, who has been diagnosed with PDD-NOS. Research into this supplement is continuing.

Probiotics

As the name indicates, probiotics are intended to counteract the harmful effects of antibiotics. As most people who have taken a course of penicillin know, these valuable medications can cause digestive distress even as they heal infection. Probiotics are substances that restore the friendly intestinal cultures that help us digest our food.

Among other things, these cultures (and other probiotics) keep the growth of *Candida albicans* yeast in balance.

Commercial probiotic supplements may combine a number of substances, such as digestive enzymes, helpful bacteria, garlic, and the like:

- *Lactobacillus acidophilus, Bifidobacterium bifidum, and Lactobacillus bulgaricus* are friendly bacteria more familiar to most of us as the "active cultures" found in some yogurts. Yogurt itself is a good probiotic, for those who eat dairy products. Another probiotic, *S. boulardii,* may be even more effective.

- **Soil-based organisms** (SBOs) are microbes found in organic soils that are believed to help the body produce important enzymes. Some people believe that modern food-processing techniques have left people deficient in these, so they take SBO supplements. These are increasingly added to probiotic supplements, and may work better than the traditional *acidophilus* supplements. Check around for a quality source of SBOs, as not all brands are the same.

- **Garlic** is said to act against yeast in the digestive tract. You can swallow whole cloves raw or take it in a supplement.

- **Caprylic acid** is a fatty acid said to act against yeast in the digestive tract. Medium-chain triglycerides (MCT oil, also called caprylic/capric triglycerides) are a liquid source of caprylic acid.

- **Biotin,** a vitamin related to the Bs, is normally produced by friendly bacteria in the digestive tract. Replenishing these flora should ensure enough biotin, but some people do choose to take it directly.

Lecithin

Lecithin (phosphatidyl choline) is a phospholipid found mostly in high-fat foods. It is much ballyhooed for its ability to improve memory and brain processes. Lecithin is necessary for normal brain development; however, double-blind studies of patients with Alzheimer's disease did not substantiate claims that it can help people recover lost brain function.

However, it's possible that increased amounts of lecithin may be one of the keys to the ketogenic diet's success in some cases of hard-to-treat epilepsy. Some people with epilepsy have also reported reduced number and severity of seizures from taking lecithin as a supplement. It is possible that extra lecithin might be needed to rebuild damaged myelin protein.

There's no hard evidence that lecithin is a good idea for people with autism, but it does not appear to cause harm, and there are some logical reasons to think it might help—especially for people who have seizures or who test positive for anti-MBP, the autoimmune agent believed to destroy myelin basic protein.

Lecithin is oil based, and it gets rancid easily. It should be refrigerated. Lecithin capsules are available, but many people prefer the soft lecithin granules. These are a nice addition to fruit juice smoothies, adding a thicker texture.

Choline is one of the active ingredients in lecithin. It is needed by the brain for processes related to memory, learning, and mental alertness, as well as for the manufacture of cell membranes and the neurotransmitter acetylcholine.

Inositol is another active ingredient in lecithin. It may help in cases of nerve damage and is required by the neurotransmitters serotonin and acetylcholine. Clinical studies have indicated that inositol supplements may be helpful for some people with obsessive-compulsive disorder,[24] depression, and panic disorder.[25] Benefits specific to ASDs have not been officially documented.

Herbal neurological remedies

Quite a few herbs have been used to treat neurological disorders through the ages. These substances are referred to as nervines, and some may prove useful for treating specific symptoms associated with autistic spectrum disorders. Of all the herbal remedies, the nervine group of plant extracts are among the strongest, and the most likely to cause serious side effects.

- **Aloe vera gel** is sometimes recommended for GI tract problems. It's a traditional remedy for ulcers. It has anti-inflammatory (steroidal), hormonal, antioxidant, and laxative effects. Many people find it hard to take internally.

- **Black cohosh** (Cimicifuga racemosa, squaw root), a nervous system depressant and sedative, is often used by people with autoimmune conditions for its anti-inflammatory effects. Its active ingredient appears to bind to estrogen receptor sites, so it may cause hormonal activity.

- **Chamomile** is a mild but effective sedative traditionally used to treat sleep disorders or stomach upsets.

- **Damiana** is a traditional remedy for depression.

- **Gingko biloba**, an extract of the gingko tree, is advertised as an herb to improve memory. There is some clinical evidence for this claim. It is an antioxidant, and is prescribed in Germany for treatment of dementia. It is believed to increase blood flow to the brain.

- **Gotu kola** is a stimulant sometimes recommended for depression.

- **Licorice** is not just for candy or sore throats—it boosts hormone production, including hormones active in the GI tract and brain.

- **Passion flower** is recommended by some herbalists for depression, anxiety, and seizure disorders.

- **Sarsaparilla**, like licorice, seems to affect hormone production as well as settling the stomach and calming the nerves.

- **Skullcap**, an antispasmodic and sedative, is found in both European and Ayurvedic herbals. It has traditionally been used to treat tic disorders and muscle spasms, as well as seizure disorders, insomnia, and anxiety.

- **St. John's wort** (hypericum) has gained popularity as an herbal antidepressant. It has the backing of a decent amount of research, but, as noted in Chapter 5, *Medical Interventions,* those choosing to use this remedy should follow the same precautions as with SSRIs and MAOIs, two families of pharmaceutical anti-depressants. It can cause increased sensitivity to light, and should not be used by those taking protease inhibitors and some other medications. See Appendix F for more information.

- **Valerian** is a strong herbal sedative. It should not be given to young children.

Herbal antibiotics

Several herbs appear to have antiseptic, antiviral, antifungal, or antibiotic properties. Obviously, if these substances are active, they should be used carefully and sparingly, despite the claims of certain manufacturers who encourage daily use for disease prevention. Those who prefer herbal remedies sometimes try cat's claw or grapeseed oil, both mentioned in the previous section on antioxidants, or one of the following:

- **Bitter melon** (Momordica charantia), an antiviral from the Chinese herbal pharmacopoeia, is the plant from which the active ingredient in some protease inhibitors (the powerful drugs used to combat AIDS) is derived.

- **Echinacea purpurea** is the plant source of another herbal antiseptic, which also dilates blood vessels and is said to have antispasmodic qualities as well.

- **Goldenseal** plants produce an alkaloid isoquinoline derivative related to the minor opium alkaloids. Its active ingredient, hydrastine, elevates blood pressure.

This is a very strong herb with antiseptic properties when taken internally or applied topically in powder or salve form. When taken internally, it acts on the mucous membranes of the GI tract.

- SPV-30, derived from the European boxwood tree, is a fairly new item in this category. It apparently includes some antiviral and steroidal (anti-inflammatory) compounds, and has become very popular among people with AIDS as an alternative to pharmaceutical antivirals.

Sphingolin

Sphingolin is a glandular supplement made from cow spinal-cord myelin, repackaged in pill form. Some practitioners recommend it for children who have tested positive for myelin sheath proteins in the bloodstream. It is used by quite a number of people with multiple sclerosis and other neurological disorders that involve demyelinization.

Although anecdotal reports indicate that some people with ASDs have had symptom reductions when taking sphingolin, there could be a hidden problem with this supplement: It could contain particles that cause the deadly neurological disorder called bovine spongiform encephalopathy (BSE), or "mad cow disease," and its human version, Creutzfeldt-Jakob disease. It is not available in the UK for this very reason—and there's no reason to believe this disease exists only in UK cattle or UK humans.

Evaluating supplement claims

No matter what kind of complementary treatment you choose, it's just as important to be a smart consumer in this area as it is with traditional medicine. Unfortunately, it can be more difficult. Prescription medications must undergo rigorous testing. Study results and detailed information about these compounds are available in numerous books, online, or directly from the manufacturers.

With "natural" remedies, that's not always the case. It seems like every week another book appears making wild claims for a "new" antioxidant compound, herbal medication, or holistic therapy. These books—not to mention magazine articles, web sites, and semi-informed friends—sometimes wrap conjecture up in a thin veneer of science. They may reference studies that are misinterpreted, that appeared in disreputable journals, or that were so poorly designed or biased that no journal would publish them.

Supplement salespeople, and particularly those who take part in multilevel marketing schemes, seem to have taken lessons from their predecessors in the days of the traveling medicine show. They have little to lose by making outrageous claims for their products and much to gain financially. Here are just a few of the unsupported claims found in a single five-minute sweep of supplement sales sites on the Internet:

- "Glutathione slows the aging clock, prevents disease and increases life."
- "Pycogenol . . . dramatically relieves ADD/ADHD, improves skin smoothness and elasticity, reduces prostate inflammation and other inflammatory conditions, reduces diabetic retinopathy and neuropathy, improves circulation and enhances cell vitality" [and, according to this site, cures almost anything else that might ail you!]
- "Sage and bee pollen nourish the brain."
- "Soybean lecithin has been found to clean out veins and arteries—dissolve the gooey sludge cholesterol—and thus increase circulation, relieve heart, vein and artery problems. It has cured many diabetics—cured brain clots, strokes, paralyzed legs, hands and arms!"

Take the time to browse your local health food or vitamin store's shelves, and you'll probably spot a number of deceptively advertised products. Some companies try to deceive you with "sound-alike" names, packaging that mimics other products, or suggestive names that hint at cures. Other colorful bottles contain substances that can't actually be absorbed by the body in oral form—for example, "DNA" (deoxyribonucleic acid, the building block of human genetic material) graces some shelves. One manufacturer of this useless "supplement" claims that "it is the key element in the reprogramming and stimulation of lazy cells to avoid, improve, or correct problems in the respiratory, digestive, nervous, or glandular systems."

Be especially cautious when sales pitches are written in pseudoscientific language that doesn't hold up under close examination with a dictionary. This is a popular ploy. For example, one product peddled to parents of children with ASDs claims to "support cellular communication through a dietary supplement of monosaccharides needed for glycoconjugate synthesis." Translated into plain English, this product is a sugar pill.

How can you assess supplement claims? Start by relying primarily on reputable reference books for your basic information, rather than advertisements or the popular press. Watch out for any product whose salespeople claim it will "cure" anything. Supplements and vitamins may enhance health and promote wellness, but they rarely effect cures. Be wary of universal usefulness claims. In an effort to make the most sales, the worst offenders in supplement advertising tout their wares as cure-alls for a multitude of unrelated conditions. When in doubt, consult with your doctor or a licensed dietician or nutritionist.

Even when you have seen the science behind a vitamin or supplement treatment, there's still the problem of quality and purity. It's almost impossible for consumers to know for sure that a tablet or powder contains the substances advertised at the strength and purity promised. Whenever possible, do business with reputable manufacturers that back up their products with potency guarantees or standards. In most European countries, potency is governed by government standards; in the US, it's a matter of corporate choice.

Diet

Parents have long observed that their children with autism have disturbed eating, digestion, and elimination habits. These problems have been attributed to severely self-restricted diets, *Candida* yeast overgrowth, food allergies, or food intolerances/ toxicities, particularly problems with metabolizing the proteins gluten or casein.

If this is the case for you or your child, a licensed dietician or nutritionist with expertise in addressing GI tract problems via dietary changes will be able to help. Effective medical treatments are also available. Medical testing can help you pinpoint the cause of GI tract distress.

Self-restricted diets can be caused by a number of factors, ranging from texture preferences to food intolerances. Paradoxically, many children with severely self-restricted diets increase their willingness to try new foods when gluten and/or casein are removed from their menu—even if the only foods they had previously been willing to eat contained these substances.

No matter what kind of dietary changes you're making, keeping a careful food and behavior diary is essential.

Casein-free and gluten-free (CF/GF) diets

Quite a number of children and adults with ASDs have experienced relief from GI tract troubles, and occasionally from some autistic symptoms as well, by removing casein, gluten, or both from their diets. Scientists espousing the opiate excess theory of autistic spectrum disorders say that peptides derived from these proteins mimic opioid chemicals. If they can slip through the gut wall because of inflammation, they slow down digestion, cause a lack of alertness and increased physical sluggishness, and producing a variety of changes in brain chemistry.[26] Some people seem to have a literal addiction to these opioids, refusing almost all foods except dairy products and gluten-containing starches.

Casein is the easier protein to avoid. It is present only in milk and milk byproducts, so you must rule out milk, cream, buttermilk, butter, sour cream, yogurt, and cheese. You also have to watch out for milk derivatives, which are hiding in many places. For example, check the ingredients label on that soy cheese: Almost all varieties are made with casein or caseinate. Ditto for most margarines, which may contain casein, lactose (milk sugar), whey, dry nonfat milk, yogurt, or buttermilk. Cookies, soups, breads, potato chips, and many other supermarket foods may contain milk byproducts.

If you aren't allergic to soy products, many excellent substitutes are available for casein-containing foods. Soy milk fortified with calcium and vitamins is widely available now, and there are also casein-free soy cheeses and soy yogurts. Tofu substitutes nicely when you want the creaminess of cheese or sour cream in a recipe, and a couple of manufacturers produce dairy-free sour cream, cream cheese, and frozen desserts. Check out vegetarian or vegan (no animal products, including dairy) cookbooks for some ideas on cooking without casein, and keep an eye out for packaged foods that are labeled "vegan." It will take four or more weeks to see if there will be any benefits from removing casein.

Gluten is a bit harder to avoid. It is the protein found in wheat, spelt, oats, rye, triticale, and barley. To avoid gluten, choose other grains instead. Gluten-free grains include corn, rice, wild rice, buckwheat, millet, quinoa, teff, and more. There are many commercial gluten-free products on the market, including baking mixes, rice flour, rice cakes, popcorn cakes, cornmeal, breads and other baked goods, frozen waffles, and breakfast cereals. As with soy, some people do have difficulties with one or more of these alternative grains. Try a wide variety of gluten-free grains, and let your experience (and your taste buds) be your guide.

Gluten is sometimes hidden in common supermarket items. Look out for malt, grain starches, textured vegetable protein (TVP), hydrolyzed vegetable protein (HVP), and vinegar, among other items. Sometimes TVP and HVP are made from soybeans, but not always.

Erasing the effects of gluten takes from six months to a year on a GF diet.

Parents report that children who respond to a CF and/or GF diet tend to exhibit clingy, whiny, irritable behavior when starting out. Some may go on a hunger strike, refusing to eat at all. This stage will pass. Positive results that follow may include a newfound ability to be toilet trained, willingness to try a wider variety of foods, and more normal bowel movements. Some parents also report that long-standing skin problems have cleared up, and that children who wandered aimlessly or even made escape attempts reduced these behaviors. Behavioral results vary widely, from none at all to almost complete disappearance of autistic symptoms. The most dramatic results are seen with very young children.

One of the great questions about CF/GF diets is how long you need to stay on them. If no positive benefits are seen from a CF diet after six months or from either GF or CF/GF after a year, and you are sure the diet has been followed to the letter in all settings (home, school, grandparents' house, and so on), the diet can probably be safely abandoned. Reintroduce foods with gluten or casein slowly—just a bite of toast or a tiny cube of cheese to start, for example—as any "new" food can cause tummy trouble. Watch out for the return of symptoms, either suddenly or over a period of time. Sometimes the diet has been helping more than you think!

If the diet does seem to be working, one school of thought says that once the gut is healed (assuming that casein and gluten peptides are only escaping into the bloodstream because of GI tract damage), these foods can return to the diet in moderation. Others say abstinence should be a lifelong project, as the sensitivities will not go away. Your best guideline is the results you get. If going casein-free and/or gluten-free seems to help, and if regression or behavior problems occur when these proteins are added back to the diet, stick with the strict diet.

Before trying the diet, you can have a urine test for abnormal metabolites of casein and gluten. See Appendix A, *Resources*.

Anti-*Candida* diets

If medical tests show that a significant overgrowth of *Candida* yeast, some dietary changes will discourage the yeast from multiplying. Remember that some *Candida* yeast is normal. Overgrowth causes the most trouble for people with serious immune system conditions, such as AIDS.

Fermented or moldy foods, yeasty foods, and sugars are the main items to be avoided. Fermented or moldy foods include cheese, alcohol, brine pickles, tempeh, soy sauce, vinegar, dried fruits, nut butters, honey, and others. Yeasty foods include all grains that have gluten, and all yeasty products, including yeast-containing baked goods, brewer's yeast ("nutritional yeast"), and beer.

It's also suggested that citrus and acid fruits, such as grapefruit, oranges, lemons, limes, pineapple, and tomatoes, be avoided for the first month of an anti-*Candida* diet. In fact, many such diet plans are completely free of fruit. All of them are as sugar-free as possible. Finally, anti-*Candida* diets should contain plenty of roughage for fiber. Most books on *Candida* overgrowth suggest starting with an allergy elimination/reintroduction diet, and then following a rotation diet. They often suggest paying attention to environmental sources of mold as well, such as damp basements, carpets, and old furnace filters.

Other anti-*Candida* measures include adding probiotics, which compete with *Candida* in the gut, and attending to sulfation problems that may allow *Candida* to establish itself on the gut wall. Medication is generally used only in severe cases.

For more information, see the many books available on *Candida albicans* or this *Candida* web site (*http://www.panix.com/~candida/*).

Feingold diet

In the 1970s and 1980s, Dr. Ben Feingold promoted a special diet for hyperactivity in children. He recommended avoiding synthetic flavorings and food colors, certain preservatives, and sometimes other additives. Interestingly, many foods forbidden on the Feingold diet are high in phenolic compounds.

The Feingold Association now supports families using this diet. Its *Pure Facts* newsletter lists commercial foods that meet (or do not meet) the restrictions. The Feingold Association also supports "The IA-USA Extended Feingold Program for Autism/PDD and Milk & Wheat Allergies," which combines the original plan with CF/GF restrictions. There is a membership charge to join this group, which can provide meal plans, food lists, information about doctors and nutritionists who support the diet, and contacts with others using the diet.

If you want to know more about the Feingold diet, see the Feingold Association web site at *http://www.feingold.org/*.

Elimination/reintroduction diet for food allergies

Diets to detect and eliminate food allergies should be carried out under the aegis of an allergist or other knowledgeable physician. Most start patients out with an elimination diet, taking out all the most common allergens: dairy products, eggs, all gluten-containing grains, corn, citrus fruits, bananas, nuts (especially peanuts), soy, and vegetables from the nightshade family (tomatoes, eggplant, potatoes, and peppers). Obviously, if you already know of or suspect an allergy to another food, this item should be eliminated as well. Most people stay on this very restricted diet for at least four weeks—some doctors recommend an elimination diet for as long as six months.

Next comes the reintroduction process: Reintroduce one previously eliminated food at a time. Eat it at every meal. If you suffer no ill effects, you aren't allergic to that food and can add it back to your regular diet.

If you do seem to have an allergic reaction to a food, eliminate it again for several weeks and then reintroduce it once more. You may need to follow this last step several times to make sure you know which food is causing the possible allergic reaction or intolerance.

Rotation diet for food allergies

Once you have identified definite food allergies or food sensitivities, allergists usually recommend following a rotation diet. This plan requires that you eat different foods each day in a four-day period to decrease the likelihood of developing new allergies. When they follow a rotation diet, people with mild food sensitivities may find they can eventually tolerate foods that once caused them distress, but reintroducing these foods should be done very carefully.

The ketogenic diet

The ketogenic diet plan is a nutritionist's nightmare. It includes almost no starches or sugars. Instead, you consume 1 gram of protein for every 4 grams of fat. The body is thus forced to burn fat for energy, rather than carbohydrates, producing waste products called ketones. The ketones somehow suppress seizure activity.

Obviously, this is not a healthy, balanced diet. It is used as a last-ditch effort to manage seizures that cannot be controlled with medication. Under no circumstances should this diet be tried without medical supervision. Not only is it potentially dangerous, it's pretty hard to make it appetizing. A medical center that specializes in epilepsy treatment should be able to provide guidance and expert nutritional advice if this option is recommended for you or your child.

Special diet or not, pay close to attention to the quality of food you choose. Everyone's health benefits from eating a variety of fresh foods without unnecessary pesticides, processing, or additives. Some people with autism do appear to have unique metabolic difficulties, such as problems with foods that are high in histamines or phenols, or an inability to tolerate certain food additives, such as aspartame or monosodium glutamate (MSG). Keeping a food diary can help you to recognize problems, or to recognize that diet is not an issue at all for you or your child.

Allergy treatments

Allergies also have an impact on dietary choices. About 5 percent of all children have classic IgE (immunoglobulin E)-mediated food allergies, but the rate among people with autistic spectrum disorders appears higher. The most common food allergies are milk, eggs, peanuts, soy, nuts, fish, and shellfish. Food sensitivities and intolerances, which are not the same as allergies, are considerably more common among people with ASDs than allergies.

The most common tests for food allergies are the skin-prick test and the radioallergosorbent test (RAST). Of the two, the RAST is preferred for young children and anyone with eczema. It is also more specific, although the skin test may actually be more sensitive. The RAST is a blood test that measures the level of IgE antibodies to specific foods. If there are no IgE antibodies present in the blood, the person does not have food allergies.

Before the RAST is administered, make sure your allergist knows what medications you or your child take. Antihistamines, steroids, and some other medicines can skew the results by inhibiting the inflammatory response.

The only sure treatment for food allergies is food avoidance. Desensitization shots are available for other types of allergens, such as pollens, but this therapy is only in its formative stages for food allergies. Some allergists are willing to try so-called neutralization shots or sublingual drops, also called low-dose immunotherapy. The efficacy of these is not proven.

Severe allergic reactions are rare, but those at risk must be extra careful about reading labels and should always carry an emergency kit. Your allergist can help you put this kit together. People who have both asthma and allergies have a higher risk of dangerous allergic reactions. Food sensitivity reactions can sometimes be cut short with a simple dose of baking soda, or commercial preparations containing bicarbonate of soda, such as Alka-Seltzer.

Eye therapies

Of all the areas you may choose to investigate, eye-related procedures are among the most hotly contested. Little hard research has been done. Accordingly, you should assess claims carefully.

Irlen lenses

As noted in Chapter 5, the use of colored lenses such as those developed by the Irlen Institute is controversial as a treatment for autism, although some have reported benefits. Glasses with colored lenses are used to remediate visual perception problems (the Irlen people call it scotopic sensitivity). Many people with autism do report visual perceptual problems, such as tunnel vision, reliance on peripheral vision, or difficulty in telling foreground from background.

Vision therapy

Also called eye training, visual training, behavioral optometry, and a host of other names, vision therapy is delivered by some optometrists and ophthalmologists. Eye exercises, and sometimes prismatic lenses, are used to address obvious eye defects such as "lazy eye" and crossed eyes. Some practitioners use these same rehabilitative methods to treat visual processing deficits that may have behavioral consequences.

As mentioned in Chapter 5, some people with ASDs have reported that vision therapy reduced their symptoms. For more information, see the Children with Special Needs web site (*http://www.children-special-needs.org/*) and the Center for the Study of Autism's visual training section (*http://www.autism.org/visual.html*).

Bodywork

The general label of "bodywork" applies to many types of therapeutic touch. When performed by a trained practitioner, none of the bodywork methods listed here should be harmful. They can relax people, and may increase flexibility and range of movement. Some bodywork boosters make more extravagant claims for their work, such as neurological or even spiritual benefits. Don't accept such claims at face value—ask to see any studies to which a practitioner refers, and do your own research before choosing either a method or a practitioner.

- **Acupressure** is similar to acupuncture, which is discussed briefly at the beginning of this chapter. Instead of using needles, acupressure employs touch on specific sites on the body. The pressure may be light or firm. Like acupuncture, acupressure does have a track record in helping with chronic pain and other disorders. Its efficacy for autistic symptoms is unknown.

- **Massage** comes in many forms, including Swedish, Shiatsu (which resembles acupressure in some ways), and more. It's relaxing and enjoyable, and one study at the University of Miami School of Medicine's Touch Research Institute showed that autistic toddlers who received a 30-minute massage two times a week for five weeks showed socialization and imitation improvement by objective measures, as compared with a control group of children who were held by a teacher while playing instead.[27]

- **The Feldenkrais method**, developed by Moshe Feldenkrais, concentrates on rebuilding sensory and movement systems, particularly through unlearning poor movement patterns. A number of Feldenkrais practitioners work with children who have neurological problems, including autism. The therapy is gentle, and some children have experienced gross motor, fine motor, sensory, and relational improvement—as have some autistic spectrum adults. A variant, Feldenkrais for Children with Neurological Disorders (FCND), is designed for this population. FCND practitioners have had additional training. For more information, see the Movement Educators web site at *http://www.movement-educators.com/*.

- **Craniosacral therapy**, discussed earlier in this chapter along with osteopathy, involves delicately manipulating the plates of the skull and the "cranial tides" of the body. Some may question the scientific basis of craniosacral work, but it is gentle and noninvasive. It has been reported as helpful by parents of many children with neurological problems, including autism. Adults with ASDs may also enjoy this approach. Most craniosacral therapists employ a certain amount of "talk therapy" along with the bodywork, which may or may not appeal to you. For more information, see the Craniosacral Therapy web site at *http://www.craniosacral.co.uk/*.

- **The Alexander Technique** is used by practitioners to help people streamline and increase the gracefulness of their movements. Clients learn new, more balanced movement patterns. Because self-awareness is an important part of this approach, the Alexander Technique is probably more applicable to adults with ASDs (especially those who have significant problems with clumsiness) than to children. For more information, see the Alexander Technique web site at *http://www.alexandertechnique.com/*.

For any bodywork method, including those not mentioned here, check the practitioner's credentials, and make sure you feel comfortable with both the person and the methodology. All the modalities listed here have accrediting bodies in most Western countries. Generally speaking, accredited, well-trained practitioners are more likely to do beneficial work than self-trained or nonaccredited practitioners.

Parents of children with ASDs, partners of adults with ASDs, and practitioners of related disciplines such as occupational therapy and physical therapy may want to get some training in one of these methods themselves. If you happen to be near a massage school or a training center for another bodywork method, inexpensive classes may be available. Some schools also operate free or low-cost clinics that allow students to practice on live patients under close supervision.

Chelation

Chelation is the process of binding heavy metals that may be present in the body and removing them via the urine. It has been the subject of much discussion among the parents of children with autism, following the revelation that many have higher-than-normal levels of mercury (and sometimes other heavy metals).

Chelation is not without risk, and is not a "do it yourself" project. Under the supervision of a competent medical doctor, however, it may prove useful. It appears to work best when nutritional and bowel problems have already been dealt with.

Before chelating, provocation testing is done. Usually either 2,3-dimercaptosuccinic acid (DMSA) or 2,3-dimercapto-propane-sulfonate (DMPS) is given, and urine produced over the next several hours is collected and analyzed by a lab. DMSA (sold under the brand-names Succimer and Chemet) is considered the safer of these two compounds, both of which are powerful antioxidants.

If the presence of abnormal levels of heavy metals is uncovered, treatment should be preceded by a basic blood test called the complete blood count (CBC) and tests for liver enzyme (ALT/AST), blood urea nitrogen (BUN), and creatinine. That's because DMSA can suppress bone marrow and have adverse effects on the liver and kidneys, and should not be used repeatedly if problems already exist. These tests can be done by any physician, and should be repeated during treatment if you do decide to try chelation.

Treatment usually involves giving DMSA in several doses of 10 to 30 milligrams, 3 to 8 hours apart, over a period of days. Treatment is then stopped for a period of days, and resumed again. The actual dose, and the length of treatment and break periods, should be set by your physician. Supplementing with 1 to 2 milligrams of zinc per kilogram of weight is recommended to enhance absorption of DMSA.

DMSA can cause side effects, typically tiredness and nausea. Rarely, more serious side effects occur.

Researchers acknowledge that these treatments may have actions other than chelation, such as antioxidant effects.

More information about chelation is available from the Autism Research Institute (*http://www.autismresearchinstitute.com*), which also offers a DMSA-based chelation protocol. Information is also available from physicians with expertise in treating toxin exposure.

Some people have also used vitamin C and E supplements, Epsom salts baths, and saunas as part of their "detoxification" efforts.

Multifaceted approaches

There are so many possible complementary approaches to treating ASD symptoms that it's hard to choose a starting point. As the story that opened this chapter indicates, most people end up trying several different options.

The Defeat Autism Now! (DAN!) protocol ("Clinical Assessment Options for Children with Autism and Related Disorders: A Biomedical Approach," available from the Autism Research Institute) is a guide to the latest research on nonpharmaceutical treatments, and is updated yearly.

Each doctor using the DAN! protocol has his or her own biases and preferences. Some eschew pharmaceuticals entirely; others practice complementary medicine, mixing both alternative and medical therapies. Some may simply be interested in the latest research, and continue to use primarily traditional treatments. For more information about DAN!, including a list of practitioners, see its web site at *http://www. autism.com/ari/dan.html*.

Evaluating alternative interventions

Desperate to find something that works to ameliorate difficult symptoms, people tend to pile on the interventions. That makes it hard to tell when something's really working—or if it would work without interference from another remedy.

To get the clearest picture of any complementary intervention, you must introduce it independent of others, and independent of pharmaceuticals or therapeutic interventions. This will often be impractical—you wouldn't stop speech therapy to see if DMG might help with speech, for example—but starting several things at once will only cause confusion.

Keep careful, *daily* records of supplements and dietary changes you introduce, when they are given and in what amounts, what brands you used, and any visible effects that you observe. If after four to six weeks you have not seen improvements with a supplement, it's unlikely that it will be of benefit. Dietary changes, bodywork, and other interventions may take much longer to bear fruit.

Remember that many people report initial problems with supplements and dietary changes, and some children may be resistant to bodywork at first as well. Don't gloss over dangerous side effects, but expect to weather some behavior problems for a couple of weeks.

If you can convince your physician to make alternative therapies part of his prescription, you're in luck. Some actively oppose them, and that may force you to find a new doctor. Whatever you do, don't operate behind your doctor's back. If you're philosophically incompatible, you should simply part ways—but you need a medical expert on your team.

CHAPTER 8

Insurance

AS THE PREVIOUS CHAPTERS HAVE MADE CLEAR, autistic spectrum disorders are not treated with medications alone. One-on-one therapeutic intervention, and often major lifestyle changes such as special diets, should be part of a well-rounded treatment plan. Treatment is a long-term affair. Unfortunately for people with ASDs and their families, paying for this kind of health care is expensive. Insurance should help, as it does for other major medical expenses, but that's not always the case.

You need not have health insurance for this chapter to be useful. It covers private insurance, including HMOs and other forms of managed care, national health plans, and alternatives to health insurance. It describes typical insurance roadblocks and shows you how to get around them. It begins by talking about health insurance in the US, but the systems of other English-speaking countries are also addressed.

How insurance companies see autism

Insurance companies operate from the basic premises that autism cannot be cured, and that there are no drugs officially approved to treat the condition. It does not seem to matter that the National Institutes of Health and other mainstream medical research bodies have identified medications and therapies that help.

Indeed, after reading the last few chapters of this book, you'll probably be surprised to learn that insurance companies feel free to ignore the proven, long-term clinical track record of ABA, floor-time play therapy, and other interventions for ASDs— interventions that have better success rates than many treatments for cancer and heart disease routinely covered by insurance. But they do.

In this author's opinion—an opinion shared by every organization campaigning on the behalf of people with ASDs—this attitude amounts to blatant discrimination. Insurance companies do make long-term therapeutic services available for schizophrenia and other neurobiological disorders, including full and partial hospitalization programs. They provide long-term speech, occupational, and physical therapy to people who have suffered impairment from stroke or traumatic brain injury. The prognosis for these individuals is not much different from that of people with autism. Untreated, a few seem to get better, whereas with assistance many more improve or recover.

One cannot help but think that somewhere at the bottom of these differences in treatment provision lie assumptions about the *value* of people with developmental disabilities and, perhaps, a lingering belief that autism is a psychological condition rather than a medical issue.

Parents and advocates have campaigned to change this situation for decades, but change has only recently begun. The passage of state mental health parity laws that specifically include autism has forced insurance companies to reconsider blanket denial of services, although covered offerings are still out of line with recommended medical practice. For example, in 2000 when California passed a new parity law that included autism and related conditions, people with these diagnoses could no longer be excluded completely from coverage. However, even in California insurance companies continue to exclude any therapy they deem "educational," a category that includes ABA, speech therapy, occupational therapy, social skills training, and more.

Insurance companies show their attitudes about autistic spectrum disorders in many ways. For example, their health education offices rarely offer written material to parents of children with autism or related disorders, or health education materials for adults with ASDs, as they do for people affected by Alzheimer's disease, breast cancer, and other conditions. Despite the increasing prevalence of ASDs, they haven't put much thought into how they might better respond, or how to support families by offering accurate and timely information.

When you choose an insurance company, assess its attitude toward ASDs in advance. You may be surprised at what you learn. An article comparing state health insurance coverage laws as they relate to autism can be found on the Web at *http://autism.about. com/library/weekly/aa022801a.htm?terms=insurance.*

The coverage question

In the US and other countries where private medical insurance is the norm, the insurance system can be hard to deal with under the best of circumstances. Each company in the industry offers multiple plans with various rates and benefits, and there's no central oversight. When insurance plans specifically refuse to cover autism, pervasive developmental disorders, any mental or neurological disorder, or any condition they deem "developmental" or "incurable," the refusal can have devastating effects.

Robin, mother of 5-year-old Nicole, says,

> *We do not have any insurance coverage. We are getting by with the bare minimum health care. Due to this situation we have never taken Nicole to a developmental specialist or neurologist, though we would like to.*

Other companies cover ASDs in a substandard way. For example, they may cover only short-term therapy programs. They may refuse coverage for necessary speech therapy, occupational therapy, or physical therapy. They may have no qualified "in plan" practitioners but refuse to make outside referrals, or they may call ASDs a mental health issue rather than a medical problem, and limit coverage accordingly.

It's mostly about money, but to some extent it's also about outdated medical notions. Take, for example, the words "developmental disorder." What this term really means is a medical condition that skews the process of normal child development. Doctors use it as a euphemism for mental retardation, and also to describe a variety of neurological, metabolic, and chromosomal disorders that emerge in childhood. Insurance companies, however, seem to think developmental disorders are either temporary conditions that the child will grow out of, or immutable conditions that cannot be helped at all. Unless state law insists otherwise, they are almost always excluded from coverage.

The idea that ASDs are incurable, and therefore not worthy of treatment, persists against all contrary evidence. If your insurance company tries this tactic, tell it that its position makes no sense, because the same standard is not applied to other conditions. For ammunition, you might ask the company what coverage it provides for children born with spina bifida. Spina bifida, a birth defect of the neural tube, is incurable, but thanks to modern medical technology, children with spina bifida can now live long and productive lives. Most need multiple operations and physical therapy, and many need a wheelchair or other orthopedic equipment. Few insurance companies have the gall to refuse coverage for this incurable, but treatable, condition. Other common conditions that are incurable but treatable are asthma, epilepsy, and diabetes.

When you argue your case for coverage, you can buttress your arguments by bringing copies or abstracts of pertinent medical studies, information from the National Institutes of Health or other official government sources, or books such as this one with you.

ASDs are eminently treatable. Many medically validated treatments are available, including medications for specific symptoms, speech therapy, occupational therapy,

ABA, floor-time play therapy, and in some cases nutritional or metabolic interventions. The success rate of early intervention using either ABA or floor-time techniques alone exceeds that of many medical treatments for other conditions that your insurance would probably cover without question. If you add more interventions to the picture, the chances of a good outcome will most likely be even brighter.

Treatment and the law

In the US, both case law and state legislation increasingly supports treatment coverage for autism and related disorders. For example, the 1988 case *Kunin v. Benefit Trust Life Insurance Co.,* settled in federal court in California and later affirmed by the US Court of Appeals for the Ninth Circuit, established that because autism has organic causes, it is not a mental illness and so cannot be used as a basis for denying or limiting insurance benefits. Cases in other states have affirmed this conclusion in relation to other neurological disorders.

Christopher Angelo, a consumer and plaintiff's trial attorney with the Los Angeles firm Mazursky, Schwartz, and Angelo, is all too familiar with the insurance problems experienced by people with autistic spectrum disorders. Angelo is the father of an autistic son, and also the author of the Autism Society of America's booklet, *For Our Children: A Lawyer's Guide to Insurance Coverage and a Parent's Call to Organize.*

According to Angelo, nearly 90 to 95 percent of insurance companies refuse outright to cover treatment for autistic spectrum disorders, although most cover the cost of reaching the initial diagnosis.[1] This refusal is rarely legal and never ethical, he adds. Parents and adults coping with ASDs need to know this, and take steps to successfully appeal such blanket denials of care. Begin by asking for a written copy of the denial of coverage or services. Make sure the reason you were given verbally is also the reason given in this written denial.

Your next stop is the insurance company's own documents. You'll need a copy of the health plan's master policy (see "Managing managed care," later in this chapter). Somewhere in its fine print you will probably find that if any of the company's policies are unenforceable under state law, they cannot be asserted. Most insurance claims adjusters know very little about state insurance law. Your job is to educate yourself, and then to educate them.

Now you need to find out what *your* state says about autistic spectrum disorders. The answer may be found in actual legislation. For example, California's mental health parity law specifically mandates coverage for ASDs. Your state may have similar laws or public policies on the books, possibly within state mental health parity laws or in laws protecting the disabled against discrimination. Your state's insurance commission (every state has its own, there's no federal insurance commission) will also have policy statements. Remember, actual state law trumps policy statements every time. State laws may be more restrictive than federal regulations, in which case the state prevails. If state laws are less restrictive than federal laws, the federal government prevails.

Your state's chapter of the Autism Society of America and other disability advocacy organizations, such as The ARC (formerly the Association of Retarded Citizens), may already have on hand the information you need. Nonprofit disability-law services, some of which are listed in Appendix B, *Support and Advocacy*, are another good resource.

If no one seems to know about insurance law regarding ASDs in your state, start researching on your own. If you have Internet access, then state laws, some public policies, and insurance commission decisions may be available online. Insurance commission staff members should be able to help. You can also call your state representative's office and ask a staff member to do research for you.

What you learn may be quite enlightening. For Christopher Angelo, research into applicable state laws led to a high-profile case, *Broughton v. CIGNA*. Angelo said he hopes this case will ensure that all US parents and patients have a right to appeal in court arbitrary and illegal health care restrictions. "If I continue to win *Broughton*, HMOs and insurance companies will have to change their practices not only statewide but nationwide," he said. The *Broughton* case, currently in litigation, may indeed yield the landmark decision for which thwarted health care consumers have been waiting.

Angelo's innovative case hinges on laws against discriminatory business practices, laws that most US states adopted after civil unrest rocked major cities in 1967. In California, this law is called the Consumer Legal Remedies Act. It prevents consumers from signing away their right to sue for relief in court when a business discriminates against them. Under the law, disability is a protected class, as are race, sex, and age. Many insurance companies say consumers can't force them to cover certain conditions, and such companies push unhappy customers into internal appeals procedures and then arbitration instead of court. If the Consumer Legal Remedies Act and similar state laws applied, this practice would be illegal.

Legal arguments of the sort needed to secure coverage can be hard for a layperson to craft. Advocacy groups may be able to help you write a well-written and persuasive letter of appeal on legal grounds.

Incidentally, Angelo adds, formal arbitration is rarely a viable solution. "Arbitration is a stacked deck," he says. "Arbitrators on average get paid $400,000 per year by health care plans, which only continue to use those arbitrators on stipulation. If it gets one arbitration decision it doesn't like, it stops using that arbitrator." Also, in arbitration consumers cannot recover their legal costs, which can range upward of $50,000. Most consumer law cases in the courts are taken by lawyers who work on contingency, meaning that they only get paid if they win—so it's hard to secure legal help for an arbitration.

The mental health exemption

If the company provides some treatment for ASDs, but only as part of a limited mental health benefit, you can also challenge that limitation. It's easy to show that autistic spectrum disorders are based on biology rather than on mental health, so you may be able to get out from under the mental health limit altogether.

Find out in advance how the company treats acquired neurological disorders, such as strokes, brain tumors, or traumatic brain injuries. If your insurance covers long-term care for these conditions, your state may mandate equal benefits for people with biological brain disorders.

Incidentally, a neurologist may be your best witness. Most people with ASDs have concrete signs of neurological dysfunction, which can't be written off as simply psychological. Some people have successfully asserted that their child is the victim of an acquired brain disorder, based on the child having developed normally and then regressed; on a documented reaction to a vaccine, medication, or environmental toxin; or on the basis of tests that show antimyelin antibodies or other substances in the blood.

The educational services exemption

After blanket denial of coverage, says Angelo, the second most frequent insurance roadblock is the educational services exclusion. "They'll say, 'We don't have to pay to teach your child how to speak, because that's education,'" he explains. "However, if a teacher wants to be a speech therapist, it requires a health care license in all 50 states, not just a teaching credential."

Sarah, mother of 2-year-old Elaine, has come up against this rule against educational services.

> *I have insurance, but as of yet I have not been able to get coverage*
> *for any speech therapy. I am now spending approximately $250 a week*
> *[for a speech-centered home ABA program]. That does not include*
> *anything that I purchase for her learning, that's just payroll.*

Angelo encourages parents to work with Early Intervention providers and school systems to force health insurers to pay for speech therapy, physical therapy, occupational therapy, home-and-hospital programs, and other services that must legally be delivered by health care professionals. He feels that schools should bill parents' health insurance for these services and sue if the insurer refuses to pay.

School districts, state health care programs, and the federal government are logical allies in the fight to force insurers to do their share, Angelo contends. "When insurers won't pay, the consumer then goes to overworked, underfunded taxpayer programs, like Social Security Disability, Medicare, the schools, regional centers, etc., to try to get funding for speech, OT, recreational therapy, partial hospitalization programs, and more, all of which should have been covered by the health care system," he says. "As soon as health care companies realize that passing the buck wrongfully to school districts and other public programs will cost them, they'll start training their claims adjusters in state law."

For now, however, Angelo's last bit of advice may be problematic for parents. Only in the past two years or so have major school districts attempted to bill insurers for services provided in school settings. Many parents rightfully fear that if the insurance companies deny payment, the school district will deny services. This is illegal, but lack of funds is one of the most frequent excuses that districts offer for refusing needed special education services. Parents persistent enough to get therapeutic services from both the school district and their insurance company fear their services will be cut in half, not augmented. Others fear that using their insurance in this way could quickly lead to surpassing yearly or even lifetime insurance coverage limits.

You can sometimes challenge denial of therapeutic services by explaining that speech or other therapeutic goals are essential activities of everyday life, useful not only in school but for functioning in the larger world. This "essential activities of everyday life" rationale is what people with orthopedic disabilities use to get the therapies they need covered by insurance.

Getting coverage for new treatments

All insurance plans bar coverage for experimental treatments. Some do have a "compassionate care" exception, which comes into play when regular treatments have been tried unsuccessfully and the plan's medical advisers agree that the experimental treatment could be workable. This exception is generally available only to people with life-threatening illnesses.

So what do you do to pay for promising new treatments for ASDs? You either pay out of pocket, or you work closely with your physician to get around the experimental treatment exclusion.

Joe, father of 7-year-old Kyle, says,

> *The HMOs won't cover any experimental tests. I switched this year to a dual medical plan where we can go out of the HMO. The insurance will pay 70 percent and we pay 30 percent. This allowed us to get tests done we knew might help find a cause (titers, allergies, yeast), and we found a flexible out-of-plan MD.*
>
> *We are very frustrated with trying to find the right specialists and having to battle our son's primary care physician for a referral.*

"Creative coding" is the term doctors use to describe billing the insurer or managed care entity for something that's not quite what was actually delivered. For example, an audiologist might be willing to bill for auditory integration therapy, which the insurance company probably would not pay for, as something else that the insurer would pay for. This is a form of fraud, and providers who do this take tremendous risks.

For immunological or GI tract–related treatments, physicians may choose to bill their services as treatments for immune system dysfunction, GI tract, or nutritional problems alone, with no mention of ASDs. Unlike creative coding, this probably will not get the physician in trouble if she has documented evidence of the conditions she is treating.

Your physician may have to prepare a "letter of medical necessity" to support your treatment request—or this task may fall to you. This letter must include the following:

- The diagnosis for which the service or equipment is needed
- The specific symptom or function that the service or equipment will treat or help
- A full description of the service or equipment and how it will help
- Supporting evidence (medical studies, journal articles, and so on) for any new or experimental service or equipment
- Well-supported reasons why less expensive or more traditional alternatives are not appropriate for this patient

Making smart insurance choices

If you have more than one insurance plan to choose from, your best bet is a plan with an out-of-network clause. These plans let you choose your own providers if you can't find the right professional within the plan. You generally pay more for these out-of-plan visits, but you won't have to run the referral gauntlet as often. Integrated HMOs that offer both medical and mental health care may offer similar advantages to their customers, although not all customers agree.

Cindy, mother of 15-year-old Jeffrey, has had problems with an integrated HMO:

> We had no insurance years ago, and I paid for some things out-of-pocket. Now I have him covered with Kaiser. It's a struggle to get them to care, to get to a specialist, to get them to take me seriously. I am trying to get chromosome studies and an MRI. It will be a challenge, I am sure.

If your employer does not offer insurance that covers speech therapy, mental health-care, out-of-network providers, or other needed services, take this up with the human resources department or, in small companies, the boss. When the cost is spread over a group, these additional benefits may not be very expensive.

Insurance for families or individuals affected by long-term disability is very hard to get in the private market. It's available, but premium costs are extraordinarily high. If you anticipate leaving a job that provides you with health insurance for one that does not, look into a COBRA plan (COBRA is the Consolidated Omnibus Budget Reconciliation Act of 1985). These plans allow you to continue your current, employer-sponsored coverage after leaving employment. You will pay the full rate, including the contribution previously made by your employer, plus up to a 2 percent administrative fee.

If you do choose a COBRA, it's important to pay all your premiums on time, as COBRA administrators are not lenient about late premiums.

A COBRA plan is not a permanent arrangement, but it can help you maintain your coverage for 18 months—or longer, if you or another covered member of your family meets the Social Security Administration definition of disabled. You can apply for Social Security Income for yourself or your child, even if you think you earn too much to qualify. Once the Social Security Administration informs you in writing that the person has been found to be disabled, send a copy of that letter to your COBRA administrator within 60 days to extend COBRA coverage for 11 months. This extension applies to the entire family, not just the person with a disability.

If your COBRA coverage cannot be extended and is nearing its end, call your state insurance commission. Some states sponsor an insurance pool for state residents with expired COBRA plans. Try to apply at least a month before your plan's end date: To avoid being locked out of insurance coverage because of pre-existing conditions, you must maintain continuous coverage. If a COBRA isn't an option, other possibilities include group plans offered by trade associations, unions, clubs, and other organizations. You may also want to look into public health insurance options, which are discussed later in this chapter.

Appendix A, *Resources,* lists several books and publications that can help in your quest to secure insurance coverage and health care. For information on managed care issues, visit the web site of MCARE, the National Clearinghouse on Managed Care and Long-Term Supports and Services for People with Developmental Disabilities and Their Families *(http://www.mcare.net/).* The National Coalition of Mental Health Professionals and Consumers also maintains a useful site *(http://www.NoManagedCare. org/).*

Mental health parity and you

The federal Mental Health Parity Act was passed in 1996, and went into effect at the beginning of 1998. This law affects only employer-sponsored group insurance plans that wish to offer mental health coverage. If adding such coverage raises the company's premium cost by more than 1 percent, the company need not comply. Companies with fewer than 50 employees are exempted from the law.

The Mental Health Parity Act raised the annual or lifetime cap on mental health care in the plans that it covers, but it does not prevent insurance companies from limiting access or recovering costs in other ways. They may, for example, legally restrict the number of visits you can make to a mental health provider, raise the copayment required for such visits, or raise your deductible for mental health care.

Many states, including Arkansas, California, Colorado, Connecticut, Indiana, Maine, Maryland, Minnesota, New Hampshire, North Carolina, Rhode Island, Texas, and Vermont have more restrictive state mental health parity laws. These laws supersede the federal regulations. Several other states have parity laws that are equal to the federal act, and others have less restrictive parity laws. California, Colorado, Connecticut, Maine, New Hampshire, Rhode Island, and Texas specifically require coverage for autistic spectrum disorders and other "biologically based" mental illnesses. This is a step in the right direction, although it remains to be seen how these laws will be enforced.

Managing managed care

Once you have health insurance, you will almost surely find yourself dealing with the dominant trend in medical care today: managed care. The managed care concept has some consumer-friendly components. In most health maintenance organizations (HMOs) and other managed care entities, providers and provider groups earn more if their patients stay healthy. An emphasis on preventive care and timely intervention can work to the benefit of many. People with long-term disabilities, however, may be perceived as obstacles in the way of profits.

There are four basic rules for managing your insurance affairs when you're dealing with an HMO or other managed care organization:

1. Make yourself knowledgeable.

2. Document everything.

3. Make your providers into allies.

4. Appeal.

Make yourself knowledgeable

Most people look at the glossy brochure for the plan and at the provider list when they get insurance, but unless something goes wrong, that's about as much as they want to know. If you or your child has a disability, however, that's not enough. You'll need a copy of the firm's master policy, the document that specifies what is and isn't covered.

To order the master policy, call your employer's human resources office (for employer-provided insurance or COBRA plans administered by a former employer) or the insurance company's customer relations office (for health insurance that you buy directly from the insurer). If this document is hard to understand, disability advocacy organizations and related web sites can help explain its provisions.

Document everything

Keep copies of all bills, reports, evaluations, test results, and other medical records. You'll also need to keep records of when and how your insurance payments are made. If you have a dispute with your health care provider or insurer, this information is essential.

Document personal conversations and phone calls. Simply note the date and time of your call or chat, whom you spoke with, and what was said or decided. You needn't tape-record these interactions, although during a dispute recording can be a good idea (make sure to let the other party know that you are doing so).

Referral forms are especially important. Most managed care firms send a copy to both the patient and the provider. This document usually has a referral number on it. Be sure to bring your referral form when you see a new provider. If the provider has not received his or her copy of the form, your copy can ensure that you'll still be seen. Without it, you may be turned away.

Make your providers into allies

Money is a motivator for doctors and other health care providers, but most of them also care about helping their patients. Your providers are the most powerful allies you have. Give them information about ASDs and about your specific concerns. Let them know how important their help is. They have the power to write referrals, to recommend and approve treatments, and to advocate on your behalf within the managed care organization.

Don't rely on your providers completely, however. They have many patients, some of whose needs will likely take precedence over yours from time to time. Another staff member, such as a nurse or office assistant, can keep your provider on track, but you'll have to return calls and provide accurate information. For example, if you're interested in a new treatment, summarize information about it on one page, and attach the relevant studies or journal articles. The doctor can then quickly scan the basics in her office, and read the rest when time permits.

Grievances and appeals

Most insurance coverage and claims denials are never appealed. However, it is worth your while to appeal. The process should be explained in the insurance company's master plan. If it is not, call the company's customer service office or your employer's human resources department for information.

A grievance or appeal is not the same thing as a complaint. Complaints do not require a legal response. Grievances and appeals do, and health care consumers are entitled to have matters presented in this way addressed.

Grievances are formal complaints about how you have been treated. If your doctor is rude, you are forced to sit in the waiting room for four hours, or your paperwork is lost, these are topics for a grievance.

Appeals are formal responses to decisions about insurance coverage or medical care. If you are denied insurance, denied coverage for a specific treatment, or refused referral for a needed service, these are topics for an appeal.

When you file a formal grievance or appeal, the insurance company or managed care entity usually convenes a committee made up of people not involved in your problem. This committee will meet to consider the matter, usually within 30 days of receiving your written complaint. Particularly in HMOs, where the committee is usually made up mostly of physicians, medical arguments may fall on receptive ears.

It's unlikely that you will be personally present when your grievances or appeal is discussed. You can send written material to support your position. It's best if your physician or care provider also writes a letter of support, explaining why he or she supports your request for coverage or a specific service.

If your initial effort is denied, ask if you can appeal the decision to a higher body. You may have the right to appear in person at this higher level hearing, to bring an outside representative (such as a disability advocate, outside medical expert, or health care lawyer), and to question the company representatives or medical practitioners involved. In other words, if a second-level procedure is available, it will be more like a trial or arbitration hearing.

If you are still denied, you may be able to pursue the matter with your state's Department of Health or Insurance Commission. If your managed care plan is part of a public insurance program (for example, if you receive state medical benefits and have been required to join an HMO to receive care), you may also have an appeals avenue through another state agency, such as your welfare office.

Tips for managing managed care

There are tactics that can help you tackle common communication problems. Here are some that others have used successfully:

- Whenever you speak to someone at your HMO, especially if it's a claims representative, ask for her full name and direct phone line or phone extension.
- If you can't get help from a claims or customer service representative, ask for his supervisor. If you're told that he isn't available, get the supervisor's full name, direct phone line, and mailing address. Simply asking for this information sometimes makes missing supervisors magically appear.
- Use humor to defuses tense situations.
- Whatever you do, stay calm.

- Make it clear that you're gathering information in a way that indicates legal action—for instance, asking how to spell names and asking where official documents should be sent.

National health care

Some US families have even more serious health insurance problems: They just can't get any. If this ever growing group includes you, publicly funded options include Medicaid, state programs for low-income residents or residents with disabilities, and county health programs.

Universal publicly funded coverage is the norm in Canada, Australia, New Zealand, western Europe, and some Asian countries, but that doesn't mean treatment for ASDs is necessarily provided or provided well. Publicly funded health care varies considerably based on your location, access to specialists, and medical philosophy.

Government health care plans in the US

The US government does supply low-cost health insurance to some citizens through the Medicare and Medicaid programs. It also has health care plans for current and former military personnel and their dependants. Some states have their own health care plans, which make innovative use of state funds and federal Medicaid payments.

Medicaid

Medicaid is the federal insurance program for those who are not senior citizens. It will pay for doctor and hospital bills, six prescription medications per month, adaptive equipment, and physical, occupational, or speech therapy. If you receive Social Security, Social Security Disability, Social Security survivor's benefits, or Supplemental Security Income (SSI), you or your child should be eligible for health care benefits as well through either Medicaid or, for seniors, Medicare. Some people receiving either Medicaid or a state plan are asked to join a managed care group.

SSI is for people with serious health impairments and either low family income (for children) or limited ability to earn a living (for adults). Chapter 10, *Family Issues and Support,* explains more about applying for SSI.

Too much family income may not always bar a disabled child from qualifying for SSI and Medicaid. In some cases, family income reduces the amount of SSI received to as low as one dollar per month, but the beneficiary gets full medical coverage. Parents may need to apply for a "Katie Beckett waiver." The parents of Katie Beckett, a severely handicapped child, wanted to care for her at home, but government regulations would only cover care in an expensive hospital setting. Her family could not bear the full cost of at-home care but had an income too high to qualify for SSI. They successfully lobbied for a program that would allow seriously handicapped children to qualify for Medicaid coverage.

Applying for a Katie Beckett waiver

The waiver program is administered at a state level. Some states have severely limited the number of Katie Beckett waivers they will allow. You must apply for SSI and be turned down to qualify. When you are denied SSI, ask for a written proof of denial. Next, contact your county department for child and family services (CFS) and ask for a Medicaid worker. Schedule an appointment with this person to apply for a Katie Beckett waiver.

This appointment will be long, and the questions will be intrusive, so be prepared. You will need copious documentation, including

- Your SSI rejection letter
- Your child's birth certificate and Social Security number
- Proof of income (check stubs, or a statement provided by child and family services for your employer to sign, and possibly income tax forms)
- Names, addresses, and phone numbers of all physicians who have examined your child
- Bank account and safety deposit box numbers, and amounts in these accounts
- List of other assets and their value, including your house and car
- A DMA6 medical report and physician referral form signed by the doctor who knows your child best (CFS will provide you with these forms)

If you have a caseworker with your county's developmental disabilities or mental health offices, or if you regularly work with someone at a regional center or in an Early Intervention program, this person may be able to help you navigate the SSI, Medicaid, and Katie Beckett waiver process.

If you have problems accessing appropriate medical care under Medicaid, Medicare, or allied state health plans, talk to a disability advocacy attorney or consult the Health Law Project at (800) 274-3258.

The problem with Medicaid and state health plans

Coverage is a fine thing, but what happens when no one will accept you as a patient? Millions of Americans who have government-provided health care face this situation. You may find yourself limited to overcrowded, understaffed, and possibly inadequate county health clinics or public hospitals, and to those providers willing to work for cut-rate fees. Public plans don't pay health care providers as much as private insurers do, and providers aren't legally required to take this type of insurance.

Jennifer, mother of 3-year-old Joseph, is coping with the public system:

> We have no insurance. We are relying on Early Intervention and special education. We are supposed to be starting OT for sensory integration soon. The funding was approved three weeks ago, but the state agency cannot find a local provider that is willing to accept the rates that they are required to pay. He is only eligible for this funding source for another three months, so I hope and pray they will be able to get this started soon.

Health Canada

In Canada, coverage is ensured for emergency and routine health care by Health Canada. Health care regulations are the same nationwide, although providers can be hard to find in the less populated northern provinces.

To initiate an evaluation, parents can go through the school system or talk to the pediatrician. Adults should see their primary care physician. The pediatrician or family doctor would then make a referral to an appropriate specialist.

Rae, mother of 13-year-old D'Arcy, says,

> Our family doctor referred us to a specialist pediatrician, who specialized in emotional problems in children. She assessed D'Arcy carefully and then referred us on to the area mental health clinic, where D'Arcy was seen by (and still sees) a psychiatrist. The psychiatrist arranged for necessary tests (EEG, CAT scan, MRI) and arranged for D'Arcy to meet regularly for about a year with a counseling psychologist.

A variety of specialists are available through the Canadian health system, with university hospitals and clinics among the best options. There are waiting lists, but calls and letters (especially if they come from a doctor) can often open up opportunities quicker than usual.

Public assistance programs can help you get expert care in the closest city if you live in rural Canada. This may include covering transportation costs, housing the patient and a caregiver during evaluation and treatment, and providing regular consultations later on with a doctor closer to home. In practice, rural Canadians with severe disabilities do sometimes have trouble obtaining adequate care.

Therapeutic services, such as speech therapy, may be delivered in a medical or school setting. There isn't much coordination between the school and health care systems, according to Canadian parents.

Canadians also report that privatization and other changes are starting to limit their access to health care. Some now carry private insurance to ensure timely and frequent access to care providers.

Canadians in border areas may wish to consult with specialists in the US. Except in rare, preapproved cases, such visits are not covered by Health Canada.

ABA and similar intensive programs may, in some cases, be funded by Health Canada. These techniques are gaining in popularity, and trained practitioners are available in urban areas. Coordinating public funding for home delivery of such services can be a chore, but some families have succeeded.

National Health Service in the UK

The National Health Service in Britain and Scotland has undergone tremendous upheaval over the past three decades. All services were once free to UK citizens, whereas private-pay physicians were strictly for the wealthy. Public services have since been sharply curtailed. Nevertheless, services for people with autistic spectrum disorders are probably better now than they were in the past, when grim government boarding schools and then institutionalization were the norm.

ASD assessment may begin with a health visitor, pediatrician, psychiatrist or psychologist, Child Development Centre, or specialist child and family guidance clinic. Adults can access a specialist through their general practitioner (GP). Referrals to specialists are sometimes difficult to obtain.

Denise Cunningham of the National Autistic Society says,

> It is very difficult for some parents to reach a specialist [due to] long waiting lists, not being able to get the referral in the first place, not knowing where the specialists are, etc. When the child does get a diagnosis, their GP is always informed of the outcome.

The National Autistic Society (NAS) was set up precisely to help parents and adult patients navigate the National Health Service and educational system in the UK. It publishes excellent materials, runs more than 50 schools and care centers, and sponsors the NAS Network, which can help parents and patients obtain direct care and other services they need. Local autism societies are also active in bringing parents and adult patients together around health care issues.

Because health care practitioners are an important part of the Statement of Special Needs ("statementing") procedure for getting Early Intervention and special education services, it may be quite practical to pursue both a medical diagnosis and statementing at the same time. Speech therapy through NHS practitioners may be delivered in a clinic or at the child's school. Occupational and physical therapy are usually done at a clinic, except in special needs schools.

ABA and other intensive programs are becoming more prevalent in the UK, although they are not normally available as in-home programs with public funding. Trained practitioners are available in most urban areas. Some schools for children with ASDs offer ABA or other intensive one-to-one programs. Social Services departments are responsible for helping parents with home needs and for creating a coordinated service plan.

Medicare in Australia

Medicare, the Australian health plan, pays 85 percent of all doctor's fees. It also qualifies Australian citizens for free treatment in any public hospital. Many general practitioners and pediatricians "bulk-bill": They charge the government directly for all their patient visits and let the 15 percent copayment slide. Specialists usually won't bulk-bill. Once a certain cost level has been reached, Medicare pays 100 percent of the bill.

Patients can see the physician of their choice without getting a preliminary referral, but many specialists have long waiting lists.

A number of programs have been set up to identify and help Australian children with developmental disabilities at an early age. Parents say that medical professionals are sometimes less than savvy about neurological disorders in general, but if you can make contact with one who is, services are available.

Kerry, mother of 12-year-old Kim, explains:

> *If a child has really obvious problems, such as clear autistic behavior,*
> *lack of language, or a physical disability, this would possibly be picked up*

*by the Infant Welfare Service (a free service where mothers can take their
toddlers to be weighed, vaccinated, screened for hearing loss, etc.) The
Infant Welfare Centres are run by nurses who are supposed to guide and
advise mothers during the first few years of their child's life. This service
has been progressively cut back in recent years. Some of the Centres are
fantastic, others mediocre, even bad. It all depends on the nursing staff,
really.*

*Less obvious problems would not be picked up at this level. The
tendency would be for the nurse to reassure the mother that the child will
"grow out of it," "is going through a stage," "all children follow somewhat
different developmental trajectories," etc.*

*In the past, the government used to provide a free screening for all
children at age 4, and again at around age 6. This would be conducted
in kindergartens, some day-care centers, and in schools. This was mainly
a medical screening, but basic developmental and behavioral differences
were sometimes picked up at this stage. Nowadays the screening is no
longer universal . . . either the parent or teacher/child-care worker has
to request it. Many children who would benefit from intervention thus slip
through the net.*

*In Australia, some pediatricians specialize in behavioral issues (the
specialty of "ambulatory pediatrics"), and at the present time children
with neurological issues end up being sent to one of these. Neurologists
and psychiatrists are not involved in the care of children, except in cases
of clear physical signs (e.g., epilepsy) or adolescent depression.*

Services such as speech therapy, occupational therapy, and physical therapy may be
delivered at home, in a school, or in a clinical setting. Parents in rural areas may have
difficulty getting access to qualified practitioners, although the emergency health care
system for rural Australia is enviable. In some situations, parents or patients in very
rural areas may be able to access professionals for advice or "virtual consultations"
over the Internet, telephone, or even radio.

Some prescription medications are not covered by Medicaid, and there is a sliding
scale copayment for those that are.

ABA and other intensive programs for people with ASDs are still fairly new in Australia, although trained providers are available in major cities.

New Zealand

About 75 percent of all health care in New Zealand is publicly funded. Care is delivered through private physicians who accept payment from the public health system. Treatment at public hospitals is fully covered for all citizens.

Health care and disability services are both provided through a central Health Authority, which is trying to improve delivery of mental, pediatric, and minority-group health care. Talk to your pediatrician or family physician about specialist referral for ASD diagnosis and treatment, or go directly to a specialist.

Urban patients may have access to group practices centered around Crown (public) hospitals, which often have excellent specialists. Maori patients may access health care and assessments through medical clinics centered around traditional tribal structures if they prefer.

About 40 percent of New Zealanders carry private insurance, primarily for hospitalization or long-term geriatric care. This insurance is helpful when you need elective surgery and want to avoid waiting lists at public hospitals. It is not needed or required to access speech therapy, occupational therapy, physical therapy, psychiatric care, or other direct health or disability services.

As in Australia, ABA and other intensive programs for people with ASDs are hard to access. People with ASDs and their families complain that waiting lists for assessments and treatment can be excessive.

For patients in need of temporary or permanent residential care, volunteer organizations (particularly churches) are heavily involved in running long-term care facilities in New Zealand. These facilities are usually free of charge, although some are reimbursed by public health.

Privatization is a growing trend in New Zealand. Public hospitals and allied clinics have been recreated as public–private corporations. However, the government still provides most of the funding and regulates health care.

Alternatives to insurance

No matter where you live, there are alternatives to expensive medical care. Those who don't have insurance, or whose insurance is inadequate, will want to investigate these resources.

Sometimes you can come up with creative payment arrangements, trading services or products for care, arranging a payment plan, or paying reduced fees based on financial need. The larger the provider, the more likely it is to have a system in place for sliding scale fees. Hospitals and major clinics may have social workers on staff who can help with financial arrangements. Sometimes small practices agree to barter arrangements.

ABA and similar intensive programs can be delivered by parents themselves, perhaps with some paid or volunteer help. Special education students, ABA providers in training, and community volunteers can often be recruited to help with discrete trials for a few hours a week, giving parents time to rest or work.

Sources of free or low-cost health care or therapeutic services include the following:

- Public hospitals and health clinics, including school-based health clinics

- Hospitals and clinics run by religious or charitable orders, especially the Shriners Children's Hospitals

- Medical and nursing schools, and associated teaching hospitals and clinics

- College programs training speech, occupational, and physical therapists

- Charitable institutions associated with religious denominations, such Catholic Charities, the Jewish Aid Society, and the Salvation Army

- Scottish Rite fraternal order (for speech and hearing)

- The Flutie Foundation (*http://www.dougflutiejrfoundation.org/*), set up to assist parents of autistic children

- Volunteer organizations, such as Easter Seals and The ARC

- United Way: This fund-raising organization is made up of many programs, and can often give referrals

In the UK, special resources outside of National Health include

- National Autistic Society

- Aidis Trust (for augmentative communication assistance)

- Mind (the National Association for Mental Health)

- Community Trust associations for autism, particularly the Tarka Home Trust (for a complete list of these organizations, as well as local autism societies, see *http://www.caritasdata.co.uk*)

- Samaritans and other charitable groups

Charlotte, mother of 4-year-old Rory, says,

> *Our insurance refused to play for Rory's out-of-school speech and occupational therapy. We receive assistance from a United Way program, and some grant funds from the state Department of Mental Retardation. As far as medical tests, etc., the insurance was no problem.*

Medical savings accounts

Medical savings accounts are a new health care payment option in the US that may have benefits for some children and adults with ASDs. A medical savings account (MSA), also known as an Archer MSA, allows families to put away a certain amount of money specifically for health care costs. This income is exempted from federal (and in some cases state) income taxes. Unused funds continue to gain tax-free interest. These accounts can be used to pay for insurance deductibles, copayments, prescriptions, and medical services not covered by insurance.

Families faced with paying out-of-pocket for an expensive ABA program or augmentative communication device might be able to use an Archer MSA to reduce their expenses by an impressive percentage. You'll need to check the regulations of the specific MSA plan to see what expenses qualify.

You can find a good consumer's guide to Archer MSAs on the Web at *http://www.jpeek. com/msa.html.*

Changing the rules

Advocating for changes in the insurance system or your national health care system is a big job. Unless you want to make it your life mission, it's probably too big for any one person. But by working together—and by working with health care providers, most of whom are just as dismayed with the current state of medical care— individuals can accomplish a lot.

Advocacy organizations can serve as the point of contact between health care consumers, insurers, HMOs, and public health. The Autism Society of America does not do any direct outreach to insurance companies, according to development and public affairs coordinator Caroline Ketchum. "It's too big an undertaking, since each state has an insurance commissioner," she said. Effective action in the US will probably be at the state level. There's a need for education, for public advocacy, for legislative action, and even for legal action. People with ASDs, family members, and caring health practitioners can all help with these efforts.

Everyone wants to see improvements in health care and in how it's delivered. By working closely with allies in the public, private, and volunteer sectors, people with autistic spectrum disorders and those who care about them can make it happen. Even insurance companies and managed care entities can be brought on board if shown the positive benefit, which include a reduced need for emergency care, hospitalization, long-term care, and expensive medications. Alternative models for care are evolving, and with hard work these new systems can be both more humane and more cost efficient.

CHAPTER 9

School

IN THE US, FEDERAL LAW MANDATES THAT ALL CHILDREN receive a free and appropriate education, regardless of disability. That means providing, free of charge, special education programs, speech therapy, occupational therapy, physical therapy, psychiatric services, augmentative communication techniques and devices, and other interventions as needed to help each child learn. So why are families around the country angry about how their children with ASDs are being (mis)educated, pulling their children out of school in frustration, or taking their school district to court? Simply put, law and reality collide daily in the schoolhouse.

This chapter offers the latest information about appropriate school placements for children with autistic spectrum disorders under the latest version of the Individuals with Disabilities Education Act (IDEA), the federal law governing special education. It presents the voices of parents and students about classrooms that work. And for those facing problems, it provides a primer on special education law, including how to appeal improper placement and make service decisions.

Lack of adequate funding, lack of information about educating children with autistic spectrum disorders, and many other factors are at work here, and these are certainly not unique to the US. School issues in the rest of the English-speaking world are covered separately in this chapter as well.

Early Intervention

The first educational placement for a young child on the autistic spectrum is usually made through an Early Intervention program. EI service offerings vary widely. They should, however, be determined by the child's needs, not just what happens to be available or customary in your area.

The document that spells out these needs and the services that will be provided to meet them is the Individual Family Service Plan (IFSP), which should be based on a comprehensive evaluation of the child (see Chapter 3, *Getting a Diagnosis*). This document should be created at an IFSP meeting, which you will be invited to attend and contribute to. Although it's a good idea for both parents and practitioners to write down ideas for goals and interventions in advance, the IFSP itself should not be written in advance and simply handed to the parents to sign.

The first page of the IFSP is for basic information on the child and on the team members present at the IFSP meeting, including contact information for each of them. It also summarizes the services to be provided, who will provide them, how often they will be provided, and where they will be delivered. The details of these services are entered on the IFSP's goals and objectives pages. Accordingly, these should not be filled in until the goals and objectives have been set. They dictate which services are required for your child, and how often they are delivered. Your cover page should be similar to the one shown in Figure 9-1.

One or more pages of the IFSP summarize the evaluation of your child. These pages should cover medical information, psychiatric diagnosis, and the results of hearing, vision, and developmental screening. This information is entered on a form similar to the one shown in Figure 9-2.

Finally, the IFSP lists specific goals and objectives for the EI team to meet, and explains how this will be done. These goals are developed by the team at the IFSP meeting. You are part of this team. You can bring your own goals to IFSP meetings, and you should make sure the rest of the team takes your ideas seriously.

There are usually goal statements in the areas of cognition, fine motor and gross motor development, communication, social skills, and self-help skills. Chapter 4, *Getting Started,* lists many general goals that may give you some good ideas. Most of these are long-term goals.

It's good to keep these overall goals in mind as you develop the IFSP, but in creating the final document you'll want to break them down into small, manageable steps. For example, you might have the long-term goal "Billy will learn to say his name." To meet this goal, the team might put sequential steps into the IFSP such as the following:

1. Billy will understand the concept of names.

2. Billy will associate his name with himself.

3. Billy will produce the sounds in his name.

4. Billy will say his name.

5. Billy will say his name when he sees a picture or mirror image of himself.

6. Billy will use his name in response to the question "What is your name?"

Individual Family Service Plan (IFSP)

Child: _____ Birthdate: _____

Parent(s)/Guardian: _____ Home Phone: _____

Work Phone: _____ Address: _____

IFSP Coordinator/Agency: _____

Resident School District: _____

Meeting Date: _____

Date Eligibility Established: _____

Review Date: _____

Annual Review: _____

Transition Plan?   ☐ Yes   ☐ No

12-Month Services?   ☐ Yes   ☐ No

Team Members in Attendance: Name/Role/Phone

_____

_____

_____

Team Members Not in Attendance: Name/Role/Phone

_____

_____

_____

Extent of participation with non-disabled peers: _____

Summary of Services

Service/Method	How Often?	Where?	Who Will Do This?	Who Will Pay?	Start Date	Stop Date

I (We) have had the opportunity to participate in the development of this IFSP.   Signature(s): _____

Figure 9-1. An IFSP sample cover page

Current Developmental Information Summary

Child's Name: _____   Date: _____

Child's Strengths and Interests: _____

_____

_____

Sources of Information in Developing This IFSP: _____

Pertinent Medical Information: _____

_____

_____

Hearing Screening: _____

_____

_____

Vision Screening: _____

_____

_____

Present Skill Levels

Cognitive: _____

_____

Communication: _____

_____

Social: _____

_____

Fine Motor: _____

_____

Gross Motor: _____

_____

_____

Self-Care: _____

_____

_____

Figure 9-2. A current developmental information form

Figure 9-3 shows a sample IFSP page for goals and objectives. Your EI program may use different forms, but they should include space for all the items shown. Each goal item should include information on what services will be provided, how progress will be measured, and who will deliver the services needed.

The IFSP can also include services needed by the whole family to help you care for your child. For example, these services might include parent education classes, the services of a behavior expert who can help you with home discipline problems, or help in finding and accessing community resources.

EI placements

Ideally, the IFSP dictates the proper placement. EI placements commonly used for children on the autistic spectrum include the following:

- **Home-based services.** Programs in this category can range from sending an SLP or parent consultant into the home once a week to implementing a 40–hours–per week applied behavior analysis (ABA) program with extensive wrap-around services. For very young children with severe impairments, such as extreme sensory sensitivity, home-based services often make the most sense. Home-based programs may include direct therapeutic and educational services, training and supervision for parents and volunteers working with the child, and assistance with medical procedures and care needed to allow education to take place.

- **Direct services.** This category includes all professional services, such as speech therapy, occupational therapy, physical therapy, and talk therapy, that are delivered independent of each other in a school (but not as part of a preschool program), clinic, or other setting outside the home. For example, the IFSP might specify that your child is to receive one hour of speech therapy three times per week at the university's speech clinic, or physical therapy for 45 minutes twice a week at a clinic. These services may be delivered by professionals or facilities under contract with Early Intervention, or by practitioners working directly for the EI program.

- **School-based services.** This category includes all services delivered as part of a public or private preschool program at the school site. Therapeutic services may be integrated into a special or typical preschool program, or your child may leave class for one-on-one or small group work ("pull-out" services).

A primarily home-based program goes the furthest to build a strong relationship between the child and his parents, which will be the building block for all later social interactions. It takes place in a familiar, nondistracting environment that has probably already been made appropriate for the child's sensory needs. It eliminates lost time

Child's Goals and Objectives

Child: _____   Date: _____   Developmental Area: _____

What we want to happen (long-term goal): _____

Who will work on it? _____   Who will keep track of progress? _____

How We Will Do It (Short-Term Objectives and Criteria)	Evaluation Procedures and Schedule	Family Resources/ Other Resources	Start Date	Review	Annual Review

Figure 9-3. A sample IFSP page for goals and objectives

and problems related to transporting a preschool child to school (many school-based EI programs actually bus infants and toddlers across town). It also provides the best stage for intensive, one-on-one intervention using applied behavior analysis, floor-time play therapy, and similar techniques.

A home-based program is also extraordinarily difficult to get approved. One tool that may help you win this battle is a thorough and accurate financial appraisal that compares the cost of an intensive home-based program in the early years to 12 years of special education services, residential placement, or private placement.

Early Intervention classrooms

For many children with an ASD diagnosis, a preschool setting with other children is the best placement. That's because one hallmark of these disorders is differences in how the child relates to others, plays, and learns. Spending time with other children in a structured setting can be very beneficial for developing more age-appropriate social skills.

Of course, an autistic spectrum child should never simply be plopped down in a room full of screaming 3-year-olds and left to fend for herself on the grounds that it's "therapeutic." Attention must be paid to your child's special needs, deficits, strengths, sensory issues, and so on.

EI preschools come in four major flavors, described next:

- **Regular preschool classroom.** Also called a full-integration setting or mainstreaming, this might be a Head Start or similar preschool classroom. Your child would attend preschool with therapeutic services, classroom adaptations, and personal support, such as an aide, as needed. These services, adaptations, and supports must be written into the IFSP.

- **Supported integrated preschool classroom.** Also called a reverse integration setting, because the nondisabled students are integrated into a special program rather than the other way around. This specially created preschool setting brings together a small group of children with disabilities and children without disabilities. Therapeutic services, classroom adaptations, and personal support are provided to each child with a disability according to his IFSP. Children in a supported integrated classroom may have a variety of different disabilities, such as developmental delay, Down syndrome, or cerebral palsy. Often autistic spectrum children are placed with children who have various speech and language disabilities, such as cleft palate, stuttering, and apraxia. Some supported integrated classrooms mix only children with ASDs and normally developing children. In these cases, the severity of autistic behavior may range from severe to mild.

- **Special preschool classroom.** This is a preschool class designed for children with disabilities only. The children may have a mix of various disabilities, or all may be somewhere on the autistic spectrum. The classroom may be part of a larger school with other types of classrooms, providing opportunities to interact with nondisabled children.

- **Special preschool.** This is an entire preschool program created specifically to work with children who have disabilities. It may be within a larger school program that also educates school age children. It may be owned and run by a public school district, or it may be a private school that contracts with the Early Intervention program to provide services. If a private program is judged to be the most appropriate setting for your child, EI and/or the school district should pay the full cost of tuition.

Each of these typical settings has positive aspects. For children who can handle inclusion in a regular preschool classroom, there are ample opportunities to model behavior and speech on that of typically developing peers.

Supported integrated classrooms offer similar benefits, with a daily program and structure that's more geared toward the child with special needs.

Special classrooms and schools generally have the most services, but provide fewer opportunities to interact with nondisabled peers. Your child's needs, abilities, and difficulties will dictate the right placement, because there is no workable one-size-fits-all approach. Here are some families' experiences with Early Intervention—and one student's fond memories.

Shayna, mother of 3-year-old Max, says,

> *Early Intervention has been a positive experience. I feel these people truly care, and I have been approached for additional services rather than having to ask for services.*

Sally, mother of 4-year-old Dhylan, likes his TEACCH-based program:

> *My son has had good Early Intervention services, which I feel is the key to his wonderful progress. He started school when he was 3 years old. It is a full-time program at a school for autistic children. It is a marvelous school, and it has benefited him enormously. They use the TEACCH program, and have a very good student-to-teacher ratio: about two students to one teacher. They have a very structured day.*

> If I had a magic wand, I would create schools for autistic children
> in every city, and the education would continue through high school.
> I dread putting him in the public school system—he learns so
> differently.

Holly says a home-based ABA program is best for her 3-year-old son, Max:

> Max received very inappropriate center-based EI for a short period,
> upon which he started exhibiting self-injurious behavior [SIB] and
> was taken out. The SIB stopped right afterward. Now he receives in-
> home, one-to-one Early Intervention and ABA services. The ABA is
> the most helpful of everything. He receives occupational therapy three
> times per week. This has effectively stopped feces smearing, and it
> helps with calming and balancing. Since movement gives him speech,
> it helps generally.
>
> In-home EI is only as good as the provider. Mine is marginal, but
> certainly better than the criminal-type behavior at the EI center.

Lesley, mother of 3-year-old Danielle, says an integrated setting has been ideal:

> Danielle is in an integrated preschool; they are wonderful with her.
> She is inconsistent with everything, so finding the right teaching style
> is difficult, though. Still, she seems really content and happy with her
> life.

William, now age 11, has happy memories of his EI program:

> I liked the teachers and my friend Linneus at Rice School [site of his
> supported integrated Early Intervention preschool]. I learned my
> ABCs. I did the sand table and the water table. I loved the water table
> and I still do! I hated circle time, it was so boring.

The right placement is indicated by the goals in the child's IFSP, and it can make a huge difference. Unfortunately, what many parents get from their school district is strictly an effort to fit their child into an existing program, with perhaps an offer to adapt the program slightly. Sometimes this approach works very well. Other times, it's absolutely inappropriate.

You may be told that only a few hours of preschool or a type of therapy are available to any child because of budget constraints, staff limitations, or other reasons. This information is incorrect. Legally, the only factor that should limit your child's access to services is her actual needs. If the EI program is having a hard time financially, it needs to find additional resources.

If a program is suggested that doesn't make sense to you given the goals and objectives in your child's IFSP, you can advocate for a better placement.

Dorthy has not been offered an individualized program for 5-year-old Jesse:

> Jesse's "Early Intervention program" was putting him in preschool for two years. That was 2 half-days a week at first, then upgraded to 4 half-days a week. While his teacher and the aides were wonderful, I really felt that he needed more time and was not given it. This year looks to be the same, with the exception that he will now be in school 5 half-days a week.

Jennifer, mother of 3-year-old Joseph, has had to fight for proper services:

> Although Joseph is now receiving a very good program, it took over nine months of fighting to get it, and now Early Intervention is almost over. The providers didn't seem to know what to do with my son because he didn't fit any of their preconceived categories. They also did not want to provide anywhere near the level of intensity that he needed. For example, speech therapy was only provided after we filed for a due process hearing.
>
> On a more positive note, he has gone from single words to 3- to 4-word communicative sentences in just over three months of therapy. But I do wonder how much more he would be talking if he had nine months of intensive therapy behind him instead of only three.

As explained in the sections on ABA and floor-time play therapy in Chapter 6, *Therapeutic Interventions*, intensive intervention is the key to helping children with autistic spectrum disorders reach their full potential. What the EI program won't offer, you'll have to do on your own, while advocating at the same time for a more appropriate level of public services. It's a tough balancing act.

Other educational settings for young children

A fourth type of setting, the diagnostic classroom, may be a joint project of the school system and a regional center or medical facility. These classrooms are for long-term medical or psychiatric observation and evaluation of children whose behavior and abilities don't seem to fit the profile of any typical diagnosis. This is not a permanent placement, but if your child's case is especially unusual, she may stay in the diagnostic classroom for quite some time.

A very few young children with ASDs are placed in a day treatment or residential setting. Day treatment centers are generally for children with very difficult behaviors (such as SIB or aggression toward other children), or coexisting psychiatric or medical problems, that make even a self-contained classroom inappropriate at this time. Good day treatment centers provide medical and psychiatric support, specially trained staff, a very secure environment, and intensive intervention. However, very few day treatment centers have experience working with young autistic spectrum children—most have until recently specialized in school age children, and in the treatment of behavior disorders. At the end of the school day, children in day treatment go home to their families.

Residential schools offer educational programming and 24-hour care for the child. For obvious reasons, residential schools are rarely considered as a placement for a preschool child. The very few exceptions are children with very severe health or behavior problems whose parents are unable or unwilling to care for them at home, and those who cannot obtain services in any other setting—for example, an isolated family living in rural Alaska, where school age children are generally either home-schooled or sent to boarding schools.

If the issue is the family itself rather than the family's location, as in cases of abuse, neglect, or abandonment, child services authorities will generally pursue a long-term placement in therapeutic foster care. These are homes where the foster parents have been trained to work with children who have special needs (in some states, a college degree in social work, psychiatry, special education, or a related discipline is required in addition to the foster care agency's own training program) and are willing to provide full-time, family-style care for these children. In some cases, parental rights are terminated and the child is placed for adoption.

Therapeutic foster homes are also an option for families who are simply unable to handle caring for a disabled child—for example, a teenage single parent; a parent with mental illness, mental retardation, or physical disability; a parent who is currently homeless or in recovery for substance abuse; or a family that already has many children or that already has one or more children with a serious disability. Most counties try to help these types of families with home-based services, but sometimes placement in a therapeutic foster home is a good option. In these cases, the foster parents and birth parents will work as a team to meet the child's personal and educational needs, with eventual family reunification as another goal. Permanent placement is generally not part of the plan.

Monitoring progress in EI

Most IFSPs are fairly lengthy, with two or more pages of goals. That makes monitoring progress hard for parents and teachers alike. It's important to talk informally as often as you can, rather than waiting three months or longer for a formal review to take place. Your child may meet some goals quickly, and these sections should be revised right away. Other goals may seem impossible to reach. These goals may need to be broken up into even smaller steps, or the team may need to come up with different teaching methods.

Using a communications notebook or daily report form works well for many families. A communications notebook can be a spiral-bound notebook or notepad that goes to and from school every day with the child. Both teachers and parents can write notes in this notebook. For example, you might let the teacher know that Jennie slept poorly last night and ran a slight fever. The teacher might let you know that Jennie did very well in speech today, is working on naming colors, and had a normal temperature when the school nurse checked it at noon.

Both problems and successes should be written into the notebook. Too often, communications notebooks are used as gripe books, and parents get the inaccurate idea that their children are performing poorly overall instead of just in certain areas. Parents also forget to let teachers know about successes at home that could have an impact in the classroom, such as the emergence of new words or skills.

All your child's goals and objectives will be revised as needed at IFSP review meetings. These are held at least once during the school year. If you think one is needed sooner, you can call the team together yourself.

If your child is in a residential setting, you may need to designate someone else to be your compliance monitor. A caseworker from the local Early Intervention program's staff, or someone from the county's child services, developmental disability, or mental health department, may be able to take on this responsibility. Some parents have chosen to pay an independent advocate. Of course, you should still get regular reports by mail or telephone and attend meetings in person with the staff and your child whenever possible.

Transition from EI to school

Children in Early Intervention make the transition into the district's special education program around 3 years of age, although in some areas the transition comes when they are judged ready to enter kindergarten (if available) or first grade. At this time, your child will be re-evaluated—for special education eligibility (see Chapter 3). This eligibility determination is made by a committee of specialists in most areas, which may be called the multidisciplinary team (M-team), eligibility committee, child study team, or a similar name. You should have input during the eligibility process.

The eligibility team will decide if your child has a condition that qualifies him for special education. Exact language differs between states, but typical qualifying categories include the following:

- Autistic
- Hearing impaired (deaf)
- Visually impaired
- Both hearing impaired and visually impaired (deaf and blind)
- Speech and language impaired
- Mentally retarded/developmentally delayed
- Multihandicapped
- Severely orthopedically impaired
- Other health impaired (OHI)
- Seriously emotionally disturbed (SED)
- Severely and profoundly disabled
- Specific learning disability
- Traumatic brain injury

Check your state's special education regulations for the list of labels used in your state.

The condition that causes the most impairment in school-related activities is usually considered the primary handicapping condition, and any others that coexist with it are secondary handicapping conditions. For example, a child might be considered eligible for special education under the primary condition "deaf and blind," with autism as a secondary criterion. In this case, the child would also qualify under the term "multihandicapped," if available.

Although the eligibility committee will take your child's medical diagnosis and the opinions of Early Intervention evaluators into account, these categories are defined by the school district or state department of education in terms of education, not medicine. Even if your child has a medical diagnosis from a psychiatrist, neurologist, or other physician, the committee can still decide that your child does not meet the educational definition of autism. This means that the committee feels your child does not need special services to take advantage of educational opportunities.

In fact, one of the stickiest educational issues related to ASDs involves the label "autism." Children with an educational diagnosis of autism, no matter how "high functioning" they may be, are automatically entitled to special education services, but children labeled as having related disorders may not be entitled to the same level of services, no matter how impaired they are. That's not to say that districts are giving autistic students enough help, either—in fact, court battles are underway in almost every state over unavailable, inadequate, or even harmful special education services.

You have a right to appeal the eligibility team's decision about the autism label or any other issue. If the team's decision prevents your child from receiving special education eligibility or needed services, you should appeal. It is helpful to prepare a list of ways your child's neurological problems affect his ability to be educated when he does not have the added help of special education services.

A child with an ASD may qualify for services under the following categories:

- Speech and language impaired, if speech is delayed or unusual
- Other health impaired, if the child has a known autoimmune condition that contributes to autistic symptoms, or has a co-diagnosis of obsessive-compulsive disorder, Tourette's syndrome, epilepsy, or ADD/ADHD
- Developmentally delayed
- Traumatic brain injury, if the child's autistic symptoms are known to be caused by infection or injury to the brain
- Seriously emotionally disturbed (SED), especially if the child has a codiagnosis of depression, bipolar disorder, and so on

Using the SED label for kids with ASDs is controversial, and obviously not proper. However, certain school districts use it as a label of convenience to obtain special placements, such as day treatment or residential slots, that are not available without this label.

You may still receive some services through an Early Intervention program while your child is under an IEP with the school district. For example, US regional centers supply many parents of older children with special supplies, including diapers and nutritional items, and may provide respite care providers.

Special education

The Individuals with Disabilities Education Act, most recently revised in 1997, revolutionized special education in the US. This set of comprehensive rules and regulations aims to ensure that all children get an adequate education, regardless of disabilities or special needs.

IDEA is the basis of a document that will soon become your close companion: your child's individualized education plan (IEP). Like the IFSP in Early Intervention programs, the IEP describes your child's strengths and weaknesses, sets out goals and objectives, and details how these can be met within the context of the school system. Unlike the IFSP, the IEP is almost entirely about what happens within school walls. There's little information about services from outside programs or parents, unless the IEP team agrees to include it.

The IEP is created in a meeting of the IEP team, which has a minimum of three members: a representative of the school district, a teacher, and a parent. The district may send more than one representative. If your child has more than one teacher, or if direct service providers such as her speech therapist would like to attend, they can all be present. If it is your child's first IEP and first assessment, one team member is required by federal law to have experience with and knowledge of the child's suspected or known disabilities. You may want to check this person's credentials in advance. The "autism specialists" employed by some school districts may have as little as one college course on the topic of autism, or even no qualifications other than the title itself.

Both parents are encouraged to participate in the IEP process. Parents can also bring anyone else they would like: grandparents or other relatives, a friend, an after-school caretaker, a disability advocate, or a lawyer, for example. The child himself can also be at the IEP meeting if the parents would like—however, to avoid disruptions it's a good idea to bring a sitter for a young child. You want to give the IEP process your full attention, and that's hard when you're trying to keep a child out of trouble.

Older teens and self-advocacy

Districts are trying to involve middle school and high school students in the IEP process more often, and this is probably a good trend. You may want to discuss the meeting with your child and elicit her suggestions in advance. Some adolescents prefer to write up their suggestions rather than (or in addition to) attending the meeting. Bring someone to help with your child if she tends to be disruptive, and bring a book or game in case the meeting gets boring. It's not beneficial to force an unwilling child to take part in the meeting.

Recently parents of older teens in special education have reported a disturbing new trend: Some school districts are trying to circumvent IDEA by making teens "self-advocates" at 18, regardless of their ability to make wise choices, and regardless of their parents' wishes. If parents agree—and only if parents agree—any child in special education who has reached age 18 can take full control of all further contacts with the school district. Needless to say, this is often a very unwise thing to agree to. In many cases, the outcome is that the child immediately leaves school and loses all services.

If your district tries this ploy, there is a way back in. As an adult self-advocate, your child can appoint another person to advocate for her. That person can be you, or if your child prefers, a professional advocate.

Special education services should continue until at least age 21, or until the attainment of a regular high school diploma (not a GED or IEP diploma).

Building an IEP

Usually the IEP meeting is held at a school or a district office. However, you can request another location for the meeting if it is necessary—for example, if your child is on homebound instruction or has severe behavior problems that make caring for him impossible away from the controlled environment of home at this time. The meeting date and time should also be convenient to you (and, of course, to the other team members).

The first IEP meeting should begin with a presentation of your child's strengths and weaknesses. This may be merely a form listing test scores and milestones, or it can include verbal reports of observations by team members—including you. You can use this time to tell the team a little more about your child, her likes and dislikes, her abilities, and the worries that have brought you all together for this meeting. Even if you're repeating information that the team members already know, this kind of story-telling humanizes your child and yourself. You'll want to keep it brief, though, so you may want to use a short outline and even practice in advance. Five or ten minutes seems about right, although you may find you need more time. If you can keep your written description to one or two pages, that would be good.

This kind of information may also be entered on an evaluation or record summary form.

The meat of the IEP is the cover sheet, usually called the accommodations page, and the goals and objectives pages. Your district may have its own bureaucratic jargon for these pages, such as a "G3" or an "eval sheet." If team members start throwing around terms you don't understand, be sure to speak up! If the wrong forms are filled out or if important paperwork is left undone, you may not have an acceptable IEP at the end of the meeting.

Accommodations

Parents tend to focus on the goals and objectives pages, and often overlook the accommodations page. That's a *big* mistake. The goals and objectives are all about what your child will do, and if they are not accomplished, there's no one who can be truly held accountable but your child. The accommodations page, however, is about what the school district will do: what services it will provide or pay for, what kind of classroom setting your child will be in, and any other special education help that the district promises to provide. This is where really important promises are made. Figure 9-4 shows a sample accommodations page.

Accommodations that your child may need include the following:

- A specific type of classroom

- Provision of other types of environments, such as a resource room for certain subjects, mainstreaming for other subjects, or an area for time-outs or self-calming

- Changes to the classroom environment to accommodate your child's sensory difficulties

- Specific learning materials or methods

- A reduced number of required courses for graduation

- Grade arrangements that take into account assignments and school days missed because of symptoms—these accommodations might include estimating semester grades based only on the work that was completed; offering the option of an "incomplete" grade to allow the student to finish the course when well; or basing grades on some combination of class participation when present, work completed, and a special oral exam

- A personal educational assistant or aide: either a monitoring aide who simply helps with behavior control, or an inclusion or instructional aide

- Therapeutic services and their frequency

Student's Name: _____ Birthdate: _____ Grade: _____ PPS ID#: _____

Home School: _____ Attending School: _____ IEP Meeting Date: _____

IEP Manager: _____ Position: _____ Projected Review Date: _____

Specially Designed Instruction

Regular PE   ☐ Yes ☐ No

Attends Home School   ☐ Yes ☐ No
If no, explain: _____

	Service Time	Date of Initiation	Anticipated Duration
☐ Adapted PE	___	___	___
☐ Independent Living	___	___	___
☐ Language Arts	___	___	___
☐ Mathematics	___	___	___
☐ Motor	___	___	___
☐ Recreation/Leisure	___	___	___
☐ Self Management	___	___	___
☐ Social/Behavioral	___	___	___
☐ Speech/Language	___	___	___
☐ Vocational/Career Ed	___	___	___

Extent of participation in general education classes/activities: _____

Modifications and/or supplementary aids and services: _____

High School Students Only

Projected Diploma: ☐ Standard

☐ Modified   ☐ Certificate

Credits earned to date: _____

Passed PALT/GST:

Math   ☐ Yes ☐ No

Reading   ☐ Yes ☐ No

Pre-Requirement Completed ☐ Yes ☐ No

Individual Transition Plan
Completed/Updated   ☐ Yes ☐ No

Social Security Number: _____

Related Services Necessary

	Service Time	Date of Initiation	Anticipated Duration
☐ Audiology	___	___	___
☐ Counseling/Interv.	___	___	___
☐ Health Care	___	___	___
☐ Occ. Therapy	___	___	___
☐ Physical Therapy	___	___	___
☐ Transportation	___	___	___
☐ _____	___	___	___
☐ _____	___	___	___
☐ _____	___	___	___
☐ _____	___	___	___
☐ _____	___	___	___

Participants in Individualized Education Program

Parent/Guardian/Surrogate: _____

_____

Teacher: _____

District Representative: _____

Student: _____

Other: _____

Other: _____

Figure 9-4. A sample accommodations page

- Adaptive communications equipment or procedures

- Other classroom equipment needed to help your child learn, such as a microphone or sound field system to help the child with auditory processing problems, a slanted work surface, or pencils with an orthopedic grip

- Preparation and implementation of a behavior plan

The cover page should also summarize any therapeutic services your child will receive, from whom, where, and how frequently.

When the IEP meeting begins, the accommodations page should be blank, because the goals and objectives dictate what accommodations are needed.

Beware: Saying that your child will do something costs the district nothing, but promising that the district will do something has a price tag attached. Be prepared to hear phrases like "I don't want to commit the district to that" over and over—and to methodically show that the accommodations you're asking for are the only way the goals and objectives the team has set can be met. With few exceptions, district representatives see their role in the IEP as being the gatekeeper. Depending on the person, the district, and the situation, this role may be interpreted as spending as little money as possible, or ensuring that children are matched with services that meet their needs. Most district representatives struggle to balance these two goals. As your child's advocate, your job is to persuade the representative to tip the scales in your child's favor.

Goals and objectives

As with the IFSP, when you fill out the goals and objectives pages you'll be working backward. Begin with big goals—"Katie will learn how to read," for example—and break them down into developmentally appropriate steps that can be accomplished in the classroom. Classroom teacher(s) and direct service providers should be the experts at this task. Often each team member sends or brings a list of goals and objectives already broken down for the whole IEP team to discuss. This saves a lot of time, and allows everyone to concentrate on the pros and cons of the ideas rather than having to actually come up with the ideas themselves at the meeting. You may choose to meet one-on-one with these team members to talk over IEP ideas before the big meeting.

There may be goals in the areas of cognition (problem-solving and preacademic skills, such as knowing the names of colors), fine motor and gross motor development, communication, social skills, self-help skills, and behavior management. There will also be academic goals. Chapter 4 lists many general goals that may give you some good ideas. Most of these are long-term goals. They will be detailed on a form similar to the one shown in Figure 9-5.

Individualized Education Program Goals and Objectives

Page: _____ of: _____

Student's Name: _____ ID Number: _____ Date: _____

Home School: _____ Attending School: _____ Grade: _____ Birthdate:____

Skill Area: _____

Present Level of Educational Performance (including test data, remedial areas, etc.): _____

_____

_____

Annual Goal: _____

√ If Objective Carried Over	Short-Term Objectives	Criteria	Evaluation Procedure(s)	Schedules

Figure 9-5. A sample IEP goals and objectives page

Academic goals

Academic goals are often the center of controversy in an IEP meeting. Schools do not want to guarantee that a student will learn certain material; in many cases, they don't even want to promise that they'll try to teach it. And if an autistic spectrum child happens to have certain academic skills that are close to being age appropriate, appropriate for his age, or even superior, it is very hard to have anything written into the IEP about maintaining or developing these skills further. Special education services are about addressing deficits, say the educators.

Parents, however, know from experience that whatever gifts or islands of competence their child may have are essential to his well-being and educational success. The child who can read well but does not speak needs to continue to develop that reading skill, as it may be his only mode of communication for now. The child with a special gift for mathematics may be offering the teacher a way, through math, to impart other lessons, from the rules of grammar to the rules of playground basketball. Parents and experienced, caring teachers can often show the rest of the team why IEP goals based on strengths can be as important as those based on deficits.

Generally speaking, children in special education programs should be educated to the same standards as all other students whenever that is possible. They should also work with the same curriculum and objectives. For example, if third-graders in your district are normally required to present a 10-minute oral report about state history, a child with a severe speech impairment that prevents an oral report from being fully understood should be allowed to present a visual report, to have her written report read out loud by a helper, or to use an augmentative communication device to deliver the report. A child with mild mental retardation might present an oral report with a simpler format or shorter length, according to his abilities.

As a parent, you'll want to talk to your child's teacher about the academic curriculum. Make sure that your child is being instructed in the skills, concepts, and facts needed to proceed in school.

In some states, children are required to meet certain benchmark standards to move on to the next grade level or to complete high school. High school diplomas are discussed further in the section "Graduation," later in this chapter, but you may be able to include a provision in your child's IEP regarding how any standardized achievement tests are handled. This may range from exempting the child from the testing requirement to insisting that the school provide extra academic help and/or test-taking accommodations.

Social opportunities

Another area often left out of IEP plans is opportunities for socialization and enrichment (see the section "Social skills training," later in the chapter). Again, you may be told that this is not part of special education. Because the primary deficit in autistic spectrum disorders is precisely in the area of socialization, however, this is emphatically *not* true where your child is concerned. The best place for children to learn appropriate social skills is in supervised activities with peers, and most schools make a plethora of these available to their students.

Linda, mother of 11-year-old William, says these opportunities have been a very important part of his development:

> William has had varying success with after-school activities and clubs, but even when the outcome fell short of our hopes we think he learned something. He tried Cub Scouts for awhile, but the meetings were not very structured. School chorus and being in school plays has been great, though.
>
> This year he helped with a large 6th-grade art project, sang in a Christmas pageant, and played soccer on a noncompetitive team. He also goes to a "homework club" after school, where he gets help with studying for his upcoming standardized tests, and he meets other kids at the library near his school to use the computers or read.

Ann, mother of 7-year-old Miles, says,

> An after-school program has been wonderful for Miles. He loves science, and they really stress sciences in this program. It has helped him with socialization, also.

In fact, under the Americans with Disabilities Act (ADA), all children with disabilities have the right to be involved in all school activities and clubs, not just classroom-based educational activities. This includes band, chess club, chorus, sports, camping trips, field trips, and any other activities of interest to your child that are school sponsored or school affiliated. If your child will need accommodations or support to take advantage of these activities, the IEP is where these should be listed. If you do not have an IEP, a 504 plan (see later in this chapter) can be used.

Socialization opportunities may also be available through community programs outside of school, such as Scouting or Special Olympics. You can write support for these activities in the IEP as well.

Signing the IEP . . . or not

When the IEP is complete, the accommodations page will include a list of each promise, information about where and when it will be met, and the name of the person responsible for delivering or ensuring the delivery of the service or accommodation. If the complete IEP is acceptable to everyone present, this is probably also where all team members sign on the dotted line.

You do not have to sign the IEP if it is not acceptable. This fact can't be emphasized enough! If the meeting has ended and you don't feel comfortable with the IEP as it is, you have the right to take home the current document and think about it (or discuss it with your spouse or an advocate) before you sign. You also have the right to set another IEP meeting, and another, and another, until it is truly complete. Don't hinder the process unnecessarily, of course, but also don't let yourself be steamrolled by the district. The IEP is about your child's needs, not the district's needs.

Needless to say, you should never sign a blank or unfinished IEP: It's a bit like signing a blank check. Certain school districts ask IEP meeting participants to sign an approval sheet before even talking about the IEP. Others are in the habit of taking notes for a prospective IEP and asking parents to sign an approval form at the end of the meeting, even though the goals, objectives, and accommodations have not been entered on an actual IEP form. This is not okay. If the district representatives insist you sign a piece of paper, make sure to add next to your name that you are signing because you were present, but that you have not agreed to a final document.

If your child already has an IEP in place from the previous year, this IEP will stay in place until the new one is finalized and signed. If your child does not, you may need to come to a partial agreement with the district while the IEP is worked out.

If the process has become contentious, be sure to bring an advocate to the next meeting. A good advocate can help smooth out the bumps in the IEP process while preserving your child's access to a free and appropriate education.

Classrooms that work

There are as many educational techniques and settings that work for kids with ASDs as there are children with these diagnoses. Some settings have a marked record of success, and parents would love to see these replicated.

Some characteristics of a successful classroom include the following:

- Caring, informed personnel
- Adequate ratio of children to classroom personnel
- Good rapport between classroom personnel, specialists, and parents
- Availability of appropriate teaching materials
- Individualized educational programming for each child with a disability
- Opportunities for interaction between children with ASDs and their normally developing peers
- Consideration for the sensory differences of autistic spectrum individuals

Most of these items take more time than money, and they can be implemented in a variety of settings. Two factors govern the choice of setting: the most appropriate educational program and the least restrictive environment (LRE). Typical special education settings follow, in order of their restrictiveness:

- **Regular classroom.** Also called a full-integration setting or mainstreaming, this is a regular classroom with nondisabled students. Your child would attend school with therapeutic services, classroom adaptations, and personal support, such as an aide, as needed. These services, adaptations, and supports must be written into the IEP. This is the least restrictive option.

- **Supported integrated classroom.** Also called a reverse integration setting because the nondisabled students are being integrated into a special program rather than the other way around, this specially created school setting brings together a group of children with disabilities and children without disabilities. Therapeutic services, classroom adaptations, and personal support are provided to each child with a disability according to his IEP. Children in a supported integrated classroom may have a variety of disabilities, such as developmental delay, Down syndrome, or cerebral palsy. Often autistic spectrum children are placed with children who have different speech and language disabilities, such as cleft palate, stuttering, and apraxia. Some supported integrated classrooms mix only children with ASDs and normally developing children. In these cases, the level of autistic behavior may range from severe to mild.

- **Special school classroom.** This is a specially created school setting for children with disabilities only. The children may have a mix of various disabilities, or all may be somewhere on the autistic spectrum. The classroom may be part of a larger school with other types of classrooms. Most districts have a range of classrooms available. There may be life skills classes geared toward teaching toileting, speech, and movement; classes for students with communications disorders; classes for children with behavior problems; and classes primarily for students who are developmentally delayed. It matters less what the class is called than what the teacher's philosophy and practices are.

- **Special school.** This is an entire school program created specifically to work with children who have disabilities. It may be owned and run by a public school district, or it may be a private school that contracts with the school district to provide services. If it is private, the school district should pay the full cost of tuition if it is judged to be the most appropriate setting for your child.

- **Home-based program.** Home-based programs are, as the name implies, delivered entirely or almost entirely in the student's home. Tutors approved by the district use appropriate curriculum to meet the IEP's requirements. Therapeutic services may be delivered in the home, or the student may travel to a clinical or school setting if possible and appropriate. For some older students on home instruction, tutors may choose to meet and work with their charges in a public library or another especially resource-rich location.

- **Hospital-based or residential care setting.** For special education students who are hospitalized or who have been placed in residential care for any reason, delivery of a free and appropriate public education according to their IEP is still mandatory.

In between these options are combination settings created to meet a student's specific needs. For example, a student with severe anxiety might be able to handle a half-day full-inclusion program in the morning, then have home-based instruction for other subjects in the afternoon. Another child might be placed in a special class for everything but art and music classes, which he would attend with normally developing peers.

Each child's needs are different, and they will likely change as your child progresses through school. The setting(s) listed in your child's IEP will be reviewed every year (or more often at your request) to ensure that the educational program is still meeting his needs, and that he is still in the least restrictive setting. Whenever possible, the current movement is toward full inclusion. This may or may not be appropriate for your child. If a less restrictive setting is proposed by the district, be open-minded enough to check it out, but don't say yes unless you're sure it's right. Inquire about supports, such as personal or classroom aides, that can be added to make inclusive settings more realistic.

Here are the experiences of several families in finding an appropriate setting for their school-aged children.

Joe, father of 7-year-old Kyle, says,

> Kyle was home-schooled this year using a modified Options Method program. We had our volunteers go from 10 to 2, so it was hard on my wife, who had to work with him all the other hours.

Linda says day treatment had both advantages and disadvantages:

> William spent a year and a half in a private day treatment program paid for by the school district. At first, we thought it would be awful because it was geared strictly toward SED kids. They had never had a child like him before.
>
> We had to work hard to ensure that his needs were met, but we had a cooperative, caring, wonderful teacher who went out of her way for him. We also had an excellent speech therapist, although there was no equipment for OT, PT, or adaptive physical education.
>
> The program was far from perfect due to high staff turnover and other factors, but since he was a "runner," the high security level was essential. It gave him a chance to stabilize after a horrible experience in a public-school "behavioral" kindergarten, get a real diagnosis, and go through some difficult medication trials in a safe environment.

Ann, mother of 8-year-old Theron, says he needs a more restrictive setting:

> My son attends a regular elementary school and has been mainstreamed in the past with only reading and math in special education. However, due to problems last school year he will be in a self-contained special education class, receiving all classes with a private tutor who has been hired exclusively for him.

Debbie, mother of 11-year-old Doug, is pleased with his special classroom:

> Doug goes to a regular elementary school, but is placed in a special life skills classroom. We are currently using the TEACCH method, and it's working very well with Doug. Also, the speech teacher started to introduce the PECS system to Doug at the end of the school year, and plans to continue with that when school starts again.

Cindy, mother of 15-year-old Jeffrey, says,

> Mainstream "full inclusion" type classes with the promise of
> modification and support were a disaster. Confined, modified
> environments (special day class with one teacher and an aide,
> one room, small class size) worked best.

Kim has found that a structured mainstream class works for 7-year-old Brad:

> Brad attends a regular, K–5 elementary school. The small group
> approach works best with Brad. The ideal situation would be for
> him to be home-schooled, due to distractions at school. If he is in a
> crowded classroom, he will zone out due to sensory overload.
>
> I would say that as far as teaching styles go, it is best for Brad's
> teacher to be strict and extremely structured. He is doing better than
> ever, because his teacher is having the kids sit down at their desks and
> do their work quietly. The disorganization of center-based learning,
> where a child learns with others at, let's say, a reading or math center,
> was disastrous.

The TEACCH method

TEACCH (*http://www.unc.edu/depts/teacch/*) stands for Treatment and Education of
Autistic and Related Communication Handicapped CHildren. Developed by Eric
Schopler in the early 1970s, this special system for educating autistic spectrum children began at the School of Psychiatry at the University of North Carolina in Chapel
Hill. It has since been adopted whole, or adapted for use, by schools around the
country. It is a highly structured program that integrates individualized classroom
methods, services delivered by outside community organizations, and support services for families.

The part of the TEACCH program most frequently implemented outside of North
Carolina is structured teaching. This approach hinges on careful classroom design,
scheduling, and using predictable teaching methods in a systematic way.

TEACCH has contributed many logical, workable ideas to the knowledge base on
educating people with autism. Nevertheless, it sometimes comes in for criticism. The
antipathy between adherents of the ABA approach and TEACCH fans sometimes
reaches a violently angry level. Certain TEACCH people have accused ABA proponents of forcing people with autistic spectrum disorders to fit into a "normal" mold

against their will, and of creating robotic rote thinkers with their repetitive drills. For their own part, ABA fans have accused TEACCH of having low expectations for autistic people and allowing school districts to base their programming on price rather than effectiveness.

The truth probably lies in neither camp. People involved on both sides have allowed their personal differences to become a vendetta, which certainly doesn't serve children. It would be far more logical to look at these approaches, and all other educational methods, in relationship to each child with an autistic spectrum disorder. The best approach for a specific child may be TEACCH methods, ABA, a combination of the two—or neither.

General classroom tips

When education majors are instructed in pedagogic technique, they're given this classroom model: control, curriculum, motivation, setting. In other words, a good teacher starts by maintaining control of the classroom, develops and/or provides an appropriate curriculum, motivates her students to do the work, and ensures that they have a good environment to do it in—in that order.

Autistic spectrum children's needs can turn this whole paradigm on its head. They often are uncontrollable unless the setting is correct, they won't pay attention to the curriculum unless properly motivated, and the curriculum itself (along with setting and motivation) is the key to maintaining control.

It can take a while for teachers to figure this out, especially teachers in newly integrated classrooms who have never before had a student on the autistic spectrum. In the meantime, chaos ensues and everyone will probably blame the child, the IEP, or the parents. See if your district can provide a regular consult service from a teacher experienced in working with children who have ASDs. This person can observe the situation, then give the frazzled teacher some good tips for turning it around.

One area where parents, teachers, and students can work closely together is developing a system for classwork and homework. Options range from using a single notebook with sections for each subject to color-coded schemes. Students with ASDs benefit greatly from homework checklists and other visual memory aids, including checklists broken down to show when parts of a long project, such as a book report, should be completed. They may need verbal reminders and increased oversight as well to successfully complete and turn in assignments.

Social skills training

Schools are the primary social venue for children, but many schools are unsure how to fit social skills into their curriculum. Community organizations that convey the social graces to nondisabled children, such as Scouting and religious youth groups, may be unprepared to deal with a child whose social skills are far behind those of his peers. And even children who interact well with their siblings may not carry these skills over easily to socializing with unfamiliar children and adults.

Not surprisingly, many children and adults with ASDs find themselves ostracized because of barbaric manners, inability to tackle the back-and-forth of playground games and conversation, and difficulty reading common social cues. It's not their fault—these skills do not come naturally to people on the autistic spectrum, and parents are usually so busy teaching other essentials that messy eating habits and such are the least of their worries. But true inclusion in the workplace and community is elusive for people without positive social skills.

Some people may be surprised to learn that many adults with ASDs are avid readers of books about etiquette, protocol, and body language. These books spell out the things that everyone else seems to know. Others take courses in psychology, or tackle self-help books that promise to teach readers how to be successful in work, life, and love. Depending on the book or course, this can be a good approach for many adults.

Skill areas that some people with ASDs may need to work on follow.

- Maintaining appropriate eye contact
- Maintaining appropriate body space
- Developing a sense of empathy for others
- Giving and receiving complements
- Sharing interests and other strategies for making friends
- Decoding facial expressions and body language
- Using facial expressions and body language
- Learning conversational techniques, including openers and closers
- Determining whether a topic is appropriate for discussion
- Learning table manners
- Understanding rules for community activities, such as riding the bus or going to a movie

- Understanding dating and sexual etiquette
- Learning grooming techniques and expectations
- Interacting with authority figures
- Using observation to determine appropriate behavior, dress, and manners in a new social situation

Developing and using self-calming techniques is one of the most important social skills. These techniques help people develop a self-righting mechanism of sorts, preventing embarrassing meltdowns that lead to ostracism.

Many schools implement friendship clubs or social skills clubs. These are small, adult-supervised groups of children brought together to help one or more children in the group learn appropriate social behavior. The adult leader—and eventually the other children—acts as a social skills coach.

Social stories are a good mechanism for teaching appropriate social behavior. This special kind of storytelling was originally developed by educator Carol Gray. Social stories provide a narrative about events that are going to happen or should happen. They are short, easy to remember, and can be told over and over to help a person internalize what's expected. A sample of a social story follows.

James Is a Good Bus Rider

When James gets ready for school in the morning, he has his coat and backpack ready before the school bus arrives.

When the bus comes, he gives his mom a hug and gets on the bus right away.

James sits in the seat right behind the driver as soon as he gets on the bus. He puts on his seat belt. Then he puts his backpack on his lap.

Sometimes James talks to his friends when he is riding the bus. They talk quietly.

Sometimes James draws pictures or looks at a book while he is riding the bus. He puts his paper, crayons, and books in his backpack when the bus gets to school.

If someone bothers James on the bus, he asks the bus driver for help.

When the bus gets to school, James gets off the bus first. He waits with Mr. Smith until all the other children have gotten off the bus, and then they walk to class in a line.

You'll notice that the story is about all the good things that James does, or should do, on the bus. It isn't a list of "don'ts," no matter how tempting it might be to add a line like "James doesn't hit or bite the other children on the bus."

"Sometimes" lines such as the ones in the story example can be very important for children on the autistic spectrum, who have a tendency to get stuck in very specific routines. These lines emphasize the idea of flexibility: Sometimes we do X, and sometimes we do Y.

Some parents and teachers like to set social stories to music, which can make them even easier to remember. Others make them into picture books with illustrations or photographs. For example, James might be asked to act out his bus social story while a teacher or parent takes some instant photos. Then the book can be written out one line to a page, with an illustration for each line. Thick paper and lamination can be used to protect social stories that children want to carry with them.

Social stories can work well for people of all ages, even teenagers and adults.

Social skills work may actually be harder today than it was 50 years ago, despite everything we've learned about behavior and human development. The rules of society are in flux everywhere, and lessons learned at home or in the classroom may not be reinforced in everyday life. As some people with ASDs take rules very seriously, this can make their lives difficult. Playgrounds are full of inappropriate language and behavior, diners at fast food restaurants wolf their food down sloppily as though no one were looking, rudeness abounds on television, and the freeway is full of drivers who break the rules. Knowing the rules is important, but you also need to know that you can't control the behavior of others.

Monitoring progress

Once you have an educational program in place, your next job is ensuring that it is delivered. You can't rely totally on the school or school district to monitor your child's progress or ensure compliance with his IEP. Keep a copy of this document and other important notes at hand, and check them against any communications notebooks, progress reports, report cards, and other information that comes home from the school or that your child tells you about activities, therapies, and results.

Of course you'll want to attend all official meetings, but make a point of just dropping by occasionally on the pretext of bringing your child her coat or having paperwork due at the school office. If you can volunteer an hour a week or so in the school (not necessarily in your child's classroom), even better.

If the school is not complying with the IEP, start by talking to the teacher and work your way up. Most problems can be addressed at the classroom level.

One area that can be especially difficult is monitoring the delivery of therapeutic services. This task may seem simple, but many parents report that their school district refuses to provide any type of checklist that parents can see to make sure their child is receiving the services listed in the IEP. If your child is verbal, just ask. If she isn't, that should clinch your need for getting this essential information in writing from the school.

Another problem area is the administration of medication at school. Some parents report refusal to deliver medication at the appointed time, mysteriously missing pills (especially Ritalin and other amphetamines), and missed or mistaken doses. Most self-contained classrooms have many children who take scheduled medications, and they tend to have processes in place. The worst medication problems seem to occur in full-inclusion settings, especially if the student is not capable of monitoring medication delivery himself. You may need to insist on a daily checklist, and increase your own monitoring efforts.

If your IEP includes academic goals, see if there are standardized ways to monitor progress. Too often parents are told that their child is participating well and learning, and then, when an objective measure is used, they discover he has not gained new skills or has actually regressed.

Be sure to praise your child's teacher and service providers when your child makes progress, even if it's small. People who feel appreciated work harder. Besides, we need to encourage the good guys!

Extended school year services

If your child needs a consistent educational and therapeutic program year round, most school districts will only provide services during summer vacations and other long breaks if you can document his need for extended school year (ESY) services. This requires special attention to monitoring how your child copes with breaks in the school routine. Teachers and service providers can help you amass the evidence you need to show that your child loses skills or regresses behaviorally after being out of school for more than a weekend. During breaks from school, keep your own log of behaviors and regressions, if any.

Some parents have also been able to qualify their children for ESY services by showing that services available during the summer satisfy parts of the IEP not addressed adequately during the school year. For example, a student might be able to get ESY funding approved for a special summer program geared toward teaching social skills or independent living skills to people with ASDs.

Dealing with behavioral dilemmas

Because of recent episodes of violence, many US schools are taking a hard line on verbal threats, aggressive or assaultive behavior, and even on the presence of students with behavioral, emotional, or neurological disorders in schools. In some cases, this campaign has crossed over from prudent caution to violating the rights of special education students. For example, some districts have announced that all assaults (a category that includes hitting, biting, and even playground pushing) will result in police being called to actually arrest the student. Students have been suspended or threatened with expulsion for angrily saying things like "I wish this school would burn down" or even for singing that traditional student song that begins with the line "Mine eyes have seen the glory of the burning of the school," which has probably been part of American childhood folklore for 100 years.

According to IDEA, students with disabilities are subject to discipline for infractions of school rules just like all other students—unless the problem is a result of the disability. For example, it would be unfair to suspend a child with Tourette's syndrome for having a spitting tic, even though spitting would normally be a rule violation. Likewise, it would be wrong to expel or arrest a student for biting a classroom aide if his assaultive behaviors were related to an autistic spectrum disorder.

At the same time, schools do have a duty to protect other students, faculty, and staff. Case law has upheld the idea that if a student cannot be safely maintained in a less restrictive setting, the district has the right to place the student in a more restrictive setting. The devil is in the details, of course. Parents in these situations find they carry the burden of proving that the district did not do all it could to keep the student in the least restrictive setting.

If you or the school suspects that your child's misbehavior is the result of her disability, a functional behavior assessment (FBA) and a functional intervention plan (FIP) are the correct response. The FBA should include the following items:

- A clear description of the problem behavior, including the pattern or sequence of behavior observed
- Time and place when the behavior occurs (setting and antecedents)
- The current consequences attached to the behavior
- A hypothesis about the cause and effect of the behavior
- Direct observation data

The FIP should derive from the FBA and should consist of guidelines for modifying the student's environment to eliminate or improve behavior, as well as ideas for teaching the student positive alternative behavior. Creating a workable FIP may require trying several hypotheses about the behavior and then testing different interventions. This procedure should be followed whenever a special education student has a long-lasting behavior problem or has any behavior problem that puts him in danger of suspension, expulsion, or arrest.

For example, in the situation cited earlier where a child has a spitting tic, the FIP could include several ideas for handling the problem. The child could go to the bathroom to spit, use a trash can, or spit into a handkerchief. Adults could see if stress is increasing tics and then reduce stress, or try a different medication for tic reduction. For the child who bites, an FBA could find out why the child is doing so, and an FIP could provide ways to prevent the behavior.

Suspension and expulsion

If a student covered by an IEP is suspended for more than 10 days in one school year or is expelled, the district is responsible for finding an appropriate alternative educational setting immediately, and continuing to implement the IEP. Suspension of a disabled student for more than 10 days requires parental permission or a court order. The district is also required to do an FBA and create a FIP if this has not already been done, or to take a new look at the existing FIP in light of the incident.

Suspensions longer than 10 days constitute a change of placement, which means an IEP meeting must be called immediately. IDEA does not spell out exactly how this procedure should work, so districts may not have a plan in place to deal with emergency placements. Parents report that many school districts respond by putting the student on homebound instruction until a new placement can be found. This may or may not be acceptable. Delivery of therapeutic services can be a problem on homebound instruction. To prevent the search process from dragging on too long, parents will probably have to get involved.

For the purpose of these protections, the category of disabled students includes not only those with a special education IEP or other formal agreement with the district, but also those students whose parents have requested special education assessment or written a letter of concern about the child to school personnel (if the parent is illiterate or cannot write, a verbal inquiry will suffice) before the incident occurred, students whose behavior and performance should have indicated a disability to any objective observer, and children about whom district personnel have expressed disability-related concern before the incident.

Expulsion is an even more serious matter. Parents must be informed in writing about the district's intention to seek expulsion, and this document must include clear reasons for this action, evidence, and information about the child's procedural rights. There must be an assessment before expulsion can take place, and parents must also be informed of this in writing. Only if all safeguards are provided and all procedures are followed can a disabled student be expelled.

Expulsion does not mean the same thing for a disabled student as it does for a garden-variety miscreant, who may simply be kicked out to rot in front of the TV at home. It's more like a forced change of placement. By expelling the student, the district has determined that the current placement is not working. It must then find an appropriate placement, which means revisiting the IEP.

504 plans

Some children with ASDs may not qualify for special education services, based on the district's evaluation. You should probably appeal the evaluation, but while you wait for the appeals process to move forward, your child is still eligible for some special services under Section 504 of the Rehabilitation Act of 1973. These services and accommodations are written into a document colloquially known as a 504 plan.

In fact, some special education advocates recommend that parents request a 504 evaluation at the same time they start the IEP process. This can mean asking the 504 coordinator to attend your IEP meetings. It may confuse your district, because it isn't a common practice, but it'll save time in obtaining services and accommodations if services are denied under IDEA and parents have to appeal.

Unlike special education eligibility, Section 504 eligibility is not based on having a certain type of disability. Instead, it is based on these factors:

1. Having a physical or mental impairment that substantially limits a major life activity, such as learning (note that, in contrast to IDEA regulations, learning is not the only activity that applies: 504 plans can cover other major life activities, such as breathing, walking, and socialization)

2. Having a record of such an impairment, such as a medical diagnosis

3. Being regarded as having such an impairment

A 504 plan can put many helpful procedures in place, such as medication delivery, exemption from timed tests, or the provision of a classroom aide. Teachers and school administrators usually do not accord 504 plans the status of an IEP, but they have equal legal weight. In fact, 504 plans have a certain advantage, because you can appeal them at a state level without going through several district procedures first, as you must with a due process complaint over an IEP.

A 504 plan can be very good for ensuring that certain procedures are followed if your child has a difficult behavior episode at school. Many children with ASDs who have progressed well enough to be in a full-inclusion setting still experience an occasional meltdown. These episodes of anxiety, rage, or unusual behavior may occur in response to stress, fear, teasing, illness, missed medications, or even from eating a food the child is sensitive to. You can develop a response plan in advance and put it in place via a 504 plan, ensuring it's there just in case. Other excellent uses for a 504 plan include medication arrangements, planning for communication between home and school, classroom accommodations, requiring certain organization systems for homework and books, requiring special training for personnel, ensuring socialization opportunities, and bringing in outside agencies as part of your education team.

If you apply for 504 status and are still denied services, appeal this decision to your state's Office of Civil Rights (OCR). If your child has been medically diagnosed with an autistic spectrum disorder, a 504 plan is the very least he qualifies for. Even students with mild ADHD or occasional asthma attacks qualify for services under a 504 plan. Under no circumstances should your child be denied this limited protection, no matter how "high functioning" he may be.

Taking on the school system

What can you do when the school district refuses your child a free and appropriate public education? Your options include the following:

- Sitting back and letting it happen (obviously, not recommended)
- Advocating for your child within the classroom and the IEP process
- Bringing in an expert to help you advocate for your child
- Requesting a due process hearing
- Organizing with other parents to advocate for a group of students with similar problems
- Working with other advocates at a legislative level
- Going to court

Most school problems can be worked out with the teacher or within the IEP system. Although some school districts have a well-deserved reputation for venality, most are simply hampered by a lack of resources and knowledge. An informed parent can make a difference. Give them information about educational possibilities, and let them know that the resource problem is something to take up with government funding sources, not to penalize children with.

Bringing in an expert can do much to tip the scales in your favor. All over the country educational advocates and self-styled IEP experts are becoming available. Some of these people work for disability advocacy organizations or disability law firms. Others are freelance practitioners. Some are parents of children with disabilities who have turned their avocation into a vocation.

You may have to pay for expert services. Services can include researching programs available in your area, connecting you with appropriate resources, helping you write a better IEP, and advocating for your child at IEP meetings and due process hearings.

Due process

The words "due process" are guaranteed to strike fear into the hearts of school district bureaucrats. In fact, some parents have gotten a lot of mileage out of conspicuously placing a folder marked "Due Process" on the table during IEP meetings. "Due process" usually refers to a due process hearing: an internal appeals procedure used by school districts to determine whether or not special education procedures have been handled properly—in other words, whether the child and his family have been given access to the processes that they are due under the law.

The due process hearing will hinge on whether the district has followed federal- and state-mandated procedures for evaluating a child for special education and setting up a program for that child. Violations can include small things, such as notifying parents of a meeting over the phone rather in writing, or major issues, such as using untrained or incompetent personnel to evaluate children or deliberately denying needed services to save money.

Issues that tend to end up in due process include disagreements over evaluations or educational labels, provision of inadequate therapeutic services, placement in inappropriate educational settings, noncompliance with the IEP, lack of extended school year services when appropriate, and poor transition planning.

Obviously, every due process case is unique. Each state also has its own due process system. All these systems have certain regulations in common:

- Parents must initiate a due process hearing in writing.
- The hearing must take place in a timely fashion.

- An impartial person who doesn't work for the district presides over hearings.
- Children have the right to stay in the current placement until after the hearing (this is called the "stay put" rule).
- Parents can attend due process hearings and advocate for their child.
- Parents can hire an educational advocate or lawyer to represent them at the due process hearing.
- If the parents use a lawyer and they win, they are entitled to have their legal fees paid by the district.

Due process hearings resemble a court hearing before a judge. Both sides argue their case and present evidence. Both sides can call on experts or submit documents to buttress their statements. However, experienced advocates know that despite the veneer of impartiality, if it comes down to your word against the district's, the district will probably have an edge.

Some districts offer a less formal procedure: arbitration, also called mediation. In an arbitration hearing, both parties agree in advance to comply with the arbitrator's ruling. You can't recover your legal fees in arbitration, and your rights are not spelled out in the law. Be very cautious about agreeing to waive your right to a due process hearing in favor of arbitration. You can pursue mediation while waiting for your due process hearing. That way, if mediation works, you're done, and if it doesn't, everything is in motion for due process.

Public advocacy

Some problems in special education are systemic, and changes are needed at the top. Parents can band together to get better services for children on the autistic spectrum. The organization Families for Early Autism Treatment (FEAT), for example, works to make ABA programs and similar intensive interventions a part of state and provincial Early Intervention programs.

You may choose to form your own organization, join an existing group covering ASD-related issues, or work with a larger group of special education parents. If you're looking for potential allies, see the organizations in Appendix B, *Support and Advocacy*. You may also find allies in teacher's unions and organizations, regular parents' associations, and elsewhere in your community.

If you're not the kind of person who enjoys conflict, advocacy and due process can be very draining. School districts count on endless meetings, criticism of your parenting skills, and constant references to their superior knowledge about your child to wear down your defenses. Be open to logical compromises and the possibility of beneficial alliances, but hold your ground when it's important.

Sarah, mother of 2-year-old Elaine, says,

> *I'm the mother, I know what my child needs! Sometimes my husband is just too easy—he would let people just have their way as not to have any type of conflict. But I want what my daughter has coming to her, and I want it now. I'm her strongest supporter. I will not let the school system push me around!*

Going to court

Due process is bad enough. Going to court is absolutely, positively your last recourse. It's something you do only when nothing else works, not even marching on a school board meeting with a bunch of disgruntled parents. Going to court is time consuming, exhausting, and expensive. The outcome is uncertain, and while the case drags on, your child may be languishing in an inappropriate setting. Sometimes it just has to happen, though, as the now infamous 1994 case *W.B. v. Matula* makes clear.

In this case, a New Jersey kindergartner was refused appropriate assessment for special education services, given a grossly inappropriate placement, and punished for actions and conditions related to his disability. He was later refused appropriate interventions based on an incomplete evaluation, from which some documents were withheld from the parents. He was later diagnosed with severe neurological impairments, including Tourette's syndrome, obsessive-compulsive disorder, ADHD, and specific learning disabilities (he also had marked symptoms of an autistic spectrum disorder, although this was not diagnosed). His mother filed for a due process hearing and won at that level, but the district refused to comply with the edicts of its own due process hearing officer.

As a result, his mother was forced to obtain evaluations and diagnostic help at her own expense, provide her increasingly emotionally disturbed child with psychiatric care at her own expense, and watch her child regress because of improper educational placement and procedures. Eventually she won a second due process hearing, after which she sued the district for violating federal education law and on constitutional grounds under the Fourteenth Amendment, which entitles all citizens to equal protection under the law. To the consternation of school districts everywhere, she won her case and a substantial financial judgment.

The *Matula* case put school districts on notice that parents of special needs children can successfully pursue them beyond the due process hearing. Besides the federal education laws and constitutional grounds used in the *Matula* case, parents may be able to ask the courts for redress under state education laws or even contract law. There are few legal precedents as yet, but the number of successful legal challenges is growing.

Private schools

As noted earlier in this chapter, school districts sometimes contract with private schools and programs to provide services that the districts do not. These programs are usually not religious in nature (there are a few exceptions, such as residential programs that are affiliated with a religious denomination), and they must be willing to comply with district regulations.

Sometimes parents have good reasons to opt for private school placement directly, at their own cost. Perhaps daily religious instruction is very important to you, or your child's siblings already attend a private school. Luckily, choosing a private school does not automatically disqualify your child from publicly funded Early Intervention and special education services.

To receive these services, your child must be evaluated and qualified within the public system. His IFSP or IEP will determine which services will be delivered, where they will be delivered, and by whom. This can get sticky, depending on your state or local district. Some districts are so cautious about maintaining separation of church and state that if several children in a religious school need speech therapy, they will deliver speech therapy in a "speech van" parked outside the school rather than allowing a public employee to help children inside the walls of a parochial school. Other districts have no qualms about sending employees to private school sites.

Unlike public schools, private schools are not required to fulfill any academic promises made in an IEP. The IEP is a contract between you and the school district only. However, private schools that wish to better serve students with disabilities are well aware of how valuable the ideas in a well-written IEP can be. Some private schools encourage teachers to be part of the IEP process. In some cases, these private school representatives have entered their own goals into the IEP, usually under the aegis of the parent. Private schools that accept any form of public funding may be subject to additional regulations. Most are also subject to the Americans with Disabilities Act.

Not everyone has a rosy private school experience. The school that served your other children well may be horribly wrong for a child with an autistic spectrum disorder. Educational programming for children with ASDs requires a certain level of knowledge and flexibility that not all schools have, public or private. You can advocate until you're blue in the face, but in the end, private schools do not *have* to take your child.

Home-schooling

Educating your children at home is legal in most US states. Each state has its own regulations about who can home-school, what (if anything) must be taught, and how (or if) children's learning will be tested. If these regulations include standardized testing, exceptions to the testing requirements for disabled children are usually not written into the law. You will want to be very careful about doing baseline testing and documenting reasons why a child may not do well on standardized tests, if they are required.

Eligible home-schooled children are entitled to Early Intervention and special education services. These services may be delivered in the child's home, at a neutral site, or in a nearby school or clinic.

Some districts have programs to help home-schooling parents create good programs for children with disabilities, whereas others go out of their way to make it difficult. In most states, home-schoolers can take part in extracurricular activities at their neighborhood public school, or even take some classes while doing the bulk of their schoolwork at home.

If you are home-schooling children with social deficits, it's important to set up socialization opportunities. Many home-schooling families share teaching duties with other parents, bringing several children together for certain lessons or activities.

If you are *forced* to home-school your child because your district cannot or will not provide an appropriate educational placement, you may be eligible to be paid to teach your child. This has been the case for certain parents in very rural areas, as well as for parents in more populated districts that could not provide a safe setting for a child with assaultive behaviors or a tendency to run away.

Transition planning

Transition planning should begin in the early years of high school, when the student's peers are beginning to gain work skills and amass credits toward high school graduation. Special education students have a right to be prepared for graduation, higher education, and work in ways that fit their needs. Most need extra support to make a smooth transition from high school to adulthood. The transition plan should address high school graduation, higher education, and work skills and opportunities. It may also include helping the student apply for supported housing and other benefits, learn how to manage his medical and psychiatric care, and gain skills such as budgeting, driving, and cooking.

Graduation

Many students with ASDs will be headed for a regular high school diploma. This usually requires passing a certain number of specified courses. If the student needs changes in the graduation requirements—for example, a speech-impaired student faced with a foreign language requirement might ask that the requirement be waived, or might ask that fluency in sign language be allowed to substitute for foreign language proficiency—now's the time to arrange for these changes.

Some students need extra coursework to make it through high school, such as special instruction in keyboarding or study skills. These abilities also help with higher education or work later on.

Some students will not be able to earn a regular diploma. A special form of graduation called an IEP or "adapted" diploma is also available. If a student earns an IEP diploma, that means he has completed all the objectives set out in his IEP for graduation.

A general equivalency diploma (GED), which is earned by passing an examination, may be an option for some other students.

Students who are headed for college may want or need to go beyond the basic high school diploma. If your state has a special diploma for advanced students, such as Oregon's Certificate of Advanced Mastery or New York's Regents Diploma, check early on about accommodations needed for the examination or portfolio process for these credentials. Some states (including Oregon, as of this writing, but not New York) have refused to permit accommodations. This is patently illegal and will surely be successfully challenged. If you don't want to be the one to bring the challenge, ask instead for special tutoring before the test.

In the UK, Australia, New Zealand, and Ireland, special help may be available to help teens pass their level exams, including modified exams in some cases. Talk to your education authority for more information about options in your area.

Work

Preparing for the world of work means gaining appropriate skills, such as typing, filing, driving, filling out forms, using tools, cooking, or lifting. These skills may be gained in school-based vocational or technical classes, in classes taken at a community college or vocational school while the student is still in high school, in a union- or employer-sponsored apprenticeship program, via job shadowing arrangements or internships, or on the job. Vocational planning is mandatory for special education students in the US by age 16, and should really be undertaken much earlier.

Transition-to-work services may include moving into the public vocational rehabilitation system, which trains and places adults with disabilities into jobs. However, in many states this system is severely overloaded, with wait times for placement ranging from three months to three years or more. Typical opportunities range from "sheltered workshop" jobs (splitting kindling wood, sorting recyclables, light assembly work) under direct supervision, to supported placement in the community as grocery clerks, office helpers, chip-fabrication plant workers, and the like. Often the person works with a job coach who helps him learn work skills and how to handle workplace stresses. In some cases, the job coach actually comes to work with the person for awhile.

School districts may sponsor their own supported work opportunities, such as learning how to run an espresso coffee cart or working in a student-run horticultural business. Many schools have vocational programs that give students a chance to have a mentor in their chosen field, and that may include actual work experience with local employers.

Some public and private agencies may also be able to help with job training and placement, such as the state employment department, the Opportunities Industrialization Commission, and the Private Industry Council. Goodwill Industries also operates a job placement service in many larger cities.

Students with disabilities should receive appropriate vocational counseling, including aptitude testing, discussion of interests and abilities, and information about work possibilities. Parents need to ensure that students are not shunted into dead-end positions that will leave them financially vulnerable as adults.

Higher education

Students planning to attend trade school, sixth-form college, a two-year community college program, or university need information far in advance on high school courses or exams required for entry. This is especially important for those students with disabilities who carry a lighter course load, as they may need to make up some credits in summer school or via correspondence courses.

Transition programs should address the move from high school to trade school, community college, or a university program. Students are eligible for publicly funded education and/or services until age 22 if needed. Tuition in some programs may be covered for some students, in full or in part. Special education services and help for students with learning disabilities are available on campus and in the dorms at many colleges.

It's against the law to deny admission to students based on disabilities; of course, other admission criteria generally must be met. Public universities and community colleges may waive some admission criteria for disabled students on a case-by-case basis if the student can show that he is capable of college-level work. For example, if his poor hand coordination made getting a high score on the SAT difficult but he will have a classroom aide available at college to make up for this problem, he might be admitted despite the low score. Standardized test requirements might also be set aside if high school grades or the student's work portfolio look good.

Schools that normally require all freshmen to live on campus may waive this requirement for a student with special needs. If living at home is not an option, a group home or supervised apartment near campus might be. Before your child leaves for college in another city, make sure that you have secured safe and appropriate housing, found competent local professionals to provide ongoing care, and rehearsed daily life activities such as grocery shopping and visiting the laundromat. You'll also want to work out a crisis plan with your child, just in case things go wrong. She will want to know who to call and where to go.

Education in Canada

The Canadian special education process is very similar to that used in the US. Provincial guidelines are set down by the national Ministry of Education and governed by the Education Act, but most decisions are made at the regional, district, or school level. Evaluations are done by a team that may include a school district psychologist, a behavior specialist, a special education teacher, other school or district personnel, and in some cases a parent, although the latter is not required by law as it is in the US.

Children between the ages of 6 and 22 may qualify for special education assistance under the Designated Disabled Program (DDP), the Special Needs Program (SNP), or the Targeted Behaviour Program (TBP), depending on the labels they receive in evaluation. The evaluation is used as a basis for an individualized education program (IEP), which is usually updated yearly or more frequently if needed. A formal review is required every three years.

Rae, mother of 13-year-old D'Arcy, says,

> *We have IEPs, but they don't have quite the same clout here that they appear to have under the US legislation. What you have to trumpet here is the legal requirement, under human rights legislation, that disability be "accommodated." For us, the school counselor is being very helpful, as is the district behavior specialist. I'm doing some research on the actual legal requirements so that I know just how much I can demand.*
>
> *I've found the most effective resource is to be a pleasant, informed, persistent, somewhat annoying pest.*

A full range of placement options is available for Canadian students, from home-based instruction to full inclusion. Partial inclusion is increasingly common, as is supported mainstreaming. Students from rural or poorly served areas may be sent to a residential school, or funding may be provided for room and board to allow the student to attend a day program outside of her home area.

If disputes arise between the school or the district and the parents, there is a School Division Decision Review Process available for adjudicating them. The concept known as due process in the US is usually referred to as fundamental justice in Canada.

Education in the UK

When a child in the UK is judged eligible for special education services, he is said to be statemented. This term refers to an IEP-like document called a Statement of Special Educational Needs. This document is developed at the council level by the Local Educational Authority (LEA), and lists the services that a statemented child needs. Usually the team that creates the statement includes an educational psychologist, a teacher, and the parents. It may also include the family's health visitor or other personnel, such as a speech therapist, physiotherapist, occupational therapist, or child development specialist. The statement is reviewed and updated annually. Disability advocates strongly urge parents to get expert help with the statementing process, as there are several stages of evaluation and provision before the process is complete.

For 11-year-old William, the statementing process took about six months:

> *We enrolled our son in a small, traditional-minded mainstream school. Although he already had test results and medical reports, he had to be evaluated by an educational psychologist and speech therapist all over again.*

He is now statemented and receiving help from an aide for a few hours each week, speech consultation services for the school through the NHS, and occasional help with social skills from a pastoral care worker at school. The school head said the process can take years, however, if you aren't persistent.

Your LEA can limit services according to its budget, even if those services are listed as necessary on your child's statement. Service availability varies widely between LEAs. Some therapeutic services, such as speech therapy, may also be available through National Health.

School placements in the UK run the gamut from residential schools to specialist schools to full inclusion in mainstream schools. There are more residential options available than in the US system, because of the English tradition of public schools.

Schools working with statemented students operate under a government Code of Practice that is analogous to, but much weaker than, the federal IDEA in the US. Parents and disability advocates can insist that LEAs follow this code when devising programs for statemented students, and have access to a formal appeals process. European human rights laws also apply in some situations.

The UK government has recently taken steps toward improving Early Intervention offerings. Currently, EI services are not mandated by law, although they are available in many areas through the Sure Start scheme, among others.

Parents report that home-schooling a child with a disability is particularly hard in some parts of the UK. Regular inspection by an educational welfare officer is required, and some of these bureaucrats are not very knowledgeable about disabilities. Parents should be prepared to document their child's educational experiences and learning progress.

The Autism UK web site (*http://www.autism-uk.ed.ac.uk/*) provides many pointers for parents.

Education in Australia

Australia's system is paradoxically looser and yet more accommodating to students with disabilities of all sorts. There is only a thin legal framework for the provision of special education services, but in the urban areas where most Australians live, these services are apparently no harder to obtain than they are in the UK. Early Intervention services are usually readily available in urban areas for children age 6 and under, including EI services specifically for students with autism. To obtain an EI evaluation, parents should contact the Specialist Children's Services Team at their local Department of Human Services.

Placement options for older children include residential schools (including placement in residential schools located in the UK, for some students), special schools for children with moderate to severe developmental delay or autistic spectrum disorder, special classrooms for disabled children within regular schools, and the full range of mainstreaming options. "Mix and match" placements that allow students to be mainstreamed for just part of the day are still rare, however. For students in rural areas, there is a traveling teacher service focused on autism and other disabilities.

There are federal regulations regarding special education, but most regulatory action takes place through each state's Department of Education, Training, and Employment (DETS), or at a local or school level. Each DETS provides information, parent services, assistive technology, augmentative communication, special curricula, and other services for students with disabilities.

The Autism Victoria web site (*http://avoca.vicnet.net.au/~autism/*) offers links to a number of excellent education-related resources throughout Australia.

Kerry, mother of 12-year-old Kim, says,

> We don't have anything like IEPs, and I think that there are some cultural factors involved in the way disability is approached here. I've been trying to put my finger on just what it is . . . I think it has to do with the fact that Australian society is less "harsh" than American society. There's a bit more sense of cooperation and caring for the underdog. People don't talk as much about "rights," don't sue each other very often, etc. (though it is happening more). Perhaps there has been less need to label kids because there is somewhat less tendency to isolate and discriminate.
>
> I'm not saying that there aren't huge problems for kids with differences (especially subtle differences which aren't at all obvious); however, I think that people here tend to expect to talk things through with schools and teachers and make informal arrangements. There's an expectation of reasonableness, in many cases. I get to know teachers on a personal level and explain about Kim's differences.
>
> On the one hand we have less bureaucratization of services and more individual innovation, on the other hand we have less services altogether.

Education in New Zealand

Students who have qualified for special education services in New Zealand are said to be "section nined" (old terminology) or "qualified for the Ongoing Resourcing Scheme" (ORS). ORS qualification is currently reserved for those children whose impairment is judged to be "high" or "very high," with the most resources going to the latter group. As of this writing, special education services for early childhood centers and home-based programs are not funded. Nevertheless, some young children with ASDs receive Early Intervention services through special arrangement, in a clinical setting, or in home-based programs.

The Ministry of Education sets up qualifying guidelines for early childhood and school-age special education services. The Autistic Association of New Zealand (*http://www.autismnz.org.nz/*) provides parent education, expert evaluation services, educational and vocational advocacy, and other direct services.

Recent news reports indicate that limited local resources and a move to push for full inclusion under the Special Education 2000 program has eliminated many special education resources that were once available in New Zealand's schools. Autistic spectrum children are said to be highly represented in the large group that is now being denied ORS funding.

School placements include a few special schools, attached special education units within regular schools, and a range of inclusion options in mainstream settings. Some students are in residential settings. Under Special Education 2000, many more schools will have a resource-room-like arrangement rather than self-contained special education units.

Since the death of an autistic girl in 1997, lifespan services for autistic spectrum individuals in New Zealand have been getting a closer look. Seventeen-year-old Casey Albury was killed by her mother, who cracked under the strain of caring for her without the availability of respite or other needed services.

Changing educational paradigms

No matter where you go in the world, there's an increasing emphasis on intensive intervention early in life and a wider spectrum of services for older children and adults with ASDs as well. At the same time, most school systems are struggling with budget restrictions.

How these conflicting forces will affect educational service offerings for children on the autistic spectrum remains to be seen.

CHAPTER 10

Family Issues and Support

THERE'S A COMMON MYTH THAT A CHILD'S DISABILITY brings a family together, but divorce rates are actually twice as high in families dealing with disability or serious illness as they are in the rest of the population. The attention and effort required tears apart parents, siblings, extended families, and friendships. Extra stress magnifies the normal difficulties that family relationships face. People often need help to work through blame, guilt, sorrow, and fear when they get in the way of healthy relationships.

This chapter looks at issues families face when a member has an autistic spectrum disorder, and coping strategies that have worked for other families. It explores how to keep talking, how to accept a partner who has a different approach, finding time for each other and for other children, and caring for older relatives when you are also responsible for a child with an ASD.

It also covers financial issues, one of the greatest stresses families coping with ASDs face, including government programs and other resources that can help. Finally, it looks at linking up with others for mutual support.

Most of the material in this chapter applies to parents or to professionals who work directly with families. Some adults with ASDs will benefit from the information on disability support programs, and may find other sections help them better understand their own family dynamics.

Welcome to Holland?

There's a parable about accepting children with disabilities that regularly makes the rounds of support group newsletters and Internet discussion groups. Written by Emily Perl Kingsley, "Welcome to Holland" (Kingsley, 1987) talks about the experience of planning a trip to Italy but accidentally ending up in Holland, which doesn't have the Colosseum or Michelangelo's David, but does have lovely tulips and Rembrandt. Holland is different, but it's good in its own way—just like your child with a disability.

Although many parents have found this fable comforting, others feel patronized by well-meaning advice that encourages them to simply accept their lot.

Krista, mother of 7-year-old Joshua, says,

> I look at that "Welcome to Holland" pap piece and think, "What the
> hell do they mean? Try 'Welcome to Bosnia'!"

When you are encouraged to accept your situation, even to see it as a gift, it can make
you think you don't have the right to be mad—but you do. No one deserves to have
a disability, and no one deserves to have their life turned upside down by caring for
someone else who does. On one level, you do have to accept the situation. On
another, you cannot, and must not if you are to have the energy and determination to
help yourself or your child.

You may feel surprisingly angry if you're told that God or nature has chosen you for
the "special" duty of parenting a child with a disability. People usually mean these
words as a compliment, but they can add to internal feelings of being trapped in a
role you never asked for, and to feelings of inadequacy.

As Krista's comments indicate, disability can turn family life into a battlefield. Looking at the carnage through rose-colored glasses isn't always an option.

Family strife

Mary Callahan's book *Fighting for Tony* is a fine portrait of how an ASD diagnosis can
affect a family. Whether you agree with Callahan's theories about the causes of her
son's autistic behavior or not, her description of a marriage disintegrating under
pressure will be sadly familiar to many. As her son's mysterious illness pitched the
Callahans into repeated battles with doctors, the school system, and each other, a solid
and loving relationship was destroyed by the pressure. This true story has a happy
ending—not only did Callahan "recover" her son, but she and her husband eventually recovered their marriage.

Another poignant portrait of autism's effects on the family is *Family Pictures,* a novel
by Sue Miller. Later made into a very affecting TV movie, *Family Pictures* chronicles
the dramatic impact of an autistic son on his affluent family.

Both Callahan's real life account and its fictional counterpart demonstrate the same
point: ASDs have a pervasive impact on both those who have them and on the people
around affected individuals.

Lesley, mother of 3-year-old Danielle, says,

> My marriage has definitely suffered, also my relationship with my older
> daughters. I find it difficult to keep it all in perspective

Every family is different, but some family problems are quite common:

- Differences over discipline
- Inability to handle problem behaviors
- Withdrawal by one parent, or by one or more siblings
- Over involvement by one parent
- Burnout
- Resentment
- "Genetic blame"
- Parental neuropsychiatric problems
- Breakdown of extended family relationships
- Community isolation/social exclusion
- Financial problems related to disability
- Sibling rivalry compounded by behavior problems

Discipline

Perhaps the number one problem in any family with children is differences of opinion about appropriate discipline. These are only compounded when a child has a neuropsychiatric disability. The behavior problems are bigger, and solving them is more difficult. Conflicts between parents become more likely.

Dr. Benjamin Spock or Penelope Leach—for many people the authorities on the normal course of parenting—did not deal with uncontrollable rages, self-injurious behavior, assaultive or destructive behavior, and communication problems between parent and nonverbal child. Grandparents and friends often haven't a clue. The usual strategies may not work at all.

Spanking and other forms of corporal punishment often spark the parent–child conflagration. For one thing, people with ASDs can have unusual perceptions of pain. There's a danger that getting through to the child with a smack on the behind won't work, and parents may then be tempted to go too far with physical punishment. In addition, hitting can reinforce a child's assaultive or self-injurious behaviors. For these reasons, parents are strongly advised to find alternative methods of discipline.

And therein lies the rub. For many children, rules, reasoning, brief time-outs, and an occasional docked allowance usually suffice. But what do you do when the child can't follow your reasoning or puts up a wall that you can't get through? This is a struggle for any parent, and when two parents are at odds it only gets worse.

It's very common for one partner to have a lower tolerance threshold, or a smaller repertoire of effective, nonviolent discipline strategies. This is where the arguments begin. One parent lets a behavior go, whereas the other is hugely annoyed by it and eventually blows up. One parent spanks, and the other rushes to comfort the child. One parent gives a time-out, and the other adds a second punishment because the time-out doesn't seem like enough.

Kim, mother of 7-year-old Brad, speaks from firsthand experience:

> My husband and I had trouble for several years because he did not
> want to admit that our son had a problem. It was just too much for him
> to face. He felt that strict discipline would overcome the hyperactivity
> and the short attention span. Finally, after my son regressed to the point
> that he didn't want to be touched and couldn't find his way around,
> [my husband] came to the party.

Differences over discipline are often deep-seated. Most of what we know about raising well-behaved children we learned from our parents, for better or for worse. Chances are that not only were your parents imperfect disciplinarians at best, but also weren't raising children with ASDs. Techniques that worked on you as a youngster may be totally inappropriate for your child.

The first key to resolving discipline disagreements is making a compact between parents. Behavior experts who work with families affected by a wide variety of neuro-psychiatric disorders agree that this compact should include, at minimum, the following points:

- The best discipline is positive, so parents must rely on providing incentives for desirable behavior before using punishment to control undesirable behavior. The "token economy" schemes used in many classrooms can be successfully adapted for home use, for example. Parents should also learn about alternative strategies for addressing the roots of problem behavior, such as relaxation techniques.

- Punishment must fit the crime. Whenever possible, the only punishment should be experiencing the natural and logical consequences of an undesirable action. For example, if Joe bites his friend Jane, Jane will go home. If Joe pours his juice on the table, Joe has to clean it up (if he is able to) and does not get another glass of juice.

- Parents must agree on basic guidelines for stopping undesirable behavior, such as whether physical punishment is ever acceptable, what form discipline will take, and under what circumstances it will be meted out.

- If physical punishment is ever to be used, it should be a last resort and used in a controlled fashion.

- Parents need a common set of effective disciplinary measures for undesirable behavior. These may include loss of allowance or privileges, addition of chores or other responsibilities, time-outs and, for older children, grounding.

- Parents must agree to avoid calling the child (or each other) hurtful names or using other verbal abuse.

- Parents need to support each other in the effort to remain calm during behavior problems. If a parent is losing control, he or she should feel free to turn the situation over to the other partner long enough to take a "parental time-out."

- Parents must not, however, give one partner the permanent role of disciplinarian. The old "wait 'til Daddy gets home" scenario lets one parent off the hook, and encourages children to be fearful and manipulative. For children with neurological problems, delayed discipline can be particularly confusing.

- If an undesirable behavior happens repeatedly, and neither incentives nor disincentives seem to curb it, parents should agree to look closer for hidden causes. The behavior analysis techniques discussed in Chapter 6, *Therapeutic Interventions,* can be very useful in this regard.

- Most importantly, parents must present a united front, even when they don't actually agree. Arguments over discipline should not occur in front of the child. If Mom thinks Joe needs a time-out for throwing blocks, but Dad thinks a reprimand is sufficient, Dad can let her know how he feels while Joe is in time-out. Next time it happens, they'll be in full agreement about the proper consequence for throwing things.

Parents do need to remember that people with ASDs may respond to discipline unevenly. A child who has rages that arise out of seizures or other neurological events may not be able to gain self-control at these times, but can do so when the behavior is a garden-variety temper tantrum. People with ASDs may be unable to control compulsive actions by force of will alone. Interventions may have to include protective devices, security measures like those discussed in the section "Tips for daily life," later in the chapter, or medication.

The bottom line is that you know your child. To be effective, your discipline must be individualized, and flexible enough to take into account your child's physical and mental abilities.

Finding help

These skills don't come naturally, so the second key to defusing the behavior time bomb is expert assistance. Behavior modification professionals, ABA practitioners, family therapists who are knowledgeable about neuropsychiatric disorders, and others can help. Usually the professional should observe the child interacting with parents and siblings at home, preferably more than once.

These professionals can help both with an overall behavior plan, much like those used in schools (see Chapter 9, *School*) and with specific suggestions. It's best when experts are available on a long-term basis, providing parents with someone to call when they run out of ideas or patience. A good family therapist can be of particular help when parents do not agree about appropriate rules and discipline (see the section "Family therapy," later in this chapter).

Your special education case manager, government mental health or developmental disabilities department, psychiatrist, or ABA provider should be able to help you find a behavior management professional.

About time-outs

For most children, time-outs are an effective way to gain the child's attention, make it clear that a behavior is undesirable, and attach a consequence to a behavior that doesn't have built-in natural and logical consequences. For some children with ASDs, they are very effective.

For others, they are not. Children who are severely socially withdrawn may actually find time-outs pleasurable, so time-outs may reinforce the behavior. For these children, ABA and behavior modification techniques are a better choice.

You may want to modify your time-out procedure to take your child's special needs into account. For children who have trouble with time concepts, for example, a timer or stopwatch can help. Children who are often given time-outs to deal with frustrated, aggressive behavior may need a space with pillows or foam bats they can safely bang around. Some families have cleared out a closet for a time-out space, removing the clothes bar and any other potentially dangerous items and adding a punching bag, beanbag chair, and other things that can help a child work out angry feelings.

Parenting classes

Parenting classes may or may not be useful. Parent Effectiveness Training, Positive Parenting, and similar courses are designed for children whose responses fit the predictable pattern. When a child has an ASD, his response to an incentive or disciplinary measure may not fit the mold. For example, your child may not grasp the concept of natural and logical consequences until a much later age than expected. As noted earlier, corporal punishment may be ineffective or counterproductive. Reasoning with a grade school child who has an ASD may be a useless exercise. Incentives that motivate other children may be of little interest.

Linda, mother of 11-year-old William, says,

> *My son's day treatment center required parents to attend a weekly skill-building group. I'm sure it was valuable for some of the families, but it just gave me a regular reminder of how far out of the mainstream we were. When I asked my first question, it was about how to handle a child in an out-of-control rage. The teacher asked me to explain what I meant. When I started talking about a child who turns bright red, falls to the floor, bites anything in reach, and can't be calmed for as long as two hours, she blanched and said, "Gee, I don't know . . . maybe you should ask a psychiatrist." The psychiatrist, of course, had suggested that I bring up the issue in my parenting class.*
>
> *We never have gotten a good answer. We definitely need parenting skills that are different from what worked with our daughter. Who can tell us what we should be doing?*

Sometimes parenting classes geared to the special needs of families with disabled children are available through local hospitals, Early Intervention or special education programs, or disability support groups. Depending on the instructor's skill level and approach, these can be very valuable. A number of good books on parenting the special needs child are listed in Appendix A, *Resources*.

Problem behaviors

What do you do when your child has a behavior that you (or your partner) simply can't handle? Echolalia, weird noises, constant humming, head-banging, pestering the pets—whatever makes you flip your lid, the child with an ASD will probably find it.

If it appears to be something neurological that you'll just have to live with for a while, try dealing with your reaction rather than the behavior. Try ear plugs, a Walkman with headphones, asking your partner if you can go for a walk for 15 minutes . . . whatever it takes to keep you sane. Likewise, if your partner is the one being driven up the wall, be willing to take over for a while and let him or her avoid the annoyance.

Alternatively, change the situation to avoid the annoying behavior. If your child's fine motor problems lead to atrocious eating habits that turn your stomach, have a kids' table and an adults' table at dinnertime, or two different times for dinner. Or serve the child foods that are harder to make a horrible mess with. Try relaxing your standards a bit—Martha Stewart does not have an child with autism at home, so you really shouldn't try to compete with her in the creative housekeeping department. Get a sitter instead of taking your child to a fancy restaurant, or choose restaurants where being messy is no big deal.

Be creative in your solutions, and don't worry about whether your family's way of coping is "normal" or not. Go grocery shopping at midnight, order clothes from catalogs, put a lock on the refrigerator, set up a cot in your room for your child who has night terrors. If it works for you and harms no one, it's all right.

Linda says,

> Our son still sleeps in our bed almost every night. I brought this up hesitantly in my email chat group, and found out that we are far from the only parents who allow this. He seems to need the extra contact, and he sleeps through the night consistently.
>
> We find other times and places to be intimate, and take advantage of those nights when he does sleep in his own room.

Withdrawal and over involvement

In some families with a disabled child, one parent tends to stay as remote from the situation as possible whereas another's involvement borders on obsession. The withdrawn parent may be just as concerned, but either doesn't have the coping skills or has delegated responsibility to the more involved partner. Generally—but not always—fathers tend to withdraw, and mothers tend to jump in with both feet.

Holly, mother of 3-year-old Max, says,

> My relationship with my husband is changed due to his (and most males', I'm finding) lack of whatever it takes to deal with this disability.

This situation is not healthy for either parent, nor does it really benefit the child. Parents need to keep the lines of communication open, even when job responsibilities and schedule conflicts force one partner to be more directly involved in activities such as in-home ABA training, attending school meetings, or talking with doctors.

Set up a time each week to talk about events and, perhaps more importantly, about feelings and frustrations. Try to find ways to actively involve the parent who has a tendency to pull back. Perhaps that parent can take part in some rambunctious play time while the other fixes dinner, or can take on a special weekend activity, such as Scouting, team sports, or a hobby. The trick is to actually schedule these activities and make sure they happen. It's a rare pair of parents who are absolutely fifty–fifty in their involvement, but for the sake of their partnership, the most involved parent needs to know that there will be regularly scheduled break times ahead.

Burnout and respite

What happens when break time doesn't happen? Burnout. No matter how much you love your child, there will be a day when your batteries just run out of juice. Single parents, and couples who have a very unbalanced system of sharing responsibility for their child with an ASD, are at high risk.

Anyone who's ever had a horrible job knows the symptoms of impending burnout. You start feeling hopeless, numb, resentful, and angry, all at the same time. You may get physically ill, suffering from an increase in headaches, bowel complaints, and fatigue. You start fantasizing about running away.

Sadly, some parents really do run away—away from their share of responsibilities, away from their marriage, even away from their child.

Cindy, mother of 15-year-old Jeffrey, says,

> His father simply saw him as flawed, and never became involved in searching for an answer or diagnosis. He abandoned me, Jeffrey, and his younger brother Jonah when the boys were 7 and 5, respectively. After I fought through the courts for support, he surfaced for occasional visits, but lives out of town.
>
> He never asks what is wrong with his son, and isn't careful with him when they are out in public. Jonah, who is 13 now, "parents" his brother when the three of them are together.

Don't let this happen to you or your partner. It's okay to say that you're overwhelmed. Only then can you look for a way to remedy the situation. If you have trouble doing it on your own, a good family counselor can help you set up a schedule that gives you some time off to clear your head, take a class, or just enjoy a quiet cup of tea or a game of golf. Usually it doesn't take much to lift the burden of your day-in, day-out duties—but you do have to ask.

Like Jeffrey's father, some parents deal with feelings of guilt, embarrassment, and shame with denial. These feelings are anything but easy to work out—particularly for men (or women) who have trouble articulating their emotions. A little understanding can go a long way.

Single parents, and couples who want their time off to be time together, should access respite-care services if they are available. Respite providers are trained to care for disabled youth and adults for the afternoon, overnight, or even during a family vacation.

Sally, mother of 4-year-old Dhylan, says,

> Dhylan is very hard to manage at times, and therefore we don't go out without him (kind of like the American Express card). We just applied for respite care and are hoping we get it. A break is so important.

Respite care may be available at no or low cost through community agencies, public or private. A county caseworker or local disability organization should be able to put you in touch with respite resources in your area.

As an alternative, perhaps you can set up an informal respite arrangement with one or more parents of children with disabilities in your area. For young children, play group co-ops can be a great idea, and they're one that many parents are already familiar with. The same concept can work with older kids and even adults cared for at home too, and can be extended to cover overnight care and occasionally longer visits.

If you have the financial resources, of course, you could hire someone with appropriate training to provide respite services in your home on occasion. If a nearby college has a special education degree program, students may be able to earn extra credit and gain valuable experience, as well as earning some money, by caring for your child.

Summer day camps, overnight camps, "parents' night out" programs, and other options are available for giving yourself some much-needed time off. It's not a selfish thing to do at all; in fact, avoiding burnout is an essential part of being a good parent for a child with ASDs. The sanity you save may be your own!

Resentment

Resentment is an ever-present emotion in families affected by disabilities. Unfortunately, it usually festers away in private, only surfacing when an argument crosses the line of civility. It's hard not to feel resentment when this diagnosis can take so much away from your life: free time, undisturbed sleep, quiet mealtimes, the ability to go places with your old friends and their "normal" children, community approval, financial security—the list goes on.

Shayna, mother of 3-year-old Max, is working toward a solution:

> My husband has had to put off finishing school and finding a career
> in order to stay with my son during the day. He feels some resentment
> toward that, but now we have the common goal of our son to keep us
> warm.

Resentment is the result of feeling like you're not getting a fair deal, so it's important that other family members validate any suffering that anyone is doing for the child's sake. No one should feel like a silent martyr (and with any luck, no one will act like one either).

Siblings may harbor more resentment toward their disabled sister or brother than they're willing to admit. See the "Siblings" section later in this chapter for more information.

Genetic blame

Family problems are often compounded by the red herring of "genetic blame": Whose crummy genes caused this ASD problem, anyway? You would be surprised at how often this unspoken issue underlies arguments that only appear to be about disciplinary methods or parenting style. When it finally comes out into the open, watch out!

Parents and relatives all need to know that ASDs are neither rare nor exclusively found in your respective families. You could not have predicted that your child would have this diagnosis, not even if you had discussed every unusual relative in your respective family trees before procreating. Nor could a professional genetic counselor have been of use, because genetic screening is not available.

It may also be useful to remind each other about what's *good* in your genetic heritage or your partner's. The same side that passed on the genes for ASDs probably also passed on many wonderful characteristics, which everyone can hope your child will also share.

Also, make an agreement with your partner early on that if your own parents or other family members try to start a genetic blame conversation, you will both nip it in the bud immediately.

Parental neuropsychiatric problems

Some real parenting issues do stem from genetic heritage. Autistic spectrum disorders are, at least in part, inherited disorders. It is not uncommon for one or both parents to have neurological difficulties of their own, and these may make it even harder to raise a child with an ASD.

Some professionals have said that a few of Bruno Bettelheim's "cold and distant" mothers of autistic children may have actually had mild forms of autism themselves. Certainly, parents of children with ASDs have a slightly higher incidence of depression and other mental disorders, as well as a higher incidence of health problems in general, perhaps related to an underlying immune system dysfunction. Some of this may be genetically based, although some may derive from being in a difficult situation.

It's best to be open about these problems with your medical provider. Medical care and counseling for your own neuropsychiatric problems can help you feel better, and that alone will make you a better parent. You will be more available to your child, more patient, and less easily stressed.

Unfortunately, it isn't always to your advantage to let state or school authorities know you are experiencing mental or physical problems. Some people in social services and education have negative attitudes about parents with psychiatric or neurological problems. They may not take you seriously when you discuss your child's needs, and in some cases may even place you in danger of losing your children (see the section "Noncustodial parents," later in this chapter).

Siblings

When a child is in crisis, the everyday problems of her brothers and sisters seem to recede into the background. Reactions differ. Siblings may become super-achievers to get their share of the attention—or they may seek negative pursuits, for the same reason.

Resentment is also a natural reaction when another child in the family takes more attention and more financial resources than you do.

Julie, mother of 4-year-old Sean, says,

> *Our child's siblings are wonderful with him; however, they do*
> *sometimes feel that he gets away with more. But so far we have been*
> *able to talk this out with them.*

Problems faced by the siblings of disabled children are beginning to get more attention. Books are available that discuss typical reactions. One of the best is *Views from Our Shoes: Growing Up with a Brother or Sister with Special Needs* (Meyer, Woodbine House, 1997). This excellent guide to sibling issues is written from the children's point of view.

Chat groups and workshops can also help. You may be able to get your other children involved in SibShops, which are part of a sibling support project that started in Seattle, Washington. SibShops and similar workshops give siblings a chance to meet other kids their age who share their situation. With a little help from adult facilitators, these workshops can help siblings talk about their feelings and fears. Friendships are frequently a nice side effect.

You can find an international directory of sibling support groups, including SibShops, at *http://www.seattlechildrens.org/sibsupp/*. This site also has links to a variety of online and offline resources for siblings.

The behaviors of people with ASDs can be difficult for siblings to deal with. If your child has behaviors that are aggressive or assaultive, handling these is the first order of business. It's not fair for your other children to be at risk for actual harm. If you need this kind of help, call a behavioral professional immediately.

You may need to take special steps to safeguard the personal property of your other children, and to ensure that they have a quiet place to get away from your disabled child's tantrums, loud noises, or intrusive behaviors. Some of the solutions are not things most parents would normally want to do. Possibilities include putting a keyed lock on a child's door, situating children's bedrooms as far apart in your home as possible, and providing niceties like a telephone, television, computer, or stereo in the child's room (or in a lockable family room) to permit their uninterrupted use. You'll have to set rules for the use of these devices that prevents the sibling from withdrawing into couch potato land, of course.

It goes without saying that a fair share of your time is far more important than possessions, space, or even privacy. It's essential to make some special time for your other children. Some parents have a meal out, go to a movie, or enjoy an activity with their other children each week, and swear by the results. Ensure that your other children can find time to talk with you about school, friends, ideas, and concerns, without interruptions from your child with an ASD. You may need to be flexible about bedtimes one night each week, allowing another child to stay up just a bit later than usual to enjoy some one-on-one time with you. Another way to carve out time is to wake one child up a bit early once a week for a cup of cocoa and some quiet talk.

Your extended family may be able to take up some of the slack. Grandparents, aunts and uncles, or older cousins might take on some minor duties, such as transporting another child to soccer practice twice a week. Some grandparents may even be willing to fund enrichment activities or take excursions together. Many families have special friends or neighbors who might be willing to get more involved, if you ask—this system can work out very well if you can recruit the parents of a sibling's friends. Family friends, and other trusted adults in the community, can act as mentors and advisers, and help your other children pursue personal interests.

Most siblings do have worries and questions about ASDs, and they may be afraid to talk to you about their fears. Children are exquisitely sensitive to family stress, and they don't want to burden you with more. It's essential for these issues be put on the table, though. Common fears include wondering if their sibling is going to die from his illness, worries about possibly dangerous medication, feeling different from other children who don't have a disabled sibling, being teased because of their sibling's odd behaviors, and fear that their parents are unconcerned with their needs because of the other child's demands.

Quality information is the key. There are some films available that can help you start the conversation. *What's Eating Gilbert Grape?* starring Johnny Depp and Leonardo DiCaprio, is a particularly good one, as is the Dustin Hoffman–Tom Cruise film *Rain Man*. Short videos for siblings may be available through advocacy organizations as well.

There are quite a few children's books on autism. For siblings of severely affected children, these can be great. For those with brothers and sisters who have milder forms of autism, these can be more frightening than reassuring. They may fear that their sibling will become "worse," like the child in the story, or they may not identify their sibling with the more severely autistic child at all. Teens often find books by high-functioning autistic writers like Donna Williams or Temple Grandin interesting and informative.

Adolescent and adult siblings may resent the very real impact on their future of having a brother or sister with a disability. As Joe's quote in the section "Financial problems and solutions," later in this chapter, illustrates, siblings may lose out on a lot, including opportunities for higher education, participation in community sports leagues, music and dance lessons, having a car, or (as explored to tragi-comic effect in *Rain Man*) receiving an inheritance.

They may also fear that as their parents age, they will be expected to take on increasing responsibilities for their sibling—and this is not an unreasonable worry. You may indeed need to pass on guardianship at some point. Your expectations should be discussed as early as possible.

As siblings approach the teen years, where family conflicts can get especially difficult, parents need to ensure that each child has activities that give him a chance to shine. School activities, religious youth groups, and volunteer organizations can be good choices if money is tight because of medical bills.

Quite a few parents interviewed for this book report that their other children have become fierce advocates for their brother or sister with an ASD. Some have even chosen careers in medicine, teaching, or psychology because of the influence of their sibling's struggles. Other parents note that siblings have been therapeutically important, particularly when it comes to helping their child with an ASD learn language and social skills. Children can insist on interaction in ways that adults can't seem to get away with. Basically, they know how to make it *fun*—and we should always let them know how much we appreciate their efforts.

Lack of family support

If it takes a village to raise a child, some families of children who have ASDs wonder where their village has gone. Sometimes their child is passed over for family activities, such as invitations to grandmother's house for Christmas or trips to the mall with siblings. Some family members even neglect birthdays for the disabled child, while acknowledging his or her siblings.

Debbie, mother of 11-year-old Doug, says,

> As far as the extended family, most of them act like Doug doesn't
> even exist. That's mainly on Doug's father side of the family. On my
> side, Doug is just kind of "there," nobody really does much with him.
> I don't have much help or support from them.

Sometimes the problem is simply a deep-seated prejudice against disabled people, and you can't do much about that. Often it's related to a lack of adequate information about the child.

It might make you feel uncomfortable to do so, but you can share evaluations from your child's school or doctor with family members who seem to question the disability's existence. Some parents have even brought a grandparent along for a psychiatrist or doctor visit, with hopes that hearing the diagnosis from an expert in a white coat will help the grandparent accept it at last. You might want to discuss this possibility with one of your most accessible professionals, perhaps asking that they deliver some suggestions for helping your child along with information about the disability.

Jennifer, mother of 3-year-old Joseph, says,

> *It has been a source of tension in the family because, with my son at least, diagnosis is not clear-cut. He is not classically autistic and is, in fact, very affectionate and related to his family, both immediate and extended. There are those in the family who think nothing is wrong and say we are stigmatizing him by seeking help. There are others who think he is just poorly disciplined and out of control.*

Community isolation

All it takes is one embarrassing episode in the checkout line or at the public park to make the average parent want to crawl under a rock. Every time the worst happens, the impulse to withdraw from public life is amplified.

Joe, father of 7-year-old Kyle, says his son's disability has limited their lives:

> *We cannot do anything with him, except go for car rides (this calms him), walk with him (he needs the motion), and bring him to the playground. He prevents people from talking to each other, with his noise and disruptions. He is not communicative, he is hyperactive, and he makes weird noises. We cannot even bring him out to eat. We try to shop in the early morning when the stores are empty.*

One of the most difficult areas for family members of people with ASDs is dealing with rude or clueless remarks from strangers. Children with ASDs are rarely beneficiaries of the sympathy factor. There's no wheelchair or leg brace to signal "This is a disabled child," so onlookers may assume they're witnessing willful misbehavior. Some are quite vocal about letting parents know it, which can do a number on your self-esteem.

Some people carry cards explaining the problem that they can give to busybodies. Others have a canned speech for these situations, such as "My daughter has a neurological problem that can cause *[insert the unusual behavior of the moment here]*. I'm sure you understand."

You may be tempted to add, "In other words, she's disabled. What's *your* excuse?" although it's probably not a good idea. You may also be tempted to avoid the problem altogether by disappearing from public view. But isolation is a breeding ground for depression, and it does a child with social deficits no favors, either. Chapter 11, *Growing Up on the Autistic Spectrum,* goes into some detail about ways that children with ASDs can break out of their isolation. But what about parents?

It's sadly true that the friends you had before your child's problems became evident may fall away. You'll have to be the judge of whether the cause is fear, prejudice, or simply the fact that you have less free time to spend with friends than you used to. On the one hand, disability support groups are frequently a source for new, and potentially rewarding, friendships. On the other hand, you may struggle mightily to hold onto friendships that have no relationship to ASDs, just to avoid having your child's disability permeate every aspect of your life.

Special interest groups, from car clubs to 4-H to volunteer organizations, may be able to find room for you, either with your entire family or as an individual participant. Be direct: Ask how your child (or your hectic schedule) can be accommodated.

Strategies that families have successfully used include assuring other adults involved in children's activities that they will be present with their child at all times if needed, educating other parents and children, and being careful to choose activities that meet their family's needs without overwhelming their child. For example, some children enjoy the crowds and lights of holiday parades, whereas others would prefer to wrap gifts for the needy with a few quiet volunteers.

In the US, the Americans with Disabilities Act (ADA) was passed specifically to ensure that people with disabilities have equal access to community life and facilities. If your child's condition is causing discrimination against your entire family, the ADA covers you, too. The European Community charter and some individual European countries have similar regulations—and legality aside, full inclusion is certainly the ideal that people everywhere should aspire to. Don't be afraid to assert the natural right that you, your child, and your family have to participate in everyday life whenever possible.

Religious activities

Activities at your place of worship can be a great venue for socializing and support—assuming that your congregation understands and accepts people with ASDs. Some religious bodies do have formal programs for including people with disabilities in services and religious life. Check at the national, regional, or diocese level to find out what's available. Religious life is one area that many parents interviewed for this book cite as an island of acceptance in the larger community, although others have had negative experiences.

Leaders and members of your group may also be able to provide help of a more practical sort. Counseling on personal, family, medical, or spiritual matters; volunteers to help with home-based therapy programs; respite care; or even housework and prepared meals when your family is in crisis are all support services that some grateful families have found.

Family therapy

Finding professional help for family problems isn't always easy when a person with an ASD is part of the equation, because few family therapists know much about neurological disorders. The wrong therapist can cause irreparable harm by once again blaming the parents for the disorder, looking around for nonexistent sexual abuse, or inflaming feelings of guilt or resentment in one partner.

As one parent puts it,

> The last thing we needed was for the therapist to goad us into a fight during the session. We are dealing with an incredible amount of stress. At the end of the hour, he got to leave. We got to go home steaming, our problems still unresolved. When we hadn't gotten around to talking about making any positive changes after three sessions, we decided to call it quits.

Parents interviewed for this book cited many negative experiences with traditional models of family therapy, particularly when sessions were conducted by inexperienced or "old school" personnel. Parents of adults with ASDs interviewed for this book had particularly heinous tales to tell from the "bad old days." But in the hands of a competent, experienced professional, family therapy can be a positive growth experience for people dealing with disability.

Dorthy, mother of 5-year-old Jesse, has found support in a family therapy group:

> My main sources of strength are the autism newslist on the Net and the other parents at therapy.

According to parents who have tried family therapy, two models seem to get the best results: (1) "whole family" approaches that may include working separately with parents, siblings, and the person with an ASD, then bringing everyone together on a regular basis to hash out interpersonal issues; and (2) group therapy sessions that involve several parents. The latter can provide families who are new to the diagnosis with a built-in support system, and participants in well-run groups report a growing sense of confidence as they, too, are able to pass knowledge on to others.

The focus of either approach should be less on "fixing" dysfunctional family systems than on empowering family members with new coping skills and providing a safe place to work out conflicts. Some therapy groups for parents operate more like parenting classes, with speakers invited in to discuss various topics of concern to the group.

Separation and divorce

As noted in this chapter's introduction, marriages suffer when a child is disabled. The legal aspects are beyond the scope of this book, but it is important that parents of a child with an ASD who do choose to end their relationship take the child's special needs into account. Issues may include the following:

- Custody arrangements that allow both parents access to the child and respite. These arrangements may constrain the parents from living too far from each other, which can be a difficult situation.

- Financial settlements that take into account the added expenditures needed to care for a disabled child, possibly including extended alimony for a stay-at-home parent.

- Financial arrangements to ensure that both parents will be responsible for the child's needs after the age of 18 (most divorce decrees only cover support until the age of legal majority).

- Written agreements about which parent will pay for medical bills, tuition, therapy, and other expenses related to the disability, and to ensure that health insurance coverage is maintained.

- Special agreements to protect the child, if the divorce is caused by abuse, neglect, or substance abuse by one parent.

Very little good can be said about families splitting up, unless it's for reasons of safety. Parents should simply do their best to ensure that each partner's relationship with their children is maintained. Professional help, either in the form of social work aid or family counseling, is strongly advised.

Single parents

Couple problems are plenty of trouble, but it's trouble that those going it alone sometimes wish they had. No matter how ineffectual one half of a couple is, a partner is still an adult sounding board and a shoulder to cry on.

Single parents also face increased financial pressure, and have a terrible time getting meetings with school districts, doctors, and other helpers to fit into their schedule. Voicemail, pagers, email, and fax machines can be the single parent's best friends. You may also try to fit several appointments (school, psychiatrist, and pediatrician, for example) into one day off work. If your child has a low tolerance level, however, the results may not be great.

Some therapists do offer evening and weekend hours, and school districts can often be convinced to hold early morning meetings. You may need to work with an advocate who can represent you at meetings. A friend, relative, sitter, or professional hired specifically for the purpose may be able to take your child to medical appointments.

And don't forget to take some time out for you—if you can find it! There's nothing like a child with an ASD to stop any semblance of a post-breakup love life. The time commitment alone may take you away from the dating world for years, and explaining what your home life is like could turn off a potential mate.

Ann, mother of 8-year-old Theron, says,

> *Theron's behavior problems keep me from finding a partner to share*
> *my life with, as his father left six years ago. His two younger brothers*
> *have many of the same problems, though not the same diagnoses, so*
> *my attention is divided fairly equally among them, none for me!*

Single parents have more reason than any others to seek allies in their extended family or community. Respite care and quality after-school care are absolute necessities. Foster grandparent programs, Big Brothers/Sisters, Scouting, religious institutions, and parent groups can all become part of your web of support.

Multigenerational living

If you're part of the "sandwich generation"—caring for children and aging parents at once—your family faces extra stress. Older relatives in the home can be a wonderful addition to your life, but if they have many medical needs of their own or can't handle the behaviors of your child with an ASD, the situation will eventually explode.

In such situations, an extra pair of hands is a must. In the US, Canada, Britain, Australia, and most parts of Europe, home health aides are available for frail or disabled elderly people, even when they are cared for by their children. Volunteer groups and religious institutions may also be able to provide assistance.

Housekeeping help can give you more time for the important stuff. Again, volunteer help or public assistance may be available in this area. Contact your government department for services to the elderly for more information, and be sure to explain that you have the extra burden of caring for a disabled child.

As with siblings, you may need to take special care to ensure that older relatives are safe from aggressive or assaultive behaviors, and that they can secure their possessions and peace of mind. Locks, latches, intercoms, and soundproofing can help in some situations.

Noncustodial parents

In some countries, and in some US states, parents are told that they must give up legal custody of their child to the state if he needs publicly funded residential services. Disability advocacy organizations, many of which are listed in Appendix B, *Support and Advocacy*, can help you sort through various options.

Giving up custody need not mean having no input. However, some programs are so unused to parental involvement that they aren't sure how to include family members in the lives of institutionalized clients. Set up a meeting to discuss the ways you can help your child, activities you want to continue to share and, if applicable, issues related to financial management and personal safety.

Divorce can also prevent parents from retaining full custody. Both parents' level of personal and financial involvement should be written into the divorce settlement. If the settlement is unsatisfactory, or you are prevented from involvement in your child's life, you need legal help to assert custodial rights.

Medical care is a frequent sticking point. If parents disagree about the right medical approach (for example, if one is totally opposed to using medications and the other is not, or if one prefers a traditional approach while the other is into alternative therapies), they may need to use the services of a counselor or arbitrator to work things out. Alternatively, parents may be able to agree on a practitioner or program, and simply agree that both will abide by the recommendations of this third party.

Worst of all is the situation of having your children forcibly taken from you. This has happened to parents of children with neurological disorders when uninformed social workers thought the child's behavior resulted from abuse, especially when the disorder had not been diagnosed before the action took place. Parental neuropsychiatric problems can be complicating factor in such cases. Of course, families of people with ASDs are not immune to abuse, neglect, or parental substance abuse, either.

If you feel you are at risk of losing custody of your child to the state or to an ex-spouse, do not delay in seeking legal (and medical) support. Disability advocacy organizations may be able to provide you with advice and, in some cases, legal assistance.

Adoption and foster care

Although hard numbers are not available because of confidentiality laws, it's well known that childhood disability is a major factor in adoption and foster care placements by natural parents. Some parents simply don't have the knowledge or resources to take care of a child with a potentially lifelong disability. Tragically, these children are among the hardest to place. Parents who step up for this duty deserve a medal—and extra support.

Roni, adoptive mother of 5-year-old Stevie, says,

> Stevie was originally diagnosed as deaf, which is why I got him, as I sign. He was 3½ years old when first diagnosed with autism. His deprivation was so severe we aren't sure just how much is the autism and how much is the deprivation.
>
> Unfortunately, Early Intervention wasn't an option in his case. All diagnosis, progress, services, schooling, etc., started 21 months ago, when he came to live with me.
>
> Finding community resources has been the biggest thorn in my side. We are hooked up with a regional center that tends to pass the buck to the foster agency or school district until the adoption is final. Our FFA

[foster family agency] has not been helpful in any way. No backup,
no help finding babysitting services, it all falls on me. I'm not
complaining, honest, I wouldn't trade my life now with Stevie for
anything!

As I am raising Stevie as a single mother, I can tell you that I have
depleted most of my savings and live hand-to-mouth many months.
Even though I receive a monthly stipend for him, it hardly covers the
cost of shoes! It's a great struggle, but I have great faith and trust in
a Higher Power . . . if I didn't, I couldn't survive.

Some foster and adoption agencies that work with special needs children have more to offer than Roni's. Private agencies for the disabled could help those that do not, but communication between the public and private sectors is apparently difficult. Parent support groups and disability advocacy groups can sometimes bridge the two.

Some parents of children with ASDs may have to place their children in a therapeutic foster home, either temporarily or permanently. This type of foster care arrangement is set up to provide specially trained round-the-clock caregivers for medically fragile or disabled children who cannot be cared for at home. Typical reasons for placement may include assaultive or aggressive behavior that endangers parents or siblings; a parent's disability, incarceration, or death; or difficult medical issues, such as tube feeding.

With temporary foster care placements, the goal is usually to wait out or find a solution for the situation that led to placement. Natural parents must stay as involved as possible—it's very important to attend all meetings and therapy sessions when your child is in foster care, even if the placement was voluntary. Lack of participation can lead to the termination of parental rights.

Natural parents also need to maintain oversight of the child's medical, educational, and personal needs during foster care placement. Foster care arrangements vary in quality, ranging from homes you wish you had grown up in to the worst of abusive environments. Most therapeutic foster parents are quite good, however.

If the foster placement is in another city, you may need to secure assistance to make regular visits, or send an advocate to make visits for you. When distance is an issue, regular communication by mail, email, and/or telephone with your child should be assured.

It's sad that in the US, foster care placement is sometimes chosen as a way to ensure the delivery of essential services to children. Foster parents merit a stipend to pay for the cost of the child's care, and the child receives publicly funded health care and mental health services. In a better world, natural parents could receive the special training provided to therapeutic foster parents, as well as the subsidies and services needed to care for difficult children. This is a goal worth working for.

Financial problems and solutions

ASDs can be a financial drain, and that's a family strain. Parents cite money woes as a major source of family stress.

Joe, father of Kyle, says,

> We've spent about $11,000 out-of-pocket in four years! We had to recently use our home-equity line of credit to pay for this, and haven't been able to save money for our older son's college (we have four kids, ages 17 through 7). We rarely can afford nice vacations, music lessons for the other children, etc. I drive a car with 200,000 miles on it because we cannot afford a replacement.

As this father's words indicate, money problems are about more than a low bank account balance. Other family members may miss out on opportunities or do without some material things. Unless the situation is thoroughly and regularly discussed with them, they may not understand why the person with ASD's needs are costing so much, and why such needs are a family priority.

Social services programs are both a source of assistance and a source of financial difficulty for many families. Job choices and saving money for future needs may be jeopardized by these programs' earning and property rules. Parents who want to take advantage of these services and still meet their responsibilities to other children (not to mention to themselves) may need specialized financial planning.

Most people dealing with ASDs have plenty of practice when it comes to squeezing a buck. Some, however, are hard put to find a dollar to squeeze. Parents with challenging children and adults with serious difficulties can have trouble securing gainful employment.

There are programs that may provide you or your family with direct financial support. The checks will be small, but with careful planning they may let you offer your child the gift of a home-based intensive program or may provide time to develop a career that meets your need to be at home more.

United States

The US stands alone in the civilized world as the only country that would rather pay strangers or an institution to care for a child than provide support for parents to do so themselves. Although all western European nations (and many others) provide family support allowances to encourage one parent to stay home with all young children, the US government has cut support even to single parents, and provides extraordinarily low allowances when allowances are available.

This policy affects the parents of children with disabilities particularly harshly.

Until recently, single, low-income parents of children with disabilities tended to receive Aid to Families with Dependent Children (AFDC, "welfare") and Social Security Income (SSI). When put together, income from these two programs permitted them to eke out a living well below the poverty line, but with some hope of obtaining adequate housing and food. For many of these families, the most important benefit was access to health care, as government health insurance coverage comes with both AFDC and SSI.

Temporary Assistance for Needy Families (TANF)

Welfare reform has changed this picture drastically. The Temporary Assistance for Needy Families (TANF) program, a system of short-term emergency supports, has replaced AFDC. All states have now imposed stringent rules, such as limiting assistance to once in a lifetime, requiring that parents work for their grants, or forcing parents into job-training schemes geared toward a rapid transition to low-wage employment. Although most states have also added child care services to their offerings to help parents receiving TANF grants transition to the workplace, affordable child care slots for children and teens with disabilities are almost nonexistent. This leaves even the most determined low-income parent at a severe disadvantage.

Federal law permits exceptions to TANF regulations for some—but not all—parents caring for disabled children, and for parents who are themselves disabled. However, caseworkers are responsible for holding down the number of exemptions to a small percentage of their clients, even though as many as half of families remaining on welfare now include either a mother or a child with a serious disability.[1] You can apply for TANF at your county's child and family services department. The program is primarily for single parents, but two-parent families are eligible in some areas and under some circumstances.

The amount of the monthly grant varies. It is determined by the county government, which administers TANF programs at the local level. You'll need to provide very complete documentation to get and retain benefits on the basis of needing to provide full-time home care for a disabled child. You can expect to have an eligibility review at least every three months, during which all your documents will be reviewed and you will be re-interviewed. Generally speaking, you cannot have savings or possessions worth over $1,000, although you may own a modest home and car. You may need to sell a late-model car and other valuables before you can receive benefits. Your grant may be reduced by the amount of other financial assistance you receive. If you find part-time work, your grant may also be reduced. Some states have work incentive programs, however. Court-ordered child support payments to TANF recipients are paid to the county rather than directly to the parent, to offset the cost of the grant.

You may be eligible for Food Stamps, "commodities" (free food), and other benefits, such as job training, if you receive TANF. People leaving TANF programs may be eligible for certain short-term benefits, such as subsidized childcare and continued health insurance.

If you need help in obtaining or keeping public assistance, contact a local welfare rights organization or advocacy group, or contact the National Welfare Monitoring and Advocacy Partnership (NWMAP) for national information and referrals (see Appendix A).

Social Security Income

SSI is a federal program that provides a small monthly stipend for people with disabilities that cause marked and severe functional limitations. Benefits range from around $300 to $400 per month for children or for adults living in another person's household to over $600 per month for adults living independently. More importantly for many, SSI recipients are also eligible for Medicaid, a federal health insurance plan. As with TANF, your assets and income from other sources must be limited, which can bring stress of its own as parents are forced to "spend down" any savings and let careers slide to become or remain eligible.

Holly, mother of 3-year-old Max, has seen both sides of SSI:

> *Staying able to get SSI and Medicaid has meant my husband could not get a better job because the pay would knock us out of contention for Medicaid. We don't care about the SSI, we just need Medicaid for therapy and vision coverage.*

Your nearest Social Security office can provide you with an application and current instruction book. You can also do a pre-eligibility screen over the phone: Just call the national Social Security hotline at (800) 772-1213. The application form is extremely long, and requires copious documentation.

The SSI application process has become increasingly adversarial over the past two decades. You may get the distinct impression that the people interviewing you think you or your child is faking a disability—and your impression may be right. The Social Security department will order an Individualized Functional Assessment (IFA), which may include seeing more doctors as well as a review of your medical documentation. You or your child may be interviewed and observed by a psychiatrist or medical doctor working for Social Security. You have the right to be present if your child is interviewed, although parents report that some doctors seem to want to exclude them from the process.

Most applicants for SSI are rejected on their first try. You have the right to appeal, however—and you should, because a high percentage of appeals succeed. In addition, successful appellants get a lump sum equal to the payments they should have received had their original application been properly approved. This sum can be several thousand dollars, and has helped many families fund things such as more secure housing, transportation, and other important needs.

If you need help with SSI (or, for that matter, with AFDC if you are applying primarily because of your own or your child's special needs), contact a disability advocacy agency (see Appendix B). This agency can help you through the application process, and most can provide legal assistance if you need to appeal. Additional information about the program is available online at *http://www.ssa.gov/disability.*

SSI is usually an income-dependent program. If you are working and earn more than the regulations allow, your child will not be eligible for SSI. However, a special income-limit waiver is available to help families who have income but whose children have expensive medical needs. See Chapter 8, *Insurance,* for information on the waiver process.

Some states, large cities, private agencies, and Native American tribes also have income support programs. A county social worker or tribal official should be able to help you find out if you qualify.

Charlotte, mother of 4-year-old Rory, has found some help this way:

> *We receive assistance from a United Way program and some grant
> funds from the state Department of Mental Retardation.*

If you have an ASD or other handicap and are parenting and receiving benefits in the US, this may work for you or against you. Some parents who have let their case-worker know about a personal neurological problem have been exempted from certain regulations. Others have lost their children to the foster care system. You should see a welfare rights organization or sympathetic social worker before making the decision to tell. They can help you ensure your children's security by approaching the issue correctly.

Canada

Welfare is available in Canada for people with disabilities, single parents, and unemployed adults with or without children. The amount of the monthly payment is set at the provincial level, varying from about $580 per month in poor provinces like New Brunswick to around $800 per month in more expensive Ontario and British Columbia. Payments to parents caring for children, single or otherwise, are higher than those for disabled adults.

To apply for state welfare benefits, visit your nearest ministry or department of social services. For disability benefits, regulations vary by state. Generally speaking, you must be 18 years of age or older and require either item 1 or items 2 and 3 of the following, as a direct result of a severe mental or physical impairment:

1. Extensive assistance or supervision in order to perform daily living tasks within a reasonable time

2. Unusual and continuous monthly expenditures for transportation, special diets, or other unusual but essential and continuous needs

3. Have confirmation from a medical practitioner that the impairment exists and will likely continue for at least two years or longer, or that it is likely to continue for at least one year and then recur

There are limits on the amount and kinds of savings and other property that a person or family receiving benefits can have.

As in the US, welfare reform is a growing trend in Canada. Some states have introduced mandatory workfare programs for single adults and for some parents on welfare. These provisions generally do not apply to people receiving disability benefits, and parents caring for disabled children may be able to have welfare-to-work requirements waived or deferred.

Some assistance for people with disabilities may also be available at the federal level, or from First Nations (Native Canadian) agencies.

Canadians who are denied benefits or who have other problems with the benefits agency can appeal its decisions to an independent tribunal.

Other direct and indirect income assistance is available, such as subsidized travel and tax benefits. For example, college students with permanent disabilities can have their student loans forgiven, and are also eligible for special grants to pay for a note-taker, transportation, and other education-related expenses.

United Kingdom

In the UK, people with disabilities have access to three major types of direct state benefits. You can apply for these programs at your local Benefits Agency Office:

- The Disability Living Allowance (DLA) is for adults or children with a disability. Parents or carers can apply on behalf of a child. Payment ranges from 15 to 35 pounds per week. The DLA forms are complex, so find an experienced disability advocate to help you fill them out if possible. Your Citizens Advice Bureau or local council can help you apply.

- Parents and others caring for a child who receives DLA can apply for the Attendants Allowance (also called the Carers Allowance) program as well.

- Any person over 5 years old who receives DLA can also get a Mobility Allowance, a small sum of money to help them get to medical appointments and meet general transportation needs.

Your local council may also have its own benefits scheme. These may be direct payments, such as a supplemental housing benefit, or council tax offsets.

A number of supported work schemes are available for people with disabilities and adults receiving other forms of public assistance. In some cases, these programs are mandatory. If you are parenting a child who may have difficulty finding work, start learning about these programs before he reaches school-leaving age.

Teens and young adults attending college or trade school may find themselves in a "Catch 22" situation: On some occasions benefits officers have decided that if they are well enough to go to college, they're well enough to work, and canceled their benefits. You can appeal these and other unfavorable decisions to a Social Security Appeals Tribunal.

Help with disability benefit issues is available from UK groups listed in Appendix B.

Republic of Ireland

Disability Allowance and Disability Benefit are available in Ireland, but are far from generous. Both are administered via the Department of Social Welfare. Disabled students can continue to receive these benefits while attending third level courses, although they may lose other types of public assistance, such as rent allowance. Maintenance Grant (a general benefit for poor families) is not affected by these benefits.

Supported work schemes are available, although your earnings may make you lose your disability benefits. The exception is work that the local welfare officer agrees is "rehabilitative" in nature.

A number of scholarship and grant programs are available to assist students with disabilities. See the report at *http://www.ahead.ie/grants/grants.html#toc* for more information.

Australia

A variety of income support programs are available to Australian citizens, including direct financial assistance for adults with disabilities, parents caring for children with disabilities, single parents, unemployed single adults, youth, and students. Programs related specifically to disabled citizens and their families include Disability Support Pension, Related Wife Pension, Sickness Allowance, Mobility Allowance, Carer Payment, and Child Disability Allowance.

Employment programs for Australians with disabilities are many and varied, including the Supported Wage System (SWS), which brings the earnings of disabled workers in sheltered workshops or other types of supported or low-wage employment closer to the livability range.

Indirect benefits may also be available under the Disability Services Act in the areas of education, work, recreation, and more.

You can find information about all of Australia's benefit plans at the Centrelink web site (*http://www.centrelink.gov.au/*). To apply for benefits or disability services, contact your local Department of Family and Community Services. You can get help with disability income and health benefit issues from the support and advocacy organizations listed in Appendix B.

New Zealand

Direct benefits in New Zealand are similar to those provided in Australia, although the payments have historically been much lower. Domestic Purposes Benefit is for single parents. Additional services are available to the disabled and their carers, including training schemes, supported employment, and recreational assistance. The social safety net in New Zealand is currently being revamped, but services for people with disabilities are actually expected to expand.

To apply for benefits or services, contact your local Ministry of Social Welfare office, which runs the Income Support program. If you need help with paperwork or appeals, Beneficiary Advisory Services (*http://canterbury.cyberplace.org.nz/community/bas.html*) in Christchurch provides assistance and advocacy, as do a number of disability advocacy groups, particularly the information clearinghouse Disability Information Service (03 366 6189 or *http://canterbury.cyberplace.co.nz/community/dis.html*).

Indirect financial help

In the US, tax deductions have replaced direct financial assistance to the poor in many cases. These benefits are less convenient, because they are provided just once a year, but families coping with the high cost of disability care should take advantage of them.

One of the most important tax benefits is the medical deduction available on your federal tax forms. You can write off not only the direct cost of doctors' visits not covered by health insurance, but also insurance co-payments and deductibles, and out-of-pocket expenses for medications, medical devices, in-home health care assistants (presumably including ABA therapists), travel costs related to medical care, and at least some expenses related to attending medical or disability conferences and classes. Special deductions for health insurance premiums are available for self-employed people.

Because medical deductions limit your federal tax liability, they will also reduce your state income taxes (state taxes are usually based on taxable income figures from your federal form). Some states have additional tax benefits for the disabled. In Oregon, for example, each disabled child counts as two dependents.

Another important federal tax benefit is the Earned Income Credit (EIC) program. This benefit for the working poor can actually supplement your earnings with a tax rebate, not just a deduction.

Mortgage interest is also tax deductible. Because your home is usually not considered an asset when determining eligibility for direct financial assistance, this makes home ownership particularly attractive to disabled adults and to families who expect to provide care for a child with an ASD into adulthood. Some banks and credit unions have special mortgage programs for low- and moderate-income families.

Given the strong financial benefits of home ownership, including the opportunity to keep your housing costs from going up in the future, purchasing a house is very advisable.

Very low income families, including adults with ASDs who rely on SSI or fixed-income trusts, may be able to get additional help to reach the goal of home owner-ship from organizations such as Habitat for Humanity.

Tips for daily life

There are a lot of things about raising a child with an autistic spectrum disorder that teachers, therapists, and doctors don't know much about. The way you live will change, like it or not.

The good news is that the behaviors that cause these changes usually don't last forever: The child who this week broke wine glasses just to hear them smash will probably not be tossing them two years from now. But if you want to avoid rushing from disaster to disaster, you must have a proactive parenting style. Avoid conflict, redirect behavior, and always be on the lookout for an alternative solution to behavior problems. The following sections present advice culled from many parents on handling typical trouble spots.

Haircuts

If you can figure out what it is about haircuts that drives your child wild, then remove that particular trigger. You may then be able to get the job done at a regular barbershop or salon, with modifications. Some common problems and solutions follow:

- **Sensitivity to barbershop or salon odors.** If this is the case, look for an old-fashioned barbershop that eschews smelly shampoos, or buy a home haircutting kit. Unscented products are often available, but you may have to buy them yourself and bring them in, or request them in advance.

- **Sensitivity to the sound of buzzing clippers or snapping scissors.** Some people can tolerate one but not the other. There are also old-fashioned hand razors for cutting hair, but it's hard to find a barber who can wield one with precision. Call around! You might also try ear plugs, or a Walkman playing a favorite tape over headphones. Your barber will happily work around headphones if it keeps the child in the chair. You might also choose to accept a longer hairstyle, if grooming is not a problem.

- **Sensory sensitivity in general.** Try brushing the head and hair frequently with a medium-soft hairbrush. This may desensitize the area in time. You may be able to have your child sit in your lap during a haircut; a tight hug may calm him down. Again, home haircuts may be your best bet. Make sure to use a neck strip and a cape to keep hair off the skin and clothes, and clean up with a soft brush and/or a blow dryer set on cool. Parents whose children are of African descent may have a particularly hard time with sensory issues when it comes to hair care. Braided styles are the most convenient when it comes to grooming, but take a long time to achieve and involve a lot of pulling. Straightening chemicals and pressing are no picnic either. Short, natural styles may be the easiest to manage.

- **Extreme hyperactivity.** One false move in the barber's chair can result in inadvertent punk-rock 'dos. Many parents swear by cutting hair while the child is fast asleep. Scissors work best for this operation. Keep a brush and comb handy, and work slowly. You may want to use a plastic bowl on the head to get an even length or, for longer styles, hair tape (available at beauty supply stores and many drugstores or chemists).

Toenail and fingernail clipping/cleaning

It may be an exaggerated fear of being cut, a desire to not lose a part of oneself, or the metallic clicking of the clippers, but many children with ASDs hate this grooming task. It's best if kids learn to do it for themselves as early as possible, although those with fine motor problems may find it difficult.

Curved toenail clippers are larger and easier to operate than smaller fingernail clippers, and can do both jobs passably. This is another job that parents can do while a child is asleep.

Bathing

This is a problem area with teenagers more often than it is with young children, according to parents. You may have to institute a schedule, or even allow gym class showers to suffice during the school year.

Even for older kids, tub toys, soap "paints," bubble bath, or other items may allow you to get them in and out of a warm tub once a week.

Contrary to popular belief, it's not necessary to bathe children daily unless there are special medical or sanitary reasons to do so. Use a washcloth to zap any particularly grungy areas daily, and schedule an unavoidable bath time for one or more days each week. A flexible shower hose can be very useful for washing the hair of children who are afraid of the big shower.

Some kids who won't go near a bathtub will go swimming, which usually comes with the added bonus of a mandatory shower. In a pinch, you can see if they'll run through a lawn sprinkler in a pair of shorts. The novelty of pools and sprinklers sometimes trumps fear of getting wet.

Clothing

What do you do with a child who strips off his clothes at every opportunity? First, you try to find out why. The most common reason is sensory sensitivity, so first talk to an occupational therapist about instituting a program of sensory integration therapy.

In the meantime, see what you can do to make staying clothed more comfortable. Verbal children may be able to explain what they don't like about wearing clothes. Common problems include chafing waistbands, itchy fabrics, "new clothes" smells, and annoying tags. Kids who can't stand regular waistbands can often handle elastic waist pants and shorts, especially those made with soft fabrics, such as sweatpants. Others can wear only overalls or coveralls with ease—and these have the added bonus of being harder to remove.

For children who wear diapers, the diaper itself may be the problem. Check for and treat any actual diaper rash (incidentally, diaper rash can be caused by a yeast infection on the skin, which may indicate a larger problem with yeast overgrowth—see Chapter 5, *Medical Interventions*). Experiment with different types of cloth diapers, various brands of disposables, and larger diapers if tightness around the waist and legs is an issue.

Over the diaper or training pants, sweatpants, overalls (especially the ones with snaps along the inseam), coveralls, and jumpsuits work well. Some parents actually stitch down the overall straps each morning, or replace easy-open fasteners with something more complex. It's possible to open overalls and coveralls for larger children along the inseam and add unobtrusive snaps or Velcro for easy toileting without complete clothes removal.

Shirts and dresses that button or zip up the back are also hard to remove.

Some children who tend to remove all their clothing in the bathroom are simply taking extreme steps to prevent getting their clothes dirty. Careful work on toileting technique and rewards for good performance can help. Some may also want to have wet wipes available to improve their after-toilet cleanup, and thereby avoid dirtying their clothes. Wipes can be purchased in small, discreet containers that fit well in a purse or backpack.

Catalogs that carry special clothing for children with disabilities are listed in Appendix A. Many items in these catalogs are especially good for older children who have toileting problems, or for children with orthopedic impairments in addition to an ASD.

Many people with sensory problems prefer soft fabrics, such as cotton jersey or terry-cloth, to stiff fabrics such as denim. If this is the case with your child, go shopping with that in mind. It can help to wash new clothing a few times before wearing it, to remove that stiff feeling as well as any unfamiliar smells.

And speaking of smells, if an aversion to clothing crops up suddenly, make sure you haven't just changed your detergent or fabric softener. There may be a smell or allergy issue going on.

Remove tags from the inside of garments as needed.

One solution that saves money and hassles is purchasing used clothes instead of new ones. These presoftened garments may already feel "just right." Again, they may need to be washed a few times to take away any bothersome scents.

Decorating for autism

The homes of most young children with autistic spectrum disorders have a certain uniformity. After a few incidents of shattered heirlooms and leaning towers of furniture, accessible areas tend to get a makeover in the direction of a simple, stripped-down look. Baby gates, locked doors, childproofing devices, and the like abound.

When shopping for new furniture, pay extra attention to sturdy, easy-to-clean pieces. You may want to use sticky-back Velcro or foam to secure a few knick-knacks, but it's best to relegate the family china and precious ornaments to an inaccessible room or a locked (and hard to overturn or shake) china cabinet.

Bunk beds and other furnishings that invite acrobatics may not be a good idea for your child. Then again, they might, if your child tends to be unresponsive to her environment, but gets excited about climbing up to an upper bunk or bouncing on a springy mattress.

Likewise, shelves that could be used as steps up to precipitous locations should be removed or very securely anchored.

Linda describes anchoring chairs:

> Even though he couldn't walk yet, William kept using our dining room chairs to climb up onto the table. Several times he made his way up there in seconds, knocking items onto the floor and risking a fall of several feet.
>
> We solved the problem by chaining the dining room chairs to the wall, one in each corner. It made visitors scratch their heads when they saw us do it, but to use the chairs at the table, we just unhooked them.

Some children seem to have a compulsion to move furniture, often using it to build ramps up to places they shouldn't be. Solutions include the following:

- Removing wheels or plastic sliders from furniture legs

- Choosing very heavy furnishings

- Weighting or blocking the movement of furniture with heavy concrete blocks hidden beneath stuffed couches and chairs

- Literally attaching furniture to walls or floor with hook-and-eye fasteners or other hardware

For the early years at least, it's good if you can learn to appreciate thrift store chic. You'll feel a lot worse if your child picks holes in a $1,000 couch than if he damages a $75 sofa from a garage sale. Slipcovers are a good idea for protecting nice fabrics.

If you want to have one or more nice rooms, either lock them or be prepared to stand guard at all times. Experienced parents can attest that the latter option is not worth it—you definitely have better things to do with your days than worrying about stains on your Persian rugs. There will probably be a time when you can enjoy some of the finer things again, but now may not be that time.

Childproofing dangerous items

Most parents of crawling babies and toddlers take pains to remove hazards from their reach. You may need to continue and even expand this program with a child who has an ASD. Funding may be available through government developmental delay or mental health departments, or private agencies, to help cover the expense of these modifications. Several catalogs with commercial childproofing solutions are listed in Appendix A. These items can pose dangers.

- **Glass items and windows.** Some children seem to enjoy the sound of broken glass. This may necessitate using window treatments that can be locked down or even boarding up some windows. Cutting a piece of foam to fit within the interior window well is an inexpensive solution that has worked for some parents. Replacing the glass in windows or picture frames with unbreakable plastic may save accidents.

- **Window blind cords.** These present a danger of hanging if the child puts her head inside the loop. Simply cut through the loop. For persistent offenders, you may want to cut the cords very short as well.

Take a walk through your house with your child's size and interests in mind. If you can notice and remove potential problems before your child sees them, you've done well. Here are some things to watch out for:

- **Exposed electrical outlets.** A variety of plugs and covers are available.

- **Exposed electrical wiring and extension cords.** Obviously, any exposed wires should be moved inside conduit or walls. Extension cords can either be eliminated by adding additional wall outlets, or stapled to the wall. Rubber channels for making them less accessible can usually be found at office supply stores.

- **Electric fans.** Box fans are less dangerous, but little fingers may still fit in. Experiment with fan placement. You might consider using ceiling fans, swamp coolers, or air conditioning instead in hot weather.

- **Stove burners.** Burner covers can eliminate the attraction of fire or glowing coils, but can also cause burns if touched when hot. Some parents remove the knobs from their stove, place a barrier in front of the stove, add a disconnect valve for the gas behind the stove or unplug it when not in use, or add locking doors to the kitchen.

- **Matches, lighters, and combustibles.** Lock these up, and watch out for guests who carelessly leave lighters or matches on tables.

- **Household cleaning supplies, paints, solvents, and other chemicals.** A securely locked cabinet is a must if your child tastes and smells everything. Some young children with autism have incurred serious brain damage by repeatedly sniffing gasoline, glue, or other solvents. Of course, adolescents and teens sometimes abuse these items as drugs.

- **Medications, including herbal remedies and vitamins.** Most people are unaware that aspirin and Tylenol top the list of medication overdose causes—in other words, keep everything that's medicine out of reach. Securely locked bathroom cabinets can work, but storing medications in the bathroom is actually not that great an idea because of the moisture level. You might install a similar cabinet in another room or use a simple lock-box. Small cash boxes work well and are available at office supply stores for a reasonable price. For convenience's sake, you may wish to keep one week's medications, supplements, and vitamins counted out in a plastic pill box, then keep the pill box in your purse or another more secure location. Be especially wary about leaving chewable medications and vitamins within reach.

- **Houseplants.** A few are out-and-out poisonous, and heavy pots coupled with tantalizing fronds and tendrils can lead to hurt heads and major messes. Use ceiling hooks to hang trailing plants well out of the way, or try using sticky-back Velcro or foam to secure pots to a flat surface.

- **Cigarettes.** You would think they'd taste too horrible to eat, but some kids will do it. Tobacco can be quite dangerous when eaten. Keep cigarettes, cigars, chewing tobacco, and full ashtrays under wraps.

- **Alcohol.** It's dangerous to mix even a little alcohol with many of the medications used for ASDs, and it has plenty of inherent dangers of its own. If you like to keep a selection of liquor, wine, or beer at home, consider a locked liquor cabinet or keeping a separate refrigerator in a locked garage or basement.

- **Cat litter boxes.** Cat feces carry disease and should not be handled by pregnant women or anyone with immune system problems. The covered boxes may or may not be less attractive to marauding children. Protect the room where the cat box is with a baby gate, or add a cat door to a locked door.

- **Stairs and stair banisters.** Baby gates or locked doors at the top and/or bottom of stairs may be enough. If the stairs need to be available to your child, make sure that any slats and banisters are too closely spaced for heads or bodies to slip through. If they aren't, you could add more slats or change the banister's style or position. Another solution is blocking access with a net, piece of fabric, or sheet of wood. Commercial stair nets are available that tie securely to open banisters and slats in a stairwell.

- **Guns and other weapons.** These do not belong in the homes of children with neurological disorders, particularly teenagers. The combination of a high potential for depression and easy access to lethal force is very dangerous, and younger children with ASDs may be at risk simply because of their impulsivity. As some recent, tragic cases have shown, storing guns in a locked box under the parents' bed or in a gun cabinet does not guarantee safety around determined teens. If you enjoy shooting sports or hunting, see if you can store your guns at a shooting range or hunt club.

- **Knives.** Sharp knives are common household tools, of course, but they also pose dangers. A drawer latch may be sufficient for keeping kitchen knives out of reach, or you may need to install a keyed lock on the knife drawer. Watch out for knives and other sharp kitchen tools that may be left in the sink, on countertops, or in the dishwasher.

Handling escape artists

Some children with autistic spectrum disorders seem to have a Houdini-like ability to escape their rooms, homes, and yards. This would be an amazing talent if it didn't cause families so much fear and heartache. Unfortunately, incidents of harm to autistic individuals are depressingly common. In recent years at least three autistic children in the US have died in drowning accidents after escaping from their homes. Another spent several harrowing days alone in the Florida Everglades before being rescued—an experience that the nonverbal child's pictures indicated may have included an encounter with an alligator.

The parents of all these children had spent considerable time and expense to secure their homes—all it took was a second for the child to slip out of view. If escapes are a problem for your family, please consider using the services of a professional security consultant. You may be able to get help from government developmental delay or mental health agencies, or private agencies, to find and even pay for these services. Most people don't wish to turn their homes into fortresses, but in some cases it's the most caring thing you can do. It could very well save a life.

Security options that parents have tried, with varying degrees of success, follow:

- Installing key locks or doorknobs with twist locks facing outward on bedroom doors can keep a child securely in his room at night. Obviously, toileting could be a problem with this solution. An intercom or buzzer to summon parents can solve this problem (as could a chamber pot, for those willing to try it).

- Latch-style locks, hook-and-eye hardware, or chain-locks installed at the top of interior doors can limit access to certain rooms, or keep a child in one room. Of course, these can be foiled easily when a child gets taller, becomes strong enough to force the door, or figures out how to stand on a chair.

- Double- or triple-bolt security doors can slow down a would-be escapee, and some types can be unlocked only from the inside with a key. Although expensive, they are tremendously jimmy-proof. Keep the keys well hidden, of course—on your person, if need be. Fire regulations may require that an exterior lock key be secured in a fireproof box or stored at the nearest fire station in case of emergency.

- Windows can be nailed or latched shut.

- Bars can also be placed on windows, as many homeowners in urban areas already do. Like key locks, these can be a fire hazard. A security consultant, or perhaps your local fire department, may be able to come up with ideas. Some types of bars have interior latches.

- Alarms are available that will warn you if a nocturnal roamer is approaching a door or window. Other types only sound when the door or window is actually opened. Depending on your child's speed, the latter may not give you enough response time.

- Obviously, fences and gates are a good idea for backyards. Some types are less easily scaled than others. Although it might seem cruel, in extreme cases a child's safety could be secured by using electric fencing (usually this involves a single "live" wire at the top of a tall fence). Electric fencing kits are available at some hardware stores or at farm supply stores.

- For gates, key locks are more secure than latches.

- Electronic locks of various types are another option, including remote control and keypad varieties. These can be used for garage doors, gates, or exterior doors.

In some cities, the local police department is sensitive to the needs and special problems of the disabled. Officers may be available to provide information about keeping your child or adult patient safe and secure, whether he lives in your home, in an institution or group home, or independently in the community. Some also have special classes to teach self-defense skills to disabled adults.

A few police departments keep a registry of disabled people whose behavior could be a hazard to their own safety or whose behavior could be misinterpreted as threatening. Avail yourself of this service if your child is an escape artist, has behaviors that could look like drunkenness or drug use to an uninformed observer, uses threatening words or gestures when afraid, or is extremely trusting of strangers.

People with ASDs can have a bracelet or necklace made with their home phone number, an emergency medical contact number, or the phone number of a service that can inform the caller about their diagnosis. Labels you might want to have engraved on this item include:

- Nonverbal

- Speech-impaired

- Multiple medications

- Medications include…(list)

- Epilepsy (or other medical condition)

Members of the general public, and even some safety officials, may not know the word "autistic." They are even more unlikely to know what autistic spectrum disorder, pervasive developmental disorder, PDD, or ASD means.

If this section has conjured up visions of a nightmarish life with your child, please remember that most people with ASDs do not experience severe problems in the home that cannot be helped with therapeutic, medical, or educational interventions. However, as experienced parents can tell you, once one problem behavior is extinguished it invariably seems to be replaced by a new one. Parents always need to keep on their toes, and it can be exhausting.

Breaking out of isolation

When a child is diagnosed with an ASD, his family has already experienced a period of prediagnosis crisis. The family has usually undergone immense stress and become increasingly isolated. Old friends have fallen away, the family may have stopped attending religious services or participating in community activities, and breaks with the extended family have often occurred. Marriages and sibling relationships have suffered. One of the most important tasks at hand is building a new support system.

This support system is likely to be very different from the old one. When your life is rolling along nicely, you seek out friends and activities for the purpose of mutual enjoyment. When you are in the throes of difficulty, however, you look for a lifeline. The old sources of support may not be adequate anymore.

Your new support system is also likely to include some paid professionals—counselors, social workers, psychologists, or psychiatrists—as well as people who are personally involved with autistic spectrum disorders as parents, adults with ASDs, support group coordinators, and advocates. It can feel pretty strange to pay for support, or to find yourself immersed in a community of people drawn together by a disability. It may not seem natural. It takes some getting used to at first, but it will be worthwhile.

Support groups

Support groups, in person or on the Internet, can help you break through the wall of isolation. Many excellent support resources are available for parents, and there are a few springing up for children or adults with ASDs as well.

Every support group is different, even local groups that are based on a regional or national model. Personalities, style, location, and local issues set the tone for each group. Typical kinds of support groups include the following:

- **Groups for parents of newly diagnosed children,** which may have a professional in a leadership or organizational role. These groups tend to be short-lived or to be an official service made available to a new set of parents each year (for example, as part of an Early Intervention program).

- **Parent groups for mutual support and for exchanging information about local resources.** These may be organized by parents themselves, or they may be provided by a school or organization. Some groups bring in speakers for each meeting, whereas others are more informal.

- **Parent groups organized around a specific topic or activity,** such as groups for parents implementing special diets, families whose children attend the same school, or those pursuing the possibility that their child's ASD was caused by vaccinations.

- **Social skills groups for children and teenagers.** These groups are usually founded by parents to organize activities that allow their children (and sometimes nondisabled peers or siblings) to get to know each other and enjoy mutual interests. While the children play, adults often find time for informal socializing and support.

- **Adult support groups,** which may include older teens or other family members as well. Some such groups are purely social, some act as formal information forums, and others get involved in advocacy projects.

- **Advocacy groups that take on specific political or educational projects.** Most developed nations have a national autism organization of some sort, and many have similar regional and local groups as well. These groups may publish informational materials for parents and professionals, sponsor conferences and classes, provide direct services to parents and people with ASDs, lobby for increased government or private funding for ASD-related services, lobby in favor of medical research, and try to raise the profile of autistic spectrum disorders.

- **Online support groups**, which may be open to all comers and unmoderated, open but moderated, or limited to approved members only.

If a group that appeals to you already exists, you can simply join in. If it's strictly a volunteer-run enterprise, you can be sure that you'll be expected to lend a hand occasionally. This isn't easy when your life is already full of work and stress, but there are small tasks available in any group that will make you a valuable contributor without taking away too much time from the rest of your life. One thing's for certain: you will get out what you put into any group. If no one's willing to put energy into an organization, it will wither away quickly.

Starting a new group

If there isn't already an organization available that meets your needs, you might consider starting your own. It's easier than you might think.

Typically, new support and advocacy groups arise in periods of crisis. If this is your situation—for example, if adequate educational services are not available in your area for children with ASDs—the stage is set. To contact other parents who might be interested, you can send flyers home with children in special education classes; publish a notice in the local newspaper; use Internet chat forums to post information; put up flyers around town; ask local religious institutions to let their congregations know about the issue; and ask doctors, psychiatrists, neurologists, and others who work with parents to pass the word. Word of mouth is also a powerful organizing tool.

Some of the best support groups are quite small, made up of just a few families coming together to share their feelings and ideas over a meal or coffee. Even advocacy groups need not be large to have an effect. All it takes is a few people with the time and vision to plan a campaign. Disability advocacy groups can often attract volunteers who don't have a personal connection to the disability. Many organizations and forums exist that help prospective volunteers hook up with groups that need them. Schools are also an excellent source of volunteers, who may even be able to earn credit for their work with your organization.

Support groups aren't always "activist" in nature. One mother tells about her favorite:

> We have a really special support group for parents in our
> neighborhood. It's so informal that it doesn't even have a name. Once
> a month we meet at an inexpensive Italian restaurant for dinner and
> talk about our troubles and our triumphs. I also go to meetings of a

national support group, but this other one makes me feel the most
nurtured. I look forward to those dinners all month.

Keeping your group alive

No matter how large your group is or what its purpose will be, a few issues will affect
it right from the start. These include the following:

- **Money.** Passing the hat suffices for coffee and copier fees, but groups that publish newsletters or pamphlets, conduct research, or do major outreach and lobby-
  ing efforts need more secure funding. In some cases, money may be available
  through a hospital, health or disabilities department, or private foundation. Some
  groups are able to tap outside donors or philanthropists. You may want to charge
  members a small fee to join, hold annual fundraising events, put penny jars at
  businesses around town, or try other methods to help the group meet its financial goals.

- **Leadership.** Your group may or may not want to have elected officials, but this
  may be required by law if you choose to have a nonprofit tax status. Generally
  speaking, members should set the direction of the group and do the work, but
  sometimes an official spokesperson or a facilitator (someone who keeps discussions on track at meetings) is needed. Larger advocacy organizations generally
  have some paid staff members, but they still rely heavily on volunteers to get
  things done. Finding and motivating volunteers, tapping new resources, and
  thinking up ideas for activities takes a special kind of leadership. Leaders are
  made, not born, and they do require nurturing. Many groups have found that
  rotating new people through leadership positions prevents burnout, spreads
  skills throughout the organization, and brings new ideas to the fore.

- **Meeting space.** Support groups may meet in members' homes, in restaurants, or
  in rented meeting rooms. Others find rooms available at no or low cost at
  schools, hospitals or clinics, mental health facilities, or churches, mosques, and
  synagogues.

- **Communication.** Phone trees, email lists, web sites that allow members to post
  and reply to messages, and printed newsletters are the main ways that support
  and advocacy groups communicate between meetings. Electronic communication
  is the least expensive, but printed newsletters have the added advantage of being
  available for anyone who can read. Many groups use a combination of communication methods. Some support groups don't have communication between meetings at all, other than notes or cards sent out to inform members of when and
  where the next meeting will be. Some groups have been able to get hospitals or

other medical facilities to send out their newsletters or announcements at no or low cost.

- **Information.** The greatest source of information in any support or advocacy group is its members. However, many groups choose to maintain a library of books, videotapes, pamphlets, documents, medical reports, and ideas for the use of all members. Some keep computer databases or files of local resources and problems, perhaps making them available via the Internet. A support group's library can be as simple as a box of books, videos, and file folders brought to each meeting. Members can look at materials during the meeting, make copies if a machine is convenient, or borrow items. Some groups work with a hospital or medical center library to maintain up-to-date files on autistic spectrum disorders.

Professional support

As the previous section indicated, support groups can be part of a range of professional services provided to parents or to adults with ASDs. These kinds of support groups may be organized by government bodies, schools, or health care organizations.

Group therapy

Group therapy is perhaps the most common type of professional support group. It brings people who have a common problem together with one or more professionals to discuss their difficulties and find solutions. This can be a empowering experience, especially when dealing with a new diagnosis.

It's also less expensive than individual therapy, so it's an attractive concept to managed care organizations concerned with mental health or neurological issues. If you'd like to see these kinds of services available in your area, the best way to begin is by contacting a health care organization or facility that might be willing to sponsor such a group. Explain what kind of help you and others are looking for, and how it might be provided in a clinical setting. Group therapy sessions may be paid for by your insurance, or each participant might pay a small fee.

Some organizations that provide mental health care sponsor support groups as a free or low-cost benefit for their clients. These groups may be able to use meeting space at a clinic after hours, and may get access to resources such as a photocopy machine, postage meter, professional library, or Internet hookup. Often a counselor, social worker, or other professional facilitates this type of support group. There may be speakers or meetings geared to specific topics, such as discipline, diet, or medication side effects, or each meeting may be a forum for free-form discussion.

Individual support

Not everyone is a candidate for support services in a group setting. Sometimes a family's problems are too overwhelming to make attending or making use of group therapy possible. Other times, people simply need individual attention. As earlier in this chapter, family therapy and respite services can be essential parts of a well-conceived support system. Other types of professional support services include the following:

- Case management services that help families manage complex medical, educational, and social programs

- Personal support and informational services delivered by a social worker or counselor

- Direct support services from professionals who help parents and patients solve specific problems

Many families have a long-term need for these kinds of services, which can be hard to find and expensive. However, if the professionals involved have the expertise to truly help, they will prevent many problems further on down the line. Volunteer-based groups—such as The ARC (formerly the Association of Retarded Citizens), Easter Seals, and Samaritans—may be able to provide referrals for low-cost services; some also supply such services directly at little or no cost. Government services for people with disabilities may also include a social work or case management component.

Advocacy groups sometimes have parent-to-parent programs available that match the parents of a newly diagnosed child with an experienced family. Others have crisis intervention help, or even case management services, available at no or low cost. You may have to be a dues-paying member to access these services, although that's not always the case.

Is there a better way?

If parents and adults with ASDs could design the perfect support system, it would be reliable, comprehensive, and adaptable to meet the changing needs of people with ASDs as they move through life's stages.

Holly, mother of 3-year-old Max, says,

> *I'd do more than you could imagine. I'd give them local resources,*
> *actually answer their questions and not fob them off onto another*

agency, be a lending library, be an IEP expert, describe the differences between one program and the next. Be a one-stop shopping resource list, but also be available to answer questions that no one thought of at the time.

Can this ideal be achieved? Probably not by any one program, but making a "cafeteria plan" of support possibilities available to families and individuals affected by autistic spectrum disorders would go a long way toward this goal. Creating and maintaining these resources will probably always fall primarily to those who are closest to the problem, but as professionals in health care and education become more aware of the value of support groups, institutional support is emerging to help people with ASDs and their caregivers better meet their own needs.

One trend that may help is a move toward giving families who use social services more choices about how to spend "their" money, sometimes called self-directed supports. Some programs are experimenting with direct grants to families or adults dealing with mental, physical, or developmental disabilities. When recipients have the power to choose, the range of services available is likely to change in response to demand.

Record keeping

Time is money, and there's no worse waste of both than losing that all- important referral slip or medical report. File every single piece of paper you get from your doctors, therapists, insurance company, service agencies, and school. This includes assessments, evaluations, diagnostic reports, report cards, test results, IFSPs, IEPs, and so on. Be especially sure to save copies of your own correspondence. You can be sure that you'll need it later, if only to impress some recalcitrant official with the extent of your organizational abilities.

A portable plastic file box with a handle can be a real boon. You can carry this box to IEP or other meetings easily and have absolutely everything right at hand. Put your documents in labeled folders or large envelopes. Typical section labels include *Educational, Financial, Medical, Psychological,* and *Social/Recreational.* If an item fits two categories, file it in one folder and make a note on the outside of the other folder about where it is. These folders can also help you keep track of relevant articles, photocopies, and computer printouts.

Try to file items as they are received. It's much more difficult to go through a whole pile of documents that have been tossed together.

Daily record keeping

It sounds time consuming to keep daily records, but that can be essential for monitoring the effect of dietary changes, medications, vitamins, or supplements. It's also important for assessing behavior patterns and sleep problems.

The easiest thing to do is use a small notebook or daily planner specifically for this purpose. This journal can also be used to keep track of medical, therapy, and school appointments.

It's more precise to bind a year's worth of photocopied pages with important items prelisted to jog your memory or to create a customized electronic journal on your home or notebook computer. You may want to include these items on your journal pages, either as fill-in-the-blank listings or checkboxes.

- Medications taken, with time and dose

- Vitamins and supplements taken, with time and dose

- Food and drink taken, with time and rough amount

- Observable reactions to any of the preceding

- Bowel movements and urination (time, amount, characteristics, and so on, as needed)

- Any medical or emotional problems observed, with comments

- ABA or floor-time therapy sessions completed, with comments

- Therapy appointments, with comments

- Medical appointments, with comments

- Recreational activities, with comments

- Self-care activities, with comments

Depending on the individual, there may be many other items to add to this list—or far fewer may suffice.

Other items that you should always have on file include a current profile of your child (strengths, weaknesses, abilities, areas of deficit), a list of current medical or psychiatric concerns, and a list of past concerns and how they were addressed.

Many parents and patients like to jot down a few personal notes in their daily journal as well, when they have the time. You might mention how you're feeling, how your relationships are faring, what stresses you're under—whatever helps you unwind and put the day in perspective.

Be sure to save your journal, even if it's just a list on your computer. You'd be surprised how handy the information you have gathered might be in the future. It will help you take a long-term look at what's worked and what hasn't. Although it's possible to become a bit obsessive about observing your child's every mood, reaction, and action, all these things may be clues to her medical condition. Playing detective may give you the key to a breakthrough someday.

When you must be self-reliant

Children and adults with ASDs who live in isolated rural areas, or who simply do not have access to appropriate health care and education services due to lack of money, face a serious struggle. They must be largely self-reliant, using their ingenuity and limited community resources to build support systems.

It can be done.

Two of the most effective interventions for children with ASDs—ABA and floor-time play therapy—can be delivered at home by parents and volunteers. No special equipment is required, just time and dedication. Books on home ABA and floor-time therapy programs are available via mail order (see Appendix A).

Obviously, medical and psychiatric care requires expertise that most of us don't have, but even there, resources are available. Bibliotherapy, the time-honored process of getting medical or psychiatric information from self-help books, is what you're doing right now.

You may also be able to get direct help from physicians and therapeutic professionals via mail or telephone. Some are even willing to make themselves available for a "virtual consultation" online. Naturally, it's best to see a doctor or medical professional in person, but if your location or financial situation prevents that, there may be ways to work things out. It never hurts to ask.

Home-schooling support

If appropriate educational facilities are not available in your area and residential schooling is out of the question, you will probably decide to opt for home-schooling. If you can possibly afford it and access it, get an Internet connection. Online support will allow you to offer your child "classes" at home in everything from geography to calculus. Compared to the cost of purchasing books and encyclopedias, the Internet is almost always a bargain, and it can put you in touch with the latest medical information as well.

Expensive equipment is not required. Internet access may be available at no charge through your public library, a nearby school, or a business or government agency that's willing to provide you with occasional access to its equipment.

Home-schooling support is also available by mail via newsletters, magazines, and parent-to-parent letters.

Books for home-schoolers can be purchased by mail order, although public libraries may have a decent selection. If you are in a very rural area, you may be able to borrow books from a library at some distance via mail.

Mail order medications

Lack of a drugstore or a limited budget need not cut you off from medications, either. If you can't get it for free (see Appendix A for resources), there are also cheaper and more convenient ways to fill your prescription than paying full price.

Online and mail-order pharmacies can fill your prescription and mail it to you, sometimes at a substantial savings. Medications may be available via mail order within your country or from overseas. The latter option can be surprisingly inexpensive and may provide you with access to medications that normally would not be available where you live. Communicating via fax, email, or telephone generally works best with these firms, which can usually send you a three-month supply in each order. Be sure to check for any customs regulations that might prohibit you from importing medication before ordering, of course, especially if the drug is not approved for use in your country. Some mail-order pharmacies are listed in Appendix A.

Some mail-order and online pharmacies accept health insurance if you have a drug benefit. A few cover your medication copayment as part of the deal.

Your doctor may have to fill out some paperwork before you can use these mail-order services. As with any other transaction by mail or over the Internet, you'll want to do as much as you can to check out the company's reputation and quality of service before sending money or using your credit card.

If you are stationed overseas with the US military, contact your Tricare health benefits representative about mail-order arrangements.

CHAPTER 11

Growing Up on the Autistic Spectrum

UP UNTIL NOW, THIS BOOK HAS BEEN VERY MUCH ABOUT medical realities. But children with autistic spectrum disorders are, first and foremost, children. They have the same basic emotional needs as all children. They need their parents' love, they need friendship, they need to play and have fun. The social deficits that are part and parcel of ASDs can make these basic needs hard to meet.

This chapter looks at childhood as experienced by people with ASDs. It includes information about gently encouraging socialization. It also features the stories of two children who have an autistic spectrum disorder.

Socialization on one's own terms

People tend to assume that all children enjoy the same kinds of social situations. They couldn't be more wrong. Even among children without disabilities, there is a wide range of preferences and interests. Accepting these differences is important, especially when likes and dislikes are based on the child's neurological makeup. Some kinds of social activities can be overwhelming, even frightening, for kids with ASDs. Others allow these children to develop new social skills and enjoy themselves without anxiety.

Many people with ASDs like being in the company of others, but without doing activities that involve a lot of social interaction. Rather than joining in games with a large group, they may prefer having a chess match with one other enthusiast, hanging out at the video arcade with two or three friends, or going on a guided nature walk with a small group.

Many activities can be adapted to fit this preference for controlled socialization. Whereas other children in a play group may play together, the child with an ASD may play beside them, only interacting occasionally. That's a perfectly acceptable place to start. Introduce more opportunities for interaction slowly and gently. Put the emphasis on fun.

Jennifer, mother of 3-year-old Joseph, says,

> *Gymboree [a children's exercise program] has been a godsend. It is based on sensory and developmental principles, and also provides a natural environment for socialization and parent–child bonding. The teachers know about Joseph's diagnosis and have always been very welcoming.*

Activities that offer opportunities for controlled socialization let children with ASDs decide how much conversation they want to take part in, how close to others they wish to be physically, and how much activity they can handle. People who are unused to group activities may hang out on the periphery for quite some time. Many never progress past the point of engaging in activity with only one or two members of the group. That's fine—you're not trying to create a social butterfly, just to help a child with an autistic spectrum disorder find an enjoyable role as part of the larger community.

This kind of socializing may not appeal as much to the parent or caretaker, but respecting the need for personal space and for self-paced involvement is important. You have to remember that social situations may feel different to the person with ASDs. Because he or she may not pick up on cues or know the rules of interaction, social activities can be confusing and fraught with opportunities for mistakes, misunderstandings, and embarrassment. The sensory input involved in noisy activities or crowds may be unbearable. Many people with ASDs are very content to limit their interactions to family and just one or two friends. It's not the number of relationships that matter, but their depth.

Charlotte, mother of 4-year-old Rory, says,

> *We treat Rory like a regular kid and take him everywhere. His grandparents adore him, especially his maternal grandmother. She has great faith in him and points out that he's a very smart little boy. And he loves her; he never wants to leave when we go to visit her.*

Sports

Vigorous physical activity has many health benefits, and it's an important part of social life for many children and teenagers. Although some children with ASDs enjoy team sports such as football and baseball, others may prefer joining a track, swimming, or martial arts team. In these groups the essential activity is individual, but there is camaraderie during training and competition. Others might enjoy working out at a gym, bowling, taking a dance or exercise class, going on group hikes, or joining in on a cleanup day at a park or beach.

You may want to seek out community activities set up especially for disabled children or adults. In the US, Special Olympics has an excellent sports program that is very accepting. There are also organized sports leagues specifically for children with disabilities, and leagues that integrate them into sports teams with nondisabled children. Challenger leagues for baseball are the best known integrated leagues, but similar groups exist for soccer and other sports.

Public parks-and-recreation departments may also have staff who can help children with ASDs participate in activities, classes, and trips that they organize. In larger cities, they may also sponsor some special activities for the disabled, ranging from trips to the bowling alley to summer camps.

School activities

As mentioned in Chapter 9, *School,* children with ASDs have the right to be involved in school clubs and activities to the extent that they wish. Many young people have become valued members of school track and swim teams, golf and tennis clubs, chess clubs, science clubs, choirs, orchestras, and theater groups, among other activities. If your child needs an aide to be successful in class, she may also need an aide to participate in these activities. Support services that make these activities possible can be written into an IEP or 504 plan.

Children with disabilities should not be excluded from school field trips, either, including overnight trips. Providing support for longer activities can be difficult, and parents may have to attend with their child.

Neighborhood activities

Most children with ASDs are not part of neighborhood street hockey games and sand-lot baseball. The political aspects of child's play are anything but simple, and navigating within large groups of fussing, pushy kids is often just too much.

Some children do take a special interest in another child who is different, especially kids whose home situation is difficult or who have some minor "differences" of their own. Should your child be so lucky as to attract a potential friend like this, take advantage of the opportunity as much as you can.

Patti, mother of 4-year-old Alyssa, says,

> *One of the best things we ever did was set up play dates for Alyssa. She usually can't handle the whole gang of little girls on our street at once, and even if she tried to tag along they might leave her behind because she is nonverbal. We've found that if it's just her and one girl, we can set up simple activities that both can enjoy, like stringing bead necklaces or baking cookies.*
>
> *The girls are learning about Alyssa and coming away from an afternoon at our house with a good feeling about her. So far this year, two girls invited her to their birthday parties and one asked her to go roller-skating. They also wave and say hi when they see her. I can tell by the smile on her face that this makes her happy.*

Not all neighborhood relationships are so great. Parents have to go out of their way to educate neighbors about their child, and not everyone will be receptive. Parents whose children have a tendency to scream or break things in a rage, or who have other unusual behaviors (such as self-injury, stripping off their clothes, or using inappropriate language), have sometimes had to deal with police or child protective services workers called in because their neighbors didn't understand.

And when the parents don't understand or even actively cause trouble, their children are likely to follow suit.

Linda, mother of 11-year-old William, says,

> *Our relationship with neighbors in our old neighborhood was not very good. They allowed their children to torment our son, then came running if he fought back. We didn't allow him to play outside unsupervised, and there were certain children that we instructed him to avoid because they were just plain mean!*
>
> *In our new neighborhood, he mostly hangs around on the periphery when they are kicking a ball around, only joining in now and again. Still, this is a step forward. We have made a point of inviting the boys over one or two at a time for a snack and perhaps to play a video game with him. My husband had a chat with two of them about teasing, and things have been fine with them since then. Now only one is still a bit of a problem, but I think it will work out on its own. William is learning to stand up for himself.*

Friends are important, and your own neighborhood is the most convenient place to find them. Those who live in very rural areas or in areas that are not safe for children to play without direct supervision may have to turn to other resources for finding friends. A playground, indoor park, organized play group, or children's club can also be the stage for introducing your child to social activities.

Different lives

Each child on the autistic spectrum has unique characteristics, interests, and abilities. What his or her experience of childhood is like depends very much on the severity of symptoms and the environment in which they occur.

Walking the line

Amy's son Miles is 7, and his differences are not always evident to outsiders. Initially diagnosed with severe ADHD at 3½, his current diagnosis is PDD-NOS. For Miles, social relationships are probably the most difficult part of childhood to navigate.

> *He knows he is different. He has a few motor stereotypies—*
> *arm-flapping is the most conspicuous—that cause him to be teased*
> *at school. He has trouble making friends, and he knows it.*
>
> *Miles does not travel well and reacts behaviorally to changes in his*
> *normal routine. Miles' behaviors impact the stress level of my*
> *relationship with my partner, in that he needs so much time and*
> *attention and his behaviors are unpleasant at times.*

Miles attends second grade in a regular public school classroom, and has pull-out sessions for speech therapy and occupational therapy. Amy credits these two interventions, and particularly sensory integration work, with his success in a mainstream setting. Schoolwork isn't a problem, as long as he's in a very structured environment.

> *Miles is very intelligent, and at the same time he has many*
> *communication and social difficulties. Some days, I see him as a*
> *research scientist when he grows up . . . some days, I worry that*
> *he will never gain the skills to be independent of me.*
>
> *This highlights the biggest issue for me, that Miles could go either*
> *way. With the proper teaching and support, he will do well; without*
> *it, he will surely fall through the cracks. He looks "typical," and he*

dances on that fine line between "our world" and "Miles's world"
every single day. Hopefully, he will use this precarious position to his
advantage someday—I am trying to give him the tools to do that.

Miles has help from many adults in his life. His parents are behind him all the way, but the professionals at his school are too, from the school nurse to his teacher and the occupational therapist who comes to work with him. With their guidance and care, his mother feels, he will go far.

Feeling different

William's diagnosis is also PDD-NOS. He had severe speech delays, and continues to have problems with motor development, social interaction, and obsessive interests. Between the ages 6 and 10, William attended school in a self-contained special education classroom. His academic skills mirrored his IQ scatter—great at math, struggling with reading but improving, hopeless in PE. He was a talented artist, and after being a very self-involved toddler and young child, began to reach out socially. His first real friendship was a very important part of his development.

> *Mickey and William have been friends since they were toddlers.*
> *Sometimes their friendship is very one-sided because they are so*
> *different, but despite the fights and arguments they still seek each*
> *other out. Mickey is the youngest in a large family, and visiting with*
> *William gives him individual attention. We have included him in our*
> *family activities whenever we can. He probably taught William more*
> *about social skills than anything we or the school has ever done.*

From this friendship, and from a formal social skills group, the desire for more social activity slowly emerged. William's 8th birthday party had just four guests. This was the largest gathering he had asked for up to that time, and he was a little nervous. With structured activities and a short time frame, the party was a success, and he said afterward that it made him feel "like a regular kid." For his 11th birthday, he invited the entire class. Nineteen children came, and they had a ball. William retreated into his room with his new toys for part of the party, but his friends carried on with playing games and eventually he joined in again.

William is intensely aware of some of his differences. His speech difficulties in particular make him a target for bullying. "Sometimes [other kids] won't share with me. Sometimes they don't want to be my friend," he says.

William's parents are working to build up his resilience by helping him have success in his areas of interest and talent. His drawings are always proudly displayed, and his skills with math, computers, puzzles, and LEGO blocks get lots of praise.

When asked at 8 years what his plans are when he grows up, he had lots of answers:

> I'm going to play basketball, live in Greece, hunt Bigfoot or the Loch Ness monster or aliens. Visit Egypt, Rome, the Himalayas, Scotland, England, and . . . where did the man in the iron mask live? Oh, yeah, France.

His parents feel that his future looks bright, considering how far he has come in the past few years.

Interpreting the world of the nonverbal child

Miles and William are both relatively "high functioning" children, but not all children with ASDs reach this level. Those with mental retardation often lead very different lives, for example. Children who never gain the gift of speech, even minimal speech, have a particularly difficult time.

Parents of "low functioning" children often wonder about their experiences. They hope their child is content and happy, but it's hard to be sure. As new communication technologies permit more nonverbal people to "speak," perhaps we will find out. What's certain is that behavior is a form of communication: If your child's actions indicate that he is happy, he probably is.

As you work to bring your child into the world of social relationships, there may be times when he feels uncomfortable and even angry. You may be tempted to leave him in his own world, where he seems perfectly content. Occasionally that's alright, but social skills are important for overall development and for a satisfying adult life.

Parents need to find a balance between respect for the essential differences that make people on the autistic spectrum who they are, and the need to fit into society. We need to help our children meet the outside world halfway, and also do our best to make society go halfway for people who have special needs.

CHAPTER 12

Adults with Autistic Spectrum Disorders

CHILDREN GROW UP. MOST PARENTS LOOK FORWARD TO THIS, but parents of children with autism sometimes dread it. They fear that their child will not have a good quality of life as an adult. They worry that without parents on hand to fight for them, they may be lost in the social services system, pushed into the margins of society by low-paid work, prejudice, and dependency.

This chapter looks at planning for adult life, and includes stories about three adults with autistic spectrum disorders. These stories illustrate the only certainties about adults with ASDs: that each is an individual, and that each can find a way of living that suits his abilities and interests.

Planning for independence

As noted in Chapter 9, *School,* transition planning services for teens in special education may include helping them arrange for financial support through work, government programs, or special needs trusts; getting young adults into medical insurance programs; helping young adults manage their own medical and/or psychiatric care; and providing other services, such as GED assistance, job shadowing, and so on.

You can also make your own transition plan. Areas that most families need to work on include the following.

- Housing, including group homes or other supported housing if needed
- Higher education (see Chapter 9)
- Work or financial assistance (see Chapter 9)
- Health care
- Health insurance (see Chapter 8, *Insurance*)
- Case management

- Long-term planning
- Legal rights
- Adult relationships
- Sexuality

Start thinking about the future while your child is still young, and revise your expectations as you go. Don't be afraid to have big dreams for your child, as starting early makes them more likely to be realized, no matter how "unrealistic."

At the same time, don't be afraid of facing reality. Most people have some degree of dependency on others at some point of their adult lives. We all rely on our families, friends, and colleagues for help at times. It's okay if your child will need extra assistance in adulthood. What's important is his happiness and safety.

Cindy, mother of 15-year-old Jeffrey, explains:

> I hope Jeffrey will be able to live in a supervised rental, with others
> his age, and be able to take care of his needs with some assistance.
> I hope he will find meaningful, satisfying work (not hauling trash
> or sweeping floors!) and be able to earn some of his own money. I
> hope he develops a physical activity he is able to do on a regular
> basis, perhaps with others, which will keep him healthy. And most
> of all, if life gets to be too much for him, I hope he will be able to
> tell me.

Housing

People with disabilities tend to have low incomes, whether they work or rely on public benefits. One of the most difficult results of this problem is trouble with finding suitable housing. To respond to this need, there are a variety of housing programs and types available. These range from subsidized housing, which is simply less expensive than housing available on the open market, to housing geared to the special needs of people with disabilities.

Apply for housing before there's a pressing need, as waiting lists for the better programs are long (up to three years for the Section 8 program described later in this chapter). This may mean applying while a teenager is still in high school.

AutismCommunity, an online discussion group (see *http://groups.yahoo.com/group/ AutismCommunity/* to subscribe) is a forum for talking about housing issues.

Subsidized housing

For many years, the main form of subsidized housing in the US was public housing: government-owned buildings intended to offer adequate accommodation at very affordable rates to people under a certain income threshold. Very little public housing has been built in the past two decades, and much of what exists has deteriorated. It is worth looking at the availability of public housing in your area, however, as some units still offer good value for money, and many cities are making great efforts to improve and even expand the existing stock of units. In most areas, people with disabilities get preference when housing units are assigned.

Some disabled people in the US are eligible for housing choice voucher programs administrated by the Housing and Urban Development (HUD) department, including Section 8 vouchers. These monthly grants can be used to reduce the cost of housing you find on the open market. This is now the main form of subsidized housing in the US.

Special housing choice grants are available for families with disabled children and for disabled adults. In some cases, you can use these grants to get housing in subsidized units normally reserved for senior citizens—these buildings are usually among the best maintained, quietest, and most secure in public housing, and so it's well worth checking your eligibility. See HUD's housing choice voucher program web site at *http:// www.hud.gov/offices/pih/programs/hcv/index.cfm* or call (202) 708-1112 for more information. HUD can put you in touch with your local public housing authority as well as tell you about voucher programs.

Some charitable organizations and churches also manage low-income housing projects or voucher programs, and may have preferential treatment for people with disabilities. If you are a Native American, there are also subsidized housing opportunities through special vouchers and tribally owned units.

When examining subsidized housing units, pay special attention to security concerns, such as locking doors and windows, having a personal telephone in case of emergencies, and the safety of the surrounding neighborhood for a person who may be particularly vulnerable to crime. Sanitary conditions may also need work, especially if you are considering an older housing project or a residential hotel. Landlords are responsible for bringing units up to code, but they may not respond until the tenant's family or a social services agency gets involved.

If you are or are about to be homeless, you may be able to move to the front of the line for subsidized housing. Contact a social services agency for help in pressing your case quickly, especially if you have children.

Public (social) housing is widely available throughout the UK and Europe, where minimum standards and ongoing building programs have largely prevented the decayed urban housing projects that blight some US cities. Be sure to look closely at any social housing you are offered, of course, because some buildings and areas should be avoided. As in the US, people with disabilities usually jump to the front of the queue for social housing.

Supported housing

Supported housing ranges from group homes with full-time staff on up to private apartments with occasional support services arranged through social services or private agencies. Options vary as widely as the people who need help: there are suburban group homes with three to five residents, large urban apartment buildings with medical and social work staff on site or nearby, and in-home services provided anywhere you choose to live.

These programs may be covered by long-term care insurance, health insurance, funds placed in trust, or monthly payments made by you or your adult child. Regional autism and mental health advocacy groups should have lists of supported housing possibilities in your area, or you can check in with a public or private social services agency.

Group homes are now the dominant form of supported housing in the US. They vary in quality. Some provide custodial care only, others are dedicated to fostering independence and a sense of community. For a look at how good they can be, check out projects sponsored by the L'Arche movement (206-306-1330 or *http://www.geocities.com/larcheusa/*).

Many adults with ASDs can live largely independent lives if their families and professional helpers lay the groundwork. Adults with ASDs should always have full input on decisions, particularly where an important issue like housing is concerned. If you are dissatisfied with a group home or other living situation, talk it over with family members, your case manager, or a trusted advocate. Many larger cities have independent living centers that can help. These self-help groups originated to assist people with physical disabilities, but they can be terrific places to find resources for adults with ASDs. Typical offerings include assistive technology help, self-care classes, and help with finding qualified home care aides. See *http://www.independentliving.org/* on the Web for some online resources as well.

Services to help you achieve the goal of independent living might include housekeeping, budgeting help, and special transportation arrangements. Don't be afraid to ask.

These basic services are generally much less expensive than group homes or other living arrangements with round-the-clock support. If they can be shared with a housemate or neighbor, the cost may be even lower.

There is a trend toward people with disabilities setting up their own shared housing arrangements. Unlike a typical group home, these households of higher functioning individuals run cooperatively, not unlike a shared house full of college students who just happen to pool funds to hire housekeeping and therapy services rather than pizza and cable TV service.

There is also a growing trend toward helping disabled adults purchase their own homes: See the National Home of Your Own Alliance web site (*http://alliance.unh.edu/*) for more information. Grants are available for down payment assistance, along with special loan programs, trust arrangements, and home buying and home ownership training. See the HUD web site listed earlier in this chapter for more information about homebuyer help for people using Section 8 vouchers. The charitable organization Habitat for Humanity (229-924-6935 or *http://www.habitat.org/*) administers many local self-help homeownership programs, as do other groups.

Farm communities

For people with ASDs who have grown up in a rural environment, moving to a big city just to get special housing is a scary idea. Many who have grown up in suburbs or cities like the idea of a quieter, safer country life.

Farm communities for people with autism are more common in Europe than in the US. You can find more information about farm communities for people with autism on the Web at *http://www.lin.ca/resource/html/Vol27/V27N1A2.htm*.

Institutional care

Today, very few people with ASDs live in large institutions, such as mental hospitals, in the US or UK. If a mental health crisis or pressing physical problems necessitate a hospital stay, know that it is just a short-term solution, and work hard to put a transition plan in place for post-hospital care in the community.

In some countries, however, long-term institutional care is still common. If you or your adult child will be spending more than a month in institutional care, find out as much as you can about the program. If you are a parent, support your child's right to make independent choices whenever possible. Stay alert and involved with his care. Visit as often as possible, and get to know the professionals involved.

Health care

You won't always be there to take your child to medical and therapy appointments, make sure he takes his medications and vitamins, and wrangle with health care issues on his behalf. Parents need to start teaching their children as early as possible about using public transportation or driving, picking up prescriptions and reading their labels, paying medical bills, and knowing where to go for help.

Some adults are never able to handle all these tasks adequately, even though they may be perfectly competent in other areas of their life. These individuals will need support to help them get appropriate medical care. Case management services, described later in this chapter, can help. A personal aide or a self-care advocate may be even better.

You'll also need to identify adult health care providers in advance as your child nears the end of adolescence. Young women will need to see a gynecologist, for example, and both boys and girls will be leaving their pediatrician for a general practitioner.

If there will be changes in how your child's health care is paid for—for example, if she will be making a transition from private health insurance to Medicaid—you may have to prospect for knowledgeable doctors in an unfamiliar medical bureaucracy.

You can help your adult child develop methods for keeping track of medications, appointments, dietary restrictions, and the like. Visual charts, calendars, and personal agenda books may be useful if appointments are filled in far in advance. Pillboxes that divide up a week's doses are very helpful.

Case management

You may continue to act as your adult child's "case manager" for many years, or he may wish to give this job to a professional. Case management services can encompass arranging for health care, connecting the adult client with community services, a certain amount of financial management (such as being a payee for SSI), and much more.

Case managers can be hired privately or found within government departments or advocacy agencies for the disabled. Some medical facilities provide health case management services for adult disabled patients.

Linda, mother of 17-year-old KayCee, says,

> What we opted for was the services of a caseworker with County
> Mental Health, who will continue to be a resource person for KayCee as
> she transitions to adulthood. He signed her up for a supplemental mental

*health insurance program available through the state that will cover any
needs that fall outside of our insurance plan, like mental health inpatient
care or extra therapy sessions. When she reaches the age of 18, she'll be
eligible for state health insurance or Medicaid, based on her own income
from work.*

Long-term planning

If you're lucky enough to have an estate that could help your child after your death,
do not put off making arrangements. Because of the laws surrounding public disability benefits, inheriting money could end up being a terrible burden rather than a
safety net.

Special trusts, usually called discretionary or special needs trusts, can make funds or
real property (such as a home) available to adults with disabilities. These trusts are set
up to keep the recipient eligible for government assistance, publicly funded health
insurance, and subsidized housing. Generally speaking, discretionary trusts require a
trustee other than the recipient to be in charge. Money in a discretionary trust can be
used to pay for items other than food, clothing, and shelter, such as education, phone
bills, and recreation, without reducing benefits. If these funds are used for food,
clothing, or shelter, a limited amount will be deducted from the person's SSI check.

You'll need to consult a financial planner and/or a lawyer with experience in working on disability issues to set up a discretionary trust. Advocacy groups, such as The
ARC (formerly the Association of Retarded Citizens), often run workshops on this
topic for families.

Legal rights

Although full independence is every parent's goal, most adults with ASDs need at
least some help and oversight long after the age of 18 or 21—and retaining a close
relationship with one's parents is valuable in and of itself. Legal issues can get in the
way, however.

Once your child has reached the age of majority, you don't have the automatic right
to determine her medical care, or to control any other aspect of her personal life. You
may find yourself shut out of important decisions about housing, food, medical care,
education, and vocational choices. If your child is able to handle these choices alone,
that's great, even if you don't always agree with her decisions.

For many families, however, problems occur when the adult child's friends, therapists, or professionals with various programs start calling the plays. You may not be sure your adult child agrees with these decisions, and sometimes individuals deliberately try to prevent you from having access to the decision-making process. Your input can help ensure your child's safety and keep his personal needs met. You may need to take legal steps to make sure you stay in the picture.

Guardianship is one option. This basically places you in full charge of your adult child's affairs. It is only appropriate if your adult child is completely unable to make his own decisions and care for himself. A court must declare the person incompetent and appoint you (or someone else) as guardian. In some areas, partial (plenary) guardianship is an option.

Less restrictive options include the following:

- A durable medical power of attorney, which allows you to step in if your adult child becomes mentally or physically incapacitated

- A limited power of attorney, which gives you the ability to make certain kinds of legal decisions for your child

- Financial planning, such as special needs trusts, limited bank accounts that you co-sign or oversee, or appointing a representative payee

Adult relationships and ASDs

Some people with ASDs do have friendships and romantic relationships, marry, and/or have children, although this is rarely the case for individuals diagnosed with autistic disorder. Accordingly, it's essential that explicit instruction be provided to all people with autistic spectrum diagnoses on meeting and approaching potential friends or romantic interests, appropriate dating behavior, avoiding domestic violence, sexuality (see later section), contraception, pregnancy, childbirth, and child rearing. This is information needed by both sexes, and should be imparted in ways appropriate to the person's age and ability to understand.

Adults with ASDs who have successful adult relationships, including marriage, report that the experience can be rocky. Professional or religious marriage counseling is invaluable, particularly before marriage, when the partners have a chance to work out areas of potential conflict in advance. Some married couples in which one or both partners has an ASD have made a long-term commitment to family therapy for this reason.

Support for the partners of adults with Asperger syndrome is increasingly available. Support groups such as ASPIRES (*http://www.justgathertogether.com/aspires.html*) and books about the common issues affected families face, such as *An Asperger Marriage,* by Gisela and Chris Slater-Walter (Jessica Kingsley Publishers, 2002) or Maxine Aston's *The Other Half of Asperger Syndrome* (Autism Asperger Publishing, 2002), can be very helpful.

Some adults with ASDs need assistance with household upkeep and parenting, which is often provided by their partner or by other family members. Housekeeping services, and ongoing parenting education and support, may also be available through government or private agencies for people with disabilities. Of course, a housekeeper or nanny can also be privately hired if you have the financial means. As with school and work, adults with ASDs may need to use visual charts and careful scheduling to assure that they meet their home and family responsibilities, from doing housework to keeping up with their children's medical appointments.

Incidentally, because autistic spectrum disorders have a genetic component, it's important to initiate early screening for the children of adults with ASDs. Social enrichment programs, such as a good preschool, can also help to close gaps in learning that young children may experience as a result of their parent's disability.

ASDs and sexuality

Many parents fear that their children with ASDs may be sexually abused or exploited, even as adults. Sadly, this fear is realistic, particularly for those individuals who are nonverbal or institutionalized. Parents and caretakers need training on recognizing signs of sexual abuse and exploitation, and all residential and day programs for vulnerable children and adults need to take into account the danger of inappropriate or predatory behavior by staff, visitors, and others. This doesn't mean denying people with ASDs the right to sexual expression—it means ensuring that sexual activity takes place in the context of consenting, non-exploitative relationships or, in the case of masturbation, in private and without negative consequences.

Parents of people with ASDs also worry about whether their offspring will be able to navigate the issues of menstruation, contraception, and both the emotional and physical aspects of sexual expression. With careful instruction about sexual function, emotions, relationships, and self-protection, the answer should be yes—but these factors are lacking in the education plans of many teens and young adults with ASDs.

A nationwide survey on sexual activity in the autistic population of Denmark[1] covered these issues, as well as the problem of public masturbation and other inappropriate sexual behaviors. This survey established that individuals on the autistic spectrum have a number of difficulties in the area of sexuality, including naive and socially inappropriate expressions of sexuality, social deficits that make sexual relationships difficult to initiate and maintain, obsessional sexual desire or behavior, and the sexual side effects of psychiatric drugs.

This survey also noted that the adults with ASDs surveyed had a higher-than-usual level of "deviant" sexual behavior, which the researchers hypothesized had some relationship to the unnatural conditions under which this population had discovered and learned about sexuality (all were adults living in group homes, and many had been institutionalized since early childhood), and also a possible relationship to the sensory disorders that can be part of autism (for example, sexual fetishism, in which certain smells or objects are perceived as sexually arousing, was fairly common). As the researchers put it, "Sexual behavior or autistic behavior is neither deviant nor disturbed, but rather an expression of social and emotional immaturity. In fact, autistic people develop inappropriate sexual behavior because of their inability to understand social norms and rules, and because of their inability in communicating and establishing reciprocal relationships."

Regarding adults with high-functioning autism, the Danish researchers' findings were particularly enlightening. They found that frustrated sexual feelings, including an inability to masturbate to a climax and thwarted desires for sexual relationships, correlated strongly with self-abusive behavior. Often this behavior had an obvious connection, such as hitting the genitals.

The message here is one that many parents and professionals find difficult: Some people need explicit instruction on how to enjoy themselves sexually. This is a basic human right, but it's often overlooked when it comes to people with disabilities. People expect that everyone will be able to simply "do what comes naturally," ignoring the fact that for some people sex does not come naturally at all. There is also a tendency to infantilize adults with disabilities, assuming that they do not experience sexual desire. If parents or caretakers don't feel comfortable with the task, the services of a professional sex therapist can be engaged to teach techniques. But because most people want to have sex in the context of an affectionate relationship, it's more natural for discussions about sex to be with parents or close friends.

There is a surprisingly large amount of literature available on the general topic of disability and sexuality, including information on facilitating appropriate sexual expression, teaching disabled adults about related health and hygiene concerns, and preventing sexual abuse. A number of states, school districts, and agencies have developed instructional materials geared toward various special populations, including mentally retarded, deaf, mentally ill, behaviorally disordered, physically handicapped, and institutionalized youth and adults. At least some of these materials could be useful for adolescents and adults with ASDs. A 1991 bibliography, *Disability, Sexuality, and Abuse,* is referenced in Appendix A, *Resources.*

Lives on the autistic spectrum

The lives of adults with ASDs are as different from one another as are the lives of people without disabilities. Much depends on the severity of the person's condition, coexisting health problems, and family situation.

Currently, more adults with ASDs than ever before are finding jobs, pursuing higher education opportunities, living more independent lives, and forming families of their own.

Side by side

Liz can't tell her own story. At 25 years old, she is still primarily nonverbal. Her 27-year-old sister Donna, however, has stuck by her side ever since her previously rambunctious and talkative 3-year-old sister developed encephalitis, which resulted in autistic-like symptoms and epilepsy.

When her little sister got a flu-like illness, Donna wasn't all that worried—but Liz kept getting worse instead of better. When the medical crisis was finally over, major changes were immediately evident. "The first thing I noticed was that she wasn't talking, really," Donna says. Liz was also having seizures, and the medications she took to control them made her violent and unpredictable.

Donna's life changed almost as much as her sister's. She took on more responsibility for her two other siblings, because her parents needed to supervise Liz very closely. Her sister's behavior kept her from bringing friends over, as well.

> *It was embarrassing. I wouldn't want to bring them home because*
> *I didn't know what kind of state she'd be in. One time she threw this*

metallic toy cymbal across the room like a Frisbee, and it sliced into my friend's face.

I became an "outside" kid. I was over at other people's houses all the time.

However, Liz's struggle made Donna more sensitive to people with disabilities.

Whenever anybody made fun of someone who was disabled, I'd say, "Stop that, my sister's like this." I was always trying to educate people.

Liz has found adult pursuits she enjoys. She works part time on a nearby farm, where she feeds and cares for the animals. She's especially fond of the horses and has learned to ride well. Liz still lives at home with her parents.

Liz communicates with sounds, some ASL signs, her own personal sign language, and expressive body and facial movements. New medications for her seizures have helped minimize her violent episodes. Donna says,

She still goes up and down quite a bit, especially around her menstrual cycle. Some days she'll have a lot of seizures and be almost catatonic, but sometimes she's very connected. She understands short, one-word things, but I think sometimes what she hears is kind of jumbled, like it's hard to process so much information at once.

The next step for Liz will probably be living in a group home, once her parents have found a safe, appropriate place with people she enjoys. She's able to take care of herself physically in most ways, but may need help in activities for independent living, such as budgeting. She may also need some level of daily supervision. As she gets older, though, her moods are more manageable, and she's able to make her own wishes known some of the time. That, along with her supportive family, bodes well for a more independent life as she gets older.

The worth of a label

Kalen, now 24, was never told that she had been speculatively diagnosed autistic at age 3. She struggled through school with social and organizational difficulties, and was finally identified as "learning disabled" when she was 14. Academics weren't a problem; it was everything else: all the daily interactions with peers and teachers, trying to process convoluted chunks of information, and being teased by her classmates. Things were a mess at home, too, with an abusive family situation adding to her difficulties.

In college, the pieces started to come together for Kalen:

> *In college I found that some teaching styles don't work for me. For example, I was taking a literature course in which the instructor had us break up into small groups during every class. I couldn't process the conversations or deal with the interaction required.*

Adult relationships were a puzzle, however. In her early 20s she became a single parent.

After doing research online, she finally found out about autism, was able to confirm clues from her early childhood, and just over three years ago was given a medical diagnosis of high-functioning autism (HFA).

> *I have spent a long time trying to figure out what's wrong with me, as well as in therapy for childhood abuse.*
>
> *On one hand, I am glad I found out I am autistic. It gives me an explanation for what I thought was laziness or not caring. It was also wonderful to find out that I am not the only person like this on the planet...although in a way I would have liked to think I was the only one. On the other hand, laziness and apathy are things that can be overcome, while autism carries with it permanent limitations. It is hard to come to terms with the fact that I have a disability and can't do everything I had always been told I could.*

For two years, Kalen attended college part time, taking courses in calculus, chemistry, physics, English, and philosophy. Although she didn't finish every course she started, her grades in completed classes were quite good. She also found some community support, both in the city where she lived and online, where she made many friends.

> *For a year I lived with an older couple who took care of my practical needs. That was nice, because I am not good at taking care of myself and the housework. It was actually the ideal situation for me: I was responsible for myself and my own money, but I had help with the things I have difficulty with. Those people still have me over for supper once or twice a month, and they fix things around my apartment.*

For a while she lived on permanent disability benefit in her own small apartment, and also had a part-time job building and maintaining a web site for the local autism society. Her daughter was in a foster care placement at that time, with her access limited to just four hours each week. During this period her life was difficult.

> *My life is pretty boring. I spend most of it on the Internet with the TV on beside me. I am currently taking a life skills course for single parents. It is extremely difficult for me to deal with the group interaction, especially the unstructured times of coffee breaks and lunch. I need a lot of time to decompress in the evenings, and if I don't have that, I fall apart.*

Eventually she regained custody of her daughter, and got engaged to a man in England whom she met online. They wrote to each other daily via email, and talked on the phone when possible. In time, she moved to England to live with him, and they now have a child together.

Despite her obvious high intelligence, Kalen has no plans to move into a career, because of her social difficulties and some additional health problems.

> *The stress of having to work in order to live would be more than I could cope with, and I would end up not working at all. Sorry to be discouraging to parents . . . I do think that a lot of this could have been remediated if I had [had] proper support as a child and adolescent. I would like to see a supported living situation for HFA and Asperger's syndrome adults. I'm working on this with the autism society here, which already has four homes for lower functioning people. It seems that I am too low functioning to get on in the world very well, and too high functioning to get any help.*

For other adults recently given a diagnosis in the autism spectrum, she has some simple (if tongue-in-cheek) advice:

> *Don't panic. There are good things about being autistic, and there are others from the home planet trying to exist here.*

Like parent, like child

When 5-year-old Nicole was diagnosed with mild autism, her mother was worried, but not crushed. She had already seen a success story, and he was sitting right across from her at the dinner table: her husband, Nicole's father.

> *The reason for my optimism is the fact that my husband was diagnosed ADHD, and probably also had high-functioning autism—behaviorally, he matched that diagnosis even more than Nicole does.*

The three local public schools kicked him out at the tender age of 7.
They did not know what to do with him! He had very supportive parents
who had him tutored from first grade to seventh grade.

Through hard work, perseverance, and many prayers, he did get
through school, attending regular mainstreamed junior and senior high.

College was an even more successful experience. He completed senior-level engineering courses, and now runs his own successful business working with computers and doing electronics repairs.

He went much further than his parents expected him to, and started
out with many of the same issues as our daughter.

Nicole is already showing signs of her father's fighting spirit.

We attend church regularly, and Nicole seems to enjoy her time there.
She also takes swimming lessons at the YMCA and loves that activity as
well. I have every reason to believe that with the same spirit of
perseverance and support that her father had, Nicole can also be
successful in whatever she chooses to conquer in her life.

Don't just hope for the best, create it

Work hard while your child is young to achieve the best outcome. Help her to gain personal strength and flexibility to handle life's ups and downs, and your job will have been done well. Do your best to understand how your child feels about things and what he wants out of life: Ask questions, and really listen to the answers. Challenge your own assumptions about what's best for him—you might try visiting the Institute for the Neurologically Typical at *http://isnt.autistics.org/*, a humorous web site created by an adult with autism, for a glimpse into how strange "normal" thought processes can seem to people who don't see things the same way.

As the personal stories in this chapter illustrate, life on the autistic spectrum can be rich and rewarding. There are challenges, as in everyone's life, but with help from friends, families, and professionals, these can be faced and overcome.

Resources

THE BOOKS, PAMPHLETS, AND OTHER RESOURCES LISTED HERE can help you further explore areas of interest related to autistic spectrum disorders. We have included addresses for printed materials that are not usually available in stores or libraries. Otherwise, you should be able to find these items in your local library or via interlibrary loan, or be able to purchase them in regular or online bookstores.

Autistic spectrum disorders

These books and publications are guides to aspects of autistic spectrum disorders.

Attwood, Tony. *Asperger's Syndrome: A Guide for Parents and Professionals.* London: Jessica Kingsley Publishers, 1998.

Autism Research Institute. *Autism Research Review International (ARRI).* This informative newsletter summarizes medical study results, and includes reports on traditional and alternative medicine for autistic symptoms. Available from ARI at 4182 Adams Avenue, San Diego, CA 92116.

Baron-Cohen, Simon, MD, and Bolton, Patrick, MD. *Autism: The Facts.* Oxford, UK: Oxford University Press, 1995.

Bashe, Patty R., and Kirby, Barb. *The OASIS Guide to Asperger Syndrome.* New York: Crown Publishing, 2001.

Cohen, Shirley. *Targeting Autism: What We Know, Don't Know, and Can Do to Help Young Children with Autism and Related Disorders.* Berkeley, CA: University of California Press, 1998.

Gerlach, Elizabeth. *Autism Treatment Guide.* Eugene, OR: Four Leaf Press, 1996. This book by a parent offers practical suggestions for addressing difficult symptoms and behaviors.

Kephart, Beth. *A Slant of Sun: One Child's Courage.* New York: Norton, 1998. This is a mother's memoir of raising a son with PDD-NOS.

Kozloff, Martin A. *Reaching the Autistic Child: A Parent Training Program.* Cambridge, MA: Brookline Books, 1998.

Leicestershire County Council and Fosse Health Trust. *Autism: How to Help Your Young Child.* London: National Autistic Society, 1995. This is an excellent introductory booklet for UK parents with a newly diagnosed child.

Schopler, Eric, and Gary B. Mesibov, editors. *High-Functioning Individuals with Autism (Current Issues in Autism).* New York: Plenum Publishing, 1992.

Sperry, Virginia Walker, and Sally Provence. *Fragile Success: Nine Autistic Children, Childhood to Adulthood.* 2nd edition. Baltimore, MD: Paul H. Brookes Publishing, 2000. This book offers fascinating profiles written over a period of years, including one follow-up report by a young man with autistic tendencies who is also profiled as a child.

Tantam, Digby. *A Mind of One's Own: A Guide to the Special Difficulties and Needs of the More Able Person with Autism or Asperger's Syndrome.* London: National Autism Society, 1991.

Wing, Lorna. *Autistic Spectrum Disorders: A Guide to Diagnosis.* London: National Autistic Society, 1993. This diagnostic guide is also available on tape.

Books by adults with ASDs

Jesssica Kingsley Publishers, a specialty publishing company, has published many books by people with ASDs. Its catalog is online at *http://www.jessicakingsley.com.*

Gerland, Gunilla. *A Real Person: Life on the Outside.* London: Souvenir Press, 1997.

Grandin, Temple. *Thinking in Pictures, and Other Reports from My Life with Autism.* New York: Vintage Books, 1996.

Grandin, Temple, and Margaret M. Scariano. *Emergence: Labeled Autistic.* New York: Warner Books, 1996.

Williams, Donna. *Nobody, Nowhere: The Extraordinary Autobiography of an Autistic.* New York: Avon Books, 1994.

Children's books about ASDs

Choose among these books for a gentle introduction to autistic spectrum disorders for siblings, young relatives, and classmates. Another good choice for helping young children understand the maddeningly literal thinking patterns common in individuals on the spectrum is the *Amelia Bedelia* book series by Peggy Parish.

Amenta, Charles A., III. *Russell Is Extra Special: A Book About Autism.* Washington, DC: Magination Press, 1992.

Gartenberg, Zachary M. *Mori's Story: A Book About a Boy with Autism.* Minneapolis: Lerner Publications, 1998. Written by a grade–school student about his brother—and very good.

Gerland, Gunilla. *Finding Out About Asperger Syndrome, High Functioning Autism and PDD.* London: Jessica Kingsley Publishers, 2000. Gerland's book is aimed at children who want to know more about their own diagnosis.

Gold, Phyllis-Terri. *Please Don't Say Hello.* New York: Human Sciences Press, 1986.

Gottlieb, Eli. *The Boy Who Went Away.* New York: St. Martin's Press, 1997.

Katz, Illana, and Dr. Edward Ritvo. *Joey and Sam: A Heartwarming Storybook About Autism, a Family, and a Brother's Love.* Los Angeles: Real Life Story Books, 1993.

Lears, Laurie. *Ian's Walk: A Story About Autism.* Morton, IL: Albert Whitman & Company, 1998.

Saguisag, Lara. *There's a Duwende in My Brother's Soup.* Manila: Lampara Books, 2001. This bilingual book in Filipino and English has super illustrations. It's a funny, sweet story about a sister's view of her brother's autism, and her attempt to understand his world.

Thompson, Mary. *Andy and His Yellow Frisbee.* Rockville, MD: Woodbine House, 1996.

Watson, Esther. *Talking to Angels.* New York: Harcourt Brace, 1996.

Werlin, Nancy. *Are You Alone on Purpose?* New York: Houghton Mifflin, 1996.

Web sites about ASDs

Much information is also available on the web sites of autism organizations listed in Appendix B, *Support and Advocacy*, and research and treatment centers, listed in Appendix C, *Research and Testing Facilities*.

Autism Resources
http://www.autism-resources.com/

Compiled by the manager of the St. John's Autism list, this includes a comprehensive book list, advice, and much more.

Autism Research Institute
http://www.autism.com/ari/

See the ARI Publications List for a wide variety of ARI pamphlets, papers, books, and videotapes on subjects related to autistic spectrum disorders.

The Maze: Jypsy's Autism Links
http://www.isn.net/~jypsy/autilink.htm

Quite possibly the largest collection of addresses for autism-related web sites around the world, and served up with a healthy helping of humor.

Online Asperger's Syndrome Information and Support
http://www.udel.edu/bkirby/asperger/

O.A.S.I.S. is Information Central for issues related to Asperger's syndrome.

"A Tiger by the Tail"
http://members.aol.com/bertvan/index.htm

This is a mother's story of raising an autistic child in the bad old days.

General disability

Exceptional Parent
555 Kinderkamack Road
Oradell, NJ 07649-1517
(201) 634-6550
Fax (201) 634-6599
http://www.eparent.com/

This magazine for parents of children with disabilities is an invaluable resource. Most issues are constructed around a theme, such as transition planning, mobility, or special education. The parent-to-parent letters section is especially useful for families trying to identify or find others with a rare disability.

Massachusetts General Hospital Neurology Forums
http://neuro-www.mgh.harvard.edu/

This web site features discussion groups (live and bulletin board–style) on almost every known neurological disorder.

Health care and insurance

American Association on Mental Retardation Publications Center. *Health Care Financing for Severe Developmental Disabilities.* Monograph. 444 N. Capitol Street NW, Suite 846, Washington, DC 20001-1512, (202) 287-1968 or (800) 424-3688, fax (202) 387-2193, *aamr@pmds.com.*

Beckett, Julie. *Health Care Financing: A Guide for Families.* Iowa City: National Maternal and Child Health Resource Center. This overview of the health care financing system includes advocacy strategies for families and information about public health insurance in the US. University of Iowa, Iowa City, IA 52242, (319) 335-9073.

The Disability Bookshop. *How to Get Quality Care for a Child with Special Health Needs: A Guide to Health Services and How to Pay for Them.* P.O. Box 129, Vancouver, WA 98666-0129, (206) 694-2462 or (800) 637-2256.

Larson, Georgianna, and Judith Kahn. *Special Needs/Special Solutions: How to Get Quality Care for a Child with Special Health Needs.* St. Paul, MN: Life Line Press, 2500 University Avenue, St. Paul, MN 55141.

McManue, Margaret. *Understanding Your Health Insurance Options: A Guide for Families Who Have Children with Special Needs.* Bethesda, MD: ACCH. This guide covers health care financing, insurance coverage, and long-term planning. 7910 Woodmont Avenue, Suite 300, Bethesda, MD 20814, (301) 654-6549.

Neville, Kathy. *Strategic Insurance Negotiation: An Introduction to Basic Skills for Families and Community Mental Health Workers.* Boston: Federation for Children with Special Needs. Single copies of this pamphlet are available at no cost, and it is very helpful if your insurance company insists on forcing you to use the mental health system rather than your regular medical benefits for care. CAPP/NPRC Project, 95 Berkeley Street, Suite 104, Boston, MA 02116.

Oreck, Stephen. *How to Get the Most Money Out of Your Health Insurance* (pamphlet). Medic Publishing, P.O. Box 89, Redmond, WA 98073, (206) 881-2883.

Peterson, Robert, and David Tenenbaum. *Fighting Back: Health Insurance Denials.* Madison, WI: Center for Public Representation. This book can help you get better coverage and combat claims denials. 121 S. Pinckney Street, Madison, WI 53703, (800) 369-0338.

Association of Maternal and Child Health Programs
1220 19th Street NW, Suite 801
Washington, DC 20036
(202) 775-0436
Fax (202) 775-0061
info@amchp.org
http://www.amchp1.org/

Contact AMCHP to locate your state's Children with Special Health Care Needs Program.

National Association of Insurance Commissioners
2301 McGee Street, Suite 800
Kansas City, MO 64108-2604
(816) 842-3600
http://www.naic.org/splash.htm

Contact NAIC to locate your state insurance commissioner, who can tell you about health insurance regulations in your state regarding ASDs.

Parenting and siblings

The Sibling Support Project
Children's Hospital and Medical Center
P.O. Box 5371, CL-09
Seattle, WA 98105
(206) 527-5712
Fax (206) 527-5705
Contact: Donald Meyer, *mdj9@qwest.net*
http://www.chmc.org/departmt/sibsupp/

This group offers information about the Sibshops support group project and the online support lists SibKids and SibNet.

Gray, David E. *Autism and the Family: Problems, Prospects, and Coping with the Disorder.* Springfield, IL: Charles C Thomas Publishers, 1998.

Greenspan, Dr. Stanley I., with Jacqueline Salmon. *The Challenging Child.* Reading, MA: Addison-Wesley, 1995. This book introduces Dr. Greenspan's concepts about tailoring interventions to each specific child.

Greenspan, Dr. Stanley I., and Serena Wieder, with Robin Simons. *The Child with Special Needs.* Reading, MA: Addison-Wesley, 1998. Highly recommended for all parents and professionals working with people who have ASDs. Greenspan explains floor-time play therapy, and discusses how to match it to your child's personality, physical needs, and diagnosis.

Kurcinka, Mary Sheedy. *Raising Your Spirited Child.* Reprint edition. New York: Harper Perennial Library, 1992. Written for parents of nondisabled but "difficult" children, this is nevertheless an excellent parenting guide to have on hand. It covers sensory issues, feeding problems, and more. An accompanying parent workbook is also available.

Meyer, Donald, and Patricia Vadasy. *Living with a Brother or Sister with Special Needs.* Seattle: University of Washington Press, 1996.

Meyer, Donald, editor. *Views from Our Shoes: Growing up with a Brother or Sister with Special Needs.* Rockville, MD: Woodbine House, 1997.

Meyer, Donald, editor. *Uncommon Fathers: Reflections on Raising a Child with a Disability.* Rockville, MD: Woodbine House, 1995.

Naseef, Robert A. *Special Children, Challenged Parents: The Struggles and Rewards of Raising a Child with a Disability.* New York: Birch Lane Press, 1997.

Schopler, Eric, editor. *Parent Survival Manual: A Guide to Crisis Resolution in Autism and Related Developmental Disorders.* New York: Plenum Publishing, 1995. Based on the TEACCH model, this book provides concrete suggestions for dealing with specific problems and general issues.

Stehli, Annabel, editor. *Dancing in the Rain: Stories of Exceptional Progress by Parents of Children with Special Needs.* Westport, CT: Georgiana Organization, 1995.

Special education

For information about local school programs, consult both parent groups and advocacy organizations in advance. They can usually tell you about specific schools or programs that have been successful in the past—and warn you away from those that may be detrimental to your child. National autism and disability advocacy groups can also help. The following are general special education resources, including information for parents and about pedagogical techniques. For more, see "Specific therapeutic interventions," later in this Appendix.

Anderson, Winifred, Stephen Chitwood, and Dierdre Hayden. *Negotiating the Special Education Maze: A Guide for Parents and Teachers.* 3rd edition. Rockville, MD: Woodbine House, 1997. Well-written and very complete, this is a good "starter kit" for beginners.

Dornbush, Marilyn P., and Sheryl K. Pruitt. *Teaching the Tiger: A Handbook for Individuals Involved in the Education of Students with Attention Deficit Disorders, Tourette Syndrome, or Obsessive Compulsive Disorder.* Duarte, CA: Hope Press, 1995. This is a *wonderful* book, full of practical suggestions, organizing aids, and ideas for teachers, parents, and students. Despite the title, it's very applicable to children with ASDs.

Fouse, Beth. *Creating a Win-Win IEP for Students with Autism.* Arlington, TX: Future Horizons, 1996.

Fullerton, Ann, editor. *Higher Functioning Adolescents and Young Adults with Autism: A Teacher's Guide.* Austin, TX: ProEd, 1996.

Koegel, Robert L., and Lynn Kern Koegel, editors. *Teaching Children with Autism: Strategies for Initiating Positive Interactions and Improving Learning Opportunities.* Baltimore: Paul H. Brookes Publishing, 1996.

National Autistic Society. *Schools, Units, and Classes.* London: NAS, 1998. This list of specialist schools and units (self-contained classrooms) in the UK for children with autism also includes addresses of county education councils.

Peeters, Theo. *Autism: From Theoretical Understanding to Educational Intervention.* Lewisville, TX: J.A. Majors Company, 1997. This book explains the techniques used in TEACCH programs.

Powell, Stuart, and Peggy Ahrenhold Gallagher. *Autism and Learning: A Guide to Good Practice.* London: David Fulton Publishers, 1997.

Quill, Kathleen Ann, editor. *Teaching Children with Autism: Strategies to Enhance Communication and Socialization.* Albany, NY: Delmar Publications, 1995.

Simpson, Richard L., and Brenda Myles, editors. *Educating Children and Youth with Autism: Strategies for Effective Practice.* Austin, TX: ProEd, 1998.

Wright, Peter W. D., and Wright, Pamela. *Wrightslaw: Special Education Law.* Hartfield, VA: Harbor House Law Press, 1999.

Wright, Peter W. D., and Wright, Pamela. *Wrightslaw: From Emotions to Advocacy: The Special Education Survival Guide.* Hartfield, VA: Harbor House Law Press, 2001. Both "Wrightslaw" titles are packed with essential information on special education law, advocacy tactics, and IEP tips.

Families for Early Autism Treatment (FEAT)
http://www.feat.org

This web site contains much information about ABA, and also has a copy of the excellent and very comprehensive California Education Department report "Best Practices for Designing and Delivering Effective Programs for Individuals with Autistic Spectrum Disorders."

HEATH: The National Clearinghouse on Postsecondary Education for Individuals with Disabilities
http://www.heath.gwu.edu/

This web site focuses on college opportunities for people with physical or learning disabilities.

Special Education and Disabilities Resources
http://www.educ.drake.edu/rc/sp_ed_top.html

This web site features information and links on US special education law, assistive technology, and related topics.

Childproofing

These are just some of the companies that sell child safety devices.

Childproofers Online
(314) 962-2229
info@childproofers.com
http://www.childproofers.com/

Child Safety Store
1085 SW 15th Avenue, E-3
Delray Beach, FL 33444
(561) 272-8242
Fax (561) 272-8289
http://www.childsafetystore.com

The Safety Store
P.O. Box 7227
Charlottesville, VA 22906-7227
(434) 973-8030 or (888) 723-3897
http://www.safetystore.com/

Special needs clothing

These companies (and many others) carry clothing designed for people who have difficulty with fasteners, mobility problems, special toileting needs, and so on.

A few of the catalogs listed include shoes, which tend to be a special problem. Slip-ons or styles with Velcro closures may be available locally; alternatively, there are a variety of items that can replace regular laces, including lace-in Velcro closures and curly elastic laces that bounce shut.

Adrian's Adaptive Closet
29571 Monarch Drive
San Juan Capistrano, CA 92675
(800) 831-2577
Fax (714) 364-4380
adrians@infostations.com
http://www.adrianscloset.com/

E-Z Clothes
P.O. Box 213
Tupelo, MS 38802
(800) 320-7889

Personal Touch Health Care Apparel Inc.
P.O. Box 230321
Brooklyn, NY 11223
(718) 375-1703 or (888) 626-1703
Fax (718) 627-0200
info@nursinghomeapparel.com
http://www.nursinghomeapparel.com/

This company has adult clothing only, including styles with easy closures.

Restart Gear
(61) 3 9781 2533
Fax (61) 3 9781 2544
http://findit.cowleys.com.au/clients/restart.htm

This firm offers very hip Australian designs for people with disabilities.

Special Clothes Inc.
P.O. Box 333
Harwich, MA 02645
(508) 896-7939
Specialclo@aol.com
http://www.special-clothes.com/

Specific therapeutic interventions

Here are some resources related to interventions discussed in this book. Web sites listed earlier may also contain useful links to online information.

Diet, vitamins, and allergy-related interventions

The Autism Research Institute's web site and publications list have a wealth of information on these topics, as does Allergy Induced Autism in the UK. Both are listed in Appendix B. There are more resources for people on casein-free and gluten-free diets in books written for people with celiac disease.

Callahan, Mary. *Fighting for Tony*. New York: Simon & Schuster, 1987. A mother's story of "recovering" her autistic son, whose behavior improved dramatically with dietary changes.

Crook, William G., MD. *The Yeast Connection Handbook*. Jackson, TN: Professional Books, 1997.

Jackson, Luke. *A User Guide to the GF/CF Diet for Autism, Asperger Syndrome and ADHD*. London: Jessica Kingsley Publishers, 2001. Featuring kid-tested GF/CF recipes and written by a highly articulate teen with AS, this is easily the most engaging and user-friendly intro to dietary interventions.

LeBreton, Marilyn. *Diet Intervention and Autism: Implementing the Gluten Free Casein Free Diet for Autistic Children: A Practical Guide for Parents*. London: Jessica Kingsley Publishers, 2001.

Lewis, Lisa. *Special Diets for Special Kids: Implementing a Diet to Improve the Lives of Children with Autism and Related Disorders*. Arlington, TX: Future Horizons, 1998. Written by the mother of a son diagnosed with PDD-NOS who was helped greatly by dietary intervention.

Meyer, Elisa. *Feeding Your Allergic Child: Happy Food for Happy Kids: 75 Proven Recipes Free of Wheat, Dairy, Corn, and Eggs*. New York: St. Martin's Press, 1997.

Rapp, Doris. *Is This Your Child? Discovering and Treating Unrecognized Allergies in Children and Adults*. New York: William Morrow and Company, 1992.

Shattock, Paul, and Savery, Dawn. *Autism as a Metabolic Disorder*. 2nd edition. Booklet. Available for £3 sterling from Autism Research Unit, School of Health Sciences, University of Sunderland, Sunderland SR2 7EE, UK.

Shaw, William, and others. *Biological Treatments for Autism and PDD: What's Going On? What Can You Do About It?* Toronto: Sunflower Publications, 1998. An in-depth introduction to biological interventions, including diet and vitamins.

Autism Network for Dietary Intervention (ANDI)
http://members.aol.com/AutismNDI/PAGES/links.htm

Founded by Lisa Lewis and friends, this is an advocacy and information site for diet and vitamins as treatments for ASDs.

Celiac/gluten-free archive
http://www.fastlane.net/homepages/thodge/archive.htm#first

Gluten-Free Page
http://www.gluten-free.org/

No Milk Page
http://www.nomilk.com/

NO-MILK mailing list
LISTSERV@SJUVM.STJOHNS.EDU

This is an open, unmoderated discussion list for those following a milk/casein/lactose-free diet. To subscribe, send email with the subject line as "SUB NO-MILK YourFirstName Your-LastName".

Applied behavior analysis

These books and online resources cover aspects of ABA and ABA-like interventions.

Fouse, Beth. *A Treasure Chest of Behavioral Strategies for Individuals with Autism.* Arlington, TX: Future Horizons, 1997.

Harris, Sandra L., and Mary Jane Gill-Weiss. *Right from the Start: Behavioral Intervention for Young Children with Autism: A Guide for Parents and Professionals.* Rockville, MD: Woodbine House, 1998.

Lovaas, Ivar, MD, and others. *Teaching Developmentally Disabled Children: The ME Book.* Austin, TX: Pro-Ed, 1981.

Lovaas, Ivar, MD, et al. *Teaching Individuals with Developmental Delays: Basics.* Austin, TX: Pro-Ed, 2002.

Luiselli, James K., and Michael J. Cameron, editors. *Antecedent Control: Innovative Approaches to Behavioral Support.* Baltimore, MD: Paul H. Brookes Publishing, 1998.

Maurice, Catherine, Gina Green, and Stephen C. Luce, editors. *Behavioral Intervention for Young Children with Autism.* Austin, TX: Pro-Ed, 1996.

The Journal of Applied Behavior Analysis (JABA)
Department of Human Development
University of Kansas
Lawrence, KS 66045-2133
(785) 843-0008
jabamlw@idir.net
http://www.envmed.rochester.edu/wwwrap/behavior/jaba/jabahome.htm

JABA is the professional journal for ABA practitioners and researchers. Its web site includes a searchable index of articles.

The Me List
rallen@iupui.edu
http://php.iupui.edu/~rallen/me_list.html

The Me List is a private, archived mailing list on ABA and related topics. It offers lots of "how to" and "how it worked" information. To subscribe, send email to moderator Ruth Allen.

Animal-assisted therapy

Dog-Play
http://www.dog-play.com/therapy.html

This site offers links related to animal-assisted therapy and therapy animals.

Island Dolphin Care
http://www.islanddolphincare.org/

One of several facilities that provide dolphin-assisted therapy.

North American Riding for the Handicapped Association
http://www.narha.org

This site provides information on hippotherapy (horse-assisted therapy) for autism and other disorders, as well as referrals to members.

Art therapy

Davalos, Sandra. *Making Sense of Art: Sensory-Based Art Activities for Children with Autism, Asperger Syndrome, and Pervasive Developmental Disorders.* Shawnee Mission, KS: Autism Asperger Publishing, 1999.

Flowers, Tony. *Reaching Children with Autism Through Art: Practical Fun Activities to Enhance Motor Skills and to Improve Tactile and Concept Awareness.* Arlington, TX: Future Horizons, 1996.

ASAFARI Gallery of Autistic Spectrum Art
http://ctrf.net/asafari/

This online art gallery is great, and includes some information on art therapy for people with ASDs.

Auditory integration and related therapies

Alvin, Juliette, and Warwick, Auriel. *Music Therapy for the Autistic Child.* Oxford, UK: Oxford University Press, 1991.

Berard, Guy, Monnier-Clay, Simone, and Rimland, Bernard. *Hearing Equals Behavior.* New Canaan, CT: Keats Publishing, 1993.

National Autistic Society. *A Visit to the Light and Sound Therapy Centre.* Pamphlet. London: NAS, 1996.

Stehli, Annabel. *The Sound of a Miracle: A Child's Triumph over Autism.* Westport, CT: Georgiana Organization, 1997. This is a mother's account of her autistic daughter's "recovery" via auditory integration.

Tomatis, Alfred, MD. *The Ear and Language.* Ontario: Moulin Publishing, 1996.

Cognitive Concepts Inc.
990 Grove Street
Evanston, IL 60201
(847) 328-8099 or (888) 328-8199
Fax (847) 328-5881
http://www.earobics.com/

This company offers Earobics, an AI-like package for home or school use.

Vision Audio Inc.
611 Anchor Drive
Joppa, MD 21085
(888) 213-7858
visionaud@aol.com
http://www.vision-audio.com/

Vision Audio provides Electronic Auditory Stimulation effect (EASe) recordings, engineered for a relaxing effect on people with auditory sensitivities.

Scientific Learning Corporation
300 Frank H. Ogawa Plaza, Suite 500
Oakland, CA 94612-2040
(888) 665-9707
Fax (510) 444-3580
info@scilearn.com
http://www.scientificlearning.com/

SLC sells FastForWord and other well-tested software for helping people with speech, language, and auditory processing disorders.

Society for Auditory Intervention Techniques
1040 Commercial Street SE, Suite 306
Salem, OR 97302
http://www.sait.org

The Tomatis Method
http://www.tomatis.com/

This web site provides information about the Tomatis method in English and Spanish, and also lists centers in the US, Canada, and Mexico.

Facilitated communication

Twachtman-Cullen, Diane. *A Passion to Believe: Autism and the Facilitated Communication Phenomenon.* Boulder, CO: Westview Press, 1998.

Floor-time play therapy and similar interventions

Hewett, David, and Nind, Melanie. *Interaction in Action: Reflections on the Use of Intensive Interaction.* London: David Fulton Publishers, 1998.

Greenspan, Stanley, MD. *Floor Time.* This videotape is about using floor-time techniques with typically developing children, but many parents and professionals will find it useful to see the method in action.

VanFleet, Risë. *Filial Therapy: Strengthening Parent–Child Relationships Through Play.* Sarasota, FL: Professional Resource Press, 1994.

About Floor Time
http://www.mindspring.com/~dgn/playther.htm

This web site explains basic floor-time concepts and ideas, and includes a question-and-answer section.

Family Enhancement and Play Therapy Center
P.O. Box 613
Boiling Springs, PA 17007
(717) 249-4707
Fax (717) 249-9479
http://play-therapy.com/

This center offers *Child-Centered Play Therapy with Risë VanFleet, Ph.D.*, a video on techniques used in child-centered play therapy (CCPT) and filial therapy.

Dr. Stanley Greenspan
http://www.stanleygreenspan.com/

Several of Dr. Stanley Greenspan's books are listed under "Parenting and siblings," earlier in this appendix. Audiotapes of his lectures on using floor-time techniques and other interventions can be ordered through his web site, as can training videotapes.

Irlen lenses

The Irlen Institute
Irlen@Irlen.com
http://www.irlen.com

The Irlen Institute's web site includes pointers to practitioners who can fit the Irlen system and a company newsletter, among other resources.

Occupational therapy and sensory integration

Anderson, Elizabeth, and Pauline Emmons. *Unlocking the Mysteries of Sensory Dysfunction: A Resource for Anyone Who Works with, or Lives with, a Child with Sensory Issues.* Arlington, TX: Future Horizons, 1996.

Ayres, Jean, and Jeff Robbins. *Sensory Integration and the Child.* Los Angeles, CA: Western Psychological Services, 1983.

Bissel, Julie, and others. *Sensory Motor Handbook: A Guide for Implementing and Modifying Activities in the Classroom.* Torrance, CA: Sensory Integration International, 1988.

Kranowitz, Carol Stock. *The Out-of-Sync Child: Recognizing and Coping with Sensory Integration Dysfunction.* New York: Perigee, 1998.

Kranowitz, Carol. *Answers to Questions Teachers Ask About Sensory Integration.* Las Vegas, NV: Sensory Resources, 2001. A video version is also available.

Reisman, Judith E., producer. Video: *Making Contact: Sensory Integration and Autism.* Glendale, AZ: Center for Neurodevelopmental Studies, 1993. Available through Continuing Education Programs of America (CEPA) at (309) 263-0310.

Reisman, Judith E., producer. Video: *Sensory Processing for Parents: From Roots to Wings.* Glendale, AZ: Center for Neurodevelopmental Studies, 1996. Available through Continuing Education Programs of America (CEPA) at (309) 263-0310.

Sensory Comfort
(888) 436-2622
http://www.sensorycomfort.com

This catalog offers therapy equipment, clothing, and other items designed for people with SI dysfunction.

Sensory Integration International (SII)
1514 Cabrillo Avenue
Torrance, CA 90501
(310) 787-8805
Fax (310) 787-8130
info@sensoryint.com
http://www.sensoryint.com/

Referrals to SII-qualified occupational therapists, books, and other materials for sensory integration can be accessed through this organization.

SI Supplies and Equipment
http://www.mindspring.com/~mariep/si/links/supplies.html

This web site has links to many manufacturers of sensory integration and occupational therapy equipment.

Secretin

Beck, Victoria, and Gary Beck. *Unlocking the Potential of Secretin.* San Diego, CA: Autism Research Institute, 1998. This is a short, parent-written book about the successful use of secretin to treat an autistic child.

ARI's Secretin page
http://www.secretin.com

The Autism Research Institute is collecting data on secretin trials and results, and presents updated data via this page.

"Autism and Secretin"
http://curry.edschool.virginia.edu/go/cise/ose/information/secretin.html

This online research paper by John Wills Lloyd also has links to related data.

The Use of Secretin for the Treatment of Autism
http://osiris.sunderland.ac.uk/autism/sec.htm

This web site includes the full text of the "Dateline" show that featured Victoria and Gary Beck and their son, references to related journal articles, and regularly updated data.

Social skills training

Gray, Carol. *Comic Strip Conversations.* Arlington, TX: Future Horizons, 1994.

Gray, Carol. *The New Social Story Book.* 2nd illustrated edition. Arlington, TX: Future Horizons, 2001.

Gray, Carol. *Taming the Recess Jungle: Socially Simplifying Recess for Students with Autism and Related Disorders.* Arlington, TX: Future Horizons, 1993.

Greenspan, Dr. Stanley I., with Jacqueline Salmon. *Playground Politics: Understanding the Emotional Life of Your School-Age Child.* Reading, MA: Addison-Wesley, 1993.

Mannix, Darlene. *Social Skills Activities for Special Children.* New York: Prentice Hall, 1993. Teacher's guide with reproducible worksheets.

Myles, Brenda, and Jack Southwick. *Asperger Syndrome and Difficult Moments: Practical Solutions for Tantrums, Rage, and Meltdowns.* Shawnee Mission, KS: Autism Asperger Publishing, 1999.

Simpson, Richard, editor. *Social Skills for Students with Autism.* 2nd edition. Reston, VA: Council for Exceptional Children, 1997.

Speech therapy and communication

Carr, Edward G. *How to Teach Sign Language to Developmentally Disabled Children.* H & H Enterprises, 1981.

Crystal, David, editor. *The Cambridge Encyclopedia of Language.* Cambridge, UK: Cambridge University Press, 1987.

Freeman, Sabrina, and Lorelei Dake. *Teach Me Language: A Language Manual for Children with Autism, Asperger's Syndrome, and Related Developmental Disorders.* Langley, British Columbia: SKF Books, 1996. A set of worksheets and forms is also available for use with this guidebook.

Lund, Nancy J., and Judith F. Duchan. *Assessing Children's Language in Naturalistic Contexts.* 3rd edition. Englewood Cliffs, NJ: Prentice Hall, 1993.

Schwartz, Sue, and Joan E. Heller Miller. *The New Language of Toys: Teaching Communication Skills to Special-Needs Children.* Rockville, MD: Woodbine House, 1996.

American Speech-Language-Hearing Association
10801 Rockville Pike
Rockville, MD 20852
(301) 897-8682 or (800) 638-8255
http://www.asha.org/

Apraxia-Kids mailing list
Listserv@Listserv.syr.edu
http://www.apraxia-kids.org/

This mailing list covers oral motor apraxia and related disabilities. The web site is also superb. To subscribe, send an email with the message "subscribe apraxia-kids FirstName LastName".

Imaginart International
307 Arizona Street
Bisbee, AZ 85603
(520) 432-5741 or (800) 828-1376
Fax (800) 737-1376
imaginart@AOL.com
http://www.imaginart.com

Speech therapy and occupational therapy materials can be ordered from Imaginart.

IntelliTools
http://www.intellitools.com/

This firm has a great catalog of assistive technology and communication devices.

Super Duper Publications
Department SD 98
P.O. Box 24997
Greenville, SC 29616-2497
(864) 288-3536 or (800) 277-8737
Fax (800) 978-7379
custserv@superduperinc.com
http://www.superduperinc.com

SuperDuper has a huge catalog of speech and language learning materials, games, videos, books, and tests. It also includes items related to augmentative communication, social skills, and sensorimotor activities.

Medical information

Baker, Sidney M., MD, and Jon Pangborn, PhD. *Defeat Autism Now! (DAN!) Clinical Options Manual.* San Diego, CA: Autism Research Institute. Written especially for physicians, this collection of data and suggestions for treating ASDs is updated regularly with information from the yearly Defeat Autism Now! conference. Parents who don't have access to a DAN! doctor may wish to buy this as a guide for their regular physician, or as a guide for setting up their own treatment plan.

Cohen, Donald J., and Fred R. Volkmar, editors. *Handbook of Autism and Pervasive Developmental Disorders.* 2nd edition. New York: Wiley, 1997. This is the most current collection of research data and papers related to autistic spectrum disorders. It compares and contrasts studies from around the world. It's in medical language, but not impossible to read. Expensive—check your nearest medical library.

Gillberg, Christopher, and Mary Coleman. *The Biology of the Autistic Syndromes.* Cambridge, UK: Cambridge University Press, 1992. Heavy-duty reading—covers brain-imaging studies, genetics, and more. A great deal has been uncovered since 1992, but this book is still useful for those who want the hard medical facts.

Medscape
http://www.medscape.com

Medscape provides a searchable, online index to hundreds of medical journals. Many articles are available in full, others as abstracts only.

PubMed

http://www.ncbi.nlm.nih.gov/PubMed/

Free interface for searching the MEDLINE medical database, which can help you find out about studies, medications, and more.

Books about medications

Chapter 5, *Medical Interventions,* and Appendix E, *Medication Reference,* cover most of the commonly used medications for ASD symptoms. However, it's important to educate yourself well. There are a number of books available that list side effects, cautions, and more regarding medications. The biggest and best is the *Physicians Desk Reference* (PDR), but its price is well out of the average parent's or patient's league. You may, however, find a used but recent copy at a good price.

Those with allergies to food dyes, or to corn, wheat, and other materials used as fillers in pills, need to consult the manufacturer directly.

British Medical Association and the Royal Pharmaceutical Society of Great Britain. *The British National Formulary* (BNF). This standard reference for prescribing and dispensing drugs in the UK is updated twice yearly.

Gorman, Jack M., MD. *The Essential Guide to Psychiatric Drugs.* New York: St. Martin's Press, 1998.

Silverman, Harold M., editor. *The Pill Book.* 10th edition. New York: Bantam Books, 2002.

Sullivan, Donald. *The American Pharmaceutical Association's Guide to Prescription Drugs.* New York: Signet, 1998.

Web sites about medications

Canadian Drug Product Database

http://www.hc-sc.gc.ca/hpb-dgps/therapeut/htmleng/dpd.html

Dr. Bob's Psychopharmacology Tips

http://www.dr-bob.org/tips/

Excellent information on psychiatric drugs, including things like the MAOI dietary restrictions and common SSRI interactions, from Dr. Robert Hsiung.

Federal Drug Administration (FDA)

http://www.fda.gov/cder/drug/default.htm

Official US information on new drugs and generic versions of old drugs, FDA warnings and recalls, and so forth is archived here.

The Internet Drug List

http://www.rxlist.com/

PharmWeb

http://www.pharmweb.net/

Mail order pharmacies

CanadaRx
14 James Street North, Suite 3000
Hamilton, Ontario L8R 2J9
Canada
(905) 528-3922
http://www.canadarx.net/

This is a consortium of Canadian pharmacies set up specifically to provide discounted prescriptions to US customers, although Canadians and others can use the service as well. You must have a valid, signed prescription.

CVS ProCare Pharmacy (previously Stadtlanders Pharmacy)
600 Penn Center Boulevard
Pittsburgh, PA 15235-5810
(800) 238-7828
enroll@stadtlander.com
http://stadtlander.com/

CVS is the new name of Stadtlanders Pharmacy, which has long enjoyed a stellar reputation in the disability community.

DrugPlace.com
2201 W. Sample Road, Building 9, Suite 1-A
Pompano Beach, FL 33073
(954) 969-1230 or (800) 881-6325
Fax (800) 881-6990
cust-svc@prefrx.com
http://www.drugplace.com/

Farmacia Rex S.R.L.
Cordoba 2401
Esq. Azcuénaga 1120
Buenos Aires, Argentina
(54-1) 961-0338
Fax (54-1) 962-0153
http://www.todoservicio.com.ar/farmacia.rex/rexmenu.htm

This South American pharmacy has deeply discounted prices.

GlobalRx
4024 Carrington Lane
Efland, NC 27243 ·
(919) 304-4278 or (800) 526-6447
Fax (919) 304-4405
info@globalrx.com
http://globalrx.com/

Masters Marketing Company, Ltd.
Masters House
5 Snadridge Close
Harrow, Middlesex HA1 1TW
UK
(011) 44 181 424 9400
Fax (011) 44 208 427 1998
info@mastersmarketing.com
http://www.mastersmarketing.com/

MMC carries a limited selection of European and American pharmaceuticals for customers worldwide.

No Frills Pharmacy
1510 Harlan Drive
Bellevue, NE 68005
(800) 485-7423
Fax (800) 522-5360
nofrills@usaverx.com
http://www.nofrillspharmacy.com/

Peoples Pharmacy
http://www.peoplesrx.com/

This chain, based in Austin, Texas, provides mail-order service and can also compound medications.

Pharmacy Direct
3 Coal Street
Silverwater, NSW 2128
Australia
(02) 9648-8888 or (1300) 656-245
Fax (02) 9648 8999 or (1300) 656 329
pharmacy@pharmacydirect.com.au
http://www.pharmacydirect.com.au

You must have a prescription from an Australian doctor to use this mail-order service, although they will ship to New Zealand as well.

The Pharmacy Shop
5007 N. Central
Phoenix, AZ 85012
(602) 274-9956 or (800) 775-6888
Fax (602) 241-0104
sales@pharmacyshop.com
http://www.pharmacyshop.com/

Victoria Apotheke (Victoria Pharmacy)
Dr. C. Egloff
P.O. Box CH-8021
Zurich, Switzerland
(01) 211-2432 (Europe) or (011) 411-211-24 32 (US)
Fax (01) 221-2322 (Europe) or (011) 411-221-2322 (US)
victoriaapotheke@access.ch
http://www.access.ch/victoria_pharmacy

Help with medications

You may be able to get medications free just by providing documentation to charitable programs run by pharmaceutical companies. In the US, the Pharmaceutical Manufacturers Association publishes a directory of programs for indigent patients, with contact details listed by company. Doctors can get a copy of the PMA's official guide by calling (800) 762-4636, and patients can browse the online version at *http://www.phrma.org/searchcures/dpdpap/*.

Most indigent patient programs require that you have no insurance coverage for outpatient prescription drugs, that purchasing the medication at retail price would be a hardship for you because of your income and/or expenses, and that you do not qualify for a government or third-party program that can pay for the prescription.

The Medicine Program
P.O. Box 515
Doniphan, MO 63935-0515
(573) 778-1118,
help@themedicineprogram.com
http://www.themedicineprogram.com/

The Medicine Program can help you sign up with indigent patient programs.

Help with medical care expenses

The Doug Flutie, Jr. Foundation for Autism
c/o The Giving Back Fund
230 Congress Street
Boston, MA 02110
(617) 556-2820
Fax (617) 426-5441
http://www.dougflutie.org/

Founded by pro football player Doug Flutie, who is the father of an autistic son, this foundation raises funds to help disadvantaged families pay for treatment and to support research efforts. It does not give direct grants to families, but a nonprofit treatment organization can apply for help to pay for your child's program.

If you need medical assistance in a location far from home but can't afford the cost of a flight or hotel, the following resources may be able to help. If you are outside North America, contact your national airline for assistance and advice.

AirCare Alliance
6202 South Lewis Avenue, Suite F2
Tulsa, OK 74136-1064
(918) 745-0384 or (800) 260-9707
http://www.aircareall.org/

AirLifeLine
5775 Wayzata Boulevard, Suite 700
Minneapolis, MN 55416
(877) 247-5543
http://www.airlifeline.org

Hope Air/Vols d'Espoir
Procter & Gamble Building
4711 Yonge Street
Toronto, Ontario M2N 6K8
(416) 222-6335
mail@hopeair.org
http://www.hopeair.org/

Miracle Flights for Kids
2756 N. Green Valley Parkway, No. 115
Green Valley, NV 89014-2120
(702) 261-0494
http://www.miracleflights.com/

National Association of Hospital Hospitality Houses
P.O. Box 18087
Ashville, NC 28814-0087
(800) 524-9730
http://www.nahhh.org/

PatientTravel.org
c/o Mercy Medical Airlift
4620 Haygood Road, Suite 1
Virginia Beach, VA 23455
(800) 296-1217
http://www.patienttravel.org/

Genetic counseling resources

Genetic counselors have special training in helping families understand the implications of having a member diagnosed with a genetic disorder. They can explain whether these disorders will be passed on to a diagnosed person's children, and help you assess associated risks. They can also provide information about genetic testing for other family members.

American Board of Genetic Counseling Inc.
9650 Rockville Pike
Bethesda, MD 20814-3998
(301) 571-1825
Fax (301) 571-1895
http://www.faseb.org/genetics/abgc/abgcmenu.htm

The ABGC credentials professionals in the field of genetic counseling, and can help you find a reputable member via phone, mail, or its web site.

GeneTests-GeneClinics
Children's Hospital and Regional Medical Center
P.O. Box 5371
Seattle, WA 98105-0371
(206) 527-5742
Fax (206) 527-5743
genetests@genetests.org
http://www.genetests.org

GeneTests and GeneClinics are federally funded genetic testing resources. The web site provides a list of genetic research and clinical laboratories, descriptions of genetic testing and counseling, and information for patients and professionals.

European Society of Human Genetics
Clinical Genetics Unit
Birmingham Women's Hospital
Birmingham B15 2TG United Kingdom
(44) 0-121-623-6820
esgh@esgh.org
http://www.eshg.org/

Human Genetics Society of Australasia
Royal Australian College of Physicians
145 Macquarie Street
Sydney, NSW 2000 Australia
(02) 9256-5471
Fax (02) 9251-8174
hgsa@racp.edu.au
http://www.hgsa.com.au/

Transition planning and adult issues

Gray, Carol. *What's Next? Preparing the Student with Autism or Other Developmental Disabilities for Success in the Community.* Arlington, TX: Future Horizons, 1992.

Debbault, Dennis. *Autism, Advocates, and Law Enforcement Professionals: Recognizing and Reducing Risk Situations for People with Autistic Spectrum Disorders.* London: Jessica Kingsley Publishers, 2001. Debbault explores problems that can happen when people with ASDs encounter the police.

Hingsburger, Dave. *Just Say Know! Understanding and Reducing the Risk of Sexual Victimization of People with Developmental Disabilities.* Eastman, Quebec: Diverse City Press, 1995.

Howlin, Patricia. *Autism: Preparing for Adulthood.* London: Routledge, 1997. Transition planning, with special attention to resources and possibilities in the UK.

Meyer, Roger. *Asperger Syndrome Employment Workbook.* London: Jessica Kingsley Publishers, 2000. Written by a person with AS, this excellent workbook can help adults understand their vocational interests and secure employment.

Morgan, Hugh. *Adults with Autism: A Guide to Theory and Practice.* Cambridge, UK: Cambridge University Press, 1996.

Mortlock, John. *The Socio-Sexual Development of People with Autism and Related Learning Disabilities* (pamphlet). London: National Autistic Society, 1993.

Slater-Walker, Gisela, and Christopher Slater-Walker. *An Asperger Marriage.* London: Jessica Kingsley Publishers, 2002. This personal story from a man with AS and his nondisabled partner illustrates issues that come up in family relationships.

Smith, Marcia Datlow, Ronald G. Belcher, and Patricia D. Juhrs. *A Guide to Successful Employment for Individuals with Autism.* Baltimore: Paul H. Brookes Publishing, 1995.

Sobsey, Dick, et al., editors. *Disability, Sexuality, and Abuse: An Annotated Bibliography.* Baltimore: Paul H. Brookes Publishing, 1991.

National Information Center for Children and Youth with Disabilities. *Transition Planning: A Team Effort.* NICHY, P.O. Box 1492, Washington, DC 20013, (202) 884-8200 or (800) 695-0285, or on the Web at *http://www.nichcy.org/pubs/transum/ts10txt.htm.*

Support and Advocacy

National autism organizations

In addition to the national organizations listed next, there are also many local support groups focused on autism spectrum disorders. Many are listed on the web site for this book, at *http://www.patientcenters.com/autism*.

United States

Asperger Syndrome Coalition of the US
P.O. Box 351268
Jacksonville, FL 32235-1668
(866) 4-ASPRGR
aspen@cybermax.net
http://www.asperger.org

Autism Society of America
7910 Woodmont Avenue, Suite 300
Bethesda, MD 20814-3067
(301) 657-0881 or (800) 3AUTISM
Fax (301) 657-0869
Fax on demand for information (800) 329-0899
http://www.autism-society.org/

United Kingdom

The National Autistic Society
393 City Road
London EC1V 1NE
44 (0)20 7833 2299
Fax 44 (0)20 7833 9666
nas@nas.org.uk
http://www.nas.org.uk/

The Scottish Society for Autistic Children
Head Office, Hilton House
Alloa Business Park
Whins Road
Alloa FK10 3SA Scotland
(01259) 720044
Fax (01259) 720051
ssac@autism-in-scotland.org.uk
http://www.autism-in-scotland.org.uk/

Republic of Ireland

Irish Society for Autism
Unity Building
16/17 Lower O'Connell Street
Dublin 1, Republic of Ireland
(071) 744684
Fax (071) 744224
autism@isa.iol.ie
http://www.iol.ie/~isa1/

Australia and New Zealand

Asperger's Syndrome Austalian Information Centre
http://members.ozemail.com.au/~rbmitch/Asperger.htm

Autism Council of Australia Ltd.
http://www.autismaus.com.au/

Autistic Organization of New Zealand Inc.
P.O. Box 7305
Sydenham, Christchurch, New Zealand
64 03 332 1038
http://www.autismnz.org.nz/

Elsewhere and worldwide

Action for Autism
T370 Chiragh Gaon, 3rd Floor
New Delhi 110 017, India
(91) 11-641-6469
Fax (91) 11-641-470
autism@vsnl.com
http://www.autism-india.org/

This English-language group is active in India and South Asia.

Autism in Africa

http://autism-alabama.org/africa/

This web site holds a collection of links to autism resources throughout Africa, including information in continental and West African French.

Autism Europe

Avenue E. Van Becelaere 26B, Bte. 21
B-1170 Bruxelles, Belgium
(32-0) 2-675-75-05
Fax (32-0) 2-675-72-70
autisme.europe@arcadis.be
http://www.autismeurope.arc.be/

Information available in French, English, and some other European languages.

AUTINET links

http://www.autinet.org/anflinks.htm

This international site has a long list of links that may lead you to advocacy and support groups in nations where English is not spoken.

Autism Network International

P.O. Box 35448
Syracuse, NY 13235-5448
http://ani.autistics.org/

This is a self-help and self-advocacy organization for people with autism.

World Autism Organisation (WAO)

Contact c/o Autism Europe
contact@worldautism.org
http://worldautism.org/

The WAO was founded in 1998 to work with the UN, UNESCO, and other international organizations to improve the lives of people with autism worldwide.

Online support groups

AUT2BHOME

http://www.paulbunyan.net/users/shannon/autism.htm

This web site can help you join an email discussion group for people homeschooling children with ASDs.

Autism-UK

owner-autism-uk@lists.ed.ac.uk
http://www.autism-uk.ed.ac.uk/welcome.html

To join this UK autism discussion group, send an email to this email address with a blank subject line and the message body "subscribe autism-uk", or see the web site.

Independent Living on the Autistic Spectrum (InLv) list
martijn@inlv.demon.nl
http://www.inlv.demon.nl/

This is an international list primarily for adults with ASDs. Some submissions are archived on the web site, and parents can benefit greatly from the perspective they present. To join, send an email to list manager Martijn Dekker about why you want to be part of the list.

OzAutism List (Australia and New Zealand)
Email Carolyn Baird at *Majordomo@hunter.apana.org.au*
http://hunter.apana.org.au/~cas/ozautism.html

St. John's AS Support list
asperger-request@maelstrom.stjohns.edu

This is a list for adults with high-functioning autism or Asperger's syndrome, and parents of children with these conditions. To subscribe, send an email about why you want to join the list, with your name and email address.

St. John's Autism list
listserv@maelstrom.stjohns.edu
http://maelstrom.stjhns.edu/archives/autism.html

This very active list is for parents of children with ASDs and for adults with ASDs. Send email with the message "subscribe autism Firstname Lastname". Past messages since 1997 are archived on the web site.

Related conditions

Several health conditions are linked to autism. If you or your child is affected by one of these, the following resources may help.

Angelman syndrome

Angelman Syndrome Foundation Inc.
414 Plaza Drive, Suite 209
Westmont, IL 60559
(630) 734-9267 or (800) IF-ANGEL
Fax (630) 655-0391
info@angelman.org
http://www.angelman.org/

Canadian Angelman Syndrome Society
P.O. Box 37
Priddis, Alberta TOL 1WO Canada
(403) 931-2415
Fax (403) 931-2415

Cornelia de Lange syndrome

Cornelia de Lange Syndrome Foundation Inc.
302 West Main Street, Suite 100
Avon, CT 06001
(860) 676-8166
cdlsintl@iconn.net
http://cdlsoutreach.org

Deafness and communication disorders

National Institute on Deafness and Other Communication Disorders Information Clearinghouse
1 Communication Avenue
Bethesda, MD 20892-3456
(301) 907-8830
NIDCD@AERIE.COM
http://www.nidcd.nih.gov/

Epilepsy

Epilepsy Foundation
4351 Garden City Drive
Landover, MD 20785-7223
(800) 332-1000
http://www.epilepsyfoundation.org/

Fragile X syndrome

The Fragile X Society
53 Winchelsea Lane
Hastings, East Sussex, TN35 4LG England
(44–0) 1424-813147
http://www.fragilex.org.uk/

The National Fragile X Foundation
P.O. Box 190488
San Francisco, CA 94119-0488
(800) 688-8765
http://www.fragilex.org/

Hyperlexia

American Hyperlexia Association
195 West Spangler Street, Suite B
Elmhurst, IL 60126
(630) 415-2212
Fax (630) 530-5909
president@hyperlexia.org
http://www.hyperlexia.org/

Canadian Hyperlexia Association
300 John Street, Box 87673
Thornhill, Ontario L3T 7R3 Canada
(905) 886-9163
Fax (905) 886-4624
cha@ican.net
http://home.ican.net/~cha/

Landau-Kleffner syndrome

C.A.N.D.L.E.
4414 McCampbell Drive
Montgomery, AL 36106
(205) 271-3947

Friends of Landau-Kleffner Syndrome (FOLKS)
3 Stone Buildings, Ground Floor
Lincoln's Inn, London WC2A 3XL
(0870) 847-0707
http://www.bobjanet.demon.co.uk/lks/fws.htm

Learning disabilities

Learning Disabilities Association of America
4156 Library Road
Pittsburgh, PA 15234-1349
(412) 341-1515
Fax (412) 344-0224
http://www.ldanatl.org/

NLDline: Nonverbal Learning Disabilities web site
http://www.NLDline.com

Mental retardation

The Arc (formerly the Association of Retarded Citizens)
1010 Wayne Avenue, Suite 650
Silver Spring, MD 20910
(301) 565-3842
info@thearc.org
http://thearc.org

Pathological Demand Avoidance Syndrome

PDA Contact Group
http://www.pdacontact.org.uk

Prader-Willi syndrome

International Prader-Willi Syndrome Organization
B.I.R.D. Europe Foundation Onlus
Via Bartolomeo Barza 1
36023 Costozza
Vicenza, Italy
(39) 0444 555557
president@ipwso.org
http://www.ipwso.org/

Prader-Willi Syndrome Association
5700 Midnight Pass Road
Sarasota, FL 34242
(941) 312-0400 or (800) 926-4797
Fax (941) 312-0142
national@pwsausa.org
http://www.pwsausa.org/

Rett syndrome

International Rett Syndrome Association
9121 Piscataway Road
Clinton, MD 20735
(301) 856-3334 or (800) 818-RETT
Fax (301) 856-3336
irsa@rettsyndrome.org
http://www.rettsyndrome.org/

Tuberous sclerosis

Tuberous Sclerosis Alliance
801 Roeder Road, Suite 750
Silver Spring, MD 20912
(800) 225-6872
Fax (301) 562-9870
http://www.tsalliance.org/

TSCTalk
http://www.tsctalk.com

TSCTalk is an email discussion group about tuberous sclerosis.

General special needs

Australian Early Intervention Network
c/o CAMHS—Southern Flinders Medical Centre
Bedford Park, South Australia 5042 Australia
(08) 8404 2999
Fax (08) 8357 5484
auseinet@flinders.edu.au
http://auseinet.flinders.edu.au/

DisabilityNet
http://www.disabilitynet.co.uk

This is a UK-based disability information site.

Federation for Children with Special Needs
1135 Tremont Street, Suite 420
Boston, MA 02120
(617) 236-7210 or (800) 331-0688
http://www.fcsn.org

This group can help you locate parents or parent organizations in your area.

March of Dimes Birth Defects Foundation
1275 Mamaroneck Avenue
White Plains, NY 10605
(888) 663-4637
resourcecenter@modimes.org
http://www.modimes.org/

National Information Center for Children and Youth with Disabilities
P.O. Box 1492
Washington, DC 20013-1492
(202) 884-8200 or (800) 695-0285
Fax (202) 884-8441
nichcy@aed.org
http://www.nichcy.org/

Legal advocacy

A complete list of state and national legal referral services and disability advocacy groups is available on the web site for this book, at *http://www.patientcenters.com/autism.*

United States

For help with Social Security Income (SSI), disability rights issues, or violations of special education law, call your state bar association and ask for its pro bono (free) legal help referral service, or contact the first group listed next.

National Association of Protection and Advocacy Systems
900 Second Street NE, Suite 211
Washington, DC 20002
(202) 408-9514
Fax (202) 408-9520
http://www.protectionandadvocacy.com/

National Welfare Monitoring and Advocacy Partnership
c/o Children's Defense Fund
25 E Street NW
Washington, DC 20001
(202) 628-8787

Parent Educational Advocacy Training Center
6320 Augusta Drive, Suite 1200
Springfield, VA 22150
(703) 923-0010
Fax (703) 823-0030
partners@peatc.org
http://www.peatc.org/

UK

Disability Law Service
c/o Network for the Handicapped Ltd.
49-51 Bedford Row, 2nd Floor, Room 241
London WC1R 4LR
(0171) 831-8031
http://www.mkurrein.co.uk/work/disablaw.html

Independent Panel for Special Education Advice (IPSEA)
6 Carlow Mews
Woodbridge, Suffolk IP12 1EA
0800 0184016 (UK free phone)
0131 454 0082 (Scotland)
01232 705654 (Northern Ireland)
http://www.ipsea.org.uk/

Rights Now Campaign
c/o RADAR
12 City Forum
250 City Road
London EC1V 8AF
020 7250 3222

Australia

For general information about the Disability Discrimination Act and disability-related legal issues, you may want to start with one of the following:

Human Rights and Equal Opportunity Commission
Level 8, Piccadilly Tower
133 Castlereagh Street
Sydney, NSW 2000
(02) 9284 9600 or (1300) 656 419 (complaints)
TTY (800) 620 241
Fax (02) 9284 9611
http://www.hreoc.gov.au/disability_rights/

Action Resource Network Inc.
266 Johnston Street
Abbotsford, Victoria 3067
(03) 9416-3488 or (800) 808-126
Fax (03) 9416-3484
TTY (03) 9416-3491

New Zealand

The Human Rights Commission of New Zealand
P.O. Box 6751
Wellesley Street
Auckland
(09) 309 0874 or (0800) 496 877
Fax (09) 375 8611
help@hrc.co.nz
http://www.hrc.co.nz/

New Zealand CCS (Waikaito)
P.O. Box 272
Hamilton 2001
(07) 838 2744 or (0800) CCS CALL
Fax (07) 839 0192
info@waikato.ccs.org.nz
http://ccs.nzl.org/

Research and Testing Facilities

THE ESTABLISHMENTS AND PRACTITIONERS LISTED IN THIS APPENDIX have been compiled from a variety of sources, including parent recommendations, ASD support groups, and official government documents on health care. We do not imply endorsement of their medical or therapeutic approaches by including them here.

Autism research

These facilities and organizations conduct or fund research into autistic spectrum disorders. They are generally not sources of ongoing medical care, but their web sites, publications, and staff may inform you about new developments.

An extensive list of medical and treatment facilities is available online at *http://www. patientcenters.com/autism,* which includes facilities throughout the US, Canada, UK, Ireland, Australia, and New Zealand, state medical agencies, and larger ABA providers.

There are, of course, many individual physicians and clinics with expertise. A local autism advocacy and support organization is usually the best source of information about where to go for both evaluation and ongoing care. Another good place to start is a nearby university that has a medical school.

Allergy Induced Autism Support and Research Network
8 Hollie Lucas Road, King's Heath
Birmingham B13 0QL United Kingdom
Fax (44) 0-121 444 6450
aia@kessick.demon.co.uk
http://www.demon.co.uk/charities/AIA/aia.htm

Autism Autoimmunity Project
45 Iroquois Avenue
Lake Hiawatha, NJ 07034
Contact: Ray Gallup, *truegrit@gti.net*
http://www.gti.net/truegrit/

Autism Research Centre
Cambridge University
Douglas House
Cambridge CB2 1TN United Kingdom
http://www.psychiatry.cam.ac.uk/arc/

The Autism Research Foundation (TARF)
P.O. Box 1571, GMF
Boston, MA 02205
(617) 414-5286
Fax (617) 414-7207
http://ladders.org/tarf/TARF.htm

Autism Research Institute (ARI)
4182 Adams Avenue
San Diego, CA 92116
Fax (619) 563-6840
http://www.autism.com/ari/

ARI publishes a research journal, and has collected data from parents of children with autism for almost 40 years. It tends to have an "alternative medicine" focus, and has been instrumental in founding the Defeat Autism Now! (DAN!) doctors' group.

Autism Research Unit
School of Health Sciences
University of Sunderland
Sunderland SR2 7EE UK
(44) 0 191 510 8922
Fax (44) 0 191 567 0420
aru@sunderland.ac.uk
http://osiris.sunderland.ac.uk/autism

The ARU's research focuses on the metabolic aspects of autism. It provides urinary peptide testing for a small fee, and organizes the annual Durham Conference on autism.

Blue Bird Circle Clinic for Pediatric Neurology
Baylor College of Medicine
Department of Neurology
6565 Fannin Street, Suite NB100
Houston, TX 77030
(713) 790-5046
http://www.bcm.tmc.edu/neurol/struct/blueb/blueb2.html

The Blue Bird Clinic has particular expertise in Rett syndrome and epilepsy.

Center for the Study of Autism
P.O. Box 4538
Salem, OR 97302
http://www.autism.org/

The Center for the Study of Autism has a special interest in Auditory Integration Therapy (AIT), but also provides information to parents on a variety of topics.

The Cure Autism Now (CAN) Foundation
5225 Wilshire Boulevard, Suite 715
Los Angeles, CA 90036
(323) 529-0500 or (888) 8AUTISM
CAN@primenet.com
http://www.canfoundation.org/

Defeat Autism Now! (DAN!)
c/o Autism Research Institute
4182 Adams Avenue
San Diego, CA 92116
Fax (619) 563-6840
http://www.autism.org/dan.html

International Molecular Genetic Study of Autism Consortium
http://www.well.ox.ac.uk/~maestrin/iat.html

Laboratory for Research on the Neuroscience of Autism
8110 La Jolla Shores Drive, Suite 201
La Jolla, CA 92037
(858) 551-7925, extension 240 (Dr. Natacha Akshoomoff)
http://nodulus.extern.ucsd.edu/

M.I.N.D. Institute Clinic
U.C. Davis Medical Center
4860 Y Street, Room 3020
Sacramento, CA 95817
(916) 734-5153 or (888) 883-0961
http://mindinstitute.ucdmc.ucdavis.edu/index.htm

The M.I.N.D. Institute carries out research into a variety of neurodevelopmental disorders, including autism and Tourette's syndrome. It provides diagnostic and treatment services on a limited basis.

National Alliance for Autism Research (NAAR)
99 Wall Street, Research Park
Princeton, NJ 08540
(609) 430-9160 or (888) 777-NAAR
Fax (609) 430-9163
http://www.naar.org/

NAAR raises and disburses funds for autism research.

The Seaver Autism Research Center
Mt. Sinai School of Medicine
Department of Psychiatry, Box 1230
One Gustave L. Levy Place
New York, NY 10029
(212) 241-2994
Fax (212) 987-4031

The Seaver Center is researching the genetics of autism. Other services may also be available.

Test facilities and programs

As discussed in Chapter 5, *Medical Interventions,* and Chapter 7, *Other Interventions,* some researchers suspect that allergies, food sensitivities, metabolic disorders, *Candida* yeast overgrowth, viral infection, unusual reactions to immunizations, and other factors may be involved. Ferreting out these causes usually requires obtaining test results on blood, urine, or stool samples. Your physician may be able to do these tests. If not, the facilities listed next, along with the Autism Research Unit listed earlier, can help. Most labs work directly with doctors, not parents or patients.

Make sure you have expert medical help in interpreting test results. The reports you receive may be unintentionally misleading if you don't know what you're looking at. If the results seem inconsistent or strange, you may want to duplicate the tests at another lab. Labs do make mistakes.

It's a good idea to speak to recent clients of a lab you are considering. Labs sometimes change management or test procedures—for better or for worse.

Accu-Chem Laboratories
990 North Bowser Road, Suite 800-880
Richardson, TX 75081
(972) 234-5412 or (800) 451-0116
Fax (972) 234-5707
http://www.accuchem.com/

Accu-Chem specializes in testing for toxic chemicals and heavy metals.

Alletess Medical Laboratory
216 Pleasant Street
P.O. Box 343
Rockland, MA 02370
(617) 871-4426 or (800) 225-5404
http://www.foodallergy.com/index.html

Alletess does testing for *Candida* yeast and allergen response (IgE and IgG).

AAL Reference Laboratories Inc.
1715 E. Wilshire Boulevard, Suite 715
Santa Ana, CA 92705
(714) 972-9979 or (800) 522-2611
Fax (714) 543-2034
http://www.antibodyassay.com/

AAL can do urinary peptide tests for IAG and compounds related to casein and gluten, among many others.

The Great Plains Laboratory Inc.
11813 West 77th
Lenexa, KS 66214
(913) 341-8949
Fax (913) 341-6207
gpl4u@aol.com
http://www.greatplainslaboratory.com/

This lab offers a variety of mail-in test kits and lab analyses.

Great Smokies Diagnostic Laboratory
63 Zillicoa Street
Asheville, NC 28801
(704) 253-0621 or (800) 522-4762
Fax (828) 252-9303
cs@gsdl.com
http://www.gsdl.com/

Great Smokies provides mail-in lab analysis for *Candida* yeast, allergies, and other health issues.

Immuno Laboratories/Better Health USA
1620 Oakland Park Boulevard
Fort Lauderdale, FL 33311
(800) 684-2231
http://www.immunolabs.com/

This firm provides mail-in test lab analysis for allergies/sensitivities.

The Genetics of Autism

RESEARCHERS ONCE HOPED TO FIND AN "AUTISM GENE," allowing for early diagnosis through genetic testing, and rapid development of treatments based on what the gene discovered actually does. Unfortunately, after a decade of intensive research this dream has been dashed. Perhaps 5 to 10 percent of people with ASDs have a problem that can be traced to a single gene, such as Fragile X syndrome, Rett syndrome, or tuberous sclerosis.

But for the vast majority of people with ASDs, the genetics appear to be mind-bogglingly complex. It now appears that there are many "autism genes," that most are relatively common, and that different combinations of these genes coupled with environmental factors are responsible for the development of autistic spectrum disorders. Like breast cancer or diabetes, autism is a multifactorial condition.

At this time, genetic testing is readily available for Fragile X syndrome, and it can be obtained through specialty clinics for Rett syndrome. Genetic screening may be done if features of an "autism-like" condition, such as Angelman syndrome, are present. It may also be done as part of a comprehensive diagnostic program, or in a research setting. There is no genetic test for diagnosing autism itself.

Every human cell has a copy of our 24 chromosomes. Each chromosome has a short arm and long arm, attached to each other at the centromere (middle). The short arm is called "p" for short, and the long arm is abbreviated as "q." Chromosomes contain multiple genes. Each gene contains the instructions for making a specific protein out of certain of the 20 amino acids. These proteins make up most of the cells in our bodies, and control all human development and function.

There are about 40,000 human genes in total. Minor genetic differences are common, usually harmless, and occasionally even beneficial. Differences can be inherited, but may also happen spontaneously. Difference ("mutations") can include duplication of a genetic sequence, inverted duplication where a sequence is repeated back-to-front, and deletion of a sequence. Occasionally entire chromosomes are duplicated or deleted, with rather serious results. Sometimes a mutation occurs in some cells but not others, a pattern called mosaicism. Some people with Rett syndrome have a genetic pattern like this, and usually have less severe problems as a result.

Several genetic differences have been found in some people with autism. These are listed in the following table. Some have been found in only a few people with ASDs, and probably represent unique conditions. They may contribute to specific individual cases or be part of "autism-like" disorders not yet understood. Others are more widely distributed.

Genes linked to disorders that seem to occur more often in people with ASDs and their close relatives may also play a role in specific cases, and are listed in three separate columns. As with the autism-linked genes listed, some of these differences have been found in only a few individuals.

Identifying genes is only the first part of the chase, of course: Next, researchers have to understand what the genes actually do. Tantalizing clues are already emerging. The HRAS gene is closely linked to the production of secretin. The RELN gene is linked to production of reelin, a protein involved in brain development and metabolism of toxic metals, and it is inhibited by viral infection. Other "suspicious areas" in the genome are involved with neurotransmitter or immune system functions.

Someday, understanding how these genes affect development, behavior, and physical health may help doctors create individually tailored treatment programs. In the meantime, knowing what genes researchers suspect will give you a better understanding of news stories about the hunt for autism genes.

	GENES			
CHROMO-SOMES	Autistic spectrum disorders	Obsessive-compulsive disorder	Tourette's syndrome	Other linked disorders
1	1p region		Translocation with Ch. 8	
2	2q region			Dyslexia: DYX3
3				
4	4p region		4q region encompassing D4S1625 and D4S1644	
5	5q22 region Duplications		Dopamine receptor 1 gene: 5q31–35	
6	6q region 6p21: complement C4 protein gene Duplications		D6S477	
7	7q31: WNT2 gene 7p15–p14: HOXA1 gene 7q22: RELN gene	7p15 region: HOXA genes	Translocation with Ch. 18	Schizophrenia, bipolar disorders: 7q22 region Speech problems: 7q31–35
8			8p: two regions bounded by D8S1106, D8S1145, and D8S136 Translocation with Ch. 1	
9	9q34 region		9p deletion 9q34	Tuberous sclerosis: TSC1
10	5-HT7 Receptor gene (HTR7)		5-HT7 Receptor gene (HTR7)	

CHROMO-SOMES	GENES			
	Autistic spectrum disorders	Obsessive-compulsive disorder	Tourette's syndrome	Other linked disorders
11	11p15: HRAS, part of the G protein secondary messenger system		D11S933 11q23.1: Dopamine receptor 2 gene	ADHD, schizophrenia: 11q23.1: Dopamine receptor 2 gene Bipolar disorders
12				12q24.1: Phenylketonuria (PKU)
13	13q region		13q region	
14			14q: D14S1003	
15	Duplication or inverted duplication of 15q11–13: GABA receptor genes			Angelman syndrome and Prader-Willi: deletions in 15q11–q13 Anxiety disorders
16	16p region			Tuberous sclerosis: TSC2
17	17q11.1–q12: Serotonin receptor gene (5-HTT)	5-HTT gene	5-HTT gene	Bipolar disorders, depression, anxiety disorders: 5-HTT gene Neurofibroma-tosis 1: 17q11.2
18	18q region		18q deletion Translocation with 7	Bipolar disorders
19	19p region		19p7	
20			20q: D20S1085	
21			21q: D21S1252	Bipolar disorders
22		22q11.2: Catechol-O-methyltransferase (COMT) gene		Anxiety disorders Bipolar disorders: COMT gene
23				
X	X-linked expression Fragile X: Duplication of sequences on Xq27.3 (FMR1) Rett syndrome: mutation of Xq28 (MECP2) Deletion of Xp	X-linked expression Xp11.4–p11.3: Genes affecting monamine-oxidase (MAO) receptors	X-linked expression Xp11.4–p11.3: Genes affecting monamine-oxidase (MAO) receptors	Turner syndrome: absence of or defect in one X chromosome
Y				

Medication Reference

THIS APPENDIX PROVIDES MORE INFORMATION ABOUT MEDICATIONS that may be prescribed to treat specific symptoms associated with autistic spectrum disorders. Being listed in this appendix does not mean that a particular medication is recommended for these disorders, but it's important to know as much as possible about drugs you may hear about or be prescribed.

Only commonly reported side effects and certain rare but especially dangerous side effects are listed. Less common and rare side effects may be associated with any medication, and you may experience side effects that no one else has ever had. If you have unusual symptoms after taking medicine, or after combining more than one medication, call your doctor right away.

The information in this chapter was taken from the *Physician's Desk Reference,* pharmaceutical company literature, and other reputable sources. It should be accurate as of this writing, but new information may emerge. Be sure to personally check out any medications you or your child takes using a detailed medication reference book, such as those listed in Appendix A, *Resources,* to ensure that you are aware of all possible side effects and interactions. You should also consult the drug reference sheet packaged with your medication by the pharmacy.

Here are some more important dos and don'ts:

- Do not start or stop taking any prescription medication on your own.

- Be careful to follow exactly instructions about dosage, time, and accompaniment ("take with food," and so on).

- If you are pregnant or breastfeeding, or if you could become pregnant, ask your physician or pharmacist about any side effects specifically related to female reproduction and nursing.

- Men who are actively trying to father a child may also want to ask about male reproductive side effects.

- Be sure to tell both your physician and your pharmacist about all other medications you take, including over-the-counter drugs—even aspirin and cough syrup can cause dangerous side effects when mixed with the wrong medication.

- Inform your doctor about your use of alcohol, tobacco, any illegal drugs, and any vitamins or supplements (other than a regular daily multivitamin).

- If your doctor is unsure how a medication might interact with a supplement, you may need to help him or her find more information about the chemical action of the supplement. Most doctors are not well informed about nutritional supplements or herbal medicines, but many are willing to work with you on these matters.

- If you suspect that you have been given the wrong medication or the wrong dosage, call your pharmacist right away. Such errors do occur, and your pharmacist should be able to either reassure you or fix the problem.

The latest data on medications

The following three tables summarize what's currently known about medications that address some symptoms of ASDs. They were adapted, with permission, from "New Findings on the Causes and Treatment of Autism," by Dr. Marc Potenza and Dr. Christopher McDougle, a 1997 article published in the medical journal *CNS Spectrums* (Copyright © 1997, Medical Broadcast Limited). They are based on information from the latest studies of human subjects who have ASDs. You can find out more about these studies by reading the original journal articles about them, all of which are listed in the Notes section at the end of this book.

You will notice that all these studies are fairly small: Of the 25 studies, 16 looked at fewer than ten people, 4 looked at only one person. None examined medication response based on ASD subgroups or individual factors. It is difficult to judge the efficacy of medications based on these studies, but they are a start.

Table E-1. Drugs with Mixed 5-HT Receptor Agonism/Antagonism Properties in Pervasive Developmental Disorders

Drug/Reference	Study Design	Number of subjects	Age (years)	Dosage (mg/day)	Duration (weeks)	Efficacy	Adverse Effects
Buspirone							
Realmuto and others (1989)[1]	Open-label with blinded comparison to fenfluramine or methylphenidate	4	Range, 9–10; mean 9.3	15	4	Improvement in hyperactivity (2/4), aggression (2/4), and stereotypy (2/4)	None
Ratey and others (1989)[2]	Open-label	14 (3 with ASD)	Range, 23–63 (25–38); mean, 35.3 (32.2)	15–45	26–52 in well-described cases	Improvement in 9/14, with decreases in aggression and ritualistic behavior, and increases in social interactions	None reported
Gedye (1991)[3]	Single-blind, ABAC design, open comparison to serotonin-enhancing diet	1	39	20	10 active	Decrease in aggression (65–76%)	None
Ratey and others (1991)[4]	Multiple-baseline, placebo lead-in, ABC design	6 (1 with ASD)	Range, 18–50 (29); mean, 28.4 (29)	15–45	9 active	Improvement with decreases in self-injurious behavior and anxiety	None reported
Ricketts and others (1994)[5]	Open-label	5 (3 with ASD)	Range, 27–45 (27–34); mean, 34.6 (30)	Range, 30–60 (30–60); mean, 49.5 (45)	6–33	Decrease in aggression (13%–72%)	None
Trazodone							
Gedye (1991)[3]	Open-label, ABAB design	1	17	50–150	10 active	Decrease in aggression (70%–79%)	None reported

Table E-2. Selective Serotonin Reuptake Inhibitors in Pervasive Developmental Disorders

Drug/ Reference	Study Design	Number of subjects	Age (years)	Dosage (mg/day)	Duration (weeks)	Efficacy	Adverse Effects
Clomipramine							
Gordon and others (1993)[6]	Double-blind crossover	12 vs. DMI 12 vs. PLA	Range, 6–18; mean, 9.7	152+/56	5	CMI > DMI, CMI > PLA for stereotypies, anger, rituals; CMI = DMI > PLA for hyperactivity	Insomnia, constipation, sedation, twitching, EKG changes (N = 1), tachycardia (N = 2), grand mal seizure
McDougle and others (1992)[7]	Open-label	5	Range, 13–33; mean, 25.2	185+/74	12	4/5 patients showed improved social relatedness and reduced repetitive behavior and aggression	Dry mouth
Garber and others (1992)[8]	Open-label	11	Range, 10–20; mean, 15.0	70+/37	4–52	10/11 patients had >50% reduction in SIB and stereotypies	Hypomania, constipation, sedation, enuresis, aggression
Brasic and others (1994)[9]	Open-label	5	Range, 6–12; mean, 9.4	200+/0.0	8–78	5/5 patients showed reduced adventitious movements and compulsions	None reported
Brodkin and others (1997)[10]	Open-label	35	Range, 18–44; mean, 30.2	139+/50	12	18/35 patients "much improved" or "very much improved," with reduced repetitive behavior, aggression, and echolalia	Constipation, sedation, weight gain, seizures (N = 3)
Sanchez and others (1996)[11]	Open-label	8	Range, 3.5–8.7; mean, 6.4	103.6	5	7 patients worse, 1 moderately improved	Urinary retention, constipation, insomnia, sedation, aggression

Note: CGI = Clinical Global Impression Scale; CMI = clomipramine; DMI = desipramine; PLA = placebo; SIB = self-injurious behavior.

Table E-2. Selective Serotonin Reuptake Inhibitors in Pervasive Developmental Disorders (continued)

Drug/ Reference	Study Design	Number of subjects	Age (years)	Dosage) (mg/day)	Duration (weeks)	Efficacy	Adverse Effects
Fluvoxamine							
McDougle and others (1996)[12]	Double-blind parallel groups	30	Range, 18–53; mean, 30.1	277+/42	12	8/15 patients "much improved" or "very much improved" on fluvoxamine, 0/15 patients improved on placebo. Reduced repetitive behavior and aggression and improved language usage	Nausea, sedation
Fluoxetine							
Cook and others (1992)[13]	Open-label	23	Range, 7.0–28.8; mean, 15.9	28.3	1.567	15/23 patients had an improvement of 1 or more on CGI Severity Rating. Reduced rituals and aggression, better eye contact	Agitation, hyperactivity, insomnia, "elated effect," decreased appetite, increased screaming
McDougle and others (unpublished data)	Open-label	42	Range, 18–39; mean, 26.1	122+/61	12	24/42 patients "much improved" or "very much improved." Improvement seen in repetitive behavior and aggression	Agitation, headaches, reduced appetite, sedation, weight gain

Note: CGI = Clinical Global Impression Scale; CMI = clomipramine; DMI = desipramine; PLA = placebo; SIB = self-injurious behavior.

Table E-3. "Atypical" Neuroleptics in Pervasive Developmental Disorders

Drug/ Reference	Study Design	Number of subjects	Age (years)	Dosage (mg/day)	Efficacy	Adverse Effects
Clozapine						
Zuddas and others (1996)[14]	Open-label	3	Range, 8–12; mean, 9.33	200–400	Improvements in hyperactivity, SIB, aggression, and communication	Transient sedation, enuresis
Risperidone						
Purdon and others (1994)[15]	Open-label	2	Range, 29–30; mean, 29.5	68	Improvements in hyperactivity, social interactions, repetitive behaviors	None reported
McDougle and others (1995)[16]	Open-label	3	Range, 20–44; mean, 31.67	28	Improvements in social relatedness, repetitive thoughts and behaviors, and impulsive aggression	None
Simeon and others (1995)[17]	Open-label	7 (2 with ASD)	Range, 11–17; mean, 14.43 (range, 13–14; mean 13.50)	14	Improvements in social interactions and aggressive behaviors	None (transient sedation at higher doses)
Fisman and others (1996)[18]	Open-label	1	14	1	Decrease in compulsive avoidances and agitation, and improved attention	None
Demb (1996)[19]	Open-label	3	Range, 5–11; mean, 7.66	13	Decreases in SIB and hyperactivity	Temporary sedation, extrapyramidal side effects, weight gain

Note: SIB = self-injurious behavior.

Table E-3. "Atypical" Neuroleptics in Pervasive Developmental Disorders (continued)

Drug/ Reference	Study Design	Number of subjects	Age (years)	Dosage (mg/day)	Efficacy	Adverse Effects
Fisman and Steele (1996)[20]	Open-label	14	Range, 9–17; mean, 12.72	0.75–1.5	Improvement (13/14) with decreases in disruptive behaviors, agitation, anxiety, and repetitive behaviors; and increased social awareness and attention	Initial sedation (5/ 14), sleep onset insomnia (1/ 14), rhinorrhea (1/14), and transient headache (1/14)
Hardan and others (1996)[21]	Open-label	20	Range, 8–17; mean, 13.35	1.5–10	Improvement (13/20) with decreases in aggression, SIB, impulsivity, hyperactivity, and psychosis	Weight gain (3/20), galactorrhea (2/20 [2/7 girls])
Rubin (1997)[22]	Open-label	2	Range, 3.55; mean, 4.25		Improvement with decreases in repetitive and aggressive behaviors, and increased social function	None
Olanzapine						
Rubin (1997)[22]	Open-label	1	17	30	Decrease in pacing and aggression, and stabilization of mood	None

Note: SIB = self-injurious behavior.

In the sections that follow, medications have been divided into the following categories:

- Antidepressants:
    - SSRIs
    - MAOIs
    - Tricyclics
    - Other
- Catapres and Tenex
- Stimulants
- Antiseizure drugs
- Neuroleptics
    - Atypical
    - Other
- Antifungals
- Antiviral and antibacterial drugs
- Other drugs

If you are not sure which category a drug belongs in, check Chapter 5, *Medical Interventions,* or use the index.

Within each category, medications are listed by US brand-name, followed by other brand-names where known. The generic name appears on the second line of each listing. Some of these drugs are not available commercially as low-cost generics. They may be marketed under other brand-names, and are not available in some countries.

Antidepressants: The SSRIs

The brain is chock-full of serotonin receptors, tiny sites that bind with serotonin molecules to move chemical impulses through the brain. One type of antidepressants, the selective serotonin reuptake inhibitors (SSRIs), block certain receptors from absorbing serotonin. Researchers believe this results in lowered or raised levels of serotonin in specific areas of the brain. Over time, SSRIs may cause changes in brain chemistry, hopefully in a positive direction. They may also cause actual changes in brain structure with prolonged use. There are also serotonin receptor sites elsewhere in the central and peripheral nervous systems, so SSRIs can affect saliva production, appetite, digestion, skin sensitivity, and many other functions.

Celexa, Cipramil

Generic name: citalopram

Use: Depression. Some doctors are, however, experimenting with this relatively new (to the US) SSRI to treat obsessive-compulsive behaviors. Although not yet FDA-approved for this purpose, limited clinical experience indicates citalopram is effective for some people.

Action, if known: Celexa increases the amount of active serotonin in the brain. It usually has a calming and/or sedating effect.

Side effects: Celexa can cause dry mouth, insomnia or restless sleep, increased sweating, and nausea. It is reportedly less likely to cause sexual dysfunction than other SSRIs. Celexa lowers the seizure threshold, and can cause mood swings in people with bipolar disorders.

Known interaction hazards: Celexa and alcohol can be a dangerous combo. Celexa should never be taken with an MAOI antidepressant, or soon after stopping an MAOI. Use Celexa with caution if you take a drug that affects the liver, such as ketoconazole or macrolide antibiotics.

Tips: People with liver or kidney disease need regular monitoring while taking Celexa.

Luvox, Faverin

Generic name: fluvoxamine maleate

Use: OCD, social phobia, depression. Luvox is FDA-approved for use by children aged 8 and older.

Action, if known: Luvox increases the amount of active serotonin in the brain. It usually has a calming and/or sedating effect.

Side effects: Luvox can cause headache, insomnia, sleepiness, nervousness, nausea, dry mouth, diarrhea or constipation, or sexual dysfunction. It lowers the seizure threshold, and can cause mood swings in people with bipolar disorders.

Known interaction hazards: Never take Luvox with an MAOI antidepressant, or soon after stopping an MAOI. Luvox's action is strengthened by tricyclic antidepressants and lithium. It can strengthen the action of many medications, including clozapine, diltiazem and perhaps other calcium channel blockers, methadone, some beta-blockers and antihistamines, and Haldol and other neuroleptics.

Tips: Avoid taking this drug if you have liver disease. Smoking cigarettes may make it less effective. Luvox does not bind to protein in the body, unlike the other SSRIs, and may have a very different effect in some people.

Paxil, Seroxat

Generic name: paroxetine hydrochloride

Use: OCD, panic disorder, social phobia, depression.

Action, if known: Paxil increases the amount of active serotonin in the brain. It usually has a calming and/or sedating effect.

Side effects: Paxil can cause headache, insomnia or restless sleep, dizziness, tremor, nausea, weakness, sexual dysfunction, or dry mouth. It lowers the seizure threshold, and can cause mood swings in people with bipolar disorders.

Known interaction hazards: Paxil should not be taken with alcohol. Never take it with an MAOI antidepressant, or soon after stopping an MAOI. Paxil strengthens the action of warfarin, theophylline, and procyclidine. It also changes how digoxin and phenytoin act in the body.

Tips: People with liver or kidney disease should be monitored regularly while taking Paxil. This medication has a short life in the body, so missed doses may be more likely to cause side effects. Some people who take Paxil for a long period and then stop suddenly experience unpleasant effects, occasionally including the onset of depression. To avoid these difficulties, always reduce your dose gradually under medical supervision.

Prozac

Generic name: fluoxetine hydrochloride

Use: OCD, depression. Prozac is also sometimes used to treat eating disorders, ADHD, narcolepsy, migraine/chronic headache, Tourette's syndrome, and social phobia.

Action, if known: SSRI—Prozac increases the amount of active serotonin in the brain. It may have an energizing effect.

Side effects: Prozac can cause headache, insomnia or restless sleep, dizziness, tremor, nausea, weakness, sexual dysfunction, dry mouth, itchy skin, and/or rash. It may cause changes in appetite and weight. Prozac lowers the seizure threshold, and can cause mood swings in people with bipolar disorders.

Known interaction hazards: Prozac should not be taken with alcohol or other central nervous system depressants. Never take this drug with an MAOI antidepressant, or soon after stopping an MAOI. Do not take OTC or prescription cold or allergy remedies containing cyproheptadine or dextromethorphan with Prozac. This drug's action is increased by tricyclic antidepressants. It strengthens the action of lithium, phenytoin, neuroleptic drugs, carbamazepine, and cyclosporine. It reduces the effectiveness of BuSpar.

Tips: Prozac has a long life in your body, and is metabolized slowly. People with liver or kidney disease should be monitored while taking Prozac.

Zoloft, Lustral

Generic name: sertraline hydrochloride

Use: OCD, panic disorder, depression. Zoloft is FDA-approved for use by children.

Action, if known: Zoloft increases the amount of active serotonin in the brain. It has an energizing quality.

Side effects: Zoloft can cause dry mouth, headache, tremor, diarrhea, nausea, or sexual dysfunction. It may cause mood swings, especially manic episodes, in people with bipolar disorders. It lowers the seizure threshold.

Known interaction hazards: Zoloft should not be taken with alcohol or any other central nervous system depressant. Never take this drug with an MAOI antidepressant, or soon after stopping an MAOI. Zoloft strengthens the action of benzodiazepine drugs and warfarin. Its action is strengthened by cimetidine. It may affect the therapeutic level of lithium.

Tips: People with liver or kidney disease need careful monitoring while taking Zoloft.

Antidepressants: the tricyclics

Before the SSRIs came along, the tricyclic antidepressants were considered the best medications available for treating depression and obsessive-compulsive behavior. Although these drugs tend to cause more side effects than the SSRIs, sometimes they are more effective for certain people. Anafranil is the tricyclic antidepressant most often prescribed to people with ASDs. Other tricyclics are listed later, but these are infrequently used.

Anafranil

Generic name: clomipramine hydrochloride

Use: Obsessive-compulsive behavior, depression, panic disorder, chronic pain, eating disorders, severe PMS. Anafranil is sometimes prescribed to treat herpes lesions or arthritis, indicating that it may also have antiviral or anti-inflammatory qualities. It is FDA-approved for use by children age 10 and older.

Action, if known: Anafranil blocks the reuptake of norepinephrine and serotonin, and works against the hormone acetylcholine. It has weak antihistamine properties.

Side effects: Anafranil can cause sedation, tremor, seizures, dry mouth, light sensitivity, mood swings in people with bipolar disorders, and weight gain. It lowers the seizure threshold, and can cause sexual side effects.

Known interaction hazards: Combining Anafranil with alcohol, MAOI antidepressants, blood pressure medications (including clonidine and guanfacine), or thyroid medication can be dangerous. Estrogen, bicarbonate of soda (as in Alka-Seltzer and other over-the-counter remedies), acetazolamide, procainamide, and quinidine all increase the activity of this drug. Cimetidine, methylphenidate, Thorazine and similar drugs (neuroleptics), oral contraceptives, nicotine (including cigarettes), charcoal tablets, and estrogen may interfere with Anafranil's action in the body.

Tips: Take Anafranil with food if stomach upset occurs. Take the bulk of your dose at bedtime to reduce sedation, if so directed.

Other tricyclic antidepressants

Brand-name	Generic name	Brand-name	Generic name
Allegron	nortriptyline	Motival	nortriptyline
Asendin	amoxapine	Norpramin	desipramine
Asendis	amoxapine	Pamelor	nortriptyline
Aventyl	nortriptyline	Sinequan	doxepin
Elavil	amitriptyline	Surmontil	trimipramine
Janimine	imipramine	Tofranil	imipramine
Lentizal	amitriptyline	Tryptizol	amitriptyline
Limbitrol	amitryptyline/chlordiazepoxide	Vivactil	protriptyline
Motipress	nortriptyline		

Antidepressants: MAOIs

A third class of antidepressants, the monoamine oxidase inhibitors (MAOIs), is also available—but they are rarely used. These medications are effective against depression by inhibiting the metabolism of the neurotransmitters serotonin, norepinephrine, and dopamine. They do so indirectly, by interfering with the enzyme monoamine oxidase (MAO).

The MAOIs have unpleasant and even life-threatening interactions with many other drugs, including common over-the-counter medications. People taking MAOIs must also follow a special diet, because these medications interact with many foods. The list of foods to avoid includes chocolate, aged cheeses, beer, and many more. If you or your child must take a MAOI, familiarize yourself thoroughly with these dietary restrictions.

The most frequently prescribed drugs in this class are Aurorix (moclobemide), Nardil (phenelzine), and Parnate (tranylcypromine sulfate). If your doctor prescribes an MAOI, read the package insert carefully, and learn more about its possible side effects from a medication reference book or your physician.

Other antidepressants

The following antidepressants work differently from the SSRIs, tricyclics, and MAOIs. They are among the newest medications that are occasionally prescribed to people with ASDs.

Reboxetine

Generic name: edronax

Use: Depression—Reboxetine tends to have an energizing effect.

Action, if known: A nontricyclic selective noradrenaline reuptake inhibitor (selective NRI), Reboxetine inhibits the reuptake of norepinephrine by cells, increasing noradrenaline availability in the synaptic cleft.

Side effects: Dry mouth, constipation, insomnia, sweating, heart irregularities, dizziness, urine retention, and sexual dysfunction are sometimes reported.

Known interaction hazards: Don't take Reboxetine with alcohol or other CNS depressants. It may interact with other antidepressants, and may change the way some antiseizure drugs work. If you take other medications, your doctor may need to adjust doses.

Tips: Reboxetine may counteract some of the interactions associated with MAOIs, and so it may be prescribed in concert with these. This combination should be monitored closely, of course. It is not currently available in the US.

Remeron

Generic name: mirtazapine

Use: Depression, anxiety.

Action, if known: Remeron is a noradrenergic and specific serotonergic antidepressant (NaSSA): it affects the neurotransmitter noradrenaline as well as some serotonin receptors. It has an energizing effect.

Side effects: Sleepiness, dry mouth, dizziness, weight gain, and constipation may occur when taking Remeron. It lowers the seizure threshold, and can cause mood swings in people with bipolar disorder. Remeron can depress the immune system, causing a lower count of white blood cells.

Known interaction hazards: Never take with an MAOI or soon after stopping an MAOI, and avoid alcohol, tranquilizers (including OTC sleep aids), and other CNS depressants when taking this medication.

Tips: If you experience fever, aches, sore throat, or infections, call your doctor. Take with food if stomach upset occurs. People with heart, liver, or kidney disease or hypothyroidism should be monitored while taking Remeron.

Serzone

Generic name: nefazodone

Use: Depression, especially if it occurs with agitation.

Action, if known: This drug blocks the uptake of serotonin and norepinephrine in the brain, and increases the levels of two natural antihistamines in the bloodstream.

Side effects: Sleepiness, dizziness, confusion, dry mouth, nausea, visual disturbances, and rashes are associated with Serzone. It lowers the seizure threshold.

Known interaction hazards: Never take Serzone with an MAOI, astemizole, propranalol, ter-fenadine, alprazolam, or triazolam. It strengthens the action of digoxin.

Tips: People with heart or liver trouble should be monitored while taking Serzone.

Wellbutrin, Zyban

Generic name: buproprion

Use: Depression, ADHD.

Action, if known: Wellbutrin is an aminoketone antidepressant: It appears to have mild effects on serotonin, dopamine, and norepinephrine. It is also a mild general CNS stimulant, affects the hormonal system, and suppresses appetite.

Side effects: Wellbutrin increases the risk of seizures. Restlessness, anxiety, insomnia, heart palpitations, dry mouth, rapid heartbeat or heart palpitations, tremor, and headache/migraine headache may occur when taking this drug.

Known interaction hazards: L-Dopa and ritonavir increase the effects of Wellbutrin. Its effects are decreased by carbamazepine. Do not use this medication with MAOIs, or with drugs or supplements that lower the seizure threshold.

Tips: Take Wellbutrin with food if stomach upset occurs. Be especially careful to start low, increase dose slowly, and limit dose size to reduce seizure risk.

Catapres and Tenex

Clonidine (Catapres) and guanfacine (Tenex) were originally developed to treat high blood pressure, but were found to reduce tics and hyperactivity in people who also happened to need treatment for hypertension. This accidental discovery has allowed many people to address these symptoms without neuroleptics or stimulants. They are particularly valuable when a person has sleep disturbance in addition to repetitive movements or hyperactivity.

Catapres

Generic name: clonidine

Use: High blood pressure, ADHD, tics/Tourette's syndrome, extreme impulsivity, migraine, drug and alcohol withdrawal aid, ulcerative colitis, childhood growth delay.

Action, if known: Clonidine stimulates alpha-adrenergic receptors in the brain and spinal cord to widen blood vessels, and stimulates similar receptors throughout the body. This reduces the heart rate, relaxes blood vessels, and may have other effects.

Side effects: This drug can cause dry mouth, dizziness, constipation, sedation, unusually vivid or disturbing dreams, and weight gain.

Known interaction hazards: Clonidine can interact with other medications for blood pressure, and its activity is blocked by tricyclic antidepressants, such as Anafranil. It can have an additive effect with certain antihistamines that also lower blood pressure.

Tips: Do not use clonidine if you have slow heart rate or AV node conduction problems, disease of the blood vessels in the brain, or chronic kidney failure. Clonidine is not recommended for people with depression. You can become tolerant of clonidine, requiring a higher dose. You should have regular eye exams, as clonidine can affect the retina. You can diminish oral clonidine's sedating effect by taking all or the largest part of your dose at bedtime. This can help people who have sleep problems. The time-released Catapres patch is far less sedating than oral clonidine for most people. Do not stop using clonidine suddenly. Your doctor can supervise a slow withdrawal program to avoid risking a sudden, dangerous rise in blood pressure. Symptoms of this problem include rapid heartbeat, sweating, nervousness, and headache. A cream version of clonidine is also available.

Tenex

Generic name: guanfacine

Use: High blood pressure, ADHD, tic disorders/Tourette's syndrome, migraines, extreme nausea, heroin withdrawal aid.

Action, if known: Guanfacine stimulates the central nervous system to relax and widen blood vessels, allowing freer blood flow and reducing blood pressure. It may also have other effects.

Side effects: Sleepiness, changes in blood pressure or heart rate, or nausea may occur.

Known interaction hazards: Alcohol and other CNS depressants plus guanfacine can cause extreme sedation. Its effects may be counteracted by stimulants such as Ritalin, many nonprescription drugs, estrogen and oral contraceptives, indomethacin, ibuprofen, and nonsteroidal anti-inflammatory drugs. It could also have an additive effect with certain antihistamines that also lower blood pressure.

Tips: If you take another medication that lowers blood pressure, your doctor will need to adjust your Tenex dose accordingly to prevent problems. Guanfacine's sedating effect can be diminished by taking all or the largest part of your dose at bedtime. This can help people who have sleep problems.

Stimulants

Stimulants are often prescribed to help with ADD and ADHD, which are fairly common in people with ASDs. However, doctors treating people with ASDs often note that they do not respond to these drugs as well as people who have ADD or ADHD alone. Indeed, adverse reactions or lack of benefit are frequently reported. These drugs have not been approved as treatments for ASDs.

If stimulants are recommended, they should be used as part of a multifactor treatment plan, including behavior management and self-organization strategies.

Adderall

Generic name: dextroamphetamine/amphetamine

Use: ADHD.

Action, if known: Central nervous system (CNS) stimulant.

Side effects: Adderall can cause loss of appetite, weight loss, headache, insomnia, dizziness, increased heart rate, and agitation. It may increase tic severity in people with an underlying tic disorder.

Known interaction hazards: Vitamin C supplements, citrus juices, citric acid, more than four cans per day of soda pop, or taking this medication with food can reduce its effectiveness.

Tips: Make sure you drink plenty of water while taking Adderall, even if you're not thirsty. Adderall is not as well known as Ritalin, but it may be a better choice for many patients. It time-releases different amphetamine compounds smoothly over several hours, resulting in a lower chance of rebound.

Cylert

Generic name: pemoline

Use: ADHD, narcolepsy.

Action, if known: CNS stimulant.

Side effects: Cylert can cause irritability, insomnia, appetite changes, or depression. It lowers the seizure threshold.

Known interaction hazards: Cylert strengthens the action of other CNS stimulants. It may increase tic severity in people with an underlying tic disorder. Vitamin C supplements, citrus juices, citric acid, drinking more than four cans per day of soda pop, or taking this medication with food can reduce its effectiveness.

Tips: You will need to have liver enzyme tests frequently while taking Cylert—those with known liver problems may need to avoid this medication. It is not recommended for people with psychosis. You can take Cylert with food if stomach upset occurs, but the dose may need to be adjusted. Make sure you drink plenty of water, even if you're not thirsty. Cylert has a long action period, but because of the potential for liver problems and other complications it is rarely used unless all the other ADHD medications have failed to have positive effects and behavioral strategies are ineffective.

Dexedrine, Das, Dexampex, Dextrostat, Ferndex, Oxydess

Generic name: dextroamphetamine sulfate

Use: ADHD.

Action, if known: CNS stimulant.

Side effects: Dexedrine can cause agitation, restlessness, aggressive behavior, dizziness, insomnia, headache, tremor, dry mouth, change in appetite, or weight loss. It may raise blood pressure. It may increase tic severity in people with an underlying tic disorder.

Known interaction hazards: Do not use Dexedrine with MAOI antidepressants. It interacts with tricyclic antidepressants, meperidine, phenobarbital, phenytoin, propoxyphene, acetazolamide, thiazides, and some medications for stomach distress. Vitamin C supplements, citrus juices, citric acid, drinking more than four cans per day of soda pop, or taking this medication with food can reduce its effectiveness.

Tips: If you are diabetic, discuss your use of insulin and oral antidiabetes drugs with your doctor, as Dexedrine may force a change in dosage. It is not recommended for people with psychosis. Make sure you drink plenty of water, even if you're not thirsty, while taking this medication.

Desoxyn

Generic name: methamphetamine, MTH

Use: ADHD, narcolepsy.

Action, if known: CNS stimulant.

Side effects: Desoxyn can cause agitation, restlessness, aggressive behavior, dizziness, insomnia, headache, or tremor. It may raise your blood pressure. It may increase tic severity in people with an underlying tic disorder.

Known interaction hazards: Never use Desoxyn with an MAOI antidepressant. Its effects may be counteracted by barbiturates, tranquilizers (including OTC sleep aids), and tricyclic antidepressants. Desoxyn may strengthen the action of other CNS stimulants, including caffeine and OTC cold and allergy medications. Its action is strengthened by acetazolamide and sodium bicarbonate (found in Alka-Seltzer and similar over-the-counter remedies), and it may interact with thyroid hormones and some medications for gastrointestinal problems. Vitamin C supplements, citrus juices, citric acid, drinking more than four cans per day of soda pop, or taking this medication with food can reduce its effectiveness.

Tips: This is the most powerful and potentially addictive of the stimulants, and is well known as a drug of abuse. For these reasons, Desoxyn is rarely prescribed for ADHD in the US. If you are diabetic, discuss your use of insulin and oral antidiabetes drugs with your doctor, as Desoxyn may force a change in dosage. It is not recommended for people with psychosis. Make sure you drink plenty of water, even if you're not thirsty, while taking this medication.

Provigil

Generic name: modafinil

Use: ADHD, narcolepsy. Approved for narcolepsy only in the US.

Action, if known: CNS stimulant.

Side effects: Provigil can cause agitation, restlessness, aggressive behavior, dizziness, nausea, or insomnia. It may raise your blood pressure. Some people experience more infectious illnesses when taking this drug.

Known interaction hazards: Never use Provigil with an MAOI antidepressant. Its effects may be counteracted by barbiturates, tranquilizers (including OTC sleep aids), and tricyclic antidepressants. Provigil may strengthen the action of other CNS stimulants, including caffeine and OTC cold and allergy medications.

Tips: This medication is not recommended for people with psychosis.

Ritalin

Generic name: methylphenidate hydrochloride

Use: ADHD, narcolepsy, social phobia.

Action, if known: CNS stimulant.

Side effects: Ritalin can cause agitation, restlessness, aggressive behavior, dizziness, insomnia, headache, tremor, or loss of appetite and/or weight. It may raise your blood pressure. It may increase tic severity in people with an underlying tic disorder.

Known interaction hazards: Ritalin should not be taken with alcohol. Its action is strengthened by MAOI antidepressants to a high degree. It strengthens the action of tricyclic antidepressants, and reduces the action of guanethidine. Vitamin C supplements, citrus juices, citric acid, drinking more than four cans per day of soda pop, or taking this medication with food can reduce its effectiveness.

Tips: The rebound effect can be bad with Ritalin, which has the shortest life of the stimulants commonly used for ADHD. Some doctors combine Ritalin SR with regular Ritalin for the smoothest effect (SR's action is said to be erratic). Make sure you drink plenty of water, even if you're not thirsty. Some people, including quite a few doctors, swear that the brand-name Ritalin is superior to its generic counterpart. It may be worth trying the brand-name version if the generic didn't work well. A time-released version of Ritalin is now sold under the brand-name Concerta. It provides smooth delivery of medication throughout the day with a single morning dose, eliminating the need for taking medication at school or work, and potentially eliminating rebound effects.

Medications for anxiety

Anxiety and related issues, such as panic attacks, are a problem for many people with autistic spectrum disorders. An SSRI antidepressant can often relieve these symptoms, but in more severe cases an anti-anxiety medication (tranquilizer) may be prescribed. Depending on your doctor's advice, these may be taken daily or on an "as-needed" basis. Often they are prescribed as a temporary measure only. These medications may be prescribed for other conditions as well, including irritable bowel syndrome, seizure disorders, restless leg syndrome, and muscle spasms.

Most tranquilizers do have a potential for addiction and abuse, so be careful about their use and storage. Some are not FDA-approved for use by children and, speaking generally, their use should be avoided unless other strategies for reducing anxiety are ineffective. They tend to be sedating, and can cause a myriad of unpleasant side effects, including blurred vision, confusion, sleepiness, and tremors. When added to other medications that also cause sedation, dangerous levels of physical and mental slowing can be experienced if dosages of both drugs are not carefully adjusted.

Brand name	Generic name	Brand name	Generic name
Ativan	lorazepam	Serax	oxazepam
BuSpar	buspirone	Tranxene	clorazepate
Centrax	prazepam	Valium	diazepam
Klonopin	clonazepam	Xanax	alprazolam
Librium	chlordiazepoxide		

Antiseizure drugs

Medication is the primary treatment for seizure disorders, usually coupled with preventive lifestyle changes. If you or your child has seizures in addition to an ASD, be sure to take your medication as directed.

Some antiseizure drugs are also prescribed to deal with behavioral issues, such as mood swings, rages, and aggression.

Cerebyx

Generic name: fosphenytoin

Use: Seizure disorders.

Action, if known: Cerebyx inhibits activity in the part of the brain where local focal (grand mal) seizures begin.

Side effects: Gum growth, confusion, twitching, depression, irritability, and many more side effects have been reported, some of which are very serious. Because of the many interaction problems with this drug, discuss it thoroughly with your doctor and pharmacist.

Known interaction hazards: Alcohol, aspirin, sulfa drugs, succinimide antiseizure medications, some neuroleptics and antidepressants, and many other drugs strengthen Cerebyx. Cerebyx increases the action of lithium, acetaminophen, and many other drugs. Its effects are changed by use of calcium, antacids, charcoal tablets, and many prescription drugs.

Tips: Do not use this drug if you have low blood pressure or heart trouble. Keep an eye out for skin rash or bruising, which can be serious warning signs. You may want to supplement with folic acid, which is depleted by Cerebyx. You will need to have regular blood tests while taking this drug. Take with food if stomach upset occurs—but not with high-calcium foods, such as dairy products, sesame seeds, or some nuts. Do not switch brands without telling your doctor.

Depakene

Generic name: valproic acid

Use: Seizure disorders, bipolar disorder, migraine, panic disorder, rages/aggression.

Action, if known: Depakene increases the levels of gamma-aminobutyric acid (GABA) in the brain, and increases its absorption. It also stabilizes brain membranes.

Side effects: Nausea, sedation, depression, psychosis, aggression, hyperactivity, and changes in blood platelet function can occur with Depakene.

Known interaction hazards: Do not take with milk, and do not use charcoal tablets. Be careful with alcohol and with any medication that has a tranquilizing or depressant effect. Side effects may increase if you use anticoagulants, including aspirin or nonsteroidal anti-inflammatory drugs, erythromycin, chlorpromazine, cimetidine, or felbamate.

Tips: Watch out for increased bruising or bleeding, an indicator of blood platelet problems. Regular liver tests are a must. Do not crush or chew tablets.

Depakote

Generic name: divalproex sodium (valproic acid plus sodium valproate)

Use: Seizure disorders, bipolar disorder, migraine, panic disorder, rages/aggression.

Action, if known: Depakote increases the levels of gamma-aminobutyric acid (GABA) in the brain, and increases its absorption. It also stabilizes brain membranes.

Side effects: Nausea, sedation, depression, psychosis, aggression, hyperactivity, and changes in blood platelet function are sometimes seen.

Known interaction hazards: Do not take with milk; do not use charcoal tablets. Be careful with alcohol and with any medication that has a tranquilizing or depressant effect. Side effects may increase if you use anticoagulants, including aspirin or nonsteroidal anti-inflammatory drugs, erythromycin, chlorpromazine, cimetidine, or felbamate.

Tips: Watch out for increased bruising or bleeding, an indicator of blood platelet problems. Regular liver tests are a must. Do not crush or chew tablets: A formulation called Depakote Sprinkles is available for those who can't take pills.

Dilantin

Generic name: Phenytoin

Use: Seizure disorders.

Action, if known: Dilantin inhibits activity in the part of the brain where tonic-clonic seizures begin.

Side effects: Gum growth, confusion, twitching, depression, irritability, and many more side effects have been reported, some of which are very serious. Because of the many interaction problems with this drug, discuss it thoroughly with your doctor and pharmacist.

Known interaction hazards: Alcohol, aspirin, sulfa drugs, succinimide antiseizure medications, some neuroleptics and antidepressants, and many other drugs make Dilantin stronger. It strengthens the action of lithium, acetaminophen, and many other drugs. Its effects are changed by use of calcium, antacids, charcoal tablets, and many prescription drugs.

Tips: Do not use this drug if you have low blood pressure or heart trouble. Keep an eye out for skin rash or bruising, which can be serious warning signs. You may want to supplement with folic acid, which is depleted by Dilantin. You will need to have regular blood tests while taking this drug. Take with food if stomach upset occurs—but not with high-calcium foods, such as dairy products, sesame seeds, or some nuts. Do not switch brands without telling your doctor.

Lamictal

Generic name: Lamotrigine

Use: Seizure disorders, Lennox-Gastaut syndrome in children.

Action, if known: Lamictal binds to the pigment melanin, stabilizes electrical currents within the brain, and blocks the release of seizure-stimulating neurotransmitters.

Side effects: Headache, dizziness, nausea, general flu-like feeling, and light sensitivity have been associated with Lamictal. If you develop a rash, call your doctor immediately as it may be a warning of a serious side effect. Lamictal may make seizures worse in some people.

Known interaction hazards: This drug interacts with Depakote, Depakene, carbamazepine, and phenytoin—your doctor will have to monitor doses carefully. Antifolate drugs make it stronger, whereas phenobarbital and primidone may lessen its effects.

Tips: This drug is not recommended for use by children. If you have heart, kidney, or liver disease, use it only under careful supervision.

Luminal, Solfoton

Generic name: phenobarbital

Use: Seizure disorder, insomnia.

Action, if known: Luminal, a barbiturate, blocks or slows nerve impulses in the brain. It is usually used in combination with another drug to control seizures.

Side effects: Drowsiness, slow reflexes, "stoned" feeling, allergy-like symptoms, and labored breathing may occur. Call your doctor if any side effect becomes bothersome, or if you develop anemia or jaundice. Luminal carries an addiction risk—taper off dose carefully if stopping.

Known interaction hazards: Alcohol, MAOIs, and Depakote/Depakene all strengthen Luminal. Alcohol should be avoided. It is neutralized by charcoal, chloramphenicol, and rifampin. Luminal makes acetaminophen (Tylenol) and the anesthetic methoxyflurane stronger. It changes the way many other drugs act in the body, including anticoagulants, beta-blockers, oral contraceptives, and corticosteroids. Be sure to go over all medicines you take with your doctor, as doses may need to be adjusted.

Tips: You may want to supplement with vitamin D when taking Luminal. People with liver or kidney disease should be monitored when taking this drug.

Mesantoin

Generic name: mephenytoin

Use: Seizure disorders.

Action, if known: Mesantoin inhibits activity in the part of the brain where local focal (partial) seizures begin.

Side effects: Gum growth, confusion, twitching, depression, irritability, and many more issues have been reported, some of which are very serious. Given the many interaction problems with this drug, discuss it thoroughly with your doctor and pharmacist.

Known interaction hazards: Alcohol, aspirin, sulfa drugs, succinimide antiseizure medications, some neuroleptics and antidepressants, and many other drugs strengthen Mesantoin. It strengthens lithium, acetaminophen, and many other drugs. Its effects are changed by use of calcium, antacids, charcoal tablets, and many prescription drugs.

Tips: Do not use this drug if you have low blood pressure or heart trouble. Keep an eye out for skin rash or bruising, which can be serious warning signs. You may want to supplement with folic acid, which is depleted by Mesantoin. You will need to have regular blood tests while taking this drug. Take with food if stomach upset occurs—but not with high-calcium foods, such as dairy products, sesame seeds, or some nuts. Do not switch brands without telling your doctor.

Mysoline

Generic name: primidone

Use: Seizure disorders.

Action, if known: Mysoline controls nerve impulses in the brain.

Side effects: Restlessness is often seen, especially in children. Dizziness, drowsiness, and rash are also reported.

Known interaction hazards: Avoid alcohol and all other CNS depressants, including tranquilizers, narcotics, and OTC sleep aids, allergy drugs, and cold medications. Mysoline may counteract corticosteroids, oral contraceptives, and blood-thinning medications. It may interact with other Depakote, Depakene, and antiseizure drugs. Do not take Mysoline with MAOIs.

Tips: People with porphyria should not take Mysoline. If you have lung disease (including asthma), kidney disease, or liver disease, you will need to be carefully monitored while taking this drug.

Neurontin

Generic name: Gabapentin

Use: Seizure disorders, especially those that do not respond to other drugs; bipolar disorder; rage/aggression.

Action, if known: Neurontin appears to act by binding a specific protein found only on neurons in the CNS. It may increase the GABA content of some brain regions.

Side effects: Blurred vision, dizziness, clumsiness, drowsiness, swaying, and eye-rolling have been reported.

Known interaction hazards: Avoid alcohol and all other CNS depressants, including tranquilizers, OTC medications for colds and allergies, OTC sleep aids, anesthetics, and narcotics. Antacids may counteract the effects of Neurontin.

Tips: People with kidney disease should be carefully monitored while taking Neurontin. Corn is used as a filler in the usual formulation of this drug, causing allergic reactions in some. A new drug under development called Pregabolin is based on Neurontin, but with fewer side effects.

Peganone

Generic name: Ethotoin

Use: Seizure disorders.

Action, if known: Peganone inhibits activity in the part of the brain where local focal (partial) seizures begin.

Side effects: Gum growth, confusion, twitching, depression, irritability, and many more side effects have been reported, some of which are very serious. Because there are many interaction problems with this drug, discuss it thoroughly with your doctor and pharmacist.

Known interaction hazards: Alcohol, aspirin, sulfa drugs, succinimide antiseizure medications, some neuroleptics and antidepressants, and many other drugs strengthen the effects of Peganone. It strengthens lithium, acetaminophen, and many other drugs. Its effects are changed by use of calcium, antacids, charcoal tablets, and many prescription drugs.

Tips: Do not use this drug if you have low blood pressure or heart trouble. Keep an eye out for skin rash or bruising, which can be serious warning signs. You may want to supplement with folic acid, which is depleted by Peganone. You will need to have regular blood tests while taking this drug. Take with food if stomach upset occurs—but not with high-calcium foods, such as dairy products, sesame seeds, or some nuts. Do not switch brands without telling your doctor.

Tegretol

Generic name: carbamazepine

Use: Seizure disorders, nerve pain, bipolar disorder, rage/aggression, aid to drug withdrawal, restless leg syndrome, and Sydenham's chorea and similar disorders in children.

Action, if known: Tegretol appears to work by reducing polysynaptic responses.

Side effects: You may experience sleepiness, dizziness, nausea, unusual moods or behavior, headache, or retention of water. Tegretol may cause low count of white blood cells. Call your doctor right away if you have flu-like symptoms or other unusual reactions while taking this drug.

Known interaction hazards: Never take this drug with an MAOI. Tegretol is often used in combination with other antiseizure drugs, but the dose of Tegretol and drugs used with it must be very carefully adjusted. Tegretol is potentiated by numerous prescription and OTC medications, including many antibiotics, antidepressants, and cimetidine. It also counteracts or changes the effect of many drugs, including Haldol, theophylline, and acetaminophen. Because these interactions can be very serious, discuss all medications you take—including all OTC remedies—with your doctor before beginning to use Tegretol.

Tips: You should have a white blood cell count done before taking Tegretol and be monitored thereafter. Do not take if you have a history of bone marrow depression. Tegretol can be fatal at fairly low doses, so all patients taking this drug should be carefully monitored, particularly because it interacts with so many other medications.

Topamax

Generic name: topiramate

Use: Seizure disorders.

Action, if known: The mode of Topamax's antiseizure action is unknown.

Side effects: Problems reported include slowed speech, thought, and action; sleepiness; tingling in the extremities; nausea; tremor; depression; and visual disturbances.

Known interaction hazards: Avoid alcohol and other CNS depressants. Topamax interacts with other antiseizure drugs, so your doctor may need to adjust dosages. It reduces the effectiveness of digoxin and oral contraceptives.

Tips: People with kidney or liver problems should be monitored while taking Topamax.

Zarontin

Generic name: ethosuximide

Use: Absence (petit mal) seizure disorders.

Action, if known: Zarontin is thought to reduce nerve signals within the brain.

Side effects: Nausea, abdominal pain, changes in appetite, weight loss, drowsiness, headache, dizziness, irritability, or insomnia may occur. Zarontin may lower the seizure threshold in some patients with mixed forms of epilepsy.

Known interaction hazards: This drug makes fosphenytoin, phenytoin, and ethotoin stronger.

Tips: You should have regular liver function and blood tests while taking this drug. Zarontin may cause systemic lupus erythematosus (a medication-caused form of lupus).

Atypical neuroleptics

The atypical neuroleptics blend functionality against psychosis, self-injurious behavior, painful movement disorders, and other major mental symptoms, with fewer side effects and dangers than older neuroleptics, which are listed in brief elsewhere.

That's not to say that these are safe, gentle drugs: Risk is still there, and they do carry side effects that can be a problem (especially rapid weight gain). The atypical neuroleptic family includes the following medications.

Clozaril

Generic name: clozapine

Use: Schizophrenia, psychosis.

Action, if known: This drug works against the neurotransmitters acetylcholine and dopamine.

Side effects: Sedation, fever (this usually passes), changes in blood pressure or heartbeat, overproduction of saliva, and tremor are among the side effects connected with Clozaril. Major dangers include agranulocytosis (a serious blood condition), seizures, neuroleptic malignant syndrome (NMS), and tardive dyskinesia.

Known interaction hazards: Alcohol, CNS system depressants, drugs for high blood pressure, tricyclic antidepressants, and similar drugs should be avoided or used with caution. The danger of NMS increases when Clozaril is used with lithium.

Tips: Weekly blood tests are recommended for the first year of use, after which every four weeks will suffice if blood levels are stable. Women, people with low counts of white blood cells, and some people of Ashkenazi Jewish descent have a higher risk of agranulocytosis when taking this drug. People with heart disease, glaucoma, prostate trouble, or liver or kidney disease should be monitored carefully. Smoking cigarettes can affect how quickly your body metabolizes Clozaril.

Risperdal

Generic name: risperidone

Use: Psychosis, schizophrenia, rage/aggression.

Action, if known: Risperdal affects serotonin and dopamine, and raises the level of the hormone prolactin.

Side effects: You may experience sedation, headache, runny nose, anxiety, or insomnia while taking this drug. Weight gain, especially in children, is a concern. Risperdal carries a risk of neuroleptic malignant syndrome (NMS), tardive dyskinesia.

Known interaction hazards: Risperdal decreases the action of L-dopa. It interacts with carbamazepine and clozapine. It may strengthen the action of, or be strengthened by, SSRI antidepressants.

Tips: Doctors recommend having an EKG before starting Risperdal, and regular heart monitoring while taking it. In some patients, Risperdal (and possibly other atypical neuroleptics) may increase obsessive-compulsive symptoms.

Seroquel

Generic name: quetiapine

Use: Psychosis, rage/aggression.

Action, if known: Atypical neuroleptic—this drug is believed to increase the availability of serotonin and dopamine at specific receptors in the brain.

Side effects: Drowsiness, dizziness, sedation, agitation, nausea, changes in appetite, weight gain or loss, or sexual dysfunction may occur. Seroquel lowers the seizure threshold. It also carries a danger of neuroleptic malignant syndrome (NMS), extrapyramidal side effects, and tardive dyskinesia.

Known interaction hazards: The effects of this drug can be made dangerously strong by alcohol and all CNS depressants, including tranquilizers, sedatives, OTC sleep aids, and narcotics, as well as the antiseizure drug phenytoin. It may interfere with the effects of drugs for high blood pressure. Seroquel's action may be increased by other drugs, including ketoconazole, erythromycin, clarithromycin, diltiazem, verapamil, and nefazodone.

Tips: This drug can cause extra-sensitivity to heat. People with liver or kidney problems, heart disease, thyroid problems, or low blood pressure should be monitored while taking Seroquel. You may want to supplement with vitamin E, which may protect against tardive dyskinesia.

Zeldox, Geodon

Generic name: ziprasidone

Use: Schizophrenia, psychosis, rage/aggression.

Action, if known: Zeldox affects the production and use of dopamine, serotonin, and norepinephrine. It also has some antihistamine effects, and is an alpha-adrenergic blocker.

Side effects: You may experience drowsiness, dizziness, agitation, tremor, nausea, reduced appetite, lightheadedness, rash, increased light sensitivity, increased blood pressure, or cold-like symptoms while taking Zeldox. It carries a risk of neuroleptic malignant syndrome (NMS) and tardive dyskinesia. Zeldox can lower the seizure threshold.

Known interaction hazards: Avoid alcohol and all CNS depressants, including tranquilizers, sedatives, OTC sleep aids, and narcotics. Zeldox may strengthen the action of drugs that lower your blood pressure, including Clonidine and Tenex. It may counteract L-dopa and similar drugs. Its action may be strengthened by carbamazepine and ketoconazole. According to its manufacturer, Pfizer, Zeldox is less likely to interact with other medications than other atypical neuroleptics.

Tips: Before starting Zeldox, you should have an EKG, as well as regular heart monitoring while taking this drug. It should not be used with other drugs that affect the QT interval, including quinidine, dofetilide, pimozide, thioridazine, moxifloxacin, and sparfloxicin. It is not recommended for people with existing heart or liver problems, or for people with altered electrolyte balance (such as people with anorexia). Zeldox is a very new drug, and just received FDA approval for US use in February 2001. According to research carried out by its manufacturer, it is much less likely to cause rapid weight gain than other atypical antipsychotics, and may be safer for people who have diabetes or high cholesterol because it has less effect on insulin and cholesterol. Zeldox capsules contain lactose, so if you are lactose intolerant you may want to use a lactose-free version if available. Zeldox may increase the risk of birth defects in the children of women who take it. Talk to your doctor if you could become pregnant.

Zyprexa

Generic name: olanzapine

Use: Psychosis, rage/aggression, tics; also used in cases of hard-to-treat OCD, depression (usually with an antidepressant), or bipolar disorders (usually with a mood stabilizer).

Action, if known: This medication blocks uptake of dopamine and serotonin at certain receptors, and may have other actions.

Side effects: You may experience headache, agitation, dry mouth, hostility, disinhibition, insomnia, or slurred speech while taking this drug. Other risks include neuroleptic malignant syndrome (NMS), tardive dyskinesia, dizziness, and seizures.

Known interaction hazards: Alcohol and carbamazepine add to the sedating action of this drug. Zyprexa strengthens the effect of medications for high blood pressure, including clonidine and guanfacine.

Tips: Zyprexa can increase your sensitivity to heat. If you smoke, you may need to take Zyprexa more frequently, as nicotine increases the metabolism of this drug.

Other neuroleptics

If the atypical neuroleptics do not work and symptoms remain very difficult to cope with, your doctor may recommend trying one of the older neuroleptics, despite their high potential for side effects. Haldol is the most frequent choice among drugs in this class. These drugs should not be used unless all other treatment options have been exhausted.

Brand name	Generic name	Brand name	Generic name
Haldol	haloperidol	Navane	thiothixene
Largactil	chlorpromazine	Orap	diphenylbutylpiperidine
Loxipac	loxapine	Pimozide	diphenylbutylpiperidine
Loxipax	loxapine	Prolixin	fluphenazine
Loxitane	loxapine	Serenace	haloperidol
Mellaril	thioridazine hydrochloride	Serentil	mesoridazine
Moban	molindone	Stelazine	trifluoperazine
Motipress	loxapine plus nortriptyline (an anti-anxiety drug)	Thorazine	chlorpromazine
		Vesprin	trifluoperazine
Motival	loxapine plus nortriptyline		

Antifungals

If a medical exam finds clinically significant overgrowth of *Candida* yeast, an antifungal drug can help. Depending on need, these may be taken internally or used in cream form.

Diflucan

Generic name: fluconazole

Use: Yeast infections.

Action, if known: Diflucan inhibits an enzyme that occurs in Candida albicans and other yeasts.

Side effects: Some patients report unpleasant "die-off" reactions as yeast in the GI tract are killed.

Known interaction hazards: Diflucan strengthens the action of certain drugs for diabetes, causing low blood sugar. It also strengthens cyclosporine, phenytoin, theophylline, warfarin, and zidovudine. It is strengthened by hydrochlorothiazide, and may cause oral contraceptives to be ineffective.

Tips: Call your doctor if you develop a rash while taking Diflucan.

Lamisil

Generic name: terbinafine hydrochloride

Use: Lamisil is used to treat fungal infection of the skin or nails, including *Candida*.

Action, if known: This drug kills fungal organisms.

Side effects: The cream can cause itching or irritated skin; headache, diarrhea, or rash can occur when taking oral Lamisil.

Known interaction hazards: Cimetidine, terfenadine, and rifampin make Lamisil stronger. It may counteract cyclosporin. It enhances the effect of caffeine.

Tips: Do not take this drug with food. People with kidney or liver disease should be carefully monitored when taking Lamisil.

Mycostatin, Mykinac, Nilstat, Nystex

Generic name: nystatin

Use: Fungal and yeast infections.

Action, if known: This drug kills fungi by chemically binding to their cell membranes, causing cell contents to leak out.

Side effects: Nausea and diarrhea are often reported. Some people note uncomfortable "die-off" reactions during the treatment as yeast in the GI tract is killed.

Known interaction hazards: None known.

Tips: None.

Monistat

Generic name: miconazole

Use: Monistat is used to treat fungal or yeast infections.

Action, if known: Antifungal.

Side effects: Nausea and diarrhea are reported. Some people note uncomfortable "die-off" reactions during the treatment as yeast in the GI tract is killed.

Known interaction hazards: None.

Tips: None.

Nizoral

Generic name: ketoconazole

Use: Nizoral is used to treat fungal infections. It is not very effective if the infection is in the nervous system, however.

Action, if known: It invades the outer membrane of fungal cells, destroying them.

Side effects: Headaches, dizziness, drowsiness, nausea, and itching are reported. It decreases the level of the hormone testosterone, so men may experience swollen breasts. It also reduces the level of natural steroids in the body, which may depress the immune system. Nizoral can cause liver inflammation—call your doctor immediately if you see signs of jaundice or have abdominal pain.

Known interaction hazards: Do not take Nizoral with antacids or histamine H2 antagonists. It interacts with corticosteroid drugs, cyclosporine, cisapride, some antihistamines, phenytoin, and theophylline.

Tips: Take this medication with food.

Sporanax

Generic name: itraconazole

Use: Sporanax is used to treat fungal infections.

Action, if known: This drug inhibits enzymes within fungi living in the body, eventually killing them.

Side effects: Nausea, rash, water retention, and sexual dysfunction may occur.

Known interaction hazards: Never take Sporanax with astemizole or terfenadine. Avoid taking it with amlodipine or nefedipine. Sporanax strengthens the action of cisapride, digoxin, some medications for diabetes, phenytoin, quinidine, tacrolimus, and warfarin. It may be counteracted by cimetidine, ranitidine, famotidine, nazatidine, isoniazid, phenytoin, and rifampin.

Tips: People with liver disease should be monitored while taking Sporanax.

Antiviral and antibacterial drugs

If bacterial infection is found, antibiotics are the primary treatment. Normally regular antibiotics are used, not the latest and strongest type.

If viral infection is found, antivirals are not customarily used. As the following descriptions indicate, these medications carry substantial risks. However, some specialists are now experimenting with antivirals as part of a treatment program for ASDs.

Ampligen

Generic name: poly I: poly C12U

Use: This drug has been tried as a treatment for AIDS, chronic fatigue immune deficiency syndrome (CFIDS, myalgic encephalopathy), fibromyalgia, and hepatitis B and C.

Action, if known: Ampligen is a nucleic acid (NA) compound that apparently heightens production of the body's own immunological and antiviral agents, such as interferon, and boosts natural killer (NK) cell and monocyte activity. It is said to inhibit the growth of viruses and tumor cells.

Side effects: Dizziness and facial flushing have been reported. Anecdotal reports from long-term users warn of heart problems and cancer risks, although these have not been proven. Ampligen is given via IV infusion, which carries minor infection risks and can cause discomfort.

Known interaction hazards: None known, but likely to be comparable with other drugs of this type.

Tips: Ampligen is experimental, and may have hazards, actions, and benefits that are as yet unknown. It is also expensive. Some patients with CFIDS and other disorders who have obtained it are staunch supporters, others report major problems. It is available in Canada, some parts of Europe, and via clinical trials.

Foscavir

Generic name: foscarnet sodium, trisodium phosphonoformate

Use: Foscavir is used to treat infection with human herpes viruses, cytomegalovirus, HIV/AIDS, and other viruses. It can cross the blood–brain barrier.

Action, if known: An immune modulator, this drug inhibits viral reproduction.

Side effects: Nausea, tremor, twitchiness, anemia, and electrolyte imbalance in the blood have been reported. Foscavir carries a toxicity risk, can cause kidney problems, and lowers the seizure threshold. Foscavir is given via IV infusion, which carries minor infection risks and can cause discomfort.

Known interaction hazards: May interact with acyclovir, amphotericin, calcium chloride, calcium folinate, calcium gluconate, co-trimoxazole, diazepam, digoxin, diphenhydramine, dobutamine, droperidol, ganciclovir, Haldol and similar drugs, lorazepam, midazolam, pentamidine, prochlorperazine, promethazine, and vancomycin—your doctor may need to adjust your doses carefully if you take one or more of these drugs.

Tips: You will need to have regular kidney function checks while taking Foscavir. You may want to take a calcium supplement. Make sure to drink extra water. Intravenous procedures should always be done in a setting where resuscitation equipment and trained personnel are available. A topical numbing agent may decrease discomfort from needle insertion.

Isoprinosine, Inosiplex, Immunovir

Generic name: inosine pranobex

Use: Isoprinosine is used to treat infection with human herpes viruses and other viruses, including cytomegalovirus, Epstein-Barr, varicella, measles, HIV/AIDS, hepatitis.

Action, if known: This immune modulator inhibits human herpes viruses and other infections by mimicking the effect of hormones produced by the thymus gland.

Side effects: Unknown, although any type of hormone or hormone analog supplementation can be hazardous.

Known interaction hazards: Unknown.

Tips: This is a relatively new drug in the potential ASD arsenal, and its effectiveness is unknown. It is not approved for use in the US.

Kutapressin

Generic name: kutapressin, KU

Use: This immune modulator is used to treat human herpes viruses, including herpes zoster (shingles).

Action, if known: A porcine (pig) liver extract, kutapressin strengthens the action of bradykinin, and inhibits human herpes viruses and Epstein-Barr virus.

Side effects: None known, but probably similar to other drugs of this type. The fact that it is an animal extract could be problematic for some due to possible antibody cross-reactivity or viruses, although there have been no reports of these problems.

Known interaction hazards: None known.

Tips: Kutapressin is administered via intramuscular (IM) injection. A topical numbing agent may decrease discomfort from needle insertion. Most doctors feel that kutapressin's effectiveness has been far outstripped by more recent antivirals.

Valtrex

Generic name: valacyclovir hydrochloride

Use: Valtrex works against herpes zoster and other herpetiform viruses.

Action, if known: Valtrex is converted into the antiviral acyclovir in the liver and intestine. Acyclovir battles the herpes viruses by inhibiting an enzyme they need to reproduce.

Side effects: Headache, bowel complaints, dizziness, nausea, and loss of appetite are reported.

Known interaction hazards: Valtrex can cause loss of energy and sedation when combined with zidovudine to create AZT. It is strengthened by cimetidine and probenecid.

Tips: Valtrex should not be taken by people with serious immune system suppression, including AIDS, except as directed by a specialist.

Venoglobulin S, Polygam, Gammagard

Generic name: intravenous immunoglobulin (IVIG)

Use: IVIG is used to treat bacterial or viral infection that does not respond to other therapies, Kawasaki disease, idiopathic thrombocytopenic purpura, autoimmune disorders, and recurrent miscarriage from autoimmune activity.

Action, if known: Gamma globulin is the component of human blood that contains antibodies. When injected into the body, it provides (presumably temporary) passive immunity to those infections for which it has antibodies, and also decreases the activity of natural killer (NK) cells.

Side effects: Fever, chills, headache, nausea, and back pain may occur. Gamma globulin could also contain viruses, despite careful screening. Some lots were withdrawn from the market in 1998 for this reason. Any intravenous procedure can have side effects ranging from mild discomfort to death.

Known interaction hazards: None known.

Tips: Before receiving IVIG, you should have a quantitative immune-globulin panel blood test to make sure you do not have a particular deficiency, that can lead to anaphylactic shock. Drink plenty of water or other liquids before, during, and after your IVIG infusion. Benadryl may help with side effects. Intravenous procedures should always be done in a setting where resuscitation equipment and trained personnel are available. A topical numbing agent may decrease discomfort from needle insertion.

Zovirax

Generic name: acyclovir

Use: Zovirax is used to treat infection with human herpes viruses, Epstein-Barr virus, varicella (chicken pox) and varicella pneumonia, cytomegalovirus, and other viruses.

Action, if known: This immune modulator inhibits the growth of viruses from within by interfering with reproduction of viral DNA.

Side effects: Sore or bleeding gums, fever, dizziness, headache, digestive trouble, diarrhea, rash, and insomnia may occur.

Known interaction hazards: Oral probenecid strengthens this drug's action. Sleepiness may occur when combined with zidovudine.

Tips: Take Zovirax with food if stomach upset occurs.

Other drugs

This section lists a few miscellaneous drugs that are sometimes prescribed to people with ASDs.

Gastrocom

Generic name: cromolyn

Use: Prevention of allergic reaction to foods.

Action, if known: Prevents mast cells from releasing antihistamines, reducing allergic reactions; may block absorption of allergens.

Side effects: Headache, diarrhea, allergy attacks.

Known interaction hazards: Do not take with food, juice, or milk.

Tips: People with heart, kidney, or liver problems should be monitored when taking Gastrocom. You can take Gastrocom with water, and you may dissolve the contents in hot water to drink it.

Habitrol, Nicoderm, Nicotrol, ProStep

Generic name: nicotine

Use: Used as an aid to stopping smoking, but sometimes prescribed to strengthen the action of neuroleptic drugs without increasing the actual dose.

Action, if known: Nicotine affects many CNS functions, and not all its actions are known. It may reduce tics and anxiety in some people.

Side effects: Diarrhea, insomnia, and nervousness may occur. Addiction is possible.

Known interaction hazards: Caffeine interferes with nicotine absorption.

Tips: People with insulin-dependent diabetes, heart problems, liver or kidney disease, high blood pressure, or pheochromocytoma should be carefully monitored when using nicotine in any form (including cigarettes).

Nitoman, Regulin

Generic name: tetrabenazine, TDZ

Use: This is the only drug currently known to help with tardive dyskinesia. It is also used to treat dystonia, Huntington's chorea, and Tourette's syndrome.

Action, if known: Tetrabenazine depletes dopamine in nerve endings in the brain.

Side effects: Depression is a well-known side effect.

Known interaction hazards: It may interact with other drugs that affect dopamine production or use.

Tips: Available in Canada, Norway, Sweden, the UK, and Japan, tetrabenazine can be obtained only through compassionate use programs in the US.

ReVia

Generic name: naltrexone hydrochloride

Use: ReVia is primarily used as a heroin/opioid and alcohol addiction withdrawal aid.

Action, if known: It is an opioid antagonist: It blocks opioid chemicals.

Side effects: Anxiety, nervousness, insomnia, abdominal discomfort, nausea, headache, muscle or joint pain may occur.

Known interaction hazards: Avoid alcohol and all CNS depressants, including anesthetics, narcotics, and sedatives. ReVia may block the effects of these substances until they reach a critical, even deadly, level.

Tips: People with liver problems must be closely monitored while taking ReVia. This drug has been tested for use in autism with mixed results.

Secretin

Generic name: secretin

Use: Secretin is used to test GI tract function. It is being tested as an experimental therapy for autistic spectrum disorders.

Action, if known: Secretin is a polypeptide hormone produced in the small intestine to stimulate pancreatic fluid secretion and biliary epithelial excretion, including immunoglobulins. It is known to target receptors in the GI tract and brain, and to affect intracellular cAMP and neurotransmitter production, probably including serotonin. Recent studies indicate that it targets the amygdala in particular. It may break down potentially aggravating peptides, such as those produced in response to gluten and casein.

Side effects: No major side effects should be expected from one-time use, but this medication has not been thoroughly tested for repeated use. Some children who have received infusions of secretin have not responded; a few have developed new and difficult symptoms. Parents have reported fever, runny noses, and coughing during the week following infusion. Some doctors have expressed concern that antibodies in porcine (pig) secretin could cross-react with human secretin, perhaps causing the body to stop producing any of its own secretin, or causing other health problems. Synthetic human secretin might be safer, but has not yet been widely used.

Known interaction hazards: None yet known, although some doctors have advised that supplements, megavitamin therapy, antifungals, antibiotics, and some medications may interfere with the action of secretin.

Tips: Intravenous procedures should always be done in a setting where resuscitation equipment and trained personnel are available. A topical numbing agent may decrease discomfort from needle insertion. Some doctors administering secretin recommend testing for certain antibodies or health conditions before and after infusion. Some also recommend dietary changes and courses of certain medication for several months in advance of trying secretin. This is a very new therapy for autistic spectrum disorders, so you will want to work closely with your physician.

It may be possible to increase the body's own production of secretin rather than administering it directly. Substances that may have this effect include phenylpentol, methanol extract of licorice root, plaunotol, and teprenon.

Supplement Reference

THIS APPENDIX EXPANDS ON WHAT'S KNOWN ABOUT HERBAL REMEDIES, nutritional supplements, some brand-name "natural" remedies or supplements, and a few over-the-counter medications that you may hear about in connection with ASDs. Simply being listed here does not imply recommendation, however: You should always explore new interventions in concert with your physician, a nutritionist, or other appropriate health professional.

As with medications, doses are specific to the individual, so you will want to consult a knowledgeable health professional. Books like *The Herbal PDR* are also helpful.

This appendix doesn't list homeopathic remedies. If you are interested in trying homeopathy, it's best to see a qualified homeopathic practitioner who can help you create a holistic treatment program. The appendix also doesn't list many Asian or Ayurvedic remedies, simply because so little is known about these in the US and Europe at this time. Much information on Chinese herbs can be found at *http://www.rmhiherbal.org/ai/articles.html,* and you can find a brief list of common Ayurvedic remedies, including a number of nervines, at *http://niam.com/corp-web/mediplnt.htm.*

The information included here was gathered from a wide variety of sources, including standard herbal references, European studies of standardized herbal extracts, clinical data from the US National Institutes of Health's alternative medicine project, the Autism Research Institute's reports on survey results, clinical trials of vitamins and some other substances and, in some cases, anecdotal reports from health care practitioners and parents. Because few of these remedies have undergone the intense scientific scrutiny given pharmaceuticals, there is less information available about possible side effects and interactions.

Aloe vera gel

Use: GI tract problems, ulcers

Action, if known: Aloe vera has nervine, anti-inflammatory (steroidal), hormonal, antioxidant, laxative, and other effects. The active ingredient in aloe vera, allantoin, is also found in cabbage juice and comfrey.

Side effects: Nausea may occur.

Interaction hazards: None known.

Tips: Aloe vera has a bitter taste, so you may want to dilute it with water or juice.

Aspirin, acetylsalicylic acid

Use: Pain, headache.

Action, if known: Aspirin thins the blood, makes compounds called lipoxygenase products, and is classified as a nonsteroidal anti-inflammatory drug (NSAID). It blocks enzymes called COX-1 and COX-2 (cyclo-oxygenase 1 and cyclo-oxygenase 2). COX-2 may damage nerve cells, is involved in the process of inflammation and fever, and is also believed to cause cancer and tumors to start growing.

Side effects: Aspirin thins the blood, and can cause internal bleeding or GI tract irritation if overused.

Interaction hazards: Aspirin is a "hidden" ingredient in many prescription and OTC remedies. Some foods and herbal remedies also contain aspirin-like salicylates. Too much aspirin can cause sudden drops in blood pressure; counteract the effects of buprobenecid, sulfinpyrazone, ACE inhibitors, beta-blockers, and diuretics; and strengthen the action of methotrexate, propoxyphene hydrochloride (Darvon) and some other narcotics, and Depakote or Depakene.

Tips: Children should not take aspirin due to the risk of Reye's syndrome, a rare complication of chicken pox or influenza B. Do not take aspirin if you have (or are at high risk for) stomach ulcers.

Beta carotene

Use: Improving energy metabolism, fighting the physical effects of stress, supporting liver function, protecting skin from the sun, supporting the immune system.

Action, if known: This fat-soluble antioxidant protects the lipid (fat) layer of cells.

Side effects: Too much beta carotene can give your skin an orange tinge.

Interaction hazards: This vitamin is counteracted by mineral oil supplements, and may interact with nicotine or tobacco products. Although beta carotene is made into vitamin A by the body, it doesn't seem to carry a risk for hypervitaminosis, as vitamin A carries.

Tips: It's best to eat your dark green leafy vegetables and yellow-orange vegetables rather than taking beta carotene supplements.

Biotin

Use: Biotin is used to improve the balance of intestinal bacteria.

Action, if known: Normally, biotin is produced by the symbiotic bacteria that live in the digestive tract. It lowers blood sugar, and may help alleviate depression.

Side effects: None known.

Interaction hazards: Biotin is counteracted by raw egg whites and alcohol. It may change your dose requirements for insulin and diabetes medications.

Tips: If you are taking acidophilus or other supplements to maintain a healthy bacterial balance in the GI tract, you should not need to supplement with biotin. You may want to use it if you are taking antibiotics, however. You should take biotin if you are deficient in magnesium.

Bitter melon, *Momordica charantia,* karela

Use: Viral infection, stomach ache, colitis, diabetes, high blood pressure. The green leaves and unripe fruit are used.

Action, if known: Bitter melon is the plant from which the active ingredient in some protease inhibitors is extracted. It has anti-oxident, antiviral, and antibiotic properties. It may also lower blood sugar and have a beneficial effect on the GI tract.

Side effects: Avoid this herb if you have low blood sugar.

Interaction hazards: This herb could add to the action of medications for diabetes.

Tips: Bitter melon is considered a delicacy in Asia and can often be found in the produce section of Asian food markets. It is also available canned. It is not known what effect processing may have on its medicinal qualities, however. It is not safe for pregnant women, according to some herbalists, because it may have tumor-dissolving capabilities that could also endanger the fetus.

Black cohosh, *Cimicifuga racemosa,* squaw root

Use: Autoimmune disorders, especially rheumatism; Sydenham's chorea; nerve-related tinnitus; sore throat. The rhizome and root are used.

Action, if known: Black cohosh has central nervous system depressant, sedative, and anti-inflammatory qualities.

Side effects: The active ingredient in black cohosh appears to bind to estrogen receptor sites, so it may cause hormonal activity.

Interaction hazards: Do not use this herb with alcohol or other CNS depressants, or with drugs that are not recommended for use with CNS depressants.

Tips: Some multiherb remedies used for seizure disorders contain black cohosh.

Caffeine

Use: Pain relief, especially with aspirin; energizing effect.

Action, if known: Caffeine stimulates the central nervous system.

Side effects: Jitteriness, excess stomach acid, increased heart rate, or insomnia may occur. In extreme overdose, caffeine can actually kill.

Interaction hazards: Caffeine may counteract calcium and magnesium. It strengthens some asthma drugs and aspirin. Its action on aspirin can cause sudden drops in blood pressure. It can counteract the effects of probenecid, sulfinpyrazone, ACE inhibitors, beta-blockers, and diuretics; or strengthen the action of methotrexate, Depakote, or Depakene.

Tips: The use of OTC stimulants containing caffeine (such as No-Doz) can cause mood swings in people with diagnosed or undiagnosed bipolar disorder.

Calcium

Use: Preventing bone loss.

Action, if known: This mineral regulates nervous system impulses and neurotransmitter production, coagulates blood, builds and repairs bone, and activates the production of some enzymes and hormones. Many people with autism have lower than normal calcium levels.

Side effects: Excessive levels of calcium (hypocalcinuria) can result in stupor.

Interaction hazards: Calcium may be counteracted by corticosteroids, antispasmodics, thyroid hormone supplements, spinach and other green leafy vegetables, cocoa, soybeans, phosphates (including soda pop), caffeine, and phytic acid (found in bran and whole grains). It interacts with antacids, and its action may be strengthened by iron.

Tips: You must have enough vitamin D in the diet or by supplement to use calcium. It is best taken with a light meal or snack.

Caprylic acid

Use: GI tract problems, including overgrowth of *Candida* yeast.

Action, if known: This long-chain fatty acid has antifungal properties.

Side effects: Some people report unpleasant "die-off" reactions when taking caprylic acid to combat intestinal yeast infections. Nausea or headache may occur.

Interaction hazards: None known.

Tips: Avoid caprylic acid if you have GI tract inflammation. Medium-chain triglycerides (found in MCT oil, also called caprylic/capric triglycerides) are a liquid source of caprylic acid. Caprylic acid also occurs naturally in coconuts. It is absorbed quickly, so try a time-released or coated version for best results. Take it with food.

Carnitine, L-carnitine, carnitor

Use: Heart trouble, muscle weakness. It is also taken to remedy inborn deficiency or to counteract depletion of carnitine from medications or diet.

Action, if known: A short-chain carboxylic acid, it transports fats from foods to the mitochondria of cells, which turn the fats into energy.

Side effects: Nausea, abdominal cramping, and diarrhea may occur. Some people report increased body odor when taking L-carnitine.

Interaction hazards: Depakote and Depakene can deplete your body's supply of carnitine, as does the ketogenic diet.

Tips: You need an adequate supply of vitamin B_6 to make your own carnitine from meat and dairy products. Some people may have an inborn carnitine deficiency, which can be discovered through testing. Carnitor is the best-known prescription carnitine supplement.

Cat's claw, *Uncaria tomentosa, una de gato*

Use: Viral infection, diabetes, lupus and other autoimmune disorders, asthma, ulcers, irritable bowel syndrome and related disorders.

Action, if known: This herb has antioxidant, antibiotic, and antiviral qualities. It contains four oxindole alkaloids that appear to boost the immune system's ability to destroy foreign cells and to increase the production of white blood cells and other immune system components. It may lower blood pressure.

Side effects: None known.

Interaction hazards: None known.

Tips: Cat's claw appears to have powerful effects, and should be used with caution. It is not recommended for use by transplant patients, pregnant women, or people with autoimmune disorders. *Note:* The traditional Mexican remedy of the same name is from a completely different plant.

Chamomile, *Matricaria recutita*

Use: Insomnia or sleep disorders, nausea, irritable bowel syndrome.

Action, if known: This sedative herb contains volatile oils with antiseizure and anti-inflammatory effects.

Side effects: It can cause allergic reaction in people who are sensitive to daisies or ragweed.

Interaction hazards: None known.

Tips: Chamomile is safe enough for occasional use by children. It may be taken in capsule form or in the traditional chamomile tea.

Choline, phosphatidyl choline

Use: Tourette's syndrome, bipolar disorder, Alzheimer's disease, tardive dyskinesia, memory loss, sleepiness, irritability, insomnia, poor muscle coordination, learning difficulties, liver problems (including alcohol-induced cirrhosis).

Action, if known: Choline helps in the manufacture of cell membranes. It also assists production of the neurotransmitter acetylcholine, which controls the parasympathetic nervous system (including the GI tract), and also has effects within the brain. It promotes metabolism of fats, and reduces the level of "bad" cholesterol.

Side effects: In high doses, nausea, gas, excessive sweating or salivation, or fishy body odor may occur.

Interaction hazards: Phenobarbital and methotrexate may counteract choline.

Tips: Choline is one of the active ingredients in lecithin. It is also found in eggs, soybeans, cabbage, and many other foods. Normally, your body should produce enough on its own.

Coenzyme Q10, CoQ10, ubiquinone

Use: Immune disorders, including HIV/AIDS; GI tract problems, including gastric ulcers; gum disease; cancer.

Action, if known: CoQ10 is an antioxidant, and is believed to boost the immune system. It is part of the cellular process that uses fats, sugars, and amino acids to produce the energy molecule ATP.

Side effects: Sleeplessness, rashes, nausea, and abdominal pain have been reported.

Interaction hazards: This drug may interact with warfarin and insulin. Its effects may be weakened by drugs for diabetes or cholesterol reduction.

Tips: If you have liver problems or take medications that affect the liver, use CoQ10 only under medical supervision.

DMG, dimethylglycine, calcium pangamate

Use: Autistic spectrum disorders, communication disorders, heart and liver problems, high cholesterol, diabetes.

Action, if known: DMG appears to boost the immune system, possibly by increasing the number of natural killer (NK) cells and white blood cells. It also helps metabolize fats, and has minor antioxidant properties. It reduces lactate levels in muscle tissue, and increases the level of oxygen in the brain. It may help reduce the number or severity of seizures in some people. It has been shown in several studies to precipitate or increase speech in nonverbal or communication-disordered children.

Side effects: Increased hyperactivity may occur.

Interaction hazards: None known, although one report indicates that it could interfere with sulfation via Epsom salts.

Tips: DMG is usually found in the body-building/athletics area of a grocery or health food store. The sublingual tablets taste lemony, and dissolve readily under the tongue. A precursor, trimethylglycine (TMG), may be superior.

Echinacea

Use: Viral or bacterial infection, epilepsy.

Action, if known: This antibiotic and antiseptic herb may also have antiseizure qualities. It dilates blood vessels, increases the production of saliva and mucus, and activates white blood cells.

Side effects: None known, although it should not be used on a long-term basis.

Interaction hazards: Echinacea could strengthen or interfere with the action of medications that dilate the blood vessels or antiseizure drugs.

Tips: This herb is not recommended for use by people with autoimmune conditions. Some doctors also tell people with AIDS or tuberculosis to avoid it because it may affect T-cell function, although it may also have retrovirus-fighting abilities. It is often mixed with goldenseal in herbal remedies for cold and flu.

Efalex

Use: Brand-name EFA (essential fatty acid) supplement made by Efamol Nutriceuticals Inc. for people with developmental dyspraxia, ADD/ADHD, and related conditions.

Action, if known: See descriptions of essential fatty acids and other Efalex ingredients elsewhere in this appendix.

Side effects: Increased hyperactivity and agitation may occur. See listing for essential fatty acids.

Interaction hazards: See listing for essential fatty acids.

Tips: Efalex contains a mixture of fish oil, evening primrose oil, thyme oil, and vitamin E. Contact Efamol (*http://www.efamol.com*) for more information.

Efamol

Use: Brand-name EFA supplement made by Efamol Nutriceuticals Inc. for people with PMS.

Action, if known: See descriptions of essential fatty acids and other Efamol ingredients elsewhere in this appendix.

Side effects: Increased hyperactivity and agitation may occur. See listing for essential fatty acids.

Interaction hazards: See listing for essential fatty acids.

Tips: Efamol combines evening primrose oil; vitamins B_6, C, and E; niacin, zinc, and magnesium.

Epsom salts, magnesium sulfate

Use: Hydrated magnesium sulfate—the traditional Epsom salts bath—is an excellent remedy for sore, aching muscles and backache. Taken internally, it is a potent laxative. Some people with ASDs appear to have positive behavioral effects from Epsom salts baths, including reduced hyperactivity, agitation, and aggression; and increased ability to concentrate.

Action, if known: Magnesium sulfate in water is said to "draw out" inflammatory compounds. Epsom salts are sometimes given intravenously in a hospital emergency room to reduce dangerous seizures, especially in eclampsia (a seizure disorder that emerges during pregnancy). It stands to reason that they may have gentler antiseizure effects when taken in other ways.

Side effects: If taken internally, Epsom salts can cause nausea and diarrhea.

Interaction hazards: None known.

Tips: Do not take Epsom salts internally except under medical supervision.

Essential fatty acids

Use: Inflammation, autoimmune conditions of the nervous system, eczema, high blood pressure, hyperactivity, irritable bowel syndrome, arthritis, mood swings. One EFA, gammalinolenic acid (GLA), is available from evening primrose oil, black current seed oil, and other sources. Oil from certain cold-water fish, such as salmon and cod, contains eicosapentaenoic acid (EPA) and docosahexaenoic acid (DHA). Lauric acid, another EFA, is found in breast milk, coconuts, and a few other places. Its glycol ester (monolaurin or lauricidin) is available in supplement form.

Action, if known: Normally, linoleic acid is converted to gammalinolenic acid by enzymes, creating hormones and hormone-like substances called prostaglandins. These prostaglandins are involved in regulating the immune system, nervous system, and circulatory system. Lauric acid is known to have antibacterial and antiviral qualities.

Side effects: Evening primrose oil may lower the threshold for frontal lobe seizures. EPA fish oil can cause fluctuations in blood sugar, so diabetics should use it with caution. Both EPA and DHA (and, to a lesser extent, GLA) thin the blood, and may increase your risk of bleeding or bruising easily.

Interaction hazards: The arachidonic acid in evening primrose oil may counteract the effects of some antiseizure drugs, whereas EPA fish oil could counteract or add to the effects of medications for high or low blood pressure, or drugs that treat heart conditions.

Tips: EFAs are available as gelatin caps or liquids; of course, EPA fish oil can also be obtained by eating cold-water fish.

Essiac tea

Use: Cancer, autoimmune disorders.

Action, if known: A number of concoctions are sold under the name "Essiac tea." The original version contained sheep sorrel and burdock root, as well as slippery elm bark and turkey rhubarb root. These plants contain lots of vitamins and are said to have anti-inflammatory, astringent, vasodilating, antibiotic, antibacterial, antiviral, and mildly laxative effects. Slippery elm is especially good for assisting the GI tract's mucous membranes.

Side effects: Diarrhea, stomach pain, nausea.

Interaction hazards: None known, although sheep sorrel and burdock root are both fairly strong herbs.

Tips: Diabetics and people with a history of kidney stones should not use this tea. You can find some noncommercial information about Essiac tea at *http://essiac-info.org/,* including cautions about poor quality (and even dangerous) products using the "essiac" name. It's best taken on an empty stomach. Do not exceed the recommended dose.

Evening primrose oil

Use: PMS, high blood pressure, autoimmune disorders, tardive dyskinesia, eczema.

Action, if known: Evening primrose oil contains linoleic acid and gamma linolinic acid (GLA), which the body converts to prostaglandin-1. This hormone-like compound increases blood flow, thins the blood, and combats inflammation.

Side effects: Headache or nausea are sometimes reported.

Interaction hazards: None known.

Tips: Evening primrose oil and other GLA-containing products are not recommended for people with temporal lobe epilepsy. Adequate amounts of vitamin C, B_6, niacin, magnesium, and zinc are needed with GLA to make prostaglandin-1.

Eye-Q (IQ)

Use: Support for eye and brain function.

Action, if known: Eye-Q (sold as IQ in Canada) is a brand-name EFA supplement made by Equazen. It contains fish body oil, evening primrose oil, and vitamin E.

Side effects: Loose stools are sometimes reported.

Interaction hazards: None known.

Tips: At press time, Eye-Q was being clinically tested for beneficial effects on children with ASDs, dyslexia, dyspraxia, and other neurodevelopmental disorders. For more information, contact Equazen (*http://www.equazen.com/*).

Feverfew

Use: Migraine, nausea, depression.

Action, if known: One compound found in feverfew, parthenolide, is a serotonin inhibitor. This compound also inhibits leukotrienes and serum proteases.

Side effects: Feverfew is irritating to the mouth if chewed.

Interaction hazards: None known, although it could counteract or strengthen medications that affect serotonin.

Tips: Use only standardized feverfew extract, as the amount of parthenolide varies widely from plant to plant.

Folic acid

Use: Depression, anemia, slow growth; needed to make B vitamins available to the body, so it's taken as part of B vitamin formulas for autistic symptoms. Also taken to counteract some of the side effects of methotrexate (Rheumatrex).

Action, if known: Folic acid is an anti-inflammatory, helps to produce white blood cells and other components of the immune system, helps to convert amino acids into proteins, and is necessary for building and rebuilding the nervous system.

Side effects: None known in proper dose.

Interaction hazards: Dilantin competes with folic acid in the GI tract and in the brain—if you take Dilantin, consult with your physician about how to get around this interaction.

Tips: Folic acid is found in green leafy vegetables, beans, asparagus, citrus fruits and juices, whole grain foods, and liver. However, many doctors (and the March of Dimes, which is campaigning against spina bifida and other birth defects linked to a lack of folic acid in the diet) do recommend taking a supplement especially if you are or could be pregnant.

Garlic

Use: Immune disorders, high blood pressure.

Action, if known: Garlic is said to be active against yeast in the digestive tract while protecting helpful flora. It may lower blood pressure slightly.

Side effects: "Garlic breath" may occur if eaten, and it causes stomach discomfort for some.

Interaction hazards: None known.

Tips: Garlic is available as a food or a supplement. Incidentally, garlic contains high amounts of the mineral germanium (see next), as does ginseng.

Germanium

Use: Viral infection, immune disorders, cancer, inflammation, high blood pressure.

Action, if known: Germanium stimulates the body to produce its own interferon, lowers blood pressure (probably by dilating blood vessels), inhibits enzymes that reduce endorphin levels, and has anti-inflammatory properties.

Side effects: Soft stools, sleep disturbance, and mood swings are sometimes reported.

Interaction hazards: None known, although it could interfere with medications for high or low blood pressure.

Tips: Germanium supplements should not be used on a long-term basis, as it can adversely affect the kidneys. Make sure you buy the sesquioxide form of germanium, or get your germanium from food sources or other herbs.

Gingko biloba

Use: Forgetfulness, dementia, depression, Reynaud's disease, tinnitus.

Action, if known: An antioxidant, Gingko biloba increases blood flow to the brain, and increases the uptake of oxygen, glucose, and neurotransmitters by neuronal cells.

Side effects: Stomach or intestinal upset, headache, or allergic skin reactions may occur.

Interaction hazards: This herb interacts with aspirin, ibuprofen, and blood-thinning drugs. Avoid using it if you take celecoxib, diclofenac, diflunisal, ketorolac, warfarin, or similar medications.

Tips: Look for Gingko biloba from reputable manufacturers, in a standardized dose.

Inositol

Use: OCD, depression, panic disorder, degenerative and autoimmune disorders of the nervous system (including diabetic neuropathy), liver disease.

Action, if known: Required by the neurotransmitters serotonin and acetylcholine, inositol helps the nerves conduct impulses correctly, possibly by rebuilding the myelin sheath. May also have sedative effects in high doses.

Side effects: None known.

Interaction hazards: Caffeine counteracts inositol.

Tips: Inositol is one of the active ingredients in lecithin. People with ASDs who test positive for antimyelin antibodies in the blood might want to try inositol.

Lecithin, phosphatidyl choline

Use: Tourette's syndrome, bipolar disorder, Alzheimer's disease, tardive dyskinesia, memory loss, sleepiness, irritability, insomnia, poor muscle coordination, learning difficulties, liver problems (including alcohol-induced cirrhosis), OCD, depression, panic disorder, degenerative and autoimmune disorders of the nervous system, seizure disorders.

Action, if known: See listings for inositol and choline.

Side effects: None known.

Interaction hazards: Caffeine counteracts the inositol in lecithin.

Tips: A phospholipid found mostly in high-fat foods, lecithin is available in capsules or granules. One of the tastiest ways to take it is by blending the granules into a fresh fruit smoothie. Lecithin is not a cure for any neurological disorder, but both anecdotal reports and recent studies indicate that it may help in some cases.

Licorice, *Glycyrrhiza glabra*

Use: Asthma, coughs, GI tract disorders.

Action, if known: Boosts hormone production, including secretin and other hormones active in the GI tract and brain.

Side effects: None known.

Interaction hazards: None known.

Tips: Medicinal-quality licorice is a lot stronger than the sweet, licorice-flavored candy familiar to the American palate. Children may not like the taste: Gel caps, powdered licorice root capsules, or licorice tea might be better tolerated.

Magnesium

Use: Insomnia, heart problems, muscle pain, high blood pressure. If you are supplementing with vitamin B_6, you will need to add magnesium as well.

Action, if known: Magnesium lowers blood pressure, and helps regulate nerve impulses and neurotransmitter production.

Side effects: This mineral blocks calcium channels. It also dilates blood vessels, reducing blood pressure.

Interaction hazards: Fatty foods may interfere with the metabolism of magnesium. Talk to your doctor about taking magnesium if you take pharmaceutical calcium channel blockers.

Tips: Magnesium is part of the ARI's recommendations for autistic symptoms.

Melatonin

Use: Insomnia, seasonal affective disorder (SAD), mood swings, regulatory disorders, anxiety, depression.

Action, if known: Melatonin is a hormone made by the pineal gland, which regulates the body's sleep–wake cycles. It is also believed to be important to the immune system and to other parts of the endocrine system, particularly for women.

Side effects: None known, although if too large a dose is taken, you may still be tired in the morning.

Interaction hazards: None known in normal doses.

Tips: Detailed information about the use of melatonin by people with autism is available at http://www.autism.org/melatonin.html.

MSM, methyl-sulfonyl-methane, sulfur

Use: Diabetes, joint pain, high cholesterol, dysentery/GI tract dysfunction, yeast infections. Some people with ASDs appear to have a metabolic error in how they process sulfur. These individuals may need to supplement with sulfur or a related compound.

Action, if known: MSM is involved in converting fats into energy; collagen production; activating and producing enzymes that aid in digestion and in protecting the mucus lining of the GI tract; and reducing blood sugar, cholesterol, and blood pressure.

Side effects: Some people are very allergic to sulfur. Others are somewhat sensitive, and may experience sulfurous intestinal gas or burping.

Interaction hazards: None known.

Tips: Sulfur is also found in egg yolks, asparagus, garlic, onions, meat, and beans. Epsom salts baths are another option.

N-acetyl-cysteine (NAC)

Use: Seizure disorders, heavy metal poisoning, aspirin or acetaminophen poisoning, viral infection, epilepsy, diabetes, movement disorders, degenerative neurological disorders, including multiple sclerosis.

Action, if known: This antioxidant amino acid increases synthesis of glutathione. It appears to have chelating effects that help remove toxic heavy metals from the body. NAC is the acetylated version of the sulfur amino acid, l-cysteine. In the body, it turns into l-cysteine, which in turn is a precursor to glutathione.

Side effects: Nausea, dry mouth, dizziness, and headache have been reported.

Interaction hazards: NAC may interfere with the absorption of magnesium and zinc. Interactions with a variety of drugs have been reported, particularly metoclopramide and nitroglycerin. Talk to your doctor before using NAC.

Tips: A report on the latest studies on NAC and neurological disorders can be found at *http:// neuro-www.mgh.harvard.edu/neurowebforum/MovementDisordersArticles/NAcetylCysteineReport. html*. This report indicates that encouraging results have been found, although NAC tends only to arrest the progression of these disorders, rather than causing improvement.

NutriVene-D

Use: Developed as a nutritional supplement for people with Down syndrome. Contains A, B, C, and other vitamins, inositol, a variety of minerals and amino acids, essential fatty acids, and other ingredients. A "nighttime" formula is also available that contains L-tryptophan and other amino acids associated with normalizing sleep patterns.

Action, if known: NutriVene-D has antioxidant action, and is based on known and possible metabolic defects resulting from this chromosomal abnormality.

Side effects: See the complete list of NutriVene-D ingredients at *http://www.nutrivene.com/,* and then see side effects for each component.

Interaction hazards: NutriVene-D should be taken under a doctor's supervision.

Tips: Take with nonprotein food or shortly after a meal.

Pepcid AC, famotidine

Use: GI tract problems, particularly acid reflux disease ("heartburn"); used to treat social deficits in children with autism with some success in one study at the St. Luke's-Roosevelt Hospital Center in New York City (Linda A. Linday, MD, and others, "Oral famotidine: A potential treatment for children with autism," *Medical Hypotheses* 48 (5), (May 1997): 381–386).

Action, if known: Pepcid AC blocks histamine-2 (H2) receptors, which should reduce inhibitory signals to the brain.

Side effects: Diarrhea may occur. Pepcid AC can mask the pain of serious GI problems.

Interaction hazards: Antacids interact with a number of medications, and H2 blockers in particular have a number of known interactions with other drugs. Consult your pharmacist before using Pepcid.

Tips: Tagamet and Zantac are two other H2 blockers. They may or may not have similar effectiveness for ASD symptoms in some people.

Proanthocyanidins

Use: Proanthocyanidins are the active ingredients in several naturally occurring antioxidant compounds. The best known of these, grapeseed oil, is just what its name indicates. Pycogenol is a brand-name formulation derived from maritime pine bark. Both have been tried by people with ASDs and other neurological disorders, sometimes with beneficial effects for seizure control, reduced aggression, and improved immune system function.

Action, if known: Strong antioxidant activity.

Side effects: Loose stools, increased hyperactivity and/or aggression in some.

Interaction hazards: None known.

Tips: Pycogenol tends to be more expensive than other proanthocyanidins, because it is a trademarked product.

Probiotics

Use: Digestive problems, chronic constipation or diarrhea, irritable bowel syndrome and related disorders, yeast infection, autoimmune disorders.

Action, if known: Probiotics are "friendly" bacteria that flourish in the intestine to help with digestion, or substances that protect these bacteria from depredation by antibiotics or other forces.

Side effects: None known.

Interaction hazards: None known.

Tips: *Lactobacillus acidophilus, Bifidobacterium bifidum,* and *Lactobacillus bulgaricus* are friendly bacteria more familiar to most of us as the "active cultures" found in some yogurts. Yogurt itself is a good probiotic for those who eat dairy products.

Sarsaparilla

Use: GI tract disorders, asthma, psoriasis.

Action, if known: Sarsaparilla appears to have steroid-like action against inflammation.

Side effects: Stomach irritation is sometimes reported

Interaction hazards: Sarsparilla interacts with digitalis and bismuth (the active ingredient in Pepto-Bismol and similar indigestion remedies).

Tips: Several different plants are known as "sarsaparilla," all with a similar, slightly spicy, taste and similar actions. Like licorice, sarsaparilla seems to affect hormone production as well as settling the stomach and calming the nerves.

Selenium

Use: GI tract disorders; increased sperm production; selenium deficiency (Keshan disease), which occurs in some people with celiac disease and other autoimmune disorders.

Action, if known: The cooperation of vitamin E and selenium produces the vital antioxidant peptide enzyme selenium-glutathione-peroxidase. Appears to help stimulate the production of antibodies, and may stimulate synthesis of protein.

Side effects: Rash, nausea, fatigue, brittle teeth and hair may occur. Muscle, vision, and heart problems have been observed in animals getting too much selenium, and could occur in humans as well.

Interaction hazards: None known.

Tips: Selenium supplements are a must for people who are fed intravenously or via tube. If you or your child experiences GI tract problems, you may want to use a supplement of this mineral, preferably in its easily absorbed chelated form (L-selenomethionine). You can also get it in the diet. It is plentiful in fish, shellfish, red meat, grains, eggs, chicken, liver, garlic, brewer's yeast, and wheat germ. Only 50 to 200 micrograms of selenium are needed daily.

SPV-30

Use: Viral or bacterial infection, including HIV/AIDS, immune disorders, tuberculosis, inflammation.

Action, if known: SPV-30 is a reverse transcriptinase inhibitor with antiviral, antibiotic, and steroidal anti-inflammatory activity.

Side effects: Stomach cramping, skin rash, and diarrhea have been reported. If cramps occur, drink more water. Some people taking SPV-30 in AIDS studies noted that taking it earlier in the day rather than after dinner prevents a possible side effect of insomnia.

Interaction hazards: None known, but it could interact with other antivirals.

Tips: SPV-30 is derived from active ingredients found in the European boxwood tree (*Buxus sempervirens*). It has shown some promise as an antiviral in AIDS medication trials.

St. John's wort, *Hypericum perforatum*

Use: Depression, anxiety.

Action, if known: There are at least 10 active ingredients in St. John's wort that have some neurological activity. Its exact method of action is not yet known, but clinical studies indicate it is an effective treatment for mild to moderate depression.

Side effects: Increased sensitivity to light may occur. St. John's wort may cause mood swings or mania in people with diagnosed or undiagnosed bipolar disorder.

Interaction hazards: This drug may interfere with the action of protease inhibitors used to treat AIDS. Follow the restrictions in diet and medication indicated for pharmaceutical MAOI and SSRI antidepressants.

Tips: Hypericin, an extract of one active ingredient from St. John's wort, may or may not be as effective as the whole herb.

Super Nu-Thera

Use: Autistic spectrum disorders.

Action, if known: This multivitamin supplement has been crafted to the specifications of the Autism Research Institute. It contains vitamin B_6, magnesium, and other nutrients.

Side effects: Increased agitation and hyperactivity are sometimes reported. If numbness or tingling occurs in hands or feet, reduce dose or discontinue use.

Interaction hazards: None known.

Tips: This product is available in liquid, powder, and capsule form. There is more than one formulation: Contact Kirkman Labs (*http://www.kirkmanlabs.com*) for more information.

Tryptophan, L-tryptophan, 5-HTP

Use: Depression, especially with agitation; insomnia; irritability; anxiety; chronic pain.

Action, if known: Tryptophan is a precursor for increased brain levels of serotonin and for the body's production of niacin. The 5-HTP version is also said to contribute to the production of melatonin.

Side effects: Appetite may be reduced.

Interaction hazards: None known, although one should be cautious about using this amino acid with any drug known to have an effect on serotonin, such as an antidepressant.

Tips: Tryptophan is not recommended for people with autoimmune disorders or asthma, or for pregnant women. It is not available in the US. However, 5-HTP, a plant-derived type of tryptophan, is available in the US, and L-tryptophan can be purchased via mail order. Tryptophan can also be obtained by eating pineapple, turkey, chicken, yogurt, bananas, or unripened cheese, preferably with a starch.

Tyrosine, L-tyrosine

Use: Anxiety, depression, fatigue, thyroid disorders, allergies, headaches, chronic pain; also used as an aid to drug and alcohol withdrawal.

Action, if known: Tyrosine is an amino acid precursor to epinephrine, norepinephrine, and dopamine. The body normally synthesizes tyrosine from phenylalanine.

Side effects: None known.

Interaction hazards: Do not take tyrosine with an MAOI antidepressant.

Tips: Take tyrosine on an empty stomach.

Vitamin A, retinol

Use: Viral or bacterial infection, GI tract disorders.

Action, if known: An antioxidant, it helps maintain the mucus lining of the intestines.

Side effects: Vitamin A can be deadly in doses of more than 25,000 units per day. Overdose indicators include headache, blurred vision, chapped lips, dry skin, rash, joint aches and pain, and abdominal tenderness.

Interaction hazards: None known.

Tips: People with celiac disease have a hard time getting enough A, and often experience a deficiency of this vitamin.

Vitamin B$_1$, thiamin

Use: Wernicke's syndrome, Korsakoff's psychosis (often seen as a complication of alcoholism), peripheral neuropathy, cardiac disorders. Thiamin levels are sometimes low in autistic people.

Action, if known: Vitamin B$_1$ is needed for the production of acetylcholine and nucleic acids. It is part of the process of impulse initiation in neuronal membranes.

Side effects: None known.

Interaction hazards: None known.

Tips: In the diet, thiamin is found in lean pork, legumes, and yeast. However, thiamin in foods is destroyed by cooking.

Vitamin B₂, riboflavin

Use: Hormonal disorders, jaundice in newborns, depression, inflammation, inborn metabolic disorders.

Action, if known: It takes part in the conversion of tryptophan to serotonin, and in the synthesis of your body's own anti-inflammatory substances, the corticosteroids.

Side effects: None known.

Interaction hazards: Chlorpromazine, imipramine, and amitriptyline inhibit riboflavin, as may some other antidepressants.

Tips: Dietary sources for riboflavin include milk, eggs, ice cream, liver, some lean meats, and green vegetables. In the US and some other countries, breads and other baked goods made with white flour are routinely enriched with riboflavin. If you follow a vegetarian or gluten-free and/or casein-free diet, you probably should add B₂ to your diet a matter of course.

Vitamin B₃, niacin, nicotinic acid

Use: Autistic symptoms, schizophrenia, high cholesterol, deficiency (pellegra).

Action, if known: Vitamin B₃ helps red blood cells carry oxygen, and is believed to reduce inflammation. It helps build tissue, including nerve tissue, raises blood sugar, and relaxes blood vessels. It's needed for fatty acid and corticosteroid synthesis.

Side effects: Flushing (red face) may occur, produced by a sudden release of prostaglandins and histamine. Skin rash or agitation are sometimes reported. Hypouricemia and liver problems are rarely seen, but possible.

Interaction hazards: Vitamin B₃ may strengthen the action of some antiseizure drugs.

Tips: Choose "no flush" (buffered) niacin if flushing bothers you. People with diabetes, gout, or ulcers should not take niacin—although nicotinamide, a closely related enzyme, is under investigation as a treatment for diabetes.

Vitamin B₅, pantothenic acid

Use: Depression, insomnia, heart problems, fatigue, problems of the peripheral nervous system.

Action, if known: B$_5$ is needed for metabolism of carbohydrates, proteins, and lipids; synthesis of lipids, neurotransmitters, steroid hormones, porphyrins, and hemoglobin. It is also necessary for normal antibody production.

Side effects: Diarrhea, agitation, or hyperactivity may occur.

Interaction hazards: None known.

Tips: Foods that are high in B$_5$ include organ meats, lobster, poultry, soybeans, lentils, split peas, yogurt, avocado, mushrooms, and sweet potato—however, heat destroys pantothenic acid.

Vitamin B$_6$, pyridoxine

Use: Seizure disorders.

Action, if known: Vitamin B$_6$ is needed for metabolism of amino acids, protein, essential fatty acids, stored starches, neurotransmitters, and glycogen. It also influences the production of neurotransmitters, particularly norepinephrine, dopamine, and serotonin. It binds to steroid hormone receptors, may regulate steroid hormone action, and may influence the immune system.

Side effects: Agitation and hyperactivity are sometimes reported. If you choose to supplement with more than 50 mg of B$_6$ per day, as the ARI recommends, do so under a doctor's supervision. If you feel a tingling sensation in your hands or feet, stop taking B$_6$ and contact your doctor.

Interaction hazards: Many medications counteract B$_6$—talk to your doctor before supplementing with this vitamin.

Tips: B$_6$ must be given with magnesium, and preferably with other B vitamins, as it increases the metabolism of riboflavin. Food sources include poultry, fish, pork, bananas, and whole grains.

Vitamin B$_{12}$, cobalamin

Use: Depression, anemia; demyelination of spinal cord; demyelination of brain, optic, and peripheral nerves; ADD/ADHD.

Action, if known: Vitamin B$_{12}$ helps build the myelin sheath around nerve fibers. It is needed for amino acid and fatty acid metabolism.

Side effects: Agitation or hyperactivity may occur.

Interaction hazards: None known.

Tips: B$_{12}$ can be deficient in people who are not making a normal amount of digestive enzymes, such as those with GI tract disorders. People with ASDs who test positive for auto-antibodies to myelin protein should definitely supplement with B$_{12}$. Vegetarians and others may want to do so as well, as B$_{12}$ is found only in meat, eggs, and dairy products. Spirulina, blue-green algae, and some other "vegetarian" B$_{12}$ supplements contain a form of B$_{12}$ that cannot be absorbed by humans.

Vitamin C, ascorbic acid

Use: Deficiency (scurvy), gum disease, fatigue, degenerative disorders, immune disorders. Vitamin C has shown benefits for some people with autism.

Action, if known: This antioxidant is necessary for synthesis of neurotransmitters, steroid hormones, and carnitine. It converts cholesterol to bile acids, and helps with metabolism of tyrosine and metal ions. It may enhance the bioavailability of iron.

Side effects: Nausea, abdominal cramps, or diarrhea may occur.

Interaction hazards: It strengthens the action of iron.

Tips: Do not start using megadoses of C and then suddenly stop. Research indicates that vitamin C should be accompanied by vitamin E. The acidic nature of ascorbic acid can also contribute to kidney stones; the buffered form, calcium ascorbate, is more easily tolerated. Food sources include citrus fruits, berries, melons, tomatoes, potatoes, green peppers, and leafy green vegetables. Vitamin C is easily destroyed by heat and prolonged storage.

Vitamin E, alpha tocopherol

Use: Immune disorders, heart disease, neurological disorders.

Action, if known: This fat-soluble antioxidant is believed to be important for proper immune system function. It influences signal transduction pathways and thins the blood.

Side effects: Thins the blood.

Interaction hazards: Do not take vitamin E with anticoagulant drugs, or if you have a vitamin K deficiency.

Tips: People who take antipsychotics, atypical antipsychotics, tricyclic antidepressants, or other medications that carry a known risk for tardive dyskinesia may want to supplement them with vitamin E. It appears to have protective and symptom reduction qualities regarding this movement disorder. Vegetables and seed oils, including soybean, safflower, and corn oil; sunflower seeds, nuts, whole grains, and wheat germ are all good sources of vitamin E.

Zinc

Use: Viral infection, common colds.

Action, if known: Antiviral action has been proposed, as has the possibility that zinc boosts production of natural interferon.

Side effects: Nausea may occur.

Interaction hazards: Citric acid (as found in orange juice—or even in some commercial zinc lozenges for colds!) may counteract the effects of zinc. Coffee and tea should not be taken at the same time as zinc.

Tips: People with GI tract problems may want supplement with this mineral in its easiest-to-absorb chelated form: zinc aspartate or zinc picolinate.

Diagnostic Tools

FOR THOSE READERS WHO NEED TO KNOW MORE about the symptoms of autistic spectrum disorders and how these conditions are diagnosed and differentiated, this appendix includes two helpful tools: the Autism Research Institute's Form E-2 Check List, and a sample from the Childhood Autism Rating Scale (CARS).

Form E-2 is a questionnaire for parents of autistic spectrum children. It was developed by Dr. Bernard Rimland, director of the Autism Research Institute. It's important to understand that Form E-2 is not a diagnostic tool per se. Its purpose is to build a large, detailed database on autism-related symptoms and behaviors. By copying this checklist, filling it out, and mailing it to ARI, you will be assisting with the longest-running research project on the topic of ASDs. Rimland hopes your answers will help researchers differentiate between disorders—many of them as yet unnamed and unknown—that fall along the autistic spectrum. By identifying subtypes, researchers may be able to suggest more appropriate treatments for people with ASDs. As of this writing, ARI's database includes information about more than 25,000 cases of autism and autism-like conditions in more than 40 countries.

Form E-2 is also available directly from ARI in French, Spanish, Portuguese, German, Italian, Hebrew, Japanese, Turkish, and Serbo-Croatian.

If you return this questionnaire, ARI will send you a brief report explaining what your answers seem to say about your child, including a computerized "score." There is no charge for this service. This report may give you valuable information, but it's not a diagnosis. Form E-2 should not be used to self-diagnose ASDs or to permit or deny entrance to programs for people with ASDs.

Please send your copied and completed Form E-2 to:

Autism Research Institute
4182 Adams Avenue
San Diego, CA 92116
Fax (619) 563-6840

Diagnostic Checklist for Behavior-Disturbed Children (Form E-2)

Has this child been diagnosed before?

If so, what was the diagnosis?

Diagnosed by:

Where?

Instructions: You are being asked to fill out this questionnaire concerning your child in order to provide research information which will be helpful in learning more about the causes and types of behavior disturbances in children. Please pick the one answer you think is most accurate for each question. If you want to comment or add something about a question, add it right next to the question, if there is room. Or circle the number of the question, copy the number on the back of the questionnaire and write your comment there. Your additional comments are welcome, but even if you do add comments, please mark the printed question as well as you can. Remember, pick just one answer, and mark it with an "X," for each question.

It would be helpful if, on a separate sheet, you would write in any information about the child and his sisters or brothers which you think may be significant. (For example: Twins, living or dead; Behavior problems; IQ scores, if known).

USE AN "X" TO MARK ONE ANSWER FOR EACH QUESTION. DO NOT SKIP MAIN QUESTIONS. SUB-QUESTIONS (NOT ALONG LEFT MARGIN) MAY BE SKIPPED.

1. Present age of child:
   - ☐ 1. Under 3 years old
   - ☐ 2. Between 3 and 4 years old
   - ☐ 3. Between 4 and 5 years old
   - ☐ 4. Between 5 and 6 years old*
   - ☐ 5. Over 6 years old (Age: ____ years)

2. Indicate child's sex:
   - ☐ 1. Boy
   - ☐ 2. Girl

3. Indicate child's birth order and number of mother's other children:
   - ☐ 1. Child is an only child
   - ☐ 2. Child is first born of ____ children
   - ☐ 3. Child is last born of ____ children
   - ☐ 4. Child is middle born; ____ children are older and ____ are younger
   - ☐ 5. Foster child, or don't know

---

* This checklist is designed primarily for children 3 to 5 years old. If child is over 5, answer as well as you can by recall of the child's behavior.

4. Were pregnancy and delivery normal?

☐ 1. Pregnancy and delivery both normal

☐ 2. Problems during both pregnancy and delivery

☐ 3. Pregnancy troubled; routine delivery

☐ 4. Pregnancy untroubled; problems during delivery

☐ 5. Don't know

5. Was the birth premature (birth weight under 5 lbs)?

☐ 1. Yes (about ___weeks early; ___lbs)

☐ 2. No

☐ 3. Don't know

6. Was the child given oxygen in the first week?

☐ 1. Yes

☐ 2. No

☐ 3. Don't know

7. Appearance of child during first few weeks after birth:

☐ 1. Pale, delicate looking

☐ 2. Unusually healthy looking

☐ 3. Average, don't know, or other

8. Unusual conditions of birth and infancy (check only one number in left-hand column):

☐ 1. Unusual conditions
Indicate which:
___blindness ___cerebral palsy ___birth injury
___seizures ___ blue baby ___very high fever ___jaundice
___ other

☐ 2. Twin birth (___identical ___fraternal)

☐ 3. Both 1 and 2

☐ 4. Normal, or don't know

9. Concerning baby's health in first 3 months:

☐ 1. Excellent health, no problems

☐ 2. Respiration (___frequent infections ___other)

☐ 3. Skin (___rashes ___infection ___allergy ___other)

☐ 4. Feeding (___learning to suck ___ colic ___ vomiting ___ other)

☐ 5. Elimination (___diarrhea ___constipation ___other)

☐ 6. Several of above (indicate which: ___2 ___3 ___4 ___5)

10. Has the child been given an electroencephalogram (EEG)?

   ☐   1. Yes, it was considered normal

   ☐   2. Yes, it was considered borderline

   ☐   3. Yes, it was considered abnormal

   ☐   4. No, or don't know, or don't know results

11. In the first year, did the child react to bright lights, bright colors, unusual sounds, etc.?

   ☐   1. Unusually strong reaction (____pleasure ____dislike)

   ☐   2. Unusually unresponsive

   ☐   3. Average, or don't know

12. Did the child behave normally for a time before his abnormal behavior began?

   ☐   1. Never was a period of normal behavior

   ☐   2. Normal during first 6 months

   ☐   3. Normal during first year

   ☐   4. Normal during first 1 ½ years

   ☐   5. Normal during first 2 years

   ☐   6. Normal during first 3 years

   ☐   7. Normal during first 4–5 years

13. (Age 4–8 months) Did the child reach out or prepare himself to be picked up when mother approached him?

   ☐   1. Yes, or I believe so

   ☐   2. No, I don't think he did

   ☐   3. No, definitely not

   ☐   4. Don't know

14. Did the child rock in his crib as a baby?

   ☐   1. Yes, quite a lot

   ☐   2. Yes, sometimes

   ☐   3. No, or very little

   ☐   4. Don't know

15. At what age did the child learn to walk alone?

   ☐   1. 8–12 months

   ☐   2. 13–15 months

   ☐   3. 16–18 months

   ☐   4. 19–24 months

   ☐   5. 25–36 months

   ☐   6. 37 months or later, or does not walk alone

16. Which describes the change from crawling to walking?

   ☐   1. Normal change from crawling to walking

   ☐   2. Little or no crawling, gradual start of walking

   ☐   3. Little or no crawling, sudden start of walking

   ☐   4. Prolonged crawling, sudden start of walking

   ☐   5. Prolonged crawling, gradual start of walking

   ☐   6. Other, or don't know

17. During the child's first year, did he seem to be unusually intelligent?

   ☐   1. Suspected high intelligence

   ☐   2. Suspected average intelligence

   ☐   3. Child looked somewhat dull

18. During the child's first 2 years, did he like to be held?

   ☐   1. Liked being picked up; enjoyed being held

   ☐   2. Limp and passive on being held

   ☐   3. You could pick child up and hold it only when and how it preferred

   ☐   4. Notably stiff and awkward to hold

   ☐   5. Don't know

19. Before age 3, did the child ever imitate another person?

   ☐   1. Yes, waved bye-bye

   ☐   2. Yes, played pat-a-cake

   ☐   3. Yes, other (_____)

   ☐   4. Two or more of above (which? ___1 ___2 ___3)

   ☐   5. No, or not sure

20. Before age 3, did the child have an unusually good memory?

   ☐   1. Remarkable memory for songs, rhymes, TV commercials, etc., in words

   ☐   2. Remarkable memory for songs, music (humming only)

   ☐   3. Remarkable memory for names, places, routes, etc.

   ☐   4. No evidence for remarkable memory

   ☐   5. Apparently rather poor memory

   ☐   6. Both 1 and 3

   ☐   7. Both 2 and 3

21. Did you ever suspect the child was very nearly deaf?

   ☐   1. Yes

   ☐   2. No

22. (Age 2–4) Is child "deaf" to some sounds but hears others?

☐ 1. Yes, can be "deaf" to loud sounds, but hear low ones

☐ 2. No, this is not true of him

23. (Age 2–4) Does child hold his hands in strange postures?

☐ 1. Yes, sometimes or often

☐ 2. No

24. (Age 2–4) Does child engage in rhythmic or rocking activity for very long periods of time (like on rocking-horse or chair, jumpchair, swing, etc.)?

☐ 1. Yes, this is typical

☐ 2. Seldom does this

☐ 3. Not true of him

25. (Age 2–4) Does child ever "look through" or "walk through" people, as though they weren't there?

☐ 1. Yes, often

☐ 2. Yes, I think so

☐ 3. No, doesn't do this

26. (Age 2–5) Does child have any unusual cravings for things to eat or chew on?

☐ 1. Yes, salt or salty foods

☐ 2. Yes, often chews metal objects

☐ 3. Yes, other (_____)

☐ 4. Yes, more than 2 above (which? _____)

☐ 5. No, or not sure

27. (Age 2–4) Does child have certain eating oddities, such as refusing to drink from a transparent container, eating only hot (or cold) food, eating only one or two foods, etc.?

☐ 1. Yes, definitely

☐ 2. No, or not to any marked degree

☐ 3. Don't know

28. Would you describe your child around 3 or 4 as often seeming "in a shell," or so distant and "lost in thought" that you couldn't reach him?

☐ 1. Yes, this is a very accurate description

☐ 2. Once in awhile he might possibly be like that

☐ 3. Not an accurate description

29. (Age 2–5) Is he cuddly?

☐ 1. Definitely, likes to cling to adults

☐ 2. Above average (likes to be held)

☐ 3. No, rather stiff and awkward to hold

☐ 4. Don't know

30. (Age 3–5) Does the child deliberately hit his own head?

☐ 1. Never, or rarely

☐ 2. Yes, usually by slapping it with his hand

☐ 3. Yes, usually by banging it against someone else's legs or head

☐ 4. Yes, usually by hitting walls, floor, furniture, etc.

☐ 5. Several of above (which? ____2 ____3 ____4)

31. (Age 3–5) How well physically coordinated is the child (running, walking, balancing, climbing)?

☐ 1. Unusually graceful

☐ 2. About average

☐ 3. Somewhat below average, or poor

32. (Age 3–5) Does the child sometimes whirl himself like a top?

☐ 1. Yes, does this often

☐ 2. Yes, sometimes

☐ 3. Yes, if you start him out

☐ 4. No, he shows no tendency to whirl

33. (Age 3–5) How skillful is the child in doing fine work with his fingers or playing with small objects?

☐ 1. Exceptionally skillful

☐ 2. Average for age

☐ 3. A little awkward, or very awkward

☐ 4. Don't know

34. (Age 3–5) Does the child like to spin things like jar lids, coins, or coasters?

☐ 1. Yes, often and for rather long periods

☐ 2. Very seldom, or never

35. (Age 3–5) Does child show an unusual degree of skill (much better than normal child his age) at any of the following:

- ☐ 1. Assembling jigsaw or similar puzzles
- ☐ 2. Arithmetic computation
- ☐ 3. Can tell day of week a certain date will fall on
- ☐ 4. Perfect musical pitch
- ☐ 5. Throwing and/or catching a ball
- ☐ 6. Other (_____)
- ☐ 7. More than one of above (which? _____)
- ☐ 8. No unusual skill, or not sure

36. (Age 3–5) Does the child sometimes jump up and down gleefully when pleased?

- ☐ 1. Yes, this is typical
- ☐ 2. No, or rarely

37. (Age 3–5) Does child sometimes line things up in precise evenly spaced rows and insist they not be disturbed?

- ☐ 1. No
- ☐ 2. Yes
- ☐ 3. Not sure

38. (Age 3–5) Does the child refuse to use his hands for an extended period of time?

- ☐ 1. Yes
- ☐ 2. No

39. Was there a time before age 5 when the child strongly insisted on listening to music on records?

- ☐ 1. Yes, insisted on only certain records
- ☐ 2. Yes, but almost any record would do
- ☐ 3. Liked to listen, but didn't demand to
- ☐ 4. No special interest in records

40. (Age 3–5) How interested is the child in mechanical objects such as the stove or vacuum cleaner?

- ☐ 1. Little or no interest
- ☐ 2. Average interest
- ☐ 3. Fascinated by certain mechanical things

41. (Age 3–5) How does the child usually react to being interrupted in what he is doing?

☐ 1. Rarely or never gets upset

☐ 2. Sometimes gets mildly upset; rarely very upset

☐ 3. Typically gets very upset

42. (Age 3–5) Will the child readily accept new articles of clothing (shoes, coats, etc.)?

☐ 1. Usually resists new clothes

☐ 2. Doesn't seem to mind, or enjoys them

43. (Age 3–5) Is child upset by certain things that are not "right" (like crack in the wall, spot on rug, books leaning in bookcase, broken rung on chair, pipe held and not smoked)?

☐ 1. Not especially

☐ 2. Yes, such things upset him greatly

☐ 3. Not sure

44. (Age 3–5) Does child adopt complicated "rituals" that make him very upset if not followed (like putting many dolls to bed in a certain order, taking exactly the same route between two places, dressing according to a precise pattern, or insisting that only certain words be used in a given situation)?

☐ 1. Yes, definitely

☐ 2. Not sure

☐ 3. No

45. (Age 3–5) Does child get very upset if certain things he is used to are changed (like furniture or toy arrangement, or certain doors which must be left open or shut)?

☐ 1. No

☐ 2. Yes, definitely

☐ 3. Slightly true

46. (Age 3–5) Is the child destructive?

☐ 1. Yes, this is definitely a problem

☐ 2. Not deliberately or severely destructive

☐ 3. Not especially destructive

47. (Age 3–5) Is the child unusually physically pliable (can be led easily; melts into your arms)?

☐ 1. Yes

☐ 2. Seems normal in this way

☐ 3. Definitely not pliable

48. (Age 3–5) Which single description, or combination of two descriptions, best character-izes the child?

- [ ] 1. Hyperactive, constantly moving, changes quickly from one thing to another
- [ ] 2. Watches television quietly for long periods
- [ ] 3. Sits for long periods
  For example, stares into space or plays repetitively with objects, without appar-ent purpose
- [ ] 4. Combination of 1 and 2
- [ ] 5. Combination of 2 and 3
- [ ] 6. Combination of 1 and 3

49. (Age 2–5) Does the child seem to want to be liked?

- [ ] 1. Yes, unusually so
- [ ] 2. Just normally so
- [ ] 3. Indifferent to being liked; happiest when left alone

50. (Age 3–5) Is child sensitive and/or affectionate?

- [ ] 1. Is sensitive to criticism and affectionate
- [ ] 2. Is sensitive to criticism, not affectionate
- [ ] 3. Not sensitive to criticism, is affectionate
- [ ] 4. Not sensitive to criticism nor affectionate

51. (Age 3–5) Is it possible to direct child's attention to an object some distance away or out a window?

- [ ] 1. Yes, no special problem
- [ ] 2. He rarely sees things very far out of reach
- [ ] 3. He examines things with fingers and mouth only

52. (Age 3–5) Do people consider the child especially attractive?

- [ ] 1. Yes, very good-looking child
- [ ] 2. No, just average
- [ ] 3. Faulty in physical appearance

53. (Age 3–5) Does the child look up at people (meet their eyes) when they are talking to him?

- [ ] 1. Never, or rarely
- [ ] 2. Only with parents
- [ ] 3. Usually does

54. (Age 3–5) Does the child take an adult by the wrist to use adult's hand (to open door, get cookies, turn on TV, etc.)?

  ☐ 1. Yes, this is typical

  ☐ 2. Perhaps, or rarely

  ☐ 3. No

55. (Age 3–5) Which set of terms best describes the child?

  ☐ 1. Confused, self-concerned, perplexed, dependent, worried

  ☐ 2. Aloof, indifferent, self-contented, remote

56. (Age 3–5) Is the child extremely fearful?

  ☐ 1. Yes, of strangers or certain people

  ☐ 2. Yes, of certain animals, noises or objects

  ☐ 3. Yes, of 1 and 2 above

  ☐ 4. Only normal fearfulness

  ☐ 5. Seems unusually bold and free of fear

  ☐ 6. Child ignores or is unaware of fearsome objects

57. (Age 3–5) Does he fall or get hurt in running or climbing?

  ☐ 1. Tends toward falling or injury

  ☐ 2. Average in this way

  ☐ 3. Never, or almost never, exposes self to falling

  ☐ 4. Surprisingly safe despite active climbing, swimming, etc.

58. (Age 3–5) Is there a problem in that the child hits, pinches, bites, or otherwise injures himself or others?

  ☐ 1. Yes, self only

  ☐ 2. Yes, others only

  ☐ 3. Yes, self and others

  ☐ 4. No, not a problem

59. At what age did the child say his first words (even if later stopped talking)?

  ☐ 1. Has never used words

  ☐ 2. 8–12 months

  ☐ 3. 13–15 months

  ☐ 4. 16–24 months

  ☐ 5. 2 years–3 years

  ☐ 6. 3 years–4 years

  ☐ 7. After 4 years old

  ☐ 8. Don't know

60. In the space below list child's first six words (as well as you can remember them).

61. (Before age 5) Did the child start to talk, then become silent again for a week or more?

☐ 1. Yes, but later talked again (age stopped____ duration____)

☐ 2. Yes, but never started again (age stopped____)

☐ 3. No, continued to talk, or never began talking

62. (Before age 5) Did the child start to talk, then stop, and begin to whisper instead, for a week or more?

☐ 1. Yes, but later talked again (age stopped____ duration____)

☐ 2. Yes, still only whispers (age stopped talking ____)

☐ 3. Now doesn't even whisper
(age stopped talking ____ age stopped whispering ____)

☐ 4. No, continued to talk, or never began talking

63. (Age 1–5) How well could the child pronounce his first words when learning to speak, and how well could he pronounce difficult words between 3 and 5?

☐ 1. Too little speech to tell, or other answer

☐ 2. Average or below average pronunciation of first words ("wabbit," etc.), and also poor at 3 to 5

☐ 3. Average or below on first words, unusually good at 3–5

☐ 4. Unusually good on first words, average or below at 3–5

☐ 5. Unusually good on first words, and also at 3–5

64. (Age 3–5) Is the child's vocabulary (the number of things he can name or point to accurately) greatly out of proportion to his ability to "communicate" (to answer questions or tell you something)?

☐ 1. He can point to many objects I name, but doesn't speak or "communicate"

☐ 2. He can accurately name many objects, but not "communicate"

☐ 3. Ability to "communicate" is pretty good—about what you would expect from the number of words he knows

☐ 4. Doesn't use or understand words

65. When the child spoke his first sentences, did he surprise you by using words he had not used individually before?

☐ 1. Yes (Any examples? _____)

☐ 2. No

☐ 3. Not sure

☐ 4. Too little speech to tell

66. How did child refer to himself on first learning to talk?

- ☐ 1. "(John) fall down," or "Baby (or Boy) fall down."
- ☐ 2. "Me fall down," or "I fall down"
- ☐ 3. "(He, Him, She, or Her) fall down"
- ☐ 4. "You fall down"
- ☐ 5. Any combination of a, b, and/or c
- ☐ 6. Combination of a and d
- ☐ 7. No speech or too little speech as yet

67. (Age 3–5) Does child repeat phrases or sentences that he has heard in the past (maybe using a hollow, parrot-like voice), what is said having little or no relation to the situation?

- ☐ 1. Yes, definitely, except voice not hollow or parrot-like
- ☐ 2. Yes, definitely, including peculiar voice tone
- ☐ 3. Not sure
- ☐ 4. No
- ☐ 5. Too little speech to tell

68. (Before age 5) Can the child answer a simple question like "What is your first name?" or "Why did Mommy spank Billy?"

- ☐ 1. Yes, can answer such questions adequately
- ☐ 2. No, uses speech, but can't answer questions
- ☐ 3. Too little speech to tell

69. (Before age 5) Can the child understand what you say to him, judging from his ability to follow instructions or answer you?

- ☐ 1. Yes, understands very well
- ☐ 2. Yes, understands fairly well
- ☐ 3. Understands a little, if you repeat and repeat
- ☐ 4. Very little or no understanding

70. (Before age 5) If the child talks, do you feel he understands what he is saying?

- ☐ 1. Doesn't talk enough to tell
- ☐ 2. No, he is just repeating what he has heard with hardly any understanding
- ☐ 3. Not just repeating—he understands what he is saying, but not well
- ☐ 4. No doubt that he understands what he is saying

71. (Before age 5) Has the child used the word "Yes?"

☐ 1. Has used "Yes" fairly often and correctly

☐ 2. Seldom has used "Yes," but has used it

☐ 3. Has used sentences, but hasn't used word "Yes"

☐ 4. Has used a number of other words or phrases, but hasn't used word "Yes"

☐ 5. Has no speech, or too little speech to tell

72. (Age 3–5) Does the child typically say "yes" by repeating the same question he has been asked? (*Example:* You ask "Shall we go for a walk, Honey?" and he indicates he does want to go by saying "Shall we go for a walk, Honey" or "Shall we go for a walk?")

☐ 1. Yes, definitely, does not say "Yes" directly

☐ 2. No, would say "Yes" or "OK" or similar answer

☐ 3. Not sure

☐ 4. Too little speech to say

73. (Before age 5) Has the child asked for something by using the same sentence you would use when you offer it to him? (*Example:* The child wants milk, so he says: "Do you want some milk?" or "You want some milk")

☐ 1. Yes, definitely (uses "You" instead of "I")

☐ 2. No, would ask differently

☐ 3. Not sure

☐ 4. Not enough speech to tell

74. (Before age 5) Has the child used the word "I"?

☐ 1. Has used "I" fairly often and correctly

☐ 2. Seldom has used "I," but has used it correctly

☐ 3. Has used sentences, but hasn't used the word "I"

☐ 4. Has used a number of words or phrases, but hasn't used the word "I"

☐ 5. Has used "I," but only where the word "you" belonged

☐ 6. Has no speech, or too little speech to tell

75. (Before age 5) How does the child usually say "No" or refuse something?

☐ 1. He would just say "No"

☐ 2. He would ignore you

☐ 3. He would grunt and wave his arms

☐ 4. He would use some rigid meaningful phrase (like "Don't want it!" or "No milk!" or "No walk!")

☐ 5. Would use phrase having only private meaning like "Daddy go in car"

☐ 6. Other, or too little speech to tell

76. (Before age 5) Has the child used one word or idea as a substitute for another, for a prolonged time? (*Example:* always says "catsup" to mean "red," or uses "penny" for "drawer"
after seeing pennies in a desk drawer)

☐ 1. Yes, definitely

☐ 2. No

☐ 3. Not sure

☐ 4. Too little speech to tell

77. Knowing what you do now, at what age do you think you could have first detected the
child's abnormal behavior? That is, when did detectable abnormal behavior actually
begin? (Under "A," indicate when you might have; under "B" when you did.)

			A	B
☐	1.	In first 3 months		
☐	2.	4–6 months		
☐	3.	7–12 months		
☐	4.	13–24 months		
☐	5.	2 years–3 years		
☐	6.	3 years–4 years		
☐	7.	After 4th year		

78. Parents' highest educational level

		(Father)	(Mother)
1.	Did not graduate high school		
2.	High school graduate		
3.	Post high school tech. training		
4.	Some college		
5.	College graduate		
6.	Some graduate work		
7.	Graduate degree ( )		

79. Indicate the child's nearest blood relatives, including parents, who have been in a mental hospital or who were known to have been seriously mentally ill or retarded. Consider parents, siblings, grandparents, uncles and aunts.

If none, check here: ____

	Relationship	Diagnosis, if known (Schizophrenia, Depressive, Other)
1.		
2.		
3.		
4.		
5.		

Form E2, Part 2

Please answer the following questions by writing "1" if Very True, "2" if True and "3" if False on the line preceding the question. Except for the first two questions, which pertain to the child before age 2, answer "Very True" (1) or "True" (2) if the statement described the child any time before his 10th birthday. If the statement is not particularly true of the child before age 10, answer "False" (3). *Remember:* 1 = Very True, 2 = True, 3 = False.

_____ 80. Before age 2, arched back and bent head back, when held

_____ 81. Before age 2, struggled against being held

_____ 82. Abnormal craving for certain foods

_____ 83. Eats unusually large amounts of food

_____ 84. Covers ears at many sounds

_____ 85. Only certain sounds seem painful to him

_____ 86. Fails to blink at bright lights

_____ 87. Skin color lighter or darker than others in family (which: ____lighter ____darker)

_____ 88. Prefers inanimate (nonliving) things

_____ 89. Avoids people

_____ 90. Insists on keeping certain object with him

_____ 91. Always frightened or very anxious

_____ 92. Inconsolable crying

_____ 93. Notices changes or imperfections and tries to correct them

_____ 94. Tidy (neat, avoids messy things)

_____ 95. Has collected a particular thing (toy horses, bits of glass, etc.)

_____ 96. After delay, repeats phrases he has heard

_____ 97. After delay, repeats whole sentences he has heard

_____ 98. Repeats questions or conversations he has heard, over and over, without variation

_____ 99. Gets "hooked" or fixated on one topic (like cars, mops, death)

_____ 100. Examines surfaces with fingers

_____ 101. Holds bizarre pose or posture

_____ 102. Chews or swallows nonfood objects

_____ 103. Dislikes being touched or held

_____ 104. Intensely aware of odors

_____ 105. Hides skill or knowledge, so you are surprised later on

_____ 106. Seems not to feel pain

_____ 107. Terrified at unusual happenings

_____ 108. Learned words useless to himself

_____ 109. Learned certain words, then stopped using them

Please supply any additional information that you think may lead to understanding the cause or diagnosis of the child's illness.

CARS: Childhood Autism Rating Scale

The following items are a sample of the questions found on the Childhood Autism Rating Scale, by Eric Schopler, Dr. Robert Reichler, and Barbara Rochen Renner (Los Angeles: Western Psychological Services, 1993), also known as the CARS. This instrument is often used to evaluate young children who may have autistic spectrum disorders. Evaluators using the CARS rate the child on a scale from 1 to 4 in each of 15 areas.

Relating to People

Rating	Behavior
1	No evidence of difficulty or abnormality in relating to people. The child's behavior is appropriate for his or her age. Some shyness, fussiness, or annoyance at being told what to do may be observed, but not to an atypical degree.
1.5	(if between these points)
2	Mildly abnormal relationships. The child may avoid looking the adult in the eye, avoid the adult or become fussy if interaction is forced, be excessively shy, not be as responsive to the adult as is typical, or cling to parents somewhat more than most children of the same age.
2.5	(if between these points)
3	Moderately abnormal relationships. The child shows aloofness (seems unaware of adult) at times. Persistent and forceful attempts are necessary to get the child's attention at times. Minimal contact is initiated by the child.
3.5	(if between these points)
4	Severely abnormal relationships. The child is consistently aloof or unaware of what the adult is doing. He or she almost never responds or initiates contact with the adult. Only the most persistent attempts to get the child's attention have any effect.

Body Use

Rating	Behavior
1	Age-appropriate body use. The child moves with the same ease, agility, and coordination of a normal child of the same age.
1.5	(if between these points)
2	Mildly abnormal body use. Some minor peculiarities may be present, such as clumsiness, repetitive movements, poor coordination, or the rare appearance of more unusual movements.
2.5	(if between these points)
3	Moderately abnormal body use. Behaviors that are clearly strange or unusual for a child of this age may include strange finger movements, peculiar finger or body posturing, staring or picking at the body, self-directed aggression, rocking, spinning, finger-wiggling, or toe-walking.

Rating	Behavior
3.5	(if between these points)
4	Severely abnormal body use. Intense or frequent movements of the type listed above are signs of severely abnormal body use. These behaviors may persist despite attempts to discourage them or involve the child in other activities.

Adaptation to Change

Rating	Behavior
1	Age-appropriate response to change. While the child may notice or comment on changes in routine, he or she accepts these changes without undue distress.
1.5	(if between these points)
2	Mildly abnormal adaptation to change. When an adult tries to change tasks, the child may continue the same activity or use the same materials.
2.5	(if between these points)
3	Moderately abnormal adaptation to change. The child actively resists changes in routine, tries to continue the old activity, and is difficult to distract. He or she may become angry and unhappy when an established routine is altered.
3.5	(if between these points)
4	Severely abnormal adaptation to change. The child shows severe reactions to change. If a change is forced, he or she may become extremely angry or uncooperative and respond with tantrums.

Listening Response

Rating	Behavior
1	Age-appropriate listening response. The child's listening behavior is normal and appropriate for age. Listening is used together with other senses.
1.5	(if between these points)
2	Mildly abnormal listening response. There may be some lack of response, or mild overreaction to certain sounds. Responses to sounds may be delayed, and sounds may need repetition to catch the child's attention. The child may be distracted by extraneous sounds.
2.5	(if between these points)
3	Moderately abnormal listening response. The child's responses to sounds vary; often ignores a sound the first few times it is made; may be startled or cover ears when hearing some everyday sounds.
3.5	(if between these points)
4	Severely abnormal listening response. The child overreacts and/or under reacts to sounds to an extremely marked degree, regardless of the type of sound.

Verbal Communication

Rating	Behavior
1	Normal verbal communication, age and situation appropriate.
1.5	(if between these points)
2	Mildly abnormal verbal communication. Speech shows overall retardation. Most speech is meaningful; however, some echolalia or pronoun reversal may occur. Some peculiar words or jargon may be used occasionally.
2.5	(if between these points)
3	Moderately abnormal verbal communication. Speech may be absent. When present, verbal communication may be a mixture of some meaningful speech and some peculiar speech such as jargon, echolalia, or pronoun reversal. Peculiarities in meaningful speech include excessive questioning or preoccupation with particular topics.
3.5	(if between these points)
4	Severely abnormal verbal communication. Meaningful speech is not used. The child may make infantile squeals, weird or animal-like sounds, complex noises approximating speech, or may show persistent, bizarre use of some recognizable words or phrases.

This sample was used with permission from Western Psychological Services and the authors. The complete Childhood Autism Rating Scale is available to qualified professionals. Please write to:

Western Psychological Services
12031 Wilshire Boulevard
Los Angeles, CA 90025

Glossary of Acronyms

AA arachidonic acid

AAC augmentative and alternative communication

ABA Applied Behavioral Analysis

ABC Aberrant Behavior Checklist

ABC-ASIEP Autism Behavior Checklist of the Autism Screening Instrument for Educational Planning

ABIC Adaptive Behavior Inventory for Children

ABR/BSER Auditory Brainstem Response/ Brain Stem Evoked Response

ADA Americans with Disabilities Act

ADD attention deficit disorder

ADHD attention deficit hyperactivity disorder

ADI-R Autism Diagnostic Interview-Revised

ADOS Autism Diagnostic Observation Schedule

AFDC Aid to Families with Dependent Children

AGRE Autism Genetic Resource Exchange

AIDS autoimmune deficiency syndrome

AIT Auditory Integration Training

ALPHA Assessment Link Between Phonology and Articulation Test

AMCHP Association of Maternal and Child Health Programs

ANA anti-neuronal antibody

ANDI Autism Network for Dietary Intervention

APA American Psychological Association

ARC Association of Retarded Citizens

ARI Autism Research Institute

ARRI Autism Research Review International

ASD autistic spectrum disorder

ASO/ASLO group A beta-hemolytic streptococcus

ASPEN Asperger Syndrome Education Network of America, Inc.

BASC Behavior Assessment System for Children

BNF The British National Formulary

BOS Behavior Observation Scale for Autism

BRIAC Behavior Rating Instrument for Autistic and other Atypical Children

BUN blood urea nitrogen

CAMP cyclic adenosine monophosphate

CAN Cure Autism Now Foundation

CAP comprehensive central auditory processing

CAPD central auditory processing deficit

CARS Childhood Autism Rating Scale

CAT computer-assisted tomography

CBC Achenbach Child Behavior Checklist

CCPT child-centered play therapy

CELF-3 Clinical Evaluation of Language Fundamentals–3

CFIDS chronic fatigue immune deficiency syndrome

CHADD Children and Adults with Attention Deficit Disorders

CMS Children's Memory Scale

CMS chronic mononucleosis syndrome

CMV cytomegalovirus

CNS central nervous system

CPA conditioned play audiometry

CRS Conner's Rating Scales

CSHCN Children with Special Health Care Needs Program

DAN! Defeat Autism Now!

DARAS Disability Access Rights and Advice Service

DASI-II Developmental Assessment Screening Inventory II

DDP Designated Disabled Program

DETS Department of Education, Training and Employment

DGLA dihomogamma-linolenic acid

DLA Disability Living Allowance

DMG dimethylglycine

DMSO dimethylsulfoxide

DNA deoxyribonucleic acid

DO Doctor of Osteopathy (Chiropractor)

DSM-IV *Diagnostic and Statistical Manual of Mental Disorders*

EBV Epstein-Barr virus

EEG electroencephalogram

EFA essential fatty acid

EIC Earned Income Credit

EKG electrocardiogram

EPS extrapyramidal side effects

ESY extended school year

FAPE free and appropriate public education

FBA functional behavior assessment

FCND Feldenkrais for Children with Neurological Disorders

FDA Federal Drug Administration

FEAT Families for Early Autism Treatment

FIP functional intervention plan

FRAXA fragile X syndrome

GABA gamma-aminobutyric acid

GAGs glycosaminoglycans

GARS Gilliam Autism Rating Scale

GI gastrointestinal

GLA gammalinolenic acid

GP general practitioner

HFA high-functioning autism

HHV6, HHV7, HHV8, HSV-1, HSV-2 human herpes viruses

HMO health maintenance organization

HNTBC Halstead-Reitan Neuropsychological Test Battery for Children

HUD Housing and Urban Development

IEP Individualized Education Plan

IFA Individualized Functional Assessment

IFSP Individualized Family Service Plan

Ig immunoglobin

IgA AGA immunoglobin A Gliadin Antibodies

IgA ARA, R1 type immunoglobin A Reticulin Antibodies

IgE immunoglobulin E

IgG immunoglobulin G

IgG1, IgG2, IgG3, IgG4 immunoglobulin G subclass abnormalities

IgM immunoglobulin M

InLv Independent Living on the Autistic Spectrum list

IPSEA Independent Panel for Special Education Advice

IQ intelligence quotient

IVIg intravenous immunoglobulin infusion

JABA *The Journal of Applied Behavior Analysis*

Kaufman-ABC Kaufman Assessment Battery for Children

LDA Learning Disabilities Association of America

Leiter-R Leiter International Performance Scale—Revised

LEA Local Educational Authority

LRE least restrictive environment

LNNB Luria-Nebraska Neuropsychological Battery

LNNB-CR Luria-Nebraska Neuropsychological Battery—Children's Revision

LPAD Learning Potential Assessment Device

MA mental age

MAO monoamine oxidase

MAOIs Monoamineoxidase Inhibitors

MBD minimal brain dysfunction

anti-MBP myelin basic protein antibodies

MCT medium chain triglycerides

MLT melatonin

measles-IgG measles virus antibodies

MMR measles, mumps, and rubella (vaccine)

MRI magnetic resonance imagery

MSD multisystem neurological disorder

MSM sulfur methyl-sulphonyl-methane

NA nucleic acid

NAAR National Alliance for Autism Research

NAC N-Acetyl-Cysteine

NAFP neuron-axon filament protein

NAS National Autistic Society

NaSSA noradrenergic and specific serotonergic antidepressant

ND naturopathic doctor

NICHCY National Information Center for Children and Youth with Disabilities

NIDS neuro-immune dysfunction syndromes

NIH National Institutes of Health

NK cells natural killer cells

NMS neuroleptic malignant syndrome

NRI Norepinephrine Reuptake Inhibitor

NSAID non-steroidal anti-inflammatory drug

OCD obsessive-compulsive disorder

OCR Office of Civil Rights

OHI other health impaired

ORS Ongoing Resourcing Scheme

OT occupational therapy/therapist

PANDAS Pediatric Autoimmune Neuropsychiatric Disorders Associated with Streptococcus

PAPS phosphoadenylyl sulphate

PAS-ADD Psychiatric Assessment Schedule for Adults with Developmental Disability

PCP primary care provider

PDD pervasive developmental disorder

PDD-NOS pervasive developmental disorder not otherwise specified

PDMS Peabody Developmental and Motor Scales

PDR Physicians' Desk Reference

PEACH Parents for the Early Intervention of Autism in Children

PEATC Parent Educational Advocacy Training Center

PECS Picture Exchange Communication System

PET positron emission tomography

PIA Parent Interviews for Autism

PIAT Peabody Individual Achievement Test

PIC Private Industry Council

PKU phenylketonuria

PPA phenylpropanolamine

PPVT-R Peabody Picture Vocabulary Test—Revised

PRT pivotal response training

PSC Pediatric Symptom Checklist

PST phenolsulfotransferase

PT physical therapy/therapist

RAST radioallergosorbent test

RET rapid eye therapy

RINTB Reitan-Indiana Neuropsychological Test Battery

SAD seasonal affective disorder

S-B IV Stanford-Binet Intelligence Test Fourth Edition

SBOs Soil-based organisms

SCSIT Southern California Sensory Integration Test

SED seriously emotionally disturbed

SI sensory integration

SIB self-injurious behavior

SICD-R Sequenced Inventory of Communication Development—Revised

SII Sensory Integration International

SIPT Sensory Integration and Praxis Tests

SPECT single photon emission computed tomography

SNP Special Needs Program

SWS Supported Wage System

SLP speech and language pathologist

SSI Supplemental/Social Security Income

SSRIs selective serotonin reuptake inhibitors

TARF The Autism Research Foundation

TEACCH structured teaching

TLC Test of Language Competence

TOLD Test of Language Development

TONI Test of Non-Verbal Intelligence

TPE therapeutic plasma exchange

TS Tourette syndrome or tuberous sclerosis

TVP textured vegetable protein

WAIS-R Weschler Adult Intelligence Scale

WAO World Autism Organisation

WISC Weschler Intelligence Scale for Children

WJPEB Woodcock-Johnson Psycho Educational Battery

WPPSI Weschler Preschool and Prima Scale of Intelligence

WRAT Wide Range of Assessment Test

Notes

Chapter 1: The Medical Facts About Autism

1. Shattock, P., Whiteley, P., & Todd, L. "Is there an increasing incidence of autism? Evidence and possible explanations." In the Proceedings of the 12th Annual International Durham Conference on Autism, Durham, England, April 2001.

2. Bauman, M. L., & Kemper, T. L. "Neuroanatomical observations of the brain in autism." In J. Panksepp, *Advances in Biological Psychiatry*, Vol. 1. Greenwich, CT: JAI Press, 1995.

3. Courchesne, E. "Brainstem, cerebellar and limbic neuroanatomical abnormalities in autism." *Current Opinion in Neurobiology* 7 (1997): 269–278.

4. Sherman, C. "Research suggests complexity of autism deficits." *Clinical Psychiatry News* 28 (5), (2000): 39.

5. Bolton, P., & Griffiths, P. "Association of tuberous sclerosis of temporal lobes with autism and atypical autism." *Lancet* 349 (December 1997): 392–395.

6. Croonenberghs, J., and others. "Peripheral markers of serotonergic and noradrenergic function in post-pubertal, Caucasian males with autistic disorder." *Neuropsychopharmacology* 22 (3) (March 2000): 275–283.

7. Lake, C. R., Ziegler, M. G., & Murphy, D. L. "Increased norepinephrine levels and decreased dopamine-beta-hydroxylase activity in primary autism." *Archives of General Psychiatry* 34 (1977): 553–556.

8. Schauf, C., Moffet, D., & Moffet, S. In D. Allen, *Human Physiology*. St. Louis: Times Mirror/Mosby College Publishing, 1990, pp. 567–573.

9. Autism Society of America. "What is autism?" Bethesda, MD: Autism Society of America, 2002. Available online at *http://www.autism-society.org/whatisautism/autism.html*.

10. Ritvo, E., and others. "The UCLA-University of Utah Epidemiologic Survey of Autism: Recurrence risk estimates and genetic counseling." *American Journal of Psychiatry* 146 (1989): 1032–1036.

11. Ritvo and others, "The UCLA-University of Utah Epidemiologic Survey of Autism."

12. International Molecular Genetic Study of Autism Consortium. "A full genome screen for autism with evidence for linkage to a region on chromosome 7q." *Human Molecular Genetics* 7 (3): 571–578.

13. Fisher, S. E., and others. "Localisation of a gene implicated in a severe speech and language disorder." *Nature Genetics* 18 (February 1998): 168.

14. Webb, T., & Latif, F. "Rett syndrome and the MeCP2 gene." *Journal of Medical Genetics* 38 (4), (April 2001): 217–223.

15. Van den Veyver, I. B., MD. "Rett syndrome, MECP2 mutations and autism." Presentation: National Institutes of Health/ACC Scientific Conference September 6, 2001.

16. Dykens, E. M., & Volkmar, F. "Medical conditions in autism," in D. J. Cohen & F. Volkmar (eds.), *Handbook of Autism and Pervasive Developmental Disorders,* 2nd ed. New York: Wiley, 1997, pp. 388–410.

17. Bolton, P., & Griffiths, P. "Association of tuberous sclerosis of temporal lobes with autism and atypical autism."

18. Warren, R., and others. "Possible association of the extended MHC haplotype B44-SC30-DR4 with autism." *Immunogenetics* 36, 1992: 203–207.

19. Allan, A. J. "Group A streptococcal infections and childhood neuropsychiatric disorders—Relationships and therapeutic implications." *CNS Drugs* 4 (October 1997): 267–275.

20. Hollander, E., and others. "B lymphocyte antigen D8/17 and repetitive behaviors in autism." *American Journal of Psychiatry* 156 (2) (February 1999): 317–320.

21. Edelson, S. M. "Overview of autism." Salem, OR: Center for the Study of Autism, 1999. Available at *http://www.autism.org/overview.html*.

22. Binstock, T. "Atypical chronic infections and other immune atypicalities in autism spectrum children: Preliminary data suggesting a new diagnostic subgroup" (monograph). Available at *http://www.jorsm.com/~binstock/chronic1.htm*.

23. Shattock, P., & Savery, D. "The role of vaccines in the causation of autism and related disorders." In the Proceedings of the 8th Annual International Durham Conference on Autism, April 1997. Available at *http://osiris.sunderland.ac.uk/autism/vaccine.htm*.

24. Singh, V. K., and others. "Serological association of measles virus and human herpesvirus-6 with brain autoantibodies in autism." *Clinical Immunology and Immunopathology* 89 (October 1998): 105–108.

25. Wakefield, A., and others. "Ileal-lymphoid-nodular hyperplasia, non-specific colitis, and pervasive developmental disorder in children." *Lancet* 351 (February 28, 1998): 637–641.

26. Weiss, B., & Landrigan, P. J. "The developing brain and the environment." *Environmental Health Perspectives* 107, Supplement 3 (June 2000).

27. Johnson, L. "Feds: Autism cluster found in New Jersey." (Brick, NJ) *Associated Press,* April 18, 2000.

Chapter 2: Categorizing Autistic Spectrum Disorders

1. Cheadle, J. P., and others. "Long-Read sequence analysis of the MECP2 gene in Rett syndrome patients: Correlation of disease severity with mutation type and location." *Human Molecular Genetics* 9 (2000): 1119–1129.

2. Newson, E., & le Maréchal, K. "Pathological demand avoidance syndrome: Discriminant functions analysis demonstrating its essential differences from autism and Asperger's syndrome." poster presentation: Psychobiology of Autism: Current Research and Practice conference, April 1998.

Chapter 3: Getting a Diagnosis

1. Costello, E., and others. "The Great Smoky Mountains Study of Youth: Functional impairment and serious emotional disturbance (SED)." *Archives of General Psychiatry* (1988): 1107–1116.

Chapter 5: Medical Interventions

1. McDougle, C. J., Naylor, S. T., Cohen, D. J., Volkmar, F. R., Heninger, G. R., & Price, L. H. "A double-blind, placebo-controlled study of fluvoxamine in adults with autistic disorder." *Archives of General Psychiatry* 53 (11), (November 1996): 1001–1008.

2. DeLong, G. R., Teague, L. A., and McSwain, K. M. "Effects of fluoxetine treatment in young children with idiopathic autism." *Developmental Medicine and Child Neurology* 40 (8), (August 1998): 551–562.

3. Steingard, R. J., Zimnitzky, B., DeMaso, D. R., Bauman, M. L., & Bucci, J. P. "Sertraline treatment of transition-associated anxiety and agitation in children with autistic disorder." *Journal of Child and Adolescent Psychopharmacology* 7 (1), (Spring 1997): 9–15.

4. Gordon, C. T., Rapoport, J. L., Hamburger, S. D., State, R. C., & Mannheim, G. B. "Differential response of seven subjects with autistic disorder to clomipramine and desipramine." *American Journal of Psychiatry* 149 (3), (March 1992): 363–366.

5. Kerbeshian, J., Burd, L., & Fisher, W. "Lithium carbonate in the treatment of two patients with infantile autism and atypical bipolar symptomology." *Journal of Clinical Psychopharmacology* 7 (6), (1987): 401–405.

6. Posey, D. J., Guenin, K. D., Kohn, A. E., Swiezy, N. B., & McDougle, C. J. "A naturalistic open-label study of mirtazapine in autistic and other pervasive developmental disorders." *Journal of Child and Adolescent Psychopharmacology* 11 (3), (Fall 2001): 267–277.

7. Hollander, E., Kaplan, A., Cartwright, C., & Reichman, D. "Venlafaxine in children, adolescents, and young adults with autism spectrum disorders: An open retrospective clinical report." *Journal of Child Neurology* 15 (2), (February 2000): 132–135.

8. Marrosu, F., Marrosu, G., Rachel, M. G., & Biggio, G. "Paradoxical reactions elicited by diazepam in children with classic autism." *Functional Neurology* 2 (3), (1987): 355–361.

9. McCormick, L. H. "Treatment with buspirone in a patient with autism." *Archives of Family Medicine* 6 (4), (July–August 1997): 368–370.

10. Realmuto, G. M., August G. J., & Garfinkel, B. D. "Clinical effect of buspirone in autistic children." *Journal of Clinical Psychopharmacology* 9 (2), (April 1989): 122–125.

11. Hollander, E., Dolgoff-Kaspar, R., Cartwright, C., Rawitt, R., & Novotny, S. "An open trial of dival-proex sodium in autism spectrum disorders." *Journal of Clinical Psychiatry* 62 (7), (July 2001): 530-534.

12. Childs, J. A., & Blair, J. L. "Valproic acid treatment of epilepsy in autistic twins." *Journal of Neuroscience Nursing* 29 (4), (August 1997): 244–248.

13. Williams, G., King, J., Cunningham, M., Stephan, M., Kerr, B., & Hersh, J. H. "Fetal valproate syndrome and autism: Additional evidence of an association." *Developmental Medicine and Child Neurology* 43 (3), (March 2001): 202–206.

14. Edelson, S. M. "Treatment tips: A brief overview of common problems and fixes." Salem, OR: Center for the Study of Autism. Available at *http://www.autism.org/quickfix.html.*

15. National Institute of Mental Health. "Methylphenidate in children and adolescents with pervasive developmental disorders." Bethesda, MD, ClinicalTrials.gov, October 2001). Available at *http://www.clinicaltrials.gov/ct/gui/c/a1r/show/NCT00025779?order=1&JServSessionIdzone_ct=o6dpjvweq1.*

16. Anderson, L. T., Campbell, M., Adams, P., Small, A. M., Perry, R., & Shell, J. "The effects of haloperidol on discrimination learning and behavioral symptoms in autistic children." *Journal of Autism and Developmental Disorders* 19 (2), (June 1989): 227–239.

17. Zuddas, A., Di Martino, A., Muglia, P., & Cianchetti, C. "Long-term risperidone for pervasive developmental disorder: Efficacy, tolerability, and discontinuation." *Journal of Child and Adolescent Psychopharmacology* 10 (2), (Summer 2000): 79–90.

18. Jaselskis, C. A., Cook, E. H., Jr., Fletcher, K. E., & Leventhal, B. L. "Clonidine treatment of hyperactive and impulsive children with autistic disorder." *Journal of Clinical Psychopharmacology* 12 (5), (October 1992): 322–327.

19. Kolmen, B. K., Feldman, H. M., Handen, B. L., & Janosky, J. E. "Naltrexone in young autistic children: A double-blind, placebo-controlled crossover study." *Journal of the American Academy of Child and Adolescent Psychiatry* 34 (2), (February 1995): 223–231.

20. Perry, E. K., Lee, M. L.W., Martin-Ruiz, C. M., Court, J. A., Volsen, S. G., Merrit, J., Folly, E., Iversen, P. E., Bauman, M. L., Perry, R. H., & Wenk, G. L. "Cholinergic activity in autism: Abnormalities in the cerebral cortex and basal forebrain." *American Journal of Psychiatry* 158 (2001): 1058–1066.

21. Swedo, S., MD, and others. "Identification of children with pediatric autoimmune neuropsychiatric disorders associated with streptococcal infections by a marker associated with rheumatic fever." *American Journal of Psychiatry* 154 (January 1997): 110–112.

22. Hollander, E., and others. "B lymphocyte antigen D8/17 and repetitive behaviors in autism." *American Journal of Psychiatry* 156 (2), February 1999: 317–320.

23. Beer, D. Interview with the author. September 1998.

24. Sandler, R. H., and others. "Short-term benefit from oral vancomycin treatment of regressive onset autism." *Journal of Child Neurology* 15 (July 2000): 429–435.

25. Corker-Vann, M. R., and others. "Frequently asked questions about antibiotic therapy." Available at *http://www.rheumatic.org/faq.htm.*

26. Weizman, A., and others. "Abnormal immune response to brain tissue antigen in the syndrome of autism." *American Journal of Psychiatry* 139 (11), November 1982: 1462–1465.

27. Singh, V. K., and others. "Antibodies to myelin basic protein in children with autistic behavior." *Brain, Behavior and Immunity* 7 (1), (March 1993): 97–103.

28. Ring, A., Barak, Y., & Ticher, A. "Evidence for an infectious aetiology in autism." *Pathophysiology* 4 (1997): 1485–1488.

29. Gillberg, C. "Onset at age 14 of atypical autistic syndrome: A case report of a previously normal girl with herpes encephalitis." *Journal of Autism and Developmental Disorders* 16 (1986): 369–375.

30. DeLong, G. R., Beau, S. C., & Brown, F. R., III. "Acquired reversible autistic syndrome in acute encephalopathic illness in children." *Archives of Neurology* 38 (1981): 191–194.

31. Stubbs, E. G. "Autistic symptoms in a child with congenital cytomegalovirus infection." *Journal of Autism and Schizophrenia* 8 (1978): 37–43.

32. Stubbs, E. G., Ritvo, E. R., & Mason-Brothers, A. "Autism and shared parental HLA antigens." *Journal of the American Academy of Child Psychiatry* 24 (1985): 182–185.

33. Heikkinen, T., Thint, M., & Chonmaitree, T. "Prevalence of various respiratory viruses in the middle ear during acute otitis media." *New England Journal of Medicine* 240 (4), (January 28, 1999): 260–264.

34. King, B. H., and others. "Double-blind, placebo-controlled study of amantadine hydrochloride in the treatment of children with autistic disorder." *Journal of the American Academy of Child and Adolescent Psychiatry* 40 (2001): 658–665.

35. Justice Awareness and Basic Support. "A Report on MMR questionnaires and personal communications." JABS. Available at *http://www.argonet.co.uk/users/jabs/mmrrep.html*.

36. Singh, V. K., & Nelson, C. "Abnormal measles serology and autoimmunity in autistic children." *Journal of Allergy and Clinical Immunology* 109 (1), Supplement 232, January 2002.

37. Brunson, A. "Researcher sounds note of caution." *Herald Journal* (Logan, UT), September 23, 2000.

38. Wakefield, A., and others. "Illeal-lymphoid-nodular hyperplasia, non-specific colitis, and pervasive developmental disorder in children."

39. Uhlmann, V., and othersand others. "Potential viral pathogenic mechanism for new variant inflammatory bowel disease." *Journal of Clinical Pathology: Molecular Pathology* 22 (April 2002). Available at *http://jcp.bmjjournals.com/cgi/data/55/1/DC1/1*.

40. Fatemi, S. H. "Reelin mutations in mouse and man: From reeler mouse to schizophrenia, mood disorders, autism and lissencephaly." *Molecular Psychiatry* 6 (2), (March 2001): 129–133.

41. Fenichel, G. M. "Assessment: Neurologic risk of immunization: Report of the Therapeutics and Technology Assessment Subcommittee of the American Academy of Neurology." *Neurology* 52 (1999): 1546–1552. Available at *http://www.aan.com/public/practiceguidelines/immun.PDF*.

42. US Food and Drug Administration (FDA). "Thimerosol in vaccines" (Washington, DC: FDA, November 2001). Available at *http://www.fda.gov/cber/vaccine/thimerosal.htm*.

43. Alberti, A., Pirrone, P., Elia, M., Waring, R. H., & Romano, C. "Sulphation deficit in 'low-functioning' autistic children: A pilot study," *Biological Psychiatry* 46 (3), (August 1, 1999): 420–424.

44. Owens, S. "Explorations of the new frontier between gut and brain: A look at GAGs, CCK and motilin," in the Proceedings of the 9th Annual International Durham Conference on Autism, April 1998, Durham, England. Available at *http://osiris.sunderland.ac.uk/autism/owens.htm*.

45. National Institutes of Health. "The utility of therapeutic plasmapheresis for neurological disorders. NIH Consensus Statement Online 1986 June 2–4" 6 (4), (June 2–4, 1986): 1–7. Available at *http://text.nlm.nih.gov/nih/cdc/www/56txt.html*.

46. Rimland, B. "Dimethylglycine (DMG) for autism." Autism Research Institute, 1996. Available at *http://www.autism.com/ari/dmg2.html*.

47. American Academy of Pediatrics, American Association for Pediatric Ophthalmology and Strabismus, American Academy of Ophthalmology. "Position statement on learning disabilities, dyslexia and vision." *Pediatrics* 90 (1), (1992): 124–125.

48. Monmaney, T. "St. John's wort: Regulatory vacuum leaves doubt about potency, effects of herb used for depression." *Los Angeles Times*, August 31, 1998.

Chapter 6: Therapeutic Interventions

1. Lovaas, O. I. "Behavioral treatment and normal educational and intellectual functioning in young autistic children." *Journal of Consulting and Clinical Psychology* 55 (1987): 3–9.

2. Scientific Learning Corporation. "Fast ForWord outcomes." Available at *http://www.scilearn.com/scie/index.php3?main=out/cp_summary1*.

3. Jacobson, J. W., Mulick, J. A., & Schwartz, A. A. "A history of facilitated communication: Science, pseudoscience, and antiscience: Science Working Group on Facilitated Communication." *American Psychologist* 50 (9), (1995): 750–765.

4. Greenspan, S. *The Child with Special Needs*. New York: Addison-Wesley, 1998.

5. Pierce, K., & Schreibman, L. "Multiple peer use of pivotal response training to increase social behaviors of classmates with autism: Results from trained and untrained peers." *Journal of Applied Behavior Analysis* 30 (1997): 157–160.

6. Atwood, T. "Modifications to cognitive behaviour therapy to accommodate the cognitive profile of people with Asperger's syndrome." Available at *http://www.tonyattwood.com/paper2.htm.*

Chapter 7: Other Interventions

1. National Institutes of Health. "Acupuncture." *NIH Consensus Statement* 15 (5), (November 1997): 1–34. Available at *http://odp.od.nih.gov/consensus/cons/107/107_statement.htm.*

2. Y. Li, Tougas, G., Chiverton, S. G., & Hunt, R. H. "The effect of acupuncture on gastrointestinal function and disorders." *American Journal of Gastroenterology* 87 (10), (1992): 1372–1381.

3. National Institutes of Health, "Acupuncture."

4. Wong, V., & Sun, J. G. "Double blind randomized placebo controlled trial of using tongue acupuncture in autistic spectrum disorder." Poster presentation at the 4th Congress of European Paediatric Neurology Society, Baden-Baden, Germany, September 12–16, 2001.

5. Sandefur, R., & Adams, E. "The effects of chiropractic adjustments on the behavior of autistic children: A case review." *Journal of the American Chiropractic Association* 21 (5), (December 1987).

6. National Council Against Health Fraud. "Homeopathy: A position statement by the National Council Against Health Fraud." Loma Linda, CA: National Council Against Health Fraud, 1994. Available at *http://www.skeptic.com/03.1.jarvis-homeo.html.*

7. Friedman, A. Summary of unpublished work (2000). Available at *http://www.gfcfdiet.com/Explanationofdiet.htm.*

8. Rimland, B. "Vitamin B_6 (and magnesium) in the treatment of autism." *Autism Research Review International* 1 (4), (1987). Available at *http://www.autism.org/vitb6.html.*

9. Hoffer, A. "Chronic schizophrenic patients treated ten years or more." *Journal of Orthomolecular Medicine* 9 (1994): 7–37.

10. Fry, P. C., and others. "Metabolic response to a pantothenic acid deficient diet in humans." *Journal of Nutrition Science and Vitaminology* 22 (1976): 339–346.

11. Rimland, "Vitamin B_6 (and magnesium) in the treatment of autism."

12. Rimland, B. "Vitamin C in the prevention and treatment of autism." San Diego: Autism Research Institute, 1998. Available at *http://www.autism.com/ari/editorials/vitaminc.html.*

13. Vogelaar, A. "Studying the effects of essential nutrients and environmental factors on autistic behavior." Presentation: Defeat Autism Now! "Think Tank" meeting, Phoenix, Arizona, August 2000.

14. Landgree, A. R., & Landgrebe, M. A. "Celiac autism: Calcium studies and their relationship to celiac disease in autistic patients." in *The Autistic Syndromes.* New York: Elsevier, pp. 197–205.

15. Waring, R. "Biochemical parameters in autistic subgroups." presentation at the 4th Consensus Conference on Biological Basis and Clinical Perspectives in Autism, Troina, Sicily, October 1995.

16. Sinaiko, R. J., MD. "The biochemistry of attentional/behavioral problems" Presentation: Feingold Association Conference, 1996. Available at *http://www.feingold.org/sinaiko.shtml.*

17. Owens, S. "Sulfation in autism: Its role in etiology and its importance in treatment." Presentation: Autism Society of America, Oakland Chapter conference, Pontiac, Michigan, April 13, 2002.

18. Stoll, A. L., and others. "Omega-3 fatty acids in bipolar disorders: A preliminary double-blind, placebo-controlled trial." *Archives of General Psychiatry* 56 (1999): 407–412.

19. Kern, J. K., and others. "Effectiveness of N,N-dimethylglycine in autism and pervasive developmental disorder." *Journal of Child Neurology* 16 (3), (March 2001): 169–173.

20. Bolman, W. M., & Richmond, J. A. "Double-blind, placebo-controlled, crossover pilot trial of low dose dimethylglycine in patients with autistic disorder." *Journal of Autism and Developmental Disorders* 29 (3), (June 1999): 191.

21. Shin-Siung Jung & Yueh-Ching Lee. "A double blind study of dimethylglycine treatment in children with autism." *Tzu Chi Medical Journal* 12 (2000): 111–121.

22. Chamberlain, R. S., & Herman, B. H. "A novel biochemical model linking dysfunction in the brain, melatonin, propiomelanocortin peptides, and serotonin in autism." *Biological Psychiatry* 28 (1990): 773–793.

23. Tazira, M., Takase, M., & Sasaki, H. "Sleep disorder in children with autism." *Psychiatry and Clinical Neurosciences* 52 (2), (April 1998): 182–183.

24. Fux, M., and others. "Inositol treatment of obsessive-compulsive disorder." *American Journal of Psychiatry* 153 (1996): 1219–1221.

25. Levine, J. "Controlled trials of inositol in psychiatry." *European Neuropsychopharmacology* 7 (May 1997): 147–155.

26. Shattock, P., & Lowdon, G. "Proteins, peptides and autism. Part 2: Implications for the education and care of people with autism." *Brain Dysfunction* 4 (6), (1991): 323–334.

27. Field, T., and others. "Brief report: Autistic children's attentiveness and responsivity improve after touch therapy." *Journal of Autism and Developmental Disorders* 27 (1997): 333–338.

Chapter 8: Insurance

1. Angelo, C. Interview with the author, 1998.

Chapter 10: Family Issues and Support

1. National Technical Assistance Center of Welfare Reform/Welfare Policy Clearinghouse. "Welfare reform and disability." Available at *http://www.welfare-policy.org/weldisab.htm*.

Chapter 12: Adults with Autistic Spectrum Disorders

1. Haracopos, D., & Pedersen, L. "Sexuality and autism, Danish Report" (1992). Available at *http://giraffe.rmplc.co.uk/eduweb/sites/autism/sexaut.html*.

Appendix E: Medication Reference

1. Realmuto, G. M., August, G. J., & Garfinkel, B. D. "Clinical effect of buspirone in autistic children." *Journal of Clinical Psychopharmacology* 9 (1989): 122–125.

2. Ratey, J. J., and others. "Buspirone therapy for maladaptive behavior and anxiety in developmentally disabled persons." *Journal of Clinical Psychiatry* 50 (1989): 382–384.

3. Gedye, A. "Buspirone alone or with serotonergic diet reduced aggression in a developmentally disabled adult." *Biological Psychiatry* 30 (1991): 88–91.

4. Ratey, J. J., and others. "Buspirone treatment of aggression and anxiety in mentally retarded patients: A multiple baseline, placebo lead-in study." *Journal of Clinical Psychiatry* 52 (1991): 159–162.

5. Ricketts, R. W., and others. "Clinical effects of buspirone on intractable self-injury in adults with mental retardation." *Journal of the American Academy of Child and Adolescent Psychiatry* 33 (1994): 270–276.

6. Gordon, C. T., and others. "A double-blind comparison of clomipramine, desipramine, and placebo in the treatment of autistic disorder." *Archives of General Psychiatry* 50 (1993): 441–447.

7. McDougle, C. J., and others. "Clomipramine in autism: Preliminary evidence of efficacy." *Journal of the American Academy of Child and Adolescent Psychiatry* 31 (1992): 746–750.

8. Garber, H. J., and others. "Clomipramine treatment of stereotypic behaviors and self-injury in patients with developmental disabilities." *Journal of the American Academy of Child and Adolescent Psychiatry* 31 (1992): 1157–1160.

9. Brasic, J. R., and others. "Clomipramine ameliorates adventitious movements and compulsions in prepubertal boys with autistic disorder and severe mental retardation." *Neurology* 44 (1994): 1309–1312.

10. Brodkin, E. S., and others. "Clomipramine in adults with pervasive developmental disorders: A prospective open-label investigation." *Journal of Child and Adolescent Psychopharmacology* 7 (2), (1997): 109–21.

11. Sanchez, L. E., and others. "A pilot study of clomipramine in young autistic children." *Journal of the American Academy of Child and Adolescent Psychiatry* 35 (1996): 537–544.

12. McDougle, C. J., and others. "Effects of tryptophan depletion in drug-free adults with autistic disorder." *Archives of General Psychiatry* 53 (1996): 993–1000.

13. Cook, E. H., Jr., and others. "Fluoxetine treatment of children and adults with autistic disorder and mental retardation." *Journal of the American Academy of Child and Adolescent Psychiatry* 31 (1992): 739–745.

14. Zuddas, A., and others. "Clinical effects of clozapine on autistic disorder" (letter). *American Journal of Psychiatry* 153 (1996): 738.

15. Purdon, S. E., and others. "Risperidone in the treatment of pervasive developmental disorder." *Canadian Journal of Psychiatry* 39 (1994): 400–405.

16. McDougle, C. J., and others. "Risperidone in adults with autism or pervasive developmental disorder." *Journal of Child and Adolescent Psychopharmacology* 5 (1995): 273–282.

17. Simeon, J. G., and others. "Risperidone effects in treatment-resistant adolescents: Preliminary case reports." *Journal of Child and Adolescent Psychopharmacology* 5 (1995): 69–79.

18. Fisman, S., and others. "Case study: Anorexia nervosa and autistic disorder in an adolescent girl." *Journal of the American Academy of Child and Adolescent Psychiatry* 35 (1996): 937–940.

19. Demb, H. B. "Risperidone in young children with pervasive developmental disorders and other developmental disabilities" (letter). *Journal of Child and Adolescent Psychopharmacology* 6 (1996):79–80.

20. Fisman, S., & Steele, M. "Use of risperidone in pervasive developmental disorders: A case series." *Journal of Child and Adolescent Psychopharmacology* 6 (1996): 177–190.

21. Hardan, A., and others. "Case study: Risperidone treatment of children and adolescents with developmental disorders." *Journal of the American Academy of Child and Adolescent Psychiatry* 35 (1996): 1551–1556.

22. Rubin, M. "Use of atypical antipsychotics in children with mental retardation, autism, and other developmental disabilities." *Psychiatric Annals* 27 (1997): 219–221.

Index

CT (computerized tomography) scans, 7
Cylert, 113, 415–416
  action period of, 113
Cytomegaloviruses, 15
  Acyclovir and, 137
  link to autism, 125

D

Daily living skills education, 85
Dake, Lorelei, 172
Damiana, 201
Dance therapy, 157
DAN! Clinical Options Manual, 93, 124
Das, 112, 416
Dating etiquette, 267
Day treatment centers, 249
D-cycloserine, 117
DDAVP nasal spray, 118
Deafness resources, 386
Decorating issues, 321–322
Defeat Autism Now! (DAN!)
  DAN! Clinical Options Manual, 93, 124
  first annual conference, 124
  treatment protocol, 214
Defiant regulatory disorder, 33
Deficits in attention, motor control, and perception (DAMP), 33
Dental care, 141–142
Dental guards, 141–142
Depakene, 110, 419
Depakote, 93, 110, 420
  for aggression or SIB, 111
Department of Education, Training, and Employment (DETS), Australia, 285
Depression. *See also* Bipolar disorder
  and adult diagnosis, 66
  on diagnosis, 73
  family history of, 13
  in parents of ASDs, 298
  sleep disorders and, 108
  tricyclic antidepressants, 106
Designated Disabled Program (DDP), Canada, 282
Desipramine (Norpramin), 106
Desoxyn, 112, 416–417
Despiramine (Norpramin), 411
Developmental, use of term, 3
Developmental Assessment Screening Inventory (DASI-II), 57

Developmental delay
  in reverse integration classrooms, 262
  and supported integrated preschool classrooms, 245–246
Developmental disorder, defined, 218
Developmental dyspraxia, 169
Developmental Dyspraxia: A Practical Manual for Parents and Professionals (Portwood), 169
Developmental histories, 63
Developmental pediatricians, 39–40
Developmental Profile II, 57
Developmental Test of Visual-Motor Integration (Berry-Buktenica Test), 59
Developmental tests, 56–59
Dexampex, 112, 416
Dexedrine, 112, 416
  beneficial effects, length of, 113
Dextroamphetamine/amphetamine. *See* Adderall
Dextrostat, 112, 416
Diagnoses, 18–20
  adult diagnosis, 66–67
  alphabet soup diagnoses, 30
  bewilderment at diagnosis, 74–75
  of cerebral palsy, 29
  of complex partial-seizure disorder, 98
  disagreement with, 69–70
  incorrect diagnosis, 19
  of Landau-Kleffner syndrome, 31
  misdiagnosis, 68
  newer classifications, 33–34
  obtaining a diagnosis, 35–70
  of seizure disorders, 97–98
  tools for, 460–484
  video diagnostic aids, 21
  of Williams syndrome, 32
Diagnostic and Statistical Manual of Mental Disorders (DSM-IV), 4
Diagnostic classrooms, 248–249
Diaper rash, 131, 320
  antifungals, 140
Diaries
  for diagnostic evaluations, 37
  maintaining, 334–335
Diarrhea, 14
Diazepam (Valium), 109, 418

Diet, 205–209. *See also* Eating issues; Food allergies
  allergy diets, 210
  anti-Candida diet, 140, 207–208
  for autistic children, 25
  for candida-caused autism, 34
  Candida control, 140
  elimination/reintroduction diet, 208–209
  Feingold diet, 208
  ketogenic diet, 209
  in naturopathy, 188
  neurotransmitters and, 11
  phenols, foods with, 196–197
  as preventative treatment, 121
  resource list, 367–368
  rotation diet, 209
  seizures and, 111
Dietary supplements, 195–203
  evaluating, 203–205
Diet pills, 113–114
Differences, dealing with, 341–343
Diflucan, 140, 428–429
Digestive problems, 14
Dihomogamma-linolenic acid (DGLA), 197–198
Dilantin, 110, 420
Diphenylbutylpiperidine (Orap, Pimozide), 114, 428
Direct services, 243
Disability Living Allowance (DLA), UK, 315
Disabled, services for, 84–85
Discipline
  family discipline, 289–293
  guidelines for, 291
  parenting classes, 293
  professional help with, 292
  at school, 271
  time-outs, 292
Discretionary trusts, 350
Divalproex sodium. *See* Depakote
Divorce, 287, 305–306
  noncustodial parents, 307–308
DMG (dimethylglycine), 443
  as immune system modulator, 137, 138
  seizures and, 111
  supplements, 198–199
Dogs, therapy with, 147–148
Dolphin therapy, 148
Doman-Delacato/Institutes for the Achievement of Human Potential, 181

Genetics, 11–14
    addressing issues involving, 121
    Angelman syndrome, 13, 30–31
    blame in families, 297–298
    Cornelia de Lange syndrome,
        31
    counseling resources, 379–380
    explanation of, 397–399
    fragile X syndrome (FRAXA),
        25–26
    Prader-Willi syndrome and, 13,
        32
    Rett syndrome and, 12, 27–28
    role of, 5
    tuberous sclerosis and, 13
    Williams syndrome and, 32
Geodon, 115, 427
Georgianna Foundation, 153
Germanium, 448
German measles. See Rubella
GGT (gamma glutamyl
        transpeptidase), 95
Gilliam Autism Rating Scale
        (GARS), 53
Gingko biloba, 201–202, 448
Girl Scouts, 260, 306
Glasses, 142–143
Glass items, 322
Glial cells, 6
Glial filament proteins, 124
Glutamatergic N-methyl-
        D-aspartate (NDMA)
        receptor system, 117
Glutathione peroxidase, 194
Gluten
    casein-free and gluten-free (CF/
        GF) diets, 205–207
    urine testing for, 132
Glycosaminoglycans (GAGs), 130
Glycyrrhiza glabra, 202, 449
Goals, 71, 78–79. See also
        Academic goals
    communication goals, 80–82
    health goals, 79–80
    Individual Family Service Plan
        (IFSP) stating, 240–243
    in individualized education
        plans (IEPs), 257–259
    multifaceted goals, 87
    plan for reaching, 88–89
    prioritizing, 77–78
    safety goals, 79–80
    social goals, 82–84
Goldberg, Michael J., 125–126
Goldenseal, 202–203
Goodwill Industries, 281
Gotu kola, 202

Government agency case
        management, 119
Graduation transition planning,
        279–280
Grains, gluten-free, 206
Grammar problems, 171–172
Grand acute lymphoblastic
        leukemia (AML) seizures,
        96
Grandin, Temple, 55, 90, 165,
        300
Grandparents, 300, 307
    foster grandparent programs,
        306
Grapeseed oil, 194
Gray, Carol, 268–269
Great Britain. See United Kingdom
Greenspan, Stanley, 4, 33, 152,
        157–159, 177
Grievances with HMOs, 227–228
Grooming techniques, 267
Group homes, 347
Group therapy, 331
Guanfacine (Tenex), 112,
        115–116, 414
Guardianships, 351
Guilt feelings, 75–76
Guns, securing, 324
Gymboree, 338

H

Habitat for Humanity, 318
Habitrol, 435
Haircuts, dealing with, 318–319
Haldol, 114, 428
    liquid form, 100
Hallucinations, 98
Haloperidol. See Haldol
Halstead-Reitan
        Neuropsychological Test
        Battery for Children
        (HNTBC), 55–56
Hand-flapping
    in Angelman syndrome, 30
    relaxation techniques and, 165
HANDLE Institute approach,
        159–160
Hand-wringing, 28
Hawking, Stephen, 154
Head-banging, 293
    as communication, 92
Health Canada, 231–232
Health care. See also Insurance;
        National health care
    for adults with ASDs, 349
    custody of children and, 308

free or low-cost care, 236
    medical savings accounts, 237
    resource list, 362–363,
        374–375
Health goals, 79–80
Health Law Project, 230
Hearing problems, 28
Heart problems
    from IVIG transfusions, 135
    in Williams syndrome, 32
Heavy metals, 15
    chelation, 213–214
    reelin, 127
Helmets, 144
Hepatitis from IVIG transfusions,
        135
Herbal supplements, 195,
        201–203
    antibiotics, herbal, 202–203
    as antidepressants, 108
    childproofing for, 323–325
    evaluating, 203–205
    issues involving, 144–145
    in naturopathy, 188
    neurotransmitters and, 11
    reference list, 437–459
    for seizures, 99
    seizures and, 111
Herpes, 15
    Acyclovir, 137
    kutapressin and, 137
    link to autism, 125
The Hidden Child: The Linwood
        Method for Reaching the
        Autistic Child (Simons),
        160
Higher education, 281–282
High-functioning autism
    capabilities in, 24
    defined, 19
High school graduation, 84
Hippocampus, 138
Hippotherapy, 148
Hiskev-Nebraska Test of Learning
        Aptitude, 61
Histamine (HA), 140
Histidinemia, 14
Histories, 63–64
HIV. See AIDS/HIV
HMOs (health maintenance
        organizations)
    appeals, 227–228
    case management through, 119
    dealing with, 226–229
    documenting with, 226–227
    grievances, 227–228
    out-of-network clauses, 224

Itraconazole (Sporanax), 140, 430–431
IVIG therapy, 123, 134–135, 433–434

J

Janimine, 103, 106, 118, 411
Jellinek, Michael S., 39
Job placement services, 281
Journals. *See* Diaries
Jump rope jingles, 182

K

Kanner's syndrome, 24–25
Karela, 439
Katie Beckett waivers, 230
Kaufman, Barry Neil, 162
Kaufman, Raun, 162
Kaufman Assessment Battery for Children (Kaufman-ABC), 57–58
Ketchum, Caroline, 237
Ketoconazole (Nizoral), 140, 430
Ketogenic diet, 209
    seizures and, 111
Ketones, 209
Kindergarten, transition to, 250–252
Kinetic Family Drawing System for Family and School, 55
Kingsley, Emily Perl, 287–288
Kirman Sales, 193
Klonopin, 109, 110, 418
Knives, securing, 325
Koegel, Robert L., 163–164
Kozloff, Martin A., 152
Kunin v. Benefit Trust Life Insurance Co., 219
Kutapressin, 137, 432–433

L

Labels, 18–20
    alternative labels, 2–3
    problems with, 3–4
Lactobacillus acidophilus, 136, 200
Lactobacillus bulgaricus, 200
Lamictal, 110, 421
Lamisil, 140, 429
Lamotrigine (Lamictal), 110, 421
Landau-Kleffner syndrome, 30
    description of, 31–32
    misdiagnosis of, 68
    organizations, 387
    seizures in, 109

Language disorders. *See* Speech disorders
L'Arche movement, 347
Largactil, 114, 428
Leach, Penelope, 289
Lead exposure, 15
Leaky gut phenomenon, 130–131
Learning disability resources, 387
Learning Potential Assessment Device (LPAD), 58
Lecithin, 200–201, 449
    seizures and, 111
Legal issues
    of adults with ASDs, 350–351
    insurance coverage, 219–221
    resources, list of, 390
Leiter International Performance Scale—Revised (Leiter-R), 58
Lentizal, 411
Lesch-Nyhan syndrome, 14
Let Me Hear Your Voice (Maurice), 149
Letters of medical necessity, 223
Librium, 108, 418
Licorice, 202, 449
Lifestyles, seizures and, 111
Limbic system, 7
Limbitrol, 106
Linoleic acid, 197–198
Linwood method, 160
Liquid medications, 100–101
Lithane, 107
Lithium, 107
Lithobid, 107
Lithonate, 107
Lithotabs, 107
Liver enzymes, 94
Living skills education, 85
Local Educational Authority (LEA), UK, 283–284
Locks, installing, 325
Long-term institutional care, 348
Lorazepam (Ativan), 109, 418
Lovaas, O. Ivar, 148–152, 174, 181
Lovaas Institute for Early Intervention, 150
Low blood pressure, 135
Low-functioning autism
    defined, 19
    retardation in, 24
Low-income families. *See also* Financial aid
    diagnostic help for, 41
Loxapine (Loxipac et al.), 114, 428

Loxapine plus nortriptyline, 428
Loxipac/Loxipax, 114, 428
Loxitane, 114, 428
L-selenomethionane, 194
L-tryptophan, 454–455
L-tyrosine, 455
Luminal, 110, 421
Lunch bunch groups, 170
Lupus, 123
Luria-Nebraska Neuropsychological Battery (LNNB), 55
Lustral, 409–410
Luvox, 105, 106, 408
Lysergic acid diethylamide (LSD), 103

M

McCarthy Scales, 60
McDougle, Christopher, 401
Mad cow disease, 135, 203
Magnesium, 195, 449–450
Magnesium sulfate, 130, 196, 444–445
Ma huang, 114
Mail order pharmacies, 336
    resource list, 376–377
Mainstreaming. *See* Full-inclusion settings
Makaton, 81
Managed care. *See* HMOs (health maintenance organizations)
Manic depression. *See* Bipolar disorder
MAOIs (monoamine oxidase inhibitors), 106–107
    reference guide, 411
Martin-Bell syndrome. *See* Fragile X syndrome (FRAXA)
Massage, 168, 211–212
    in naturopathy, 188
Matches, 323
Matricaria recutita, 201, 442
Maurice, Catherine, 149, 150
Mayo Test for Apraxia of Speech and Oral Apraxia— Children's Battery, 61
MCare Web sites, 225
Measles, 15. *See also* MMR vaccine; Rubella
MeCP2 gene, 12
Mediation with schools, 276
Medicaid, 87, 229–230
    for adults with ASDs, 349
    Health Law Project, 230

Mutism, selective, 29
Mycostatin, 140, 429
Myelin, 124
Mykinac, 140, 429
Myoclonic seizures, 96
Mysoline, 110, 422

N

N-acetyl-cysteine (NAC), 130, 196, 450–451
Nail clipping/cleaning, 319
Naltrexone (ReVia), 116, 435–436
  for self-injurious behaviors (SIBs), 144
Name-calling, 291
Nardil, 107
National autism organizations, list of, 382–391
National Autistic Society (NAS), 233, 382
National Center for Homeopathy, 188
National Certification Commission for Acupuncture and Oriental Medicine (NCCAOM), 187
National Clearinghouse on Managed Care and Long-Term Supports and Services for People with Developmental Disabilities and Their Families, 225
National Coalition of Mental Health Professionals and Consumers, 225
National health care, 229–235
  in Australia, 233–234
  in Canada, 231–232
  in New Zealand, 235
  in United Kingdom, 117, 232–233
  in United States, 229–231
National Health Service (UK), 232–233
  clinical trials information, 117
National Home of Your Own Alliance, 348
National Institute of Ayurvedic Medicine, 187
National Institute of Mental Health
  PANDAS treatment protocol, 134
  Ritalin study, 112
National Institute on Disability and Rehabilitation Research, 154

National Institutes of Health (NIH), 14–15
  acupuncture studies, 186
  clinical trials information, 117
National Welfare Monitoring and Advocacy Partnership (NWMAP), 312
Native Americans, subsidized housing for, 346
Natural killer (NK) cells, 134
  DMG (dimethylglycine) and, 137
  IVIG transfusions and, 135
Naturopathy, 188–189
Navane, 114, 428
Nefazodone (Serzone), 107, 412–413
Neighborhood. See Community
Nephrotic syndrome, 135
Neuro-immune dysfunction syndrome (NIDS), 34
Neuroleptics, 114–115
  atypical neuroleptics, 115, 425–428
  reference list, 425–428
Neurologists, 50
Neurology, 5–11
Neuronal proteins, 124
Neuron axon filament protein (anti-NAFP), 15
Neurons, 6
  in autistic spectrum disorders, 7
  structure of, 9
Neurontin, 110, 111, 423
Neuropsychiatric tests, 54–56
Neuropsychologists, 35
NeuroSPECT scans, 7, 133
  chronic fatigue immune deficiency syndrome (CFIDS), 126
  for seizure diagnosis, 98
Neurotransmitters, 8–11
  antidepressants affecting, 104–105
  medications affecting, 104
  neuroleptics and, 114
New York's Regents Diploma, 280
New Zealand
  autism organizations, 383
  Early Intervention programs in, 41
  financial aid in, 316–317
  legal advocacy resources, 391
  national health care in, 235
  schools in, 286
Nexcare "Tattoos" bandages, 116
Niacin, 191, 456

Nicoderm, 435
Nicotine (Habitrol et al.), 435
Nicotine treatment, 117
Nicotinic acid, 191, 456
Nicotinic receptors, 117
Nicotrol, 435
Nilstat, 140, 429
Nitoman, 435
Nizoral, 140, 430
Noncustodial parents, 307–308
Nonverbal children, 343
Norepinephrine, 10
Norpramin, 106, 411
Nortriptyline (Aventyl, Pamelor), 106, 411
Notes (chapter), 490–496
Notes on prescriptions, 101
No Time for Jello (Bratt), 181
NTX, 116
Nursery rhymes, 182
NutriVene-D, 198, 451
Nystatin (Mycostatin et al.), 140, 429
Nystex, 140, 429

O

Obsessive-compulsive disease
  and adult diagnosis, 66
  diagnosis of, 29
  family history of, 13
  PANDAS project research, 122–124
  streptococcus bacteria and, 14–15
  tricyclic antidepressants, 106
Occupational therapists, 50
Occupational therapy, 161–162
  for autistic children, 25
  resource list, 371–372
  test instruments, 59–60
Office of Civil Rights (OCR), 274
Olanzapine (Zyprexa), 115, 427–428
Oligomeric proanthocyanidins (OPCs), 194
Omega-6 fatty acids, 197–198
OmegalBrite, 198
Ongoing Resourcing Scheme (ORS), New Zealand, 286
Opioid blockers, 116
Opportunities Industrialization Commission, 281
Options Institute method, 162–163
Optometric Extension Program Foundation, 142

About the Author

MITZI WALTZ has been a professional author, journalist, and editor for over a decade, covering topics ranging from computers to health care. She has been heavily involved in parent support work, and has also advocated for special-needs children within the medical, insurance, and education systems. She is currently completing her PhD in England with the University of Sunderland's Autism Research Unit.

Ms. Waltz has also authored *Bipolar Disorders: A Guide to Helping Children and Adolescents, Obsessive-Compulsive Disorder: Help for Children and Adolescents, Partial Seizure Disorders: Help for Patients and Families, Tourette's Syndrome: Finding Answers & Getting Help,* and *Adult Bipolar Disorders: Understanding Your Diagnosis & Getting Help* for the Patient-Centered Guides series.

Colophon

Patient-Centered Guides are about the experience of illness. They contain personal stories as well as a combination of practical and medical information.

The cover of *Autistic Spectrum Disorders* was designed by Kristen Throop of Combustion Creative. The warm colors and quilt-like patterns are intended to convey a sense of comfort. The use of repetitive patterning was inspired by tile work seen by the designer on a trip to Turkey. The layout was created on a Macintosh using Quark 4.0. Fonts in the design are: Berkeley, Coronet, GillSans, Minion Ornaments, Throhand, and Univers Ultra Condensed. The design was built with tints of three PMS colors.

Rad Proctor designed the interior layout for the book based on a series design by Nancy Priest and Edie Freedman. The interior fonts are Berkeley and Franklin Gothic. The text was prepared using FrameMaker.

The book was copyedited by Linda Purrington and proofread by Marianne Rogoff. Tom Dorsaneo and Katherine Stimson conducted quality assurance checks. Katherine Stimson wrote the index. The illustrations that appear in this book were produced by Rob Romano. Interior composition was done by Rad Proctor.